Essential Journalism

This book is a practical guide to all aspects of modern journalism for anyone seeking to study for the National Council for the Training of Journalists (NCTJ) Diploma in Journalism and become a qualified journalist in the UK.

Written in collaboration with the NCTJ, *Essential Journalism* outlines everything you need to know about the journalism industry today, from its ethical framework to its practice across print, television, radio, online and social media. It looks at the core principles and the skills that are required of journalists across all platforms, helping students develop an overall understanding of the business and examining the application and adaptation of traditional best practice to the demands of the digital age. This is a unique one-stop shop for anyone who wants to understand the nature and purpose of journalism, and how it is changing and evolving in today's digital newsrooms.

This book is a core resource for journalism trainees and undergraduates, as well as for seasoned practitioners and lecturers.

Jonathan Baker is an award-winning journalist and journalism teacher. His first foray into journalism was during a gap year spent on the *Ashbourne News Telegraph* in Derbyshire. He joined the *Liverpool Daily Post and Echo* as a graduate trainee and passed his NCTJ Proficiency Test there before joining BBC Radio in London. He held senior positions in BBC radio, television and multimedia newsgathering. He was variously Executive Editor of the Radio Newsroom, Executive Editor of Radio 5 Live News Programmes, Editor of the BBC One o'Clock and Six o'Clock Television News, Editor of the BBC Ten o'Clock News, and World News Editor. For four years he was Head of the College of Journalism, responsible for the training of the BBC's 8,000 journalists. His last role at the BBC was Head of Newsgathering. He was appointed Founding Professor of Journalism at the University of Essex, where he devised and delivered an NCTJ-accredited undergraduate course in multimedia journalism. He is a winner of the NCTJ Chairman's Award for outstanding contribution to high standards of journalism training.

Essential Journalism

The NCTJ Guide for Trainee Journalists

Jonathan Baker

Routledge
Taylor & Francis Group

LONDON AND NEW YORK

First published 2021
by Routledge
2 Park Square, Milton Park, Abingdon, Oxon OX14 4RN

and by Routledge
605 Third Avenue, New York, NY 10158

Routledge is an imprint of the Taylor & Francis Group, an informa business

British Library Cataloguing-in-Publication Data
A catalogue record for this book is available from the British Library

Library of Congress Cataloging-in-Publication Data
Names: Baker, Jonathan (Professor of journalism), author. | National Council
for the Training of Journalists (Great Britain), issuing body.
Title: Essential journalism: the NCTJ guide for trainee journalists / Jonathan Baker.
Description: London; New York: Routledge, 2021. | Includes bibliographical references and
index. | Identifiers: LCCN 2020056938 | ISBN 9780367645908 (hardback) |
ISBN 9780367645892 (paperback) | ISBN 9781003125341 (ebook)
Subjects: LCSH: Journalism—Handbooks, manuals, etc. |
Journalism—Vocational guidance—Great Britain.
Classification: LCC PN4775 .B255 2021 | DDC 808.06/607—dc23
LC record available at https://lccn.loc.gov/2020056938

ISBN: 9780367645908 (hbk)
ISBN: 9780367645892 (pbk)
ISBN: 9781003125341 (ebk)

Typeset in Goudy
by codeMantra

For all my fellow travellers in journalism. And especially for Carol Frost, who started me on my own journey

Contents

Foreword

Strap yourself in. You are about to have the ride of your life. It will be like no other – frustrating and exhausting but also exhilarating, immensely fulfilling and rewarding. You will quickly learn your most challenging task as a journalist is to get to the truth – and often truth can be *and is* interpreted very differently, depending on which way you are looking. You will be given signposts on your journey to get there which may be inadvertently misleading, and could be downright wrong or even malevolently provided. Your job is to analyse those signs and work out which are honest and which are not. You've got to have 20/20 vision and be alert to the human frailty of seeing just what you *want* to see. You've got to have the stamina to dig and dig and then when you think you cannot dig any further, ready your journalistic shovel and dig even deeper. You've just signed up to a career where there are no money-back guarantees and no clear paths but which will never be dull. You may meet with politicians and Presidents, the impoverished and the plutocratic elite – and all the training you are learning now will help you cope with it all. My first morning walking into the Newcastle HQ of the Thomson Regional Newspapers office in the Bigg Market, as an 18-year-old journalism trainee, started with tutor Walter Greenwood going around the room asking us all what "stories" we had noticed or picked up on the way in. Everywhere there are stories waiting to be investigated and worth telling, and as a journalist you may be the only way that story is ever going to be told. It is a huge responsibility as well as a tremendous privilege. Soak up every bit of knowledge that you can from this book, because nothing you are learning now will ever be wasted. Journalism is a lifelong educational rollercoaster. Whether you end up trying to scribble shorthand in the back of a bouncing armoured personnel carrier in the middle of the Democratic Republic of Congo or you find yourself trying to remember what international laws are applicable whilst interviewing a despot or dictator, you should spend every waking hour as a journalist learning more, delving deeper and thoroughly appreciating being in one of the toughest but most gratifying professions there is. This is just the beginning of your training. Love every minute of it. You won't regret it.

Alex Crawford, Special Correspondent Sky News and Patron of the
National Council for the Training of Journalists

Preface

This book is for students on journalism or media studies courses, and anyone else who wants to become a journalist. It is a practical primer, designed to introduce newcomers to all aspects of modern journalism. Some sections will also be valuable to established journalists who want to move between media – say from print to radio, or from radio to television or from anywhere to digital platforms.

The book carries the stamp of approval from the National Council for the Training of Journalists (NCTJ), the UK's principal training body. As such, it should be of particular value to students on courses accredited by the NCTJ. The majority of those students work towards the NCTJ's Diploma in Journalism, and the book is aligned to the Programmes of Study, or syllabus, laid out in the Diploma.

The Diploma is made up of compulsory and optional modules. The titles and content of the modules are kept under constant review, as the nature and demands of the industry evolve and change. The compulsory elements or "core study units" are as follows: **Essential Journalism** (including a portfolio of work); **Essential Journalism Ethics and Regulation**; and **Essential Media Law and Regulation**. Media law is comprehensively examined in a separate NCTJ publication, *McNae's Essential Law for Journalists*. This book covers all the compulsory elements of the Diploma syllabus other than law – looking across the full range of skills young journalists are expected to have at the outset of their careers.

A number of the elective, or optional, modules of the Diploma, such as Radio Journalism, Television Journalism and Data Journalism, build on the basics set out in the core study units. Much of the material in this book will also be relevant to those non-compulsory modules. Other optional modules – such as PR and Communications – are not covered here. The focus is on those skills designated by the NCTJ as 'essential'; it is not a set of pass notes or a revision guide for all elements of the Diploma syllabus.

The practice of journalism today is no longer compartmentalised. Not that long ago, you were a print journalist, an online journalist, a radio journalist or a television journalist. You could move between the sectors, but for the most part you worked in only one of them at any given time. There was little or no overlap between them, even within the same organisation. For many years, BBC Television News and BBC Radio News were separate organisations based in newsrooms five miles apart across London. BBC News Online began life in a tiny office several floors away from the television newsroom.

All that has changed, and continues to change apace. The buzzwords now are "multimedia", "multiplatform", "multiskilling" and "digital". This reflects the fact that journalism is now delivered across a broad range of platforms, and that many journalists now operate in at least two media, of which online/social is almost certainly one. Their work ranges across several of the traditional frontiers between sectors.

Although digital is the word on everyone's lips, the extent to which journalists operate online and on social networks varies hugely. The NCTJ's 2018 study *Journalists at Work* found that print remained the main platform for around half of the estimated 73,000 journalists working in the UK. Many others worked principally for radio or television. Those working wholly for online or digital platforms constituted only a small proportion of the whole. They represent the direction of travel, however, and things are clearly shifting further in the digital direction. Significantly, the 2018 survey also showed that some form of working online as a *secondary* or supplementary activity was the norm for most journalists (85 per cent). So a digital journalist might interpret the survey findings as evidence that more journalists are working online than anywhere else. However you look at it, almost everyone is operating somewhere in the digital space to a greater or lesser extent. The barriers are down.

The book attempts to reflect this mixed economy. It looks at the core principles and the skills that are required of all journalists; then it takes each of the different sectors in turn, with analysis of the specific craft skills required of online, radio, television and print journalism. The intention is to help students develop an overall understanding, but also to see how each of those platforms works on its own. It is a virtuous circle: it is necessary to be familiar with the nature of each platform and the differences and similarities between them in order to be able to see the big picture. In many ways, digital journalism brings everything together. The skillset of the digital journalist includes elements of all forms of traditional journalism, as well as a range of new competencies.

Much of what is in these pages represents the fruits of my own 40 years in journalism, taking in weekly and regional daily newspapers, radio, television and multimedia newsgathering. The level at which it is pitched stems from my experiences setting up and then teaching an NCTJ-accredited undergraduate course in Multimedia Journalism at the University of Essex.

My experience at Essex, reinforced by conversations with counterparts in other universities, was that students often come to undergraduate or postgraduate courses with little prior knowledge about the practicalities of journalism. Many are attracted to journalism primarily because they enjoy writing. They are interested in what is going on in the world, but probably know little of how news works. Most have no idea what branch of journalism they might wish to pursue. If this sounds like you, don't worry. It is a perfectly natural place from which to embark on your journey. With this book you will be introduced to the basics of journalism, but also, I hope, be enthused about journalism as a calling, and the stimulating and varied career path it offers.

Your NCTJ course will probably contain a mix of academic theory and a large amount of learning through practical exercises and work experience. Journalism students love practical work, which, in the case of Essex, began with the first class on the first day of the first week of the course. If you have been used to sitting in a school library trying to pad out a 3,000-word essay, you may be disconcerted to learn that research for journalism is largely done by talking to people, and that a word count of 300 will often be considered generous. But when you have got your head around it, you will find it liberating – and fun.

The book assumes very little in the way of prior knowledge, and the focus is on the fundamental and the practical. It is not an academic work. It adopts an ABC approach to explaining in detail how and why things are done and then applies that to practical examples. It also tries to convey a sense of how it feels to be a journalist, and what everyday life is like in the modern newsroom – what kind of tasks a young journalist can typically be assigned, what sort of skills and level of competence will be expected. It explains how you are expected to behave in a variety of professional situations.

The central thesis of the book is that the craft of journalism today is essentially the same as it always was. At root, it is about gathering information and then disseminating and explaining it. That was the function of journalism when print was its only medium. It remained so through the arrival and growth of both radio and television. It remains so today in the age of the internet, social media and all the digital platforms. The purpose and function are the same. There are many more ways of gathering information now, and many more ways of presenting it to readers and audiences at ever-greater speeds. But the essentials are unchanged.

It follows that the things that made journalism good or bad in the pre-digital age are still good and bad today. The core values of best practice in the past are the core values of best practice now. None has been rendered obsolete or irrelevant by 24-hour news or the march of digital. People still need journalism that is rooted in proper research, checking and corroborating, devotion to accuracy, fair dealing and ethical behaviour, good writing for all platforms, good spelling and good grammar. In the Wild West of the digital world, people need good journalism more than ever.

There is no change in the ethical approach either. The Editors' Code of Practice, governing the print and digital conduct of many newspapers, may now be overseen by IPSO, but has obvious lineage from the precepts previously followed by the Press Complaints Commission. The IMPRESS Code of Conduct, to which smaller titles have signed up, is similarly rooted in long-recognised standards of behaviour. The thrust of the Ofcom Broadcasting Code and the BBC's Editorial Guidelines, between them embodying broadcasting best practice, has not changed radically since their first publication, and has remained constant through several iterations. These codes inform responses to the new challenges of the digital era. The philosophy and culture they collectively represent is reflected in the syllabus of the NCTJ Diploma, and in all the learning materials freely available to anyone through the NCTJ's Journalism Skills Academy.

All this underlines that it is not the principles of good journalism that have changed; it is the environment and the manner in which they are applied. To meet the challenges of digital journalism and the world today, we should rely on the principles and standards that have always been acknowledged as the basis of good practice.

That can create an issue of perception: to the digital generation, talking about the value of time-honoured and traditional working practices can sound complacent, backward-looking and out of touch. It is a perception that university journalism educators will recognise. I offer three points in response:

– Understanding the fundamentals of good journalism, and the individual skills that make up the best print and broadcast output, will make you a better digital journalist. The more you understand about constructing a print story or the principles of television and radio news, the better equipped you are to flourish in the digital space. You need a raft of other skills too of course. But we do not have to reinvent journalism to respond to the new challenges.

– As the 2018 survey showed, not everyone is yet a full-time player in the digital world. Although few are untouched by it, there are still thousands of journalists whose principal efforts are directed at one (or two) of newspaper and magazine journalism, television and radio. For them, the traditional core skills are as relevant as they always were, although digital and other technical developments make possible new applications of them, such as mobile journalism. The individual analysis of these skills is therefore of strong relevance to many whose principal output is not web-focused.

– It is risky to generalise about the speed and take-up of the digital approach. Traditional practices and job titles long abandoned by those at the cutting edge of digital journalism survive unmolested in other places. My own personal observations of representative examples of local, regional and national journalism brought this home to me very forcefully. Not everyone is moving at the same pace. Some are streaking ahead, others are barely warming up at the starting line. That will not always be the case – indeed, may not be the case for much longer. The future of newspapers looks particularly parlous. But a mixed economy of some sort is likely to be with us for some time yet. It seems inevitable that everyone will have to head for the same destination eventually. But for the moment, a guide to essential journalism must reflect the fact that all are at different stages of the journey and many different working practices apply. I have attempted to reflect this varied picture, and to be guided by the promise implicit in the title of this book: *Essential Journalism*.

Your course probably recognises the importance of tried and tested principles, by introducing you very early to the basic unit of journalism and news reporting: the news story, of the sort you might routinely find in a newspaper or on a website. A couple of hundred words, attractively written, telling you what you need to know about something that has happened. It might not seem like an obvious starting point for a career in a world of digital journalism. But that basic unit of storytelling is at the foundation of all journalism, and if you can grasp what is required to research and produce a lively and accurate account, you will be well on your way, wherever you are working. True, there are lots of shiny new digital tools – but they too are employed with an eye to the time-honoured values of good journalism.

Journalists are opinionated and argumentative animals, so I do not expect my judgements and recommendations to meet with the agreement and approval of all journalism lecturers or students. That is as it should be. Where we differ, perhaps I will at least have provided talking points for class discussions.

There are many excellent books about journalism, and among the titles and links in Further Reading are those I have found most useful both in developing my teaching at Essex and subsequently in writing this book. I acknowledge my debt to them, only mentioning them by name in the text where I quote from them directly. Many of them go into much more detail about specific aspects of journalism than I have been able to do in this general study. Areas that I cover in one or two chapters are the subjects of entire books in some cases. So further reading is to be encouraged. My aim has been to bring together in one place the information and knowledge students need in order to understand and master the practical skills required by the core elements of the NCTJ Diploma.

One publication that demands specific mention is *Essential Reporting* by Jon Smith, which is the forerunner of the book you hold in your hand. Smith's book was published in 2007. The digital revolution, then only in its infancy, was soon to make its presence felt. As a result, the scope of this book, its successor, has had to be much wider and multi faceted. Yet so much of Smith's wisdom, common sense and explanations of the basics of good, accurate, ethical journalism remain highly relevant and applicable today. I am grateful to the NCTJ and to Jon Smith for allowing me to transfer so much of that wisdom to this book.

Acknowledgements

I must first thank Joanne Butcher, Chief Executive of the National Council for the Training of Journalists (NCTJ), for encouraging me to write this book and subsequently giving it the NCTJ seal of approval. The NCTJ trained me, and their endorsement means a lot. Will Gore of the NCTJ read the drafts with the shrewd and discerning eye of both a critic and a sub-editor, and made countless corrections and improvements. The book is much the better for his insights, and I thank him for his eagle eye, and for his support and encouragement.

My thanks are also due to those – whose names are unknown to me – who vetted sample chapters and then the entire manuscript as part of the peer review process. They too made valuable suggestions and put me on the right track in a number of areas where I had strayed. Any mistakes that have survived the rigours of this process are my responsibility. Margaret Farrelly and Priscille Biehlmann at Routledge were unfailingly helpful and supportive.

Some of the chapters are based on classes I taught on the BA Multimedia Journalism course at the University of Essex. I thank my fellow tutors, Tim Fenton, Paul Anderson, Karen Gooch and Fatima el Issawi for their comradeship, and apologise for any gems I may have subconsciously stolen from them without acknowledgement.

I am grateful to Anthony Reuben, Mark Wray and Deirdre Mulcahy who shared their knowledge and expertise for individual chapters, and then gave their expert feedback on the results. I am particularly indebted to Cordelia Hebblethwaite of the BBC and Steve Jones of PA Media for their enormous contributions to the chapters covering digital journalism. I would have been lost without them. I received invaluable help from Rebecca Curley on the reporting of local politics, and from Ross McCarthy on court reporting.

I am grateful to the specialists whose thoughts and insights about their roles and craft feature in the chapter on specialist journalism: Roger Harrabin, Eleni Courea, Paul Kelso, Jeremy Laurence, Simon Walters, Emily Beament, Will Gompertz, Adina Campbell and Chris Morris.

For access to working newsrooms, and taking time out to discuss their work with me, my thanks to James Preston of the *Maidenhead Advertiser*, Anna Jeys of *Birmingham Live* and Simon Walters of the *Daily Mail*.

The Editors' Code of Practice is reproduced by kind permission of the Regulatory Funding Company and is ©2021 The Regulatory Funding Company. Thanks also to Ofcom and IMPRESS for permission to reproduce their Codes, and to the BBC for permission to quote from Editorial Guidelines and other policy documents.

Finally my love and thanks to my wife Diane for her forbearance during the inordinate and unexpectedly lengthy amount of time I spent closeted away on the computer keyboard during the construction of the book.

Part one

Journalism and journalists

1
The journalism landscape

The world you are entering

Journalism is on the move. Since the turn of the century, technological and other developments have forced journalists in all media to reassess the fundamentals of what they do and how they do it. The result has been a revolution in the newsroom and beyond. The speed and scale of change over a sustained period has been unrelenting, and journalism has often struggled to keep pace. It was largely slow to react to the new digital world, and is still coming to terms with what digital means for the business of gathering and disseminating rapid and reliable information in the ways that people require and are prepared to pay for. Long-standing business models and working practices are being swept aside, as journalism competes with a million other demands on the time and attention of an audience it was once able to take for granted. It must fight to win and hold public trust and support, and lead the counter attack against disinformation and fake news.

This is the chaotic and dynamic world into which you are stepping. Do not be disheartened! As we shall see, the role of the journalist in this changed world is ever more important – and in many respects, ever more exciting.

Many of the changes have been reactive, a response to new technical possibilities, to new players on the media scene, and to the ways in which the information economy now behaves. The ever-increasing sophistication of the internet and the development of digital and mobile phone technology have been two of the biggest drivers of this revolution. Social networks have done much to destroy the old certainties.

There have been profound consequences. Consumers are no longer reliant on traditional news providers – "the mainstream media" – delivering news in a manner and at a time of their own choosing via a one-way channel of communication. Through the internet, more than four billion people have instant access to information from an infinite number of sources at any moment of the day or night. Well over half of them use smartphones as their means of access, consuming on the move. The flow of information now travels in multiple directions, because as well as receiving content, anyone can create and share it at the drop of a hat. It is largely unmoderated and unfiltered. The consumers of content are also the makers of it. They are, in the words of influential media critic Jay Rosen, "the people formerly known as the audience". Everyone is a reporter now. To quote the title of commentator Clay Shirky's book about the phenomenon: "Here Comes Everybody".

With powerful new players such as Facebook, Twitter, Instagram, YouTube and the rest, professional providers of news and information risk being bypassed or pushed to the margins. Consumers have at their disposal the tools of gathering and publishing that were once the preserve of journalists alone. It is not surprising that there has been a drift away from traditional news providers, now that the levers of control have been wrested from them. Consumers simply started going elsewhere, and in due course it dawned on journalism that they would not be coming back. It had to follow them if it was not to become an irrelevance.

Most media organisations of any size now operate on several platforms. Newspapers and radio and television stations all have websites, and their journalists are expected to produce material across platforms, including social networks. Realising that many people first hear of breaking news through the smartphones that they are checking constantly, the media have reassessed their workflows and systems of news management, with priority given to publishing online – on web pages and across social networks. Newspapers may still hold back a big story for next day's printed product, but no one can afford to be slow with breaking news online. This is also reflected in staffing, with many people employed to keep web pages and social accounts fuelled and up to date. This has become an increasingly important recruiting ground for young journalists in the early stages of their careers. Those with well-honed digital skills are eminently employable.

When it comes to social media, a presence on Facebook, Twitter and Instagram is now the norm for news providers. The material published there usually tries to tempt people to seek more content on the publisher's main platforms, but it has to be self-standing as well. Although Twitter tends to be the platform that attracts the attention – not least when the most powerful politician in the world makes it the vehicle for policy announcements – Facebook is by far the larger and more influential player. Establishing a credible presence on these platforms, and on new ones as they emerge, is a further recognition by mainstream media of the simple fact that the audience has moved. When news is available around the clock, people see less and less point in paying for a newspaper that may be out of date before it hits the streets, or waiting until bedtime for a television news bulletin. True, there is still a substantial market for that kind of journalism. Older people still cling to the reading, listening and viewing habits of a lifetime, and journalism is about more than breaking news. But a mixed economy has emerged, and the balance is changing all the time. Millennials and Generation Z growing up in the digital age have never formed those habits in the first place. They get their information online, and often not from recognised news providers. They keep up to date by looking at what their friends and those they follow are sharing on social media. If that is where consumers are, that is where news providers have to be too.

Alongside the new platforms, new providers have emerged, often operating solely online – the likes of *HuffPost* and *Vice* – and, at a more grass roots level, hyperlocal news websites serving community needs. At the same time, there have been heavy casualties. The regional newspaper industry – traditionally the place young journalists cut their teeth – has been particularly badly hit. The internet has accustomed people to free content. Fewer of them buy a printed newspaper, and the circulation of most papers is in long-term decline. One national newspaper, *The Independent*, stopped printing altogether, and exists only online. Trinity Mirror tried to reverse the trend by launching a new daily newspaper, *The New Day*, in 2016. It closed within two months. Archant's *The New European* has proved more enduring.

Income from advertising, more important than sales, has also collapsed. The likes of eBay and Gumtree offer much larger markets for buying and selling than printed columns of classified advertisements. Many print titles have closed, and others have been swallowed by large conglomerates such as Newsquest, Reach and JPI Media, between them the owners of hundreds of local newspapers. Operating on a large scale like this enables them to reduce their costs and make a more compelling offer to advertisers, especially online. Some publishers have set up websites reporting regional news across the catchment areas of a number of their newspapers, with no corresponding printed product. Various means have been tried to monetise the digital product, through sponsorship, advertising or charging for "added value" content. The overall picture is one of fewer journalists, each with a broader range of skills and perhaps working for more than one title in a group. Reporters on weekly and provincial daily papers can expect to take their own still pictures for the printed newspaper while gathering and editing audio and video to illustrate the stories they write for the website. Multiplatform and multiskilling are the order of the day.

More than 200 newspaper titles have disappeared since the turn of the century, and the number of regional journalists has halved. The coronavirus pandemic of 2020 exacerbated the situation and brought local journalism to the brink. More than half the population now has no access to a "local" daily or weekly print title. This has a detrimental effect on community engagement and the reporting and scrutiny of local government. Competition between regional or weekly titles covering the same area is non-existent in many places.

Even the mighty BBC is not immune to the aftershocks of the digital revolution. The case for funding the BBC through a tax – the licence fee – is increasingly difficult to make when so many people are getting their news and entertainment elsewhere, sometimes for nothing. Even with the very large income the licence fee delivers, the BBC is finding it more and more difficult to compete with the budgets of Amazon and Netflix when it comes to making new drama, and the pockets of Sky when it comes to bidding for sports rights. It has to make big savings, and the News division takes its share of the pain.

This revolution, unfolding over a period of years rather than overnight, has not met with universal acclaim. Not everyone is enamoured of the noise and chaos of the new realities. Some believe the imperative for speed, and for news delivered in easily digestible chunks, has led to superficiality and the dumbing down of journalism. They no longer feel sure that the information they are receiving is reliable and trustworthy. Journalism has never enjoyed unqualified public confidence, and certainly cannot take trust for granted. Indeed, it has had to put its own house in order more than once. In 2011, already reeling from the challenges posed by these brash new online arrivals, UK journalism was hit by a scandal that further undermined what faith the public may have had in its integrity, honesty and basic morality. It was revealed that at least one and perhaps several national newspapers had been systematically and deliberately breaking the law by hacking into the mobile phones of well-known people in all walks of life. The resultant scandal was a shattering blow to the reputation of newspaper journalism – a reputation that had never stood particularly high in the first place.

A new and different front was opened up with the election of Donald Trump as President of the US in 2016, with his persistent attacks on the media as purveyors of lies and "fake news". In its proper meaning, fake news has nothing to do with journalists, but is literally fabricated and peddled by non-journalists with an unsavoury variety of motives. But Trump's constant elision of fake news with what he saw as bias in the mainstream media – essentially anything critical of himself – had an insidious effect. It has become more widely fashionable to dismiss as "fake" any inconvenient truth that does not tally with the accuser's own preferences and opinions. This is detrimental to public discourse. What is more, politicians and others have the capacity to target and appeal directly to the voters, bypassing the filters of question and challenge provided by the mainstream media.

Throughout this book, you will hear a piece of advice repeated with numbing regularity: think about the audience. Unless I am talking specifically about a readership, I use the word "audience" to describe all consumers across all platforms – print, web, social, television and radio. They are the customers, the people at whom your work is aimed. Always consider their wants and needs. Data analytics make it possible to find out who they are and what they are doing in much greater detail than in the past. Commercial news providers have an obvious imperative to do this, because if they do not serve their customers, they risk going out of business. The BBC as a public service broadcaster acknowledges it too. One of its many mantras is "audiences are at the heart of everything we do".

Thinking about the audience is one of the ways in which journalism must respond to the seismic changes that are still reverberating. It needs to understand that audiences are not the same as they were. They are more diverse, they inhabit different spaces, they behave differently, they communicate differently, they form their opinions on the basis of different sources. Paradoxically, they have access to thousands of times more information, and yet show signs of becoming less open-minded and less accepting of points of view that do not chime with their own. Public debate has become more polarised and less tolerant of shades of opinion or different perspectives – coarsened, as some describe it. Journalism needs to find ways of re-connecting with consumers in a way that for a long time it was painfully slow to do. It needs to be where they are, to understand what they are now looking for from a news provider and to establish a trustworthy presence. Now that audiences have the power to speak as well as to listen, journalism must give them the means to be heard. It must accept and come to terms with the disruptiveness of social media platforms that have so loosened the grip of the mainstream media, and find the best way of bringing authority and trustworthiness into the social world. This places a responsibility on every individual journalist, however junior. This will be your world – and your responsibility.

A pessimist might discern in all of this an industry in terminal decline, overtaken by events and no longer trusted or needed by its audience: a marginalised and outmoded business, thrashing about helplessly, and incapable of asserting itself in a world turned inside out within the working lives of a single generation of journalists. But all is very far from being lost. Fewer people buy a daily newspaper, it is true – but plenty still do. Many more read and view news and current affairs from the mainstream media online and on their phones. Millions of people still tune in for television news bulletins. Radio remains a healthy me-dium. And there is much brave and revelatory investigative work being carried out in all media in the finest traditions of journalism. The bad and the corrupt are still being exposed. There is still courageous reporting from the front lines of conflicts or natural disasters. Politicians and chief executives are still being held to account. The fact-checking or reality-checking teams employed by most big media organ-isations are collectively doing more to expose the weak, the spurious and the downright dishonest than has ever been the case before. Data journalists with analytical skills are finding more and more powerful stories online. Bright lights are still being shone into dark places. These are the things the best journalism has always been about.

It is into this complicated world that you are taking your first tentative steps as a young journalist. This book attempts to prepare you for it, by describing how today's newsrooms work and offering practical advice across the whole range of media platforms and roles. The situation just described is the big picture. But the bulk of this book takes you directly to your desk in the newsroom – or to your kitchen or spare bedroom if you find yourself part of the increasing trend towards working from home. It helps you with the detail of the tasks you can expect to be given. When you have your NCTJ Diploma, you will work in ways very different from your predecessors of only a decade or so earlier. Thanks to your NCTJ course and what you learn from this book, you will possess a wide range of skills across media platforms, and be able to move easily between them. You will understand how to operate within an ethical framework, redrawn and given renewed impetus in the aftermath of the phone hacking scandal. You will have a survival guide for the new environment.

The NCTJ syllabus is rooted in the traditional values that have always been a part of good journalism practice and remain so, no matter what storms have been raging outside. In a world in which professional journalism can feel under siege from all sides, this should be seen as a reason to be cheerful. Journalism's principal defence, or perhaps its most potent weapon of counter attack, is to keep faith with those val-ues, and to stand by the time-honoured dedication to accuracy, inquiry, fair dealing and the provision of trustworthy well-founded information of the sort needed by every citizen in a democratic society. It needs to understand the relationship between best practice and new practice, and to minimise the gap between them. The overall picture may seem gloomy. But professional journalism has the chance to show that it is more important than ever in the modern world.

You are part of that mission. How trustworthy news is produced and distributed may have changed pro-foundly in the last few years; but as the Preface argued, the core values that underpin the best journalism have not changed. The challenge for today's journalists is to reaffirm those values and understand how they can best be applied in a world turned topsy-turvy by an unprecedented amount of change in a very short time. That is a large part of what this book is about – identifying good practice and understanding how to apply it in radically changed circumstances.

Prior to the coronavirus pandemic, it seemed unlikely that the next ten years would see change across the board on the same scale as the previous ten. That looks less certain now. The head of one large regional newspaper publishing group reported that they had done more work on their digital offer in the first three months of coronavirus than they had in the whole of the previous five years. There is also a feeling of adaptation and stabilisation, as journalism explores and exploits the immensely powerful tools that we all now have at our fingertips, and attempts to reassert its worth, re-establish its reputation and develop a secure long-term financial industry model. Old models of sales and advertising are being replaced by new ways of developing a profitable business around a specific audience. Industry players old and new will aim to offer a safe and dependable haven – both online and still, in many cases, off it – for those who find the speed and volume of the wider digital world too much to handle, and the information overload both bewildering and burdensome.

It is a dynamic, fast-moving, risky time, and not everyone will survive unscathed. But do not be daunted. This book will also aim to convey what any journalist will tell you: that journalism is an exciting, challenging and above all fun way of earning a living, one that few would be prepared to exchange for any other. You should find it energising to be entering a world in which so much is going on, in which so many options are open to you and in which you have a genuine opportunity to be part of the new journalism that emerges.

The UK media scene

The media landscape in the UK is complex and mature, and probably second only to the US in its size. The sheer scope of the industry is astonishing: around ten national newspapers published every day, with hundreds more regional and local dailies and weeklies; a huge magazine sector; continuous television news services and built news programmes across several mass-audience channels; hundreds of radio stations with news as the spine of their output; countless apps and websites; and the whole panoply of social networks. It adds up to a huge volume of news available on multiple outlets. As consumers, we are literally spoilt for choice. That sheer weight of options can be intimidating, and it is not always easy to know where to go for the best and most trustworthy information. As a journalist, you must stay informed. But it is not physically possible to read and watch and listen to all this news output.

This section aims to help you understand the market better, by looking in more detail at some of the principal sources of news. We will take a short tour of the UK media scene, to help you develop some knowledge of what is out there, and which sources are likely to be of most use to you. Armed with that knowledge, you will be offered some suggestions about how to pick and choose in such a way that you remain fully informed, without your entire life being taken over by the consumption of news.

Newspapers

We will start with the oldest form of news provision – the printed newspaper. As we shall see, broadcasters are required by law to be balanced and impartial in their coverage. Newspapers labour under no such obligation. As long as they observe the codes of practice we will be looking at in Chapter 4, they can be as opinionated and as partisan as they wish. You can see this in action most clearly in the sphere of political coverage, with most newspapers unabashedly supporting one political party over another. The overall picture is not balanced: there are more traditionally Conservative-supporting papers than there are Labour, which can count only on the *Daily Mirror* for steadfast endorsement. Neither was the picture balanced when it came to the most important and divisive political issue of recent years: Britain's continued membership of the European Union (EU). The issue cut across political allegiances, and a majority of the national newspapers – including the two with the largest circulations, the *Sun* and the *Daily Mail* – were strongly in favour of Britain leaving the Union. Their relentless promotion of the Leave cause, and their coverage of successive General Election campaigns, will have had an influence on their readers – the voters – and therefore on the ultimate results of these polls. How much of an effect, it is difficult to measure.

The habit of reading a physical daily newspaper – or perhaps more than one – is rapidly disappearing. People seek faster and more easily accessible ways of keeping up with the news. Younger people seldom buy a newspaper, and often read one only if they find a discarded free sheet left on the bus or the train. The circulation of most newspapers of all kinds has been in steady decline for years, largely because of the availability of constantly updated information on the internet. Even so, the nationals still sell millions of copies a day between them, and still boast considerable political influence. And almost all of them have embraced the internet to potent effect, with some of their apps and websites popular around the world. Models vary, especially on the key question of whether to provide online content free or to charge for it.

Old hands see the decline of the printed newspaper as something to be lamented. They maintain that those who read their newspapers online are missing something. A newspaper in your hands offers a different, more tactile and more leisurely reading experience, and there is always the serendipitous possibility of happening upon a well-illustrated story or article that you might pass over online, but which you are glad to have discovered. No doubt there is something in this – after all, people of all age groups are still prepared to part with much larger sums of money to buy periodicals or magazines devoted to both general and special interests. But there is no room in commerce for sentiment, and for newspapers, continuing decline looks inevitable.

Even so, as a young reporter you should make it your business to look at the newspapers as often as possible, in their printed form if you can, as well as online. You will find that most other daily news journalists do at least to some extent, and it is important to be part of the newsroom conversation, especially as editorial calls are being made. All forms of journalism constantly watch and feed off each other.

What follows is a brief look at each of the national newspapers, giving some sense of their size, history, ownership and political stance, so that when reading them you get a sense of where they are coming from, and why they express the opinions they do. I quote circulation figures to give an idea of the size of each paper's readership relative to the others. Those figures are changing all the time – and the movement is all downwards. They are collated by the Audit Bureau of Circulations. Figures quoted below are from its 2021 reports, unless stated. They reflect the fact that the pandemic had a huge effect on circulation across the board.

The national newspapers are generally divided into two or three categories. The "quality" or "broadsheet" papers, supposedly offering more serious and intelligent content, are *The Times*, *Financial Times (FT)*, *Daily Telegraph*, *Guardian* and *Independent*. The latter now exists only online, publishing a newspaper-like app edition to retain a sense of its former printed self. The word "broadsheet" is a printer's term referring to the actual physical size of the printed page: only the *Daily Telegraph* and the *FT* are still broadsheet in that strict sense, but the term is still used to refer generically to the higher end of the market.

The other newspapers are printed in a smaller format known as "tabloid". Some of the tabloids – the *Daily Mirror*, *Sun* and *Daily Star* – are also sometimes known as "red tops" because of their scarlet front-page mastheads. These are high-circulation papers aimed at a mass audience, with an emphasis on bold headlines, strong colours, big pictures, striking stories and a commitment to entertaining readers as well as informing them.

Somewhere in the middle we find the *Daily Mail* and the *Daily Express* – tabloids in the technical sense of size, but seeing themselves as appealing to a rather more sophisticated market than the red tops. Their readership is sometimes referred to as "middle England". This is usually taken to mean the aspirational middle class, a large section of society occupying the political centre. The votes of these people swing elections, so they are heavily courted by all the major parties, giving these papers a particularly powerful influence at election time.

Prior to the pandemic, one newspaper – the *Metro* – had a readership bigger than all of these, in spite of being only 20 or so years old. It is a middle-market tabloid that is distributed free across major towns and cities throughout the UK, excluding Northern Ireland. This model made it particularly vulnerable to the effects of national lockdowns.

The national newspapers are still often referred to collectively as "Fleet Street", after the street in London where most of them once had their headquarters. None of them is based there now, but the label survives.

THE TIMES
- Founded 1788
- Sister paper: *Sunday Times*
- Owner: News Corp (Rupert Murdoch)
- Political stance: moderate
- Circulation: c360,000 (2020)

The *Times* is one of the oldest and most distinguished British daily national newspapers, and retains a respected reputation in the market. With The *Sunday Times*, it is owned by the media tycoon Rupert Murdoch (who also owns the *Sun*). Though traditionally a moderate newspaper and sometimes a supporter of the Conservatives, it supported Labour in the 2001 and 2005 general elections. The *Times* urged readers to vote Remain in the EU referendum of 2016. It endorsed the Conservatives in 2019.

THE DAILY TELEGRAPH
- Founded 1855
- Sister paper: *Sunday Telegraph*
- Owner: Telegraph Media Group (For sale at time of writing)
- Political stance: Conservative
- Circulation: c360,000 (2019)

The *Daily Telegraph* is politically Conservative, to the extent that it is nicknamed "the Torygraph". Even when public support for the Conservatives slumped during the ascendancy of Labour in the early 2000s, The *Telegraph* remained loyal to the party. It was one of the most ardent of the Eurosceptics, consistently arguing for a British exit from the EU. As Boris Johnson was its star columnist, The *Telegraph* unsurprisingly supported him in the 2019 election.

THE GUARDIAN
- Founded 1821
- Sister paper: *Observer*
- Owner: Guardian Media Group (Scott Trust)
- Political stance: centre left
- Circulation: c110,000

The *Guardian*, which was known as the *Manchester Guardian* until 1959, describes itself as a paper of the centre left. It supported the Liberal Democrats during the 2010 general election, and the Labour Party in 2015 and 2017. In the 2016 EU referendum campaign, it urged readers to vote Remain. The Guardian Media Group is owned by the Scott Trust, which exists to secure the paper's financial and editorial independence. It is sometimes referred to as "the Grauniad" – a reference to a past weakness for spelling and typographical errors.

THE FINANCIAL TIMES (FT)
- Founded 1888
- Owner: Nikkei (Japanese media company)
- Political stance: various – pro-Coalition 2015
- Circulation: c100,000

The *FT*, as it generally known, specialises in news for the business community. The circulation figure above is for UK sales of the distinctive pink broadsheet, but the *FT* is an international publication with a large worldwide readership. It claims to have more than a million paying subscriptions, most of them subscribers to the digital version. Politically, it sided with the Conservatives in 2017, and backed the Remain campaign for continued EU membership.

THE INDEPENDENT
- 1986–2016: since then, digital only
- Sister paper: *Independent on Sunday*
- Principal owner: Lebedev family
- Political stance: independent

The *Indie*, as it is popularly known, was the first national newspaper in recent times to have stopped publishing in hard copy and to exist only online – a decision taken in 2016 because of falling circulation. It is owned by the Russian tycoon Alexander Lebedev and his son Lord (Evgeny) Lebedev, who also own the London *Evening Standard*. The *Independent* is not associated with any political party, and its editorial and comment pages reflect a range of views with a broadly progressive and liberal character. As its name suggests, the paper originally described itself as "free from party political bias, free from proprietorial influence". This banner was dropped from the front page in 2011.

THE i
- Founded 2010
- Owner: Daily Mail and General Trust
- Political stance: independent
- Circulation: c140,000

The *i* was a spin-off from The *Independent*, published as a tabloid daily and carrying the news in a digest form. It is however regarded as being a part of the "quality" press. The *i* soon achieved a larger circulation than the main paper. When The *Independent* ceased print publication, The *i* was sold to the regional newspaper group Johnston Press, and subsequently to the publishers of the *Daily Mail*.

THE DAILY MAIL
- Founded 1896
- Sister paper: *Mail on Sunday*
- Owner: Daily Mail and General Trust
- Political stance: Conservative
- Circulation: c950,000

The *Daily Mail* is a middle-market tabloid created by Lord Northcliffe, the father of popular journalism. It jostles with the *Sun* for the title of the UK's biggest-selling paid-for daily newspaper. Like many of its readers, the *Mail* has traditionally been a supporter of the Conservative Party, and has endorsed it in all recent general elections. While the paper retained its support for the Conservatives in 2015, it urged Conservatively inclined readers to vote tactically for the UK Independence Party (UKIP) in constituencies where Labour was the main challenger. The *Mail* was a strong voice in the EU Leave campaign – although its sister paper The *Mail on Sunday* was in the Remain camp.

THE DAILY EXPRESS

- Founded 1900
- Sister paper: *Sunday Express*
- Owner: Reach plc (also owners of the Daily Mirror and Daily Star)
- Political stance: Conservative, UKIP
- Circulation: c240,000

The *Daily Express* is another middle-market paper with a similar readership and outlook to that of the *Mail*, and was founded at about the same time. Before the 2001 election, when it backed the Labour Party, the newspaper had supported the Conservatives in every election since the Second World War. An enthusiast for the Leave EU campaign, it supported UKIP in 2015, returning to the Tories in 2017.

THE SUN

- Founded 1964
- Sister paper: *Sun on Sunday* (successor to the News of the World)
- Owner: News Corp (Rupert Murdoch)
- Political stance: Swing voter
- Circulation: c1.4m (2019)

The *Sun* is one of the younger dailies and has the largest circulation. Like The *Times*, it is owned by Rupert Murdoch, giving him influence at both ends of the market. The *Sun* made its name with bright, bold and brash journalism that attracted a large working-class readership. The *Sun on Sunday* was launched in 2012 after the *News of the World* was closed down in the wake of the phone hacking scandal.

The *Sun* does not have a fixed political creed and likes to think of itself as a kingmaker in British politics. It has campaigned for both the main parties. In spite of their profile, many of the readers of *the Sun* are Conservative voters, or have voted at various times for both Labour and the Conservatives. The paper throws its whole weight behind whichever party it decides to back at election time. On the morning of the 1992 general election, the paper urged readers to vote for the Conservatives and reject the Labour leader Neil Kinnock. Its front page read: "If Kinnock wins today, will the last person to leave Britain please turn out the lights". Labour had been leading in the polls, but were defeated – convincing the *Sun* that its intervention had swung the election. In another famous front page it declared: "It's the Sun wot won it!"

Five years later, the *Sun* joined the Labour bandwagon, and supported Tony Blair as he went on to win three elections in a row. By 2010, it was back in the Conservative camp, where it remains. The *Sun* backed the Leave campaign in the EU referendum.

THE DAILY MIRROR

- Founded 1903
- Sister paper: *Sunday Mirror*
- Owner: Reach plc (formerly Trinity Mirror)
- Political stance: Labour
- Circulation: c365,000

The *Mirror* was originally aimed at a middle-class readership but transformed itself into a working-class newspaper after 1934. As such it has traditionally and consistently backed the Labour Party, and was the only tabloid to campaign for a Remain vote in the EU referendum.

THE METRO
- Founded 1999
- Owner: Daily Mail and General Trust plc
- Political stance: none
- Circulation: c600,000 (the worst-hit by the pandemic: the 2020 figure was c1.4m)

The *Metro* is owned by the Daily Mail Group and has the highest circulation of any UK print newspaper. It is published Monday to Friday in a tabloid format, and distributed free on public transport and in airports and hospitals in major towns and cities across England, Wales and Scotland. It has never endorsed any political party or candidate and describes itself as politically neutral.

THE DAILY STAR
- Founded 1978
- Sister papers: *Daily Express, Daily Star Sunday*
- Owner: Reach plc
- Political stance: none
- Circulation: c220,000

The *Daily Star* emulates the bold and eye-catching format of the *Sun*, but is much less a vehicle for telling the news and simply aims to be an entertaining read. It carries little political coverage and has rarely expressed support for any particular party.

National/regional press

The national dailies publish separate editions in the different nations and regions of the UK, and the nations have their own publications – Scotland, for example, has The *Scotsman*, the *Daily Record* and the *Herald*. Most big towns and cities have their own newspapers, many of them publishing daily. Those with the biggest circulations are:

– *Wolverhampton Express and Star*
– *Aberdeen Press and Journal*
– *Manchester Evening News*
– *Liverpool Echo*
– *Belfast Telegraph*
– *Dundee Courier*
– *The Irish News (Belfast)*
– *Eastern Daily Press (Norfolk)*
– *Glasgow Herald*
– *Hull Daily Mail.*

Only two of these are independently owned – the others belong to larger media conglomerates that publish many regional daily and weekly newspapers. Three of the titles listed above (those in

Manchester, Liverpool and Hull) belong to Reach plc, formerly Trinity Mirror, which also owns national daily titles.

Periodicals

Prominent among magazines that feature extensive political and current affairs coverage are:

The Economist: targets highly educated readers – many of them overseas – and claims an audience containing many influential executives and policy-makers.

The New Statesman: has a left-of-centre political viewpoint.

The Spectator: has a right-of-centre political stance, and is the oldest continuously published magazine in the English language (founded 1828). Editorship of *The Spectator* has often been a step on the ladder to high office in the Conservative Party – in the case of Boris Johnson, the highest office of all.

Private Eye: sometimes called the house magazine of Fleet Street, the "Eye" was founded in 1961 as a satirical current affairs magazine specialising in inside track investigative stories and gossip from the worlds of politics and journalism among others.

All of these publications can also be read online to a greater or lesser degree, though may require payment of a subscription for some or all of the content.

Television

National and international television news channels, many of them streamed online, make it easy to catch up with the news at any time. Most of these channels offer regular updates of the news of the day, and will sustain lengthy periods of continuous coverage of breaking stories as they happen. (See also Chapter 17.)

The main 24-hour television news channels are:

- **Sky News**
- **BBC News Channel** for UK audiences
- **BBC World** serves international audiences
- **CNN** the first 24-hour channel, based in the USA
- **CNN International** for international audiences
- **MSNBC** part of NBC News, USA
- **Bloomberg** global business channel
- **Fox News Channel** often accused of slanting the news in favour of the US Republican Party and conservative causes
- **Al Jazeera English** based in Qatar; news from an Arabic perspective.
- two new UK television news channels launch in 2021: Rupert Murdoch's **News UK TV** and **GB News**, fronted by former BBC anchor Andrew Neil

In addition, there are English-language channels such as RT (Russia Today), sponsored by foreign governments in order to promote their own perspectives to international audiences.

Within the UK, the most-watched continuous channels are those specialising in the UK and world news: Sky and the BBC News Channel. Both are streamed online. It is a good idea to dip into each of them every now and then during the day, to catch up with what is happening and to compare and contrast the different ways in which they tackle and rank stories. There are news summaries at the top of every hour.

Traditional television news bulletins, in which the day's news is packaged into programmes of about half an hour in length, still deliver large audiences. Rather like printed newspapers, these traditional formats remain popular with older audiences who watch them as they are broadcast (rather than through catch-up services) and so keep what media analysts call an "appointment to view" with their favourite news programmes.

The main "built" bulletins are:

– **BBC News** at Six o'Clock
– **BBC News** at Ten o'Clock
– **ITV** Evening News (at 1830)
– **News at Ten** (ITV).

Channel 4 News (at 1900) is a longer programme, combining news with interviews and other current affairs elements. The news bulletins for ITV, Channel 4 and Channel 5 are made by Independent Television News (ITN).

Newsnight at or soon after 2230 on BBC2 is the BBC's late night current affairs programme.

In addition, there are regional television news programmes of around half an hour on BBC1 (at 1830, after the national news) and on ITV (at 1800, before the national news). And there are longer-form current affairs documentary strands such as Panorama and Dispatches.

Sunday is the day for the heavyweight interview-based political programmes, which frequently create news lines for the later news bulletins.

Do not feel the need to watch all of these programmes exhaustively, but try to catch at least some television news every day, even if you do not watch a programme from beginning to end. Have a look at the BBC news one day, and then try ITN the following day. Compare Channel 4 News with Newsnight. As well as keeping up, you will get a sense of their different agendas and the different ways in which they approach and present stories, as well as a feel for some of the techniques of television news reporting.

Radio

There are a number of national 24-hour news-dominated radio stations, (see also Chapter 15). Among them are:

LBC News, a commercial sister station of LBC (originally the London Broadcasting Company), was launched in 2019 as a national station of rolling news, travel and weather.

talkRADIO, a sister station of talkSPORT, is a national talk station with regular news updates.

BBC Radio Five Live is a 24-hour news and sport channel combining live coverage of sporting events with a semi-formal, magazine-style service of news, discussion, interactivity and analysis.

BBC World Service is an international news channel with a global agenda, broadcast to audiences around the world, although it can also be heard in the UK. The channel enjoys a high degree of prestige and respect in many parts of the world, especially in the former Soviet Union and totalitarian states where it is, or has been, the only source of independent news available to the population. The World Service broadcasts in more than 40 languages.

Times Radio is a digital news station owned by News UK, and was launched in June 2020.

Radio 4

Outside these channels, most radio news programming is broadcast by the BBC on its main speech network, Radio 4. The daily current affairs programmes, or "sequences" as they are known, are broadcast at regular points in the daily schedule. The main programmes are:

Today

0600–0900 Monday–Saturday. The most influential news programme on the radio, with a large and discerning audience. *Today* reports the overnight news to a breakfast audience, but also likes to think of itself as setting the agenda for the day ahead, previewing and discussing the stories that are likely to unfold later. There are bulletins of news at the top of each hour – listening to one of them is a great way of briefing yourself and preparing yourself for the news day.

The World at One

1300–1345 Monday–Friday, 1300–1330 on Sunday. Begins with a news bulletin and then discusses the main stories of the morning and what will follow later, often with a strong bent towards domestic political issues.

PM

1700–1800 Monday–Friday, with a different format on Saturdays. A news magazine programme with reportage and discussion of the day's news.

The Six O'Clock News

A 30-minute bulletin of straight reportage, read by a newsreader (as opposed to a journalist or presenter) and carrying a wide range of reports and analysis from correspondents. If you manage to catch only one news programme in the evening, you could do a lot worse than choose this one.

The World Tonight

2200–2245 Monday–Friday. A news and discussion programme, with a more international and slightly more discursive bent.

The Midnight News

The same format as at six o'clock for those coming in late who have missed the news of the day. Again, half an hour of straight news reports.

Radio 1

In addition to the Radio 4 provision, Radio 1 has its own news team producing **Newsbeat** for a younger audience. The network broadcasts two 15-minute editions of *Newsbeat* each day, at 1245 and 1745.

As with television, you need to be selective, depending on where you are and your availability to listen. Vary your listening day by day, to contrast styles and treatments. Catching some of *Today* is a good way of briefing yourself for the day ahead.

Websites, social media, apps

You will have access to some or all of the news sources mentioned above via apps or live streams on your smartphone. You will also be monitoring your favourite social networks, which are an excellent source of news alerts, even if you go elsewhere for a more detailed account of events. A few minutes spent first thing on a news website such as the BBC, Sky, *The Times* or *The Guardian* is a very quick and efficient way of starting your news day, and these are also good places to find short backgrounders and explainers to the main stories if you are not familiar with them.

There are also a number of online-only news providers, most of them providing free content, with a heavy emphasis on video, and funding themselves through advertising. They have not been immune from the economic pressures that have affected traditional providers.

HuffPost (formerly the *Huffington Post*) was the first internet newspaper when it was launched in 2005. As with most other news providers, it aims to offer breaking news, original journalism, and reporting on the real lives of its readers.

BuzzFeed News is part of the larger digital media company BuzzFeed, which was founded in 2006. It prides itself on its investigative reporting as well as its core news coverage, and claims a global audience of around 650 million, 70 per cent of them accessing the content on mobile phones.

Vice News is a part of the larger Vice Media Group, and publishes through a website and a YouTube channel. It was launched in 2013, claiming to specialise in "under-reported stories".

Keeping informed: your news day

Clearly there is far too much output for any one person to keep across everything. You would go mad if you tried. You will want to select a manageable range of reliable sources and revisit them regularly. This is increasingly how audiences in general behave – where once they might have got all their news from one source, they are now more likely to use more than one medium across the day. If you get into the habit of doing that, keeping up will soon become a natural part of your daily life, and you will hardly notice that you are doing it. You don't have to watch, listen to or read everything – just give yourself a good range of tasters every day.

You have two objectives:

– To keep up with what is happening, so that you can be sure you are not missing anything. You probably do this already – checking your feeds, social networks or favourite apps at regular intervals. It will sometimes take no more than a few seconds to satisfy yourself that nothing significant has happened since you last looked.
– To have a basic understanding of what each story is about: the key facts, the issues, the arguments. This can be achieved with some selective consumption across a range of outlets – not sticking to the same ones all the time.

By varying the sources by which you keep up to speed, you will also be educating yourself in multimedia journalism, noting how the same stories receive different treatments according to the medium, time of day, likely audience and so on. It will help familiarise you with the different techniques of print, digital and broadcast.

With all that in mind, here is what your news consumption might look like on a typical day:

First thing

When you wake up, check one or two of your news apps and social accounts to see what has happened overnight and what seems to be creating most interest. While you are getting yourself organised for the day, catch half an hour of *Today*, including a news bulletin.

Morning

Have a look at a newspaper or more than one if you have the chance – preferably in hard copy form, but otherwise online, where you will also find digests of what is in all the papers. Some news outlets charge for online access – subscribe to one or two if you can.

Keep a regular eye on your news feeds and/or continuous TV channels.

Lunchtime

Try to catch some television news (BBC or ITV) or some radio news (*World at One*) – both on at 1300.

Afternoon

Keep a regular eye on your news feeds and/or continuous TV channels. Check live pages on news websites for new developments on the big stories. The afternoon is when many stories emerge, so there may be events to keep across – such as statements in the House of Commons or press conferences. They will probably be carried live on continuous channels on both radio and television, as well as on new websites – where live blogs provide instant analysis alongside the coverage.

Evening

Between 1700 and 2000, take in some of *PM* or the *Radio 4 Six o'Clock News*, and one of the television bulletins or some of *Channel 4 News*. Hop around – you don't have to stick with any of them all the way through if you don't want to, and it is useful to compare and contrast the way different outlets select and treat stories.

Late evening

Watch some of the ITN or BBC bulletins at ten o'clock, and some of Newsnight after 1030.

All this might still seem a lot, and the time you have available to do it will vary according to what else you are doing. But this is not an unusual level of consumption for a working journalist. It may well reflect the way you already behave, checking in frequently on your smartphone. All you are doing is expanding your range a little by listening to some radio and watching some television. It might add up to a couple of hours a day, but it is broken up into short segments. If you miss all of this programing because you have other things to do, a lot of it is available, sometimes for limited periods, via catch-up services.

Set yourself up at the start of the day with some knowledge of the stories that are around, and then update and top up as the day goes on. Think of this not as a chore, but as integral to your daily routine and a key part of your job. As a journalist, you have a responsibility to know and understand what the big stories are and some of the background behind them. It is intrinsic to a professional approach to the job and your ability to do it well.

Skimming the papers

We have referred to the diminishing role the printed press plays in the news business. But newspapers still have a powerful influence on the way the entire news industry discusses and responds to stories. Reviews of what the papers are saying feature in a lot of late evening and early morning broadcast output, and there will be sets of papers in their printed versions in many newsrooms.

Looking through a whole set of morning editions can feel like quite a big investment of time and effort, especially at the weekend, when there are so many weighty sections and supplements. But if you know your way round a newspaper, you can skim one quite quickly, only lingering over stories that catch your eye if you have the leisure to read them.

Here is a quick guide to the constituent parts of the typical newspaper.

The front page

This is where the paper presents what it considers to be its main story of the day – the "lead" or "splash". It will appear under a large headline, often accompanied by a picture. Some of the tabloids devote so much space to the headline and picture that there is room only for a few words of text – one or two paragraphs at most, trailing to the rest of the story on an inside page. This has the advantage – to them – that if you want to read the full story you have to buy the paper.

Front pages are also used to trail the content inside – features, reader offers, sports coverage and so on. So in every sense, the role of the front page is to persuade you to part with money to buy the paper and savour the treats inside.

Page three

When you turn the pages of a newspaper, book or magazine, your eye is naturally drawn to the right-hand side first. Page three is the first one you will turn to, and it is the place newspapers often place stories they think readers will find appealing, even if they are not the strongest in hard news terms. These may be picture-led stories, lurid court reports or anything that is just plain interesting. The *Sun* famously invented Page Three Girls, although these days there is less interest in and tolerance for pictures of half-naked women.

Page two

Note that by contrast, page two is usually a place for more prosaic stories, or the completion of stories that begun on the front page. Much less effort goes into the design and presentation of page two, simply because our eyes are naturally focused elsewhere.

News pages

The next few pages will normally be devoted to British news, followed in the broadsheets with some pages of world/international news.

Leaders/op eds/opinion pieces

Most papers devote a column to expressing their own views on the big story or stories of the day. This is called the "leader", or the comment or editorial column. On the same page, or the facing page, or both, there will be further comment columns – "op eds" (as in "opposite the editorial") by staff correspondents or guest writers – politicians, polemicists or subject experts. These are the elements in which the newspaper's political stance is evident. The articles will often appear below provocative headlines.

Letters

Most newspapers still make space for letters from their readers, and they are always worth a glance. They can give you an insight into the sort of people who read the paper, what their views are and what is exercising them. If the letter writers are well-known people or in positions of authority, they might well be potential interviewees on a story, now or in the future.

Features

Then there are the general feature pages, of longer-form, softer pieces, including reviews. There will usually be plenty of puzzles and brain teasers. Crosswords have long been a staple of the daily paper, and there are Sudoku, Codewords, horoscopes and quizzes as well. These are popular with readers and may occupy several pages.

Sports

Sport is a huge seller of newspapers, and many publish separate supplements every day. Business and financial news might also have dedicated sections.

So if you just want to get the bones of what is in the paper that day, have a look at the lead story and page three, flick through the news pages to see what catches your eye and then read the leader column and some of the "op ed" coverage. You will learn to skim, and this will not take many minutes. Try to look at more than one paper in this way every day, for the purposes of comparison. You do not have to read every paper every day. But try to spread your reading and avoid always looking at the same ones.

In sum, you can keep yourself fully informed by a "little and often" approach through the day in a way that does not have to take over your life. Get a sense at the start of the day of what the main stories and talking points are, and then check for updates in the hours that follow. You probably look at your phone every few minutes anyway – have a look at your news feeds while you are there. Choose a small number of apps that you like and trust, and use them as the basis for these regular update checks and for your wider consumption. Dip in regularly to as many sources as you can, so you maintain a sense of different media, different political perspectives, different treatments and so on. Not only will this help you keep up with how the stories are developing, but it will also enable you to absorb useful insights into the nature of the various news providers, their viewpoints and the way they operate. All this will be helpful when you come to write your own stories.

2

The nature of journalism: the nature of news

what is journalism?.... what is journalism for?....exercising and defending freedom of speech.....holding power to account.....exposing wrongdoing.....giving a voice to the voiceless.....unearthing hidden stories.....what is news?.....is it news?.....journalism and news: the same or different?

You have decided you would like to become a journalist. Good choice. It is an endlessly fascinating and stimulating business in which no two days are the same, and you will find it both enjoyable and rewarding. If you are interested in people and in the world around you, you could not have made a better decision.

It is a choice you might have made for a number of reasons: a love of words, or the process of writing and storytelling perhaps; an itch to find things out; an urge to understand why things happen, and how events relate to each other; a desire to communicate, and to report the news.

You might also have given some thoughts to the wider role of journalism, its mission and responsibilities, and its importance in underpinning the rights of the citizen in a free country. These are more theoretical ideas about journalism serving a particular social purpose, and as the world changes, and journalism changes with it, they need constantly to be reinforced and reasserted.

An understanding of the purpose of journalism, what it is actually *for*, is an important preliminary to learning how to do it, and how to do it properly and well. In this chapter, we will address some fundamental questions about the business you are joining. What is journalism? What is news? Are they the same things? What are their purposes?

This is an important starting place. But it need not entangle us too deeply in theory or philosophy. Indeed, journalists have a near-pathological fear of anything that sounds pretentious or pseudo-intellectual. Most do not regard themselves as following a "profession". The former newspaper editor and distinguished BBC broadcaster Andrew Marr wrote a book about his life in journalism. He called it "My Trade". To others it is a craft – a skill to be developed – or simply a job or an occupation. In the British culture at least, there is a reluctance among journalists to over-intellectualise what they do. They scorn pretentiousness, pomposity and unnecessary complexity.

What is journalism?

As all journalists should, we will keep things simple, with a basic, clear, neutral and factual definition:

Journalism is the activity of gathering, assessing and presenting news and information.

This is a good start. An even pithier comment, by the celebrated American editor and publisher John S Knight, emphasises that what you present needs to be accurate:

> Get the truth and print it.

The veteran BBC journalist, Jeremy Paxman, former long-time presenter of the current affairs programme *Newsnight*, puts it equally straightforwardly:

> Journalism is basically finding things out and telling people about them.

As a brisk and unambiguous description, that is also hard to beat. A similar thought seems to have been in the mind of Tom Brokaw, a long-serving American news anchor who presented *NBC Nightly News* for more than 20 years. He said:

> It's all storytelling. That's what journalism is all about.

And this next definition, taken from the forerunner of this book, *Essential Reporting*, makes the same point, but goes a little further – introducing the idea of journalism having an obligation to promote understanding, as well as simply report what is happening:

> The media's most important role is to tell the public what is going on, and why.

Again, as a one-sentence summary of the role of journalism, this is pretty good. There are lots of different forms of journalism, fulfilling lots of different purposes, but at its heart it is about gathering and conveying useful information. But those two little words at the end: "and why" are also very significant. Not only is it the role of journalists to *report* the news, they also have a duty to try to *explain* and make sense of it, to provide "news you can use". In a complex world, and one in which misinformation can take root swiftly on social media, the explanatory role of journalism is more vital than ever.

In the mission statement of the BBC, one of the world's foremost providers of news and journalism, this process is seen as being about educating audiences:

> To inform, to educate and to entertain.

This is the mission statement of the whole organisation, not just the news division. But it applies particularly to news – yes, even the reference to "entertaining". If your news is not interesting and engaging, no one will take any notice of it, and you are wasting your time producing it.

All these definitions have slightly different emphases, but the same core theme is common to all: journalism is about finding things out, and reporting and explaining them in an interesting, accessible way. That holds true in the age of the internet and social media.

Of course, not everyone sees journalism and journalists as deserving of unqualified admiration. They suffer from low public esteem, way down near the bottom of the pile, with estate agents, car salesmen, bankers and, of course, politicians. There is a stereotype of journalists as ruthless, amoral and rather grubby creatures who are prepared to trample over anyone or anything in pursuit of a story. And sometimes – more often than we might like to admit – there is some truth in that characterisation.

This jaundiced view of journalism is not new. For evidence of that, we need look no further than a famous little rhyme written in the 1920s by a British poet, Humbert Wolfe. No doubt he spends a lot of time turning in his grave, because although he wrote reams of other stuff, this oft-quoted verse is pretty much the only thing for which he is remembered now:

You cannot hope to bribe or twist
Thank God! The British journalist.
But seeing what the man will do
Unbribed, there's no occasion to

Unscrupulous, unfeeling, economical with the truth. That is the cliché of the hard-bitten, hard-drinking hack reporter with a dirty raincoat and a foot in the door. There is a degree of general cynicism about news values and priorities as well – what journalists consider worthy of reporting. Here is the American politician Adlai Stevenson:

Newspaper editors are men who separate the wheat from the chaff – and then print the chaff.

His is another common criticism, again not without force – that journalism tends to focus on the trivial and the sensational at the expense of the significant, which can be difficult, complicated and perhaps a bit dull as well.

GK Chesterton, an English writer and sometime journalist who was active at the start of the 20th century, took a similar view about the banality and irrelevance of much of the popular journalism of the day:

Journalism consists largely in saying 'Lord Jones is dead' to people who never knew Lord Jones was alive.

Oddly, some of the most cynical observations about the business emanated from a man who could lay claim to be the father of popular journalism. Alfred Harmsworth, later Lord Northcliffe, the founder of the *Daily Mail* and the *Daily Mirror* among others, was a pioneer of mass-market tabloid newspapers for readers of all classes. Judging by this remark, he did not regard it as a high calling:

Journalism: a profession whose business is to explain to others what it does not understand itself.

A century on, and with a very great deal of water having passed under the bridge, there is still more than a grain of truth in these observations. But whatever its shortcomings, it is widely acknowledged that journalism has an important and serious role to play in society, and especially in a democracy. So much so that the news media are sometimes informally referred to as "The Fourth Estate", implying equal status with the three great pillars of the state – the Executive (government), the Legislature (Parliament) and the Judiciary (law courts).

What is journalism for?

To help us begin to explore that role further, here is another famous, and more charitable idea, reflecting that more serious character:

Journalism is the first rough draft of history.

It is often attributed to Philip Graham, publisher of the *Washington Post* in the 1950s, although there are suggestions that it was not original to him. On this definition, journalism is an attempt not just to report, but also to analyse and contextualise events more or less as they happen – which of course can have a big influence on the way people react to them.

This next extract is from an online guide to journalism compiled by the American Press Institute (API), which supports good practice and the development of journalism:

News keeps us informed of the changing events, issues, and characters in the world outside.

teachers and lawyers. More than 150 journalists were arrested by an increasingly authoritarian regime as part of a crackdown on freedom of speech.

Virtually all the journalists under arrest were charged with "membership of a terrorist organisation", "spreading terrorist propaganda", "attempting to overthrow the government" or spying. The practice of silencing journalists through the abuse of the criminal justice system, and expanding the scope of the definition of terrorism to use it against dissidents or critics, are among the violations frequently cited in human rights reports. The rest of the world saw this crackdown on the media as a clear sign that democracy was under threat in Turkey. Freedom of expression and a free media go hand in hand; the latter is the manifestation and defender of the former.

The threats to freedom of expression in the UK are on nothing like the same scale as in Turkey or those countries at the bottom of the Index. But British media organisations, acting alone or together, will often react if they feel this basic right is being challenged. As you might expect, they respond particularly vigorously to anything they see as restraining their own activities. The media will often challenge specific injunctions and legal rulings preventing the publication of information that, they argue, should be disclosed as a matter of public interest. The phone hacking scandal of 2011 revived perennial debates about the extent to which the print media could be relied upon to regulate their own activities, or whether they should be constrained by legislation. When regulation underpinned by law was proposed, the newspaper industry remonstrated loud and long about threats to press freedom, and every major player declined to cooperate with the regulatory framework that was eventually established. This episode and media regulation are discussed in greater depth in Chapter 5.

Acting in what they see as their wider role as guardians of free speech, journalists will also challenge anything that might appear to give too much power to those who might not be fully accountable, and who might misuse it. In the internet age, for example, there are plenty of concerns and arguments about privacy, and how much information about individuals should legitimately be held by governments, security services, retailers and social networks. Media coverage ensures that these are open and live debates.

This issue of freedom of speech was thrown into tragic focus by an attack in Paris in January 2015 on the offices of the French satirical magazine *Charlie Hebdo*. Islamist gunmen entered the building and shot dead 12 members of staff. The magazine had a reputation for irreverence and secular beliefs, ridiculing religions of all sorts, Islam among them. It printed cartoons of the Prophet – sacrilege in the eyes of Muslims.

Opinions were divided as to whether the magazine had operated within its rights in a free country, or whether good taste and respect meant there should be limits to freedom of expression – limits that might include the lampooning of religious beliefs. With rights come responsibilities, but how they are met and interpreted is a matter of opinion.

In any event, the public response to the killings was extraordinary. Millions demonstrated in Paris and elsewhere in defence of the principle of freedom of speech. The phrase *"Je suis Charlie"*, or "I am Charlie", was adopted by demonstrators as a mark of solidarity with a publication that had in their view done nothing more than exercise its absolute rights to free speech and freedom of expression.

History was tragically to repeat itself in France in October 2020, with the savage murder of a schoolteacher who had showed the cartoons to his class as part of a discussion about freedom of speech prompted by the *Charlie Hebdo* case. Once again, there were large public demonstrations reinforcing France's determination to stand by its core national values – freedom of expression among them.

Holding power to account

One of the jobs of a free media is to make sure that politicians and people in public office, or people who manage public money, behave as they promised they would or as they are supposed to. This idea is often referred to as "holding power to account". Over the years, there have been very many stories exposing hypocrisy, wrongdoing or corruption by those in power, sometimes with momentous results. Here are some outstanding examples:

Watergate

The most famous, not least because of its seismic consequences, was the *Washington Post*'s long investigation into corrupt and criminal behaviour in the early 1970s, by those working on the campaign to re-elect Richard Nixon as US President. The tenacious and painstaking efforts over many months by two reporters in particular, and the editor who backed them, led eventually to the door of the President himself. Nixon was forced from office in 1974 – the only US President to resign. The scandal was known as Watergate, because the *Post* was first alerted to the story by a burglary at the Democratic Party offices in a building of that name. The tag "-gate" has been added to many scandals since then.

MPs' expenses

More recently, in 2009 the *Daily Telegraph* published the details of thousands of bogus expenses and allowances claims made by British Members of Parliament. These stories were based on confidential information that had been leaked to the paper. The *Telegraph* set up a special team to spend weeks combing through hundreds of thousands of documents, and published its findings day after day, leaving many MPs ridiculed or discredited. Members and former members of both the House of Commons and the House of Lords resigned, were sacked or retired early. Several were prosecuted and went to jail.

Edward Snowden

The Guardian and *Washington Post* newspapers among others pursued stories stemming from the revelations of Edward Snowden, a former contractor for the CIA. He left the US in 2013 after copying and leaking details of extensive internet and telephone surveillance by American intelligence agencies. He gave the material to a group of journalists who later worked with a number of newspapers in different countries to publish it. *The Guardian* stories revealed that the US National Security Agency (NSA) was collecting the telephone records of millions of Americans, and that British intelligence was doing the same in the UK. It was later revealed that the NSA was spying on European Union offices and was reported to have listened in on conversations involving the German Chancellor – supposedly a key American ally.

These are just three among many examples of the way in which the media can hold to account those in power, and bring about far-reaching change.

Exposing wrongdoing

There are also thousands of examples of the media exposing bad, corrupt, immoral or illegal behaviour.

The thalidomide scandal

One of the most celebrated was an exposé by The *Sunday Times* in the 1960s about a drug called thalidomide, which was prescribed to pregnant women to alleviate the symptoms of morning sickness. Several thousand women who had taken the drug later gave birth to babies with malformed limbs and other deformities. The drugs company denied liability. The *Sunday Times* spent years campaigning for compensation for the victims, providing case studies and evidence of the side effects. In 1968, the company agreed to a multi-million-pound compensation scheme.

Phone hacking

An investigation by *The Guardian* uncovered the hacking of thousands of mobile phones owned by celebrities, members of the Royal Family, politicians and others by the *News of the World* and other newspapers. This was an instance of one newspaper exposing the illegal practices of others. The story that started it all was a report that journalists had hacked into the voicemail messages of a missing schoolgirl – wrongly encouraging her family to believe that she was reading her messages, and so was still alive. The revelation catapulted the issue from the front page of *The Guardian* to a full-blown public scandal that resulted in criminal trials, the payment of tens of millions in out-of-court settlements and the closure of the *News of the World*.

Boston sex abuse

Journalists on the Spotlight investigative team at the *Boston Globe* newspaper uncovered a scandal involving the sexual abuse of minors by Roman Catholic priests. Their stories, published in 2002, led to the prosecutions of a number of priests, and the exposure of other cases elsewhere. This eventually became a worldwide crisis for the Roman Catholic Church.

Jimmy Savile

Television has its own track record of investigation. It was an ITV programme, *Exposure*, that first broadcast claims in 2012 of the serial sexual abuse of underage girls by the charity fundraiser and television presenter Sir Jimmy Savile, who had died the previous year. After the programme, hundreds more women came forward and claimed they had been abused or assaulted by Savile. Many more cases of historic child abuse involving other well-known names also came to light, resulting in a number of convictions of prominent people. A pattern was established of a handful of revelations about individuals prompting other victims to break cover and to tell their stories. More recently, the high-profile exposures of Jeffrey Epstein and Harvey Weinstein followed a similar pattern.

Nor have the new digital-only players been slow to embrace this role. In 2012, *HuffPost* became the first digital media enterprise to win a prestigious Pulitzer Prize for a series highlighting the struggles of severely wounded war veterans and their families. *BuzzFeed News* has claimed a number of scoops, including publication of a draft dossier containing allegations of improper contacts between the Russians and Donald Trump's presidential election campaign team in 2016.

Hollywood has not been slow to see the dramatic possibilities of some of these historic investigations, and some great films have been produced – all well worth watching. Try *All the President's Men* (1976) the story of Watergate; *Spotlight* (2015), the story of the Boston sex abuse scandal, which won the Oscar for Best Picture; and *The Post* (2017), the story of the *Washington Post's* efforts to publish The Pentagon Papers – classified documents about America's involvement in the Vietnam War.

Giving a voice to the voiceless

A lot of these stories involve newspapers or media organisations taking up the cudgels on behalf of people who do not have the power, means, influence or ability to pursue justice or redress for themselves. This is another means by which journalism can exert a positive impact on society, giving a mouthpiece and an outlet to those who have no other means of being heard. These stories may be about individuals who are the victims of injustice, or groups of people who are having difficulty resolving their grievances. The thalidomide campaign falls into this category. Or they may simply bring to light the plight of those on the fringes of society – the homeless, the destitute, the addicted, the sick.

Unearthing hidden stories

Later in this book we will talk a lot about data journalism – the art of finding stories that are hidden, often in plain sight, on the internet. A problem with researching stories these days is not that there is not enough information around, rather that there is too much. There is a lot of important and potentially newsworthy information online, but it is buried in out-of-the-way places or in thousands of pages of documents. It is not always easy to find – and sometimes of course, it has been deliberately obscured. A relatively new but rapidly expanding role for journalism is delving deep into the internet to try to find those stories.

We have now assembled an impressive list of the contributions that good journalism can and should make to citizenship, and to the functioning of a democratic society. We have answered our two fundamental questions: What is journalism? What is it for?

- Telling people what is happening in the world
- Explaining, analysing, contextualising and making sense of events
- Providing accurate and trustworthy information produced to a high standard
- Bolstering citizenship and underpinning democracy
- Protecting and defending freedom of speech
- Holding to account governments and those in positions of power
- Exposing crime, corruption and wrongdoing
- Giving a voice to the voiceless and campaigning for social justice
- Unearthing hidden stories.

Of course, not all journalism is fine and upstanding, and fulfils any or all of these functions. Standards are sacrificed, corners are cut and mistakes are made. We will look in Chapters 4 and 5 at how and why things sometimes go awry.

Even so, the functions in our list are important and significant. But they cannot exist in a vacuum. They have to be recognised and accepted by the public. Here is another quotation from the API:

> While journalism occupies a much smaller space than the talk, entertainment, opinion, assertion, advertising and propaganda that dominate the media universe, it is nevertheless perceived as being more valuable than most of the 'stuff' out there.

This suggests that the service journalism is performing is valued and trusted to a greater or lesser degree. "Trust" is a key word in the business – if people do not believe they can rely on what you are putting in front of them, they will go somewhere else and they will not come back. But amid the noise and distractions that surround us all nowadays, people generally do feel that they need to keep informed and to understand what is happening. The majority still turn to the mainstream media in times of crisis and uncertainty for dependable information and explanation. They instinctively understand and support some of the key functions of a free press that we have been discussing.

What is news?

So far we have talked about journalism and news as more or less synonymous. But are they? Let us look at a few definitions of news, as opposed to journalism, and see if we can draw out some distinctions.

Here is perhaps the best-known and most quoted definition of news:

> Dog bites man: that's not news…………
> …….man bites dog: that's news

The thought underpinning this is that news is something that is unusual, or out of the ordinary. But that is only a part of it.

> News is people.

Most stories are about people, what they have done or said, or what has happened to them. And as human beings, it is stories about people that we are most interested in and that we most respond to. This might sound obvious, but it is an important piece of knowledge for a journalist, and one you forget at your peril. If you read or hear or watch a piece of news that seems lifeless and lacking in colour, the chances are that it is because the human element is missing. As consumers, we need something to relate to, and that something will almost always be the human factor. As you start to write your own stories, you should always remember that. We call news items "stories" not because they have been invented, but because they tell you about something that has happened, they have a plot and a narrative and they have human interest. That is why journalists will often define news as what might interest their mothers, or their friends – when they meet in the pub or share on social media. Something can be news simply because it is interesting and unusual.

Here is our cynical friend Lord Northcliffe again.

> News is what people do not want you to print. All the rest is advertising.

This thought is also attributed to George Orwell, substituting "public relations" for "advertising". In both cases, the point is that news will often mean publishing things that the people involved would like to keep out of the public domain: that there is an investigative and perhaps intrusive nature to news. Finding things out and telling people about them, to repeat Jeremy Paxman's words, will often mean finding and publishing things that people want kept concealed, for any number of reasons.

Think of news from the perspective of the audience. They probably never stop to think about it, but they will have their own conscious or subconscious ideas about what they consider newsworthy. A list might look something like this:

> Something I did not already know
> Something surprising, unexpected, amusing

Something I want, or need, to know about
Something that directly affects me, my family and friends
Something that helps me understand the raw facts and make sense of the world
Something that helps me form my own opinions and make decisions about my life
Something that – once I have heard it – I want to tell someone else about.

In the age of social media, this last point is particularly worthy of consideration, because it offers a whole new range of opportunities to push your journalism to a very wide audience.

A list made by *journalists* would probably reflect those criteria to a large extent. Their ideas of what makes news might look something like this:

It has (just) happened
It is about to happen
It is significant – people need to know about it and understand it
It is surprising or unexpected
It is odd, eccentric, unusual, intriguing, funny
It is dramatic
It is relevant to the lives of my audience
It is something someone of note has said
It is an announcement/decision/appointment
It is something my mum/my mates/my audience will be interested in
It involves conflict and argument
It is a new angle or development on an old story
It throws new light on a subject.

If you think about the news that we read and see and hear every day, it is the same dozen or so subjects that make the headlines most of the time:

– **Conflict**: wars, strikes, revolutions, the power battles of politics, religion
– **Argument/debate**: political exchanges in particular are about arguing the case for viewpoints, courses of action, public policy. Moral and ethical issues also feature prominently
– **Power**: people in powerful positions or large and influential companies and organisations
– **Disaster/tragedy**: air crashes, train crashes, oil spills, volcanic eruptions, earthquakes, famines – human tragedies
– **Security and terrorism**: at home and around the world
– **Crime**: small-scale crime can be news at a local level, but bigger crimes like robbery, corruption, fraud, rape or murder will make national headlines
– **Money**: the economy, school fees, taxes, the Budget, food prices, mortgages, wage rises, inflation, interest rates. Big media organisations have business, economics and personal finance correspondents, with dedicated sections for coverage of these issues
– **Health and science**: this includes the state of health provision across the country. But many people are also concerned with their personal health, so are interested in stories about traditional remedies, medical research, diseases, drugs, diet and exercise, as well as a range of other science stories
– **Sex**: all societies are interested in sex, whether or not they talk about it openly. News stories about sex may be prurient but they can also involve morality, social trends or behaviour that goes outside society's generally accepted standards
– **Weather/climate change**: don't confuse the two! The weather may affect daily routines, travel and leisure plans, and is of interest when it behaves unusually. Global warming is part of a wider environmental story that also commands a great deal of coverage

- **Entertainment/celebrity/personalities**: what people in the public eye do, the lives they lead and what they look like, are all of interest. You can dismiss this as gossip or trivia, but there is a huge market for it. It is especially newsworthy when celebrities fall from power, lose their money, fall in love, fall out of love or are involved in scandal
- **Culture**: films, books, music, theatre, art, food, wine
- **Sport**: millions participate in sport and millions are spectators. They all want to know results, statistics, news of sportsmen and sportswomen and their achievements
- **Human interest**: there are as many stories as there are people. Examples might be fundraising for a child going abroad for life-saving surgery; a pilot recovering from injuries sustained in an air crash and determined to fly again; or a man with a collection of 10,000 picture postcards.

The lower half of this list in particular reminds us that something might be newsworthy even if it is not, strictly speaking, important. It might just be quirky, interesting or amusing.

The balance between these stories will vary according to the media outlet and its audience or readership. In general terms, however, there has been a long-term shift away from the predominance of a more earnest, reportage-driven agenda and towards more personal and celebrity-dominated stories. For example, there are far fewer foreign news correspondents working for UK media outlets than there used to be, and much more coverage – even in the more "serious" publications and news programmes – of cult television viewing such as *Strictly Come Dancing*, *The Great British Bake-Off* and *I'm a Celebrity – Get me Out of Here!*

Is it news?

All the subjects on our list have strong news potential, but not everything that happens, even if it falls under one of these headings, is news, or *newsworthy* – that is, worth reporting today, or as it stands. Old hands will tell you that they might not be able to define a news story, but they know one when they see one. That is not much help as you try to learn how to know one when *you* see one. If you are not sure whether something is newsworthy or not, try using this simple checklist:

- **Is it new?** Have you, or has your audience, heard this before? If yes, it probably is not news. However, even on stories that are known about and have been around for a while, there is always the possibility of new angles or information emerging that will make that story newsworthy once again. Often your job will be trying actively to find these new leads, to keep a good story going.
- **Is it unusual?** This is the Man bites Dog/Dog bites Man question. Whatever your audience would find unusual, surprising, out of the ordinary, different from the norm is likely to be news.
- **Is it interesting?** Not everything unusual is interesting. It is a subjective judgement. Would your audience think it was of interest?
- **Is it significant?** Is this important information that people need to know, either for their own use (a rail strike, a rise in interest rates, a change in government policy) or because it is part of my general duty to keep them informed about big events?
- **Is there a strong human element?** News is about people. Every story will involve people, and they will usually be at the centre of it. A personal account can be hugely effective as a story on its own, or as a way of illustrating and humanising a bigger story.

And at the back of all of these questions is this one:

How does this affect the lives of my readers, listeners or viewers?

You will have noticed repeated mention of the audience as we were going through the checklist. These are the people your news is serving. If it affects them directly, it is a news story. In a globalised world, more and more things that seem to be far away can have consequences on our doorsteps. A fall in oil production in the Middle East can push up petrol prices in East Anglia. An erupting volcano in Iceland can send a cloud of ash across northern Europe and ground aircraft. Pollution in China or India can worsen the climate crisis for all of us. A deadly virus that emerges in a Chinese city can be in your home town within weeks. But events that do not have direct impact can be strong too – coverage of a famine in Africa can spark a fundraising relief effort in your local community.

Always think about those you are addressing. We talked about definitions of news earlier: some journalists saying that the news is what their mum wants to hear, or what they would tell their friends in the pub. Visualising an audience helps you make decisions about what is newsworthy for that audience. There is no one-size-fits-all answer. What makes a lead story for one outlet might be of no interest at all to another. You will know, or should have an idea of, the sorts of people who are reading, watching or listening. Think about what they want and what they need – while remembering that those are not always the same things. Think about what they know or are likely to understand: not many people slavishly follow every twist and turn in a news story, and will need help and reminders. Awareness of who is out there, and what they want and need, will also influence how you tell those stories once you have selected them.

Journalism and news

So: are journalism and news the same thing?

Assembling the facts and conveying them – telling people what is happening and what is new – are essential parts of journalism. We might categorise those elements of journalism as reporting. But the internet means that people can get news anywhere now, and they do – even from sources that they suspect are unreliable and in which they have little faith. You can often pick up something from a random post on Twitter long before any official sources or traditional news providers begin reporting it. It is free, it is fast and quite a lot of it is inaccurate or untrue. So journalism needs to uphold its standards of accuracy and speed, but it has to do more than simply report. What is that "more"?

This is how the American media commentator George Snell tackles that question:

> Reporting is an important element of journalism. But the web has changed the way we get our news. Proper journalism is more than just reportage. It puts news into context and explains its relevance.

Snell makes a distinction here. There is *reporting* – that part of the business that gathers and conveys basic information – "the news". And there is *journalism*, which is the wider process embracing all of the added value that we have talked about in this chapter. It also includes a great deal more than the reporting of hard news, such as features, profiles, entertainment. Confusingly, the terms "reporter" and "journalist" are often used interchangeably. But, essential and fundamental though it is, news is just one part of the wider business of journalism, which takes the raw materials and turns them into something of use and value. As Snell puts it:

> Journalism is getting beneath the news. It's investigative analysis and thoughtful commentary. It's in-depth expository reporting.

And when journalism does that, and does it well, it fulfils those vital social and democratic functions that we talked about earlier.

In looking at societal responsibilities and at distinctions between journalism and news, we have inevitably adopted a rather narrow view of journalism. It is not just about daily news, and much of it has nothing to do with the hurly burly of the news agenda. Journalism that caters for special interests, for example – there are hundreds of magazines that do exactly that. But what they all have in common is that need to understand the wants and the needs of their audiences. Journalism does not exist in some self-indulgent vacuum: it is offering a service to the people who consume it. Never lose sight of the people you are writing for.

3
You, the reporter

essential qualities.....desirable qualities.....help yourself to become a better reporter.....practical steps..... tools of the trade

The last chapter was about definitions of news and about journalism as an occupation. This one is about the people who ply it – the journalists themselves. In spite of the stereotypes, there is of course no such thing as a typical journalist. But there are some qualities that you will need to have, or be able to demonstrate to some degree. No-one has all of them, but understanding what they are and why they might be important should be useful as you make your way in journalism – recognising the skills and qualities you already have, and others that you might need to develop in the future. This chapter offers some practical ideas as to how you can improve your reporting skills without the need to undergo a complete personality change. And it catalogues the kit you will need to operate as a multimedia, multiplatform reporter.

We have noted some of the rude things people have had to say about journalism as a whole. It should not come as any surprise to know that they have been no more flattering about journalists as individuals. And, again, some of the most biting comments come from journalists themselves. This often-quoted observation was made by Nicholas Tomalin, a prominent journalist who was killed when covering a war in the Middle East in 1973.

> The only qualities essential for real success in journalism are rat-like cunning, a plausible manner and a little literary ability.

A lot of journalists would not have too much argument with that.

Here is a very modern-sounding quotation, but it actually comes from a 19th-century German philosopher, Arthur Schopenhauer. Clearly, a journalist had upset him at some point.

> Journalists are like dogs. Whenever anything moves they begin to bark.

Most dogs – and not a few journalists – might take that as a compliment.

The writer Stella Gibbons clearly did not have much time for journalists or their literary abilities:

> The life of a journalist is poor, nasty, brutish and short. So is his style.

And even Mother Teresa – who saw good in most people – shrank from dealings with journalists:

> Facing the press is more difficult than bathing a leper.

Since Mother Teresa achieved fame, and sainthood, by founding a charity to help those with leprosy, tuberculosis and other diseases of the poor, she is perhaps the only person in history able to make this claim with any degree of authority.

From the sublime…..Dave Barry, an American columnist and writer, makes no bones about the superficiality of some journalism:

> I can write hundreds of words on virtually any topic without possessing a shred of information. Which is how I got a good job in journalism.

Again, many journalists would regard this as a back-handed compliment. The ability to master a brief at speed, or to stretch very few facts into a lengthy exposition are prized skills. A talent for making a lot out of a little is generally regarded as something of which to be proud rather than embarrassed.

Nearly all journalists start as reporters. This is where they learn the basic skills of the craft. Some never want to do anything else. Others move into production roles, into editing or management, into specific areas of journalism like politics or sport or into writing features. Specialisms in data journalism or audience engagement are increasingly common destinations too. But most start in the same place – very often as junior reporters on local newspapers, junior producers on local radio stations or junior web content creators. That is why this chapter, and indeed much of the book as a whole, tends to talk about reporters rather than journalists. Reporting embodies many of the essential core skills of the craft, without which it is much harder to move up the career ladder.

Essential qualities

Like humanity, journalists come in all shapes and sizes, with different combinations of different qualities. But there are some things that most of them have in common. Without a good dose of these, it is hard to make much headway in journalism.

Accurate

There is no room for compromise here. From the beginning, you need to develop a passion for accuracy, and a commitment to getting things right. It is the most fundamental rule of journalism. Check everything, even the most basic facts such as the spelling of names. If you write a brilliant story, but you spell the name of the main character wrongly, the whole thing is devalued. Check and double-check. A reputation for accuracy and reliability is hard-won and easily lost. But it is a great asset, and it will be rewarded. If you are slipshod and make silly mistakes, you will lose the trust of your editor – and he or she will assign you less interesting stories, or possibly decide to dispense with your services altogether. Get the basics right, make sure you get the general tone and emphasis right and never make any assumptions: they will almost always be wrong. The vast majority of errors are avoidable, and are the result of carelessness or haste. Set yourself high standards in this regard and be hard on yourself if you fall below them.

Articulate

An obvious requirement is an ability to express yourself, both verbally and on paper. A joy in writing is what attracts many people to journalism. If you are good at setting out your thoughts clearly and logically and in an attractive way, you are in a good place to embark on a career in the business. If you find that pleasurable, and enjoy the challenges involved in gathering information and setting it out coherently and concisely – and often quickly – so much the better.

The ability to articulate verbally is obviously vital if you have ideas of becoming a broadcast journalist, and appearing on radio or television. But you also need a facility with words in order to undertake some of the more fundamental areas of all forms of reporting, such as gathering information and persuading people to talk to you. It also helps you pitch ideas to time-pressured editors.

On no account disqualify yourself from a career in broadcasting because you think your voice or your appearance will not be acceptable to broadcast platforms. Practice and training can do wonders, and very few people are genuinely incapable of broadcasting at least adequately. Do not assume that you are one of those people: you almost certainly are not.

Curious

If you ask any seasoned journalist for a list of the most important attributes for a practitioner, they will invariably put this in their top three, and often make it their number one requirement. Curious, inquisitive, questioning – perhaps downright nosey. Call it what you will, it is the primary attribute of all good journalists. A natural desire to know what is going on and to ask questions. What has happened? Why? What are the details? What does it mean?

We will have more than one encounter ahead with what are sometimes called the 6Ws (even though they don't all begin with W), which are the key questions you ask about any story: who, what, when, where, why and how. Good reporters are always asking these questions about everything that is happening around them.

Desire to tell stories

When reporters find something out, they are desperate to share that knowledge. As Tom Brokaw told us in Chapter 2, journalism is about storytelling. Reporters, like other sorts of writers, are tellers of stories. In fact, social media has made everybody a storyteller. Facebook, Twitter and Instagram are the digital equivalents of the person who bursts into the room exclaiming "you'll never guess what!" or "have you heard the latest?" For many reporters, the thrill of the chase – *finding* the story – is what the game is all about. But most take an equal or greater pleasure in the telling of it, setting out what they have learned in a clear and effective narrative. So another key characteristic is the urge to disseminate information and knowledge.

Interest in people

As we have heard, journalism is primarily about people and their stories, so it follows that you will have a strong interest in your fellow human beings and what makes them tick. Every single person has his or her own story. An American cop series of the 1940s, set in New York, always concluded with the words: "There are eight million stories in the naked city. This has been one of them". Recognising that everyone has a story is the first step to wanting to find out what those stories are and reporting them. Personal and human details are at the heart of any story, the things that bring it to life. Good reporters see everyone as potential subjects, and they find them all fascinating.

Desirable qualities

We can argue about whether some of the next list of qualities are essential or desirable. Suffice it to say that they are commonly found in good reporters. In each case, I will try to explain why – if they do not come naturally to you – it might be worth you being conscious of that, and recognising that there will be times when you have to get out of character and out of your comfort zone and show that you are capable of demonstrating them. Most of us have some of them, and you can cultivate others with practice and experience.

Sceptical

A healthy mistrust of people in authority – politicians, spokespeople, press officers and so on – is crucial. All these people have agendas: ask yourself what those agendas are, and why they might be saying what they are saying. Don't take anything at face value. Question it. At the extreme, there is the oft-quoted maxim of a distinguished foreign correspondent named Louis Heren (sometimes attributed to Jeremy Paxman) who said: "when a politician tells you something in confidence, always ask yourself: why is this lying bastard lying to me?" You might argue that this is bordering on cynicism, which is not the same thing. A cynic, as Oscar Wilde observed, is one who knows the price of everything and the value of nothing. Many grizzled and hard-bitten journalists do become cynical, but that is not a good place to be. Not everyone is a lying bastard: many people who enter the public service, as MPs or councillors or civil servants, do so from honourable motives – to make a difference, help people and change things for the better. If they mess up, it is perfectly legitimate to hold them to account. But they are not all venal or self-serving. So sceptical, certainly; cynical, no.

Tenacious, resilient

Good stories do not fall into your lap, ready to go. They have to be worried away at and worked on, sometimes over a long period. In these days of instant news, it is often hard to chisel out the time to look more deeply and get at the heart of the story. That is why investigative reporters and programmes are so valuable. You need to be persistent and determined, and prepared not to take no for an answer. Editors hate reporters who say they can't find things out, or track people down. You will spend a lot of time approaching people, making phone calls, trying to find out how to get hold of people, being stonewalled and blanked and knocked back. Keep going, and use your imagination. There is nearly always a way round.

Courageous

There are many forms of reporting, and not all of them require you to be physically or morally brave. But some do, and not just reporting from war zones. If you are working on a sensitive story, you may find yourself in a hostile or even threatening atmosphere, and it takes guts to carry on. And if you are working abroad, there is an increasing number of places where you are under genuine threat of injury or death – what the industry calls hostile environments. Most areas of the Middle East, for example, can be very dangerous to work in most of the time. In war zones, journalists are not regarded as neutral observers in the way they once were, but as legitimate targets. Your bosses should not send you there anywhere dangerous without proper training, equipment and back-up. And they should not send you at all if you do not want to go, for whatever reason.

At a more routine level, it sometimes takes a lot of courage to confront an overbearing or uncooperative interviewee, or to put difficult questions to people to their faces. Are you guilty? Are you corrupt? Have you been having an affair? Did you lie? These are not questions many of us would feel comfortable about putting to strangers. But sometimes it is necessary to do so. In Chapter 8, we look at techniques for asking difficult questions.

Even if they are not actually physically threatening, people will be rude to you, or dismissive, sometimes with good reason. You have to be thick-skinned and resilient – and brave.

Motivated

Editors love reporters who are enthusiastic about stories and want to get stuck into them. And they like to see hunger – people volunteering to do things, and ready to go the extra mile to help bring the story home, on their own or as part of a team. In most newsrooms now there will be an imperative to produce a steady stream of content to keep websites and social channels full and up to date. A good number of stories might not be original or exclusive to your outlet – but even if you are rewriting someone else's material you should always do your best to add something new, so that your version stands out. And when you do get the chance to do some of your own stories, be proactive – get out of the office if you can, and speak to people. Don't wait for the story to come to you. Show keenness, and put yourself forward for tasks. You will always learn something, however mundane they may seem.

Questioning

This builds on what we said about the importance of curiosity. Journalists spend an inordinate amount of their time asking questions. It is the principal means by which they find things out. And sometimes those questions may be pretty stupid or seem blindingly obvious. The people you are dealing with talk in jargon, use short cuts or acronyms, don't always express themselves clearly or deliberately dissemble. Always ask them to spell things out for you, and never be embarrassed by asking what sounds like a silly or obvious question. People don't mind on the whole, and it is part of your commitment to accuracy and to getting the story right. If they smile at your naiveté, so what? That is better than getting it wrong. The really stupid people are those who don't ask questions and then make mistakes, or find they have not asked enough questions to allow them to write an intelligible story.

Inexperienced reporters often find this one of the most difficult aspects of the job. We are not used to walking up to complete strangers, or cold-calling them on the phone, to ask what may be unwelcome questions. If this is the way you feel, you will simply have to get over it. If you don't ask you won't get. People expect reporters to ask questions, and as long as they think you are genuinely interested in their story and getting it right, they will generally not mind answering them. Dealing with people directly and actually speaking to them in person is the best way of establishing a rapport and getting the best possible material from them. Emailing or messaging them and using a written reply in your story is a very poor substitute, and should be a last resort. It will strike a false note and make the story feel wooden. Even if it does not come naturally to you, it is essential that you steel yourself to speak to people and ask them questions. It will soon become second nature. You will not produce any decent stories if you don't.

Outgoing

Plenty of good reporters are introverts. But you will find that many, if not most, are outgoing and sociable by nature. That is one reason they used to have a reputation for sinking heroic quantities of alcohol. That is much less the case now. But when you are dealing with strangers, and seeking to establish a rapid rapport with them, it helps if you are able to get on with them and encourage them to confide in you. Use humour as much as you can, and be resourceful in worming your way past over-protective assistants, press officers or people who don't want to speak to you.

Empathetic

An extension of the same thing, and linked to an ability to listen and react appropriately. You may be hot on the trail of your story, but you should still treat people decently and as human beings. Some of them may be talking to you about traumatic or upsetting things that have happened to them, and you need to respond in an empathetic manner. A voice in your head may be telling you excitedly that this is going to make a snorter of a front-page story, but you do not want that to be apparent in your manner. Make yourself a good listener. The more you empathise, the more you will get out of your subject, as we will see in Chapter 8 when we discuss interviewing techniques. Try never to lose your basic humanity or sense of what is right and decent. Be principled and professional. This is related to what we were saying about being interested in people. If you are interested, show that you are interested. Listen to what they have to say, and make them feel that you are on their side.

Good reporters also have a strong sense of natural justice. They instinctively back the little person against authority, get angry at unfair treatment and – as we saw in the last chapter – want to give a voice to people who cannot speak up for themselves for whatever reason.

Competitive

This is a highly competitive business. Less so than it used to be in the print industry perhaps, when even quite small towns once boasted two or three rival papers. But the battle for listeners, viewers and eyes online is still fierce – perhaps fiercer, since everyone can, in theory, reach the whole world. You should always want to get the scoop, beating others to a story: but if you can't do that, make sure your report is the best. If you have the trust of your subjects, you improve your chances – especially if there are other journalists chasing the same lead, when the demands of competition mean some probably won't be behaving as well as they should.

Work quickly

If you can deliver at speed, that is a big bonus. You will often be writing to a deadline that means you cannot spend as long as you would like gathering material and crafting it. But remember that however brilliant your story is, if you miss the deadline and it does not appear, it is worthless. Meeting the deadline is your first priority. You can add to, or polish the story, or find new angles for later versions. Speed trumps everything except accuracy. Most news organisations would rather be second and accurate rather than first and wrong. But time pressures are often intense. In the words of a senior journalist on the *Times*: "to the question 'do you want it good, or do you want it now?' there is only ever one answer". Teaching yourself to gather and turn round your material quickly will stand you in very good stead.

Absorb information quickly

That need for speedy writing means you have to absorb and process facts and information at top speed as well. If you are given an official report to read, you will often find there is a summary of its findings, or a list of conclusions. Start with those: you will not have time to read the whole thing in detail. Teach yourself to skim read. You can help yourself with preparation if you know you are going to cover a story, reading round the subject, being clear about the key issues and maybe even drafting a few choice phrases. Journalism is all about getting quickly to the heart of a subject and extracting the core elements. Watch the top television news anchors, who are receiving information in their earpieces while they are presenting live. They manage to absorb what they are being told and then repeat it on air with great authority as if it was something they had known all along.

Flexible, adaptable

Ideally, you might have half a dozen stories on the go at any one time, as you wait for your calls to be returned and information to come back in. On a local paper or news website, you might write a dozen stories a day of various lengths. You need to be able to keep all these plates spinning, and adapt to circumstances as they change. A story that looked as if it would make 500 words can begin to fall away, and be superseded by something else or perhaps dropped altogether. Another, that looked to be worth no more than a couple of pars, will suddenly get a lot more interesting, and shoot up the running order. This variety and unpredictability is part of the attraction of the job for many reporters.

Up to speed

Journalists like to be the first to know things and hate feeling that they are behind the curve. Make it your business always to be up to date with stories on your patch, or with a wider national, even international, agenda. There is nothing worse than suggesting a story for your newspaper, website, programme or station, only to find that it has already recently been done. In Chapter 1, we looked at a number of tips about how to stay in touch at all times.

Technically adept

No matter what branch of journalism you enter, you are going to need a modicum of technical knowledge and experience. The carefree days when a pen, a notebook and access to a telephone were pretty much all you needed are long gone. Do not despair. You will already have many of the required skills. You should already know your way around the internet and the various functions of a smartphone, for example, and will probably have an active social presence online. These are vital in all areas of modern journalism, in both gathering and distribution. Other skills are more specific to the medium or individual platform on which you are working at any given time. But in most cases you will probably be expected to know how to record good quality video and audio material, and possibly to edit and publish it; how to take good quality still pictures; how to use the content management and production systems employed at your place of work; how to gather information effectively and present it in suitable form for newspapers, websites, social networks, radio and television.

This is not an exhaustive list, but of course you will not be doing all of these things all of the time. It feels daunting, but your NCTJ course, and this book, will introduce you to many of these skills and should give you plenty of opportunity to experiment and acquire practical experience. When you pass your NCTJ Diploma, you will be able to do many of these things to a solid level of competence. Others you will pick up on the job, with or without formal training, when you start work. Journalists are not renowned for their technical prowess, but most are able to master the protocols and systems that exist in their particular workplace. Those who excel will improve their chances of rapid progression.

Professional

Finally this. It is a word that could encompass a whole range of things, including dress, appearance, manner, attitude and general behaviour. We will come in Chapter 4 to codes of conduct and standards, and the values and principles of the best journalism. Whether or not journalism is a profession is irrelevant: its practitioners must behave in a professional manner. Set high standards for yourself, and do everything you can to live up to them. Remember that the people you deal with are sharing with you key moments and aspects of their lives. That is a privilege. Treat them and what they tell you with respect, not just as fodder for your story.

There is one quality missing from this list, an omission that you might find surprising. There is nothing about having to be brainy or brilliant. Of course, you need to be bright enough to recognise a story and understand often quite complicated concepts and issues. You have to be able to summarise and condense and present them in an interesting and engaging way. You have to be able to absorb the more academic elements of the NCTJ syllabus, such as Law and Public Affairs. You need to know your way around technical equipment and systems. You need to be streetwise to be able to operate effectively as a reporter. But you do not have to be a genius or academically outstanding. We have been talking mostly about the human qualities and characteristics that are displayed by many good reporters – not levels of academic achievement. In the days before university courses or pre-entry training schemes, most trainee reporters joined local papers straight from school, some at age 16. They would not have been academically anything like as well qualified as today's journalism students, and they learned on the job, studying for their NCTJ qualifications along the way. But if they had at least some of the qualities we have been discussing, they could go on to be great reporters and great journalists, and many did.

Help yourself to become a better reporter

You may be getting worried that none of this sounds like you. But it would be very unusual if you had come this far without possessing at least some of these qualities, or the potential to develop them. And with instruction and practice, they can be learned and developed. Some great reporters may be born not made, but even the best of them will be improved by training, practising the craft and honing their skills in the light of learning and – very importantly – of experience. And there are plenty of things you can do to help develop your own reporting skills and make yourself better than you are, and as good as you can be.

Trust your instincts

Believe in yourself and learn to follow your gut feelings. Most reporters do, and develop a knack for sniffing out the phony, the overblown and the exaggerated.

Be open-minded

Be prepared to put that instinctive response to the test. Always be open to considering other arguments or perspectives, and seeing how your own thoughts match up against them. Every reporter will tell you that the more you find out about a story, the more your view of it changes and becomes more nuanced. For that reason it is very important that you do not embark on a story with a preconceived notion of how it will turn out or – worse – how you want it to turn out. Be flexible and open to following new lines, or doing things in a different way if the facts take you there.

Don't assume anything

If you make assumptions, as likely as not they will turn out to be misplaced or plain wrong. They are the results of first impressions, ignorance, prejudice or jumping to conclusions. As above, keep an open mind and be ready to let the facts speak for themselves.

Set high standards for yourself

Even if you are not being held to high standards by your bosses, make sure you always live up to the mark you set for yourself. Do not cut corners or let others do the spadework for you. Be satisfied that whatever you produce is the best it can be, and the best you can do in the circumstances.

Ask for feedback, and act on it

People always say they want feedback, but unless it is unqualified praise they do not always react well to it. If it is not offered, seek feedback from those whose views you respect. You will not always agree with it, and sometimes it might be painful. Take it on the chin. If it is offered in a constructive and helpful spirit, it will be worth heeding.

Someone giving you feedback will often put their finger on something that deep down you knew was not quite right. If you are lucky enough to get good advice, act on it. The best reporters are the ones who are most open to advice, because they know the value of another, impartial perspective, and they are always striving to be better. Be prepared to give honest feedback too, if you are asked for it.

First impressions

Whether in person or on the phone, even by email, the initial impressions you make are massively important. We make up our minds about people almost instantly, and those prejudices can take a lot of shifting. Make sure you make the right impression. Dress smartly, or appropriately for the story. Don't turn up to the Lord Mayor's Banquet in a Hawaiian shirt and a pair of sandals. You want to merge with your surroundings, not stick out like a sore thumb. Think about your appearance. Behave courteously and don't lose your temper – it will not get you anywhere. Remember, people do not have to talk to you if they do not want to. It is part of your job to make them want to. Treat them courteously, but persevere. This is all part of your professional approach to your work.

Practical steps

These are all things that you can do on your own – and at no expense!

Understand your craft

A lot of your most valuable learning will be on the job or on work experience placements. As the most junior person on the team, you will be given lesser tasks and sometimes feel that you do not have enough to do. Use any downtime to observe and soak up as much as you can about what is going on around you, how people are talking about stories and making decisions about them and how people are going about their business. If you do not understand something, do not be afraid to ask. As long as you pick your moment, people will usually be prepared to stop and explain. For a good online resource for all aspects of journalism, have a look at *The News Manual* https://www.thenews-manual.net/index.htm a free online guide to the principles and practices of journalism. It also has an extensive glossary of terms that you can consult if you do not understand some of the jargon flying about the office.

Develop your news sense

Any journalist can talk up or talk down a story if they are so minded. So how do editors determine what stories to cover and what to ignore? How do they decide when something becomes a story? How do they decide the prominence they give stories? Read and listen to and watch as much news as you can, and try to do so with a critical eye: Why is this is a story? Why are they giving it so much prominence – or so little? How have they put it together? How else could it have been done? If you attend editorial meetings, listen to the way stories are pitched, assessed and judged.

Analyse how others do it

If other journalists have been working on the same story as you, look at how they have covered it. Have they done better than you? Have they thought of better angles, got better quotes, written it more compellingly? If so, analyse how they did that. Do the same with other stories that have been covered by more than one reporter. Compare and contrast their work, and try to put your finger on why you think one approach is better than the other. Try to deconstruct the way stories have been put together. If you see a technique or a trick that you like, squirrel it away for future use.

Keep informed

Make sure that you always know what is going on in the world, and in the particular area where you work. This does not mean having an encyclopaedic knowledge of every single story, but it does mean having a general awareness of what is in the news, and the key elements of the most important subjects, or stories that crop up on a regular basis. You should always be able to provide an answer when your less well-informed friend asks you: "All this fuss about X. What's it all about?"

Learn where to find things

The internet is fantastic of course, and the most potent tool you could wish for. But it cannot do everything. It cannot always replace old-fashioned reporting techniques known as "phone-bashing" or "shoe-leather journalism", where you go round knocking on doors. Develop your research capabilities, and know what useful information is in the public domain – the electoral roll, for example, or the names of company directors. Familiarise yourself with the mechanics of Freedom of Information requests (discussed in Chapter 7) and some of the many tools that will help you to mine data (discussed in Chapter 14).

Understand the news business

Be aware of who the big industry players are, who the owners are, what the political affiliations are, and the trends and current issues in the business of journalism and the media.

Practice working under pressure

We have talked a little about absorbing information quickly and writing to deadlines. You don't want to experience those pressures for the first time when it is for real and you cannot afford to fail. Give yourself little private tests. Listen to a speech or a news conference or a news item, and jot down a few notes to test how much of it you can remember. Train yourself to do things within a set time, even if it is something trivial. It is sometimes hard to get a sense of what you can accomplish in five minutes, or ten, or half an hour.

Be well organised

Lots of reporters, even the best – especially the best – are hopelessly disorganised. It's a cliché that reporters never seem to have a pen or paper on them when they need them. Their cars and their desks are often a disgrace. They can never put their hands on anything they need, and they are surrounded by dirty coffee cups and half-eaten sandwiches. If this sounds like you, try to do something about it. The better organised you are, the less cluttered you are both in body and in mind, the more efficiently you will operate.

Behave professionally

To reiterate: behave in a professional manner. Learn what behaviour is expected of you as a professional, and observe it. Different newsrooms have different expectations, even when it comes to basic things like dress codes.

Tools of the trade

There are a few simple and largely inexpensive things you need in order to function efficiently as a reporter. Some – like high-end video cameras – should be provided by your employer if you need them to do your job. Some you will have to buy yourself. The good news is that you can kit yourself out relatively inexpensively.

A pen

Yes, I know. Goes without saying. Except that journalists are notorious for being unable to find a functioning pen at the critical moment. Having to borrow one from your interviewee will not improve your credibility. A highlighter pen will also be useful when you are going through your notes looking for the best bits.

An A5 spiral-bound notebook

These are sometimes called "reporter's notebooks". Even if you don't have a stationery cupboard in the office, you can buy them very cheaply. In the interests of speed, you will find it easier to write on one side of the paper only. When you reach the end you can turn it round and use the blank pages. When a book is full, write on the cover the dates it covers, and then keep it for at least a year. You might need your notes if a story is challenged, or if you have to give evidence in court.

Smaller notebooks that fit in your pocket or bag are handy and more discreet, but fill up more quickly and can feel fiddly. Lined A4 pads are handy in the office, but can be unwieldy in the field.

Even in the age of smartphones and miniature recorders, pen and paper remain your most reliable tools, especially if you have shorthand. With decent notes, you will not have to worry about batteries going flat, or recordings turning out to be inaudible when you come to play them back. If you are interviewing someone for a few short quotes, writing them down will also be much quicker than playing back and transcribing a recording. This is important in a business where time is often of the essence. Indeed, if you are a broadcast reporter, you might need to do a "live" immediately after a press conference; having accurate shorthand notes in that scenario is more or less essential. In some reporting environments, notably the law courts, you are not allowed to record anyway.

A contacts book

Essential. You will amass far too many contacts to store efficiently on your phone. Buy an A4 book with tabs down the right-hand side showing separate pages for each letter of the alphabet. Again, these are not expensive. Write your name and address in it straight away so that people know where to return it if you lose it.

Start putting contacts in your book immediately, and never throw anything away. Write legibly, and have a system for entries. Cross reference if appropriate – for example, by entering people twice, by organisation and by individual name; this may seem dull, but it is worthwhile and may save you time as well as saving your bacon. Enter the names, addresses, email addresses and phone numbers of all sources. Put in *everyone* – you may think you will never need to speak to them again, but you never know when their details might come in handy.

Put in contacts even if you have not spoken to them yourself or don't have all details – for example, someone you think might be a good source at some time in the future. You can paste business cards directly into the book, but it might get too bulky. Keep those cards, but store them somewhere else.

Make useful lists – so that, for example, you have local contacts for all the emergency services, police, fire and ambulance, on one page. Bring together details for local hospitals and schools, to make ring-rounds easier and quicker. Consider copying your whole book every now and then in case of loss. Remember though that you are collecting personal data, so be aware of the requirements of data protection legislation in terms of keeping your book secure and up to date.

You can of course create an online contacts book, but it will take a lot of time and effort, and is not necessarily as convenient as a book that you carry round with you.

A diary

This is useful not only as a way of keeping your life in order and arranging your schedule, but also as a prompt to take you back to stories and follow them up. It could be a physical book, or a diary you keep on your laptop, tablet or phone.

Apart from the obvious things you would put in a diary, mark down dates of known upcoming events such as trials, inquiries, report publications and so on. If a court case you are covering is adjourned, or councillors defer a decision, record in your diary the date the case is due to resume or the councillors will reconvene. After big local stories, make a note for yourself in the diary 6 or 12 months ahead, to prompt you to see if updates are appropriate or whether it is worth thinking about anniversary coverage. Write reminders to yourself to check on progress of stories you have done and of which you want to retain a degree of ownership.

A dictionary

Do not rely on spell check! It can fool you with American spellings that are not the same as UK spellings. If your spelling is iffy, check on your phone or buy a pocket dictionary so that you can look up anything you are not sure of. There is no excuse for spelling something wrongly.

A thesaurus

Sometimes called "Roget", because his was the first, a thesaurus is a dictionary of synonyms, or alternative words. It can help you when you are stuck for new ways of saying things, or when you want to avoid repeatedly using the same word. Available in book form or free online.

An atlas

Get a good world map with boundaries and capital cities clearly marked. You may not be travelling the world yourself, but people in your coverage area will, and if they get into trouble of some sort while abroad, you need to be able to find and describe where they are.

A UK road map, and a good map of your local area

Not just for helping you move around, but to help you cover stories. They will help you put places in perspective and get a sense of their size and where they are in relation to each other.

A smartphone

Of course, you can do nearly all of the above with a phone. But you might want to use it for other things at the same time. It might go flat, have no connection or get lost or stolen – and a book can often be easier and quicker to use. However, a smartphone is probably the single most useful tool you can have for both gathering and publishing.

A recording device

Again, a smartphone will make audio recordings for you, but a professional recording machine is very useful if you are going to work with audio a lot and want to be able to edit quickly and efficiently in broadcast quality. If you are doing an interview and just want to have a serviceable recording for checking against, you could buy a Dictaphone, which is smaller and more discreet. It may not record in broadcast quality. A reliable recording device will enable you concentrate on the questions and establish better rapport and eye contact with your subject – though listening back and transcribing do take time.

A stills camera

Your phone will have one of course, but there is no harm in having a separate device, for a better range of options and as a back-up.

A video camera

Again, your phone will serve, but your phone cannot do everything all the time and is not great for close-ups. If you are going to be regularly producing television pieces or video material for digital output, a small easy-to-use camera is a good investment.

A cuttings box

Cut out, or print, or file in your inbox, stories or snippets that interest you, or you think might be worth further investigation at some point. They may also be useful backgrounders on big stories that encapsulate the key points and will act as instant briefing notes. Or basic information, such as a list of your local councillors, with their responsibilities, wards and political affiliations. Delve into your box when you are stuck for ideas for stories. Keep a record of your own work too, both to build up a portfolio and to prompt you to investigate follow-up stories later.

4
Ethics

————————

the importance of ethics and values….why things can go wrong….. constraints on journalism…..who regulates you?…..The Editors' Code…..'the public interest'…..the IMPRESS Standards Code…..the NUJ Code of Conduct…..the Ofcom Broadcasting Code…..BBC Editorial Guidelines…..BBC values ….. common themes…….what this means for you

This chapter describes the manner in which all journalists – print, broadcast and online – are expected to behave, and the standards against which we are held accountable. If we fall below them, we abuse and jeopardise the extensive freedoms and privileges that journalism enjoys in a democratic society. Unethical behaviour is reprehensible in itself, but it also provides ammunition for those who are always ready to demand greater controls and restraints on the operation of the media.

The material in this chapter and the next relates directly to the National Council for the Training of Journalists (NCTJ) modules *Essential Journalism* and *Essential Journalism Ethics and Regulation*. The NCTJ Diploma requires you to pass a paper in print regulation – which also applies to the digital operations of most newspapers; or, if you are taking a module in broadcast journalism, in broadcast regulation. You will be asked to flag ethical issues in other papers too. Your e-portfolios will be scrutinised for evidence that you have gone about your work in an appropriate manner. This chapter and the next one cover everything that is contained in the Programmes of Study for those modules in terms of ethical behaviour, codes of conduct and regulation.

The importance of ethics and values

It is easy to think about ethical matters in isolation, as exceptional knotty issues that emerge from time to time, to be resolved only after much soul searching and head scratching. Real life is not like that. There is an ethical dimension to everything you do as a journalist, in every decision that you make. Often those decisions will be made against the clock, without the luxury of time fully to weigh the arguments. Once your ethical consciousness has been developed, you will make a lot of these decisions without even thinking about them.

The way you behave is of a piece with the sort of journalist you are. You will already know and care about the importance of accuracy, of getting the story right, of the need to deal decently with people and produce fair reporting. These are all part of the make-up of the ethical journalist. An ethical approach to the job means you should also care about the people whose stories you are telling, and treat them not as props and news commodities, but with respect and humanity. You want to be able to look at yourself in the mirror and know that you have not crossed any moral boundaries, and that your successes have not been achieved at the cost of unnecessary distress to others.

This might sound rather high-minded and idealistic, as well as being a far cry from the hack of popular perception, that caricature of the hard-bitten news reporter we met in Chapter 2. But it is the approach that all the various industry codes of conduct seek to encourage and foster. The codes are rooted in the conviction that ethical journalism is good journalism.

There are several such codes. In this chapter, we will examine and compare the principal ones and discuss their implications for the way we are expected to behave. We will not dwell on philosophical discussions about ethics and morals, but look in detail at the practical provisions of the codes, and what they mean for you as a working journalist.

At every level, journalists are routinely confronted with difficult decisions and editorial dilemmas, and these ethical codes provide the framework within which we are expected to resolve them. Through regulation, the industry seeks to ensure that standards are observed, and it can impose sanctions if they aren't. The system of regulation is described in the next chapter.

The ethical environment within which journalism works is intended to encourage good practice. It is not meant to act as a brake upon enterprise or bold and effective journalism. You can produce great stories without breaking the rules. But it does give you a point of reference. When things go wrong, it is usually because the principles have been misapplied or ignored altogether.

No rules and regulations can cover every contingency. What they can do is help you get your head in the right place to make good calls. An understanding of journalistic values and principles should help guide you to sound and well-founded editorial decision-making. This will help you build experience and judgement, even though you will almost always have the option of referring up to a more senior person, and should never be embarrassed about doing so.

After reading this chapter and learning about how the industry attempts to codify good behaviour, you should be able to:

> understand which of the codes of practice apply to you personally and the medium in which you are working

> recognise where ethical issues are involved – so that an alarm can go off in your head when you are tackling something potentially tricky, morally ambiguous or ethically difficult

> understand the impact that journalism can have on peoples' lives – either during the gathering of news, or the effect of publication. Some of the principles and rules are about protecting the public from sharp practice and unscrupulous behaviour

> understand how your actions reflect on you, your employer or journalism as a whole. If you make a mistake, the repercussions can be far-reaching

> recognise that with rights come responsibilities: we live in a democratic society with a free press and freedom of expression, but those privileges have to be respected and demand responsible behaviour in return

> understand that you can do challenging and brave journalism in a legal, ethical and responsible manner; and that ethical awareness is not about stopping you doing things, or taking the safe and easy way out.

This may all sound a bit self-evident, sanctimonious even. Why wouldn't you want to produce fair, responsible and bold journalism? Why wouldn't you behave well?

Why things can go wrong

Sadly, not everyone does behave well all the time. That is not always deliberate. There are a number of pressures that can lead even the most principled and well-meaning of us off the straight and narrow. Here are some of them:

Time

There is never enough of it – there are deadlines, editors shouting, no time to check, no time to make the calls. It adds up to a temptation to cut corners.

Space

There can be too little of that as well. You don't have room for all the angles or all the perspectives, and you struggle to get everything in, and to achieve the right overall tone and emphasis. The result may be a piece of work that is distorted or imbalanced.

Vanity

We all want to look good, make a splash, do well, get on: that can lead to a temptation to take short-cuts or liberties with the facts, to overwrite and oversell our material.

Arrogance

We think we can get away with it. It is a calculated risk, and we take it. It is worth a punt. They probably won't sue. No one will be any the wiser, will they?

Competition

Reporters compete fiercely with each other – even if they work for the same employer. Reporters and producers have been known actively to sabotage or undermine each other's stories.

Commercial pressures

Editors do not want to lose their audiences or their jobs, and take drastic steps to hold on to both. News is largely a commercial enterprise and that means it needs to turn a profit. Owners, shareholders, advertisers all have to be satisfied. Circulation figures, page views and ratings are pored over. Even non-commercial operators like the BBC are interested in healthy viewing and listening figures, and the factors that deliver them.

Culture

For the above reasons and others, there has occasionally been a culture in some workplaces that gives a low priority to observing ethical boundaries. You may feel you are putting your career or prospects at risk if you stand up against this kind of attitude – but it is the right thing to do.

News desk pressure

Reporters feel enormous pressure to get the story, and to make it better than anything the competition has produced. When you are given an assignment, you might also discover that your news desk has already decided what the story is and exactly what you are expected to write about it. You might find yourself pushed to write it that way, even if what you later find out conflicts with that approach.

You might have telephoned or knocked on the door of a potential interviewee and been told they do not want to speak to you. Your news desk may tell you that you haven't tried hard enough, and send you back to try again. It may be that they are right and that you need to be more persistent; but unwanted badgering could amount to harassment.

Finally, there is the sense that the end will justify the means – and that the message from the desk might be literally, or in effect: "do whatever it takes". This can put you in a very uncomfortable place indeed.

Inconveniences

You will often think a story is coming together nicely. Then you get a quote, or a statistic or some other piece of information that points the narrative in a different direction entirely. It can be tempting to omit or underplay material that does not "fit" with the story you think you are writing, or dilutes it in some way. Hence, the tongue-in-cheek saying "never let the facts stand in the way of a good story".

Lost in translation

A story can pass through many hands. The reporter writes it; the news desk or content editor might rewrite it; someone else updates and puts it into the content management system; it is copied and pasted into another story without the context – and so on. Sometimes the original reporter will be horrified by what eventually appears with his or her name attached to it. It might have been butchered, turned on its head or completely rewritten, and bear little relation to what they wrote in the first place.

Any or all of these things can lead reporters and editors to overstep the boundaries of what is ethical and decent, even if subconsciously or inadvertently. Things can and do go wrong, and journalism will sometimes fall short of those high-minded ideals that we considered in Chapter 2 – the important functions of journalism in a free society. When we consider an ethical approach, it is to ensure that these functions can be carried out to best effect. Here is a reminder of what they are:

> Telling people what is happening in the world
> Explaining, analysing, contextualising and making sense of events
> Providing accurate and trustworthy information produced to a high standard
> Bolstering citizenship and underpinning democracy
> Protecting and defending freedom of speech
> Holding to account governments and those in positions of power
> Exposing crime, corruption and wrongdoing
> Giving a voice to the voiceless and campaigning for social justice
> Unearthing hidden stories.

When journalism behaves itself, and does its job properly and ethically, its value is beyond dispute. When it does not, the extent of its privileges and freedom of action is called into question.

Constraints on journalism

Freedom of speech, freedom of expression and the rights of a free press do not mean that newspapers and broadcasters can do and say anything they want. There are a number of constraints on media activities:

The law

Although enjoying many freedoms, the UK's media, like its citizens, are subject to the rule of law. There is a raft of legislation covering the sort of issues in which journalism often finds itself involved – privacy, libel, copyright and so on. Tony Harcup in *The Ethical Journalist* talks of around 60 laws that impinge on the way journalists gather and disseminate information. The law is an absolute: it sets out what you can or cannot do, with the threat of prosecution and punishment if you fail to observe it.

Industry codes of practice

These set out what you ought to do, or ought not to do, but do not have the force of law. Even so, those who enforce them have the power to punish offenders, with sanctions such as fines or directions to publish apologies. The bulk of this chapter will be devoted to looking at these codes, because they define to a large extent what is meant by an ethical and values-driven approach to journalism.

"The way we do things around here"

This is about the culture in the office. Each workplace is a different environment, with different ways of doing things. The culture at the *News of the World* – and maybe others – during the phone hacking era was that the law and the rules were there to be bent and broken, and that nothing should be allowed to stand in the way of getting the story. At the other end of the spectrum, some organisations have their own in-house regulatory systems, publicly setting out their ethical stance and the steps they will take if they fall short.

Personal morality

We each have own moral compass, a sense of what we feel in our gut to be right or wrong. In a practical sense, this will often be in evidence in the way in which we deal with the people with whom we come into contact as reporters. They provide the fuel for our stories. How well do we treat them? How much do we respect them? In this we are our own referees: only we know when we have breached our personal standards. We have to satisfy our own consciences and our sense of what is decent, reasonable and humane.

Who regulates you?

If you work in print, your employers might well subscribe to the Editors' Code, which is followed by members of the Independent Press Standards Organisation, or IPSO. Most of the main newspaper publishers are signed up. Alternatively, they might work to the IMPRESS (Independent Monitor for the Press) Code. Or they might have their own in-house policies as well as, or instead of these. Find out which one applies to you!

If you work in radio or television you will be liable to the strictures of the Ofcom (Office of Communications) Broadcasting Code.

If you work for the BBC, you will be expected to observe the provisions of the Ofcom Broadcasting Code *and* the BBC's own Editorial Guidelines.

If you work on digital output, the regulatory picture is confused. Because the internet and social media know no borders, effective regulation across the board is well-nigh impossible. The IPSO and IMPRESS Codes cover the online content of newspapers and magazines, as well as the print versions. Some online-only outlets are regulated by these two bodies.

Some countries are bringing in laws to try to prevent the publication of harmful content online. In the UK, responsibility for enforcing this will fall to Ofcom, the regulator for broadcasting. The IPSO or IMPRESS Codes are broadly similar as we shall see. Outside broadcasting, use them as your guides if you are not sure how to behave, even if you are a digital journalist not formally covered by either.

If you are a member of the National Union of Journalists (NUJ), you will already have agreed to observe the NUJ Code.

The codes

The Editors' Code of Practice (sometimes known as the IPSO Code)

In the rest of this chapter, we are going to look in detail at the second of the limiting mechanisms, after the law: industry codes of practice. The print and broadcast industries work to different codes – regulated voluntarily in the case of most of print, and by statute in the case of broadcast. But all the codes are attempts to identify and define what constitutes good practice in a variety of journalistic situations, and what is considered unacceptable – and, possibly, liable for punishment.

From 1991, newspaper and magazine publishing in the UK was largely governed by a Code of Practice drawn up by the Society of Editors, and overseen by the Press Complaints Commission (PCC). The PCC no longer exists, having come in for strong criticism during the phone hacking scandal, but its Code has been adapted and adopted by the new Independent Press Standards Organisation. IPSO now regulates much of the activity of the printed press. Its code is usually referred to as The Editors' Code, and it has 16 sections.

The Editors' Code is intended to set the framework for the highest professional standards that print publications subscribing to IPSO have pledged themselves to maintain. In its preamble, the Code describes itself as "the cornerstone of the system of voluntary self-regulation to which they [the printed press] have made a binding contractual commitment".

It continues:

> It balances both the rights of the individual and the public's right to know. To achieve that balance, it is essential that an agreed Code be honoured not only to the letter, but in the full spirit. It should be interpreted neither so narrowly as to compromise its commitment to respect the rights of the individual, nor so broadly that it infringes the fundamental right to freedom of expression – such as to inform, to be partisan, to challenge, shock, be satirical and to entertain – or prevents publication in the public interest.

This is the key balance that all of these industry codes seek to maintain: that between individual rights (to privacy for example) and freedom of speech and the public's "right to know".

The preamble concludes:

> It is the responsibility of editors and publishers to apply the Code to editorial material in both printed and online versions of their publications. They should take care to ensure it is observed rigorously by all editorial staff and external contributors, including non-journalists.

So that is the purpose and the aspiration of The Editors' Code. Let us look at what it actually says – how those aspirations are achieved and applied in practice.

1. Accuracy

    i) The Press must take care not to publish inaccurate, misleading or distorted information or images, including headlines not supported by the text.
    ii) A significant inaccuracy, misleading statement or distortion must be corrected, promptly and with due prominence, and – where appropriate – an apology published. In cases involving IPSO, due prominence should be as required by the regulator.
    iii) A fair opportunity to reply to significant inaccuracies should be given, when reasonably called for.
    iv) The Press, while free to editorialise and campaign, must distinguish clearly between comment, conjecture and fact.
    v) A publication must report fairly and accurately the outcome of an action for defamation to which it has been a party, unless an agreed settlement states otherwise, or an agreed statement is published.

2. *Privacy

    i) Everyone is entitled to respect for and correspondence, including digital communications.
    ii) Editors will be expected to justify intrusions into any individual's private life without consent. In considering an individual's reasonable expectation of privacy, account will be taken of the complainant's own public disclosures of information and the extent to which the material complained about is already in the public domain or will become so.
    iii) It is unacceptable to photograph individuals, without their consent, in public or private places where there is a reasonable expectation of privacy.

3. *Harassment

    i) Journalists must not engage in intimidation, harassment or persistent pursuit.
    ii) They must not persist in questioning, telephoning, pursuing or photographing individuals once asked to desist; nor remain on property when asked to leave, and must not follow them. If requested, they must identify themselves and whom they represent.
    iii) Editors must ensure these principles are observed by those working for them and take care not to use non-compliant material from other sources.

4. Intrusion into grief or shock

    In cases involving personal grief or shock, enquiries and approaches must be made with sympathy and discretion and publication handled sensitively. These provisions should not restrict the right to report legal proceedings.

5. *Reporting suicide

    When reporting suicide, to prevent simulative acts care should be taken to avoid excessive detail of the method used, while taking into account the media's right to report legal proceedings.

6. *Children

    i)   All pupils should be free to complete their time at school without unnecessary intrusion.
    ii)   They must not be approached or photographed at school without permission of the school authorities.
    iii) Children under 16 must not be interviewed or photographed on issues involving their own or another child's welfare unless a custodial parent or similarly responsible adult consents.
    iv)   Children under 16 must not be paid for material involving their welfare, nor parents or guardians for material about their children or wards, unless it is clearly in the child's interest.
    v)   Editors must not use the fame, notoriety or position of a parent or guardian as sole justification for publishing details of a child's private life.

7. *Children in sex cases

    The press must not, even if legally free to do so, identify children under 16 who are victims or witnesses in cases involving sex offences.

    In any press report of a case involving a sexual offence against a child,
    i)   The child must not be identified.
    ii)   The adult may be identified.
    iii) The word "incest" must not be used where a child victim might be identified.
    iv)   Care must be taken that nothing in the report implies the relationship between the accused and the child.

8. *Hospitals

    i)   Journalists must identify themselves and obtain permission from a responsible executive before entering non-public areas of hospitals or similar institutions to pursue enquiries.
    ii)   The restrictions on intruding into privacy are particularly relevant to enquiries about individuals in hospitals or similar institutions.

9. *Reporting of crime

    i)   Relatives or friends of persons convicted or accused of crime should not generally be identified without their consent, unless they are genuinely relevant to the story.
    ii)   Particular regard should be paid to the potentially vulnerable position of children under the age of 18 who witness, or are victims of, crime. This should not restrict the right to report legal proceedings.
    iii) Editors should generally avoid naming children under the age of 18 after arrest for a criminal offence but before they appear in a youth court, unless they can show that the individual's name is already in the public domain, or that the individual (or, if they are under 16, a custodial parent or similarly responsible adult) has given their consent. This does not restrict the right to name juveniles who appear in a crown court, or whose anonymity is lifted.

10. *Clandestine devices and subterfuge

    i)   The press must not seek to obtain or publish material acquired by using hidden cameras or clandestine listening devices; or by intercepting private or mobile telephone calls, messages or emails; or by the unauthorised removal of documents or photographs; or by accessing digitally held information without consent.
    ii)   Engaging in misrepresentation or subterfuge, including by agents or intermediaries, can generally be justified only in the public interest and then only when the material cannot be obtained by other means.

[**Note** that this does not mean that journalists cannot record telephone calls that they themselves make or receive. This is not the same as intercepting and listening in on someone else's call. It may be necessary or desirable to record your own calls in case you later need proof that the call took place and that you reported it accurately. You do not have to tell the other person that the call is being recorded – but you would normally do so, or at least make clear that you are a journalist, unless there are good reasons not to.

Note that this clause does not prohibit the use of secret filming, provided there is a *prima facie* case to suspect wrongdoing of some sort. See the "public interest" section below. Most organisations require senior editorial sign-off for clandestine recordings.]

11 Victims of sexual assault

The press must not identify or publish material likely to lead to the identification of a victim of sexual assault unless there is adequate justification and they are legally free to do so.

12 Discrimination

i) The press must avoid prejudicial or pejorative reference to an individual's race, colour, religion, sex, gender identity, sexual orientation or to any physical or mental illness or disability.

ii) Details of an individual's race, colour, religion, gender identity, sexual orientation, physical or mental illness or disability must be avoided unless genuinely relevant to the story.

[**Note** that this does not mean that you cannot include some of these details, as appropriate, in your reporting. The key consideration is as to whether this would be "prejudicial or pejorative" and whether such details are relevant to the story].

13 Financial journalism

i) Even where the law does not prohibit it, journalists must not use for their own profit financial information they receive in advance of its general publication, nor should they pass such information to others.

ii) They must not write about shares or securities in whose performance they know that they or their close families have a significant financial interest without disclosing the interest to the editor or financial editor.

iii) They must not buy or sell, either directly or through nominees or agents, shares or securities about which they have written recently or about which they intend to write in the near future.

14 Confidential sources

Journalists have a moral obligation to protect confidential sources of information.

15 *Witness payments in criminal trials

i) No payment or offer of payment to a witness – or any person who may reasonably be expected to be called as a witness – should be made in any case once proceedings are active as defined by the Contempt of Court Act 1981. This prohibition lasts until the suspect has been freed unconditionally by police without charge or bail or the proceedings are otherwise discontinued; or has entered a guilty plea to the court; or, in the event of a not guilty plea, the court has announced its verdict.

i) Where proceedings are not yet active but are likely and foreseeable, editors must not make or offer payment to any person who may reasonably be expected to be called as a witness, unless the information concerned ought demonstrably to be published in the public interest and there is an over-riding need to make or promise payment for this to be done; all reasonable steps have been taken to ensure no financial dealings influence the evidence those witnesses give. In no circumstances should such payment be conditional on the outcome of a trial.

ii) Any payment or offer of payment made to a person later cited to give evidence in proceedings must be disclosed to the prosecution and defence. The witness must be advised of this requirement.

16 *Payment to criminals

i) Payment or offers of payment for stories, pictures or information, which seek to exploit a particular crime or to glorify or glamorise crime in general, must not be made directly or via agents to convicted or confessed criminals or to their associates – who may include family, friends and colleagues.

ii)   Editors invoking the public interest to justify payment or offers would need to demonstrate that there was good reason to believe the public interest would be served. If, despite payment, no public interest emerged, then the material should not be published.

This adds up to a very comprehensive list of the things journalists can and cannot do in a variety of common situations. It is deliberately legalistic in places – some of the provisions are designed to prevent journalists falling foul of the law. The general tenor is around fairness and respect for people who are caught up in news stories and who may be vulnerable for a number of reasons, especially children.

"The public interest"

You may have noticed that 10 of the 16 Clauses were marked with an asterisk (Clauses 2, 3, 5–10, 15 and 16). In these areas of reporting, it is stated that there may be exceptions to the bald statements of what is acceptable and what is not. These exceptions are based on a concept known as "the public interest". If you can demonstrate that even though you have broken the rules, your reporting was in the public interest, you may be able to make a successful defence of your behaviour.

So what is "the public interest"? The Code says it includes, but is not confined to:

Detecting or exposing crime, or the threat of crime, or serious impropriety.

Protecting public health or safety.

Protecting the public from being misled by an action or statement of an individual or organisation.

Disclosing a person or organisation's failure or likely failure to comply with any obligation to which they are subject.

Disclosing a miscarriage of justice.

Raising or contributing to a matter of public debate, including serious cases of impropriety, unethical conduct or incompetence concerning the public.

Disclosing concealment, or likely concealment, of any of the above.

These are areas in which, it is asserted, the public has a "right to know". The Code also says there is a public interest in freedom of expression itself. Note that this public interest defence does not apply to Clause 1 – Accuracy. No asterisk there, and no compromise. No one would argue that inaccurate journalism is in the public interest.

These judgements are subjective, and in recent years many of the debates about the public interest have related to complaints about invasion of privacy. As we have seen, the Code seeks to balance both the rights of the individual and the public's right to know, but there will always be disagreement about where the balance lies in particular instances. Are revelations about the sex lives of footballers or film stars matters of legitimate public interest? Or are they simply satisfying an unsavoury appetite for tittle-tattle, and a cynical attempt to attract more readers or viewers? As ever, the answer will depend on context. It may well be in the public interest to expose the adulterous affair of a politician who makes a habit of promoting the importance of family values. It probably won't be in the public interest to reveal a romantic relationship between two well-known and otherwise unattached people simply because they are well known.

Editors who want to defend stories on the grounds of the public interest need to demonstrate that they reasonably believed that publication – or journalistic activity undertaken with a view to publication – would both serve and be proportionate to the public interest. They need to explain how they reached that decision at the time. They need to produce a paper trail as evidence that the appropriate processes and considerations informed their decision-making. In the case of the provisions relating to children, whose interests are regarded as paramount, they would have to be able to argue exceptional grounds for breaking the rules.

The Code does not tackle issues of taste and decency. These are regarded as areas in which judgements will always be subjective, and so it is not seen as helpful to try to codify them. As we will see, this is not the case with broadcast content.

There is a clear echo in all this of what we have been saying about the societal responsibilities of journalism. If journalists are acting in the public interest, they have more latitude – because they are discharging those important functions that we discussed in Chapter 2, and reiterated above. If they are exposing crime or hypocrisy, say, they may be able to justify conduct that might otherwise be regarded as unethical. This concept of acting in the public interest is an important one, and while it may introduce scope for ambiguity, disagreement, subjective judgements and all kinds of grey areas, it serves to emphasise just how important those societal functions are – important enough to outweigh usually accepted standards and the rights of individuals.

The IMPRESS Standards Code

For reasons set out in the next chapter, on Regulation, IPSO is not the only regulatory body overseeing parts of the UK print media. There is a second organisation called IMPRESS, to which a number of publications are affiliated, albeit none of the major ones. No one is associated with both IPSO and IMPRESS.

IMPRESS has developed its own ethical guidelines which it calls the Standards Code, and which are intended to work in conjunction with legal obligations on journalists. This Code evolved from, among other things, a study of 56 different standards codes around the world, and input from more than 2,000 members of the public.

Like The Editors' Code, the IMPRESS Standards Code talks about reporting in the public interest – in other words, where the public interest in publishing is more important than some or all of the usual requirements of good practice, such as respect for privacy. Its definition of what may fall into this public interest category is similar to that of the Editors' Code, and builds on it in places:

(a) The revelation or discussion of matters such as serious incompetence or unethical behaviour that affects the public
(b) Putting the record straight where an individual or organisation has misled the public on a matter of public importance
(c) Revealing that a person or organisation may be failing to comply with any legal obligation they have
(d) The proper administration of government
(e) Open, fair and effective justice
(f) Public health and safety
(g) National security
(h) The prevention and detection of crime
(i) The discussion or analysis of artistic or cultural works.

The IMPRESS Code has ten sections. Although some of the section names are a little different, you will note that – as you would expect – there are substantial similarities with the IPSO Editors' Code. There are some new ideas too, such as the references to attribution and plagiarism in Section 2.

Section 1: Accuracy

1.1. Publishers must take all reasonable steps to ensure accuracy.

1.2. Publishers must correct any significant inaccuracy with due prominence, which should normally be equal prominence, at the earliest opportunity.

1.3. Publishers must always distinguish clearly between statements of fact, conjecture and opinion.

1.4. Whilst free to be partisan, publishers must not misrepresent or distort the facts.

Section 2: Attribution and Plagiarism

2.1. Publishers must take all reasonable steps to identify and credit the originator of any third-party content.

2.2. Publishers must correct any failure to credit the originator of any third-party content with due prominence at the earliest opportunity.

Section 3: Children

3.1. Except where there is an exceptional public interest, publishers must only interview, photograph, or otherwise record or publish the words, actions or images of a child under the age of 16 years with the consent of the child or a responsible adult and where this is not detrimental to the safety and well-being of the child. While a child should have every opportunity to express his or her wishes, journalists have a responsibility to consider carefully the age and capacity of the child to consent. Unless there is a detriment to the safety and well-being of a child, this provision does not apply to images of general scenes.

3.2. Except where there is an exceptional public interest, publishers must not identify a child under the age of 16 years without the consent of the child or a responsible adult unless this is relevant to the story and not detrimental to the safety and well-being of the child.

3.3. Publishers must give reasonable consideration to the request of a person who, when under the age of 16 years, was identified in their publication and now wishes the online version of the relevant article(s) to be anonymised.

Section 4: Discrimination

4.1. Publishers must not make prejudicial or pejorative reference to a person on the basis of that person's age, disability, mental health, gender reassignment or identity, marital or civil partnership status, pregnancy, race, religion, sex or sexual orientation or another characteristic that makes that person vulnerable to discrimination.

4.2. Publishers must not refer to a person's disability, mental health, gender reassignment or identity, pregnancy, race, religion or sexual orientation unless this characteristic is relevant to the story.

4.3. Publishers must not incite hatred against any group on the basis of that group's age, disability, mental health, gender reassignment or identity, marital or civil partnership status, pregnancy, race, religion, sex or sexual orientation or another characteristic that makes that group vulnerable to discrimination.

Section 5: Harassment

5.1. Publishers must ensure that journalists do not engage in intimidation.

5.2. Except where justified by the public interest, publishers must ensure that journalists:
   a)   Do not engage in deception.
   b)   Always identify themselves as journalists and provide the name of their publication when making contact.
   c)   Comply immediately with any reasonable request to desist from contacting, following or photographing a person.

Section 6: Justice

6.1. Publishers must not significantly impede or obstruct any criminal investigations or prejudice any criminal proceedings.

6.2. Publishers must not directly or indirectly identify persons under the age of 18 who are or have been involved in criminal or family proceedings, except as permitted by law.

6.3. Publishers must preserve the anonymity of victims of sexual offences, except as permitted by law or with the express consent of the person.

6.4. Publishers must not make payments, or offer to make payments, to witnesses or defendants in criminal proceedings, except as permitted by law.

Section 7: Privacy

7.1. Except where justified by the public interest, publishers must respect people's reasonable expectation of privacy. Such an expectation may be determined by factors that include, but are not limited to, the following:
   a)   The nature of the information concerned, such as whether it relates to intimate, family, health or medical matters or personal finances
   b)   The nature of the place concerned, such as a home, school or hospital
   c)   How the information concerned was held or communicated, such as in private correspondence or a personal diary
   d)   The relevant attributes of the person, such as their age, occupation or public profile
   e)   Whether the person had voluntarily courted publicity on a relevant aspect of their private life.

7.2. Except where justified by the public interest, publishers must:
   a)   Not use covert means to gain or record information
   b)   Respect privacy settings when reporting on social media content
   c)   Take all reasonable steps not to exacerbate grief or distress through intrusive newsgathering or reporting.

Section 8: Sources

8.1. Publishers must protect the anonymity of sources where confidentiality has been agreed and not waived by the source, except where the source has been manifestly dishonest.

8.2. Publishers must take reasonable steps to ensure that journalists do not fabricate sources.

8.3. Except where justified by an exceptional public interest, publishers must not pay public officials for information.

Section 9: Suicide

9.1. When reporting on suicide or self-harm, publishers must not provide excessive details of the method used or speculate on the motives.

Section 10: Transparency

10.1. Publishers must clearly identify content that appears to be editorial but has been paid for, financially or through a reciprocal arrangement, by a third party.

10.2. Publishers must ensure that significant conflicts of interest are disclosed.

10.3. Publishers must ensure that information about financial products is objectively presented and that any interests or conflicts of interest are effectively disclosed.

10.4. Publishers must correct any failure to disclose significant conflicts of interest with due prominence at the earliest opportunity.

The NUJ Code of Conduct

The NUJ has had a Code of Conduct for more than 80 years. All journalists joining the NUJ have to sign it, and agree that they will strive to adhere to its principles. It is brief and to the point, and covers much of the ground we have already looked at:

A journalist

- At all times upholds and defends the principle of media freedom, the right of freedom of expression and the right of the public to be informed.
- Strives to ensure that information disseminated is honestly conveyed, accurate and fair.
- Does her/his utmost to correct harmful inaccuracies.
- Differentiates between fact and opinion.
- Obtains material by honest, straightforward and open means, with the exception of investigations that are both overwhelmingly in the public interest and which involve evidence that cannot be obtained by straightforward means.
- Does nothing to intrude into anybody's private life, grief or distress unless justified by overriding consideration of the public interest.
- Protects the identity of sources who supply information in confidence and material gathered in the course of her/his work.
- Resists threats or any other inducements to influence, distort or suppress information and takes no unfair personal advantage of information gained in the course of her/his duties before the information is public knowledge.
- Produces no material likely to lead to hatred or discrimination on the grounds of a person's age, gender, race, colour, creed, legal status, disability, marital status or sexual orientation.
- Does not by way of statement, voice or appearance endorse by advertisement any commercial product or service saves for the promotion of her/his own work or of the medium by which she/he is employed.
- A journalist shall normally seek the consent of an appropriate adult when interviewing or photographing a child for a story about her/his welfare.
- Avoids plagiarism.

The union believes a journalist has the right to refuse an assignment if it would involve breaking the letter or spirit of the Code.

There are a number of areas that are common to all three Codes: accuracy, privacy, harassment, discrimination, inappropriate payments, the protection of sources and the protection of children. Note in particular the priority given to accuracy.

The Ofcom Broadcasting Code

Those then are the rules that apply to most UK newspapers and magazines, and their digital content, and some online-only outlets. Broadcasters are covered by a separate code developed by Ofcom. Ofcom is the independent regulator of the activities of UK broadcasters. It is required under the Communications Act 2003 to draw up and enforce a Broadcasting Code for television and radio, covering standards in programmes across a range of areas, including the protection of children, harmful and offensive content, impartiality, fairness and privacy.

The Code is set out across ten sections, each based on a *principle* and a series of *definitions*. The principles are there to help broadcasters understand the overall objectives of each section when applying the rules. The definitions offer guidance on how the principles should actually be applied in practice, and explain the thinking behind key concepts. The Code goes into much more detail than the print codes we have examined so far. It explains and expands on the principles in a way that the print codes do not, and it runs to more than 70 pages. But like its print counterparts, the Code does not seek to address each and every instance that could arise. The principles and definitions offer a framework intended to help broadcasters make appropriate judgements in all situations.

The Ofcom Code covers everything that is broadcast, not just journalism. Entertainment, documentaries, sport – anything that goes out on the television and radio falls within Ofcom's remit. In the context of journalism, the ten sections cover much of the same ground as print codes, and explain the criteria against which potential breaches are judged.

Broadcasters are required to be impartial in their output, and free of commercial influences, in a way that newspapers are not. So the Code also covers areas that are *not* part of the print codes: these include reporting of elections, maintenance of due impartiality and the regulation of commercial references in broadcast programmes on both radio and television.

Another major difference between the two codes is that The Editors' Code concentrates on *behaviours*, and stipulates what is acceptable and what crosses the line. The Ofcom Code looks at these areas too, but the emphasis is much more on *outputs*, and the *content* of broadcast programmes. It covers both the ethical production of content and what is actually transmitted, to whom and when, and what its likely effect on audiences may be.

The Code is too long to be reproduced in full here, although you can study it in detail on the Ofcom website. We will pick out some of the provisions most relevant to broadcast journalism.

Section 1: Protecting the under-18s

While the other Codes begin with assertions about the need for accuracy, Ofcom seems to take that requirement as read. The first section of the Broadcasting Code is about the protection of children and young people from harmful content. It introduces some of the ideas that later sections pick up when examining the same issues as they relate to adults.

Each of the separate sections of the code is introduced by a Principle setting out what the section aims to achieve. They are straightforward enough. The principle for protecting the under-18s is, as you might expect, "To ensure that under-eighteens are protected". The Code also refers in some places to "children", whom it defines as being under 15. So you should think of this section as protecting children under 15 and young people aged 15–18. For convenience, I will use "children" to refer to both groups.

Section 1 is about making sure that children are not exposed to content that is not suitable for them. This refers not only to what is actually in the programmes, but also to the times of day they are broadcast. Children are more likely to be watching during the day than they are late at night. So material that might be harmful to them should not be shown in the daytime. Ofcom calls this "appropriate scheduling".

What is "appropriate" is judged according to:

the nature of the content of the programme

the likely number and age range of children in the audience, taking into account school time, weekends and holidays

the start time and finish time of the programme

the nature of the channel or station and the particular programme

the likely expectations of the audience for a particular channel or station at a particular time and on a particular day.

All of this can be summarised as representing the *context* in which a programme is shown. Context is always a major consideration in the assessment of a potential breach of the Ofcom Code.

What this might mean, for example, is that if you were covering a crime or a court case in which there was a lot of graphic and potentially distressing detail, you would have to think carefully about how much of that detail to report if you thought that children were likely to be in the audience when it was aired.

An important part of appropriate scheduling is a concept called "the watershed". The watershed applies only to television, and it states that material unsuitable for under-18s should not, in general, be shown before 2100 at night. So those distressing details that you might omit from a teatime news report could potentially be included in a report that was broadcast after nine o'clock.

The concept of the watershed does not really work for the pattern of radio listening. So Ofcom tries to achieve an equivalent degree of protection in radio by saying that broadcasters must use their discretion and good sense, and have special regard to "times when children are particularly likely to be listening". This would cover breakfast time and the school runs, but might include other times as well, during the school holidays, for example.

The Code says that the introduction of more adult materials such as bad language or the portrayal of sex and violence must not be unduly abrupt after the 2100 watershed (in the case of television) or after the time when children are particularly likely to be listening (in the case of radio). For television, the strongest material should appear later in the schedule.

Armed with those definitions, Ofcom goes on to classify Protecting the Under-Eighteens in 30 paragraphs. The key sections refer to representations of things that Ofcom does not want children watching, and perhaps copying – such as drug, alcohol or substance abuse and smoking, physical or verbal violence, dangerous behaviour, offensive language, representations of sexual intercourse and nudity.

There is an exception here: some of these things may be allowed "when there is editorial justification". This is rather like the public interest exemptions we saw in the print codes. If broadcasters breach the Code, they need to be able to demonstrate that the editorial benefits of doing so outweighed the potential damage. So for example, you might justifiably show people smoking in a programme that was intended to show the dangers of smoking. But just as with the public interest exception in print, "editorial justification" leaves open the potential for grey areas and subjective decisions. It reminds us that an ethical approach is often about exercising discretion and judgement rather than hard and fast rules that can be rigidly applied to any set of circumstances. The threshold is high: when children are involved, Ofcom is likely to take a lot of convincing that there is a public interest in broadcasting material that is potentially harmful to them.

The key paragraphs state, in summary:

1.4. The watershed must be observed.
1.5. Radio broadcasters must have regard for times when children are likely to be listening.
1.6. The transition from pre- and post-watershed (and radio equivalent) must not be too stark.
1.10. Children's programmes must not feature drug, alcohol, substance abuse or smoking, and these activities must not be condoned, encouraged or glamorised in other programmes likely to be accessed by under-18s.
1.11. Violence, its after-effects and descriptions of violence, whether verbal or physical, must be appropriately limited in programmes broadcast before the watershed or when children are particularly likely to be listening, and must also be justified by the context.
1.12. Violence, whether verbal or physical, that is easily imitable by children in a manner that is harmful or dangerous must not be featured in programmes made primarily for children unless there is strong editorial justification.
1.13. Dangerous behaviour, or the portrayal of dangerous behaviour, that is likely to be easily imitable by children in a manner that is harmful, must not be featured in programmes made primarily for

children unless there is strong editorial justification, and in any case must not be broadcast before the watershed or when children are particularly likely to be listening unless there is editorial justification.

1.14. The most offensive language must not be broadcast when children are particularly likely to be in the audience.

1.15. Offensive language must not be used at all in programmes made for younger children except in the most exceptional circumstances, and.....

1.16. ...none is to be broadcast frequently pre-watershed.

1.20. Representations of sexual intercourse must not occur before the watershed (in the case of television) or when children are particularly likely to be listening (in the case of radio), unless there is a serious educational purpose. Any discussion on, or portrayal of, sexual behaviour must be editorially justified if included before the watershed, or when children are particularly likely to be listening and must be appropriately limited.

1.21. Pre-watershed nudity must be justified by context.

You may think it unlikely that much of this is going to be relevant to your reporting, and you may well be right. But remember that Ofcom regulates not just journalism but all broadcast content. That covers a vast range of programming. And it is always worth bearing in mind viewing and listening habits when compiling your reports.

More pertinent perhaps are the next two clauses, which move away from the protection of young people from harmful material, and concentrate on the duty of care broadcasters must have in their dealings with young people who take part in programmes.

1.28. Due care must be taken over the physical and emotional welfare and the dignity of people under-18 who take part or are otherwise involved in programmes. This is irrespective of any consent given by the participant or by a parent.

1.29. People under-18 must not be caused unnecessary distress or anxiety by their involvement in programmes or by the broadcast of those programmes.

In summary, protecting children and the under-18s means making sure as far as possible that they are not exposed to inappropriate content in these sorts of areas, either as the result of the nature of the content itself or the time it is broadcast. There are occasional caveats that breaches can sometimes be permitted if the editorial considerations are very strong. But the bar is set very high.

Section 2: Harm and offence

Here is the principle that is applied when looking at harm and offence:

> To ensure that generally accepted standards are applied to the content of TV and radio stations so as to provide adequate protection for members of the public from the inclusion in such services of harmful and/or offensive material.

This echoes some of the concerns we have been considering with relation to under-18s. Now though, we are talking about listeners and viewers of all ages. To understand the thinking behind this section, we need to know what is meant by "generally accepted standards", and what is meant by "harmful and/or offensive material".

The concept of "generally accepted standards" is another of those definitions that help interpret the Code. It is based on a judgement of what *reasonable people* would regard as being acceptable. Ofcom also has a list of materials it defines as potentially harmful and/or offensive:

> offensive language, violence, sex, sexual violence, humiliation, distress, violation of human dignity, discriminatory treatment or language (on the grounds of age, disability, gender reassignment, pregnancy and maternity, race, religion or belief, sex and sexual orientation, and marriage and civil partnership).

The Code says inclusion of these things needs to be justified by context. So now we need to know what Ofcom means by "context" in this connection. It is a similar approach to the one adopted for under-18s. Context is defined by:

> The content of a programme or series
> The service on which it is broadcast
> The time of broadcast
> The programmes scheduled before and after
> The degree of harm and offence likely to be caused
> The size, nature and expectation of audience
> The extent to which audiences have been alerted to what they are about to see or hear
> The effect on those who come on the material unawares.

In deciding whether or not material is harmful or offensive, Ofcom will consider not only the material itself, but also the people who are likely to be watching and listening to it; and what those people would expect to see or hear on that particular programme or channel at that time of day. If the material is in keeping with those expectations, it might not be in breach – or if it were, the severity of the breach would be diminished.

The rest of the section looks at more specific areas where there is a strong possibility of causing harm and offence. Some examples are:

2.4.   Material must not condone/glamorise violent, antisocial or dangerous behaviour or encourage imitation.
2.5.   Material must not show methods of suicide or self-harm unless justified editorially or in context.
2.6.–2.8. Demonstrations of exorcism, the occult and the paranormal must be objectively handled.
2.10.   Simulated news must not look too much like real news.

This last is about programmes that do reconstructions, or dramas, often police and crime series, that include mock news bulletins, scenes involving reporters, television presenters and so on. The Code says it has to be obvious that we are not watching real news, but that it has been reconstructed or presented for dramatic effect.

2.12 Warnings of flashing lights for those with photosensitive epilepsy

This applies in particular to news reports that contain a lot of flashing images, such as strobing or flash photography, because for people with this condition, such images can trigger epileptic fits. Ofcom accepts that this is usually editorially justified, but says that some form of warning – verbal or on screen, or both – should precede any item in which there are flashing images of any sort. You hear and see such warnings in television news programmes every day.

Section 3: Crime, disorder, hatred and abuse

This is the principle behind the provisions of this section:

> To ensure that material likely to encourage or incite the commission of crime or to lead to disorder is not included in TV or radio services.

The preamble to this section says that the rules are intended to reflect the right of the broadcasters to freedom of expression and the right of the audience to receive information and ideas. In other words, the Code seeks to strike a balance between censorship on the one hand, and protecting the audience from harmful material on the other. Broadcasters may wish to interview or report on organisations with extreme views as part of news and current affairs programmes, and it is often in the public interest for them to do so. But they are obliged to do so *in context* – that word again, a big favourite of Ofcom. Everything depends on the circumstances in which material is presented; very often as with Sections 1 and 2, it is not the material itself that is the potential problem, but the context in which it is broadcast. You can justify what you do if you do it responsibly.

Some of the specific elements of Section 3 are:

3.1. Material likely to encourage or incite the commission of crime or to lead to disorder must not be broadcast, nor must…..
3.2. …..hate speech, unless justified by context, or……
3.3. ….. abusive or derogatory treatment of individuals, groups, religions or communities.

"Hate speech" is any form of expression that spreads, incites, promotes or justifies hatred based on intolerance of disability, ethnicity, gender, gender reassignment, nationality, race, religion or sexual orientation. Unless justified by our old friend: context. What does context mean here?

> The content of a programme or series
> The greater the potential to offend, the greater the obligation to justify
> The extent to which material is challenged in the programme
> The service on which it is broadcast
> The size, nature, expectation of audience.

These are ideas that we are already familiar with, with one or two new ones.

For instance, we are introduced to the concept of proportionality. The Code says that the greater the risk of harm and offence, the greater the need for contextual justification. In other words, the nastier something is, the more you need to be able to present it in context to justify reporting it. This can be measured by, for example, the extent to which repugnant views or actions are challenged, or set against contrasting views, and – as before – when and where they are broadcast and what the audience is likely to expect.

More specific clauses, familiar to us from the other codes, are:

3.4. There should be no descriptions or demonstrations of criminal techniques that could lead to a crime being committed.
3.5. There should be no payment to criminals for programme contributions about their crimes – unless it can be shown to be in the public interest.
3.6. There should be no payment of witnesses….
3.7. …. or potential witnesses, unless there is a clear public interest.

Section 4: Religion

After all you have heard already, you should not be surprised by anything in Section 4. Here are the principles behind it:

> to ensure that broadcasters exercise the proper degree of responsibility with respect to the content of religious programmes

> to ensure that religious programmes do not involve any improper exploitation of any susceptibilities of the audience for such a programme…

> …and do not involve any abusive treatment of the religious views and beliefs of those belonging to a particular religion.

These principles cover the contents of the seven paragraphs of this section, which is about respect and religious tolerance, with a caution that religious programming should not seek to make converts by stealth.

Section 5: Due impartiality and due accuracy

We have already noted that this is a subject not tackled by the Editors' Code or the Standards Code, because print publications do not have any obligation to be impartial. They are expected to observe the need for accuracy and fairness, but they can be as partial and as opinionated as they choose. Broadcasters are committed to providing unbiased and independent information in a way that the print sectors are not. If they are not impartial in their coverage, they are in breach of the Code. This is a critical distinction between the regulation of print and broadcast material.

This section sets out Ofcom's view of what this commitment to impartiality means in practice. Here is how it is summarised as a principle:

> To ensure that news, in whatever form, is reported with due accuracy and presented with due impartiality and to ensure that the special impartiality requirements of the Communication Act are complied with.

The little word "due" is important here. It means that not everything has to be given the same amount of airtime or accorded the same degree of significance. It is up to broadcasters to weigh differing viewpoints and perspectives, assess the relative weight of each and, while not excluding any of them, reflect that in the way they are reported. This means judging where the balance of opinion lies and the merits of the various arguments under discussion.

"Due impartiality" is not an easy concept to grasp, and often very difficult to put into practice. Even the Code finds it easier to say what it is not, rather than defining what it is:

> "Impartiality" means not favouring one side over another

> "Due" does not mean equal time to every view or argument

> Approach may vary according to the subject, programme, channel, expectation of audience, signposting of content.

So due impartiality is not just about a neutral approach, or about achieving a crude balance on a "he said, she said" basis. The section is aimed at programmes that tackle major issues of controversy or policy. For lighter topics, impartiality might not matter anything like so much. For significant topics – often those covered by news programmes – it is about apportioning the appropriate time and weight to the arguments according to what they are perceived to deserve. This is what is meant by the word "due".

A good example to illustrate this is coverage of climate change. You might produce a radio report in which one person claimed that global warming was a big problem and that mankind was to blame for it, while another claimed that if it existed at all it was a natural phenomenon and we should stop worrying about it. Such an item might achieve balance of a sort in that you would be setting opposing opinions against each other.

But it would not pass the test of "due" impartiality. The overwhelming majority of scientists who study climate change believe that it is a reality, and that it is at least partly due to human activity. Climate change deniers represent a vanishingly small constituency, at least as far as the scientific community is concerned. It is a debate in which 99 per cent of opinion is on one side, and only one per cent on the other. So a discussion that featured a climatologist and a denier would not give the audience an accurate – or duly impartial – view of the status of the debate about climate change. Your coverage would have to make clear the nature of that 99-1 split of scientific opinion.

Political coverage is another area in which this debate is active, and a thorny one at that. Is it right to assume that every political party, regardless of its size, be given the same amount of airtime? That might seem like a fair and balanced approach, but would not represent due impartiality– or even basic common sense. We know a lot about the size of political parties, the amount of support they command at any given time, how many candidates they field at elections and so on. All of this data is used by broadcasters to decide what constitutes proportionate – or "due" – coverage when it comes to reporting politics. Put crudely, the big parties will command more airtime than the small ones. It is very far from being an exact science of course, but it is an attempt to reflect reality in as sophisticated a way as possible. We need something more nuanced than simple balance.

Here are the specific provisions of the Impartiality section, intended to build on this concept of due impartiality.

5.1.   News must be reported and presented accurately and impartially
5.2.   Significant mistakes must be acknowledged and corrected quickly
5.3.   No politician to act as reporter or newsreader unless editorially justified
5.4.   The views of channel owners on politics and public policy to be excluded
5.5.   Due impartiality can be achieved within a programme or over a series
5.6.   Where programmes are linked, that should be made clear to the audience
5.7.   Views and facts must not be misrepresented
5.8.   Any potential conflict of interests involving reporters or presenters to be made clear
5.9.   Alternative viewpoints to be encouraged
5.10. Clarity where personal or authored views are being broadcast
5.11. Due impartiality applies to "matters of major political and industrial controversy and major matters relating to current public policy"
5.12. A wide range of views is to be canvassed and given "due weight"
5.13. No views should be given undue prominence.

Section 6: Elections

This section, as the accompanying principle makes clear, is to ensure that the rules on impartiality are taken particularly seriously when it comes to reporting elections. Again, this is something not covered in newspaper Codes. Here is the principle:

To ensure that the special impartiality requirements in the Communications Act 2003 and other legislation relating to broadcasting on elections and referendums are applied at the time of elections and referendums.

This applies during what is known as the "election period" or "pending period" which can vary between different sorts of elections and referenda, but in essence refers to the final weeks before polling day.

As discussed in relation to Section 5, Ofcom applies the idea of "due weight" to an election and begins by saying that it must be applied to parties and independent candidates. In deciding what due weight is, broadcasters must look at evidence of past electoral support (such as the results of previous elections) and current support (such what the opinion polls are suggesting). They will also look at how many candidates each party is fielding. When they have gathered all the data, they come to a conclusion about which parties will receive most coverage and which least. In a British General Election, this will usually mean equal coverage for Labour and the Conservatives, and a little less for the Liberal Democrats. There will have to be separate calculations when it comes to the nationalist parties such as the Scottish National Party or Plaid Cymru. Those calculations will be different for a UK broadcaster and a Scottish or Welsh broadcaster. It is not up to Ofcom to make these decisions. Ofcom's role is to monitor output if it thinks it necessary, and to rule on complaints that a broadcaster is not providing fair, proportionate and duly impartial coverage.

All on-air discussion and analysis have to finish as soon as the polling stations open. While people are voting, broadcasters can discuss only the weather and the turnout and show important people casting their votes. Nor can they – or indeed any other media – publish any opinion polls or exit polls on election day until after the polls have closed.

If you are reporting from an individual constituency during an election period, your report must be internally balanced. You must invite every candidate to take part – although if they refuse, you can go ahead without them and report that they declined. In any case, you have to give the audience the full list of everyone who is standing at the end of your report. On television, this list is often shown on screen at the end of the report. On radio it may be read. In both cases, the audience is usually also directed to the list online.

Section 7: Fairness

This section, like the next one on Privacy, is different from the others in that it applies to how broadcasters treat individuals or organisations directly affected by programmes, as opposed to what the general public sees and hears as listeners and viewers. As such these sections are directly comparable to some of the provisions of the Editors' Code.

The principle of Fairness is:

To ensure that broadcasters avoid unjust or unfair treatment of individuals or organisations in programmes.

This is achieved by something called "practices to be followed" – another of Ofcom's definitions. If these practices are not followed, and unfair treatment results, that will be a breach of the Code. The practices are designed to make sure that programme contributors are fully aware of what they are signing up to, and are happy to agree to it – a process known as "informed consent".

The "practices to be followed" to ensure informed consent state that contributors should be made aware of the following:

- The nature and purpose of the programme, what it is about, why they have been asked to take part, when it is going out
- What sort of contribution is being asked of them – live, pre-recorded, interview, discussion, edited, unedited
- Areas of questioning
- The names of other contributors
- Information about any changes of plan as they occur
- Information about contractual rights
- Information about whether they will be able to preview the programme and suggest changes
- Information about any potential risks arising from their taking part that might affect their welfare, and any steps the programme maker intends to take to reduce them.

If you tell contributors all this, and they agree, they are deemed to have given you informed consent that they will take part on these terms. You will ask them to sign a form confirming that they have given such consent.

This might feel like quite an elaborate procedure, and it will not always be possible or necessary in the more pressured and unstructured environment of on-the-day news. You do not need to worry about it for every news interview you do, although you will normally tell people where you are from and what you are doing. It applies much more to planned programmes being made over a longer timescale. Even so, you are obliged to tell people as much as you can about what you are doing and what you want them to do. This is called "fair dealing".

Some specific clauses are:

7.4. You should not interview under-16s without parental consent, and not interview them at all about anything about which they are unlikely to be able to give you an informed opinion.
7.5. If someone over 16 cannot give consent for some reason, then someone over 18 can give it on their behalf – say, someone with primary responsibility for their care.
7.6. When a programme is edited, it should be done fairly and give a fair representation of the interview and issue.
7.7. If you promise anything up front like confidentiality or anonymity, then make sure you honour it.
7.8. If your material is going to be used in another programme or for a different purpose, or you yourself use material from somewhere else that's been recorded for a different purpose, make sure you do not create unfairness in your use of it.
7.9. Factual programmes should be sure that material facts have not been presented, disregarded or omitted in a way that might be unfair, and that everyone who should be allowed to contribute has been invited to do so.
7.10. The same applies to dramas, especially those based on actual events. They need to be fair.
7.11. If a programme makes allegations about wrongdoing, incompetence or anything else, those accused must be given the opportunity to respond (this is called "right to reply").
7.12. If you do give them such an opportunity, and they decline, you should make that clear, and give their explanation if they offer one.
7.13. This calls for fair portrayal of the views of people or organisations that are not part of the programme.
7.14. This says that you should not try to secure material or agreement through misrepresentation or deception. This might include set-ups, pranks or wind-up calls – not something you are likely to do in a journalistic context. But it may be that you have to resort to questionable methods if there is no other way of getting what you want. The Code says that might be warranted if it is in the public interest.
7.15. This says broadcasters should consider the welfare of contributors who might be at risk of significant harm as the result of taking part in a programme, because they are vulnerable or for any other reason (see 8.22 for a definition of "vulnerable").

Like much of the Code, the Fairness section attempts to put down in writing what most of us would regard as normal, reasonable and decent behaviour.

Section 8: Privacy

Much the same is true of this section, which can often overlap with Section 7. Here is the principle on which it is based:

> To ensure that broadcasters avoid any unwarranted infringement of privacy in programmes and in connection with obtaining material included in programmes.

As with Fairness, the approved behaviours under Privacy are called "practices to be followed". The Code says that people have a "legitimate expectation of privacy", and that infringements of privacy in obtaining material must be warranted. We need to unbundle these two ideas of before we can understand the thinking here.

The Code says broadcasters would have to show that an infringement of privacy was warranted on the grounds that they were acting in the public interest, and that this consideration outweighed the right to privacy. Examples of things that might justify breaching someone's privacy would be revealing or detecting crime, protecting public health or safety or exposing misleading claims.

What about "legitimate expectation of privacy"? This is a concept that we have already seen in the print Codes, both of which call it "reasonable expectation of privacy", and it derives from a legal concept.

What is legitimate or reasonable is hard to define. Ofcom says it will vary according to the place, the activity being reported, whether or not information is already in the public domain, or whether the individual concerned is already in the public eye.

There may be circumstances in which people can have an expectation of privacy in a public place, where filming or recording might be an infringement – at a funeral, for instance. And even people in the public eye have the right to retain a private life for themselves and their families. So for both print and broadcast, whether or not a breach of privacy is warranted is also going to be a subjective judgement. Journalists trying to defend such breaches would have to show that they had weighed all these factors in the balance before deciding to proceed. You will usually refer to more senior people when you are dealing with a story that requires you to consider the public interest.

There are many clauses in this section fleshing out and giving further guidance about the application of this principle. They reflect the subjective nature of the judgements involved – and make liberal use of the caveat "unless it is warranted" (my emphases in these references).

8.2. Information disclosing the location of someone's house or family should not be revealed without permission – **unless it is warranted.**
8.3. People caught up in news events still have rights to privacy at the time and later – **unless infringement is warranted.**
8.4. Even material filmed or recorded in a public place may be regarded as being private enough – say a private conversation – to require consent to broadcast – **unless broadcasting without consent is warranted.**
8.5. Infringements of privacy in the making of a programme should be with the consent of a person or organisation – **unless warranted.....**
8.6. ..... and the same applies to its actual broadcast.

8.7. More on consent – if someone's privacy is being infringed and they ask for recording to stop, those recording should agree, **unless it is warranted** to continue…..

8.8. You will want to get prior consent before filming in institutions, organisations or the like. But if you are recording in sensitive places like ambulances, hospitals, schools prisons, police stations, you will normally want to seek the separate consent from individuals – **unless it is warranted** to film or record without permission.

8.9. The means of obtaining information should be proportionate to the subject matter of the programme.

8.10. This echoes a clause from the previous section about re-use. If your material is going to be used in another programme or for a different purpose, or you yourself use material from somewhere else that's been recorded for a different purpose, make sure you don't create an unwarranted infringement of privacy in your use of it.

8.11. Before doorstepping you should have asked for an interview by conventional means – although it is usually fine to approach people in the news if they are out in public.

8.12. If you think you're going to want to record and broadcast a phone call, you need to have identified yourself, explained the purpose of the call and that it is being recorded for possible broadcast. If you didn't do those things and want to use an extract, you will need to get consent before broadcasting – **unless not to do so is warranted.**

8.13. The same applies to surreptitious filming. You will always need senior approval to do this and to get it you will need to show that you have got some evidence of a story that is in the public interest and that you could get more evidence by secret means.

8.14. Having done it, you need to think about **whether it is warranted** to use it.

8.15. It is about secret recording and filming for entertainment shows as opposed to factual programming.

8.16. Worries about footage or audio of people caught up in emergencies, who are the victims of accidents or suffering personal tragedies even if they are in a public place. It says that could be an infringement of privacy **unless it is warranted** and sometimes you might ask for consent.

8.17. None of these people, or those in a state of distress, should be pressured to give interviews.

8.18. Broadcasters should not reveal the identities of people who have died in accidents or as the result of crime/terrorism etc., unless they know that next of kin has been informed.

8.19. If you are returning to a previous story, or planning a reconstruction – which could be a drama as well as a factual programme – you will normally try to inform surviving victims or families and tell them when it is going to be broadcast to minimise potential distress.

8.20. Ofcom is particularly worried about the privacy of the under-16s. They do not lose their rights to privacy because of what their parents may have done, or because of something that happens in their school, for example.

8.21. If they are involved, then you need their consent, and/or that of a parent – unless it is a trivial matter and you feel you don't need it.

8.22. Finally, under-16s and vulnerable people should not be questioned about private matters without the consent of a parent, guardian or suitable person. "Vulnerable people" may mean those with learning difficulties, mental health problems, the bereaved, the traumatised, the terminally ill, the demented.

All in all, this is clearly something of a minefield, and although it gives a strong sense of the sort of behaviour that is expected, it is still essentially a matter of you making judgement calls in specific circumstances and checking your decisions against that criterion about whether your actions are "warranted". In practice, a young journalist would be well advised to seek advice and direction from further up the chain when dealing with a lot of these dilemmas.

Sections 9 and 10: Commercial references in television and radio programming

The Code concludes with two sections about commercial references. The same principles apply to each, but one is specifically for television (Section 9) and one is for radio (Section 10). The principles are:

> to ensure that broadcasters maintain editorial independence and control over programming (editorial independence).
> to ensure that there is distinction between editorial content and advertising (distinction).
> to protect audiences from surreptitious advertising (transparency).
> to ensure that audiences are protected from the risk of financial harm (consumer protection).
> to ensure that unsuitable sponsorship is prevented (unsuitable sponsorship).

These sections of the Code build on these principles with general overarching rules that apply to all commercial references in television programming. It also contains specific rules for different types of commercial activity (such as product placement, programme-related material, sponsorship), and whether it is carried out by, or on behalf of commercial or non-commercial entities.

The rules ensure that the principles of editorial independence are maintained: stress the distinction between advertising and editorial content; address transparency of commercial arrangements; and consumer protection.

This is a very long section but for the purposes of this summary, we will look at the features of just a handful of the key paragraphs.

9.1–9.3. are all about making sure that programmes are not distorted by any commercial interests, that broadcasters maintain their independence, that there is a clear line between programme content and advertising. Surreptitious advertising is prohibited. This is defined as a reference to a product, service or trademark within a programme, where such a reference is intended by the broadcaster to serve as advertising and this is not made clear to the audience.

9.5. No undue prominence may be given in programming to a product, service or trademark. Undue prominence may result from the presence of, or reference to, a product, service or trademark in programming where there is no editorial justification; or the manner in which a product, service or trademark appears or is referred to in programming. This is sometimes called "product placement": which has a legal definition. It is the inclusion in a programme of, or of a reference to, a product, service or trademark where the inclusion is for a commercial purpose, and is in return for the making of any payment, or the giving of other valuable consideration.

There is also something called "prop placement". This is about products that are given prominence even if no money has changed hands.

9.8. Product placement must not influence the content and scheduling of a programme in a way that affects the responsibility and editorial independence of the broadcaster.

9.9. References to placed products, services and trademarks must not be promotional or unduly prominent.

9.11. Product placement of all smoking products (including e-cigarettes) and prescription-only medicines is banned.

9.12. Product placement is specifically not permitted in religious programmes, consumer advice programmes or current affairs programmes.

9.13. Also banned is product placement of alcoholic drinks, foods or drinks high in fat, salt or sugar (HFSS), gambling; infant formula (baby milk), all medicinal products, cigarette lighters, cigarette papers or pipes intended for smoking.

9.14. Product placement must be signalled clearly, by means of a universal neutral logo.

You probably will not find yourself swimming in these waters very often, but the whole Code is included in the NCTJ syllabus, so it is worth being aware at least of the general desire to prohibit the promotion of products, especially if done in a surreptitious way.

The radio regulations are based on the same principles and concentrate on creating clear dividing lines between advertising content and editorial or other content ('programming'), to ensure that the listener is clear which is which and there is no blurring of the lines between the two.

10.1. Programming that is subject to, or associated with, a commercial arrangement must be appropriately signalled, so as to ensure that the commercial arrangement is transparent to listeners.

10.2. Spot advertisements must be clearly separated from programming.

10.3. No commercial reference, or material that implies a commercial arrangement, is permitted in or around news bulletins or news desk presentations.

10.4. No commercial reference, or material that implies a commercial arrangement, is permitted on radio services primarily aimed at children or in children's programming included in any service.

10.5. No commercial arrangement that involves payment, or the provision of some other valuable consideration, to the broadcaster may influence the selection or rotation of music for broadcast.

Summary

So that is the Ofcom Broadcasting Code. There are areas of overlap with both print codes, and where they do overlap, thankfully the codes all point in the same direction, with a few differences of emphasis. As noted, Ofcom's remit covers all types and genres of television and radio programmes. It is as concerned with the way in which material is broadcast and when, as it is with the way that material is gathered and assembled. The print Codes largely keep a focus on how journalists work; the Ofcom Code is there to cover standards more widely and to represent and protect the interests of the viewer and listener. The different approaches to the question of impartiality are critical. Ofcom goes into more detail in explaining the concepts and definitions that it has developed, which helps with the interpretation of the Code – and with the manner in which it assesses complaints that the Code has been breached.

These codes take a broadly similar approach to ethical behaviour, based on trying to get things right; remedying matters when they go wrong; treating people – in particular the young and vulnerable – in a fair and respectful manner; and obeying the law.

BBC Editorial Guidelines

The Ofcom Broadcasting Code covers all radio and television broadcasting licenced by Ofcom. Since 2017, that has included the BBC. Before 2017, the BBC, the largest and most influential broadcaster in the UK, sat outside the aegis of Ofcom. Its management was accountable to a board called the BBC Trust, and so the BBC was essentially self-regulating. It maintained a large department to handle complaints from listeners and viewers, with the Trust as the ultimate arbiter of its conduct.

As a result, the BBC has its own extensive code of values and standards, contained in a 390-page book called Editorial Guidelines – in essence a bible of what the BBC considers to be fair, proper and ethical behaviour. All BBC staff – journalists, producers and everyone else – are expected to abide by them. They are also publicly available online and are regularly revised and updated to take account of changing circumstances. They were last fully revised and reissued in 2019.

When the operations of the BBC came under the wing of Ofcom in 2017, this mechanism was retained. Complaints about BBC programmes are considered first within the internal processes of the BBC, and referred to Ofcom only if they cannot be resolved satisfactorily.

Even if you do not work for the BBC, it is worth looking at the ethical philosophy that it has evolved over a century of public service broadcasting. It devotes enormous effort to codifying its moral, cultural and ethical position, and to sharing with licence fee payers a detailed analysis of the standards by which it expects to be judged. Because the BBC is such a big player on the British media scene, no examination of ethical behaviour in journalism would be complete without a consideration of some of the pillars of this philosophy.

BBC Values

We noted in Chapter 2 the BBC's overall mission statement, "to inform, to educate and to entertain". We also looked at what the BBC calls its Public Purposes, putting flesh on the mission statement and adding some detail about what the organisation believes it is for. The ethical approach it takes while delivering on those Purposes is set out in a series of Values:

BBC Values: truth and accuracy

This is perhaps the most fundamental and important principle of all for a news organisation, let alone a public service broadcaster. We have seen that accuracy is the subject of the very first clauses of both the print codes. The BBC says it will always strive to establish the veracity of what it is reporting as best it can. It says its journalism will be based on the highest possible levels of accuracy and precise, unambiguous language. There is no place for opinion: the BBC does not have any opinions or a point of view of its own. Everyone pays the licence fee, so everyone is entitled to have his or her views articulated and respected, without the BBC favouring one over the other.

This value is also about being open and honest about what you do not know. Journalists hate admitting that they do not know something – but often, especially in the age of 24-hour news, a lack of knowledge is perfectly understandable and justifiable. News stories are messy, incomplete, unresolved. It is not a sign of weakness to admit that you do not know some of the details, or where the story is going. You are doing a disservice to the audience if you pretend otherwise. With a story that is just breaking, saying what is not yet known is very important. It helps you avoid the temptation to lurch into conjecture and speculation, and by definition it highlights the questions that remain to be answered. If you do not know, say so. Do not guess or bluster.

BBC Values: serving the public interest

This is also about being searching and rigorous in your journalism. The BBC says it will try to make its news interesting and relevant to all audiences. And it will pursue all those other high-minded purposes we talked about in Chapter 2, like holding to account people in power or positions of authority, and exposing criminality or wrongdoing.

An element of this aspiration is getting beyond the simple reporting of facts, to inform audiences of all the things they need to know in order to understand the story properly. That means employing and interviewing people with specialist knowledge and expertise to bring authority and clarity to difficult subjects.

It also means being fair and open-minded but tough in asking searching questions of those who hold public office, and reporting what it is in the public interest to reveal.

BBC Values: impartiality and diversity of opinion

If the BBC is seen to be advantaging or disadvantaging one group or opinion, then it forfeits its claim to a licence fee paid by everyone. Impartiality means neutral reporting of the facts, understanding their context and explaining it, offering guidance to audiences – but never offering opinions. As already discussed under Section 5 of the Ofcom Code, reporting a range of opinions might not necessarily be impartial if the audience is not told about the relative strengths of, or levels of support for, differing points of view. This is where we looked at the idea of "due" impartiality, in which that sort of critical analysis was a part of the journalism, albeit offered without opinion or promoting one view over another.

Impartiality is also about keeping an open mind and being willing to consider all strands of opinion, especially if they conflict with your own. You should be ready to explore the widest range and conflict of views. The BBC thinks that testing a range of views is essential if it is to give its audiences the best opportunity to decide for themselves on the issues of the day.

Offering breadth and diversity of opinion does not apply only to the political fault lines between left and right. It may include reflection of the variations between urban and rural, older and younger, poorer and wealthier, the innovative and the status quo, and so on. It may involve exploration of perspectives in different communities, interest groups and geographical areas. Impartiality, especially when linked to the other BBC Values, adds up to a commitment to fairness, open-mindedness and a willingness to reflect and to weigh as many different points of view and perspectives as you can.

BBC Values: independence

Impartiality and independence are probably the two most important words in the BBC lexicon. Its independence and distance from government are guaranteed by the licence fee, which means that it is accountable to the public rather than the government or Parliament. It is not to be swayed by state and partisan interests, and tries to be an independent monitor of powerful institutions and individuals.

BBC Values: accountability

Sometimes things go wrong. While the BBC is not accountable to the government, it has to be accountable to someone – and that someone, as we have seen, is the audience. The BBC says its first loyalty is to viewers and listeners, and it must earn and retain their trust. Trust is hard to win, easy to lose; and once lost, very difficult to win back. The BBC says it aspires to act in good faith at all times, by dealing fairly and openly with audiences, and with the people who contribute to its output. When it makes mistakes, its policy is to admit to them and to apologise for them. This is part of a culture that believes admitting your mistakes and showing a willingness to learn from them is a sign of strength, not a sign of weakness.

The BBC is not alone in articulating its own set of values within the wider industry framework. Others do so too – the *Guardian*, *Financial Times* and the *Independent*, for example, most of them building on the provisions of the Editors' Code.

Data protection

It may be that during the course of your work you find yourself in possession of personal or otherwise confidential information. There are strict rules governing the protection of such data, and large penalties for personal data breaches. These rules are set out and enforced by the Information Commissioner's Office (ICO). The General Data Protection Regulation (GDPR) requires you to report a breach within 72 hours of becoming aware of it. Definitions of what constitutes a breach include:

Loss of personal data
Destruction of personal data
Disclosure of personal data
Passing on of data without authorisation

If you are worried about the sensitivity or security of data that you are holding, seek advice and/or go to the ICO's website for guidance.

Common themes

These are the guidelines and rules against which journalistic behaviour is judged, and each of them contributes ideas as to what ethical journalism should look like. Taken together, The IPSO Editors' Code, the IMPRESS Standards Code, the NUJ Code of Conduct, the Ofcom Broadcasting Code and the BBC Editorial Guidelines and Values set out a clear view of the sort of ethical approach and fundamental values that should underpin all responsible journalism. They overlap in places, there are changes of emphasis and the approaches are slightly different: but all of them are clearly pointing in the same direction in terms of a decent and fair approach to journalism, which observes the law but also recognises the rights of the individual to be treated according to what Ofcom calls "generally accepted standards" – with decency and respect. They also back strong and responsible journalism, with their declarations that the public interest may on occasion override other considerations. At best, these values represent a decent and human way of approaching the job without undue hurdle or hindrance; at worst, they keep you out of the courts.

What this means for you

This may feel like a lot to take in. But if you understand these common themes and the thinking behind them, you will usually be able to come to good and sound decisions about whatever particular editorial dilemma rears its head. We have looked at all the various codes; but don't forget that you are likely to be working only to one of them at a time (two if you are in the NUJ), depending on whether you are a print/digital or broadcast journalist, or whether you are working for an organisation that has its own in-house Code and does not subscribe to any of the others.

Never forget that there is absolutely nothing wrong with seeking help and advice from someone more senior and more seasoned than yourself. Do not worry about being seen as needy, or incapable of making your own decisions. Any senior journalist worth his or her salt will know only too well that nothing is black and white and that some situations are really hard to resolve – and perhaps cannot be resolved at all without recourse to a least worst option. It is always worth referring up, even if only to have endorsement and support for a position you have already reached for yourself. Do not forget that there are many situations in which it is not your responsibility to make the call, but which should always be passed up the chain of command.

But it is still worth thinking about how, in practical terms, these guidelines might affect your behaviour in the sort of situations that you are likely to meet as a general reporter. In this role, you will be producing a lot of stories and interacting very extensively with members of the public. The last part of this chapter, therefore, has some specific thoughts about how you would apply the ethical approach in these interactions.

The area demanding greatest focus is around privacy, intrusion and harassment. Along with inaccurate reporting, these are things that people complain about most after their contacts with reporters. Complaints may refer to the way in which information has been obtained, or what is actually published, if it is private or confidential information such as medical records. Most complainants will not have the means or the energy to pursue a case through the courts, but some will – and costs will soon rack up. And it does not cost anything to complain to media regulators and seek redress in that way.

We have seen in the codes a general acceptance of the idea that people have a reasonable/legitimate expectation of privacy. This is further defined in The Editors' Code (Clause 2) as the idea that "everyone is entitled to respect for his or her private and family life, home, health and correspondence, including digital communications". The Code also says: "It is unacceptable to photograph individuals, without their consent, in public or private places where there is a reasonable expectation of privacy".

You might think there should be no problem photographing someone in a public place because there would be no reasonable expectation of privacy. That may be so. But the regulators say that it depends on the circumstances – a couple dining in a restaurant or even strolling in the park may be in a public place, but they may still be entitled to a degree of privacy. If you barged in and started taking pictures or trying to interview them, you would expect be found guilty of intrusion and invasion of that privacy. There have in the past been several complaints by celebrities and members of the Royal Family about the taking of photographs using long lenses, typically when they are on holiday or otherwise "off duty". They might be in a public place at the time – a beach, say – but this would be regarded as intrusive behaviour.

What about the time-honoured journalistic practice of "doorstepping"? This is when a journalist turns up unannounced and without prior warning and tries to obtain an interview or pictures. This is a common practice, and when people find themselves in the news they may discover a whole posse of reporters and photographers camped outside their front door. Politicians are especially vulnerable to this sort of treatment. As long as the press pack keeps its distance – staying in the street, say, rather than literally standing on the doorstep – this will usually be acceptable. Investigative reporters will often doorstep people whose misdemeanours they are trying to expose, if requests for an interview have been turned down or are obviously not going to be granted.

You will usually do a doorstep on your own only if you have already tried more formal methods of contact – telephone call, letter, email – and received no response or been fobbed off. It may be that you are happy to take a "no comment" and write your story anyway. But if you feel the need to give someone a right of reply, or to confront them with whatever evidence you have assembled against them, you might try to catch them when they are out or about – or, literally, on the doorstep. It might be wise to refer up before you do so, depending on the circumstances.

If people are being doorstepped or otherwise seeing their privacy under threat, whether by one person or the whole press pack, they are entitled to ask journalists to desist. If journalists ignore such requests, they might find themselves accused of harassment. The Editors' Code, as we have seen, has a whole clause on this (Clause 3), stating that "journalists must not engage in intimidation, harassment or persistent pursuit". It says they must not persist in questioning, telephoning or pursuing people if they have been asked not to. They must leave private property when asked to do so. And they must identify themselves and their employer if asked to do so. The Ofcom Code has similar provisions. This guidance around harassment is recognition that a refusal to answer questions or cooperate with journalists should be respected. Journalists can sometimes forget that people are under no obligation to speak to them if they do not wish to do so.

The codes also emphasise the need for careful and sympathetic treatment of people who may be in vulnerable situations for whatever reason: those caught up in accidents, natural disasters or major incidents such as terrorist outrages; the bereaved, or people at funerals; people in hospital. People in shock or suffering from trauma must be approached and handled sensitively, and reporters should be careful about their use of harrowing detail or graphic images.

Children, as we have seen, are granted special protection under all the Codes. Perhaps the key thing to remember here is that you must not interview or photograph/film children under the age of 16 unless you have the permission of a parent or other responsible adult.

There is an increasingly prevalent issue with the publication of material gathered from eyewitness journalism – in other words, provided by members of the public – or from social media websites, which are routinely searched by journalists seeking images or details of people in the news. This material needs handling with care and sensitivity, because publication may result in a breach of privacy and a breach of copyright as well.

This is the conduct that members of the public are entitled to expect from you when you approach them for interviews or permission to film or photograph. You have the right to make those approaches; they have the right to decline. If they do, you must respect that.

In almost all of these cases, there can be exemptions if activities are "warranted" (Ofcom) or because they are "in the public interest" (Editors' Code). We looked earlier at what that meant and how it was defined. Think twice before deciding on your own that you are acting in the public interest. Would a regulator, or a court, see it that way? As a rule of thumb, if you are thinking of doing something that might be in breach of a Code or otherwise ethically dubious, seek some advice from higher up in the editorial chain. It is the safest way to proceed and the best way to learn about how the codes work in practice. Don't forget that if things go wrong, it is your editor rather than you who is going to have to clear up the mess – and carry the can. Your editor will be even less pleased with you if he or she had no idea in advance of what you were up to. The perils of serious mistakes can include huge fines or an appearance in court.

The combined impact of looking at so many rules and regulations may be to give the impression that journalism is impossibly hamstrung in the way it works, and ties itself up in knots while trying to decide what should be allowed and what should not. Yet journalists are resourceful and enterprising animals with energy and imagination, always looking for ways of getting to the story. The codes are there to remind them that there are limits and protocols to be respected, but not to make them timid, risk-averse creatures who give up at the first hurdle for fear of being hauled up before a regulatory body or a judge. That is not the intention at all. The idea is to create a framework of behaviour that commands consensus within the industry and engenders public trust in a journalism that is robust and confident and fully capable of fulfilling its vital democratic functions. This will be integral to all that you do. That is why we have addressed ethical issues at such an early stage in this book. Ethical journalism is not tame, quiescent and unquestioning journalism. It is good journalism.

5
Regulation

regulation of newspapers and magazines and their digital output........regulation of the broadcast media.....regulation of online media.....how regulation works: IPSO, IMPRESS, independents, Ofcom

There is no point in having the grand ethical aspirations we discussed in the last chapter without any means of enforcing them, mechanisms through which breaches can be brought to light, investigated and – where necessary – punished. This system of governance and enforcement is known as regulation. Regulation of the journalism industry has been a knotty subject for many decades. The picture today remains messy and is not fully resolved.

Regulation of newspapers and magazines, and their digital output

The printed press has always strongly asserted that it is perfectly capable of regulating its own affairs, and that any attempt to do so from outside – say by government legislation – would be a threat to the basic democratic right of freedom of expression. This is all well and good in theory; but numerous examples of unlawful, unethical and immoral behaviour over the years, principally by the tabloid newspapers, have prompted regular calls for government to legislate against malpractice – and occasional warnings from government that such action is under active consideration. More than once, the press have been warned that they are "drinking in the Last Chance Saloon".

Media activities are regulated to some extent by the laws of the land, such as libel. But there are no such controls over ownership – except perhaps when one proprietor or corporation is seen as controlling so much of the market as to hamper competition. Beyond that, anyone can own or run a newspaper or magazine, or operate a website, and as long as they abide by the law, there is no obligation to worry about issues like impartiality in the way that we have seen the BBC and other news broadcasters doing. Newspaper owners and editors can use their pages to be as opinionated as they like about political or social issues, or to launch campaigns and crusades for change as the mood takes them. This can lead them to adopt fixed positions on the major issues of the day, and to pursue agendas in the confident knowledge that they can print whatever they like as long as they keep within the law. They do recognise, however, that if these rights are routinely abused by irresponsible behaviour, the media as a whole risk being regulated by statute, to which they would all be violently opposed.

In 1991, partly to keep this threat at bay, the print industry created a body called the Press Complaints Commission (PCC). The PCC replaced the Press Council, which had been set up in similar circumstances in the 1950s. A Code of Practice was drawn up, which came to be known as The Editors' Code. We looked at its provisions in detail in the previous chapter. The PCC functioned fitfully for 20 years, although it was never able to escape criticism that the industry was in effect marking its own homework – judging complaints made against itself and, in the eyes of many, being soft or ineffective in redress and sanctions.

The issue of regulation came to a head in 2011 as a result of the appearance of a story in the *Guardian* under this headline:

News of the World hacked Milly Dowler's phone during police hunt

There had already been a number of stories about journalists hacking illegally into the voicemail messages of peoples' telephones – or employing specialist hackers to do it for them – as a way of sourcing stories about the rich and famous. One journalist, the *News of the World* royal editor Clive Goodman, had even been sent to jail in 2007 for intercepting mobile phone messages within the Royal Household. Glenn Mulcaire, the man who had helped him do it, was also jailed. The paper insisted that this was an isolated offence, and that phone hacking was not a common practice in its newsroom.

But the story above, by the *Guardian* journalist Nick Davies, suggested otherwise. It claimed that journalists on the *News of the World* had managed to gain access to the voicemails of a missing schoolgirl named Milly Dowler. When Milly's family discovered that the messages had been listened to, it convinced them that she was still using her phone, and so must still be alive. Sadly, this was not the case; Milly was later found dead.

The *News of the World*, founded in 1843, was one of Britain's oldest newspapers and at one time sold more copies than any other English-language newspaper anywhere in the world. It had long been notorious for publishing sensational stories about the seamier side of the lives of those in the public eye. It was in some ways a British institution, still selling well over two and a half million copies every Sunday in 2011. But it would not survive the public outcry that followed the *Guardian's* revelations.

After the *Guardian's* story the phone hacking scandal broke in earnest, with revelations about a large number of potential hacking victims, including actors, politicians, celebrities, sportsmen and women and members of the Royal Family. All pointed to the conclusion that the illegal hacking of phones was a routine means of newsgathering at the *News of the World*. Within three days of the *Guardian's* story appearing, News International, the paper's owners, announced that the next edition would be the last. They were closing it down. The all-powerful media mogul Rupert Murdoch underwent a humiliating interrogation by a committee of MPs. Suddenly, the whole of the tabloid press was in the line of fire.

The government's response was to set up a judicial public inquiry to examine press standards – exactly the sort of scenario the printed press had spent decades striving to avoid. The inquiry was to be chaired Lord Justice Leveson, and was to be in two parts. Part 1 was to address:

> the culture, practices and ethics of the press, including contacts between the press and politicians and the press and the police; it is to consider the extent to which the current regulatory regime has failed and whether there has been a failure to act upon any previous warnings about media misconduct.

Leveson Part 2, which was postponed until ongoing police investigations into phone hacking were completed, was to examine the role of the police in providing News International journalists with information. In fact, Part 2 never happened, and was formally abandoned in 2018.

Among the 300 witnesses to give evidence over 18 months of Part 1 hearings were alleged victims of press intrusion as well as journalists, newspaper executives and proprietors, police, communications advisers and politicians. More than 50 prominent people, or people who had suddenly found themselves in the news – such as the Dowler family, who also gave evidence – were revealed as victims of phone hacking.

The inquiry uncovered widespread evidence of illegal hacking and other illicit or questionable behaviour, with strong implications that this sort of activity had not been restricted to the *News of the World*.

Leveson produced his 2,000-page report at the end of 2012. He concluded that the PCC, the main industry regulator of the printed press in the UK since 1991, was not fit for purpose. He said that when chasing stories, journalists had caused "real hardship and, on occasion, wreaked havoc with the lives of innocent people". This had happened to both famous people and members of the public. He said such behaviour "can only be described as outrageous".

Leveson went further. He said politicians of all parties had developed "too close a relationship with the press in a way that has not been in the public interest".

The relationship between politicians and press over the last three decades had, in his view, damaged the perception of public affairs. He found no evidence of widespread police corruption – the other area of his inquiry.

Leveson made broad and complex recommendations relating to the way the press should be regulated in the future. He said:

> Newspapers should continue to be self-regulated – and the government should have no power over what they publish.

> But there should be a new press standards body created by the industry, with a new code of conduct: It should take an active role in promoting high standards, including having the power to investigate serious breaches and sanction newspapers.

> That body should be backed by legislation, which would create a means of ensuring regulation was independent and effective, and to assess whether it was doing its job properly.

> The legislation would enshrine, for the first time, a legal duty on the government to protect the freedom of the press.

Legislation of this sort would for the first time take press standards out of voluntary self-assessment and regulation, and into a legal framework. Leveson denied that this amounted to statutory regulation of the press. He argued that it would give the public confidence that their complaints would be handled seriously.

Leveson said the new standards body should be independent of current journalists, the government and commercial concerns, and not include any serving editors, government members or MPs. It should encourage the press to be as transparent as possible in relation to sources for its stories, if the information was in the public domain. A whistle-blowing hotline should be established for journalists who felt under pressure to do unethical things.

Supporters of the recommendations, who unsurprisingly included many of the victims of media intrusion and phone hacking, said such a framework would guarantee that the press would behave better in the future.

Opponents, the newspapers themselves foremost among them, denounced it as an attack on press freedom, giving the government an element of control over media activities that compromised the principle of freedom of speech. Prime Minister David Cameron, who had set up the inquiry, welcomed many of Leveson's findings but said he had serious misgivings about using the law to implement them.

After a period of stalemate, a cross-party political consensus emerged. It was agreed that a new body would be created, called the Press Recognition Panel. Anyone who wanted to set themselves up as a regulator of the press could apply to the Panel to become a "recognised regulator" provided they met specific criteria. Once approved, they would have the power to impose fines of up to a million pounds and demand prominent corrections and apologies from UK news publishers. As an incentive to join the regulatory regime – or rather, a disincentive to opt out – newspapers that declined to participate would potentially be liable for hefty damages if a legal claim against them were upheld.

To much of the newspaper industry, this still looked like a system of statutory regulation by the back door, and all the major titles remained steadfast in their opposition to it. Their response, in March 2014, was to create a body of their own called the Independent Press Standards Organisation, or IPSO. This body would replace the PCC and exist outside the arrangements proposed by government, thus preserving the principle of self-regulation. IPSO adopted The Editors' Code as the foundation for its operations, but made it clear that it would not seek accreditation by the new Press Recognition Panel.

Though operating outside the approved system, IPSO regards itself and behaves as a regulator, affirming its commitment to "professional standards and an edited, regulated product". It claims to be more rigorous than the PCC. Critics complain that IPSO is not what Leveson called for and that, like the PCC before it, it is too close to its financial backers in the industry. For them, it doesn't solve the main problem that existed with the PCC: that journalists are in effect judges and juries when considering their own work – even though IPSO's complaints committee has no serving editors among its members.

The majority of the newspaper industry is now part of IPSO, which has more than 2,500 members, including many of the national titles. Of the major print players, only the *Guardian*, the *Financial Times* *(FT)*, the *Observer* and the online-only *Independent* and *Independent on Sunday* have not joined IPSO, and maintain their own processes for handling complaints. Digital players such as *HuffPost* and *Vice* are also outside the IPSO system.

IPSO aims to hold newspapers and magazines to account for their actions, protect individual rights, uphold high standards of journalism and help maintain freedom of expression. It is funded by its members, but says it works separately from and completely independently of them. It says its logo, with the slogan "For Press Freedom with Responsibility", is a kite mark of good practice and the enforcement of ethical and other standards. IPSO declares:

> in an era where the public's trust in journalism has been undermined because of the rise of 'fake news', the IPSO mark is a way in which the 2,500 newspapers, magazines and websites can show that they embrace high editorial standards and public accountability.

So IPSO operates without formal recognition because newspapers did not like, and refused to countenance, the ideas proposed by Leveson. Most of all, they abhorred the idea of a system of regulation backed by the law.

However, one regulator has emerged from within the new system – in other words it has applied to become a recognised regulator and been approved as such. This organisation is called IMPRESS – Independent Monitor for the Press. It applied to the Panel for recognition in January 2016 and was recognised in October of that year. The IMPRESS Code is also set out in the previous chapter.

IMPRESS has struggled to attract members in the same numbers as IPSO, especially among front-rank national publications. It has around 150 members, all from the regional and hyperlocal press, many of them digital-only publishers.

The Leveson inquiry into press standards uncovered all sorts of serious issues, many of them acknowledged and accepted by the newspapers themselves. But if the diagnosis was justified, the prescription has been largely ignored. Leveson has failed to lead to the creation of a universally recognised and adopted form of regulation of the printed press. Most print publications are part of IPSO, even though it does not have official regulator status. Some regulate themselves. Some are within the official system through their membership of IMPRESS. It is an untidy and fragmented picture. However, The Editors' Code in some form or another is still regarded as the base on which good or bad behaviour is judged, regardless of the banner under which the judging is being conducted.

Regulation of the broadcast media

The picture is much more clear-cut when it comes to the broadcast media. As we have seen, the big difference from the regulation of print is that there *is* a legal framework in place here, and it is adhered to by all the broadcasters. Ofcom, the Office of Communications, is an independent regulator created by an Act of Parliament, and all broadcasters are bound to abide by its requirements and rulings.

Why is this? It seems bizarre that something that is absolute anathema to the print media – legally binding regulation – seems to be acceptable to the broadcast media and to operate without provoking anything like the same sort of outrage and indignation.

The reason probably stems from the general view that broadcast material – in particular television images – has a greater power to influence audiences and to cause harm and offence than printed text and still pictures. There was a particular concern about the effects on the young of emotionally charged and graphic images of sex or violence. Harrowing images are the more harrowing if they are broadcast on television, the dangers of unfair treatment or invasions of privacy are seen to be greater and there are all sorts of dangers associated with live broadcasting. Broadcast media are on the air around the clock. All of these are regarded as persuasive arguments for tighter controls than exist with the print media.

Developments in the 21st century have done much to dilute the force of these arguments. Audio and video are no longer broadcast only by radio and television stations – they are features of a huge amount of online reporting and social media interchanges, much of it coming from the print media.

There is another very important distinction between the way in which print and broadcast are expected to behave. We have noted that anyone can run a newspaper and use it as a vehicle for any sort of opinion or crusade, as long as it stays within the law. The same is not true of broadcasting. Broadcasters are individually licenced by Ofcom and must remain neutral and impartial on important matters of public debate – principally political and social issues. As we saw in the last chapter, this imposes a legally enforceable obligation to observe "due accuracy", and offer properly weighted coverage that does not disproportionately favour one agenda or perspective over another. This obligation extends to all Ofcom licensees, with a particular emphasis on "public service broadcasters", or PSBs – notably the BBC, Independent Television News (ITN), Sky, Channel 4 and Channel 5. This requirement of impartiality would be difficult to achieve by voluntary self-regulation.

Regulation of online media

Regulation has signally failed to keep pace with the development of the internet – although that is hardly surprising given the breakneck speed and profound nature of that development. For one thing, the internet and digital technology know no borders, so there can be no fully effective UK-only solution to online regulation.

The problem of regulating journalism on the internet can be summed up by this question: should what appears online be regulated as though it was print material or broadcast material? Without some clarity around that, it is hard to decide where a comprehensive system of online regulation might even begin. On top of that, the international accessibility and sheer scale and volume of internet content – most of it produced not by professionals, but by people who would not be caught by any sort of regulation – render the task impossibly daunting.

There is no national or international framework in place to control what is posted online, although domestic law is available in some cases, such as that covering the publication of pornographic images. In the UK, there are moves towards legislation to prevent what are called "online harms" – a limited attempt to tackle some of the most offensive materials. Responsibility for enforcing any such legislation will rest with Ofcom. In the meantime, the biggest social media publishers such as Facebook and YouTube are under increasing pressure to prevent harmful material appearing in the first place, and removing it more rapidly when it does.

How regulation works: IPSO

As we have seen, IPSO is an independent regulator operating outside the system brought in following Leveson, and not recognised by the Press Recognition Panel. IPSO has adopted the provisions of The Editors' Code as its criteria for standards. This is what IPSO sees as its principal functions:

> We make sure that member newspapers and magazines follow the Editors' Code.

> We investigate complaints about printed and online material that may breach the Editors' Code.

> We can make newspapers and magazines publish corrections or adjudications if they breach the Editors' Code (including on their front page).

> We monitor press standards and require member newspapers and magazines to submit an annual statement about how they follow the Editors' Code and handle any complaints.

> We can investigate serious standards failings and can fine publishers up to £1 million in cases where they are particularly serious and systemic.

> We operate a 24-hour anti-harassment advice line.

> We provide advice for editors and journalists.

> We provide training and guidance for journalists so they can uphold the highest possible standards.

> We provide a Whistleblowing Hotline for journalists who feel they are being pressured to act in a way that is not in line with the Editors' Code.

> We work with charities, NGOs and other organisations to support and improve press standards.

IPSO considers complaints and claims that publications may be in breach of the Code. If it finds against them, it has a number of sanctions at its disposal. It can:

- Require a member to publish an adjudication, which may include a requirement to address the concerns raised.
- Impose a fine of up to £1 million.
- Require the member to pay the reasonable costs of the investigation.
- Terminate membership of IPSO.

Because it is still a relatively new organisation, IPSO is still evolving and building up its case law. In the 'Rulings' section of the IPSO website you can look at the complaints it has considered so far under each of the 16 Clauses of The Editors' Code, and the results of its investigations. New judgements are added as they are made. It is a good idea to be aware of the sorts of complaint that IPSO is receiving and how it is responding.

How regulation works: IMPRESS

IMPRESS is the only regulator currently recognised by the Press Recognition Panel. Its stated ambitions include ensuring quality journalism in the digital era:

> IMPRESS is at the vanguard of a new, positive future for news publishers, ensuring quality independent journalism flourishes in a digital age. We help to build understanding and trust between journalists and the public – and provide the public with trusted sources of news.
>
> We are a regulator designed for the future of media, building on the core principles of the past, protecting journalism, while innovating to deal with the challenges of a digital age.

Here is what IMPRESS considers to be its most important functions:

- Award a "Trust in Journalism" mark to publishers that meet our standards for membership.
- Maintain a progressive Standards Code, and assess any breaches of this code by our members.
- Provide an arbitration scheme which is free to all parties and protects publishers against the risk of court costs and exemplary damages.
- Support the development of news publishers, through partnerships and collaboration.

IMPRESS assesses complaints against its Standards Code, which we looked at in the previous chapter. Where it upholds a breach of the Code, it has a number of sanctions to hand. These include:

- Fines: IMPRESS can issue fines of up to 1 per cent of publisher annual turnover, up to a maximum of £1 million.
- Corrections: IMPRESS can direct the nature, extent and placement of corrections.
- Apologies: IMPRESS can direct the nature, extent and placement of apologies.

How regulation works: the independent approach

We noted that some of the big names in the newspaper industry are not members of either IPSO or IMPRESS. Each of those has its own internal system for dealing with complaints and offering redress if need be.

The *Guardian* has employed a Readers' Editor and followed its own Guardian News & Media Editorial Code since 1997. The Readers' Editor represents the interests of readers and is the first port of call for people unhappy with the paper's coverage. The role also covers the *Guardian*'s sister paper, the *Observer*, and online content. The paper's Editorial Code takes the Editors' Code as its base.

The paper's policy is to correct substantial errors as soon as possible. Corrections appear on the relevant web page and/or in the newspaper, and significant corrections are collated in special columns in both the *Guardian* and the *Observer*.

Much the same is true of the *FT*, which employs its own editorial Complaints Commissioner to consider complaints about what appears in the paper and to uphold the *FT* Editorial Code. This Code embraces the contents of The Editors' Code, and adds extra provision specific to dealings with sensitive market and other financial information.

The *Independent* has also drawn up a code of ethical conduct for its staff, covering the same areas that we have already studied elsewhere.

All of these Codes can be viewed on the websites of the respective titles.

How regulation works: Ofcom

Ofcom looks into complaints lodged by members of the public, and also has the capacity to initiate its own investigations if it thinks they are warranted. Complaints are assessed against the provisions of the

Broadcasting Code. If they do not involve breaches of the Code, or are not considered sufficiently serious to raise matters of concern, they may not be taken forward. For those complaints that are considered, Ofcom will ask the relevant broadcasters for their views before reaching a preliminary decision. That decision is shared with both the complainant and the broadcaster, whose responses are further considered before a final position is reached.

Complaints about BBC coverage are considered initially by the BBC's own internal complaints procedures, a system known as BBC First. Only if the BBC cannot resolve the complaints are they referred to Ofcom for further investigation.

Ofcom considers complaints against the various sections of the Broadcasting Code. It publishes its rulings, and can impose sanctions if breaches are found to be "serious, deliberate, repeated or reckless". The penalties it can impose are these:

> Direction not to repeat a programme or advertisement
> Direction to broadcast a correction and/or statement of Ofcom's findings
> Shortening of a licence period or suspension of licence
> A fine
> Removal of licence to broadcast.

Ofcom regularly publishes the results of its investigations, and details can be found on its website.

Part two

Storyfinding and storytelling

6
Storyfinding: the general reporter

every reporter's banker questions....press releases.....the calls.....births, marriages, deaths.....anni-
versaries, big birthdays, retirements......25, 50, 100 years ago.....demonstrations and marches.....
speeches.....press conferences.....vox pops.....ring-rounds.....follow-ups.....doorsteps.....death
knocks.....the weather.....embargoes.....patch reporting .....pictures.....breaking news.....eyewitness
journalism.....interviewing children.....diversity.....taste and decency.....health and safety

The number of routes into professional journalism has increased in recent years, but for many the starting
point is as a junior reporter/producer on a newspaper or a local radio station, or as a content producer
on a news website working full time on digital output. If you are fortunate, you will not be chained to
a desk in the office, but will be given some opportunities to get out and about and do some first-hand
reporting. That will give you early experience of a whole range of situations that enable you to cut your
teeth rapidly in the real world of journalism. You will find yourself doing some of the tasks described in
this chapter. You will learn to produce a lot of stories and to turn them round at speed. You will meet and
talk to real people. Learning to establish a rapid rapport with people and encouraging them to speak to
you is an essential skill that will stand you in good stead wherever your career takes you thereafter, and
however stratospheric it becomes.

Not all stories take us by surprise. Much of the news is known about in advance. You have prior access
to court lists and council agendas, sporting fixtures are scheduled months ahead, press releases tell you
of imminent launches or give you early details of soon-to-be-published surveys. There are any number of
other ways in which media organisations learn of forthcoming events that will be newsworthy, but which
have not yet taken place. This makes it easier to plan coverage in a way that by definition you cannot
do with breaking news. All these forthcoming happenings will often be entered in an online diary with
shared access. Hence the phrase "diary stories" – known about in advance and the sort of thing to which
you can expect to be assigned. Many are routine, but they are stories nonetheless and each one has the
capacity to produce an interesting or unexpected angle. This chapter will provide suggestions for how
you tackle some of those recurring stories, and handle a range of other situations in which you might find
yourself. Court reporting and council reporting are looked at separately in Chapters 22 and 23.

As the office junior, you can expect to be assigned the menial tasks to begin with. Don't complain: if you
show a willingness to turn your hand to anything, you will learn more quickly and are more likely to be
given a chance when something juicier comes along. It is also very likely that you will be asked to update
a story with new information, or to rework a story from another publication. No editor likes a competitor
having something they haven't. You'll hear these stories described as "rewrites" or "write-throughs": they
are not as much fun as doing your own original journalism, but no less important to do well. It is still
important to try to find a new angle, or fresh piece of information, so that what you produce is distinctive.

With all stories, whatever the medium, make absolutely sure you have got the basic essentials of information: names, addresses, ages, occupations, etc. And make sure they are all accurate.

Every reporter's banker questions

The basis of most of your information gathering will be asking questions – and the questions you ask will not vary enormously from story to story, from platform to platform, from one style of writing to another. We look at this area in more detail in Chapter 8 on interviewing, but we will introduce the basic concepts here.

Start with the obvious questions, the ones to which you will almost always want to find the answers. Somewhere in your finished report you will need to set out those answers.

- Who?
- What?
- When?
- Where?
- Why?
- How?
- With what result?
- What next?

Obviously there are plenty of other things you can ask, and you will develop your own method of approaching and speaking to people. But these questions will usually help you set off in the right direction. You will note that nearly all of these are open questions – they invite the person you are interviewing to give you more information, and to expand on what they have said. We will expand on some of these in Chapter 8.

Take people through a story step by step:

What happened? What happened next? Then what?

Your first priority will be to establish the narrative, and be clear in your mind about the sequence of events. Go through the whole story in chronological order and find out exactly what happened. That will open up other questions that will enable you to add detail and colour to your basic story. Use "what happened next?" and "then what?" rather than more detailed questions while you get a good sense of the order of events.

Can you take me through it from the beginning?

If it all comes out in a jumble, with the story darting backwards and forwards in time, go back over the ground. Lead the interviewee a little more the second time round: "Can I just make sure I have got all this clear?" "Can I go over this bit again with you?" "Can you repeat what you said about x?"

How do you know that?

Remember to exercise due scepticism and not to believe or take at face value everything that you are being told. "How do you know that?" or a slightly less brusque variant such as "did you actually see/hear this yourself?" is intended to establish whether someone is telling you something they personally have seen or know – in other words that they are a **primary** source – or whether they are just passing on what they have heard, or what someone else has told them. That would make them a **secondary** source, which would mean checking out what they have told you and trying to confirm or corroborate it elsewhere. See Chapter 7 for how to assess the reliability of your sources.

"Really?"

is a very useful question. It can suggest surprise or wonder, but it also makes people feel that they have to substantiate or qualify what they have been saying. This could give you more confidence in them – and also some good quotes.

Is there anyone else I can speak to?

Five people describing the same event will give you five slightly different – or even very different – accounts. Ask if there are others who were involved, who can verify or add to what you're being told (without suggesting that your informant is lying of course).

What do you make of it all?

Then you want to ask them for their own opinions and feelings. If you're not careful, these questions will seem crass and insensitive: "you've just lost your brother in a car crash: how do you feel?" Most of us would feel pretty awkward asking that question, and we would hardly expect it to go down well. But we want to know the answer; we do want to know how this poor person feels. There are slightly gentler ways of getting to the same result: try something open and empathetic – "I can't imagine what that must have been like". This is not actually a question, rather an invitation to share some insights and thoughts. If it elicits an answer like "I feel numb and I don't know how I will cope without him", then, at the risk of sounding heartless, you have a good quote that will strengthen your story. And you have obtained it without sounding insensitive and unsympathetic.

In the same way, there are other bland, but broadly sympathetic ways of asking for a response or opinion: "what was it like?"; "I don't suppose you've had time to think about what this will mean for you"; "you must still be coming to terms with this". They show that you are sensitive to the feelings of the person you are interviewing, and understand that they are in a bad place. Our bereaved sister might volunteer that there have been car crashes on this spot before, and it is time someone looked at improving the road surface or the signage. And then you have your story. "What was it like?" invites people to describe what happened in terms of their own reaction to it, in a way that the balder "what happened?" does not.

Remember, especially if you are recording something for broadcast, that you want an answer in the form of a complete sentence, so keep your questions open and try to avoid leading your interviewee unless they really need prompting. An exchange that goes like this......

> You: "You must feel terrible."
> Interviewee: "Yes I do."

....is all right for a newspaper because you can write that X said they felt terrible. But if you want to use it as an online clip or on television or radio, it won't work unless you include the question as well – which isn't as effective, and reveals that you have led the person on to say something. That is why: "what are your feelings about that?" or its equivalent is so useful. It requires the person to answer with a complete sentence, which makes a much better clip for your piece.

And?

Don't be afraid of silence. If someone is slow to respond to your question or seems to be searching for the words, give them time. And if they do not respond at all, pause as long as you decently can to give them a chance to do so. We all know that people feel obliged to fill a silence by saying something, and that something could well be worth waiting for, especially if it is unplanned and off the cuff. Similarly, when someone is describing something to you, an occasional "and?" will encourage them to keep going without breaking their train of thought – and is easily edited out afterwards.

Can I just recap on what you've told me?

A final reminder. Make sure you have the whole sequence of events absolutely straight in your head and that you have a clear idea of what your interviewee thinks or feels about it, as appropriate. Never be afraid to go back over same ground or ask for clarification. Usually preceding your question with "can I just make sure I have got this exactly right" will encourage the person to be patient and to cooperate.

If you discover later that an important piece of your jigsaw is missing for some reason, see if you can find it – call people back and ask if you can check something with them, or be clear about something you thought you had grasped but are now finding it hard to get down. If you apologise for disturbing them again and make clear that you are doing so only in the interests of quoting them accurately, or conveying their perspective clearly, they won't usually mind.

Treat all stories the same – however slight, they all deserve the same commitment to accuracy and proper storytelling. And always look for a story – in even the most unpromising situations. If you get talking to people, and show a genuine interest, you will invariably find one.

With that approach in mind, we will now examine a range of typical reporting tasks and situations that you can expect to encounter at some point along your reporting journey.

Press releases

Press releases pour into the offices of all media organisations, by post or, more often, by email. The people who send them are not always very discriminating about their targets, and even a small newspaper can receive several hundred press releases a week, the majority of them of no interest whatsoever. The senders hope the contents of the release will appear in the paper as a news item – which will be cheaper and carry much more plausibility than an advertisement.

Press releases will often look and feel like authentic news stories. This could well be because the press officers who have written them are themselves former journalists whose careers have taken them into public relations or marketing. The vast majority of releases will have little or no news appeal. Only a few have any prospect of making it into print, but some will contain a kernel of interest – even if the story needs a bit of uncovering.

A press release is typically topped with a bold headline and a newsy-looking introduction. Look out also for any reference to an embargo – the date and time the information can be made public. You should not break an embargo, but if you think the story is a good one and you don't want to wait, you can sometimes negotiate an earlier release time.

After the body of the release, which will often contain direct quotes that you can use if you wish, press releases often finish with a section described as "Notes to Editors" or similar. This will usually consist of a few paragraphs of background and context to the contents of the release.

Finally, every press release should include a name and contact details, telling you who to get in touch with for further information. If this is missing, you might feel sceptical about the contents and where they come from.

There used to be a golden rule in newsrooms that no press release would ever appear in print until a reporter had investigated and rewritten it. That remains best practice. But in offices where resources are stretched, press releases can often find their way into the paper or on to the website pretty much untouched. When that happens, it means you are unquestioningly accepting the line you are being offered and, in effect, giving someone uncritical free publicity at the possible cost to your own reputation.

So if you are given a press release to look at, always try to find a few minutes to investigate further. You will probably find that there is a story – it just isn't the one that is in the first paragraph of the release, the one they want you to swallow.

Always call the contact number provided if you can. They will give you a fuller explanation that will enable you to understand the story better – and may give you other lines to pursue. If you get some information that was not in the release, you will be a step ahead of the competition. Plus, you will have gained a contact that might come in useful at a later date.

Press releases from official bodies such as councils or government agencies will very often contain something of interest to your readership or audience. These are bodies making decisions that will directly affect your area and its inhabitants. You might need to make quite a few calls fully to understand the story, and dig out the local angle or some reaction. But it will usually be worth the effort, and you will have some quotes and extra information that will give the story more substance.

People who send out press releases generally have something to promote or an agenda to pursue – and perhaps an axe to grind. So be careful. Adopt the approach set out in Chapter 7 on sources. Ask yourself what lies behind the content of the release. What is their agenda? Where are they coming from? Their news and views may be perfectly legitimate and worth reporting, but they should be treated with caution. A story deriving from a press release is like any other story. It may need balancing with views from others with a contrasting perspective, or with a response from people being criticised or called upon to take action.

Some releases from commercial organisations will just be advertising in disguise, and thinly disguised at that. But there may also be proper stories lurking behind the launches of new products, local expansion which will bring new jobs, financial performance and so on. Keep the interests of your audience in mind.

Always be ready to make some calls to gather more detail. It will almost invariably be worthwhile – even if the only outcome is a decision not to touch the story. As noted, in many organisations the people picking up the phone will be former journalists themselves. They will understand where you are coming from, and although they have an agenda it is their job to help you, so don't feel embarrassed about calling them.

Here are some extracts from a small sample of the dozens of genuine press releases received within a 48-hour period in the offices of the *Colchester Gazette*, a newspaper in Essex that publishes daily Monday to Friday. Imagine you are a reporter on the *Gazette* and ask yourselves these questions about each of them:

Is there a story here?

Is it of interest to my audience?

What is the agenda of the people who have sent the release?

Is there something buried away that might be worth exploring?

Is there a local angle – or can I create one?

What questions would I need to ask, and what answers would I need, in order to make it something worth using?

At the very least, it should become clear from these real-life examples that no press release should ever go into the paper unless it has been rewritten.

1. The UK's fertility watchdog, the Human Fertilisation and Embryology Authority (HFEA), has recently published its first set of independent figures for Simply Fertility. The HFEA reports the IVF

clinic in Chelmsford (with satellite clinics in Colchester and Romford) has achieved a 40 per cent live birth success rate, making it the number one performing clinic across the South and East of England, and in the top three clinics in the UK.

2. As the reopening of the Mercury Theatre in Colchester draws ever closer, representatives from major funders of the redevelopment project and local and national government took a tour of the site to see its progress so far. The £9.8 million Mercury Rising project will see three new rehearsal and studio spaces, a fully refurbished main auditorium and new front of house facilities. With the reopening scheduled to take place in the autumn, the Mercury Rising campaign is nearing its target with £300,000 still to raise. If you would like to be part of this exciting project and support its completion, visit our website to find out more.

3. The Perrywood Garden Centre team visited the offices of Colchester Hospital on Friday with a donation of £350 worth of houseplants. Staff from the hospital were ready and waiting for this special delivery! It is well known that houseplants can be hugely beneficial to health – they boost concentration, improve air quality and reduce stress levels. A splash of green foliage is also the perfect way to brighten up any indoor space – either an office or home.

4. "The government's proposals to strengthen police powers against trespass could make criminals of innocent people visiting the countryside." This is the fear of the Open Spaces Society, Britain's oldest national conservation body, which has responded to the Home Office consultation on the criminalisation of trespass in England and Wales.

5. Essex County Council's £400 million construction programme will include BAM Construction, the historic firm that recently built the new multi-storey car park at Stansted Airport. BAM built its first scheme in Essex in 1879, and is known as one of the UK's leading education contractors, having been named "contractor of the year" at the recent Education Estates Conference.

6. Residents of Bures and surrounding villages who want to find out about local services and activities are invited to a community Information Session, on Monday 23rd March from 12 pm to 2 pm, at the Eight Bells Pub, Colchester Road, Bures. The free one-off event will provide information around keeping active and healthy, managing on a low income and how to protect yourself against scams and frauds as well as tips for staying safe in your home.

7. The NSPCC are celebrating the 125th birthday of the charity's Essex branch by asking local groups and organisations to raise £125 for the charity through fundraising.

   [This is a naked appeal for funds, although the target of £125 seems rather modest. But in the tenth and last par of the release we learn that they are looking for 125 individual companies to take up this challenge, and raise £125 *each*. Someone forgot to make this clear in the intro.]

8. Improving the digital skills and connectivity of small- and medium-sized businesses (SMBs) could add up to £106 million to the local economy in Essex Haven Gateway, a new report – The Digital Opportunity for Small Businesses – from Intuit QuickBooks today reveals.

   I'm quoting this next one at length because I think it is so extraordinary. See if you can guess who sent it out.

9. As the UK's dog lovers celebrate the canine world's finest pooches at Crufts, The National Lottery reveals some of the lavish lifestyles and heart-warming stories that a lottery win makes possible for winners' four-legged friends. As a nation of dog lovers – 26 per cent of the UK adult population have a dog – it should come as no surprise that National Lottery winners only want the best for their Man's (and Woman's) best friend. With nearly half (42 per cent) of all National Lottery winners owning a dog, it seems lucky winners don't just treat their nearest and dearest human friends and relations but make sure their pooches are very much a pampered part of their lottery-winning family too. When lottery millionaires Susan Richards and Barry Maddox from Essex first saw their Husky puppy, Sarna, it was love at first sight. Fast forward a couple of years and life changed very quickly for everyone, including Sarna, when Susan scooped £3 million on a scratchcard from The National Lottery. Susan said:

   The win meant so much could change in our lives for the better – new homes and cars, plenty of holidays and a more relaxed lifestyle – and Sarna has definitely benefited from it too. I still work as a carer, it's a job I love and am proud to do, but I have cut my hours dramatically so I'm at home with Sarna a lot more.

That release came from Camelot. I think even the most resourceful reporter would struggle to find a story here. You can almost feel the desperation of the person who had the misfortune to be saddled with writing it.

10. Ride for Helen is back for 2020 taking place on Sunday 17th May for its seventh year and promises to be one of the region's biggest and best cycling events for Helen Rollason Cancer Charity!
11. Author Julia Firlotte has announced the publication of *Trust In You*, the first novel in her new romantic suspense series *Falling For You*, which will be available on Amazon from April 6. A first love summer romance full of intrigue, lust and lies, Firlotte recognises the empowerment of women within modern society, reflecting what readers also want to see in romantic fiction. With this in mind, in the first novel of the series the reader sees the world through the eyes of its heroine Ella, who develops self-confidence and maturity when thrown into a criminal underworld as a young woman.
12. Britain is suffering from energy inequality, as lower income households pay significantly more for their energy than those with more money. According to new research from comparethemarket.com, lower income households spend on average £60 more every year on their energy bills than higher income households.

A reminder that all of these are genuine examples. Which would you try to turn into stories for the *Gazette*?

News of local activities

Some emails or documents might contain news from non-professional local organisations telling you about their activities – dramatic society productions, quiz nights, results and match reports from local sports teams. They will not be formal press releases, and will probably have been written by the club secretary or someone else involved. The copy may be a bit rough and ready, but this is the core content of any local news provider and the reason many people will buy the paper, visit the website or tune in to the station.

The calls

Stories involving the activities of the police, fire and ambulance services form a large component of the diet of any local news provider, and are important to the nationals too. You may therefore find yourself dealing on a regular basis with members of the emergency services. One of the things newsroom reporters are routinely asked to do is a ritual known as "the calls". This is shorthand for a series of checks with the emergency services to see if anything is happening on the patch that is worth reporting or following up.

Pretty much anything that you get from these calls is going to be of interest. Audiences like to hear about crime, accidents, fires and the like. "The calls" always used to be actual phone calls, and depending on how newsy a patch it was, and how close you were to publication or airtime, you might have made them several times a day. Nowadays, police incident rooms and duty officers are less available to take press calls. Instead, the police, fire and ambulance websites publish reports of incidents online, so you need to check constantly for new information being posted. These websites are not there specifically for the benefit of the press – they are open to any member of the public to browse. That means that from the reporter's point of view, the information posted will often be no more than a starting point. It almost certainly won't tell you everything you want to know, and might not be very up to date either. You will need to follow up with a phone call to the press office to get more detail.

Depending on the geography and nature of the patch, these regular calls might also include coastguards, mountain rescue centres, river police or transport police. And you might have more than one police, fire or ambulance service to check in with if your patch crosses jurisdictions or county boundaries.

The relationship with the police in particular is a really important one. The police are a vital source of information, but they won't tell you everything they know, especially if they feel constrained by legal considerations, or if it might prejudice their inquiries. On the other hand, when they are looking for witnesses or other help from the public, the media are a massive resource for them, and they will be more than ready to cooperate with you in issuing appeals.

The police will usually tell you about crimes, accidents and traffic problems, and might offer warnings against con men operating in the area, or public service information about crime prevention. They will report on the outcome of court cases – especially if they have resulted in a guilty verdict – and anything else that reflects positively on them or acts as a deterrent to crime. They will use you to appeal for witnesses, or other people they want to interview. They will ask you to help with initiatives such as a campaign to encourage people to improve their security at home. For a local paper, website or radio station, this is all good stuff – the sort of thing readers and audiences are interested in.

To give you a flavour of this, here is a list of the stories available on the website of one county police force on a day chosen at random:

> Man jailed for dangerous driving on motorway
> Actions of officers recognised at awards ceremony
> Boy charged with aggravated burglary and attempted rape
> Eight charged following dawn drugs raids
> Drugs and weapons seized
> Have your say on policing and community safety
> Detectives appeal for fresh information about rape and murder victim
> Two new town centre patrol teams announced
> Man banned from town centre for anti-social behaviour.

The fire and rescue service will also have a press office to tell you about their operations, which are not always about fighting fires. Remember to find out how many units attended an incident, and how many firefighters were involved: these details help give an idea of the scale of an operation. Find out whether traffic or other problems such as road closures or diversions have resulted from a fire or road traffic accident (RTA). You may have to look at other websites for extra details about the roads affected and the levels of disruption being caused.

Here is a list of the stories available on the website of the fire and rescue force of the same county on the same day:

> Fire in roof of large two-storey property
> Eighteen new firefighters join team
> Man freed from lorry following road traffic collision
> Year 9 students thank Fire and Rescue service for "inspiring" visit
> Firefighters issue safety advice after petrol used on bonfire
> Have your say on how fire service delivers its priorities.

The ambulance service will tell you about accidents – sometimes the same as those reported by the police, but others too, that have no criminal element.

Here is a list of the stories available on the website of the ambulance service of the same county on the same day:

> Quick-thinking Jamie commended for saving a life
> Have you ever considered becoming a paramedic?
> Restart a Heart day to be bigger than ever

Eleven new recruits bring life-saving skills to the streets
Dementia-friendly ambulances hit the road
Chemical incident at factory: statement
Man meets the emergency crews who saved his life.

You can imagine that if you were the calls reporter on this particular day, you would have plenty of stories to follow up across all three services. Nothing here to make a splash on the front page perhaps – but lots of solid stories with masses of appeal for a local news audience.

You can call hospitals directly to ask about their patients, but they will be duty bound to respect patient confidentiality. But if you have the name of the person you are asking about, they may give you a "condition check" – a brief description of how the patient is doing. This will enable you to convey how serious and possibly life-threatening the injuries or illness might be. The sort of descriptions you will get may be a single word such as "serious", "stable", or "critical". Injuries are sometimes described as "non-life-threatening" or "life-changing" which, while you do not have the specifics, help you convey the gravity of the patient's condition.

Births marriages and deaths

These remain a staple of local news, and like many stories that crop up frequently, they can feel parochial and mundane, tempting you to slip thoughtlessly into a well-worn formula. To do so is to short-change both your audience and yourself. You must guard against getting into that kind of a rut, and be resolved to tackle each task you are given with enthusiasm and a determination to make something of it. And with these particular stories, you will very often find something of interest if you ask a few questions. Remember that every person has a story: it is your job to find it and tell it, if it is worth telling. Put in the effort, and with the help of some pictures, you might get a good spread in the paper, online, or on social, or a really nice radio package. With a decent hook, a good local story can go viral on social networks.

That is not obviously the case with births. But newborn babies can be the subjects of stories: the mother who gives birth in the back of a taxi on the way to the hospital, or whose baby is delivered by a neighbour. The woman who was told she could never conceive and later gives birth to "my little miracle". The mother of twins who already has another pair of twins. The sisters who give birth on the same day. We have all seen stories like these. They are strong and engaging because they are full of human interest, and they will often be the most-read pieces of the week. Don't turn your nose up at them. They are fun to write, and they are great opportunities for you to exercise your reporting skills.

Weddings may also look unpromising, but like deaths and funerals they are often featured in local papers in the sure knowledge that they are good for sales. Papers used to print a picture and a full list of the bride and groom, both sets of parents, bridesmaids and best man, with lots of details of the dress, the cake, the honeymoon destination and so on. With funerals you would see lists of the mourners – the relations of the dead person – and others who attended. That doesn't happen much now. But births and marriages still make great picture stories, and obituaries of locally well-known people are also of interest to your audience.

The most routine stories can be lifted by an interesting detail; it might be the location of the wedding, since ceremonies can now be held in all sorts of strange venues – even underwater; it might be some interesting details about the life of a well-known local figure who has died. Give your full attention to any story you are writing – regardless of how slight or important you think it is. It may seem mundane to you – but you are describing really important events in the lives of those involved. The need for accuracy is as great as in everything else you do. Getting a key fact wrong about someone who has died, say, is enormously embarrassing and will make people very angry.

Anniversaries, big birthdays, retirements

All are further examples of commonly occurring local stories. This might typically be people reaching the age of 100, or couples celebrating Golden or Diamond Jubilees. Invariably you will ask them for the secret of a long life or a happy marriage. It is a clichéd question, but it usually produces an interesting or amusing answer. Sometimes you will need to tease the story out of people gently. Having a younger relative present to prompt them will often help.

Older people, or those retiring after long careers, will also have long memories. Ask couples how they met, or retirees how old they were when they started work. What was the world like then? How much was in their first wage packet? How much was a pint of beer in those days? What did the wedding dress cost? Ask them how they think things have changed and, if they have lived locally all their lives, how the town has changed. What are their early memories of it? Members of your audience will have vivid memories of these things too, and it will make for good copy. You can also get creative with a spread of pictures, some from the archive of the town as it was all those years ago.

25, 50, 100 years ago

Many local papers run weekly spreads of pictures taken from their archives. This requires a little research and some inventive caption writing. It is a simple task that might not feel very taxing of your abilities, but the results go down very well with the readership.

In the same way, anniversaries of particular events – tragedies, crimes, sporting successes – are worth noting. If the anniversary is being marked in some way, you might at least get a short news piece. But even if nothing is planned, a little research might deliver you the material for a really good feature.

Demonstrations and marches

These are rather more demanding events which can be chaotic, so it is wise to be prepared. Talk to the organisers in advance to get the background to the event and why it is taking place. Find out who is going to be speaking, and when. Arrange a time and a place to meet the organisers afterwards so that they can give you their reactions to how it went, and their estimate of how many people attended. This might well be an over-estimate, so try to get an independent estimate too, say from the police. Check also with the police for any trouble or arrests. Mingle with the demonstrators and chat to them – why are they there and how far have they come? Why do they feel so strongly? You will get some great colour for your story. Be aware that events like these can be unpredictable, and can degenerate into something of a shambles, or even violence. Keep a weather eye out for trouble, and make sure you always have the means to get quickly to a safe vantage point, or to get away altogether if things turn nasty. If you have a colleague with you, such as a photographer, work together and look out for each other. Some big organisations offer their staff special training in dealing with public order events if they are likely to encounter them regularly. Always carry your press card.

Speeches

Sometimes you will be asked to cover a speech, or an address that someone is making – the local MP, or a visiting bigwig addressing a meeting in the town for example. You need to develop a strategy for this. Even with the best shorthand, you cannot make a perfect verbatim note over 20, 30, or 60 minutes.

You can ask beforehand if you can make a recording of the speech. If you are working for a text-based outlet, you can make clear that you will use the recording only for note-taking and checking exactly what was said. If you are working for a broadcast or digital medium you may want to put extracts of the speech on the air or online. Make sure that everyone involved knows that this is your intention when they agree that you can record it, and that the speech is not an off-the-record briefing or in any other way confidential or not for broadcast.

If you are intending to air some extracts, or clips, you'll need to take more care with the recording, and ensure that what you come away with is in good broadcastable quality. You will probably get a better re-sult using a recording device to do this rather than relying on your smart phone. You may be able to plug your device directly into the audio output to get a clean recording.

Even if you are recording, you should still make notes as you go along, marking what seem to you the best or more newsworthy sections, with the time that they occur – either the time on the clock or the time from the beginning of the speech. Going through the whole recording again can be a lengthy and tedious business, but if you have already earmarked the best bits it will be much easier.

Another possibility is to ask for an advance copy of the speech. If it is a less formal event, there may not be a script – the person may be talking without notes. If there is a script though – and there usually will be if the speech is being made on the national stage – speakers or organisers may be happy to give you advance copies of either the whole speech or extracts from it, on the understanding that you do not use any of it until it has actually been delivered. This is very helpful as it enables you to identify the best bits in advance and, if you are writing to a tight deadline, to rough out a draft of your story on the basis of what you already have.

If you have been given something in advance, make sure you check it against delivery – in other words, make sure that the speaker actually utters the words that are on the paper. Sometimes a speaker will de-part from the script, or make a comment about something that has happened since the speech was first drafted. Pay particular attention to these sections: they are topical, and if they are unscripted the speaker is more likely to make an off-the-cuff remark or speak less guardedly, and you might well find that these passages offer you the best news lines in the speech. Pay attention to any bits of the original script that are *not* delivered, and ask yourself why they might have been omitted.

If you cannot get any advance help, you will need to listen to the speech carefully. Don't try to get the whole lot down. That is impossible. You will need to get the general sense of it and some specific quotes that you can put in direct speech, in quotation marks, and that reflect what you see as the main news points. These must be the exact words that were spoken. You can often sense from the speaker's voice or body language when they are working up to a good quote, so when you think one might be imminent, make sure you get it down verbatim. This is one of those occasions when your shorthand really comes into its own.

Beyond quotes, which are vitally important, treat a speech like any other story, looking for the key points and noting any facts and figures that are used to support an argument. You may want to check them out with an independent source. Mark in the margin the bits you will want to return to. If there are important things you think you have missed, or have not managed to get down in full, be prepared to approach the speaker afterwards to clarify and check.

You can ask the speaker to give you a few minutes to answer any questions you might have about what he or she was saying. You may be granted your own interview, which you are able to record and use. If so, take the opportunity. The chances are that the speakers will summarise their arguments more effectively, saying in one minute what took them ten minutes in the speech; if you are a broadcaster, you will also have an extra option when it comes to what you select as your clip, and you will have something exclu-sive to you. Your own interview may give you a news line that others will not have.

A speech is the expression of the speaker's viewpoint or agenda. There is almost certain to be someone else who has a different point of view or a different agenda. Reflecting those differences and getting quotes from those people is part of your duty as a reporter to give a balanced and well-rounded account that does not just give one side of an argument. So be ready to look for people to react to what has been said: you may be able to prepare them in advance by arranging to speak to them after the speech has been delivered.

Press conferences

The news conferences we see most often on the television news are either political set-pieces or police events called to give information about ongoing crimes, often involving appeals for witnesses. But "pressers", as they're called, are held for all sorts of other reasons and to make different sorts of announcements – such as, say, an appointment, a resignation or a charity giving details of a relief effort. Football managers hold press conferences on a very regular basis.

You will usually be able to record these pressers. They have after all been arranged specifically for the dissemination of information, so the organisers will be looking for as much coverage as they can. The usual pattern is for a prepared statement to be read out, followed by questions. Don't be afraid to ask questions yourself, and don't be embarrassed if they seem obvious or even very basic – such as asking for spellings to be repeated.

Listen to the questions that others are asking – reporters will often ask deliberately provocative leading questions in the hope of extracting a quote-worthy response. "Are the police looking for a maniac here?" "Would you describe this as a miracle cure?" "Is time running out for you?" "Is Saturday's match a must-win for you?" "Is your job on the line?" These may seem crass and crude, but they will often elicit a newsworthy response that everyone can use, and you sometimes need to be blunt in order to extract something from a dull or defensive interviewee. Even a "no comment" can be put to use. "Police would not comment on suggestions that they were searching for a maniac." Again, there will often be opportunities afterwards for you to follow up with press officers or the principals, and you may be able to secure your own interview.

The best access is not always given to the most important outlets. A press conference called to appeal for information about a missing child on your patch may attract a load of reporters from the nationals, and from network broadcasters. This need not make you feel inferior by comparison. You can often argue, and the police will often recognise, that it is much more important for them to speak to the local newspaper, website or radio station. They have the audiences who are more likely to have useful information, and it is those outlets that will give the story greater prominence and stay with it after the news caravan has moved on.

Vox pops

Vox pops, or "voxes" – from the Latin *vox populi*, "voice of the people" – are used every day in every form of journalism. They involve you approaching people in a public place and asking them to comment on the question of the day, national or local. Are food prices too high? Should the council be building new houses on green land? Are fortnightly bin collections acceptable? Are we letting too many foreigners into Britain? Should we switch off our street lights at midnight to save energy?

Vox pops have no definitive editorial value – they are a random selection of views, unscientifically gathered. But they add a bit of colour and texture to the presentation of a story and they put real people into it, and they are very widely used as a consequence. If you are asked to go and get some vox pops, grit your teeth and get on with it. If you are lucky, it won't take you very long. Be prepared for people to refuse to speak to you, or to ignore you, or even to be rude to you. They may consider that you are the rude one, pestering them in public. Be prepared also to be bored stupid by someone telling you their life story, to be offended by unpleasant views or to be told in no uncertain terms that journalists are the lowest form of life. Take it all in your stride, and keep your good humour. It is all part of life's rich tapestry for a reporter. And you will get some colourful material.

With a typical vox pop, you will be looking to record, or to write down, maybe half a dozen decent comments to add to a topical story or even to make into a separate sub-story. You will usually want the names and some brief details of the people you are speaking to, and you may want to take their photograph.

Approach two three people together – it is often easier to persuade them to talk, and they may interact with each other, which works well for television and radio. Look for people who will find it harder to avoid you – a bus queue, for example, is a captive audience, and people there cannot walk away. Try also to get a range of people and a range of views if you can. You will want to reflect a number of perspectives – and that might mean asking more people until you get what you need. However, if absolutely everyone is saying the same thing, you can make that your story – "everyone we spoke to criticised the leisure centre plans".

Ring-rounds

The ring-round is another journalistic staple, and as the name suggests will usually be done on the phone. You will be given a current story and asked to get some local opinions from people who will be affected by it, or who will have the practical knowledge to give you a pertinent opinion. The difference between this and a vox pop is that you are targeting individuals who have a handle on the story, rather than gathering random comments. The government announces more help for small businesses? Do a ring-round of some small businesses on your patch and see whether they welcome the news. House prices rising/falling/stagnant? Call your local estate agents to see how busy they are, and how they see the next few months. And so on. You can nearly always find a local angle on a national story, and vice versa, if you are prepared to put in a bit of spadework, and the ring-round is one good way of achieving it.

Follow-ups

After your story has been published, take a minute to think about whether or not it might have more mileage in it some time in the future. There may well be follow-up stories that will stem from it, the next day, the next week, even months later. Use your diary as a means of reminding yourself of convenient times to go back to the story and find out what has happened since. An alert newsdesk should be doing this anyway, but if you want to retain ownership of the story, make sure you do it too, and let it be known that you want to follow it through any future phases.

If you do a story, for example, about the launch of an appeal to raise money to send a child to the US for life-saving surgery, make sure you stay in touch with the family and check in with them for regular updates on progress, or to hear about fund-raising events you might wish to cover. If a campaign is launched to extend the opening hours of a library, or save it from closure altogether, keep tabs on how it is going, and update your audience whenever there is a new development. Something as simple as the anniversary of a big story might be a good enough reason to return to it and see what has happened over the subsequent 12 months. When there is not much news around, revisiting and updating previous stories is a very good way of generating some – and audiences like stories being followed through, and being told how they are resolved.

Doorsteps

The literal meaning of doorstepping is to hang around on a doorstep in the hope of getting a comment from an organisation or individual in the news. This can sometimes be a group exercise, with numerous reporters and cameramen camped outside a house or place of work, hoping to get a snatched quote as the subject of all the interest arrives or leaves. When the press are operating in a pack in this way, they may organise themselves into an impromptu pool – dividing their numbers, for example, to cover more than one entrance or exit, with those who strike lucky sharing whatever they have been able to get with the rest.

Solo doorsteps are rather different. Typically you will be working on a story that requires a comment from one of the main characters – probably someone with a case to answer. You want to give them right of reply, but they haven't returned your calls or answered your messages. You find out where they live or work, knock on the door and ask them directly for a comment. You may have a recorder or camera running to catch them as soon as they open the door. Even if the door is slammed in your face, you have good material for your story.

There are a number of ethical considerations to observe about doorsteps, all covered in the various codes of conduct, and partly intended to ensure that legitimate journalistic inquiry does not turn into harassment. We considered these in Chapter 4. Before you resort to a doorstep, you will usually have exhausted all other means of trying to contact the subject by phone, email or letter. It is usually worth making sure that your editor approves of what you are planning to do.

Death knocks

The most dreaded of all reporting jobs. You are sent to interview the friends or grieving relatives of someone who has just died. As it is a news story, the chances are that they have died in tragic or unexpected circumstances. Worse still, but thankfully rare, are the occasions when you turn up and realise that while you know about the death, the family has not yet heard about it. This is a horrible situation in which to find yourself, and it also presents you with a dilemma: breaking the news to them yourself might be a breach of the codes of conduct. If it is unavoidable, be as sensitive as you can and retreat as soon as possible.

It is hard to prepare yourself for a death knock, but you cannot shirk it. It is part and parcel of the job. If you can find a friend or neighbour of the family to go with you, or even a police officer, that will help cushion the possible shock or anger at your appearance on the scene. Be respectful, serious and professional, and if it is clear that you are intruding or not wanted, then step away.

You may be sent packing with some choice language. But most reporters with experience of death knocks will tell you that this kind of reaction is actually the exception. People will often be pleased to have someone to talk to, or gratified that the dead person is going to be publicly recognised in some way and their death formally marked. They will be pleased to talk about his or her personal qualities.

Be honest when you make your enquiries. If you give the impression that your report is going to be positive but it ends up being critical of the deceased, however justifiably, you may well find yourself on the receiving end of a complaint.

Your approach is to identify yourself, express your condolences, apologise for disturbing the family at such a time and gently ask if you can have a few details – and, ideally, a photograph. If they give you a picture or pictures, make sure they are returned. And if they ask you to leave – leave. You can ask if there is another member of the family you can talk to, or perhaps whether it might be convenient to return at another time. But this is one occasion when you must take no for an answer.

The weather

Just as the weather is an inexhaustible topic of conversation, so it also offers a continuous supply of stories. These days, there is the added element of climate change, and arguments about the extent to which extreme weather events are linked to global warming. But weather stories function at a much lower level as well. In essence, anything meteorological that disrupts the normal pattern of life is a strong local, and often national, story. It is guaranteed to interest the audience of any news provider.

This means that a weather round-up is a regular task for reporters at local, regional and national levels. Your contacts book should contain a lengthy list of entries under Weather, and your story will contain some or all of the following elements:

- **Conditions**: a description of the weather itself, be it extreme heat, cold, wind, rain or snow. You will need a weather forecaster to explain what this weather is doing and why, and how it compares in severity with previous weather events or the seasonal averages.
- **Forecast**: you will also need your forecaster to tell you what is going to happen in the days ahead.
- **Damage and injuries**: check with the emergency services for news of accidents, injuries, rescues, damaged buildings, fallen trees, blocked roads.
- **Transport disruption**: the transport infrastructure is notoriously vulnerable to severe weather. Check the airports, trains (and ferries if appropriate) for delays and cancellations, and roads for traffic jams, speed restrictions or trouble spots.
- **Power**: bad weather can bring down power lines, leaving people without telephones or electricity. The power companies can tell you how many people are affected and when repairs will be finished.
- **Closures**: if people cannot get to work or conditions are very bad, that can mean schools closures, shops and factories hit, sporting and other events cancelled.
- **Human stories**: be on the lookout for stories that illustrate the effects of the storm: people stranded, farms cut off, unusual ways of getting supplies to people or rescuing them; church halls turned into community centres, soup kitchens or dormitories, the organisation of emergency food parcels and so on. Weather stories are a good source of pictures, not all of which will be about suffering: children tobogganing because schools are shut by snow, or skating in a supermarket car park that has become an ice rink in the big freeze.
- **Advice**: are there any warnings to people not to travel unless they have to? Or any advice about what precautions to take?
- **More information**: tell people how they can stay in touch with all of this (preferably from you and your own organisation) and where they can get the latest information.

Embargoes

A story that is embargoed is one that is given to the media ahead of publication on the understanding that nothing will be published until the release date or time. So a press release that you receive on a Monday that is headed: "Embargoed until 0900 hours, Friday 14th" means that you cannot publish or broadcast the details until nine o'clock on Friday morning. The main purpose of this is to give you and other journalists time to plan and prepare your coverage so that when the release time arrives you are ready to go, and you are not suddenly scrambling to throw something together. In the case of the release of a big report, for example, you have time to find and interview people affected, such that you will have case studies to support your reportage. You can make contact on a confidential basis with people whose reaction you will want when the release time arrives. The most common embargo time is 0001 – in other words, one minute after midnight. The idea of that is to keep the story fresh for the morning newspapers and the early morning radio and television programmes in the hope of securing prominent coverage for a peak audience.

Because embargoes generally assist the smooth operation of journalism, you will respect them, and you will expect your competition to do so as well. You can seek to have an embargo lifted or brought forward. If your paper comes out on a Thursday, for example, you can ask for a Friday embargo to be relaxed so that you can run the story the day before and not have to wait a week – by which time you will probably have lost interest in it. The person setting the embargo might agree, in the interests of getting a good show for the story. If not, there isn't much you can do. Occasionally, embargoes are deliberately broken. If one organisation breaks an embargo, then it no longer holds, and everyone else will consider themselves free to break it as well.

Patch reporting

You may be given responsibility for looking after a patch – in other words, a district within your catchment area. Your patch might be an area of the town or one or two surrounding villages. In larger organisations that might cover a wide area, reporters may be based full-time in their districts. National news organisations have their equivalents outside London, such as a Scotland correspondent, or North of England correspondent.

Whatever your focus, the key to your success is your contacts. Make sure you know everyone who might possibly supply you with news from your patch: councillors, parish councillors, community leaders, businesses, voluntary groups, the scouts, the emergency services, sports teams, schools, shops and so on. Keep in regular touch with them, and make sure they know how to get in touch with you. Many of these people want to feature in the paper or on your radio station and are pleased to have you reporting or promoting their activities. You will find that once you have established your lines of communication, there will be a constant stream of information coming in. You might not be able to use all of it, but make sure you keep in touch with all your contacts on a regular basis, until you are satisfied that nothing remotely newsworthy can happen in your patch without you knowing about it.

Pictures

Photojournalism is a specialist branch of professional journalism. But these days reporters at all levels and in all media are expected to gather images to illustrate their stories, be it stills or video, or both. Photographs sell papers, and still and moving images are essential online, for both websites and social output. Local and regional newspapers employ far fewer specialist photographers than they once did, and the onus is usually on the reporter to take the pictures that will run with the story. You can take good quality stills on your mobile, but you may decide to invest in a digital camera and/or video recorder that will give you more options and leave your mobile free for other functions.

If you are working with a dedicated photographer, make sure that you share the details of the story with them and discuss what the best images might be. They are the experts when it comes to the technical business of taking pictures, but you know more about the editorial demands of the story and should be making suggestions and discussing ideas with them. Take the opportunity to absorb any tips or techniques that you observe, which will come in handy when you are taking the pictures yourself.

Your photographs will almost always include people. Don't cram too many of them into the picture and try to have them engaged in some sort of activity rather than lined up in a row looking at the camera and wearing vacant smiles. Make sure the main focus is off centre. And when you have taken the picture, make sure you have all the details of the people who are in it, and who is who. By the time you get back to the office, it will be too late to try to identify them or work out which face goes with which name. This is really important if you are working with a staff photographer who is expecting you to gather the details and write a caption for the picture. Sometimes the photographer will take a picture and head off to the next job, leaving you struggling to gather names as the subjects disperse.

Here are some of the most common picture requirements:

– **Group pictures** – pictures of people engaged in activities that you are covering such as fund-raiding events, local awards ceremonies, mayoral visits. This might be a group of half a dozen people or more doing nothing more interesting than standing round and looking pleased with themselves. You will do lots of these, and they will often tax your imaginative powers. Look for a background that might provide an interesting frame for the shot, or some activity that the subjects might engage in that has a relevance to the occasion. Take people outside if appropriate – an outside setting is usually more interesting than a function room.
– **Ceremony/event** – much of the above applies. You might be dealing with larger groups of people here. Again, you have the problem of trying to create engaging images from unpromising situations such as events in large rooms with audiences. The solution will usually be to focus on individuals and close-ups rather than take big panoramic shots that are unlikely to work well.
– **Weather pictures** – usually people reacting to vagaries of the climate such as sunbathing and eating ice creams on a hot day in February, children tobogganing when snow has closed their schools. Action shots, people-focused.
– **Character studies** – pictures of individuals who are the subject of news stories and features, that endeavour to capture their character, or a sense of the environment in which they live and what it is like. You can try to be a bit more artistic here. Look for props – your subject might be holding up a winning lottery ticket, a prize onion, a wartime service medal or the cup they have just won.
– **Slideshows** – sequences of pictures that can be used for newspaper spreads or as a picture gallery online to illustrate the progression of a story.

Breaking news

Breaking news stories are the ones that get the pulses racing, when you really come into your own as a reporter. How you prepare and what you do when sent out to cover a breaking news story will not vary much across all media. The objectives are the same: get to the scene, get the story and report it as quickly as possible.

Readiness

Keep a grab bag in the office or in your car, so that you can reduce the time you need to get up and running when the call comes. The bag will contain any technical equipment you might need over and above what you will carry around with you on a routine day – extra batteries, extra leads and cables, spare memory cards, a phone charger. A detailed street map of your town or area is still useful, especially if you are not familiar with the scene of the story – if transport is disrupted you may need the means of finding an alternative route to the one advocated by your satnav, and digital maps are not always easy to scale on your phone. A separate bag might hold a change of clothes in case you are away overnight, some basic toiletries, a high visibility jacket and some warm clothing. It can be cold at night at any time of year. Have a stash of emergency provisions on hand too, such as a box of energy bars and a bottle of water.

Arrival

In the thrill of the chase it may be the last thing on your mind, but be aware that you may be entering a hazardous environment. Keep your own health and safety in mind before you dive in. Remember too that you do not have the automatic right to be recording and filming just because there is a story happening – in fact the authorities might be very keen that you do not. If you need permission, get it if you can. If you can't, use your discretion.

Reporting the story

When you get to the scene you have two priorities: finding out what is happening and gathering material; and filing reports back to base. It may seem self-evident that you do the one before the other, but the two activities will often come into conflict with each other. As soon as you get there, your radio station or television channel or website will be desperate for a live report from the scene, even if you arrived only two minutes previously. Your outlet's social media accounts will all want feeding too. Editors will not much care that you have not yet had time to find anything out. They want audiences to know that they are reporting from the location as events unfold, and this is the place to be for the very latest developments on the story. The name of the game is speed, and they want you on air or filing copy describing what it is like on the ground.

If you have a colleague or colleagues with you, it should be possible to organise a sensible division of labour, so that someone is feeding the machine while someone else is out newsgathering. If you are alone, you will feel stretched every which way. In either case, the best policy is to put yourself in the hands of your newsdesk. You have got plenty on your plate: let them decide what the priorities are on that story at that time of day – whether you should be filing or gathering – and direct you accordingly. You will obviously contribute to this process – "I think the police are holding a presser in a few minutes, so I need to be free to go to that". But beyond that, let them take on the burden of decision-making while you get on with your job.

The quickest way of servicing as many demands as possible in a hurry is to get some raw material filed quickly so that your editors have something to work with. Use your camera or smartphone to take some still pictures, and shoot as much raw video as you can; record a brief unscripted live report as you film – sometimes called a "standupper" or "action rant". You will be out of vision, providing a soundtrack to what you are filming.

This might take you no more than ten minutes. It might seem a drag on you when you have only just arrived and are not yet fully across what is happening, but it buys you the time to go and find out. If your newsdesk is operating as efficiently as it should, it can use the material you have sent to create the first illustrated reports from the event on all platforms: someone in the office can write a quick online story using your recorded reports as source material and your pictures or video; breaking news material can be put out on all social networks. They have something to be getting on with. It is raw, unpolished and a bit rough around the edges, but that is only to be expected in the early phase of a breaking story.

Once you have bought yourself a little breathing space, you have time to go and do some reporting. Try to do a deal with the news or content editor that all calls about the story within the organisation are channelled through them, and you are not getting individual phone calls from half a dozen different colleagues, all of whom believe they have first call on your time. Ask the desk not to call you for half an hour or an hour unless it is absolutely necessary, while you find out what is going on.

You are now in a gathering phase. On a breaking story, gathering information and illustrative material may be one and the same thing. Record lots more wild track and natural sound. Try to find someone who looks as though they are in charge and see if you can grab a few seconds with them for an update – bearing in mind that they will be frantically busy. Trot alongside them as they go if need be, recording what they say. Even a few words will be really valuable at this stage. Approach anyone who looks as though they might be able to help you, including possible witnesses.

When you have gleaned a little more about what is happening, it is time to repeat what you did when you arrived: recording and filing an up-to-date voice piece or action rant, and any new stills or video you have assembled, including any interviews. You can also record a piece to camera on your phone. In a broadcast operation, the newsdesk may now decide that you can spend some time doing individual two ways with various outlets. For others, the priority might be a brief written account for the website or paper. And that cycle continues until you are relieved, reinforced or the story comes to an end.

There is more about mobile journalism and specific radio and television skills in later chapters.

Breaking news from the office

If the story is too far away, or you cannot be spared from the office, you might not be able to go to the scene in person. You then have to chase the story from your desk. That will involve a lot of telephone calls. Depending on the story, you might want to speak to one or more of the emergency services, and keep calling them regularly as the situation develops. Watch and listen to any other news outlets covering the story, to make sure they have not unearthed news lines that you have missed. Try to find people near to the scene who may have witnessed something or be able to tell you what is happening now. Some of them may well be posting material on social media, and a well-directed search may lead you to valuable information or video. There is a section on advanced internet and social media searching in Chapter 14. Use your own website, social accounts or airwaves to appeal for people to get in touch with you if they are nearby or have seen anything. Encourage them to send you any material they have or can obtain – making very clear to them that they must on no account put themselves into a position of danger when so doing. (See below, and also Chapter 14, for matters to be borne in mind when seeking eyewitness media.) You will need to be ready to record phone conversations with witnesses for use as audio clips on the air or online. In the early phases of a breaking story, television outlets will often use audio interviews with a still picture on the screen to keep the coverage going until the cameras arrive.

Eyewitness media

Someone on the scene may well have taken some still or moving images on their mobiles before you arrived. If you are on location, ask around in the hope of tracking some down. This material is known as eyewitness media or user-generated content (UGC), and it could be gold dust on a breaking story. Your witnesses might even have footage of the event itself. Most organisations have a protocol for formally obtaining permission to use these pictures or video and for how long, and the circumstances in which they are prepared to pay for the rights. Typically you will be asking the owner of the material to confirm that they own the copyright – in other words that they filmed or created the content themselves; and that they are happy for it to be broadcast or published. Your company might have a standard form that people are asked to sign in such circumstances. If you have not got one, writing something down on a piece of paper on the spot and getting it signed is better than nothing.

Start off by asking for exclusive rights – then you will have the material, and no one else can use it. Or get your newsdesk to ring them direct and work out how to transfer the material and what if anything is to be paid for it. Although some key footage on big stories can command high prices, especially if a bidding war develops, that does not apply in most cases, and usually people are just happy that their material will be used, especially if they are promised that their names will appear alongside the images.

Acquiring eyewitness material can require some sensitivity and an awareness of ethical issues. Depending on the story, it could be that the people who shot the pictures have been shocked or even traumatised by what they saw. They may even be in a position of danger, whether they are aware of it or not. You should encourage them to move to a place of safety and be clear that you do not want them gathering material for you if to do so would put them in harm's way. However keen you are to get your hands on the material, remember to behave with courtesy and respect.

The Eyewitness Media Hub is a not-for-profit organisation that advises on best practice in this area. It publishes a regular newsletter, and has a website at eyewitnessmediahub.com. This is what the organisation regards as the appropriate way to behave when dealing with someone whose footage you would like to secure – what it calls "the etiquette of consent":

> Introduce yourself
> Enquire about the safety or wellbeing of the person who shot the footage
> Ask if they shot it themselves
> Ask for permission to use it
> Be clear about how and where it will be used
> Ask if they would like to be credited, and if so how.

Remember someone can give you permission to use an image or video only if they took it. Only then will they own the copyright. So it is essential to establish this at the outset. Ask them directly.

There is advice about how to track down eyewitness media online and on social networks, in Chapter 14.

Interviewing children

You will recall from Chapter 4 on Ethics that there are strict and clear rules about the way journalists conduct themselves when interviewing children – even on seemingly innocent light-hearted subjects like pets and pocket money. It is essential that you observe these. Refer to the codes and refer to your editor when working in this very sensitive area.

Diversity

Very often, you will have no choice when it comes to the people you interview for your stories or features. You might need to speak to a particular MP, or business leader, or celebrity, and for whatever reason, no-one else will do. But a lot of the time, you will be talking to people from a wider pool. In those circumstances, it is worth thinking about representation, and whether or not you or your employer is conscious of the need to reflect the nature of your local area or the country as a whole through the range of people you feature in your coverage. Some organisations exercise positive discrimination to a greater or lesser degree, reflecting the overall make-up of the population. The BBC's 50:50 Project, for example, is dedicated to ensuring that as many women as men appear in its programmes.

The UK is a diverse and multicultural society, and its journalism should be conscious of that. We need to see and hear from people of all ages, backgrounds, races and faiths, and have fair representation of minority groups such as people with disabilities. Make a conscious effort to open your reporting up to as many different perspectives as you can, and in particular to reflect the nature of the area in which you are working. This is not just about making sure that all perspectives are covered. You will naturally want to speak to someone with disabilities if you are doing a story about disability. But that person will not want to be defined solely by their disability, or compartmentalised in any way. They will also have views on any number of other general subjects – the cost of living, education, crime and so on – and are just as entitled as anyone else to have those views heard on those subjects too. Just as your reporting reflects a range of opinions, so it should reflect a range of people and perspectives as well.

To help you develop a sense of what is appropriate, here are a few key facts about the make-up of the UK, taken from the 2011 Census for England and Wales:

> 51 per cent were female, 49 per cent male.
>
> 21 per cent were aged under 18 years, 29 per cent aged 18 to 39, 27 per cent aged 40 to 59, and 22 per cent aged over 60.

86 per cent were white. 7.5 per cent were from Asian ethnic groups, 3.3 per cent from black ethnic groups, 2.2 per cent from mixed/multiple ethnic groups.

Religion was a voluntary question. Of those who answered: 59.3 per cent identified as Christian, 4.8 per cent as Muslim, 1.5 per cent as Hindu, 0.8 per cent as Sikh, 0.5 per cent as Jewish and 0.4 per cent as Buddhist. 25 per cent of those who responded to this question said they had no religion.

18 per cent (10 million people) had some form of disability that limited their daily activities.

Taste and decency

You will remember what the codes had to say in relation to graphic and shocking material. Once you have been working with some violent audio or video material for a while, you can lose your sense of how appalling and offensive it might be to an audience seeing or hearing it for the first time. Try to remember your own reaction when you first saw it, and edit accordingly. Refer anything about which you are even remotely uncertain to your editor. Even in written reportage, you need to make a judgement about just how detailed and graphic your account needs to be. Consider whether children might be reading, hearing or watching it. The basic rule across all platforms is to give no more detail than audiences and readers require in order to understand the horror of the situation; go too far, and you may produce a sensational report that appears designed to shock. It can be very hard to draw the line: what is acceptable to some consumers is horrific to others. If necessary, attach "health warnings" to potentially distressing content, for example: "some readers/viewers/listeners might find the details/images in this report distressing".

Health and safety

Your employer has a duty of care towards you, whether you are in the office or out on assignment. Most will offer basic health and safety advice and training. If you are working in the field, that might extend to specialist training, such as how to react in a civil disturbance, or work with maximum safety in a war zone or other hostile environment. You may also be issued with Personal Protective Equipment such as masks, hard hats, steel-capped boots, helmets, stab vests or flak jackets, depending on the nature of the assignment. You might be required to fill in a risk assessment for any assignment that is potentially hazardous, and this has to be signed off before the job can be approved. Most organisations allow you to decline assignments with which you are uncomfortable on security or safety grounds. Never allow yourself to be ordered or persuaded to go out on a job when you feel too scared to do it. There is no shame in this. If you yield, you become a danger to your colleagues as well as to yourself. If you feel you are being put under undue pressure, or that you are undertrained or underequipped, you must speak up. The same is true about Post-Traumatic Stress Disorder – about which there is more in Chapter 14.

7
Storyfinding: sources

Why we need reliable sources

Sources are the places we get our information. If a lot of journalism is about finding things out, sources are the places where they are to be found. There are lots of such places, official and unofficial, open and secret. They are the lifeblood of the news business. A journalist is someone who may not know the answers, but knows how to find them – and quickly. But you need to be discriminating about where you go to get those answers. If you are to publish and broadcast accurate and reliable information, then you must be satisfied that your sources are themselves accurate and reliable. You must use what you know about the source and about the story to weigh the information; assess its value; decide what you can use (and, by extension, what you cannot), how it can be used and how much reliance you place on it in your finished story.

Something you will hear very often in a newsroom is the question – usually asked by a content editor – is: "where have we got this from?" Or: "who is saying this?" In other words: what is the source? They want to be reassured about the information on which a story is based, and to be confident that the story in front of them is justified by the information that has been gathered.

Attribution

More often than not, it will be helpful to share the nature of the source with the audience. This is called "attribution". Audiences have the right to know where you are getting the material you are reporting to them. If you are quoting directly from your source – "She told a news conference that truancy levels were at their highest ever" – then they feel confidence in what you are reporting. There is a clear and uncomplicated link between the statement and its source, and as long as the reporting is accurate, the story will feel solid. If your sources are less specific, or cannot be disclosed for some reason – "sources close to the actor said he would deny the charges", or "it is understood that new measures will be announced tomorrow" – then you will be asking the audience to trust you. You are telling them that you have done your homework, tested your sources and are reporting what you consider to be reliable information. But you are not telling them exactly where you got that information for some reason – perhaps because you have promised your sources that you will respect their anonymity. The more open you can be about your sources, the more credibility your work has, and the more audiences are able to draw their own conclusions about what they are being told. In terms of audience understanding of a story, knowing the source of the information can be almost as important as the information itself.

Different types of source

You will gather information from many places. It is important to be able to discriminate between sources, so that you can decide how much credibility to attach to each. You will usually be looking for more than one source.

Ideally, you will base your reporting on *primary* sources. These are the ones you will feel are the most reliable. They are first-hand sources, telling you things that they have seen or are in a position to know. Less reliable, although still vital, are *secondary* sources. They are second-hand – things that others are reporting, for example, or information that people without direct personal knowledge are passing on to you. It may simply be rumour or gossip. That does not invalidate secondary sources – but it does mean that you will want to check them further, and see if you can corroborate or confirm what they are telling you.

So once you have answered the question "what is the source?", you will have further questions about the authenticity of that source and how much store you can set by it. This is particularly important with some internet sources, the provenance of which it is sometimes hard to establish.

Primary sources

Primary, or first-hand sources are the ones we trust most. The best possible source you can have, one that you know to be true and that you will always believe, is the evidence of your own eyes. If you have seen or heard something yourself, that is a primary source. You do not need anyone else to back it up and corroborate it or confirm it – you can go right ahead and report it. "I was there, and this is what I saw and heard." You might need to add context and background of course, but you can be sure of the foundation on which your story is based. There is nothing better, and no substitute for, something that you have seen yourself. Some of the most powerful examples of journalism down the years have been eyewitness accounts written by reporters who were on the spot and who saw the events at first hand.

You will also expect to trust a first-hand account from a colleague – someone else working for the same organisation, and therefore operating to the same standards as yourself.

The next best thing to seeing something with your own eyes is to find people who have seen it with theirs – in other words eyewitnesses. If they are able to tell you what they have directly seen or heard, then they are primary sources. But you will not necessarily take everything they say as gospel. Ten people who witness the same event will give you ten different accounts of it – and there may be significant variations, even on basic points of fact. People forget or misremember. If what they have seen was distressing, they may be too confused or upset to have clear recall. Memories fade over time. And of course they may have their own motives for disclosing some details and not others, or for putting a particular interpretation on what they have seen. So treat witnesses with care. Try to corroborate their account with others who were also there, and make sure that anything you use that is reliant on an eyewitness statement is attributed.

Primary sources are those where you are getting the news straight from the horse's mouth, and there is no barrier or filter between you and the information. So as well as witness accounts, they can be public events like speeches or news conferences, information that you extract from an on-the-record interview, or information you obtain from a well-placed contact who has direct knowledge. They may be published reports or anything else that is made available on the record. If you are formally being given information by people who are in a position to know the facts, and who have the authority to disseminate it, then you are working from primary sources. Information coming from the police, fire and ambulance services would fall into this category. Information that you find in reputable reference books might also be regarded as a primary source.

Even if you have a source you consider impeccable, you should seek out others as well. Everything you get from your sources will need supporting with context, reaction and fact checking. But primary sources give you confidence that your story is accurate and well founded. Share that confidence with your audience by telling them what those sources are.

"Reliable" sources

News agencies. From primary sources, with which we can generally feel comfortable, we come to something that I call "reliable sources". These include the material provided by agencies that make their money from delivering a service of reliable news to their subscribers. In the UK, the main news agency is PA Media, formerly known as the Press Association and usually referred to in newsrooms as "PA" or "the PA". International agencies of note are Reuters, Associated Press and Agence France-Presse. In national newsrooms, journalists will have access to some or all of these at the desktop. They are not primary sources in the strictest sense, because they are the products of someone else's journalism rather than your own. But they are treated as primary sources. Media organisations pay for access to them and treat them as extensions of their own operations. They trust the information that they receive from them.

These news agencies are sometimes known as wire services, or "the wires" – because they originally distributed their content by wireless telegraph. They are fully professional journalistic organisations operating to high standards. If they were not dependable, no-one would subscribe to their services. They have their own reporting staff and production desks. They offer hard news, features, sports news, business news, pictures and so on. Some have specialties – in the case of Reuters, financial information such as share and commodity prices. PA Media will put out racing results or football league tables – data that clients can transfer directly into a page.

This saves a huge amount of time and effort. News providers can in effect copy and paste whole pages of financial information or sporting results without the need laboriously to find them for themselves and then type them all out. And subscribing to a company like Reuters, which has a worldwide reporting staff, massively increases the reach of the journalism without the enormous costs of having your own people based permanently in these places.

At a local level, there are many news agencies run as commercial enterprises on a much smaller scale – perhaps employing only a handful of people. The quality of their work will be variable, although some are excellent. They might have a contract with local news outlets to provide a service of court reporting, say, or they might make their money by selling individual stories as they find them.

BBC Monitoring. A further good source for some international stories is BBC Monitoring – essentially a newsroom of its own within the BBC, based in London, but with international offices in Europe, Russia, Asia, the Middle East and Africa.

BBC Monitoring employs native speakers from many countries, and they listen to and watch international radio and television broadcasts, and read official newspapers and websites, from 150 countries in more than 70 languages. They provide audio and video extracts for BBC news outlets, in the original language and in translation. BBC television and radio news programmes often use this material in news stories, and interview the monitors on air as experts on affairs in their native countries.

In some countries, such as China and North Korea, the media is controlled by the state, and there is no free flow of information or comment. Understanding what state-controlled media are saying will therefore often give you an insight into official government policy – and be as close as you can get to a primary source. The information provided by BBC Monitoring is essential to the telling of many stories, and may sometimes offer virtually the only hard information you can get your hands on.

Secondary sources

As the name suggests, information that you get from a secondary source is at one remove from primary sources. Typically, this will be a report of what has happened or been said. It may be a tip-off, or just something you have been told by a friend, that you have read or maybe even overheard. You will not want to rely completely on such sources. You will always want to check the information, and try to substantiate it for yourself. To put it at its simplest: everything that is not a primary source is a secondary source.

Perhaps the most used of all secondary sources is other peoples' journalism. All newsrooms keep a constant eye on what the competition is doing. Media organisations – be they television, radio, print or online – usually start their day with a morning editorial meeting to talk about the stories that are around. One of the key functions of the meeting is to monitor what everyone else is reporting, and to make sure that no stories or angles are being missed. So the early part of the working day is spent scanning and discussing what is in the morning papers – whether through their websites or social accounts, or in hard copies – looking at other news websites, checking television news, listening to the radio news and trawling social media.

A lot of stories appear first on social media, in particular Twitter. Some of them are valid; you would be happy to quote and attribute comments that came from an individual's verified personal Twitter handle. However, a lot of the content is wildly speculative and inaccurate. Either way, Twitter is often the place where the first inkling of an upcoming story can be found, and all journalists use it as a sort of tip-off service, indicating what people may be thinking and as a source of potential breaking news. The same is increasingly true of other social platforms.

The content of the newspapers is a central feature of all these morning meetings. Newspaper circulations may be falling as more and more people get their news from other sources, but they remain massively influential within the news business in setting the agenda across the entire media landscape.

All of the output being monitored in this way comes from secondary sources. It is other peoples' journalism. You would not rely on it for your own reportage, but it can point you in all sorts of new directions and give you confidence that you are not missing big stories or good angles.

Sometimes news outlets can themselves become primary sources: if you heard a minister being interviewed on the radio, or saw a piece written by him or her in a newspaper, for example, that would be a *primary* source, because you would be hearing from them directly in their own words and could report accordingly – preferably with the source. "The minister told Radio Anytown: 'we are looking into this as a matter of urgency'." "Writing in the *Times*, the minister said it was a top priority for the government." But if you heard a Radio Anytown reporter giving a summary of the interview they had done with the minister, that would be a *secondary* source, because you would be relying on that reporter's interpretation and understanding of what had been said. You would want to go back and listen to the interview in its original – primary – state.

All these national media are also looking at local newspapers and other regional media to find stories that might be strong enough for national coverage. And exactly the same process happens in reverse at a regional and local level, with provincial daily papers, weeklies, websites, regional television and local radio stations. They are always looking for local angles on national stories. Then there are freelances and local news agencies, picking up ideas from each end of the food chain. Everyone keeps a constant eye on everyone else. It is a competitive and incestuous business, and no-one wants to miss a good story, or to be scooped by their rivals.

Other sources

The internet

The internet is an unimaginably powerful tool, and an almost infinite potential source of stories for you. We will look at advanced internet research separately and in detail in Chapter 14. The internet does need treating with caution, however. It can be easy to forget that something convincingly presented online is not to be taken at face value. Websites, blogs and much else of what you find there are frequently the opinions of individuals, pressure groups or people with entrenched views or vested interests.

When searching online, always bear in mind the distinction between primary and secondary sources, and be clear about what you are dealing with. There are plenty of primary sources online, but they tend to be buried in statistics and spreadsheets, and can take some uncovering. Primary sources such as official reports, company results, releases of official statistics and so on can be many hundreds of pages long and look boring and intimidating. Most reporters read only the summary and the conclusions. There are usually other and better stories buried away inside if you have the energy and the patience to look for them. This has given rise to a whole new offshoot of journalism, and a whole new breed of journalist called data journalists. Some knowledge of data journalism is fast becoming an essential part of every journalist's tool kit. We will also look separately at data journalism in Chapter 14. For non-primary sources, use the net as an initial alert, then do your follow-up research elsewhere, perhaps using other online sources – but preferably by talking to real people.

Social media

Much of this is true too of social media, where these health warnings also apply. You can conduct highly sophisticated research on platforms such as Twitter with tools such as Tweetdeck. Again, more in Chapter 14. Social media search tools can be brilliantly effective in helping you find people who may be involved with, or have a perspective on, current stories. In general though, social media reports from unknown individuals need treating with care. They may have gone viral, but that does not mean they are any the more credible. Unless your inquiries take you to primary sources, or you can verify them, never rely on them alone. There have been countless instances of false information and stories being planted on social media, and of news organisations being taken in by them.

Email alerts, RSS feeds

Setting up personal news feeds offers you the opportunity to create your own news agency, tailored to alert you the sort of stories in which you are interested. Using Google Alerts or one of the alternatives, you create a search that will alert you when new results come in, categorised by subjects, institutions, locations, named individuals and so on. In the same way, you can set up RSS feeds to deliver you results from a range of sources such as press offices or government bodies. You can choose from a number of RSS readers to create a dashboard showing all the feeds you want to follow.

Press offices

Press officers are paid, in theory at least, to provide you with information about the organisations they represent. Use them. These days you can find a lot of stuff very quickly on the internet, but we all know how much time you can waste trying to find exactly what you want from a source with which you are comfortable. There is a whole world of public relations officers and information officers out there, many of them former journalists, whose job it is to provide quick and factual information about a host of things. They can also provide you with direct quotes. Some, inevitably, will be a lot more helpful than others.

Your internet search will probably turn up their contact details from the organisation's web pages. Do not email them. That is far too slow and unreliable a means of getting what you want. Ring them up. Young journalists used to spending a lot of time online are often reluctant to call people directly on the phone, but it is where a lot of work is done, both in terms of researching stories and securing quotes. It puts you in direct contact, and is often much quicker. Press offices are there to answer your calls, and you will find yourself phoning lots of other people as well in connection with stories. If you persevere, you will soon get comfortable with the idea of calling people you don't know and getting into conversation with them. With press offices and others, you will get more, and more useful, information on the phone, and the chances are you will get it at least as quickly as you would online. And you will very probably get something else as well – other stuff that is interesting and that you did not even know you were looking for. Do not forget of course that press officers have an agenda – they are employed to project the best possible view of their organisation, and to defend it when it is under threat. They might not always be as candid and as forthcoming as you might like. But that does not mean that they cannot furnish you with useful facts, background and perhaps interviewees.

Trade associations

Most trades and industries have professional bodies associated with them, to preserve standards or to be a public advocate for the work of that sector or organisation. Many are large enough to have local or regional offices. They can give you in-depth expert information and contacts with authoritative interviewees.

Experts

There are also people who make it their business to find and put you in touch with experts on everything under the sun. Professional institutions, trade organisations, museums and universities will often have resident experts to whom you can speak. The beauty of these people is not only that they know what they are talking about, but also that they are real people giving you real quotes – they are not just an anonymous "spokesperson said". If you quote them by name and title in your story, you add authenticity and authority to what you are writing. And unlike press officers, experts do not usually have an agenda. Their main interest is in telling you about the subject and helping you understand it better. So they are brilliant for background, quite apart from anything else.

Spend some time trying to find the right person to give you the answer to the question you are asking. The right questions are no good if you are putting them to the wrong person – someone for whom this is not really a subject of special knowledge, for example.

If you are working in regional or local news, it is a good idea to cultivate local experts to talk about subjects that crop up frequently in the news. As long as you are happy with their credentials, this is a good way of giving a local feel to a national issue. Many local radio stations or weekly newspapers will have frequent contacts with academics at local universities, or have locally based health, transport, science or other expertise to call on.

Under your nose

There is also potential in the non-news sections of the websites and print versions of local newspapers. Most of the "small ads" have now migrated from print to the web, but you can still find items of possible interest if you are prepared to look – Lost and Found posts, for example, people offering – or seeking – eccentric items for sale, people looking for homes for unusual pets.

Announcements may alert you to people about to celebrate their 100th birthday, or their 60th wedding anniversary, or bring you news of the death of a person well known locally – the sort of stories that, as we saw in the last chapter, remain popular with readers. A local firm advertising a host of new jobs could be a sign that business is booming and they are expanding – it might be worth following up. Or there may be an ad for an unusual-sounding job that could be worth a phone call or two.

Councils and other official bodies such as utilities and transport companies are obliged to publish notice of upcoming changes or planning applications – even road works – which again will be of local interest.

Other media

It is often a good trick to buddy with local newspapers or radio stations in other regions or countries that are not in competition with you. If you work for one of the big groups that has a large stable of newspapers or radio stations, you can use that network to share information and contacts with your counterparts in other parts of the country. There may well be internal systems to facilitate that sort of cooperation. If you are in Bristol, you may be able to have a mutual exchange of information with a reporter in Sheffield who works for the same company, if there has been a crime in Bristol and someone from Sheffield is being sought in connection with it. You are both chasing the same story, but you work for the same employer and have no audience overlap, so it is a non-competitive environment. If you are chasing a story abroad but have no local contacts, a phone call to the nearest newspaper or radio station is a good and quick way to get started – faster even than an appeal on social media. Local journalists, especially in the media-savvy US, will often be happy to be interviewed about their stories, and might even help you with contact numbers, for the local sheriff's office, for example.

Leaks and tip-offs

You may be offered confidential documents, or receive them anonymously. They probably won't say Top Secret in big letters on the top, but they might well be of interest. And they have the advantage of potentially being a primary source – the sort we like best. Remember that one of our definitions of news was something that somebody somewhere did not want to see published. Material contained in leaked documents is very likely to fall into that category. You may be excited to be in possession of confidential information, but do not get carried away. You will still want to know who is giving you the information and why. What do you know about your source? What is their motive in leaking the information? Are the documents genuine? Ask for proof of authenticity, and, again, research around the story to see where the piece of the jigsaw you hold might fit into the whole. If you cannot verify the source of the information yourself, get some expert advice.

Some leaks are deliberately mischievous. Politicians will often leak details of a policy they are thinking of introducing, just to test the public reaction. If there is an outcry, they can quietly drop it and say it was only ever a first draft, or an idea that was being discussed hypothetically. Newspapers and others can be sometimes willing, sometimes unwitting, vehicles for this kind of deliberate leaking. You will often see stories on the front pages of the Sunday newspapers that exactly fit this description. Quite often you will hear nothing more about them ever again. This practice is sometimes known as "kite flying".

Whistleblowers

Whistleblowers will often be people who work or have worked for a company where they see things going on that they regard as unethical or possibly illegal, and decide to expose them. They may be acting with the best of intentions: they may have ulterior motives – they may be, to use the cliché, "disgruntled former employees.' Think about that possibility before you accept them unquestioningly as a primary source. You are going to want to check out and verify anything they tell you. Explore their motives and whether their job or their access means that they are in a position to know first-hand what they are telling you.

Whistleblowers have a degree of legal protection if they expose wrongdoing. But you still see many stories about people who claim they were victimised because they brought malpractice to light – whether it is illegal activity or inappropriate behaviour in the workplace. Victims may be sacked or denied promotion, or otherwise given the cold shoulder. We will say more about how you handle whistleblowers later in the chapter.

Reference books

If the internet or your smartphone cannot find just what you want, reference books can sometimes help. There may even be a few tattered copies lying around in your office – street maps of your area, a dictionary, a thesaurus, an old *Who's Who* perhaps, with its details of famous people, where they live and how to contact them; or a *Whitaker's Almanac*, which is stuffed full of useful facts and figures of all kinds. *Willings Press Guide* is a directory of all print publications, with editions for the UK and the rest of the world. *Crockford's Clerical Directory* is the place to find Church of England clergy, with their names and telephone numbers. All these and other good reference books and directories also exist online of course, but many of them require a subscription before you can use them. Your company may be a subscriber. If not, your local library might have hard copies.

Archive/library

News organisations tend to use these terms synonymously to refer to their own past coverage of a story, whether in print or broadcast form. Newsrooms often used to maintain libraries or archives of past newspaper coverage. These were known collectively as the "the cuttings" or "cuts" – usages you will still hear even now in the digital age. Librarians would snip out and file useful morsels from a range of newspapers and when you came cold to a story, that was often the first place you would look to help read yourself in and get yourself started. But the cuttings are now online, and you don't need a librarian to explore them. The library is also many times larger. Remember that just because a previous story is still available online, that does not magically turn a secondary source into a primary source. The story might not have been accurate in the first place, and you might even be looking at a version that was later corrected.

The electoral roll

If you are trying to track down an individual, the electoral roll may help. It is a register of everyone who is eligible to vote in elections, listed by their addresses. You can consult the roll online, and in town halls and libraries.

Freedom of Information requests

The Freedom of Information (FOI) legislation gives anyone the legal right to seek information held by official bodies, and compels them to disclose it unless there are genuine reasons for not doing so. These bodies include Parliament, government departments and agencies, councils, schools, exam boards, NHS Trusts, the courts, the armed forces, police and fire services – around 25,000 in all. It is open to everyone to use, and is obviously a great tool for journalists – a brilliant way of securing access to first-hand primary sources, and getting stories that are exclusive to you. There have been hundreds of very powerful stories based on the results of FOI requests.

Every public body has an online facility for receiving FOI inquiries. They are allowed to take up to 20 working days to reply, so do not expect a rapid turnaround. They are also able to reject requests if it will take them too long or cost them too much to find the answers. This will influence the way you frame your request.

It is not difficult to come up with ideas for FOI requests. All audiences are likely to be interested in revelations about the activities of public bodies, such as how long it takes ambulances to answer emergency calls or how much the council has earned through parking fines. Look at the news on any given day and ask yourself what more you would like to know about the background to it. You can also look at revelations that have stemmed from past FOI requests, and run the same exercise again to see if anything has changed.

If you spot a story that you think is worth exploring through FOI, the first thing to do is to check that the information you want is not already freely available. Public bodies tend to publish much more than they used to, and it is embarrassing, not to say a waste of time, if you try to use FOI to compel them to disclose something that they have already made public.

Using FOI:

> Your right to information covers only what is recorded – that is, held on computers, in emails and in printed or handwritten documents as well as images, video and audio recordings.

> Your submission can be in the form of a question, rather than a request for specific documents, but the authority does not have to answer your question if this would mean creating new information.

> If you are planning to send the same request to multiple locations – say every council or police force in the country – start with one or two as trial runs. Then if there any wrinkles in the request, or it is not delivering the results you were looking for, you can refine and improve it before you send it out to everyone else.

> Be precise about the data you want. If you ask for figures going back too far, say more than five years, councils may reject the request on the grounds that collating them would consume too many resources. Include details like dates and names if you can.

> It might help the authority deal with your request if you are prepared to explain why you are making it.

> Avoid catch-all requests such as asking the authority to send you everything they have about a certain subject. Don't fish for information by sending very broad or random requests in the hope that it might turn up something newsworthy. They might decline to cooperate – or send you so much material that you cannot derive anything meaningful from it.

Different authorities gather and report the same data in different ways. If you are submitting requests to multiple bodies, frame them in such a way that you can be sure you are able to compare like with like when you have assembled your responses.

Specify the format in which you would like to receive the information.

If you are gathering information from a number of sources, make a spreadsheet to track responses, and to allow you to interrogate the data.

If you are not sure what information an authority might hold, you can contact their FOI Officer for advice and assistance. For example, you may not be sure whether the information you want is held by a district council or the county council. Authorities must give reasonable advice and assistance to anyone asking for information. Some will be more helpful than others.

Authorities are often very slow to respond. Keep chasing them if they have not responded within the deadline. Some have a reputation for being dilatory, and may be hoping you lose patience and go away. Don't. This is information you are entitled to have, and they are obliged to give you. If you think information is being unreasonably withheld you can appeal to the Information Commissioner's Office (ICO).

Don't stop researching when you have the data. Look on that as the first step only. Remember that it is people who bring stories to life. However strong your data, it will be made stronger as a news story if illustrated with case studies and reactions.

Read the section on Data Journalism in Chapter 14: there is quite a bit of overlap in the techniques involved.

There are some things that authorities are not obliged to reveal, such as information that could prejudice national security or damage commercial interests. For some exceptions, known as "qualified exemptions", the authority must consider whether the public interest in withholding the information outweighs the public interest in releasing it. If it decides that the information cannot be released it must tell you and explain why. If you disagree, you are free to argue back that release *would* be in the public interest.

You can challenge a decision not to respond to your request, and they have up to 40 days to review that decision. You can appeal to the ICO if you think their refusal does not fall within the rules. Even if the authority is entitled to withhold some of the information you have asked for, you might need to press for the rest of it, if you think other elements are not exempt.

Often the authority will respond to your request, but give you only partial information or something that falls short of what you think you asked for. You can reduce the likelihood of this if you are careful about the way you word your request in the first place. But you always have the option of going back with a further FOI request.

If you are not confident about lodging an FOI request, speak to your editor or to someone in the office who has experience of doing it. There is also a public website called *WhatDoTheyKnow.com* that will do it for you. However, the site publishes all requests and the responses, meaning your potential scoops will be there for all to see. So it is best to work off your own bat if you can. Even so, you should be aware that some authorities automatically make public the requests they have had and the answers they have given. You will want to run your story before they tell everyone else about it.

Assessing the information your sources give you

So there are very many places from which you can derive information, some primary sources, some secondary. Once you have gathered it, you need to assess what more you need to do before you feel ready to use it.

Editorial style guides and codes do not have much to say about assessing and verifying sources. One that does is the Editorial Guidelines, the bible for BBC producers. This is what it says:

> We should try to witness events and gather information first hand. Where this is not possible, we should talk to first-hand sources, and where practicable, corroborate their evidence. We should be reluctant to rely on a single source.

This is essentially a list of priorities for the gathering of news, and it holds for all journalism, not just the BBC. It underlines that the best and most reliable way of getting information is to see something for yourself. The most vivid reportage in any medium is someone – reporter or witness – describing what they themselves have personally seen and experienced. You should always try to find the people who know – first-hand sources, or primary sources of the sort we have been discussing. If you were not there yourself, find someone who was.

A lot of the time you will hear things second or third hand. You will see them on social media or elsewhere, or someone will tip you off about something. You will not feel confident about publishing a story on the basis of these sources. You will, as the BBC says, "be reluctant to rely on a single source". So you will look for another – speak to others who will know about the story, or be in a position to judge whether or not it is true, and give you more information. Always try to get a second source if you can, to back up what you are being told. It will make you feel more confident about the story you are writing, and it will make that story more rounded and better-informed.

Even if the source is good, you need to build a story around the information it is providing. If one of your contacts is the leader of your local council, say, and she tells you about a new policy she is about to launch, then that is a story from a good first-hand source. You can report it, and attribute it by name, without the need to corroborate with any other sources. But you will have told only half of it. You will still want to talk to other people around the story. You might want to see whether the leader is actually implementing the policy, and has set aside funding for it, or is just making a vague promise. You will also want reaction – what political opponents, those affected, or the public, may feel about that course of action.

The BBC Editorial Guidelines again:

> We should normally identify on-air and online sources of information and significant contributors, and provide their credentials so that our audiences can judge their status.

This reinforces the point about attribution, and again is a good general rule for all. Make clear where you are getting our information from – especially if you have been unable to verify material fully. You are in effect saying to the audience, or the readership: I have done my homework on this story as best I can, and this is what I believe to be the truth of it. Here are the people I have spoken to and the sources I am using to reach that conclusion. Now it is up to you to decide what you think.

Confirmation, corroboration, verification

We have already noted that however good your source, you will almost always want another perspective or some contextual material to put in your piece, and you need to go elsewhere for that. Your source may have told you the truth, but it might not be the unvarnished truth and it might be tainted by their personal point of view. You will need to be sure that nothing important is missing, and that you have not been given a highly coloured and perhaps even distorted account.

The business of checking and corroborating is part of the process of building the story around what your source has told you. You do this by seeking further supporting information. Again, it is largely about finding a second source. Look for people with first-hand knowledge of your story, or expertise, or a relevant view or opinion on the subject. They might be able to help you confirm and corroborate your story. Even if they can't, they will help you put it in perspective.

Ask official sources or spokespeople for a comment – they might not confirm your story, but if they do not deny it outright, or give you an equivocal reply, you might feel more confident about it. Have a look online for supporting material or sources, or places you can go to make further inquiries. And use your social media accounts to try to track down someone or something that can bolster your story.

If you cannot, in the jargon, "stand the story up" – that is, substantiate what you have been told – then you should not be publishing it. Dig deeper or drop it.

These days, with so much material posted online by millions of people, new roles have emerged in many big newsrooms for journalists whose principal job it is to try to verify sources. Often the material they are scrutinising is pictures or video rather than text or verbal statements. Potentially newsworthy pictures are posted online all the time. But we need to be sure that they really show what they purport to show, or that they were filmed when it is claimed they were filmed. It is a kind of detective function that has become an essential role in journalism as the result of the explosion of non-professional video and other content that is published on the web every day – and of course the insidious development that is fake news.

Some journalists work full-time on this function, trying to clear material for potential broadcast or reporting, and to filter out anything the provenance of which looks suspicious. They have developed special skills in the advanced use of the internet. At a more fundamental level, some familiarity with the skills needed to do this sort of gathering and checking, at least at a basic level, has become an essential for every journalist. We look at advanced tools for verification and confirmation in Chapter 14.

Using sources, weighing, verifying and corroborating what they tell you and deciding what to use is an integral part of the general business of both newsgathering and story writing – the fundamentals of good reporting. The general rules around accuracy, fair dealing and impartiality, all apply.

Here is a basic checklist of questions that you should be asking yourself about your sources when evaluating them and what they tell you. If you keep it in mind, you will not go far wrong. You will not always get clear-cut and straightforward answers – news can be a messy and subjective business. But these questions should help you weigh what you have got, and judge what kind of a story you are able to produce, what you feel you can say and what you cannot substantiate.

Who is telling me this? Always the key question. What do I know about the reliability of my source? Are they in a position to know?

Is my source impartial? Where are they coming from? What is their motive in telling me this? What is their agenda?

Does it sound/feel right? Sometimes you will have a gut feeling that something does not quite add up. There is a joke in journalism that a story can be so appealing that it is "too good to check". In other words, it looks like a cracking story, but if we ask too many questions about it, we suspect it is going to fall apart in our hands. It is just that, though: a joke. Nothing is too good to check. If a story looks too good to be true, it probably is.

Is it on the record? If someone asks to speak off the record for no obvious good reason, you might have cause to be worried about why that might be.

Can it be confirmed or corroborated? Can I check it? How? If I cannot verify it, can I use it?

All these are related questions about how you verify what it is that you have got, and how you get other sources for what you want to write.

Have I attributed? Very important, as we have discussed. Apart from anything else, it is a way of signalling to whoever is reading it that you have done your job properly.

Cultivating your own sources

Remember that members of the audience now have access to a lot more information, so you need to be careful not to tell them things they already know. Football supporters, for example, can scour their team's official website, watch the manager's press conferences live, subscribe to fanzines and follow all the latest transfer rumours online. They have direct and open access to many of the same sources as you. This makes your job a little more difficult: you need to look deeper, cast your net more widely, make connections and offer extra value. One way of doing that is by developing your own sources. Having your own sources can deliver stories that are exclusive to you, and you will do yourself a lot of favours by developing a reputation, inside the office as well as outside, as someone who can deliver "off-diary" stories – that is, stories that are not available to everyone through open sources.

Sometimes the news just happens, and all you have to do is gather some details, report them, and try to explain and put them into context. But most stories are the result of journalistic effort to a greater or lesser extent – resourcefulness, instinct, persistence, digging, research, simply asking questions or a combination of some or all of these. It has been truthfully said (I'm not sure by whom): "I've met a lot of lucky reporters. I've never met a single lazy lucky reporter". No story worth its salt ever drops into your lap fully formed and ready to go. They all need some worrying away at to get a good finished product.

Good journalists know where to look, who to speak to and what questions to ask. These are skills that you will develop. And there are things you can do to help make them happen – to find good sources and contacts and encourage them to trust you and to confide in you.

As a general rule, try to speak to people face to face. They will tell you much more than they would on the telephone or in an email or social exchange.

Keep your eyes and ears open. If you are sent to cover an event, get there early and hang around afterwards. That is when people will speak to you, and you will find things out. Other reporters have yet to arrive or have left, people are more relaxed, they let their guard drop. If they think your website, paper or station is going to tell their side of a story or reflect their perspective, they will often be very keen to talk. They will be less keen when there are hordes of other reporters swarming around. Try to get them on their own, or arrange to meet them later.

You will remember that in Chapter 3, we stressed how important your contacts book should become to you. To repeat: collect contacts and their numbers obsessively. A well-maintained and detailed book of contacts, physical or virtual, with all the different ways of getting in touch with them can be your best friend and get you out of many a hole. You will find out how good yours is when you are working late at night and you need some vital information. You might well be able to find a promising interviewee by a trawl of LinkedIn, but they might take a long time to reply to you, if they reply at all. If you have home numbers and/or mobile numbers, you will be able to get hold of people outside working hours – and if they cannot help you, they may give you the names and numbers of those who can.

You will make contacts with every story you cover. If you are working on local or regional outlets, you will bump into the same people over and over again: councillors, court officials, local business people, secretaries of local organisations, hospital administrators, head teachers, police and fire officers. Anyone you meet on any particular story might be a useful source of further information or local knowledge in the future.

You will have some key contacts who are useful to you and help you find and understand stories. Make sure you cultivate them. Don't ring them only when you want something from them, but keep in regular touch with them. Pass the time of day and ask them what is going on in their world. They may tell you something that they had not thought newsworthy, but you do. And they may remember you and call you when they do have something they think worth passing on. They will also remember you if, when they do give you stories, you report them fairly and accurately. Or the reverse.

Handling your sources

Dealing with these sources, and others too, can throw up some tricky dilemmas.

Beyond one immutable rule about anonymity, which we will come to later, there are no accepted codes, no specific rules and regulations to govern how you behave when dealing with your contacts. In general, the standards set out in the chapter on ethics should cover most circumstances. But there are always variations, depending on how you operate, the sort of story you are working on and the sort of contact it is. Here are a few rules of thumb for dealing with contacts.

Identify yourself as a journalist (if they don't already know who you are and where you work)

Pretending to be someone else, or otherwise deceiving the person you are dealing with, is not only highly unethical, but it is also dishonest and could even be dangerous. It can sometimes be justified in difficult and sensitive investigations, but on those occasions it will be done with the knowledge and approval of senior figures in your organisation. Telling people you are a reporter up front may make them more guarded and less cooperative; but that is preferable to tricking them and telling them half-way through, or not at all. They will not be very pleased when they do find out – and they might well start to retract or modify what they have already said, or tell you that it was all off the record. This puts you in an extremely awkward position. So be straight from the off.

Fair dealing

As in life, the way to get what you want is not by blustering and hectoring, but by behaving in a reasonable and decent way. Be friendly, open and honest. If you are doing a story in which your source has been criticised or accused of something, put those points to them and give them time to respond – and make space in your story for that response. Don't wade right in with: "There are demands for you to resign. Will you?" Say: "I'd like to give you the chance to put your side of the case". Don't forget that it is very likely that you will have to deal with people again, sometimes very regularly if they are local MPs or councillors. So the straighter your dealings with them and your treatment of them, the more likely they are to trust you and cooperate with you in the future.

Retain editorial control

Sometimes the people you interview will ask if they can see your story once it is written. This is known as "copy approval" – "copy" being the way journalists refer to the scripts of their stories. You should be very wary about agreeing. Usually the answer is an out-and-out "no". It is your piece, not theirs, however much they would like to be able to control what you write. Even if they say they only want to look at it and check it for accuracy, they will invariably find something with which they disagree, or – worse – that they wish to re-word or retract altogether. That puts you in an invidious position. If you think you might have got something wrong and you want to be absolutely sure it is accurate before you publish, or you need to go back and double-check quotes or facts, that is fine. That is not the same as presenting the whole of your finished work for approval or clearance. You want to avoid anything that looks as though anyone has the capacity to censor your piece or alter it, other than by correcting factual errors. You need to act independently and be seen to do so. This can sometimes be a particular issue when you are interviewing people for features. Potential interviewees can try to make copy approval a condition for agreeing to talk to you. We discuss this in the next chapter, on Interviewing.

Retraction

This is where somebody says something to you that they later regret and want to retract – in effect asking or instructing you not to use it. If they do so immediately, that is probably fair enough. And if they want to correct errors of fact, then you should allow them to do so. Beyond that, if the interviewee has a change of mind later – hours or days later – that is more complicated. If they volunteered something in a properly conducted and open interview, you are entitled to use it. It is possible they may have a good reason for changing their mind. You will want to consider that. Use your common sense and instinct for what is fair and decent. Anything you feel uneasy about should be referred up to your editor. Again, there is more on this in the next chapter devoted to Interviewing.

Payment

The decision about whether you should pay for information or material is another that you can expect your editor to take. It is not your money after all. These days, media organisations will sometimes pay for newsworthy stills or moving pictures taken by members of the public. They try to avoid doing so if they can, but some key footage can be so valuable that they are prepared to pay large sums for the rights to use it. Such footage may well be a very strong primary source, and will have huge competitive value. Tabloid newspapers will still pay for tip-offs – that is how they secure stories ahead of their rivals. In general, though, you will not expect to pay for information. Paid-for information is no more reliable, and may well be a lot less reliable; it risks creating a market, and an expectation that you will pay. Always refer up any request for money unless it is something very basic like a bus fare home or the price of a coffee or a glass of wine while someone tells you their story – something you might be able to justify under the heading of "hospitality" or legitimate expenses.

Non-attribution

We have talked several times about sharing with your readers or broadcast audiences the sources you used in writing your story. But sometimes your sources will not want to be quoted directly. They are happy to give you some information. Sometimes they may even be happy to be quoted in direct speech. But they ask you not to use their names. They do not want the story to be traceable back to them. If the information is good, and you are in danger of losing the story if you refuse, you may be prepared to agree. If so, you will need to find some way of convincing your readers that what you are saying is soundly based, even if you cannot give the name of your informant. This is when you will have to resort to phrases such as "sources close to" or "well-placed sources" or "an informed source who did not wish to be named".

On and off the record

Always try to persuade your sources to speak to you on the record – which means that you can attribute the information to them by name. This is particularly important for broadcast news outlets, which like to be able to carry audio or video clips of interviewees. A reporter who simply quotes "sources" is going to have trouble making a lively piece of television or radio.

Off-the-record conversations are to be avoided if possible. Part of the problem is that there is no single definition of what constitutes on/off the record, so you and your source may come away from a conversation with a completely different idea of what each of you means by what you have agreed. If you have been told something off the record, can you use any of it? If so what, and how?

It is essential that you sort out these ground rules in advance. In fact, anything not agreed in advance about information being off the record should mean an assumption that it is all on the record. Sources cannot say at the end of the conversation: "by the way, all that was off the record". But sometimes they do just that, which is very annoying and puts you in a quandary. Can the terms of trade be altered retrospectively?

Point out to them that they were speaking on the record. They had not previously suggested otherwise, so that was the basis on which you did the interview. Tell them they cannot change their minds halfway through, or retrospectively. Ask the reason for the change of heart. If you cannot shift the source, ask your editor for advice. In the end, if the interview was conducted in good faith, you are entitled to ignore their request if you see fit. Ignoring their wishes might of course result in you falling out with your sources. In the case of regular informants, you might want to consider whether that is a risk worth taking if it is going to destroy a conduit that could be useful to you again in the future. And of course, you will want to know the source's reason for wanting to go off the record. If they are potentially putting themselves in danger by speaking out, say, you are bound to consider that.

Experienced interviewees might give you an on-the-record interview, but every now and then ask you to regard a particular bit of the interview as off the record. This means that you can use it, but not attribute it directly to them. That is acceptable, as long as you are both very clear what is being said on the record and what off. If in doubt, ask.

Don't give up at an initial refusal to go on the record. Keep asking and making the arguments. It may be that after giving you a lot of background information unattributably, you and your source might be able to negotiate some elements at least on which they would happy to be quoted by name.

If you do agree to speak to someone off the record, you both need to be absolutely clear about the terms and conditions. Here are two questions that should help you clarify the position before the interview begins. First:

> This interview is off the record. I understand that to mean that I can use anything you tell me, as long as I do not report that it came from you. Do you agree?

This is what most people would understand to be meant by an off-the-record conversation. Your source is agreeing that you can use the information, but not say who gave it to you. You can hint of course, as we have suggested: "sources close to the actress……" "friends of the disgraced businessman…." You see this all the time, and although these signals don't involve names, they offer the audience reassurance that your story is based on sources who have access to primary information and therefore know what they are talking about.

If the answer to that question is not "yes", then you will need to probe further and discover exactly the basis on which your source thinks he/she is talking to you. Then you may have to negotiate before deciding whether you can accept these terms.

If the answer *is* yes, move on to your second question:

> Are you giving me hard information – something of which you have direct knowledge; or are you giving me a tip-off that I will need to confirm elsewhere before I can use it?

This question is important because your source may just be passing on to you a titbit of information they have picked up second or third hand, which they think you might be interested in following up. In other words, they are a secondary source. It is all too easy for a misunderstanding to arise in which you think the source knows something for a fact and is a primary source for the story.

Putting sources at their ease

We talked about the need for you to identify yourself up front and be clear who you are. That stands. But if your next steps are too forceful and direct, you might frighten off a potential source, especially if they are not used to talking to the media, or are worried about telling you anything in the first place. So adopt a softly-softly approach. Don't come right out and say "I am doing an exposé of X, and I want to interview you". The effect of that on a nervous or uncertain interviewee would not be helpful.

Start gently. "I'm trying to find out some more about what's happening with X, and I understand you might know a bit about it. Is there any chance I could have a chat with you to help me understand what's happening?" This would also work if you have to approach someone via email or on the phone rather than face to face.

Whipping out a notebook, smartphone, audio recorder or camera is another surefire way to put off someone who is uneasy about what they are doing. Talk to them first and put them at their ease. If necessary, engage in a bit of inconsequential chat before working your way round to the things you really want to ask about. Slip out your notebook when you feel that they have warmed up a bit and are a little more at ease. If they react, just say something like "do you mind if I jot some of this stuff down, to make sure I've got it right, to refresh my memory later" or something similar.

Shorthand is a boon in this situation, because it allows you to spend less time writing and potentially distracting your interviewee, and more time maintaining eye contact and engaging directly with them. But even so, written notes only take you so far if you are required to produce something more than a written story. What you really want is some sort of on-the-record broadcast interview that can be used on the website, social accounts and broadcast outlets. You may have to talk to your contact for quite a while before you broach the subject. This might actually be an advantage because it means that you will have gleaned a clear picture of the story, what your interviewee knows about it, and what will be the best questions you can ask.

It is hard to produce a microphone or camera subtly in the same way you can a notebook. Even if you are recording on a smartphone, it is tricky to start doing so without attracting some sort of attention (and you should not be doing so secretly). So you need to say something before doing so. "Would you mind if I got you on tape saying some of this?" If they decline, keep trying. If they really want the story to come out, remind them that as a broadcast report it is going to be much more effective if you have real people speaking into the microphone. If they agree but want to impose conditions, find out what those conditions are. A common condition is a refusal to answer questions in some specific area. You might well feel able to agree to this – unless of course those are the key questions that you really have to ask if you are to get your story. If so, then keep negotiating. Try everything you can to influence and persuade. There may come a point when this becomes counter-productive – you are annoying your source and actually making them more reluctant to talk, rather than less. If so, back off. You can return to them later, maybe even in a day or two – or a week or two, depending on the lead time of your story.

Be politely persistent and don't take no for an answer. Adopt an open and honest manner; make it clear you are interested and engaged; make sure you listen to what's being said; and where appropriate, empathise with the subject. Do everything you can to keep them talking, consistent with what the Editors' Code has to say about harassment of people who have made it clear they do not wish to speak to you.

Requests for anonymity

Sometimes your informants will want promises and undertakings that go beyond simply stipulating that what they are telling you is unattributable. They want a guarantee of anonymity that goes well beyond simply omitting their name. Such people might be whistleblowers, or anyone who feels they may be at risk of reprisals of some kind if it is revealed that the story came from them.

They still want the story to come out because they believe that such information – relating, for example, to corruption, misgovernment or the activities of organised criminals – should be made known to the general public, to expose wrongdoing or to stimulate public debate on the subject. But they make total anonymity a precondition for their willingness to speak.

Anonymity can be at different levels – it may be enough to ensure that contributors are not readily identifiable or recognisable by the general public. But sometimes it may be necessary to ensure they cannot even be identified by friends and family. For broadcasters, both picture and voice may need to be disguised, or actors used to reconstruct the interview.

Obviously a source you can name is better than one that you can't. If the source is named, it is easier for readers to assess his or her credibility and motives. But some important information would never reach the public if journalists were unable to guarantee confidentiality to their sources.

In general, if you promise anonymity you have to be sure that you can deliver it – including the need to resist a court order if need be. You must agree with the source how they are to be described, because you will need to give the audience some information about them if you can, to show why you think they are credible and their story worth reporting.

Protecting the identity of your source

If an organisation carries a big story based on an anonymous source, then everyone immediately wants to know who the source is. Those with an interest in trashing the story may suggest that anonymity is being used to disguise the fact that the source is lying, or not credible, maybe even that the source doesn't exist. Sometimes media organisations are taken to court in attempts to compel them to reveal their sources.

It is an article of faith that they do not do so, and that they protect the anonymity of the source. Protecting sources is a key principle of journalism for which some journalists have gone to jail. This is the immutable rule to which I referred earlier. It is a fundamental matter of ethical practice. You will remember that Clause 14 of the Editors' Code says: "Journalists have a moral obligation to protect confidential sources of information".

There is some legal support for this position. The Contempt of Court Act (1981) recognises the need to protect journalistic sources in a free society, and presumes in favour of journalists who choose not to reveal them. Courts may consider whether or not this principle is outweighed in individual cases by the interests of justice, by national security or to prevent a crime.

However, on one occasion when a court did decide against the journalist, the case was taken to the European Court of Human Rights. The European Court overturned the decision of the UK court, saying it was a breach of Article 10 of the Human Rights Convention, guaranteeing freedom of expression.

The case was Goodwin v United Kingdom (1996). Here are some of the key points of the European Court's ruling.

> An attempt to force a journalist to reveal his source for a news story violated his right to receive and impart information, and hence the right to freedom of expression. The Court considered that orders to disclose sources reduce the flow of information, to the detriment of democracy and are, therefore, only justifiable in very exceptional cases.
>
> Protection of journalistic sources is one of the basic conditions for press freedom.... Without such protection, sources may be deterred from assisting the press in informing the public on matters of public interest. As a result the vital public-watchdog role of the press may be undermined and the ability of the press to provide accurate and reliable information may be adversely affected.

The European Court intervened again in 2009 when the UK court ordered the *Financial Times* and other newspapers to reveal documents that could have exposed their source for a story about a company takeover. The European Court again overturned the ruling.

These decisions take us right back to the very fundamentals of journalism and its purpose in a democratic society, which we have discussed several times in previous chapters. The courts have tended to see the rights of journalists not to reveal their sources as part of the exercise of these functions.

Keeping records

At every level, from off-the-record conversations to much bigger exposés, good note-taking is very important, ideally in shorthand. You must take accurate, reliable and contemporaneous notes of all significant conversations and other relevant information. If you cannot write it down straight away for whatever reason, make as detailed a note as you can as soon afterwards as you can. That is what is meant by "contemporaneous" – notes made at the time or as close to the time as possible. A recording of course is even better. Keep all recordings, including the bits that you did not actually use in your final report.

You should also keep records of research, and all previous contacts, including written and email correspondence, background notes and documents. You must keep accurate notes of conversations with sources and contributors about anonymity. You may need this in case your story is challenged, in case your editor wants to see the basis on which your story stands or – in extreme cases – in case you need to produce it in court. Bear in mind that in the event of challenge, you might have to surrender all emails and any other records of conversations relating to the story. Sometimes these emails will give you defensive cover – sometimes you would rather they were not being made public. It is worth bearing that in mind when you commit anything to email or any other recoverable message.

8
Storyfinding: interviewing

types of interview and interviewee…..interviews by telephone…..interviews by email…..when it goes well, and when it goes badly…..interviewing for news reports…..interviewing for long-form features: setting up the interview; research and preparation; your questions; the first five minutes; asking the questions; delicate and sensitive areas…..active listening and observing…..they think it's all over….. pen and paper or tape recorder?….. retractions…..copy approval

Journalism is all about asking questions and getting answers. The most important single method of obtaining information is by talking to people. The job of a reporter is to identify the people who know the answers, track them down and put the questions to them. News reports and features are all heavily dependent on quotes and information from people to whom the writer or broadcaster has spoken in the course of researching the story. The ability to get on with people, and to persuade them to give you the information or comments that you seek, is clearly a very important part of the skillset of any journalist, regardless of the sort of journalism in which they are engaged.

In this chapter, we will be looking at how you develop interviewing skills across a range of different circumstances and formats. What you do with the material you gather – how you write up the interview – is covered in later chapters.

Types of interview and interviewee

You carry out interviews for three principal purposes:

– Information. You are seeking basic facts about your story, an account of what happened or expert background knowledge to help your understanding of it. This is what a lot of news reporting is about. It is unlikely that a long-form feature interview would be purely informational.
– Comment. You are looking for a view, reaction, perspective or comment to a story. "What do you think about X?" "What is your reaction to Y?" The basis for a lot of news reporting and longer form pieces too.
– Feelings. You want to know from someone what an experience was like and how they responded to it on an emotional level. Used in all forms of journalism – which is, as we know, about people.

In news reporting, your interviews will often be short, transactional and businesslike. They might last no more than a few minutes – just long enough for you to get the information and quotes you require as part of your wider story.

In a feature, a single interviewee may well be the subject of the whole piece, and so your interview will be a much more formal affair – arranged in advance, ideally face to face, and lasting much longer as you ask more detailed questions in an extended conversation.

In either case, you will interview all sorts of different individuals:

People in power

You will recall that one of the key functions of journalism in a healthy democracy is holding power to account. Anyone in a position of authority is answerable for what they do, and how they exercise that authority. People in power include elected officials – members of the government, Members of Parliament, councillors; but also heads of businesses, institutions, charities and other organisations; and at a more local level, council officers and head teachers. We might call these people "professional interviewees", because we interview them by virtue of the positions they hold, and the responsibility and accountability that go with those positions. They represent institutions, organisations or groups of people, and speak on their behalf. Such interviews will have an element of challenge: the reason you want to speak to them may well be because something for which they are answerable has gone wrong or been called into question. These are sometimes called "adversarial" interviews, because with the challenge may come a hint of combat. It is likely the authority figure will have been interviewed many times before, and some may even have had formal training about how to deal with questions from the media. They will know how to avoid or deflect questions they do not want to answer. When that happens, you need to be dogged and to resist being deflected.

Experts

As part of your research for stories and features, you will want to speak to people with the detailed knowledge and expertise that will help you understand the subject matter better. Sometimes, expert opinions will be at the centre of the story – such as during the coronavirus outbreak of 2020, when leading scientists were at the heart of policy-making. More commonly, you will find yourself embarking on a story about which you know next to nothing, and which feels quite complex and difficult. But journalism is not all about what you know: it is about what you can find out, and how quickly. You may find your experts through press offices and internet searches. They may be in universities or in industry. Sometimes you may use them simply as sources of information, to ensure that you are well briefed – you might never actually refer to them in your story. At other times, you will want to quote them to add authority and extra context to your piece. There is no adversarial element here – you are tapping into their specialist knowledge and informed opinion, not subjecting them to challenge.

"Ordinary people"

By contrast with professional interviewees, lots of people find themselves involved in news coverage by chance, as victims or witnesses, or relatives and friends of people in the news. They need treating with care, especially if their involvement is something that is likely to have left them traumatised or otherwise emotionally affected. You are talking to them when they are at their most vulnerable, and you need to be sensitive to their feelings. It may be that you are the first journalist they have ever spoken to. Unlike professional interviewees, they do not know the rules of the game. Adopt a patient and empathetic approach. Do not treat them as props or commodities in your story.

It is not all gloom. Such people may be the subjects of happy stories too – lottery winners, say, or people who have received awards or achieved their lifetime ambitions.

Vox pops and surveys

Few reporters actively enjoy approaching people in the street to ask them for their views on some topical issue, but you will be almost certainly have to do it at some point. Though much maligned, vox pops are still very widely used to add colour to coverage and try to get a sense of the public mood, however unscientific the method is. Gathering vox pops, or "voxes" is a good test of your persistence and determination, your ability to strike up a rapport with people in double-quick time and to persuade them to talk to you and give you good quotes.

Celebrities

As a feature writer, you will often produce a whole article on the basis of a single interview. Very often the subjects will be what can loosely be categorised as celebrities. You will usually want to arrange a sit-down interview with them if you can, or perhaps a phone chat if not. We look in detail at these longer form interviews later in the chapter.

It is possible to produce a profile without actually speaking to the subject, using research and speaking to people who know them. This might be necessary if you cannot secure an interview with the subject, or it might be the result of a deliberate editorial decision, because you want to take a dispassionate look at someone: *"What do we know about the new Governor of the Bank of England?" "Jane Smith is the new head of the National Theatre. We profile her and look at the task ahead." "A year ago we had never heard of her; now Saffron Stapleton is acting's latest hot property. Who is she and where has she come from?"*

You may find yourself writing features not about the celebrities themselves, but about their lifestyles – they may be sharing their beauty tips, favourite recipes, idea of the perfect weekend or things they wish they had known when they were young. Dozens of these pieces appear in newspapers and magazines every week, and they are also popular with radio and television shows. They help sate our endless curiosity about the lives of famous people.

Interviews by telephone/videolink

Ideally, you will conduct your interviews face to face. This is especially desirable if you are writing a longer piece based on a single interview. Not only can you put your questions to your subject directly, but also you can see their expressions and reactions, interpret their body language and develop a relationship with them. That is harder to do if you have to interview them on the telephone. With a telephone interview you are more reliant on the quotes because there is not the same opportunity to observe the subject and form a detailed overall impression of them as a person. You cannot describe their appearance, their surroundings or the way they react to your questions. A phone exchange is still vastly preferable to an exchange by email.

News interviews of all kinds are routinely conducted on the phone. Local radio stations and local newspapers are increasingly located on the outskirts of town rather than in the centre. A diminishing staff of reporters under pressure to produce a large number of stories finds it harder and harder to get out of the office to talk to people. Telephone interviews are cheaper and more convenient for both parties. And if your interviewee is miles away or even in another country, then a face-to-face meeting is clearly out of the question.

An alternative to the phone, if a physical meeting is impossible, is to use any of the many means available to connect via video link, so that you can see as well as hear each other. It still will not be as good as sitting down together in the same room, but it will be a substantial advance on an audio-only call. You will be able to see your interviewee reacting and pick up a degree of body language. During the coronavirus pandemic, when face-to-face interviews were not possible, doing things remotely was the only option. All the more reason to get comfortable with the phone and video calls.

All journalists would much prefer to speak face to face, but print and radio will probably be satisfied with a phone or video-link alternative. Broadcast journalists would obviously prefer video call to phone, because it gives them moving pictures of the interviewee. But in extremis, such as the early stages of a breaking story, television will run an audio-only interview accompanied by an on-screen still image and caption.

Conducting interviews successfully over the phone is a skill in itself. The only form of communication you have is your voice, so you need to work hard to establish a rapport, keep the conversation going and try to assess how the interviewee is reacting – whether they are bored, animated, distracted, suspicious or simply going through the motions. If a telephone interview is not "working", it is hard to turn things around and make a success of it.

You can record a telephone conversation if you wish, to make sure that you get the quotes and other details word perfect when you listen back. You do not have to tell the person at the other end of the line that you are doing this, but you might think it would be open and respectful to do so. They should certainly be made aware if you have any intention of broadcasting any part of the recording. If someone finds out at a later date that you recorded them without their knowledge and permission, even if you do not broadcast any of the interview, they may well feel they have been used or misled.

Interviews by email

The least satisfactory form of interview is when you submit your questions in advance, or conduct the interview via email or other electronic means. The answers come back in the same format, and there is no human interaction at all. This is a soulless transaction, very likely to produce a story that is lacking in spontaneity, and feeling flat and inauthentic.

The only format in which this even begins to work is the one designed for it, often with a title such as "60 second briefing with……", in which a series of questions are put to the interviewee and they offer brief and often not very illuminating responses. The questions are not designed to extract anything very revelatory. They may be nothing more than listing a favourite film, favourite food, pet hates and the like. These pieces fill space usefully enough, but it is a bit of a stretch to call them interviews. There is no interaction between interviewer, or question setter, and the person providing the answers – who may even be a public relations person anyway.

Even if this is not the format, over-protective public relations offices or personal assistants may still ask you to submit your questions up front. That might not be an issue if all you want to know is where they went on holiday or the first piece of music they ever bought. For anything more stretching, resist if you can. It is fine to send an outline of the sort of areas you would like to cover in the interview, but you do not want to show your hand fully, or find that an interview you were hoping to do in person is being conducted by email instead.

When it goes well, and when it goes badly

In the ideal interview, you meet your subject in person and quickly strike up a rapport. The interviewee talks freely and entertainingly. You ask relevant and well-judged questions that produce good quotable replies. You listen carefully and adapt or ditch your prepared questions if you feel the conversation is taking an interesting and unexpected turn. You ask questions appropriate to this new ground, and respond with challenge or empathy or whatever may be required. You get some great material and you and your interviewee part company on good terms.

Not all interviews are like that of course. Weighing the odds in your favour takes preparation and practice, and plenty of things can go wrong. You will interview people who express themselves poorly, who seem determined to tell you next to nothing or who are downright hostile. Others will overwhelm you with a torrent of verbiage from which it is difficult to extract anything of worth. Some will say things that are not true, or are distorted versions of the truth. You find that you and your interviewee are talking at cross purposes. You will not always recognise the significance of something you are told, or be able to put all the pieces together to complete the jigsaw. Communication is not always free and transparent. You may take a dislike to each other. Interviewees can get angry, upset, flustered or tongue-tied. They can take umbrage and walk out. Like life itself, the process is messy, unpredictable and frequently unsatisfactory. But if you work at it, you will extract something from even the most difficult encounter. Preparation is usually the key: it certainly improves the chances of the interview going well. So don't stint on your advance planning.

Interviewing for news reports

Short-form interviewing for news quotes

For news reports, you want to speak to as many people as you can whose testimony or opinion is relevant to your story. You will expect to quote at least two or three of them, reflecting different perspectives and viewpoints. Space constraints mean you will not be quoting any one person at great length. You are probably looking for two or three meaty quotes that you can report as direct speech, while you summarise the rest of what that person has to say in reported speech. There is no point talking to someone for an hour when all you need is a few sharp quotes. Indeed, people may be more willing to speak to you if you make clear you will be troubling them for only a few minutes. For these short interviews, you need to think in advance about the thrust of the story and the place of the interviewee within it. What information do you need from them? What area or school of opinion do you need them to reflect if you are to produce a balanced and comprehensive piece? To put it crudely, what sorts of things do you want them to say?

This is not about prejudging or distorting their views, or putting words into their mouths. It is about keeping in mind why you want to interview them at all, and what function you envisage for them in the structure of your final piece. Are they a champion of the scheme, or the loudest voice in opposition to it? Are they on the attack or on the defence? Are they providing the contextual background that gives some proportion and perspective to the arguments? Knowing the role of each interviewee within the story will enable you to prepare well-focused and relevant questions designed to draw out the quotes you need.

Example

A resident of a street in the town has contacted your paper to complain about potholes. She says her local councillor promised to have them repaired but hasn't done so and the state of the road is a danger and a disgrace. The news editor assigns the story to you.

These are the people you will want to speak to and the questions you will want to ask:

Resident(s)

– Can you describe the state of the road for me?
– How long have the holes been there?

– Have they caused any incidents, such as cars getting flat tyres or swerving to avoid the holes, people tripping up?
– Have you seen any of these incidents?
– Do you know anyone who has?
– What did the councillor promise to do?
– What do you think about this state of affairs?

As well as seeking information, these questions are designed to draw out some good colourful quotes.

The councillor

– What is your view about the state of the road?
– Do you think it is acceptable?
– I spoke to some residents and this is what they think; what is your reaction to that?
– What did you promise to do about it?
– What have you done?
– What was the response?
– What will happen now?

The council

– Why have the holes not been repaired?
– When will they be repaired?
– How many potholes are awaiting repair across the whole town?
– What is the target waiting time between the reporting of a pothole and its repair?
– What is the actual waiting time between the reporting of a pothole and its repair?
– What is the budget for pothole repairs?

With these last four questions – and you will be able to think of others – you are exploring whether there is a bigger story here: a general problem with repairing potholes across the whole town. The street where you started could then become a case study in a wider piece, and that one phone call from a resident might have given you a very strong story about a big local issue. But even if it is an isolated case, it works perfectly well as a story on its own.

This is a relatively straightforward story, which you will write up in no more than 500 words, perhaps a lot less. But it still involves a trip to the location to take pictures and speak to people, at least three interviews and a couple of dozen questions. You can see why it is important to stay focused and not to waste time. The nature of the story is going to dictate the approach you take when you come to conduct the interviews. You do not want free-ranging conversations that wander all over the place. You need to keep it tightly controlled, sticking to the points that you want to cover. Do not be afraid to put the same question more than once if you need to, and do not hesitate to bring the discussion back to the main point if it shows signs of veering off. If this happens, it doesn't necessarily mean your interviewee is being evasive – he or she may genuinely not know exactly what it is you want and what is of most interest to you.

This example illustrates the basic form of interviewing for news reports: you want to elicit information, reaction, background and opinion in a businesslike and economical way, until you have what you need for an accurate, well-balanced and attractive account.

Make sure that your reporting is neutral, and, if strong views are expressed, that they are attributed. In our pothole story, it is not up to you to say that the council's record on repairing potholes is a disgrace, or that the residents are guilty of exaggeration and overreaction. You must not express your own opinion. But if your interviewees say these things, you are free to report them, and attribute the criticism.

Ideally you will have been to the road and spoken to the residents before you do any other interviews. This means you have seen the situation for yourself and gathered views, so you are in a better position to put informed questions to the councillor. But you will often find that for practical reasons you are doing your interviews in the "wrong" order – in other words, not the order that is the most logical.

You will need to adopt an interview technique known as "playing devil's advocate". In each interview, you test the position of your interviewee by putting the opposing argument to them. In doing so, you make it clear that you are not taking sides. You preface your questions with phrases like: "some people might take the view that….", "your critics would answer that by saying…..", "how would you respond to those who say……". In doing so, you reinforce your role as a neutral reporter seeking to understand all sides of the story and tease out the various positions. It means you saying the equivalent of "this is not my opinion, but someone might take this view and I need to put it to you for comment." You are asking questions on behalf of the public.

You can use shock tactics and go straight in, and it may yield good results. But it is a risk. It exposes you to accusations that you are not only unnecessarily belligerent, but also partial, prejudiced and pursuing an agenda. Here are some examples of the direct approach, followed by the approach you might take if you were playing devil's advocate. The direct approach might work best if your interviewee was being evasive or defensive. The devil's advocate lines of questioning may be weaker, but they protect your impartiality and make you sound less aggressive. As with so many things, it is a matter of judgement, depending on the circumstances.

DIRECT: You're fiddling the figures aren't you?
DEVIL'S ADVOCATE: The opposition would say you are massaging the figures.
DIRECT: Your strategy is backfiring isn't it – it's doing the opposite of what you wanted?
DEVIL'S ADVOCATE: There is another way of looking at this, which might suggest that your strategy is having exactly the opposite effect of that intended.
DIRECT: That is a very cynical and callous response.
DEVIL'S ADVOCATE: Some people might say that is a very cynical and callous response.

Short-form interviewing for news clips (broadcast)

The audiovisual equivalent of the direct quote is the clip, also known as a cut or soundbite. It is a short extract from a recorded interview. Space is at an even greater premium in broadcast formats, and in a typical radio or television news report you will probably have room only for about 15 seconds of comments from each of your interviewees. The same will apply to an audiovisual package for digital platforms, where space may not be at a premium but audience attention is. This means you need to be even more focused on getting exactly the clip you want, with the interviewee covering precisely the ground that you need for your report.

That said, the basic approach is the same. The story does not change, the format through which it is being told does. So if you were covering our pothole story for radio or television, the people you would speak to and the questions you asked would be pretty much exactly the same. But you do need a sense of what you want the content of your clips to be – what you want each of your interviewees to say, in general terms. In the pothole story, for example, you will probably want your resident's clip to be an expression of disgust about the state of the road. A good clip might have a resident saying: *"It's a disgrace. It's been like this for months. They promised to fix it and nothing has happened. We're all completely fed up"*. There is not much here by way of hard information, but the clip conveys the level of feeling and sets a strong tone for the report.

Achieving a nice clip like that is very often easier said than done. You may find that your interviewees start an answer well and then tail off lamely, or wander off the point. They may stumble and lose their thread. You may get exactly the answer you want, but at twice the length you can accommodate in your report. None of this is a problem for a journalist producing a text report – you simply select the phrases you need and discard the rest. But video and broadcast journalists are looking for a self-contained extract that makes sense and gets the point across, and sometimes have to work quite hard to get it. Be ready to ask the same question a number of times in order to get the result you require. Explain why you are doing this: the interviewee will not necessarily understand the finer points of broadcast production, and may be puzzled and disconcerted if you keep asking the same question without explaining why. If you do want them to have another go at the answer, make sure you put the question to them again, rather than just asking them to start again. That way, they will respond more naturally, as they would in a conversation.

You can of course make an edit to ensure that your clip is the right length or contains the best of what the speaker had to say. But try not to rely on this too much – edits do not always sound right if the intonations do not work, or the background noise has changed, or the speaker is talking more loudly in one bit of the clip than in another. Internal edits do not work well in television because you can see the join in a jump cut. You overcome this problem with cutaway shots – but it is far preferable not to have the problem in the first place.

There is more on interviewing for broadcast clips in the later chapters on radio and television reporting.

Interviewing for long-form features

Setting up the interview

If you are planning to write a profile of an individual based on an interview with them, then clearly you need to get them to agree to speak to you. If you cannot make contact with them, or they refuse, you don't have too many places to go. Often you will find you are not even dealing directly with the potential interviewee, but with a publisher or press handler or personal assistant. This may involve you in many conversations over a lengthy period as you try to secure your interview. You may be under pressure to submit your questions in advance, to promise to stick to certain subject areas and to avoid others, and to submit your draft feature for approval before publication. You will not want to do any of these things. But if you really want the interview, you should be prepared for some tiresome and protracted negotiations, and you will need to decide what compromises are acceptable to you, if any. If you are worried about the conditions being placed on you, you should refer up to your editor. Some conditions may be acceptable without compromising your integrity, but it is always worth questioning them and pushing back as hard as you can.

Interviewees will not always be in a mood to cooperate. They may have an innate suspicion of the media, based on previous experience, and not wish to engage. They may not want to disclose the information you are seeking, because they regard it as private and confidential and they do not want to see it splashed across the newspapers. They may be suffering from shock, or grief, because of something that has happened to them or someone close to them. For any number of reasons, they might not want to speak to you at all. It is important to recognise that they are perfectly within their rights if they choose not to do so. No-one is obliged to speak to a reporter if they do not want to. Remember what the various ethical codes had to say about harassment and reasonable expectations of privacy. The IPSO Code says: "Journalists…must not persist in questioning, telephoning, pursuing or photographing individuals once asked to desist".

However, unless the refusal is uncompromisingly blunt, try not to take no for an answer straight away. Sometimes a little persistence and charm, a subtle appeal to the vanity of your target or the offer to tell "your side of the story" will secure the access you are looking for.

When you first make contact, assuming you are not working undercover or on an investigative piece, be open about who you are, who you work for, why you are asking for the interview, what ground you hope to cover, your deadline if you have one and how much time you think you would need. There is no point approaching people in any other way. If they feel you are trying to trick them or change the rules as you go along, they will simply withdraw their cooperation.

Research and preparation

You have secured the interview. Well done. Now it is time to do some more research and think in detail about what you would like to get from it, and the questions you will need to ask in order to achieve that.

The process of planning and researching is examined in more detail in Chapter 21, which is about writing features. You can only do as much preparation as you have time for. In the case of a feature, you might have quite a long time to do your research and brief yourself fully.

The better briefed you are, the better equipped you are to push back against interviewees who say something debatable, or even deliberately misleading. If you have done your homework, you are in a position to step in to challenge them – and perhaps get a new line or indeed a proper story.

INTERVIEWEE: And of course we have increased the collections so that bins are being emptied every week instead of every fortnight.
YOU: But that policy hasn't been rolled out yet has it? As I understand it, it is still an aspiration and you haven't yet found the money to pay for it.
INTERVIEWEE: Yes that's true, but we are still confident that we will be able to do it by the end of this year as we promised.
YOU: But the promise was that it would begin before the end of the financial year wasn't it – not the calendar year? So it will be nine months behind schedule. Assuming you find the money.
INTERVIEWEE: We'll find the money from somewhere, even if it means cutting something else.
YOU: Really? Like what?

You cannot push back and challenge in this way if you have not done your homework in advance.

Interviews associated with the news of the moment may not afford you the luxury of a lot of preparatory time. All seasoned journalists will have tales about being sent out to interview someone at no notice, and with no information about the story. In the age of the mobile phone and the internet you should always be able to carve out enough time to gather a little basic information about your interviewee, even if you do it on the way to the meeting. You can risk throwing yourself on their mercy, saying that you have only just been handed the story but have not been told very much about it. They are unlikely to be impressed, but they may take pity on you if you look sufficiently miserable and hapless.

Your questions

Given time though, you can work on a list of the questions you want to ask. These will be based on:

– The reason you wanted the interview in the first place
– The nature of your interviewee
– What you want your piece to achieve
– Anything that has been thrown up by your research
– A sense of what your audience is likely to be interested in, or needs to know.

Before you begin to craft subtle and sophisticated questions, do not lose sight of the tried and tested basic questions of journalism: who, what, when, where, why and how. Some or all of them will be relevant in any interview you do. Start off with the straightforward questions that will yield the basic facts that you need to know about your interviewee. This may include how they spell and pronounce their name, their job title, their age and their address. Even here there may be follow-up questions such as their actual role in their company, and what the company does. Getting these basic questions out of the way early serves two purposes: it means you can be sure that all the personal information you have about your interviewee is accurate, and it is neutral territory that helps break the ice.

Next, start to list the more substantive questions you propose to ask – framed to add substance to the theme and intent of your piece. There are two schools of thought here. One says that you should have only a handful of key questions, and play it by ear on the day – relying on your ability to frame follow-up questions as you go, depending on the answers you are getting and the direction the conversation takes. This forces you to listen properly to the answers and gives you the flexibility to pursue whatever angles seem to be the most useful. For short-form interviews, this will usually be the policy you adopt, because you will not have a great deal of time, and three or four questions will probably cover the ground you need. It is a riskier strategy for longer interviews that are going to form the basis of lengthy features. Suppose the answers you get on the day are not very interesting, and do not prompt much in the way of following up? Suppose the interviewee is not very cooperative and not fully engaged? The conversation might dry up disconcertingly quickly. So the second school of thought says: have plenty of questions – lots more than you think you will need. Even if you don't use them all, it is reassuring to know you have something to fall back on if the conversation falters, or if you are getting very brisk answers. Your list can be made up of bullet points or trigger words – you don't need to write the questions out word for word, because it will sound unnatural when you read them out. And you don't have to ask them in the order you have written them. Be ready to move things around if the conversation changes direction.

A combination of the two approaches is probably the best. Good questions do not necessarily produce good answers, so you do need to give yourself options for changing tack if you find one line of questioning is not getting you anywhere. But being flexible, and spotting the opportunity for following up when your interviewee says something interesting, is a vital skill. It depends on active listening, about which we will say more later. Sticking rigidly to your list of questions, regardless of the answers, will make you sound like an automaton and like someone who doesn't much care what the answers are. This will alienate your subject and make the experience deeply unsatisfying for both parties.

Bear in mind that many of the people you meet will have been interviewed umpteen times before, and have probably been asked the same questions on dozens of occasions. They will rattle off stock answers and possibly show indications of irritation and boredom. If you must ask those obvious questions, try to think of a less obvious way of posing them. Better still, think of some new ones that might jolt your subject out of their comfort zone and make them think before answering.

Taken together, the questions you prepare should be designed to give you the basic information you need, a clear understanding of the story or the person, and some good colourful details and quotes. If you have a theme for the interview, or there is a topical reason to be doing it, work on the questions in that area. If you have a number of things you want to cover, group the questions so that you can finish one line of inquiry before you move to another. Anticipate the replies you might get and how you will follow up. Often, the best and most effective follow-up question will simply be: "why?" Or: "why not?" It is disarmingly straightforward, yet challenges the interviewee to justify their previous answer and build upon it.

This is also a good resort if you get stuck, or your mind goes blank. Play for time. Ask the interviewee to expand on an earlier answer, or give some examples of what they mean. You may get some unexpected and useful materials. Even if you don't, you have bought yourself some thinking time to regroup and decide what you are going to ask next.

Good questions are:

– **Unambiguous** – it is clear exactly what you are asking.
– **Simple** – one question at a time.
– **Open** – they require more than yes or no answers (see below).
– **Specific** – designed to yield evidence and examples rather than generalisations.
– **Well-researched** – your interviewee will appreciate it if it is evident that you have done your homework.
– **Invitations to provide colour and evidence** – seeking examples or anecdotes that add texture to the basic information.

Weak questions are:

– **Over-complicated** – the interviewee either misinterprets them or provides an equally over-complicated response, or both.
– **Multiple questions in one** – "Were you aware of this? Shouldn't you have been? Why weren't you? What are you going to do about it?" These are four questions in one, and the interviewee can escape from the hook by simply answering the last of them, or none of them. There is nothing wrong with these questions: they just need asking one at a time.
– **Closed** – allowing the interviewee to get away with a one-word answer.
– **Too general** – yielding no evidence or examples to help you illustrate the point.
– **Ill-informed** – betraying the fact that you are under-prepared.
– **Too factual** – discouraging the interviewee from offering colour and evidence.

The first five minutes

The first few minutes after you meet your interviewee are very important in setting the tone for what follows. We all know that people form lasting impressions of each other within a few seconds, so try to make sure the impression you make is a good one. Never, never, be late. Make sure you are appropriately dressed and you have all the equipment you need for the interview and that any recording devices are working. Failure on any of these fronts demonstrates a lack of professionalism and respect and gets you off on the wrong foot. The interview may never fully recover.

When you meet, make good eye contact, thanking the subject for giving you their time. Adopt a friendly, open and confident tone, even if you do not feel confident, without being too familiar.

The first couple of minutes will be occupied by organising where you are both going to sit and the usual inconsequential small talk. You will talk about the weather, the journeys you have both had to get there, what the venue is like and so on. If you can, identify something you have in common, which you might have picked up from your research. It might be something utterly insignificant, but if it gives you something to talk about as you get comfortable with each other, then it serves its purpose. "You were born in Nottingham? I went to school there." This is your opportunity to establish the easy rapport that you will hope to carry through the interview itself, and it is also a chance for you to settle any nerves you may have. You can busy yourself finding somewhere to hang your coats, making sure the interviewee is comfortable, asking them if they would like a drink or some sort. If you are lucky enough to be meeting them on their own turf – their home, their office – then these roles are reversed somewhat, because the interviewee is the host. Be as undemanding a guest as you can. Say: "a coffee would be great, thanks" and not: "I'll have a skinny decaf latte with an extra shot".

At some early point, you will need to sort out the practical details – the parameters of the interview. If you want to record the discussion, make sure the interviewee is happy for you to do so. Make it clear whether you are doing so in the interests of accuracy, so that you can quote precisely, or whether you intend to broadcast anything. That will be pretty obvious if you work in television or radio, but recordings made by other journalists have a way of becoming public in the digital age, and your interviewee may want some reassurance on that point. If you are using a recording device, you need to be sitting quite close together so that both voices are picked up by the microphone. Sitting at right angles is preferable to face to face, and both are better than side by side, which makes eye contact difficult and could mean the interviewee will be able to see what you are writing down.

If you are filming the interview, it will take a little time to decide on the best layout and set up the camera. If you have a separate camera operator, you can use this time to continue to chat and build a relationship while that person is setting up. If you are setting up on your own, explain why you are moving the furniture around or drawing the curtains. People are usually interested in the mechanics of television and videojournalism, and again, it helps create a friendly atmosphere.

In this preliminary chat, set out the general areas you hope to cover, and confirm that the interviewee is happy with them – if the meeting has been set up by a publicist or third party, the subject may not be aware of all the prior discussions. They may be more relaxed about areas of questioning than their over-protective agents were. Finally clarify how long you have got: if you are expecting to have an hour and your subject thinks it is only half an hour, now is the time to find out about that and adapt your plans accordingly.

Even if you have a short time slot, it is still worth making an effort to go through this process of developing a basic relationship and establishing what both sides are expecting to happen. If you are good with people and quick rapport comes easily to you, you should not have any problem with this, or with getting your subject into a relaxed frame of mind and ready to talk. If you find this does not come so naturally to you, it is something you will have to work at. Develop some simple techniques that will work in most situations. If stuck, just ask the interviewee questions about themselves – house, family, work, hobbies, it doesn't really matter as long as you are avoiding awkward silences. And sometimes from this inconsequential chat, you will hear something that you will want to pick up in the interview proper.

These early exchanges also help you ready yourself for the interview. *You* need to feel at ease too. If you are really nervous, and feel you are betraying your nerves, you can admit as much: saying something like "I'm sorry, you'll have to forgive me, I'm a bit nervous: I'm a big fan and it's amazing to meet you in person". It may seem fawning or gauche, but it will probably flatter your interviewee, and make him or her feel superior and ready to be graciously condescending – and possibly less guarded in what they say.

And when all this is done, it is up to you to signal that the preliminaries are over and it is time to get down to business. Try to do this without breaking the mood that has been created:

> Shall we make a start? Let me make sure this thing is recording properly.
> Actually that was one of the things I wanted to ask you about – so shall we begin?
> If we only have half an hour, perhaps we had better get going.
> Are you ok to begin now? I'm conscious of the demands on your time.
> Can I get you some more water/tea/coffee before we dive in?

Any of these invitations signal that you are ready to go – and that even if you have not been up to now, you are now in charge of the process.

Asking the questions

By now your interviewees should feel relaxed and at ease. You have warmed them up. Keep doing so as you embark on the interview proper. Start with general and unthreatening questions. You may not use any of the answers in your final piece, but you are getting the interviewee into talking mode, and that will help when you want to move on to the areas you really want to cover. You will have to judge when it is time to do that. Your interviewee may obviously be ready to go, in which case there is no point hanging about. If not, an opportunity may naturally present itself. But if it doesn't, you can use what you have learned with your factual questions, or something you have read about the subject, to move the discussion on to the main point of the interview. "I believe you were brought up in a Cornish fishing village. Is that why the sea is such a recurring theme in your work?" "I've read that when you were a student you had a holiday job in a chicken processing plant. Is that what persuaded you to become vegetarian?" Making these connections will move you easily to the main point of the interview without any nasty gear changes, and without disrupting the rhythm you have established.

We will look now at some techniques for use in all sorts of interviews: how you actually ask the questions. We have talked in a hard news context about the blunt, head-on approach, which might be appropriate if you are dealing with an experienced and slippery interviewee, and you are up against the clock. But bear in mind that many distinguished interviewers believe that a more subtle and less confrontational approach will often yield better results. For long-form interviews, you have time to work your way up to what you see as the key questions. If you have the tools at your disposal, you can make a judgement about which ones to use and when:

Leading questions

Leading questions are closed questions that push the respondent in a certain direction, and are intended to make them go further than simple agreement or disagreement. They can often be effective in drawing out quotable answers. But beware of overuse, as it can feel as though you are being unnecessarily provocative or putting words into the interviewee's mouth.

> These people who accuse you of being a hypocrite: they're right aren't they?
> And you still claim you knew nothing about this?
> You must have reacted angrily to that.

A variation on this is the leading question that carries within it an assumption that the interviewee will feel obliged to deny:

> When are you going to stop misleading the public on this issue?
> How are you proposing to improve on your deplorable record?

Shock tactics

These are even more deliberately provocative questions, which also hope to coax the interviewee into a strong reaction. In response, they are likely to rebut the premise of the question, but may then go on to say more than they intended, or speak in a less circumspect way.

> How do you respond to those who say you've presided over a complete shambles here?
> Your opponents say you promised to fix this problem and instead you've made it worse haven't you?
> There have been calls for your head over this. Will you resign?

And the double whammy:

> What your critics say is that either you knew about this and did nothing about it, in which case you failed to do your job properly. Or you didn't know about it, in which case you weren't on top of your job and were incompetent. Which is it?

Note that these questions, though direct, still adopt the devil's advocate approach, distancing you personally from the criticism: "How do you respond to those who say…" "Your opponents say…" "There have been calls…" "Your critics say…"

Long-form interviews are not always adversarial and indeed may contain no element of challenge at all. For the most part, you just want your interviewee to talk about themselves and their personal stories – something most of us are willing to do without much prompting. Here are some techniques more suited to that sort of exchange:

Closed and open questions

Closed questions invite an answer of yes or no, or some other short reply. They have their place, for example if you are simply eliciting basic information:

> How many brothers and sisters do you have?
> Where do you go to school?
> How long did you work there?
> How old were you when you became interested in this?

They are less useful if you want a fuller answer – because in effect, the question includes the answer and does not require the interviewee to do more than agree or disagree. In fact, the following are not really questions at all, they are statements with question marks tacked on at the end. Look how unsatisfactory the answers are:

> Q So you did that by changing the shift pattern?
> A That helped, yes.
> Q So that happened because someone took their eye off the ball?
> A Possibly.
> Q So you decided to become an actor after being in the school play?
> A That's right.
> Q And your evidence for that is the half-yearly sales figures?
> A Partly.
> Q And you are unhappy about the way the debate has developed?
> A I wouldn't say that.

Monosyllabic replies are not helpful, and will sound terrible in a broadcast interview. Open questions are those that encourage the respondent to reply with more than a simple yes or no. So use open questions to elicit detailed information. This is how the five questions above could have been better phrased:

> How did you do that?
> Why do you think that might have happened?
> What made you decide to follow this career?
> What evidence do you have to back that up?
> What are your thoughts about the way this debate has developed?

Each of these should produce a more useful answer. And if you feel you would like more detail, there are various ways in which you can encourage people to expand on what they have said so far. You can add little flattering phrases that show you are interested in what you are hearing and are eager for more:

> That's an interesting thought. Can you say some more about that?
> You must have been terrified. What happened next?
> What an amazing story! And did you ever hear from them again?

Confirming and clarifying

Use questions as you go along to make sure that you are getting your facts right, and that you understand what you are being told. It is invaluable for you, and it gives interviewees confidence that you are going about your business in a careful and professional manner. For that reason, they will seldom object, unless you are being particularly dim. You should never feel embarrassed or self-conscious about asking people to repeat themselves or explain things in more detail. You want your work to be accurate above all else.

> So this was before her father died, is that right?
> As I understand it, this person was your boss at the time?
> So the head office was in Birmingham, but you were based in Coventry?
> The machine that performs this task – can you explain to me again how it works?

If names, acronyms or other references that you don't recognise come up in the conversation, get them spelled out or explained for you as you go. It will be awkward to return to them at the end, and you will probably forget anyway. Have jargon or technical terms explained as they arise.

> You say you contacted the CPL – who are they, and what do they do?

You can also pause to summarise, either as you go along or at the end.

> Can I just make sure that I have got this sequence of events right?
> Am I right in inferring that you are strongly opposed to this plan in principle?
> If I've got this right, your argument is.......
> I'm sorry to go back to this, but I want to be sure I've got it straight.

Getting your interviewee to summarise or simplify is also a good idea, especially if they are discussing difficult concepts. It will help you understand and explain when you come to write your piece, and it will help you appreciate what the interviewee thinks is the most important aspect of what he or she has been saying. On a practical level, asking people to summarise will often be the source of the crispest and most focused quotes. It is particularly useful in broadcast journalism, when you are hunting for concise, self-contained clips:

> Could I just ask you to sum that up for me?
> What does that mean in layman's terms?
> Of all the issues you have described, which do you think is the most important?
> In a sentence, what is your view on this?
> If the Prime Minister walked into the room now, what would you say to them?
> What is your message to the people responsible for this?

Finally, do not be afraid to ask the interviewee if there is anything that you should have asked but have failed to raise. They know much more about what they are talking about than you do – that is why you are speaking to them. You might easily omit something important out of ignorance. It is worth trying to insure against this, especially if your interviewee is cooperative:

> That's great thank you. Have we covered everything do you think?
>
> Is there anything I haven't asked that you think is worth mentioning?
>
> You're the expert. What is the question I haven't asked you but should have?
>
> If I have any queries when I go back over my notes/if I discover there is something I should have asked but didn't/if I need to check something, can I come back to you? What is the best way of doing that?

Silence and nudges

Silence can be an amazingly effective strategy in any sort of interview, but especially when you are discussing human feelings and reactions. When your interviewee pauses or finishes an answer, your instinct will be to press on with the next question. Resist it. Wait a few seconds before moving on, especially if it is clear from the interviewee's body language that they are still thinking about the answer that they have just given. Very often, they will start speaking again, and what they say now will often be more thoughtful and revelatory than what has gone before. They probably won't even notice that you deliberately left a pause. So give them the opportunity to go on by leaving a few seconds before you pick up again.

This can even work on very short news clips. Say you are interviewing a fire officer at the scene of a pile-up. You are looking mostly for a factual news clip, and you get one when you ask what happened and your fire officer says something like this:

> There were two cars involved and we had to cut four people out of the wreckage. Both vehicles were very badly damaged.

So far so good. You have got the facts. But you pause for a moment and the fire chief carries on talking:

> You never get used to this sort of thing. I've been doing this for more than 20 years and this is one of the worst crashes I have ever seen. It was horrendous.

By saying nothing, you have managed to get a much stronger clip, with context and emotion. And if it is for broadcast, think twice before editing out the pause in between the two sentences. You may destroy the effect.

If leaving a silence does not work, try saying the minimum possible to encourage the person to keep talking. Very small interventions will not disrupt their narrative, and these can be edited out later if need be. Your most valuable questions in this context are: "and?", "then what?", "go on" or "what did you do?"

You can encourage an interviewee to keep talking by the occasional "uh-huh" or "right" or "ok", but this can be annoying – and if you are a broadcaster, it can be difficult to edit out later. You can produce the same result without talking by nodding your head. If you watch television news interviews where the reporter is in shot, the chances are they are nodding away like mad to encourage the interviewee to keep going.

"How do you feel?"

Journalists are always criticised as heartless and insensitive when they ask this question, and often with good reason: it seems a particularly callous and crass question to put to someone who is obviously feeling terrible because something awful has happened to them. It is less of a problem with someone who has won ten million pounds on the lottery, but even then it is pretty obvious what the response will be.

The trouble is, it is the question which we all probably want answering. We really do want to know how people feel in these circumstances, what it is like to be them at that moment. So the question is still asked: print- or text-focused reporters may ask it because they only have to quote the response – no-one need ever know *that* question was asked in order to get the quote. Broadcasters sometimes risk using it, hoping they too will be able to snip it out when they come to edit the recording. But it is risky. There is a strong chance that it will nettle the person you are asking, and will only produce the angry answer: "How do you think I feel?"

There are gentler ways of finding out how people are feeling, essentially by not asking the question but preparing a space for the answer:

> I can't begin to imagine what that must have been like.
> Have you ever experienced anything remotely like this before?
> You must have been shocked/appalled/knocked sideways/horrified.
> Do you have any words to describe your feelings at that moment?

Flattery and humour

There is nothing like a bit of pandering to someone's ego to get them talking, even if they are fully aware that this is exactly what you are doing. It is a good tactic in the early stages of the interview while you are still getting into your stride, and you want to get your subject into a receptive and talkative mood. Stroking their vanity and encouraging them to talk positively about themselves is a more or less guaranteed way of doing so. It will be more successful still if it is sincere and grounded in evidence. Praise for someone's latest film or book will carry more conviction if you have read it or seen it and can comment on something specific.

You can use flattery to maintain the subject's flow: "what a great story!" "That's amazing – what an extraordinary life you lead!" "Is that true? It can't be!" "Did you really say that?" As long as you don't gush in too sick-making a manner, they will probably lap it up and feel an obligation to keep going – and maybe even to raise the bar of their performance.

Similarly, flattery can be used to disguise or cushion some more difficult and searching questions.

> The public obviously adored the book, but the critics were less enthusiastic. Why do you think that was?

> You have a reputation for telling it like it is, and many people admire that – but do you think you might have gone too far on this occasion?

> You are one of the most compelling voices in the calls for action on climate change – but you yourself must have a pretty big carbon footprint.

Humour too, or a little tongue-in-cheek banter, may also be a great way of keeping your subject sweet and making the interview seem more like a gossip between friends. But be careful. You will sometimes be dealing with self-regarding people with prickly egos. They will not necessarily like you poking fun at them, however gently, or appearing not to take them seriously. It could backfire. If in doubt, don't.

"Get out of jail" cards

Simple questions about favourite films, books and food are a familiar element of celebrity and other profiles. Sometimes the entire feature is based on Q+A versions of such questions: "The Two Minute Briefing", "The Sixty Second Interview" and so on. You might find it useful to have a selection of these banker questions up your sleeve in case the interview gets stuck, there is an awkward pause, you run out of other things to ask or you feel you have failed to extract anything very interesting from your interviewee. True, you might not get any interesting answers. But then again you might get one that triggers a whole new conversation that turns out to be quite fruitful. If you discover that a senior politician likes building models out of matchsticks in his spare time, or a film star has founded a youth club in the area in which she grew up, or a famous wine expert likes nothing better than a pint of real ale, you will have uncovered something you can pursue that will help bring your subject to life. Rather than throwing out a few well-worn questions, however, try to relate them to the subject and encourage a counter-intuitive response. Then follow up with "why?"

> Ask **authors** not what their favourite food is, but what they are reading now, or what book most influenced them growing up.

> Ask **actors** not where they take their holidays, but what other actors or directors they would most like to work with.

> Ask **chief executives** what they do to relax.

> Ask **anyone** to name their secret passion or the one luxury they could not do without (it works for Desert Island Discs and it may work for you).

You can think of dozens of these, but if you can match a question to your interviewee in such a way as to optimise your chances of an interesting response, you might be in business and the interview might regain its momentum.

Delicate and sensitive areas

Your interviews will often stray into tricky areas. Sex and drugs and rock and roll, bribery and corruption – these might indeed have been the reason you wanted the interview in the first place. Your subjects may have been implicated in criminal or immoral behaviour, for example, or you may want to discuss their personal background in some way – medical, sexual, romantic and so on. They may have been affected by a traumatic event.

It could be that they are happy to discuss these highly personal matters, which might have been flagged at the setting-up stage. If so, then you don't have a problem introducing the subject, although you do have to think about how you handle it. On the other hand, the interviewee might not want to answer these questions – and might have stipulated in advance a refusal to do so. This might not be a problem if the areas they want to steer clear of are not central to your piece, and would not be of particular relevance to you anyway. But if that is not the case, and you feel you will not have done your job properly unless you ask some difficult questions, then you should do so – while being prepared to retreat if necessary.

Here is an example:

– You are sent to interview an actor who has the leading role in a new play. Your brief is to write about the play, but also to produce a personal profile of the actor. He has long been the subject of specu- lation about his sexuality, but has always refused to comment. Recently, he has been photographed several times in public in the company of a young man, and social media are once again rife with rumours. You have secured the interview, but the actor has made it clear he will talk only about the play.
– You can of course respect that, and steer clear of the public speculation. But you may feel, and your editor will almost certainly feel, that people reading your piece will wonder why you have not ad- dressed the elephant in the room. You decide you must raise the subject. Whatever the response, you will have something you can use, and you want your piece to show that you have not shirked the question that your audience wants answered. Yet you have been told not to ask it, and you know the actor does not want to answer it. What is your plan?
– Take it slowly. Don't go charging in, but ask about the play and the role first, and in some detail. You may want to leave the delicate stuff to the end, so that if your subject storms out, you still have the first part of the interview to work with – and you have a nice dramatic ending for your piece. When you feel the time is right to tackle "the elephant", do so by acknowledging that you are entering forbidden territory:

> I know you want this interview to be about the play, but I can't let you go without asking you about all these pictures that have appeared in the papers recently, and the comments they have prompted.

– This, you will immediately note, is not a question. It is a cautious broaching of the subject, done in a way that gives the interviewee the opportunity to say anything he wants to say on the subject. If you get a dusty answer, you might feel your honour is satisfied and you can leave it at that. But you may feel that the tone and nature of the reply emboldens you to have another go, using the same softly-softly approach.

> I don't have to tell you that you have been getting a lot of play on social media lately – but most of it is not about your role in this play. Is that a frustration for you?

Or, more directly:

> You must find all this endless speculation about your sexuality very tiresome.

– This is you colluding with the subject, in effect saying: "I sympathise with you. I'm on your side". Again, you might draw a blank with this matey approach. Or you may just unleash a torrent of frustrated rhetoric that only required that gentle nudge to set it off. If so, you have a scoop on your hands.

A similar approach might be a flattering appeal to the actor's vanity:

> Do you feel this endless speculation about your sex life draws attention away from a proper assessment of you as a leading actor, and what you are trying to achieve as an artist?

– The question is there, but it is asked indirectly, smuggled in with a wave of flattery. You can see how by ostensibly asking about the great man's talent, you might draw him into the area you would like him to address.

– By coming at the issue in a very gentle and unthreatening way, you give the actor the opportunity either to say something about the speculation or to keep quiet without torpedoing the entire interview. When you think you have got as much as you are going to get, you can gracefully move on to some of your other less controversial questions, and restore the equilibrium in the conversation.

– Whatever the reaction, you have done your duty as a journalist by asking the question your audience would want and expect you to ask. And even if you draw a complete blank, you can still make this clear when you come to write your piece. Like this perhaps:

> I suggest that he cannot be unaware of the continued speculation about his personal life. "Nothing to say", he replies at once. "Move on."

> I point out that he has had a lot of newspaper coverage recently, and none of it has been about the new play. "I don't want to talk about that," he says. "My private life is no-one's business but my own."

> I ask him whether he is aware of all the social media chat about him since the play opened. "I never look at that stuff", he says. "Got better things to do."

In each of these examples, you have managed broach the taboo subject, and even though you have extracted only a single short quote and a paragraph of copy, you have demonstrated to the reader that you have not backed away from asking the difficult questions. The elephant has not been ignored.

It is not always easy asking people you have just met for the intimate details of their personal or business lives. But try not to show your apprehension and embarrassment. Be empathetic of course, because you want to encourage confidences. But do not reveal your discomfort by shifting in your seat, humming and hawing, taking ages to get to the point or using euphemisms or circumlocutory language to ask your question. Just get it out there. If you have something to ask, then ask it – as clearly as possible, and with whatever degree of sensitivity and empathy feels appropriate.

Be prepared to back off if need be. You may want to press on if you are confronting someone who has embezzled millions by raiding his company pension fund. But it is not the same when you are asking people about deeply personal matters – if they are suffering from an illness, have just been bereaved or are in the middle of a messy divorce. Ask the questions you feel you need to ask, but if you get the message either directly or indirectly that this is ground you should not be treading on, then retreat. There is a fine line between persistence and harassment, legitimate inquiry and intrusion. Stay on the right side of it. Your interviewee is a human being. So are you.

Active listening and observing

The most important part of the interview is the answers you get. So make sure you listen to them!

This sounds obvious, but there are quite a lot of other demands on your attention during an interview:

> You are conscious of the need to make good notes, or of making sure your recording device is still running.

You are thinking about how things are going – whether you are getting what you need, and if not, what you are going to do about it.

You are wondering what your top line is going to be when you come to write it up, because you can't help drafting the story in your head from an early stage. This might not be a bad thing if it helps keep you focused on the overall aim of your piece.

You are glancing surreptitiously at your list of questions and deciding what to ask next.

You are registering whether your interviewee is engaged and participating, or looks bored and is just going through the motions.

You are keeping an eye on the clock.

All of these distractions, though largely unavoidable, are barriers to effective listening. But you must try to make yourself concentrate on what is being said. The interviewee's words are the currency of your feature, so you want them to be as valuable as possible. Beyond that, the answers should be influencing the direction in which you take the interview. Interviewees rarely stick precisely to the point, and would be rather dull if they did. Their answers will wander all over the place, referring back to things you have discussed earlier, throwing in new thoughts, going off at a tangent to tell a story and so on. Your job is to decide whether or not any of these meanderings is worth following up, and you cannot do that unless your ears are pricked and you are listening intently. If your interviewee is saying things that are genuinely interesting and can form part of your piece, then encourage them with follow-up questions and see where they take you. In rare cases, you may feel that what you are hearing is much more interesting than anything you had prepared, and you can throw out all your carefully planned questions and devote yourself to this new direction. If not, try to decide what question you want to ask next and how it can be phrased in such a way as to make it sound like a natural continuation of the conversation.

In short, as we have already discussed, you are faced with the constant dilemma of deciding whether to go with the flow, because the subject seems animated and interested and is potentially giving you more and better material than you expected, or whether to try to bring them back to the original question and the areas you really wanted to discuss. It can be difficult to make the call. It would be a dull interview indeed if you simply ran through your list of prepared questions and received workmanlike but rather uninspiring responses to them. But there are some things you will feel you really must ask, and it is easy to feel that things are slipping out of your grasp. Consciously or not, the interviewee has taken control of the discussion and is still in the middle of a lengthy anecdote with only five minutes left and you still have half a dozen questions that you really want to get to. How do you butt in and wrest back the steering wheel without seeming rude and inattentive?

If it needs to be done, you just have to go for it, and do it as elegantly as you can without giving offence. Self-deprecation and blaming yourself is a good start.

Gosh look at the time! We've got carried away here, and I haven't got round to asking you half the things I wanted to know. Do you mind if we quickly go back to some of them before we run out of time?

That's an amazing story. I'd like to hear more about that. But do you mind if we just return quickly to the subject of.......

What you were saying there reminded me of one the things I wanted to ask you about.........

How did we get on to this? I was asking you about......

In desperation:

Forgive me, but I really must haul you back to what we were talking about before, namely......

Really interesting. But do you mind if I change the subject? We have so much to get through and the clock is ticking.

As well as listening to what is being said, you also want to be monitoring *how* it is being said and the body language that is accompanying it. If the two do not match, your antennae should be alerting you to the need to probe a little further.

We all give a lot away with our appearance, our clothing, our hand gestures, our facial expressions – especially our eyes – the way we sit and so on. This is a very powerful reason for doing face-to-face interviews whenever you can. People who say things like "it was a difficult time for me, but I am completely over it now" will be less convincing if they are blinking back tears and wringing their hands at the time. A little nudge from you: "I'm sorry, this must bring back painful memories for you" might bring forth a fuller and more honest answer.

Be aware of, and use, your own body language. Show that you are interested in, and concentrating on, what you are being told, and maintain eye contact as much as possible. Your own facial expressions can be used to respond appropriately without interrupting. Do plenty of nodding to encourage your interviewee to keep talking, and lean in towards them. Lean back again and stop nodding if you want them to stop.

You might be prepared to push back if you feel an interviewee is not really telling you the full story. It might genuinely be too painful for them, which you should respect. But it might also be because they are being evasive or hostile, or deliberately giving you monosyllabic answers. Have a go at reflecting back to them. It is risky, and it depends a bit on the nature of the relationship you have managed to build up, but it can work:

> You sound as if you are not quite sure about that.
> I get the impression that this is something you are not comfortable talking about.
> That doesn't really answer my question if I may say so. What I was asking you was…..

Oddly, offering to stop may have the effect of encouraging your subject to say more:

YOU: "I can see this is painful for you. Shall we move on?"
SUBJECT: "No, it's fine."

Similarly, expressing surprise or mild scepticism can suggest to someone that you don't quite believe them – which can prompt them to back down, or back up what they have said.

SUBJECT: "We're doing incredibly well. We're already turning over five million pounds a year."
YOU: "Five million! How on earth have you achieved that?"
SUBJECT: "Well it's a projected figure at the moment, but if we get the orders we are hoping for we will be well on course to achieve that, or something pretty close to it anyway."

A show of emotion

Your interviewees will by definition be talking about things that are important to them, and about which they may feel strong emotions. It is not uncommon for people to break down in tears as they remember or describe traumatic events. They may also become angry or indignant. All of these emotions can subsequently render them sullen, monosyllabic or uncooperative.

Confronted with a show of emotion, your best response is to look as empathetic as you can, but to say very little. It is fine to offer a tissue to a weeping interviewee, but you would not put your arm round them and seek to comfort them. Nor would you urge someone who was angry to calm down. This makes angry people angrier still. There is no getting away from the cynical fact that when they are experiencing extremes of emotion, people will be more open and unguarded, which from your point of view is all to the good. So bide your time while they calm down. But don't let them off the hook. Give them a chance to process those emotions and play themselves out, but continue to pursue your line of inquiry. Try some sympathetic responses like these; they show empathy, but they do not take the delicate subject off the table; rather they keep it there for further exploration:

> I'm sorry. This is painful for you. Do you want to take a moment?
> Take your time. I know it is hard for you to relive what happened.
> You are obviously still very upset about what happened.
> It sounds as though you were very badly treated.
> Has anyone got in touch with you to see if you are ok?
> Have you had any offers of help and support?

They think it's all over

Signal when the interview is at an end, and proffer your thanks and some feedback. But don't stop listening. Interviewees relax when they think it is all over, but they don't necessarily stop talking. What they say in that unguarded post-interview period can be very revealing.

> I know I said he was a good boss, and to be fair he did get good results. But he was a nightmare to work with. I wouldn't trust him as far as I could throw him.

> I thought you might ask me about Jack. Good job you didn't. I could tell you some things about him. Did you know he and I were an item back in the day?

> I hear on the grapevine that the company is in big trouble and is about to lay off a whole load of staff.

> Pity I didn't have time to tell you the story about the time I was stuck in a lift with her. She completely lost it.

The interview is over, so the interviewee now thinks he or she is chatting to you informally off the record. But when you hear remarks like this, you will want to learn more and get back on the record as soon as you can. Get your notebook or recorder out again if you need to, but make it clear that the interview has in effect restarted. Otherwise you will be left with the ethical dilemma about whether you can use something your interviewee told you freely but on the tacit understanding that it was not part of the interview and that you therefore would not use it.

Pen and paper or tape recorder?

If you are doing a lengthy interview, you may prefer to record it, especially if you are not confident of the reliability of your shorthand. That way you know you have a full account of what was said, and you will make no mistakes with your quotes. It also means you are free to give your full attention to your subject, which is hard if you are trying to take a full shorthand note with a notepad perched on your knee. Even the best shorthand cannot keep pace with the speed at which most people speak over a prolonged period. Ask the permission of the interviewee if you want to record. The physical presence of a recording device may constrain them at first, but they will soon forget it is there.

You should still have your notebook out even if the recorder is running, because it allows you to do a running log of the interview, flagging the times of the best bits for when you come to listen back to the recording. If you record a 45-minute interview, it is going to take 45 minutes to listen back to it, and even if you skip over some bits, there will be others that you need to play more than once while you transcribe your quotes or make sure you understand fully what was said. That makes for a lengthy process. Doing a rough log of the interview as you go along will save a lot of that time.

Retractions

One of the trickiest things to handle is a change of mind on the part of your interviewee. We touched on this in relation to dealing with sources in Chapter 7. They have second thoughts about something they have said to you, and ask you not to use it. This puts you on the spot, because nine times out of ten the matter in question will be something that you very much do want to use.

If you are not sure about how to respond, ask your editor or a senior colleague. The editor was not at the interview and can take a detached view about what to do. Making difficult calls goes with their territory.

You are not obliged to agree to retract any material that was legitimately gathered. If your interviewee told you things of their own accord at a transparent interview, and made no attempt to suggest you should not publish them, then you are entitled to do use them. That is your default position.

If someone asks you not to include something, your instinct will be to refuse. But you will sometimes be willing to agree. Bear these things in mind:

– **Why are they asking?** It may well be that the request comes from a genuine motive – not to hurt someone else's feelings, not to disclose information that the interviewee had promised not to reveal. You may decide it is a good enough reason to agree. Suppose an interviewee got a little carried away when describing the breakdown of their marriage and revealed personal details of the split, while making disparaging remarks about the behaviour of their ex. On reflection, they might worry about the effect on the couple's children if those comments appeared in print. You would probably be inclined to agree that this was a fair point, and that you would not want to jeopardise the welfare of the children. But if there is no valid reason such as this, stand firm.
– **How much time has elapsed since the interview?** If an interviewee says something and then says straight away "oh please don't print that, I shouldn't have said it", or "that didn't come out quite right, let me rephrase it", then you would probably agree: they have changed their minds on the spot, the way we all do. The same might apply if the request came at the end of the interview, while the matter is still fresh – especially if it is simply a request to rephrase. Asking you to disregard something significant is more problematic, although if it comes during the interview you might think it is reasonable.

     If the interviewee calls you up a day later, or a few days later, to say they have had second thoughts, you are entitled to take a rather harder line. Again, you will want to know the reason for the change of heart. You could of course say your piece has already been written and submitted. But you could just dig your heels in. They said it, it was on the record, you didn't force them to say it and you are going to use it. Your interviewee may well go over your head and appeal to directly to your editor. So even if you have not referred up, tell the editor of the request you have received by way of forewarning. In the end, you must judge each case in its merits.
– **How important is this material to your piece you are planning to write?** The last consideration is a rather commercial one. If it is not central to your piece and you can sacrifice it without compromising the whole, then it does not cost you anything to agree graciously. If you really want to use it though, and believe it is an integral part of what you want to write, then it is back to the previous two considerations, and probably to your editor.

Copy approval

We also looked briefly at this issue in Chapter 7. Your interviewee, or publicist or agent acting for them, requests or insists on the right to look over your piece before it is printed. This is called "copy approval". Your starting position should always be to refuse. You have editorial control over anything you have legitimately gathered, and you are under no obligation to submit your work for the approval of anyone you have spoken to during the business of doing that gathering. If you do agree, you will find your script returned with multiple objections and corrections, leaving you in the invidious position of having to decide which of them to accept and which to reject. The only reason you might consider offering extracts for comment is if you want to make sure you have fully understood some aspect of the story and explained it properly. Otherwise, say no.

In the burgeoning world of the celebrity interview, there is a growing trend for agents to demand the exact questions in advance of the interview and copy approval afterwards. Some publications agree, fearful of losing the interview if they do not. You should not automatically agree to preconditions like this, and refer them to your editor if you are asked to do so. If an agreement is reached after negotiation, you are then duty bound to abide by it.

Writing up the interview

You have successfully completed the interview, and have the material for a cracking long-form feature. For some thoughts about putting it together, go to Chapter 21.

9
Storytelling: anatomy of a news story

hard and soft news.....hard news stories.....how a story is built.....constituent parts of a story.....soft news

In this chapter and the next, we will consider the theory and practice of constructing a basic news story – the constituent parts you need to assemble, and how you put them all together. No two news items are exactly the same, and most will lend themselves to a variety of different approaches when it comes to the business of storytelling. In addition, the techniques required for effective storytelling will change according to the medium in which you are working – print, radio, television online – and the audience for whom your work is intended. Even so, we can identify some building blocks and principles of good practice that hold good for most situations. These will provide you with a solid foundation from which you can experiment as you develop your own individual style of reporting and adapt to individual platforms.

In these two chapters, we will take print and online news – the written story – as our focus. Much of what we say about them also applies to scripting for television and radio news; but techniques specific to broadcast news are explored in more detail in later chapters.

Hard and soft news

Journalists draw a distinction between what they call hard news and soft news. Hard news is the stuff that occupies most of the first few pages of a newspaper, the top items on a website and most of the content of television and radio news bulletins. It might include:

– A report of something that has (just) happened
– A report of something happening later that day or in the near future
– A report of a speech someone has made, or other newsworthy comments
– A development on a running story
– A press conference or other form of public announcement
– The release of a new report, poll, survey, official figures
– Financial results
– Any other material of significance, especially if it will have an impact on the world, the nation or the lives of the audience. This can be in any field – politics, economics, arts, sport and so on.

All of this is news that is literally "new" and so will be reported in a style that is factual, immediate and lacking in frills, with short sentences and short paragraphs.

"Soft news", which we will return to later, is pretty much everything else. It may be a longer interview or feature on anything – not necessarily a subject that appears in the news pages. This includes lifestyle, fashion, health, culture, celebrity and so on. These stories can also appear on news pages to add texture and variety. But they will typically be on the feature pages – longer and with a more leisurely style, and with more peripheral detail. They will often allow for more of the personality of the writer to come through.

Comment journalism – editorials, opinion columns, political commentary and the like – sits somewhere between the two. It is highly topical because it is usually about some aspect of the news of the day; but it is less a news report, more an expression of someone's point of view, or interpretation. Although you may have aspirations to be a columnist, and to have a vehicle for offering your own take on the issues of the moment, you probably need to restrict that sort of writing to your personal blog for now. As a news reporter, you are a neutral and unbiased observer. You are telling the audience what is happening and helping them understand it. But you are keeping your own views to yourself.

The distinction between hard and soft news is useful in making an initial assessment of a story and suggesting how it might be approached. But its value does not go too far beyond that. Any story can be written in either a hard way or a soft way, and you will consider each story on its merits and decide on the best method of treatment. We are not talking about major differences in style, or radically different ways of writing. The differentiation is more about helping you decide which is the most appropriate way of presenting the information.

Hard news stories

In Chapter 2, we listed the dozen or so main subjects for news stories, hard and soft:

– Conflict
– Argument and debate
– Power
– Disaster/tragedy
– Government action
– Security and terrorism
– Crime
– Money – the wider economy and personal finance
– Health, fitness and diet, science
– Sex
– Weather
– Entertainment and celebrity
– Culture
– Sport
– Human interest.

We will concentrate first on hard news – the sort of stories you are most likely to be tackling in your early days as a news reporter.

When you are gathering information for your story, and later, when you are putting the story together, remember the key questions that any story should answer – and the needs and interests of the people who will be reading it.

What?

What has happened, or what may be about to happen? Is it important or significant, interesting or amusing to your audience?

Who?

Who has it happened to? Who did it, or said it? Is this a story about people generally, or about certain individuals? If the latter, are they already well known to the reader or do they suddenly find themselves in the news because of something that has happened to them? Depending on the answer, you may need to tell your readers more about them – age, occupation, credentials, addresses and any other relevant contexts.

When?

Today? Yesterday? Tomorrow? In the distant past or in the future? In general, the more immediate something is, the newsier it is. A timeline, or a description of how developments relate to each other in terms of time, is often an important element in telling or understanding a story.

Where?

Sometimes the location of a story can be of particular significance. Even if it is not, it is part of the context of any story that you write and should be included.

How?

Your story is going to have to explain how this happened. The audience will want to know the circumstances that brought us to this point.

Why?

You are also going to have to go into the factors and the reasons behind the story, put it into context and offer some background and guidance.

These are the so-called 6Ws – even though only five of them actually start with a W – the answers to some or all of which will be the foundation of everything you write, hard or soft. And we might add some other questions, the answers to which will often strengthen your story:

What next? You may be able to give some indication of what subsequent developments in the story might be.

How do we know? This is about being clear about your sources. We talked a lot about transparency and attribution in Chapter 7. Make sure your sources are included in your story, so that your readers can judge their strength and credibility for themselves.

How much? The amount of money involved is a feature of many stories. It is of interest to the audience, and it helps provide context.

So that is what most stories are about, and the questions they attempt to answer. Let us dissect a typical story to understand how it is made and built up.

How a story is built

The headline

This is what the readers see first. Often it will be the only part of the story they do see. The eye sweeps across the page of a newspaper or website, and the brain makes rapid decisions about the stories it is interested in and those it isn't.

So your headline has a lot of important works to do. It must:

> Catch the eye.
> Give an outline of the story.
> Sell the story.
> Convey urgency and importance.

To do this, it will use strong and active words. It may be clever or amusing, if appropriate, with perhaps a play on words (though do avoid the obsession of some newspapers with bad puns). Headlines do not need to be complete sentences – other than for broadcast outlets -- and they do not need to tell the whole story. But they should be dramatic and full of impact, encouraging the reader to explore further. Their prime purpose is to be, literally, eye-catching.

The length of a headline will vary widely. The front page lead on a national newspaper will be in a large typeface that will allow very few characters and words for a headline. Sometimes a single word in very large letters will be used for impact: "Betrayal!" "Victory!" "Disgrace!" Headlines like this will usually be supported by a secondary heading in a smaller typeface giving the bare details of the story. Lesser stories on inside pages will have headlines in smaller fonts, which provide the space for more words. The length of online headlines depends on house style.

The person whose responsibility is to write the headline will vary between organisations. In newspapers, it always used to be the preserve of the sub-editors after they had reworked the reporter's material to their satisfaction. Nowadays it is just as likely to be added by a content editor. Online reporters will be expected to provide a headline when they file their stories, and perhaps a separate headline for use on social media. This is something we will look at in the digital chapters.

The introduction

The introduction, or "intro", is the first paragraph of your story. It is the place you encapsulate in simple language the main point and the thrust of the story. Again, you must be aware of the short attention span of readers. They may read the headline and then the start of the story, but there is no guarantee that they will go on to read the rest of it as well. It is your job to make sure that they do – that the intro is arresting and interesting enough to make them actively want to read on.

So you are still in the business of selling the story to the reader. If the headline was the start of the sales pitch, the intro continues the work, trying to draw the reader into the story. If no-one reads your story, you are wasting your time. So your intro needs to maintain the hard sell, continue with the use of simple language and short words and of course give readers a concise summary of the story.

Think of the headline and the intro working together to reel in the reader. They need to complement each other, with the intro building on the brevity and impact of the headline. They should not repeat individual words or say exactly the same thing.

In a traditional production process, the story will be written first, and the headline added later once the page has been designed, the location and shape of the story decided and the amount of space for the headline allocated. In this model, the reporter writes an intro with no idea of what the headline will be. It is the responsibility of the person adding the headline to ensure that it is a good fit with the intro and does not contain duplication. Sometimes editors will come up with what they consider to be a good headline, which then necessitates recasting the intro, to make the two fit together snugly and eliminate repetition. If you are writing the headline yourself, the responsibility for making it work well with the intro is yours.

Characteristics of the perfect intro

- Builds on the headline.
- Is brief and to the point.
- Gives you the guts of the story.
- Is accurate.
- Feels fresh and relevant.
- Can be understood immediately.
- Makes you want to read on

Paragraphs 2–4

You have given readers an outline of the story by means of a striking headline backed up by a crisp intro. Now you need to add flesh to the bone, filling out some of the gaps in the summary you have provided so far, and adding more detail.

This is where you begin to build on the intro by working in some of the following:

- Supporting evidence or quotes
- More details/information
- Attribution – giving the sources for the story, if you haven't already mentioned them
- Background material which gives a little necessary history and helps the reader understand the story in a wider context

The rest of the story

How much more you write depends on the strength of your story and the amount of space that has been allotted to it. Space in a printed newspaper is at a premium, but an online story in theory has no limit in terms of length. That does not mean it is a good idea to write hundreds of words. Think of the readers: they probably won't be prepared to stay with you that long, and may well give up. So even if you are not under pressure of length, do not abandon your commitment to a concise, clear and informative narrative that excludes extraneous details and is no longer than it has to be. If you do have a word count to aim for, make sure you stick to it, whatever the platform.

These later paragraphs will be used to flesh out further the skeleton you have already provided, with more background material, more details, more quotes and more explanation. But remember: everything that is essential to the story must already have been said higher up. Never leave an important fact or detail until late in the story, or the very end. If people have stopped reading before they get to this point, they will miss a key element – worse, they may leave with a completely misleading view of the story.

There is also the danger, primarily with print, that if your story is too long to fit into the space allowed for it, someone further along the production chain will simply remove material from the end until it does fit. This process is known as "cutting from the bottom". So if you write an account of a court case and leave it until the last paragraph to report that the defendant was found not guilty, you will look rather foolish (and perhaps get into hot water) if that paragraph is cut before it gets into the paper, the verdict is not reported and the readers are left thinking someone is guilty when they are innocent.

Constituent parts of a story

Facts. The information you are conveying is obviously the most important part of the story – its *raison d'être*. Make sure you have worked out what is required and that you have assembled everything you need to know about the story before you start to write it. The end product needs to contain plenty of hard information, and to be accurate and balanced. Can you answer those basic questions: who, what, when, where, why and how?

Quotes. Quotes offer the reader the evidence on which your story is based, turning it into a first-hand account of events. They give your story colour and authenticity, while telling the reader where you are getting your information. They also help break up the pace and texture of the narrative, especially in direct speech. If quotes are colourful and interesting, they can give the story a massive lift. They might even be strong enough to become part of your intro. That is why it is always worthwhile pushing your interviewees, maybe asking the same question in a number of different ways until you get something that sounds interesting and attractive.

Look at these two intros for the same story, one lifted by a vivid and apposite quote, the other relatively flat without one.

> Newtown bin collections came in for criticism at last night's council meeting, as councillors criticised them as unreliable.

> Newtown's bin collections are "a load of rubbish" councillors were told last night.

Background and context. This can be summarised as anything that helps make sense of the story for your readers. That might take many forms – more information about the players in the story, relevant recent developments, historical perspective, statistics that offer useful comparisons and so on.

Colour. Journalists use this word to mean illustrative detail that might not be key to the story but which gives it life and readability – attracting readers, helping them form an image of what is being described or relate to what they are being told. Colour is what turns the printed word into a picture conjured up in the mind's eye. People often talk about a journalistic eye for detail. Good reporters know that very small things – a telling phrase, a strong image, a close observation – will lift a person or an event off the printed page and give the reader a powerful image or signal with which to connect. If you are pushed for space, colour is the thing that you might be tempted to chop out because it does not add materially to the narrative. Be wary of doing so. The pertinent detail and the striking quote are the things that make readers want to read on. They are just as important – perhaps more important – in a serious and difficult story as they are in a lighter one.

Chronology. Your intro highlights the main point of the story, which means a report will seldom start at the beginning and go through the sequence of events chronologically to the end. But at some point – as part of your *how* and *why* – you may want to remind readers of the chain of events that brought us to this point, especially if your narrative shifts between different times. This might be a par beginning, either literally or in effect: "it all started when......"

A well-balanced story will have some or all of these elements, pieced together with the key information in a seamless and easy-to-read narrative. Its structure will keep changing direction and pace. Stories that jam all the quotes together, or leave all the background to the end, look dull and uninviting and will not be pleasurable or easy to read.

Here are two simple diagrams (Figures 9.1 and 9.2) which illustrate this basic story structure and the elements that go into it. This well-known model is known as the "inverted triangle" or "inverted pyramid".

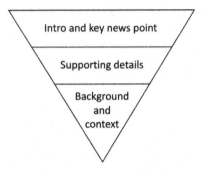

Figure 9.1

The intro will start with the most newsworthy material that answers at least some those key questions – almost certainly *Who* and *What*. Then it is backed up with important supporting details. Then other information or description adds body or texture, or helps the reader understand the story. The triangle/pyramid is inverted to indicate that the content diminishes in importance the further you read into a story.

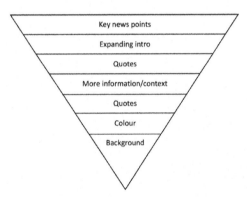

Figure 9.2

The second pyramid is designed to illustrate the indicative structure of the story-telling process and how the different elements can be combined to make a well-constructed piece.

Again, the most important detail is right up there at the top. That is not going to change. Then it is backed up with more information that substantiates the introduction. Then you might start to feed in a quote, more detail perhaps with some colour, more quotes, perhaps a run-through of the chronology of the story from the beginning, until you have worked up a logical, clear and easily readable account of what has happened.

Soft news

We will look in much more detail at this area in Chapter 21. The word "soft" in this context can mean either the subject matter of the story or the treatment of it. Just because a soft story lacks the hard-hitting immediacy of hard news, do not think of it as being in some way inferior or less important. The readers do not see it that way – for many, the non-hard news sections are the most appealing and attractive parts of the paper or website. As Lord Northcliffe said: "It is hard news that catches readers. Features hold them". Weekend newspapers are swollen by any number of sections dedicated entirely to "soft" subjects such as property, travel, gardening, the arts, sport, health and lifestyle. These supplements help sell papers – indeed some people do not buy a paper in the week, and do so only at the weekend.

Softer stories are frequently to be found on the news pages – they are not marginalised on the feature or special interest pages. Many will be high in human interest, and help create that rich mix of material that is important for any newspaper or news website. As we saw in Chapter 1, page three of a national newspaper will often be dominated by an offbeat or quirky story that has little or no significance in a hard news context. And if you want to see how soft news can attract a mass audience online, look no further than the *MailOnline* homepage.

Such stories will still answer the six or more basic questions, but offer much more scope for presenting the material. The main point of the story does not necessarily have to be in the first line of the intro, for example. The language may be more relaxed and unhurried, the style more discursive and less breathless. But the responsibility remains to engage readers early and to hold their interest – and of course, to be accurate.

10

Storytelling: writing a news story

preparation: how much do they want? by when?.....taking command.....what goes into the intro? what can you leave out?.....crafting the intro.....different approaches to storytelling.....paragraph 2 and the body of the story.....choosing the best quotes.....time to check.....the sub editor.....what is subediting.....headlines.....text breaks.....captions.....style

Now you understand the basic anatomy of a typical news story, you are in a good position to start creating your own. You have assembled all your facts, done your interviews, researched the background and are ready to move from the gathering of information to the organising and presentation of it: the writing of the story. The process is fundamentally the same whether you are producing digital, print, radio or television content. Content for the internet requires you to think about the use of key words to make your story easier to find via search engines. We look at this in detail in Chapter 13.

For each story you need to think – preferably before you start writing – about how it should be structured; what you need to include and omit; and how you combine the various elements of quotes, colour and background to get the best possible value for your newsgathering efforts. As with so many things in life, preparation and planning are critical. In particular, you need to get the intro right. That is the most challenging part, but once you are happy with it, everything else should feel much easier.

In this chapter, we look at the necessary preparation, at honing the intro and complementing it with supporting information and at the range of different storytelling techniques that you have at your disposal. We will discuss some of these issues with real examples culled from the pages of national newspapers – where, as we shall see, not every story is an unqualified success.

Preparation

You will almost always be working under the direction of someone else – perhaps a news or content editor or a senior producer. That person will have an opinion about your story and its individual merits, but also a wider overview of all the other stories that are around, the relative significance of each and how they are all going to fit into the finished product. For your part, you should be thinking only about your own story and about making the best possible job of reporting and presenting it.

Before you start, you need two critical pieces of information.

How much do they want? The first thing you need to know is how much prominence in terms of length the decision-makers in this process are planning to give your story. You might get any one of a number of different answers to this question. You might just be told to "let it run" or give it "what it makes', which invites you to use your own judgement about how much to write. You might be asked for a number of paragraphs, or be given a word count. In broadcast, you will be given a duration in time. Local practice may require you submit your story on the basis of what you think it is worth, leaving content managers to worry about how much room to allocate to it once they have it. But if you can, try to get at least a rough idea of what might be considered an appropriate length. It is no use producing a beautifully crafted 750 words if there is only ever going to be room for 250. Shorter is usually better than longer, with no important details too far down the story in case they are chopped out in the editing process.

With online stories, there is in theory no limit to the length that can be accommodated. But that is not a licence to waffle. While newspaper editors will measure a story's worth by the amount of space they have available, or are prepared to make available, web editors will be thinking about how to persuade readers to stick with the story all the way to the end. That will suggest an optimum length to them. Whatever instructions you are given about length, make sure you heed them.

When do they want it by? It is a truism that even the best story in the world is worthless if it is not ready in time. Make it a point of honour always to meet your deadlines. This is important whatever medium you are working in. Often that will mean that you do not have time to craft the story as much as you would like, and it might look a bit rough and ready. No matter. You simply must get it in on time. You might have the chance to tidy it up for later versions. Missing a deadline is a huge professional sin, and you must on no account commit it.

The answers to these two questions – *How Much?* and *By When?* – set the parameters of your story. You know how much you are going to write and how much time you have to write it. Now you should be asking yourself a secondary set of questions, which you can answer on your own, with a bit of research. These are:

> Have we done this story before?
> If so, when most recently?
> What did we say then?
> Does my story move things on from the last report?

You should always check whether your story is new, and if not, when it was last carried and what was said about it then. Ideally, you will have done this before you even started work on the story, as part of your information gathering. In local or regional journalism, dozens of stories on the same subject may be carried over a period of months or years. Every town will have its own long-running issues, such as planning sagas, which create one news story after another.

You need to brief yourself on where the story stood the last time your audience was told anything about it. This will help you calibrate the story you are writing today. It will help you write a story that looks new and is an advance on the previous position. And it will help you avoid producing a rehash of stuff we already knew and have heard before. There is no point coming up with a story that looks remarkably similar to the one that ran yesterday, or last week. So if it is a story that has been covered before, make sure you are briefed on what the status of the story was when it was last covered and how much your audiences have already been told about it. They will still need reminding of this history when you write your story – that will form part of your background material. All this gives you good context for what you are about to write, and will inform the way you compose your story.

Taking command

The most important part of writing is what happens inside your head between the end of the newsgathering process and putting the first words down. Before you begin, you should assemble your material; make an overall assessment of it; and decide what your story is about, and what you want to do with it. As David Randall puts it in *The Universal Journalist*:

> Composition is not merely the business of arranging words. It is the business of organising thought.

The job of the words is to express as clearly and cogently as possible the thoughts you have about the story. The thoughts come first!

Randall quotes a reporter he knew who talked about this process in terms of "taking command of the material". It is a good way of describing what happens when all that material has been assembled. You need to bring a clear narrative voice to it, an order and structure that includes only what is necessary, discards what is not and makes an attractive and compelling read. This means absorbing your research, making sense of it, ordering the main points in your head and deciding on the line you are going to adopt when it comes to writing it.

With a hard news story, how you do much of this may be obvious and straightforward. But lots of stories are complicated and difficult, especially if you do not have as much information as you would like, have not spoken to all the people you wanted, or if your story represents a development on one that has been running for some time. By the same token, you may have masses of information, but only 250 words into which to squeeze it, which can require some brutal decisions.

Taking command also means reacquainting yourself with some old friends, those key questions that are always worth keeping in the forefront of your mind. Here they are again, this time in the form of a little ditty by Rudyard Kipling – a great storyteller, and also a journalist.

> I keep six honest serving men
> (They taught me all I knew)
> Their names are What and Why and When
> And How and Where and Who.

Just as you tried to answer all these questions as you were gathering information, so they will serve you again when you come to write your story. Your story needs to answer those questions on behalf of the audience. You have found out the answers; now you have to convey those answers in your written account. If you think of the whole thing as a logical process like this, the relationship between storygathering and storytelling becomes much more obvious. It all boils down to you answering these questions as clearly, as fully and as succinctly as you can.

Remember to keep the interests of audiences in the forefront of your thoughts. These are the people your story is aimed at. Never forget who your story is for, and always put yourself in their shoes before you start: what do they want and what do they need? (Remember these are not always the same things.) How much do they know about this already? How much do they need to know? If I was telling this story to my friend, or my mum, what questions might they ask me? Would I know the answers? Do I know and understand enough to explain the story to them? Before you can explain something to others, you need to be sure you understand it yourself.

The point of running through this simple checklist of the basic questions your story will answer is to make sure that you have the knowledge you need to be able to write it properly, and to remind yourself to answer these questions when you do write it. If you have a hole in your knowledge, it is better to discover that and fill it before you start writing.

So, you have got your story, you have thought about how it fits together, you know how much you have to write and you know your deadline. You have thought about your story in the context of past coverage, and borne in mind the questions you will be answering on behalf of the audience. A few more tips that will save you time and make the job of writing easier still:

Go quickly through all your notes again to make sure you are carrying the whole story in your head and are clear about the key points.

Underline or highlight the bits you know you are going to need. You can then find them again quickly, and check quickly at the end that you have not left any of them out. Cross out or otherwise mark any material that you know you are not going to need.

Identify your best quotes, and make sure you can read your shorthand or your handwriting. If the time comes for you to include the killer quote and you find that you cannot read it, or you are not sure you have got it word perfect, it is going to knock a hole in your confidence – and a hole in your story.

All of this will help you write fluently and efficiently without having to pause while you try to find the bit you want, or read a word you cannot decipher. Your writing will be better and will flow more naturally if you are not stopping every few moments to check something out.

It may be helpful to sketch out a very quick outline of your story, and the order in which you are going to arrange the information. This may just be bullet points or a couple of words about what each paragraph is going to contain. Think of it as a route map or a miniature essay plan. If you know where the story is going, and the order in which you are planning to introduce information, your writing will develop momentum and again you will write without holdups.

All this may seem a bit of a performance, a rather cumbersome palaver to go through when you are up against a deadline. But it will save you time in the long run, because you have taken the trouble to get everything clear in your mind before you start – and when you do start writing, you know where the narrative is going and the location of the milestones along the way. As you become more experienced, a lot of this will become second nature and you will do it instinctively and at ever-increasing speed. But always make time for some preparatory thinking, however tight your deadline is. Time spent in preparation is never wasted.

In the days before computers, stories were bashed out on typewriters or dictated down the telephone to copytakers. If you made a mistake typing your copy, or had a change of mind, you had to start again – or, if you were dictating, you had to try to rescue things as you went along. It was a good discipline. You quickly learned to make sure you had thought in advance about what you wanted to say, and you learned to get it right first time. With a computer, you do not need to do that. You can manipulate the text in any way you want, and it is all too easy to start writing a story or a sentence without having much of an idea how it is going to end. Yes, you can always delete or move material around, and you may have a perfect-looking script at the end of it all. But you have probably wasted a lot of time with rewrites and cutting and pasting, and all because you did not get your thoughts in order in the first place.

What goes into the intro? What can you leave out?

The intro is the most important element of your story, and the hardest to get just right. Again, it is worth spending time thinking about it and playing with several ideas, because once you have written your intro, everything else should flow logically and relatively effortlessly from it. As well as giving the key facts, it is your chance to pitch the story to your audience – and how well you do that will determine whether people read it all the way through or allow their attention to wander off somewhere else.

The most obvious and important function of the introduction is to set out in a few words *what the story is*. If a bus has overturned injuring 20 schoolchildren, it is pretty obvious what the story is and what your intro will look like. But if it is a subtle development or a twist in a long-running story, or it is based on a speech someone has made about something technical like monetary policy or European regulation, then it can be tricky to grasp the main point and to convey it briefly in an engaging way. The decisions about what you leave out, or save for later in the story, are as important as the decisions about what you put in.

With complex issues, you will never be able to encapsulate the whole story intelligibly in the opening sentence, and you should not try. Ask yourself what your angle is on the story, and what you feel is the most effective way of getting into your narrative.

You may already have had to do this work when trying to engage interest in the story from your boss – your opening sales pitch. Editors do not want to be swamped with a mass of detail when you outline a proposed story to them. They just want you to cut to the chase, and they will say things like this:

> What's the top line?
> What's the headline?
> Give me the short version
> What's the intro?
> What's your angle?
> *Why do I care?*

What they are in effect saying is:

> Summarise the story for me, and tell me why I should run it.

They don't need the full detail. They don't need the names and ages. They want to know the core of the story and where you got it from. And the core of the story is what is also going to be in your intro; in effect, it *is* the intro. Imagine that you are sending a text about the story or tweeting it, and you are being charged £10 a word. That is quite a good discipline for capturing the kernel of your story in a few words – and again, those few words will form the basis for your intro.

If you can give a good, concise and crisp answer to your editor's questions, you are more than half way to creating your intro. Now refine those words until it looks and sounds right.

Remember what we said in the last chapter about the characteristics of the perfect intro:

It is brief, and to the point – some editors of newspapers and websites will not tolerate intros of more than 15 or 20 words. Even if yours does, it is not a bad discipline to try to keep within that. But don't get hung up on it. If your intro is good and it works well, no one is going to complain about its length. But the longer it is, the more complicated it will be, and the harder to grasp at once.

It gives you the guts of the story – it should be self-contained. In other words, if this were the only thing you read, you would have a reasonable indication of what the story was about, even if a lot of the detail was not there.

It is accurate – this should go without saying.

It feels fresh and relevant – it is attractively written.

It can be understood straight away – simple, simply expressed and completely unambiguous.

It makes you want to read on.

The intro must carry the bones of the story; but that does not mean there is no place for drama, human interest, telling detail and other imaginative ways of getting the story across. Do not forget the final point: "it makes you want to read on". You are selling the story to the audience, as well as giving the guts of it. This is the stuff of effective news reporting – conveying information in engaging and interesting ways. Your story must be accurate, well-researched and well-ordered – but it has also got to be interestingly, even entertainingly, presented. The audience must be hooked quickly, want to read it and enjoy reading it.

It is unlikely you'll be able to include answers to every one of your key "serving men" questions in 15 words or so. But it is possible. Here is a generic example.

> Trade unionists marched through London yesterday to protest against cuts in public services.

This answers nearly all the basic questions in just 13 words, without sounding particularly false or contrived.

> Trade unionists (WHO) marched (WHAT) through London (WHERE) yesterday (WHEN) in a protest against cuts in public services (WHY).

If you haven't the space to answer all the questions, you will have to decide which are the most important. This will nearly always include *what* – because that is point of the story – and very probably *who*. But treat each story and the context of each story, on its merits. Depending on the context, the *when* or *where* or *why* might be important enough to merit being included in the intro.

We will look in a moment at other means of getting into a story, but the simple, informative, newsy introduction is the most basic set-up and the one that news reporters employ most frequently on all platforms. As per the pyramid diagrams, the next part of your story will build on what you have sketched out in the intro, and give more detail. The next par or pars will carry the bulk of the story and what has happened.

Here's an example of this process in action: imagine you are a reporter in Newtown and your local police force releases some information about a serious incident last night. This is their statement:

> At 11.10 pm last night in West Street, near the junction with Queen Street, Newtown, a motor vehicle was in collision with a group of pedestrians who were waiting at a bus stop. Police and other emergency services were in attendance at the scene at 11.21 pm. Four persons were taken by ambulance to St Mary's Hospital, Newtown. Their condition has been described as 'critical'. At the present time, we are not in a position to release any of the names of those injured. Three were adults, two males and one female, and one was a male 12 years of age. The car involved in the incident was a BMW sports car that had been reported stolen earlier in the day. One of the injured persons is the driver of the vehicle. He is reported to have lost control of the vehicle and left the road. He was freed from the vehicle by members of the Newtown Fire and Rescue Service. Anyone who witnessed the incident is asked to contact Newtown Police Station.

Clearly, this is a strong story for Newtown's local news outlets. This imaginary statement is not untypical of the sort of factual, chronological narrative that is released by the police. It actually contains a lot more helpful detail than you might sometimes receive – news of the condition of ill or injured people is usually given by hospitals, not the police. But it also contains words that we would not use in everyday speech – or in our news stories: "a motor vehicle was in collision with…" "in attendance at the scene", "persons", "at the present time", "a male 12 years of age". The statement is careful and factual, which – if you are a police officer – is exactly what you want it to be. But much of the drama has been drained out of it as a result. It is your job as a reporter to turn this rather workmanlike prose into a sharp and arresting narrative.

Journalism students at the start of their course, given these details, will often start their stories something like this: "At 11.10 last night, near the junction of…" In other words, they start at the beginning and describe the sequence of events from there – rather like the police press release. That is fine for the police; they are not trying to attract readers. It does not serve for the news reporter. It is not storytelling. A hard news intro will begin with the most striking or important information. In this instance, the time of the incident is not the most important thing about it – so do not start with it. In fact, it is not really very important at all, except insofar as it indicates that it would have been dark at the time, and perhaps less busy than at an earlier hour. In any case, we would not say "11.10" if we were telling someone this story in conversation, or in a news report. We would say "ten past eleven", or "just after eleven o'clock".

What are the most important facts here?

– A car has run into a group of pedestrians.
– They were waiting for a bus in West Street.
– Four people were critically injured.
– One was a young boy and another the driver of the car.
– The car had been stolen.

Let us try to put all that important details into one sentence – in other words, make a first attempt at an intro to our story.

> Four people, one a boy of 12, are critically ill in St Mary's Hospital in Newtown after a car that had earlier been stolen ran into a queue at a bus stop in West Street near the junction with Queen Street at ten past eleven last night.

This is factually accurate, and contains the main facts, ordered in a more newsworthy fashion. It answers most of the key questions. It begins with the main news point: four people are critically ill. This is more important than the time it happened, because it gives us a strong indication of the scale and severity of the accident. But this intro is still rather heavy going and – because of the amount of detail it contains – not that easy to read and absorb. You might have to read it two or three times before you took it all in. The tone is very matter-of-fact, and does not reflect the seriousness or drama of what happened. That may sound callous, but reporters are storytellers and they must tell their stories to best effect. That does not mean being tactless or insensitive: but it does mean making the most of the material to hand.

In this first attempt, the reader is being offered too much information in one go. It needs to be presented clearly and logically as part of a narrative that is easy to understand and to pick up at a single reading. That means breaking down into bite-size chunks. Let us take out some of the detail, and just stick with the most important elements.

But what do we leave out? Imagine someone tells you that there has been a serious accident in the town. What are the first questions you would ask?

> What happened?
> Was anyone hurt?
> Where was this?
> When was this?

Our story needs to answer most of those questions, probably in that order. So a revised intro might read:

> Four people, one a boy of 12, are critically ill in hospital in Newtown after a stolen car ploughed into a bus queue.

This new intro is 23 words but it moves along at a good pace and does not feel especially long. Only two words are more than two syllables, and the language is clear and active.

What have we left out of the first version?

– The name of the hospital
– The exact location of the accident
– The time it happened.

All of these are important elements of detail, but they do not need to be in the intro. We can include them later, when we go into more detail about what happened.

In this new version, we have briefly answered those first two questions anyone might ask, and probably done more than enough to encourage people to read on. The simple addition of one word, 'stolen', introduces what is clearly going to be an important element of the story; again, we can return to it later and do not need to elaborate on it at this point. Saying that this accident happened in Newtown (the *where*) is important, because if we live in or near Newtown, we are likely to be very interested in knowing more. If this accident happened in a town 30 miles away, we would still be interested, but less so.

Paragraphs 2–4

Our next couple of pars might answer the rest of our initial questions – the *when* and *where* of this story.

> It happened near the junction of West Street and Queen Street at just after eleven o'clock last night.

Now we can add some more information.

> The casualties were taken to St Mary's Hospital. Police say the car driver was one of those injured.

With that "police say", we are sharing with our audience the source of our information. The audience now knows quite a lot about the story, and has been presented with the information in a digestible way.

These three paragraphs between them take more words than our first single-paragraph effort to convey roughly the same information. But they are much more readable and the information is much easier to absorb in these smaller portions. They will look much better on a web page or a printed page, or in a social post. So this is not always about using fewer words. It is about clear storytelling that audiences can follow easily, as they are guided in a logical and measured way from one piece of information to the next.

In our next paragraph, we might start explaining what we know about the sequence of events – being careful to attribute our knowledge to the police statement, which is our source for the story.

> Newtown police said a BMW sports car that had earlier been reported stolen was driving at high speed along West Street when the driver appeared to lose control. The car left the road and struck a number of people waiting for a bus.

I planted a deliberate mistake in there. Did you spot it? Read it again.

It was the reference to the fact that the car was travelling "at high speed". There is nothing in the police statement about the speed of the vehicle. I made an assumption that if the driver lost control and left the road he must have been driving too fast. That might not have been the case. It is very important not to assume, not to embroider and not to make anything up. Let the facts speak for themselves: don't try to "improve" them. Giving an energetic and colourful account of what happened is good storytelling; making assumptions, exaggerating, sensationalising or, worse, making things up is just bad journalism. So we will remove the phrase "at high speed".

What comes next?

That apart, the audience now has a pretty clear idea of what happened, and after adding anything else that we may know about the circumstances, we can start introducing further supporting material. This might include the elements we looked at in the last chapter under the heading "constituent parts of a story".

> Quotes
> Background and context
> Colour
> Chronology.

Crafting the intro

The pyramid diagrams offer templates for a straightforward news story – a report on something that has happened. They identify the elements that go into the make-up of such a story, and show how they work together to create a clear and readable account.

But of course that is not a rigid formula. There are many different ways of presenting the same information, and all reporters will have their own personal style. There may be a wrong way of writing a story, but there is no single right way. What follows are some examples of this.

It is worth reiterating the distinction between hard news and soft news. Hard news is the stuff that appears on the main news pages and home pages of websites, the stories about recent events, often of a serious or significant nature. These are the stories we have been discussing so far, the ones that tell you what has happened and why. Soft stories may also appear on the news pages, but tend to be "interesting" rather than significant, and are there to create a good mix of items on the page. Most longer form articles such as features will usually be regarded as "soft". This is not a term of disparagement, it is merely used to differentiate them from hard stories.

With hard news reporting, we usually get straight down to business and cut the story down to its bare essentials. The angles and details can wait until later. We give the basic facts in a clear and unambiguous way, and present them in such a way as to interest the audience.

Let us take a look at how the professionals do it. Here are some examples, all of them taken from national newspapers. First, a simple story about the recall of chocolate bars, with intros from two papers:

> Millions of Mars, Snickers and Milky Way chocolate bars are being recalled because of safety fears. (16 words)

> Choc giant Mars last night urged Brits to return six of its most popular products over contamination fears. (18 words)

Similar in length, and the top news line – the recall of products – is obvious. The only real difference in terms of information offered is that the first version specifies some of the brands being recalled – a good way to get the reader to relate to the story, especially as these are household names. The second refers to the "most popular products" made by Mars. Does the person in the street know what those products are, without being told? Probably not. Version 1 is also written in a more natural and conversational way that makes it easier to read. The second one is full of journalese, words that we wouldn't normally use in everyday conversation – "choc giant", "Brits". It looks like an intro that has been generated by a computer rather than a human being. Both intros do the same job at the same length – but one does it in a smoother and more informative way than the other.

Take a look at these intros for another story, about the cause of death of the singer George Michael. There had been much speculation surrounding his death, and these reports are from the inquest that recorded the official verdict about the cause. Every national newspaper sent a reporter to cover the inquest. Here is how five of them reported that same story:

1. George Michael died of natural causes from dilated cardiomyopathy with myocarditis and fatty liver, a coroner has said.
2. George Michael died of heart disease and a damaged liver, it was announced yesterday after months of speculation.
3. George Michael died from heart and liver disease, officials revealed yesterday.
4. Singer George Michael died of heart disease and a build-up of fat in his liver, a coroner has said.
5. George Michael died of natural causes from heart and liver disease, a coroner revealed yesterday.

This is a story that needs an intro containing *who* and *what/how* – who has died and the cause of death. The *who* is obviously George Michael and the *what* is the verdict, which also contains the *how* – death by "natural causes". This is the news line and it is common to all five intros. Only Version 4 thinks it is necessary to explain that George Michael was a singer – the rest assume their readers will be fully aware of who he was.

Version 1 gives us the full medical detail of how the singer died. It is not often you see the phrase "dilated cardiomyopathy with myocarditis" in a newspaper intro. There is a good reason for that. It is a cumbersome construction, and it does not really help the reader. Do you know what dilated cardiomyopathy with myocarditis is? Neither do I. Nor will the vast majority of the audience for whom this story is intended. Unless it is explained to us, it is useless as a piece of information. We are not even given a clue. So Version 1 breaks several of our rules for the perfect intro.

All the other versions talk about heart and liver disease in some way or another: that is something we can all understand. But only two of them also give us the important detail that George Michael died of natural causes. This puts paid to a lot of that lurid speculation about drink or drugs, and so is the top news line. Its absence from some of the intros is a bad miss.

All of these stories tell us the source of this information: this is the definitive and official judgement about cause of death in the form of the verdict of a coroner at an inquest. The correct way of describing the outcome here is that the coroner "reached a conclusion" or "recorded a verdict". (A jury "returns" a verdict.) None of these intros use the proper wording. The phrase "officials revealed" in Version 3 is a very odd construction. This must refer either to the coroner or the medical experts who gave evidence, or possibly both. None of these people is properly described as an "official".

I would suggest that the sharpest and best intro to this story would have been:

> George Michael died of natural causes, a coroner concluded yesterday.

If you had been following the story, as millions had, the key news point is not what he *did* die of, so much as what he *didn't* die of, given the speculation about overdoses and the like. We want to know as soon as possible that this is the final and definitive view about his death, which is why in this case we put the source of the story in the intro.

The George Michael inquest illustrates the point made earlier about the fact that a story template takes you only so far when it comes to writing your intro. There is still plenty of scope for flexibility and variety even if the basic story angle is clear. Here we have a single story with an obvious top line – but in the hands of five different reporters, we have five different accounts. I suggest that none of them hit the bullseye. Version 5 comes closest, although "revealed" is the wrong choice of word. Either "ruled" or "concluded" would better describe what the coroner actually did.

Let us conduct the same experiment with a different type of story. This one definitely falls into the category of "soft", and although it appeared on the news pages, it clearly lends itself to an imaginative treatment. Sadly, it doesn't really get it from anybody. Here is how five of the national newspapers reported it:

1. Almost half of people have never seen a hedgehog in their garden according to a survey that suggests more declines for the garden visitor.
2. Almost half of British people have never seen a hedgehog in their garden, according to a survey which suggests a decline in the creatures.
3. The number of people who saw hedgehogs in their gardens last year fell by 10 per cent, providing more evidence of their decline.
4. Almost half of Britons have never seen a hedgehog in their garden, a survey looking into their decline has found.
5. Once a common sight in hedgerows and gardens, there are fears that hedgehogs may be dying out.

We cannot really say that these reporters have distinguished themselves here. Versions 1, 2 and 4 start in an identical fashion. That is unlikely to be a coincidence. It suggests that they probably got their story from the same source, possibly a press release. The release was probably written by whoever conducted the survey, and these three reporters have more or less copied it word for word. That is lazy. This is a perfectly decent little story that will appeal to many readers. With a very small amount of effort it could be turned into a very attractive treatment.

"*More declines for the garden visitor*" (Version 1). What on earth does this mean? It isn't even English. Surely you have only one decline, and who has ever heard anyone describe a hedgehog as a "garden visitor"? There is a simple reason for this bizarre description. The writer wants to avoid using the word "hedgehog" twice in the same sentence, and has come up with this peculiar alternative description. It isn't very good though is it? It strikes a false note. Version 2 runs into the same problem, and settles for "creatures" in its second reference.

Version 5 is the only one that makes an effort to rewrite the press release – but there is nothing in this intro that refers to the survey and its findings – and that, after all, is what this story is based upon. The story employs the "drop intro" – saving the news point until the second or third par. This is a legitimate technique, which we will explore more fully later, but here it removes all the information that makes the story current. This piece could have been written on any day in the last 20 years; we need to know why it is being written today.

Reporters could have had a bit of fun with this story, but they have not really put their backs into it. These versions are stilted and lacking in imagination.

There are two potential news lines here:

1.   Half the people in Britain have never seen a hedgehog in their garden.
2.   A new survey finds hedgehog numbers are still in decline.

Four of our five versions have kicked off with the former, and they do not read well. You do not have to be a pedant to want to know whether we are talking about half the total population, or half of those who own a garden. But let that go. Version 4 is the one that comes closest to combining these two points.

This story could be made to work well using the two news lines in either order.

> A new hedgehog survey has found numbers continuing to fall. Nearly half of us have never seen one in our garden.

> Nearly half of us have never seen a hedgehog in our garden. A new survey has found their numbers are continuing to fall.

Note that these versions give each news line its own sentence – and yet they are still only around 20 words in length. If you want to include two angles in a single sentence, make sure there is proper connection between them:

> Hedgehog numbers are declining so much that nearly half of us have never seen one in our garden.

> Nearly half of us have never seen a hedgehog in our garden – and new findings suggest that's because their numbers are in freefall.

In my opinion – you are free to demur – any of these is better than anything that actually appeared in print. They may be a little matter-of-fact, but have the virtue of being expressed clearly and simply. They do more to help hold on to the reader: talking about "us" and "our", for example, is far more inclusive and natural-sounding than "British people" (Version 2) or "Britons" (Version 4). This example also underlines the fact that there are very many ways of presenting the same information.

This is a game that anyone can play, and newspapers and websites provide fresh material on a daily basis. Here are two different intros to a hard news story:

> Four people were feared dead last night after a building collapsed at a decommissioned power station. (16 words)

One person died, five were injured, and three still missing last night, after a power station collapsed. (17 words)

Again, both convey the same basic information, and begin with the consequences of the accident – the casualties – as we did in the hypothetical exercise we did earlier in this chapter. They are of similar overall length.

I would suggest that there is a quality gap between them though, and that the first is superior. It reads far more smoothly and feels more immediate, because it is not bogged down by all the commas we see in the second version. By combining the single known fatality with three feared ones, the first version is able to start with the rather more striking words: "Four people were feared dead". The second version needs twice as many words to report the casualties; three times the reader is held up by commas in the course of reading the sentence. The first intro also contains a vital piece of information that is missing from the second, through the inclusion of the single word "decommissioned". This is an important context in helping us evaluate the story – this is not an operational power station, so there is no likelihood of widespread power cuts, for example. Compare also "a building collapsed at a power station" with "a power station collapsed". Which gives you a better and more accurate idea of the scale of this incident?

Sometimes it is hard to be concise in your intro if you are reporting a new angle in a story that is already in the news. This next intro appeared two or three days after news that three British holidaymakers had been drowned in Vietnam.

The tour guide who led three Britons through the Datanla waterfalls in Vietnam has said he tried to stop them venturing towards the whirlpool that swept them to their deaths. (30 words)

The reporter has done well in newsgathering terms – managing to locate the tour guide and extracting from him a good news line that he tried to persuade the tourists not to go, but they pressed on. Three days on, that is a very good new top line for the story, and a good reason for revisiting it. The problem is that before revealing the new news line, the reporter has had to find space in the intro to recap and remind readers of the original story. The intro has to contain both the new angle and the old one. The result is an intro of a whopping 30 words. It reads well enough, but it is quite a long time before we get to that new part of the story – that the tourists decided to go to the falls in spite of being warned not to do so. That is the news line for today's story, so an alternative approach might be to bring this detail higher up the intro:

Three British holidaymakers who drowned in Vietnam ignored safety warnings, their tour guide has said.

This is a little less than half the length of the first one, and gets us to the core of the story more quickly. If it feels a little workmanlike, you could add some drama and colour without overwriting.

Three British holidaymakers swept to their deaths in a whirlpool in Vietnam ignored warnings, their tour guide has said.

An intro is too long if it contains too much information or too many superfluous words. In either case, the chances are that the reader will not be prepared to do the work required to unbundle it and make sense of it. That is the job of the reporter. Here is an example of a reporter completely abdicating that responsibility:

Recent European migrants claim 10 per cent of in-work benefits given to low-paid workers, even though they make up six per cent of the workforce, according to a Government White Paper outlining the new agreement reached in Brussels over the UK's relationship with the European Union.

Just to repeat, in case your credibility is now being stretched: I did not make this up. I copied it from a "quality" newspaper. It is hard to understand how it made it into print. It is all but impossible to grasp at a single reading what is going on here. The whole story is actually contained in the first two lines – the rest is the source, set out in a level of detail that could be held until later on. Indeed, the description of the source is longer than the outline of the story itself. And do readers know what a White Paper is? Probably not. They need to have it explained to them.

Let us first fix this by trimming the description of the source:

> Recent European migrants claim 10 per cent of in-work benefits given to low-paid workers, even though they make up six per cent of the workforce, according to a Government policy document.

It is still very hard to understand at a single reading. There is still a lot of fibre to chew through. We have got 10 per cent of one thing and 6 per cent of another. One way of helping might be to take out the percentages at this stage. Figures and statistics are really useful journalistic tools, but they need handling with care and they need explaining clearly. Let us try to write an intro that summarises what the figures show, and – again – return to the detail later in the story as supporting evidence and information that backs up the intro.

> Immigrants coming to Britain receive more than their fair share of benefits, according to government figures. (16 words)

This may not be perfect. It is perhaps over-simplified, and the rest of the story is going to have to include a fair bit of detail to justify this intro. But at least we are now looking at something that feels as though it might be a proper story. We have a manageable and intelligible sentence that tells the basics of that story and does not get entangled at this stage with too much detail. There is a hint of unfairness and injustice. You might, just might, read on.

So the usual solution to fixing an intro that feels too long to absorb quickly is to take out some of the information it contains, and split the detail over two or three shorter linked pars – making sure that the critical material is still in the top par. Sometimes this is simply a question of hacking away at subordinate clauses or extraneous detail that we do not need in the opening sentence. Here is a good example of exactly that:

> Vital HIV prevention and support services are facing closure **after being earmarked for cuts by local authorities, leaving potentially thousands of people with the virus cut adrift** at the very time the transmission rate is increasing. (37 words)

At 37 words, that is very long. The key news content that we need in this intro is that HIV support services are disappearing. What makes the story stronger is that this is happening at a time when the need for them is increasing. Two news lines with a clear connection between them. We can say all that much more concisely at the stroke of a metaphorical pen by simply removing all the verbiage printed in bold – in other words, removing the middle of the sentence and joining the beginning and end together. With this result:

> Vital HIV prevention and support services are facing closure at the very time the transmission rate is increasing. (18 words)

We have not lost anything important here. We have not even changed the order of any of the surviving words. We have just tightened up the writing and come up with a much more effective and attractive way into the story. Take away the unnecessary detail, and return to it later if you need to.

Or, as in this next case, take away unnecessary context:

> The government's pledge to cut Britain's debt share this year is in jeopardy after official figures showed the economy is smaller than previously thought. (25 words)

The new information and the guts of this story is in the second half of the intro, here:

> Official figures show the economy is smaller than previously thought. (10 words)

Why start with 15 words of background, especially as you need the information in the second half of the sentence before you can understand the whole? Again, this asks the reader to do a lot of work. The writer may justifiably feel that the context – explaining why this is important – is worthy of inclusion in the intro. But it should come *after* the main news point rather than before it.

> Official figures show the economy is smaller than previously thought, threatening to knock government spending plans off course.

You do not have to agree with all of my assessments. In fact it would be healthy if you did not had your own ideas about the most effective presentation of some of these stories. There are some who defend the idea of "double" or "umbrella" intros containing more than one thought, on the basis that sometimes both thoughts are equally important. I would not necessarily argue against that, if there were a genuine connection between the two elements, as in our HIV story above. I would take issue with it if it were simply a way of avoiding making a decision about what the top line of the story was.

It may come down to a matter of taste or circumstance. But whatever your treatment, it should still reflect the key principles we have set out about the necessary clarity, brevity and sharpness of the best intros. In sum: don't cram the whole story into one sentence; divide the material up into a succession of shorter, clearer, linked sentences. Take the readers by the hand and lead them through the narrative.

The best intros for news stories are concise, compact, self-contained and grab the interest. They must get off on the right foot from the word go. To give yourself the best chance of achieving this, think twice before starting a news story with any of these:

> **A subordinate clause**. It will get you off to a slow start, and holds the reader up. You will be giving detail or background in advance of revealing what it relates to.
>
> **A quote** – however striking. Again, we need to know more – in this case, who is talking – before we understand the significance of the quote. A quote doesn't mean much to us if we don't know who the speaker is.
>
> **A question**. Or anything else that needs to be explained.
>
> **A number**. It does not usually work to start with a number, but if you must, spell it out in words. Digits look very ugly.
>
> **The name of an official body, or a lengthy job title**. It lays a dead hand on the story. It is more acceptable, and sometimes unavoidable, in broadcasting.
>
> **Where, when, how and why**. They will usually be less important than Who and What. The context will tell you.

Different approaches to storytelling

Soft news stories, and some hard ones, lend themselves to a wider range of writing techniques, because it is not so important to have the key facts right up in the intro. The intro can be longer, more discursive and not even reveal the story at all – it will often be designed to draw readers in, and to make them want to read on. There are plenty of news stories written in this way too, with the main point in the second or even third paragraph. You will see this range and flexibility even more with longer form articles such as features, which might have no obviously "newsy" angles at all. We look at them in detail in Chapter 21.

People reading longer form features or softer stories are much more disposed to give a story room to develop, and are prepared to invest a bit more time waiting for it to get to the point – provided it is well written and holds their attention. This means that you can bend or break some of the rules we have established for hard news stories. But there are some compromises you must not make. You still want your intro to attract interest and attention. It should still be imaginative and enticing and set up the story to come.

Here are some alternative storytelling techniques, followed by some real examples of how they have been employed in practice. There are more examples in Chapter 21.

Drop, or **delayed drop.** We have already come across this. It describes a story in which the key point, or "nub", of the story is not revealed at once, but is built up to over two or three or even more pars of scene setting. It is a very familiar technique in all forms of storytelling, and works equally well for both softer news stories and longer pieces. You would not employ it for a hard news story such as those we have been discussing, when it is important to come to the point as soon as possible.

The delayed drop works as a sort of tease, trying to hook the reader and prepare for a surprise – the "reveal". There are similarities between this technique and the structure of a classic two-line joke: a set-up and then a resolution via a punchline. The analogy simply underpins the fact that good reporting is all about good storytelling.

Narrative. A narrative story will start telling the story at the beginning and run through the whole sequence of events in chronological order. You will remember that this is something we decided to avoid for hard news stories, in favour of putting the most important information in the first sentence. A narrative approach can sometimes work for newsier stories too, but is usually more appropriate for softer ones, in which *how* or *why* something happened – the build-up or combination of circumstances – might be as important or interesting as the happening itself. Don't delay the main point for too long though – readers might get bored, and be disappointed with the climax when they finally reach it.

Anecdotes. This can be a good way of getting into a story, introducing a character or situation, bringing in some telling detail or illustrating some key feature of the story that will follow. Again, do not wait too long before you explain why you are recounting the anecdote, and relate it to the thrust of your piece.

Scene setter. A description of the weather, the buildings the landscape and so on creates an atmosphere before you hone in on the particular, the point of the story. Again, do not leave it too long.

Narrative, anecdotal and scene-setting approaches are also examples of drop intros, because it takes some time before you get to the punchline, the point of the story.

A single terse sentence. It can tease, or create tension or atmosphere. It can have particular impact on important news stories. "Britain has left the European Union." "Rock legend David Bowie is dead." "Coronavirus deaths are past their peak." When it comes off, it is highly effective; but use sparingly – when it does not, it can look crass and melodramatic.

First-hand reportage. It is when you bring yourself into the story, describing something you have seen with your own eyes. Though you will usually maintain your reporter's detachment, it is permissible to make yourself the subject if you are an eyewitness to a news event: "I watched as the soldiers advanced and fired tear gas at the protesters".

Let us look at some examples of these techniques in action, and see how successful we think they are.

The Pony Club's very name conjures images of Norman Thelwell's cartoon children being bounced out of the saddle by their roly-poly steeds. And it knows it.

This is an example of a drop or delayed drop intro being used on a softish news story of the garden hedgehog variety. The intro sets up the reader for a punchline in the second or third paragraph. In this case, the news line is that the Pony Club wants to change its image. The writer has begun by telling us about its current image. The story takes a risk by assuming that readers will know not only what the Pony Club is, but will also have heard of Norman Thelwell and be familiar with his cartoons. Since he died in 2004, this is quite a big assumption for a large proportion of any general readership.

Might a "newsier" intro using the same sort of thought work better? You decide.

> The Pony Club wants to shed its image of cartoon children being bounced out of the saddle by their roly-poly steeds.

Here's another example to look at:

> This is Aidan Matthews.

This four-word intro, accompanied by a picture of Aidan, shows several different techniques at play at the same time – drop intro, single short sentence, anecdote.

It goes on:

> He is five, but he knows how to operate the washing machine.

We still don't know what the story is, but we are getting more interested. Not many five-year olds do the family washing.

> He also knows that if mummy's lips go blue and there is nobody else around, he should call 999 immediately.

We *still* don't know where all this is leading. We probably do want to know by this time, but we don't want to be kept waiting much longer.

> Aidan is one of a growing number of infant school carers....

And here, at last, is the "nub", or "reveal". We learn that this is a piece about young children who act as carers in the home. We are going to find out more about that, with young Aidan as the example that brings the story to life for us. It is an effective way into a longer piece on this theme.

Here is another drop intro, but one that doesn't work anything like as well:

> It's the scene of countless family squabbles as husbands and wives argue over what to buy and which till queue is the quickest.

This does not seem terribly convincing. Are there really countless marital squabbles about the food shopping and which queue to join? Let's see how the story develops:

> But now the secret of a stress-free speedy supermarket shop has been revealed.
> To wait as little time as possible, the responsibilities should be divided between the sexes, with men finding the trolley and choosing the checkout queue and women doing the actual shopping.

We can see now why the writer tried to get us interested in the story with all that contrived guff about arguments in the supermarket: it was to disguise the fact that the actual story is unutterably feeble and needs all the help it can get. If you are going to delay your punchline, the punchline had better be worth waiting for. In this case, it really isn't. Not entirely the reporter's fault. The story is based on one of those vacuous surveys. It is drivel, and should have ended up in the bin, rather than in the pages of a national newspaper.

Here is another analysis of how a much better story was treated by two different reporters, also on national newspapers. It is about a £32 million lottery winner who found out he had won, but waited a week before claiming the prize. The story was in all the papers, and they nearly all presented it as a delayed drop. Here are a couple of them:

Version 1

> Most lottery winners endure intense stress and sleepless nights while they wait for their tickets to be verified.
>
> But when Gerry Cannings discovered that he and his wife had won more than £32m, he calmly popped the slip in his wallet and waited for nearly a week while the decorators finished painting their home.

This works well.

Version 2

> Peckish Gerry Cannings bought five lotto lucky dips while waiting for his fish and chips – and scooped £32,543,188.
>
> And after learning of his huge win, the retired teacher, 63, walked round with the winning ticket in his pocket for a week because he was too busy having his house decorated to meet lottery bosses.

We sense a failure of nerve here: it starts off with a conventional hard news intro, but then there is a drop in the second par, which is where we find what both writers seem to think is the best angle on this story – that he held on to the ticket for a week and said nothing. This reporter wasn't able to make up his mind about how to present this story. His intro suggests the best line in this story is that Gerry Cannings bought his winning ticket at the chip shop. He is also impressed by the exact worth of the ticket. Then, he changes direction and picks up the (much better) line about the delay in claiming the prize. This writer did not do the preparatory work discussed earlier, deciding what the story was and how he (and it was a he) wanted to structure it before he sat down to write it. Either way, does "peckish" feel like the right word to begin this story?

Here is a specimen version that – for the purposes of comparison – reports this story as though it was hard news, without a drop.

> A retired teacher kept a £32m winning lottery ticket tucked away in his pocket for a week while he waited for workmen to finish decorating his house.

It is clear and factual and carries the main news points – but it does lack something in terms of energy and excitement and it is a bit matter-of-fact. You can see why the reporters working on the story thought it could be built up into something more attractive.

With this next example, we have excruciating evidence that a drop intro does not always work. It looks like a sick joke. For that reason, I have changed the unfortunate lady's name.

> When 88-year-old Jean Blackshaw was driving to the hairdresser and found the country lane blocked, a helpful binman offered to drive her car round the obstruction.
>
> Unfortunately his good deed turned to tragedy when he ran her over with her own Nissan Micra and killed her, a court heard yesterday.

I think we can agree that a conventional treatment would have been far preferable here. This is a bizarre sequence of events, but it certainly isn't funny. It is not appropriate to present it as what journalists sometimes call a "fancy that!" story.

Here is a story that draws four different approaches from four different reporters, with one of them using the drop intro technique. Again it probably comes from a press release – but this time, the reporters have tried a bit harder:

1. Most people in their 60s say they are approaching the age of 70 with increased confidence.
2. From aches and pains to worrying about our pensions, getting older is something many of us find a bit daunting. But there's good news – research suggests we get happier as we progress through our 60s.
3. Don't worry about getting old – experts reckon hitting 70 will leave you feeling fabulous.
4. Bad backs, arthritis and high blood pressure are no barrier to happiness, according to a study that finds the first baby boomers are more cheerful as they hit 70 than they were at 60.

You can take your pick. These examples show that with a bit of effort and imagination, even simple stories can acquire life and interest. They also show that there are many ways of presenting a story, and there are few definitive rights or wrongs. You should try doing this sort of exercise for yourself – take any story you see in print and try rewriting the intro using a number of different techniques. It is good practice and will help you develop an instinct for what sort of treatment works best for what sort of story.

This next one is an example of the anecdotal approach:

> In February 2002, Judy Murray drove a minibus containing her two sons and their coach, Leon Smith, from Stirling to Birmingham's National Indoor Arena, venue of the Davis Cup match between Great Britain and Sweden.

We've got a lot of detail here – far more than we would ever include in the intro to a hard news story. But this is a longer feature, and the writer is purposely including all those details to create an effect – and to make us want to see where it is leading. The "reveal" comes in the next par – this trip marked the start of a preoccupation with the Davis Cup for Judy Murray's son Andy.

Suppose the story had been written as a hard news intro:

> Andy Murray's obsession with winning the Davis Cup dates back to the first tie he attended – as a spectator.

This would be a workmanlike effort and is fine, but the writer of the first one wanted to create an atmosphere and set the scene for a longer piece about the Murray family's love affair with the Davis Cup. In that context, it works better than the more hard-nosed one. Your choice of treatment depends on the sort of story you're writing.

Here's another story that combines a number of the techniques we have been examining:

> It is May 1887.
>
> Florence Hunt, a kindly upper-class charity worker, ventures out of her well-to-do west London neighbourhood to visit her client, Lavinia Manley, in the slums of Fulham – a far cry from the yummy mummy enclave of today and a world away from her usual social orbit.

We start with a very short sentence, containing only the *when*, and establishing what period we are in with this story. So far so good. Contrast that spare opening to a very wordy second par that contains a massive amount of detail to set up the story. A short sentence followed by a long one – or vice versa – can be very effective, although this one is *very* long and contains about four separate thoughts spanning more than a hundred years. Even with a feature, it is best to stick to one, or at most two thoughts, until you are up and running and have the reader with you. This par asks rather a lot of us as readers. Having waded through it, we still have no inkling what the story is – and you might think that the writer is rather trying our patience here.

I am not going to reveal what the story was about. Do you care? I suspect not. On that measure, this intro doesn't work as well as it should, because although it sets the scene well, it doesn't really engage us and give us a thirst to know more. That's a shame, because if you look these names up online, you will find that there is a fascinating story to be told here.

Here are two famous examples, quoted by David Randall, of the use of a very short sentence to convey a story of momentous importance. The first begins an account of the death of Hitler:

> The most hated man in the world is dead.

Then an account of a major earthquake in California that all but destroyed a city:

> San Francisco is gone.

You can see how the story needs to be very big indeed for this approach to work to the greatest effect. And since they are examples from 1945 and 1906, respectively, you can see that these techniques have been around for a very long time.

Don't get stuck. The point of the intro, whatever form it takes, is that it encapsulates or sets up the story, and your thinking about how it can best be told. But if you can't get it just right, write some of the rest of your story, maybe the background or context sections, and then come back to the intro when your thinking might have crystallised somewhat. You will see it in a different light, and may quickly find a solution that eluded you earlier.

With practice will come a feel both for an effective hard news intro, and for the most appropriate way of tacking softer stories. Experiment, and see what works and what does not. Read stories in the papers or online, decide whether or not you like the treatments and try to analyse why they work or where they fall short. Don't be tentative: as you have seen from many of the real examples quoted above, the professionals do not always do a great job. If you understand why some of their efforts were not successful, or can think of a better approach, the chances are you will soon be writing crisp, clear and confident stories of all different shapes and sizes.

Paragraph 2 and the body of the story

We have spent most of this chapter considering the intro because it is the most important element of any piece of journalism. As we have seen, it is loaded with responsibilities to set out the story and sell it, and if it fails to fulfil those functions effectively, the reader may never make it to the second paragraph. We have also noted that once you have your intro sorted out, the rest of the story should flow relatively easily and quickly.

We looked in the previous chapter at what comes after the intro, and how the inverted pyramid models illustrate the way a story is built once the foundations have been laid.

The job of the second par is to reprise the intro, supplementing it with supporting evidence or information that fills some of the gaps it has left. In ensuring that our intro is crisp and engaging, we have included only the most essential details of the story – just enough to signal the main news point and what it is about, and to make the reader want more. That means that we have left out quite a lot of the details – names, ages, addresses, times, locations, sources and so on. At least some of that detail will go into the second paragraph. It will flow logically from the intro, filling out the story, supporting what we have said in the intro and possibly introducing another angle and moving things on.

Let us return to our fictional story of the car that ploughed into the bus queue. We started off with a lengthy and cumbersome intro that covered the whole story, before breaking it down into three separate paragraphs:

> Four people, one a boy of 12, are critically ill in hospital in Newtown after a stolen car ploughed into a bus queue in the town centre.

> It happened near the junction of West Street and Queen Street at just after eleven o'clock last night.

> The casualties were taken to St Mary's Hospital. Police say the car driver was one of those injured.

Our intro sets out the main point of the story in outline terms. It tells us the *what*, and it gives us something about the *who* and the *where*. And it conveys some of the drama of the incident.

Our second paragraph adds more specific detail to the *where* – Newtown people reading this story will be familiar with the town centre, so the street names will enable them to establish exactly where the accident happened. This paragraph also tells us *when* the accident happened.

The next par gives us more detail still. From here, we will probably go back to the beginning and describe as best we can from the information we have exactly what happened, and the sequence of events that led to the accident.

This is by no means the definitive way of writing this story. There are no rights and few wrongs. Once you have put the main points into a sharply written intro, you will usually have choices about where to go next. As long as the second par clearly follows from the first, it will be a matter of taste – your personal view on the most effective way of telling the story. Our second par here could just as easily have said something like this, following the same intro:

> Four people, one a boy of 12, are critically ill in hospital in Newtown after a stolen car ploughed into a bus queue in the town centre.

> Police said the driver of the car was reported to have lost control and mounted the pavement. Fire crews had to cut him free from the wreckage.

In this version we have decided to give more *what* and *how* details before filling in the details of time and place. You might prefer this version.

With some of the storytelling techniques we have examined, you will have even more choice. If you are adopting a delayed drop approach (which you would not do on an action story like our example), you can choose how long you build up the suspense before revealing your punchline.

If you have a story with more than one strong angle, and you cannot comfortably accommodate them all in the intro, you can use the second paragraph to introduce a second line, which you will return to and expand upon later in the story. As we have discussed elsewhere, rather than cramming everything into a lengthy and indigestible intro, break it down into two or three sentences, with a different angle for each. That will work well, as long as it maintains a relationship with the intro, and doesn't look as though you are embarking on another story altogether. It will make it much easier to read and understand.

There can be no absolute rules about what you put in your second or subsequent pars. But each par after the intro should add to, or build on, the information we have already been given, without repeating any of it.

To adapt an example we have already looked at:

> Official figures show the economy is growing more slowly than expected.

The second paragraph of this story would tell us what those figures were and where they came from. Let us say that they had come from the Office for National Statistics. We could of course have put that in the intro:

> Figures from the Office for National Statistics show the economy is growing more slowly than expected.

But putting the whole cumbersome name at the start of the story acts as a drag on the pace of it, so we went for the shorter and perfectly accurate description: "official figures". That means we need to report as soon as possible exactly where those figures come from.

And what about the details of what the figures show? Let us say they show that the economy had grown by 0.2 per cent in the previous quarter, against a forecast growth of 0.4 per cent. We could have shoved all that into the intro too:

> Figures from the Office for National Statistics show the economy grew by 0.2 per cent in the last quarter, below the predicted growth rate of 0.4 per cent.

But we decided that we did not want to clutter up our intro with that level of detail. However, we now have an obligation to include it as soon as possible, because it is the evidence that supports what was said in the intro.

So our story might go something like this:

> Official figures show the economy is growing more slowly than expected.

> Latest figures from the Office for National Statistics show growth of 0.2 per cent in the last quarter. This was well below the predicted growth rate of 0.4 per cent.

Instead of putting all the information into one sentence, we have divided it into three, and made it easier to read and understand. From here we will probably move to an examination of the reasons for the lower growth rate. And now is perhaps the time to consider the possible consequences – the material that was in the intro of the original story as published. So Par 3 might say:

> The figures cast doubt on the government's ability to meet its target of reducing the debt burden in this financial year.

The second par – and possibly the third and fourth as well – gives evidence and information that supports what we have read in the intro. It does not simply repeat the intro, or, worse, change the subject altogether. Nor does it hit the reader with too much extra material. It is the next component in a logical process that builds the story in a readily digestible and easy-to-read way.

If the story contains an allegation or an accusation, then report the response immediately afterwards. This is especially important in a court case: "Smith faces six counts of robbery. He has pleaded not guilty to all the charges".

Later paragraphs will be used to fill the story out further with more background materials, more details, more quotes and more explanations. The order in which you introduce them is up to you. You can if you wish introduce a narrative or chronological approach, taking the reader back to the beginning and guiding them through the rest of the story. This will mean a par beginning with a phrase such as "it all started when….", or "the day began with…". Keep the same style and tone throughout. Just because we have now brought the reader with us into the body of the story, that does not mean we can suddenly give up trying, and throw in several paragraphs of dense background or lengthy quotes.

News reports seldom have the luxury of elegant pay-offs or rounded conclusions. The editing process means that they tend to just come to a halt. It is different for features or longer form pieces, as we shall see in a later chapter. The key thing for a news report, as we have already discovered, is that no important information is left to the very end of the story. It may be cut, and never make it into print. Even if it does, the reader may never read that far – often the case with online stories. In news reports, never save anything juicy or significant for an ending, however classy. It is too risky.

Here is a simple example of the whole process in action, a basic hard news story taken at random from the pages of the *Daily Telegraph* and following the pattern of the inverted triangle. As it is rather a sad story, I have changed some of the names and details.

> A British soldier serving in Afghanistan has died in a suspected suicide.

A good crisp intro of only 12 words that sets out the story very clearly. There are no names, no attributed sources, no details, just the bare facts. We would probably want to read on. We have been given the *who* and the *what*, which are usually the two most important elements of the intro. We also have the *where*, which is obviously important here.

> Private Arthur Brown, from Stoke-on-Trent died at the end of the last month while on deployment in Kabul.

More details that build on what we have already been told in outline. We have the soldier's name, where he came from – more *who* – and then we are given the *when* and more details of the *where*:

> The Ministry of Defence announced that that the 24-year-old from Second Battalion, the Parachute Regiment, died of a "non-battle injury".

We are now given the source of the information – a primary source. We will feel confident about writing the story on the basis of a statement from the Ministry of Defence. We also have the soldier's age and regiment, so the picture of him is slowly building.

The writer did not need to take three pars to convey this basic information. Here is what might have happened if she hadn't, and had shoehorned it all into one:

> A British soldier, 24-year-old Private Arthur Brown from Stoke-on-Trent, died while serving in the Afghan capital, Kabul, at the end of last month in a suspected suicide, the Ministry of Defence has announced, describing it as a "non-battle injury".

Too long. Too much detail. Hard to take in at a single reading. It also takes too long to get the element of this story that makes it particularly newsworthy: that he killed himself while on active duty. Instead, the reporter has let the story unfold at a pace we can easily keep up with. You can see how much better the unpacked version is.

Back to the story as printed:

> It comes after the veterans minister voiced concerns that there had been a rise in the number of suicides this year among former soldiers who had fought in Afghanistan between 2002 and 2014.

> So far this year 14 former and serving British personnel are believed to have died by suicide.

This is context and background. It doesn't tell us anything else about our story, but sets it against a background of previous suicides of soldiers who had served Afghanistan. We might deduce from this that serving in Afghanistan is particularly stressful for the military. This is not developed further in the story, but might suggest a follow-up piece.

> In a tribute to Private Brown on the British Army Homepage, it described him as a soldier who "served with distinction".

> "His soldiering skills were widely recognised and he was characterised as an optimistic, capable and compassionate soldier. He was highly respected, bit by his chain-of-command and by his peers", it said.

> "He will be remembered for his passion, determination and selfless attitude."

Some direct quotes now to break up the narrative and tell us a little more about Private Brown the man, in the shape of glowing tributes to him – although none offers any hint as to why he might have taken his own life. In fact, the questions yet to be answered in this story, the *how* and the *why*, are never addressed. Perhaps we do not know. The writer could have signalled her recognition of this with a sentence saying something like: "the circumstances surrounding Private Brown's death have not been made known". This at least tells the reader that the paper realises these details are missing, but has been unable to obtain them.

> He was also described as "popular throughout the battalion" with "an impressive career" ahead of him.

The story finishes by returning to the tribute, which is lengthy and exceptionally full. It does not add a great deal to the quotes we have already read, and so this story is eminently cuttable from the bottom. There is nothing in these late pars that should have been reported higher up. But you can see how this story follows the models illustrated by the inverted triangles we met in the last chapter.

Choosing the best quotes

When you write up your story it will be with a combination of direct and reported speech. To achieve the greatest impact, you want to put the best lines from your interviews into direct quotes, to give the story authenticity and energy, and so that the audience is hearing exactly what the person said. To do that of course, you need an accurate note, because anything that appears in inverted commas has got to be as close as you can get to the actual words used. If you are not confident that you can do that, you will have to use indirect or reported speech – summarising what was said in your own words. You will also use reported speech to fill in background and to summarise those parts of the interview that do not need to be in direct quotes.

The quotes you select for direct reporting in full should be relevant to the story and help with the overall narrative or the picture you are painting. In a news story, they will probably summarise the speaker's viewpoint on the subject at issue. You should also look for quotes that have spontaneity and colour and bring both the speaker and the story to life.

Look for a strong image or telling phrase. If a speaker uses an analogy or makes a point through an anecdote, that will almost certainly make the best quote. Consider this quote:

> For the moment, we have been told we have to stay indoors and only go out when it is absolutely necessary. It wasn't so bad when that was the case for everyone, but it feels weird now it is just us. We are managing ok, but it is hard sometimes. It is like watching everyone having fun at a party to which you haven't been invited. Or being at a party when everyone is getting steadily drunk and you are stone cold sober.

The speaker here is making only one point, but if you wanted a short sharp quote to summarise what is being said, you would surely use the second half of his comments, not the first. The speaker has come up with a couple of great analogies that really bring the situation to life. If you are a broadcaster, that is the bit you would include in your soundbite. It makes the speaker's key point in a vivid and engaging way.

Quotes that do not express the speaker's view or add to the texture of the piece can safely be put into reported speech. There is no point in putting basic information into direct speech. It looks odd: "Mr Smith said: 'we will be meeting again to discuss this matter a week on Thursday'." "'The firm was founded in 1971 and now has 35 employees,' said Mrs Jones." Look for the quotes that add value.

Here is an imaginary example. You are doing an interview with Jordie Jamieson, a teenage vlogging sensation who has rapidly achieved celebrity with her own *YouTube* channel. She posts regular videos, mainly focused on cosmetics, lifestyle and beauty. The main news point for your interview is that she has just been signed up to launch her own brand of cosmetics. But you also want to ask her about how it all began.

You had intended to record this interview on your phone, but when the time came you discovered your battery was flat, so you had to rely on a written note. If you had made a recording, this is what you would hear Jordie actually saying when you played back this part of the interview:

YOU: All this started because one day you decide to post a video!

JJ: Yeah, it's mad isn't it? Seems like ages ago now but actually it was only last year. Was just a short thing about a day out with friends. I was only…..I mean I was just like filming bits on my phone. I do that all the time. I never meant…..I wasn't even thinking I would ever do anything with it.

YOU: So why did you?

JJ: So it wasn't straight away, it was maybe like the next day or…..we were back at school and looking all our social media stuff and saying…..like, there's loads of stuff there obviously but…….it didn't seem like, I don't know, there wasn't anything …..there wasn't anyone out there who was like us if you get me. Does that seem ridiculous? We sort of felt we were not being represented, girls like us at our age.

YOU: So you decided to fill the gap?

JJ: Yeah, no I suppose so. I got the idea in the bath actually. I get all my best ideas there! I was thinking about it…..and then I suddenly thought like maybe we could do something ourselves. Or I could. Came to me in a flash of light! I got really excited about it straight away and I jumped out of the bath and sat in my room making a video of our day out with my hair still dripping wet!

YOU: I guess you weren't prepared for what happened next?

JJ: No way! It was a bit scary actually. So I just shared the video round our group and I wasn't really planning…. I mean I thought that would be the end of it. But somehow it got shared and liked and passed around and suddenly everyone was like, hey that was great, where's the next one? It seemed……before I knew it, I was like making stuff every few days and loads of people I never even knew were following me. That's when I set up the YouTube channel, and after that it was crazy.

YOU: Over a million subscribers now.

JJ: Yeah, I just cannot get my head round that. And loads more on Instagram too. Sometimes it feels like all this is happening to another person. Why little old me? It just took off and I was completely knocked out by it. It's mental.

She talked quickly and – like everyone else – in broken sentences, her words following where her thoughts took her. You did your best to keep up, but it was not possible for you to get down every word. When you come to write up this section of the interview, this is what your notes look like:

YOU: how start?

JJ: mad isn't it? Seems like ages ago actually only last year. just a short…..day out with friends. was just filming bits on phone….didn't think would ever do anything with it.

YOU: why?

JJ: not straight away maybe the next day or…..at school and looking at social media stuff….loads of stuff there obviously nothing….no-one like us if you get me. ridiculous? felt not being represented, girls like us

YOU: fill gap?

JJ: idea in bath. best ideas! suddenly thought maybe we could do something, or I could. flash of light! really excited jumped out of bath and made video with hair still dripping wet!

YOU: not prepared for reaction?

JJ: a bit scary actually. just shared the video round among group and thought end of it. But somehow it got shared and liked and everyone was like, hey that was great, where's the next? Before …. was making stuff every few days. loads following me. Set up YT channel and after that. crazy.

YOU: over one million.

JJ: just cannot get my head round that. Instagram too. Sometimes feels like all happening to another person. little old me? just took off and completely knocked out. It's mental.

So you haven't got everything, but you have got the main points, and you have enough to write a few lively paragraphs for your feature with some direct and indirect quotes. What are the best points she made – the ones about which you want to quote her directly?

I would suggest there are probably four of them:

> how she spotted a gap in the market
> how she got the idea of filling it
> how it took off
> how she reacted to the response.

This is what the relevant sections of your notes has to say in those three areas:

> at school and looking all our social media stuff….loads of stuff there obviously nothing….no-one like us if you get me. ridiculous? felt not being represented, girls like us

> idea in bath. best ideas! suddenly thought maybe we could do something, or I could. flash of light! really excited jumped out of bath and made video with hair still dripping wet!

> just shared the video round among group and thought end of it. But somehow it got shared and liked and everyone was like, hey that was great, where's the next?

> just cannot get my head round that. Sometimes feels like all happening to another person. little old me? just took off and I was completely knocked out. It's mental.

Not only are these the key points of this section of the interview, they are also the areas in which you have extracted the best quotes – even if you have not got every one of them down verbatim. You still have enough for a write-up of this section that could look something like this.

> Only a year or so ago, Jordie was just like any other teenage schoolgirl, hanging out with friends and checking her social media accounts. Now she is a star vlogger with her own YouTube channel and more than a million subscribers, with half as many again following her on Instagram.

> "It's a bit scary actually," she says of this amazing rise to fame. The first video she made – of a day out with friends – was not intended for anyone outside her own circle. "But somehow it got shared and liked and everyone was like, hey that was great, where's the next one?

> "Before I knew it, I was making stuff every few days and loads of people were following me. It was crazy."

> The idea stemmed from a feeling that there was nothing out there that felt directly relevant to Jordie and her friends. "There was no-one like us if you get me. We felt we were not being represented, girls like us."

> The notion that she could fill that gap came to her in the bath. "I get all my best ideas there! I had a flash of light and suddenly thought I could do something. I jumped out and made a video of our day out with my hair still dripping wet!"

> She is still coming to terms with what happened next. "I just cannot get my head round it. It's mental."

There are any number of ways of doing this, and this is only one suggestion. But it illustrates a few key points around note-taking, picking quotes and your subsequent write-up.

As we have said, if you are not recording the interview, you need to be sure that you have some good quotes that you can put inside inverted commas. Even with shorthand, it is not easy to get down every word – so concentrate on the key words that will enable you to reconstruct the full quote later. So for example, the note: "idea in bath. best ideas", is enough for you to reconstruct the full quote: "I got the idea in the bath. I get all my best ideas there".

If you are recording, obviously it is much easier to write your quotes word for word. If you have plenty of time, that is not a problem. If you don't, it can be – going back over a recording of even a few minutes, moving backwards and forwards to find the best bits and then transcribing them can be a laborious process.

You do not have to follow the chronology of the interview. In the example, you took Jordie through her identification of a gap in the market, her idea for filling it, how she did that, how it took off and how she felt about her success. Perfectly logical, and the best way of doing it. But in the written version, you can move about if you want to. In my specimen version, I began with her current fame and then worked backwards to when it all began. It is a matter of choice and personal style.

It will not always be possible for your direct quotes to be 100 per cent accurate. People do not speak in perfectly formed sentences. You may find that you need to tidy things up a bit, removing all the ums and ers and false starts. That is fine, as long as you are faithful to the sense. You can construct a quote by taking a bit from one part of the interview and joining it on to a bit from another part. That is acceptable too, as long as you are doing this simply to make the story read and flow better and make it easier for the audience. What you must avoid at all costs is putting words into peoples' mouths, or moving things around so that you distort the original tone and meaning, and do not give a faithful representation of what was said and the context in which it was said.

Time to check

When you have finished writing, however tight you are for time, do some basic checks. Sometimes if you print your story and read a hard copy, you may spot things that you had not noticed on the screen.

Check that you have correctly spelled names, addresses, place names and any other proper nouns.
Check your other spellings.
Check you have accurately recorded ages and any numbers.
Check that you have transcribed your quotes accurately.
Check that the story as a whole feels as though it has the sort of tone and character that you wanted to try to achieve.
Check that it seems to read well. Reading it aloud can help, even with a newspaper/online script. Is everything clear and unambiguous? Do some of the longer sentences need chopping into two? Are some of the paragraphs too long?
Check that you have answered the questions a reader might want to ask.
Check that it is the length you were asked for.

The sub-editor

In a traditional newsroom, your finished story would be approved by the newsdesk and then sent to the sub-editors. The subs desk that once formed the beating heart of most print newsrooms has now largely disappeared in all but the biggest operations. The sub-editors had a variety of roles, from basic checking through rewriting and the addition of headlines to the layout of the final page.

Technology and a decline in staff numbers have changed the way these operations work, although the pace of change varies from one organisation to another. In many, the name "sub-editor" does not exist any more as a separate job description. Away from the nationals, sub-editing functions are now more likely to be performed by "page finishers" within a content management team that checks and publishes stories across a number of platforms.

What this means is that as a reporter, you may well be expected to carry out some of the duties that in the past would have been the domain of the sub-editor. So it is as well to be aware of what those duties are, and how you can help the machine run smoothly and efficiently.

What is sub-editing?

Whoever is responsible for it, and whatever the job title of that person, the business of subbing involves, among other things:

– Detecting mistakes that the reporter has made: spellings, names, dates, "facts", grammar, typos.
– Removing slang, journalese, clichés, jargon.
– Cutting stories to the required length if need be.
– Rewriting completely or in part as necessary. Sometimes this might be to combine two different reports into one, or to incorporate new information into the original story (a "writethrough").
– Updating or adding useful additional information in a secondary format – a fact box, a link, a panel with more background.
– Ensuring the story is legally sound – possibly by checking with a lawyer.
– Making sure everything conforms to the house style.
– In a print operation, fitting the stories into the page templates; writing headlines, standfirsts and adding other design features.
– For digital output, looking for keywords and widgets and other devices that will help extend the findability and reach of the story.
– Cropping and scaling pictures.
– Making sure that the whole offer is visually attractive as well as being journalistically sound and easy to read.

Some of this is about applying a second pair of eyes to the content, to look for anything that feels wrong or might have been missed. It is about bringing a close focus and critical eye to everything that is going to be published and subjecting it to meticulous and thorough scrutiny. If you have done your job properly as a reporter, then few changes will be required from the finishers. Always look at your work after it has been published, in whatever form, to see what changes have been made to it. Make sure you understand the reasons for those changes, so that you can avoid repeating any mistakes you have made.

Headlines

Depending on the practice where you work, you might be expected to write a headline for your story, especially if it is destined for publication on a website. The most basic requirement of a headline is that it fits the space available. Although all headlines are designed to draw the eye and sell the story, different factors apply when writing for print or for online. In print, a teasing headline or a pun might work well. Online, your headline is selling the story in a different way through keywords, and those puns will very rarely work. Aim for the clear, unambiguous and instantly accessible. (See the section on search engine optimisation in Chapter 13.)

Some style pointers:

– News headlines give the essence of the story, but in even more truncated form than the intro.
– Headlines do not end with full stops, also known as full points, although they can use commas, dashes, question marks or ellipsis (…) Inverted commas are always single.
– The headline and the intro should not be too similar. If you have got a brilliant headline, but it echoes too much of what the intro says, consider keeping the headline and rewriting the intro. It is the headline that first draws the reader to the story.
– Lots of short words that work well in headlines have become journalistic clichés – bid, row, probe, quiz, shock, axe, hit, fury, blast. Avoid them if you can.
– Headlines should not repeat words that are in other headlines on the same page.

Headlines often work with standfirsts, or sub-heads/decks. You are in effect writing two headlines, the second building on the first, and at more length. Here is an example:

Brexit saves MPs from the boundary chop
Plans to cut the number of constituencies by 50 are shelved as members now have "greater workload".

If you have a standfirst like this, adding some story detail, the headline does not need to carry so much of the burden of explaining the story, and can be written more with impact in mind:

Brexit boost for MPs
Plans to cut the number of constituencies by 50 are shelved as members now have "greater workload".

Standfirsts are widely used in features, and will often include the byline – the writer's name. Here is an example:

Now is the time to dig in and get gardening
Whether you have beds or a simple window box, outdoor space is more important than ever, says Debora Robertson.

A subsidiary or supporting headline placed above, rather than below the main headline, is called a strap, or strapline. It performs a similar function to the standfirst, but this time will usually be shorter than the main headline rather than longer. Here is an example:

Lib Dems call for return of concessions
Bring back free parking, council urged.

Text breaks

A big slab of text, even if split up into short paragraphs, can look very uninviting to the eye as it skims across the page deciding whether or not to read a story. A dense mass can be broken up, and the page made more visually appealing, in a number of ways:

– **With a pullquote**, or pullout quote. A few eye-catching words are copied from the main body of the report and pasted into a gap between pars in a larger typeface – and probably a different font. They break up the text and help persuade the reader to commit to the story. Pullouts can be used in other parts of the page too, to add interest and visual appeal, especially if the pictures are not very strong.
– **With a crosshead or sidehead** (assuming your template allows for them). Both are differing forms of sub-headings. Crossheads are centred, sideheads ranged left. They are one or two words inserted between pars at appropriate points, again to reduce the density of the copy.

Captions

All still photographs and embedded online video require captions, describing what we can see or are about to see. In a newspaper, an extended caption of 100 words or so may be the whole article – it is a self-contained story linked to the picture. It is up to the reporter to provide the details for the caption. In a picture spread, that will often be little more than a list of the names of those featured, with some details about when, where and why the picture was taken. Make sure you get the names down properly, and in the correct order.

Style

This chapter and the last have deliberately taken a rather mechanical approach to the business of writing a story – deconstructing the basic model and then putting it back together again. Once you have mastered the principles, you will want to bring your own style and character to what you write, especially with longer pieces that give you a little more latitude. You will find some thoughts about developing a distinctive writing style in Chapter 21.

11
Storytelling: language and style

a living language…..house style…..grammar…..use of language…..general points of style…..pronunci-ation…..spelling…..American English…..punctuation…..loaded words…..journalese…..cliché.

English is a rich, flexible and complex language that is constantly evolving. That versatility is one of its strengths and glories. Words fall out of use or change their meanings. New ones emerge, often prompted by new technologies, and the need to invent the terminology to describe them.

The evolution of language, written and spoken, gives rise to perennial and frequently tedious debates between purists who want to maintain standards, as they would see it, by preserving traditional usages, and those who take a more relaxed view of the fluidity of the language, and are happy to let it develop as it will. For every person who writes indignant letters to journalists about misplaced apostrophes and split infinitives, there is another urging those people to "wake up and smell the coffee", or "get with the programme", which no doubt provokes the complainants to new depths of fury. Relax, is the message. Embrace the swirling currents of usage that have characterised our language for centuries.

The "relaxed" camp never fails to observe that English is in any case an amalgam of many languages and dialects, principally Anglo-Saxon, Latin and French, and is all the richer for it. Over the past three centuries, Britain's colonial past and multicultural present have introduced West Indian, African and Asian influences. In the modern age, the dynamism and creativity of American English is by far the greatest influence on changes to the mother tongue. When we talk of English as the global language, we are really talking about American English. Historically, we have welcomed new words and sayings with open arms. We are often spoilt for choice among many words that have essentially the same meaning. If you look at historical documents and writings, it is clear that spellings, too, change over time, sometimes quite dramatically.

Most recently, social networks have had a big effect on our language, and arguably a less benign one. Here the rules of spelling, grammar and punctuation command little or no respect. This is very much part of the ephemeral character of these platforms, where speed and immediacy are everything, and nothing is intended to last very long. What we might describe as proper or traditional English usage goes out of the window, and that is partly the point. For the moment at least, this grammatical anarchy is largely confined to cyberspace. It should not be an excuse for journalists to abandon their standards, even though they increasingly swim in these waters. While keeping pace with change, journalism should do nothing to encourage the coarsening or degrading of the language.

Unless you are a keen student of these matters, there is no particular need to get entangled in this debate. Journalists sit at the crossroads of the argument: they must be able to write and speak proper and correct English; but they must also show that they are alert to new trends in the language, and incorporate them in what they write and broadcast. It is part of remaining relevant to their audiences. Beyond that, both written and broadcast journalism aim for an easy and accessible style, uncomplicated, unambiguous and capable of immediate comprehension. It tolerates a certain informality that often involves bending the rules and sometimes breaking them. But it does not condone sloppiness or rank bad grammar.

For all the changes, the ability to write well is still a fundamental journalistic necessity. That means having a good working knowledge and grasp of what is sometimes called "standard English", its rules and conventions, its rights and wrongs. You do not necessarily need to understand the technical definitions of pronouns and prepositions, imperfect tenses and subjunctives, in order to be able to write and express yourself in a clear and correct manner. If English is your first language, you will have absorbed its rhythms and cadences from birth. Your education should have filled in at least some of the supporting theory, and schooled you in the effective use of the written word.

So your style can and should be informal and conversational, but it must also be rooted in the essential rules of English and what is generally regarded as good practice. You can split the odd infinitive with a degree of impunity, but if your writing is full of grammatical gaffes and errors of punctuation and spelling, your prospects in journalism are likely to be somewhat limited.

When it comes to committing words to the page, you can do no better than refer back to one of our golden rules. Write, and broadcast, for your audience. Think about who they are, what they know already and what they don't know, what they want and what they need. Beyond that, consider how they speak and think, and the best way to communicate with them. Then, within the parameters of the medium in which you are working, write accordingly. Always ask: have I been clear about what I mean to say, and will my audience understand it? By "understand" we do not mean whether or not they are clever enough intellectually to grasp the story; rather, whether it has been presented to them in such a way as to make it easy for them to consume and absorb. If it hasn't – or if something sounds or feels not quite right – the solution is simple: rewrite it.

Spelling is much more of a black and white issue than grammar – social media aside, there are clear rights and wrongs. It is easy to check spellings in a way that is not readily possible with grammar and punctuation, so transgressions are less forgivable. With a pc or a smartphone, you can check a spelling (and a precise meaning, which might be just as important) within a matter of seconds. There is no excuse for spelling mistakes. Good spelling is less about proper usage and more about the basic accuracy that lies at the core of good journalism. Accuracy with spelling is as important as accuracy with facts and figures. Poor spelling will drive your editors and sub-editors wild and – if they reach the page – irritate your readers beyond measure. It undermines the authority and trustworthiness of your work every bit as much as factual errors. You should make it a point of honour never to be guilty of spelling mistakes in your work.

In sum: take it as read that you need to understand the basic rules of grammar and punctuation – in the sense of being able to apply those rules, rather than being able to define them in technical terms. Once you are in that position, you can experiment with the language as you develop your own style. But look on good spelling as a non-negotiable requirement.

It is not part of the purpose of this chapter to teach you good grammar; there are plenty of other places you can go for that, and where you can study good English and good writing for journalists. The books of Wynford Hicks are particularly recommended (see Further Reading). So are the *Economist Style Guide* and the *Times Style Guide*, both brilliantly clear-thinking and comprehensive companions to those tackling issues of grammar, spelling and style in a journalism context.

House style

Most newspapers and broadcasters have a house style governing the way they spell certain words if alternatives exist, whether or not they capitalise or hyphenate them, whether they use "%" or "per cent" and very many other points of detail. Stylebooks are designed to reflect good practice and to ensure a consistent approach. They are also great sources of knowledge and wisdom that will help keep you out of trouble, if, for example, you are not sure about the difference between Islamic and Islamist or principle and principal. Some – like the *Economist Style Guide* and the *Times Style Guide* – are printed, or available online.

House styles do vary between organisations, and if they do not produce formal guidelines you may have to pick up custom and practice as you go along. If you are working for an organisation that has a guidebook setting out house style, make sure you are familiar with it, and abide by its strictures. Occasionally, as we shall see, there is no definitive "right" way of doing things.

Grammar

Singular/plural

Some words, especially collective nouns, are singular but can look and sound better when used in the plural. Most political writers, for example, refer to the government as plural: "the government have decided to….", although "the government has decided…" is fine too. You can use either: the key thing is to conform to house style and to be consistent throughout the story. So:

"The government **have** begun to implement **their** economic strategy"   Fine.
"The government **has** begun to implement **its** economic strategy"   Fine.
"The government **have** begun to implement **its** economic strategy"   Horrible.
"The government **has** begun to implement **their** economic strategy"   Horrible.

This crops up a lot in sport. A sports team, for example, is singular, because "team" is a collective noun. But you are much more likely to hear "*England **have** drawn the first Test against Australia*" than "*England **has** drawn….*". You are more likely to hear "*Manchester United **have** won the FA Cup*", than "*Manchester United **has** won….*". The conventions of sporting language, and the fact that the plural version simply feels better, point you to plural usage. If you want to use the singular, you will not be wrong – although you may sound to a sports fan as if you lack authority. But having decided one way or another, be consistent all the way through.

Remember that contractions such as "none" are singular. "None" is short for "no one" or "not one". But you will often hear: "*Of all the British players to qualify, none **have** made it into the second round*", which is not right. You would not say: "*Of all the British players to qualify, no one **have** made it into the second round*". "Have" should be "has" in both these cases. The same is true of "each", "everyone", "everybody", "nobody" and "someone". All of these are singular. None is plural.

"Me" and "I"

Should it be "you and I"? Or "you and me"? There is a rule here, and some people get very aerated about this, but since both versions are in common use I personally don't think it matters. If you or someone who employs you thinks otherwise, go and look up Subjective and Objective Pronouns.

Also

"Also" means "as well as". So it does not make sense to use it in the negative, as in this sentence: "*Mr Smith did not turn up for the meeting, and Mr Jones was also not there*". Use the "neither/nor" construction instead: "*Neither Mr Smith nor Mr Jones turned up for the meeting.*" Or "*Mr Smith did not turn up for the meeting. Mr Jones wasn't there either.*"

Apostrophes

Oh dear. I do not propose to venture too far into this murky area other than to offer the general rule that:

> you DO need an apostrophe when you are talking about the possessive, or something belonging – 'John's pen', 'Jane's book'.

> you DO NOT need an apostrophe when you are talking about the plural, or more than one of something – 'The pens', 'The books'.

A very common error is to write "MP's" when referring to more than one MP. It should of course be "MPs". The same applies to references to decades. It is the 1970s, not the 1970's.

Beyond that, be careful to distinguish between the contraction (where the apostrophe takes the place of a missing letter) and the possessive in these common instances:

> 'Your' (belonging to you) and 'you're' (short for 'you are')
> 'Their' (belonging to them) and 'they're' (short for 'they are')
> 'Its' (belonging to it) and 'it's' (short for 'it is')
> 'Whose' (belonging to someone unknown: "whose coat is this?") and 'who's' (short for 'who is').

Even if you type it correctly, spell checking systems will often unhelpfully change things back to the wrong version for you when you are not looking. Keep an eye on them.

There are always exceptions waiting to trip you up. So "yours" and 'theirs' – referring to something belonging to you or them – do not require an apostrophe.

Tautology

A tautology means saying the same thing twice – using extra words you do not need because the words you have already used have done the job on their own. Common examples, with the redundant words in bold type:

– The reason **why.** Worse, "the reason **why** is **because**….": a double tautology.
– The minister said he may **possibly** resign.
– They are **equally** as good as each other.
– The town was **completely** surrounded by flood waters.
– The consensus **of opinion** is in favour.
– The recipe comprises **of** just six ingredients.
– The news came without **advance** warning.
– All that is **past** history now.
– He had an **exact** replica made.
– The **future** prospects are bleak.
– He announced a raft of **new** initiatives.

Note also that the centre is the middle of something. So a dispute may centre *on* a certain issue, but it cannot centre *around* it.

Conjunctions

Grammarian zealots don't like it, but there is nothing wrong with starting a sentence with "And" or "But" or "Because". And since you will be trying to avoid long sentences, you will find that you very often do so, as you divide one longer sentence into two short ones. These are the words that will link the two sentences, and make it easier for the audience. Purists object, but it is widely accepted in journalism. However, do not start a sentence with "Also".

Modifiers

The subject of the first part of a sentence must relate properly to the second part.

Crossing the road, a car struck her. It wasn't the car that was crossing the road, it was the poor woman who was hit by it. This should read: *She was crossing the road when she was struck by a car.*

Born in Manchester, Smith's parents were both schoolteachers. It was not the parents who were born in Manchester, it was Smith. *Born in Manchester, the son of schoolteachers, Smith....*

Mistakes of this kind are very common. They are called hanging, or dangling participles or modifiers.

From/to, between/and

"From" must always be followed by "to", "between" by "and". This often crops up when referring to dates:

The First World War lasted from 1914–18	Wrong.
The First World War lasted **from** 1914 **to** 1918	Right.
The First World War was between 1914–18	Wrong.
The First World War was between 1914 and 1918	Right.

"Only"

To avoid confusion, place it next to the word/phrase it refers to:

So not: *You can **only** take advantage of the offer if you are a member.*
Rather: *You can take advantage of the offer **only** if you are a member.*

Split infinitives

We tend to take a more relaxed view of these than was once the case. The infinitive form of a verb is "to walk", "to talk", "to live". You split it if you put an adverb between the two words: "to quickly walk", "to loudly talk", "to happily live". As their name suggests, adverbs should *follow* the verb, not precede it. But a split infinitive is usually an offence against style rather than grammar. It just doesn't feel or sound right a lot of the time. If you think it sounds or feels fine, then don't worry about breaking the rules.

Trying

You try *to* do something, not try *and* do something.

Metaphors

It is easy to mix metaphors almost without realising it, because our language is so rich and idiomatic, and many metaphors are so familiar to us that they are simply part of our normal everyday speech. If this is a crime, we are all guilty.

If you can think of an original metaphor, good for you. If not, try to resist the temptation to fall back on well-worn and often tired images that have long ago lost their colour and vividness. Better just to use simple straightforward English. The more metaphors you use, the greater the likelihood that you will mix them, offering your bewildered readers a whole host of different images and clashing ideas. It might look colourful and colloquial, but it is unlikely to be much of an aid to understanding.

Many of the metaphors we use in everyday speech almost without thinking, come from the military, from the weather and from sport. There is nothing wrong with them for the most part, as long as they are appropriate, and as long as they are not all mixed together. The frequency with which they are used means some are hackneyed and should be avoided.

Football and cricket in particular have given us hundreds of metaphors. And considering how relatively little enthusiasm there is in the UK for the American game of baseball, it is remarkable how many baseball images have found their way into everyday English usage:

– Step up to the plate
– Reach first base
– Knock it out of the park
– Ballpark figure
– Take a raincheck
– Three strikes and out
– All bases covered
– Curve ball
– Whole new ball game.

Pool is not as big a game here as it is there, but we often talk about being "behind the 8 ball" – in other words, in a tricky situation. Other sports have terms for the same dilemma – one can be snookered, stymied or on a sticky wicket.

If you want to use these images, fine – as long as you are satisfied that you know what they mean and are therefore employing them appropriately, and – critically – that your audience will also know what they mean.

He/she/it/them

Make sure when you use these words that it is clear who you are referring to.

> He told the court he had seen his brother that day but not his cousin, and he had asked him what he was doing and if he had seen him.

Who asked who what?

It is common practice to break the rules of grammar so as to avoid endless repetition of his and her. I have done so throughout this book. It is correct to say: "If the listener hears something he or she likes, he or she is likely to remember that when he or she tunes in again". Correct, but somewhat wearisome to read if repeated like this. It is technically *not* correct to say: "If the listener hears something they like, they are likely to remember that when they tune in again". But it is clearer, less fussy and reflects common usage. And most importantly, it is readily understandable.

References to individuals should generally use the personal pronouns they use to describe themselves. This is a sensitive area. If in doubt, refer up.

After/following

These can suggest a sequence of events that did not happen. "He was badly hurt after/following an accident." He was injured in the accident, not after it.

Verbalisation

There is probably no such word. I use it to describe the horrible modern tendency to turn all sorts of innocent nouns into verbs. It may be that this battle is lost, and that we must get used to seeing words such as impact, access, action, progress, trial, leverage and bus used as verbs.

Still, there is no verb "to hospitalise", at least not on this side of the Atlantic. People who need medical treatment are taken to hospital.

Direct speech and indirect speech

Reporting accurately what someone says is a core journalistic skill, but it is surprising how many journalists get themselves in a tangle over direct and reported speech: when to use quotation marks and when to change tenses.

Direct speech is when you are quoting the exact words that someone has said, and putting them inside quotation marks: *Councillor Jones said: "This is an outrageous waste of public money which is not in the best interests of the town."* Direct quotes are a vital element of a story, because they are primary sources – we are being told exactly what was said, without adornment, interpretation or spin. They give your reports immediacy, and, visually, break up the blocks of text. But if you use direct quotes, the words must be those that were uttered. You must on no account paraphrase or summarise what someone has said, and then put those words in direct quotes. Never make up a direct quote that you think captures the gist of what was said. You can also report people unfairly if you quote them accurately but choose partial or unrepresentative quotes.

With indirect or reported speech, you have more latitude. Here you can summarise or abridge remarks. But you must reflect fairly the thrust of what was said. If you take too many liberties, and distort the argument by oversimplifying it or being unduly selective about what you report, you will not be producing an accurate account.

Traditionally, when you put something into reported speech rather than direct, you move everything back a tense. *Councillor Jones said it was an outrageous use of public money, which was not in the best interests of the town.* That was once an unbreakable grammatical rule, but these days you see it broken as often as not, and the present tense employed. *Councillor Jones says it is an outrageous use of public money, which is not in the best interests of the town.* This is now regarded by some as acceptable, especially if your report appears on the same day that Councillor Jones made his remarks. The present tense gives them immediacy. But there is a subtle difference in meaning between the two. *Councillor Jones **said** it **was** an outrageous use of public money* clearly indicates that this is what Councillor Jones said at the time. *Councillor Jones **says** it **is** an outrageous use of public money* implies that the councillor is simply reaffirming a position he has previously taken on the issue. Traditionalists prefer the change of tense in the interests of clarity and good grammar. It is certainly preferable when you are reporting court cases and public events. But, as with so many other things, the key is consistency. If either form is acceptable, mixing the two is not. *Councillor Jones* **said** *it* **is** *an outrageous use of public money which, he* **added,** **is** *not in the best interests of the town* is inconsistent and muddled writing.

You can, of course, combine the two forms – and may have to if your shorthand lets you down mid-quote. *Councillor Jones said: "This is an outrageous use of public money." He said it was not in the best interests of the town.*

Tenses

Building on the previous section, you will often have a choice of which tense to use when writing your story. Normally you will be reporting something that has happened, and so the past tense will be the default. But use of the present tense can sometimes add immediacy and drama to your story, and it makes it sound as though you actually witnessed what you are describing. "The car comes to the junction. The driver isn't concentrating on what he is doing and pulls out without looking. He runs straight into a lorry." If appropriate, it can be effective, but it can also be wearisome if overused, especially in straightforward news pieces.

Sports pundits often use something called the historic present to describe incidents during matches. "He's beaten his man on the outside and gone to the byline. He's crossed the ball and Smith has nodded it home." It might be all right for live commentary, but it doesn't work for a written report. The choice of tenses is another weapon in your stylistic armoury. Think about what works best for each particular story. If in doubt, stick with the past tense.

Adjectives

Be ruthless. Do you really need them? All of them? Are they adding anything to your description? Or are you just using them to add a bit of artificial weight to your story? Adjectives like "big", "huge", "bumper", "massive", "astonishing" are all used in this way. Ask yourself whether your story would be any the worse without them – or whether it would be preferable to use a different adjective that actually imparted some genuine information. Beware of adjectives that contain value judgements: "tragic", "incredible", "amazing", "astonishing", "fabulous", "miraculous", "fantastic", "unfortunate", "sad".

If you are putting two words together to make an adjective – "well-known", "high-scoring", "extramarital" – remember to join them with a hyphen to indicate that they represent a single thought. Otherwise you change the meaning. Dramatically so in the case of extra-marital.

Brackets/dashes

Avoid brackets. They hold the reader up. If you must use a parenthesis – and sometimes you might – use dashes instead, as in this sentence.

Dashes are also useful in intros in building tension, creating contrasts or adding a dramatic pause before an unexpected resolution.

Mary Jones described yesterday how she ran the marathon in a personal best time – only three weeks after having a baby.

The Chancellor has hinted that income tax will be going up in the Budget – only a week after saying that tax rises were out of the question.

Sensitive areas

Words change their meaning and application over time, and we all need to be sensitive to changing usage. Words that were once considered acceptable – such as "coloured" to describe some BAME people – are not acceptable now, while others – like "immigrant" – need careful handling. It is very easy to give offence, and although you might be accused of excessive political correctness, it is usually best to err on the side of caution.

Race

You can refer to a person's race or ethnic background if it is relevant to the story. If it isn't, ask yourself why you are mentioning it and if you cannot come up with a good answer, remove it. If you have the opportunity, ask people how they prefer to be described.

Disability

Refer to disabled people as disabled or having a disability. "Deaf people" is better than "the deaf". Refer to people as having learning difficulties or mental health issues rather than using words like handicapped or backward. If such people are in hospital, it is a psychiatric hospital rather than a mental institution. Again, if appropriate, ask people how they prefer to be described.

Sex/gender/sexuality

The same applies to gender and sexual orientation. Ask people how they would like to be characterised. "Gay" is now a generally accepted term for a homosexual of either sex and does not give offence. Other words referring to sexual orientation still carry pejorative meanings. Likewise, referring to a trans person by the sex they were assigned at birth is considered offensive and may lead to a complaint about inaccuracy and discrimination.

It may sound obvious, but do remember that not all members of the emergency services are policemen, firemen and ambulancemen: use gender-neutral words like officers, crews or firefighters. If the chair of a meeting is a man, call him a chair or chairman; if a woman, a chair or chairwoman. Avoid chairperson. If someone speaking for a company is a man, call him a spokesman; if a woman, call her a spokeswoman. Only use spokesperson if you do not know the sex of the person making the comment, if it is a written statement, for example.

General points of style

Time references

Time references will often be an important part of your stories, especially if they have a narrative element – the *when* on our list of basic journalistic questions. If you are writing for television, radio, the web or social media, you will not usually need to use the word "today" in your reporting. It is a fair assumption that you are reporting things that are happening that day. Only if that is not the case do you need to say so, or if you are contrasting what happened today with what has happened on another day. You can put in more specific on-the-day time references – "this morning", "this afternoon" – if appropriate.

If you are writing for a newspaper, your story may not appear until the following day, or several days later. Your time references need to reflect the time your audience will be reading the story, not the time you are writing it. So if you are writing a story for tomorrow's paper about a police press conference you have attended today, you will need to say "at a press conference yesterday, the police said…."

If your story moves about between past, present and future, or is referring to events that are happening or have happened over a period, you need to be very clear about what happened when.

> Ministers have agreed the details of a new plan to tackle hospital waiting lists. They held an emergency meeting at Number 10 **this morning** to discuss **last week's** report showing that many hospitals were missing their targets. **Yesterday** the Prime Minster said the government was determined to tackle the problem. At **today's** meeting, it was decided that…..

He said, she said

There is nothing wrong with the verb "to say" to describe comments made by people. It is short, simple, neutral and unambiguous, and you can repeat it as often as you like. It is also the verb we are most likely to use in everyday speech. So use "said" in preference to "stated" which is not a word you would use in conversation, and avoid words that are neither short nor neutral, such as "commented", "asserted", "insisted". Never use "shared". If you feel that you are overusing "said", then use non-loaded words like "went on", "continued" or "added".

Repetition

It is good practice not to repeat the same word too often, and certainly not within a sentence. However, repetition is preferable to alternates that sound forced and artificial. We saw this with the hedgehog story in Chapter 10. A fire is a fire. You can use "blaze" as an alternative if you must, although it is not a word you would probably use much in normal speech. But "conflagration"? No. Better to repeat "fire".

Another aspect of this is the avoidance of repetition by giving the reader more details instead. But it looks and sounds ugly and unnatural.

> A Manchester man has won £10 million on the lottery.
> Builder James Green bought his lucky ticket only an hour before Saturday's draw.
> The 28-year-old father of three was celebrating last night with his family.
> Didsbury resident and self-employed plasterer James, a keen tennis player, said…

This kind of journalese feels false and is exhausting to read.

Consistency in names

Decide whether or not you are going to refer to people by their first names or their surnames, and then stick with that through the story. The nature of the story will help you decide which is the more appropriate. But don't mix them up.

> Builder James Green bought his lucky ticket only an hour before Saturday's draw.
> James was celebrating last night with his family.
> "It's a dream come true," said Mr Green.

Puns

No-one seems quite sure who first said puns were the lowest form of wit. Whoever it was had it right. If you write headlines for a tabloid or for sports reports, harmless puns are part of the convention and you will probably find yourself producing rather a lot of them. If you aren't, leave puns well alone. They are seldom clever, seldom funny.

Commonly confused/misused words

Words with similar spellings are frequently confused with each other, though their meanings may be very different. Make sure you know the meaning of the words you use. Here are some commonly confused pairs:

Refute	Reject/rebuff
Immensity	Enormity
Flout	Flaunt
Affect	Effect
Founder	Flounder
In effect	Effectively
Alternate	Alternative
Full	Fulsome
Mitigate	Militate
Complement	Compliment
Historic	Historical
Flair	Flare
Disinterested	Uninterested
Imply	Infer
Impractical	Impracticable
Lay	Lie
Dependent	Dependant
Principal	Principle
Uncharted	Unchartered
Bail	Bale
Curb	Kerb
Desert	Dessert
Discreet	Discrete
Illicit	Elicit
Faze	Phase
Councillor	Counsellor
Formally	Formerly
Stationary	Stationery
Practise	Practice
License	Licence.

Fewer/less

"Fewer" denotes a smaller amount of individual items or people: *Fewer than ten people turned up. We sold fewer items today than yesterday.*

"Less" denotes a smaller amount in terms of quantity or proportion: *He bought the painting for less than a thousand pounds. It is less than a mile to the pub from here.*

Use "more than" rather than "over" to denote a larger number. *He owed the taxman more than half a million pounds.*

Appeal/protest

English usage is to appeal or to protest *against* a decision/verdict. Missing out the word "against" – as in "they said they would appeal the decision", or "the strikers were protesting wage cuts" – is American usage.

Postpone/cancel

To postpone means to put off until a future date.

To cancel means to scrap something altogether.

Records

Never say something is the fastest, longest, tallest, heaviest or anything "-est" unless you are sure it is true. It often turns out not to be. Safer to say "what is believed to be the biggest" or "one of the biggest…."

Play it again, Sam

If you are going to use any sort of quotation in your work, whether from proverbs, catchphrases, speeches, plays, films or books, always take a moment to check that you are quoting correctly. Very many famous quotations – like the one above – are actually misquotations, but we have become so used to them that we can unwittingly repeat the error. It only takes a moment to make sure that you are quoting something accurately. If you make a mistake, rest assured that someone will point it out, and you will not look anything like as clever and well-read as you might have hoped.

The United Kingdom

"The UK" is an acceptable alternative to "the United Kingdom". "The UK" is short for "the United Kingdom of Great Britain and Northern Ireland", formed by an Act of Union in 1707. So when you talk about "the UK" you are talking about all the four nations – England, Wales, Scotland and Northern Ireland. It is acceptable to use "Britain" or "Great Britain" as a synonym for the UK. "The British Isles" is technically fine too, though not in common usage.

Remember that many powers are now devolved from UK central government in Westminster to Scotland, Wales and Northern Ireland – and that no two models are the same. So be precise in your usage. Each of the nations has its own health service, for example, so if you refer to "the NHS", what do you mean? If you mean the NHS in England, you need to specify that. Some powers are the same across England and Wales, but different in Scotland and Northern Ireland. Scotland has always had a different legal system.

For most sports, there are separate teams for each of the four nations. But the UK sends a combined team to the Olympic Games – Team GB.

If you are not sure, then check. It is a common mistake for English people to refer to "England" and "the UK", or "British" and "English", as if they were one and the same. At a time when the debate about Scottish independence from the UK is current, this is a particularly insensitive and reprehensible error to make. Not only is it inaccurate and slovenly; it absolutely infuriates non-English audiences, who rightly regard it as a sign of arrogance or ignorance, or both.

Foreign phrases

Hundreds of foreign words and phrases are in everyday English usage, many of them French or Latin. On the whole, it is best to avoid them, unless they really do represent *le mot juste* – in other words, there really is no English equivalent. It is not safe to assume that your audience is familiar with them or their meaning. Overuse of foreign words can make your writing look affected and pretentious, and the consequences will be embarrassing if you do not fully understand their meaning yourself and use them inappropriately. Translate them into English instead.

When reading foreign words on the air, Anglicise the pronunciation unless you want to sound pompous and superior. Use English pronunciations of place names – so, Paris, not Paree.

Latin plurals

Strictly speaking, words that are taken from the Latin, like referendum, stadium, syllabus, terminus, formula, should follow the Latin when they are put into the plural: referenda, stadia, syllabi, termini, formulae. But this can feel pedantic these days, and Anglicised plurals are increasingly acceptable: referendums, stadiums, syllabuses, terminuses, formulas. We retain some Latin plurals however: criterion/ criteria, medium/media, cactus/cacti.

French genders

Some words derived from the French retain their male and female forms in written English. Common examples are blond (male) and blonde (female), fiancé (male) and fiancée (female).

Acronyms

Spell them out in the first reference, or at least describe what they mean. For "NEU", for example, you don't have to say "the National Education Union". "The teachers' union, the NEU" is fine. A few acronyms are sufficiently well known to stand alone without explanation: NATO, UN, EU, USA, UK, BBC. Acronyms that can be read as words like NATO or AIDS are sometimes written with only the first letter capitalised – Nato, Aids. Check house style.

Jargon, official speak

Explain it or avoid it. Jargon need not necessarily be technical language. As we discuss elsewhere, some people talk a language that, while recognisably English, is peculiar to their profession or calling. The languages of official documents, of police statements, of academics are examples. It is your job to make sure you understand what they are talking about, and then to translate for your audience by putting it into plain language.

Here are some of the words routinely used by the emergency services, and the alternatives that more closely reflect the way we speak.

Sustained an injury	Was injured; was hurt
Was declared dead on arrival (DOA)	Died before reaching hospital
Fatally injured	Killed
Lacerations and contusions	Cuts and bruises
Rendered assistance	Helped
Extinguished	Put out
In attendance	There/at the scene.

Slang and swear words

Colourful and colloquial language that mirrors the way people actually speak is fine. But there is a line between vigorous and energetic images, and slang or crudity. Use your judgement about where that line is to be drawn. House style may dictate that certain forms of everyday slang – booze, fags, dope, kids, mums and dads, kiddies, teens, the box – are perfectly acceptable, indeed stylebooks may not regard them as slang at all. But these words will be too informal for other palates. You may feel it is cool to use modern or street slang because it shows that you are up to date. That may be so, but it will not be useful if your audience does not understand what you are talking about.

Your employer will have a policy on swear words and what Ofcom calls "the most offensive words". It will state which words can appear in print and which require the ugly and not easily read use of d----s or a********s; or which may be spoken on the air and which must not be used, or bleeped. There may be considerations of context that might prompt you to break those rules occasionally – for example, if you are using direct quotes. But don't make a decision like that on your own: refer up.

"Ironically"

This is a word much loved by journalists, and almost always employed erroneously. They use it when they mean "oddly", "coincidentally", "unusually", "surprisingly", "funnily enough" or any one of a host of other words that would serve perfectly well in its place.

The proper application of irony is in a situation in which a person appears to be mocked by fate. The irony in most genuinely ironic stories is usually obvious, and does not need emphasising.

"Literally"

The misuse of this word can lead to some hilarious images. "Literally" means something that has actually happened, and the speaker or writer feels the need to add the word for emphasis, or as a plea to be believed.

"Quite literally" is felt to have greater force still. *The trains were all cancelled and I was quite literally hours late for work* is fine, even if the qualification of "quite literally" is redundant, and used purely for emphasis; so is *it rained so hard that in five minutes I was quite literally drenched*. Problems arise when people use it to report things that very clearly have not actually happened, and never could. *The train was so crowded, people were literally standing on top of each other. It was literally raining cats and dogs. I literally laughed my head off.*

My favourite example is from a BBC Radio Newsroom stylebook in which the writer noted: "I once heard an excitable presenter preface an interview with the words: 'Mrs X is a woman who has literally been to hell and back.' I wondered briefly why the programme hadn't led on it".

"Hopefully"

"Hopefully" is an adverb meaning full of hope. It should not be used to mean: "it is to be hoped that". Using it in that sense also injects an editorial judgement – it suggests that you are hopeful, when you should be expressing no opinion at all.

> "They will try to better next time", he said hopefully

is fine

> Hopefully they will do better next time

is not

"Crucial"

A favourite in sports reporting or to describe any sort of negotiations. Is it crucial though? Really?

Tidying up the quotes

Even when using direct quotes, it is acceptable to correct any small slips the speaker may have made, in order to avoid making him or her look silly, and to aid understanding. So if the actual words are "we was walking down the street" it is fine to change them to "we were walking down the street" when you quote them in your story. Your reporting must be faithful, and this can be a slippery slope. But you don't need to reproduce every "er" and "um", "like" and "you know".

Pronunciation

Most dictionaries and pronunciation guides will use what is called Received Pronunciation (RP) as the basis for advising on how words should be pronounced. It is also called Oxford English, or the Queen's English. RP is a sort of imaginary model based on the way upper-class and middle-class people are expected to speak – or may have spoken in times gone by. Today, a lot of standard pronunciations have changed, partly because regional accents are now much more of a feature of the broadcast scene. Regional or overseas accents are no longer considered a barrier to being a successful broadcaster. This is to be welcomed: the only criteria for a broadcaster should be that they should speak clearly and confidently, regardless of their accent or where they come from, and that their voices should not be a distraction to the listener.

That means we often hear the same word pronounced in different ways on the radio and television, depending on the background of the person speaking it. As long as we can understand what is being said, there is no particular problem with that. But if there is no definitive "right" way of pronouncing some words, there is often a very evident wrong way, and all broadcasters need to respect the conventions of that indefinable thing, "good English". This is especially true of the pronunciation of proper names and place names. Getting them right is about basic accuracy, which is not negotiable.

The pronunciation of some words has changed over time in ways that it is usually impossible to trace. As with grammatical issues, this infuriates some and is a matter of indifference to others. Here are some common mispronunciations. See if you care about any of them.

You should in theory say:

– CONtroversy not ConTROVersy
– HArass and HArassment, not HarASS and HarASSment
– ReSEARCH not REsearch
– Project (with O as in "box") not Project (with O as in "so") when using the word in the sense of a plan or assignment
– MISchievous not MisCHIEVous
– ConTRIBute and DisTRIBute, not CONtribute and DIStribute
– PRImarily not PriMARily
– FORmidable not ForMIDable
– ADversary not AdVERSary
– DECade not DecADE
– SHEDule not SKEDule
– COMprable not ComPARable
– DisPUTE not DISpute
– LEEverage not Leverage (where Lev rhymes with rev).

Say "seated" not "sat"

Say "lying" not "laying"

Say "standing" not "stood".

There is no such word as "pronounciation" or "mischievious". Say "pronunciation" and "mischievous".

Spelling

Commonly misspelled words

– Accommodate
– Ageing
– Gauge
– Focused
– Benefited
– Consensus
– Supersede
– Debatable
– Diarrhoea
– Benefited
– Glamour/glamorous
– Siege

– Cemetery
– Embarrass
– Fulfil
– Harass
– Liaison
– Install/instalment
– Publicly (very common – there is no such word as publically)
– Recommend
– Occurred
– Seize
– Manoeuvre
– Mischievous
– Separate
– Targeted
– Unnecessary
– Led (often written as "lead" when referring to those following a leader)
– Receive
– Niece
– Unparalleled.

Very occasionally, you can take your pick: acknowledgement and acknowledgment, and judgement and judgment (with or without the middle "e") are all acceptable. Spellcheckers usually omit the middle "e". If your house style prefers it included, remember to overrule the computer. And be consistent.

American English

Be careful not to import American spellings into your work (which your computer may often invite you to do) unless you are writing for an American audience or you are following house style.

> Many American spellings prefer a 'z' to the 's' that is more commonly used in the UK: realize, summarize, recognize.

> Many American spellings take English words ending 're' and switch to 'er' instead: center, theater, fiber, meter.

> Many American spellings drop the ends off English spellings: catalog, analog, gram, program (though we do use program in English when referring to computer programs).

> Many American words take English words ending 'our' and drop the 'u': color, labor, ardor, valor, behavior, favor.

American usage often adds redundant words. Resist any temptation to do the same. Avoid "head up", "off of", "outside of", "meet with", "check out". Say "different from" not the American "different to".

Creeping into British usage is the American way of expressing likelihood:

– British: *it is likely to rain tomorrow.* American: *it will likely rain tomorrow.*
– Ditto this: British: *may I have a latte please?* American: *can I get a latte?*

Some common words have different meanings on opposite sides of the Atlantic. A wallet in the UK is a purse in the US. Trousers become pants. Cots in the UK are camp beds in the US. A UK vet is a veterinary surgeon who looks after sick animals. A US vet is an ex-serviceman (veteran).

If you are working as a freelance, look at the stylings used by whichever publication you are working for. If in doubt, default to English spellings and overrule your spellchecker. The person you are working for will not want to spend their time correcting basic details that should be your responsibility.

Punctuation

We tend to use punctuation a good deal less these days. As you will be writing in short concise sentences for the most part, you should not need too much of it. Some people use commas more than others, and those who are into punctuation like nothing better than a good old ding-dong about the relative values of colons and semi-colons. Much of it is a matter of taste, but if in doubt, think about what punctuation is for: it is to make your writing easier to read and understand. Too many commas can be a barrier to a smooth and flowing reading experience; too few, and your reader might have to go back and start the sentence again in order to make sense of it. So as ever, your watchword should be to do whatever you can to make your work a trouble-free, pleasing and elegant read.

In brief:

- **The comma** (,) divides words of the same kind, typically a list of adjectives, or words that mark a pause in the sentence (after "however", "for example", "of course", "on the other hand"). If you read a sentence out loud, you will see where those natural pauses are, and they will usually be marked on the page with a comma.
- **The semi colon** (;) divides a sentence in two, linking two related thoughts but offering the reader a slightly longer pause in order to absorb them. As journalists, you will often find that a full stop is a better and more effective alternative in the interests of simplicity and energy, especially in news reports.
- **The colon** (:) is a way of introducing something, such as a list or a quote: "the Prime Minister said: 'I will not stand for this'." It can be used as a bridge between two connecting thoughts: "Some people eat to live: I live to eat".
- **The full stop** (.) or "full point" ends a sentence. You don't use it in headlines and the practice of using full stops in abbreviations, such as a.m. and p.m. or r.s.v.p. has fallen away. You seldom see Mr and Mrs followed by a full stop any more, as was once invariably the case. What was once "Mr. J.C. Baker" is now "Mr JC Baker".

Quotation marks

You may have a house style decreeing when you use double quotation (or "quote") marks – properly called inverted commas – and when single. If you don't, you can use either – but be consistent. For quotes within quotes, you can use double quotes inside single or the other way round, just as long as you stick with the choice that you have made.

Paragraphs

In news stories, it is customary to start a new paragraph ("par") for each sentence. This is partly because newspaper stories are set in narrow columns, so even a single sentence can create quite a deep and dense-looking paragraph. If you are writing for the web this consideration does not generally apply. But it is still good practice to avoid long and detailed paragraphs, especially when it comes to the intro. Short paragraphs help convey immediacy and urgency, look more attractive on the page and are easier to read. That all helps draw in the reader. No par should be longer than two or three sentences.

Exclamation marks (screamers)

Annoying! Use very sparingly, if ever! Let the impact come from the writing!

Loaded words

Lots of words carry inferences or suggestions that you may not intend. They are not neutral, and so misusing them can threaten your accuracy and your impartiality. Words that can be properly used in some contexts will carry special significance in others, where they have been hijacked to serve a political purpose. The language of the politics of the Middle East is a good example. Be alert to the extra baggage that certain words carry.

Be aware too that words that you throw in without too much thought, and which look innocent enough, are also loaded, because they imply an opinion on your part. So avoid "hopefully, "tragically", "miraculously", "luckily", "unfortunately", "alarmingly", "shockingly", "remarkably" and the like. They very seldom add anything to the story anyway.

Journalese

The media, and newspapers in particular, have a language all their own. It is characterised by the short words that sub-editors reach for when they are writing headlines and are pushed for space. As you will be aware by now, I encourage the use of direct and clear language that is active and energetic. The trouble is that many of these headline words are not in common everyday usage, and so when they seep out of the headlines and into the body of stories, they can look unnatural and artificial. When broadcasters, whose job it is to sound conversational, fall into the same trap, the results can be dire. Call it journalese, call it tabloidese, call it cliché: but try to avoid using the following words: there is almost always a more elegant and more commonly used alternative, as offered here. (Note how many of them can be replaced by the word "criticise".)

– Axe (sack, fire)
– Bid (attempt)
– Blast (criticise)
– Blaze (fire)
– Blow (setback)
– Boost (increase)
– Chief (leader)
– Clash (dispute)
– Drama (event)
– Dash (hurry)
– Dub (describe, nickname)
– Feud (quarrel)
– Hike (rise, increase) Hike is an Americanism
– Hit out (criticise)
– Lash out (criticise)
– Hammer (criticise)
– Oust (replace)
– Probe (inquiry)
– Quit (resign, leave)

– Quiz (question)
– Rap (reprimand)
– Rock (surprise)
– Row (argument, dispute)
– Set to (ready to, or likely to)
– Shock (surprise)
– Slam (criticise)
– Slash (reduce)
– Soar (increase)
– Swoop (raid)
– Threat (possibility)
– Unveil (launch, announce)
– Vow (promise).

At the other extreme, there are pretentious or pompous words and phrases, euphemisms and circumlocutions, that you also want to avoid on the same grounds: they do not reflect the way people speak. Some are meaningless phrases, others are examples of French or other derivatives for which shorter Anglo Saxon versions are preferable.

Here are a few obvious ones, with their briefer alternative:

– At this precise moment in time (now)
– Additionally (also)
– At the earliest possible opportunity (soon, as soon as possible)
– With reference/regard to (about)
– Deceased (dead)
– Pass, pass away, pass over (die)
– Endeavour (try)
– As a consequence of which (as a result; because of)
– In order to (to)
– In spite of the fact that (although)
– In view of the fact that (since)
– At the end of the day (in the end)
– The fact of the matter is (almost always followed by something highly debatable. Avoid altogether)
– Was of the opinion that (thought)
– Expressed the view that (said).

Clichés

It is itself a cliché to observe that all clichés were new once and carried a certain freshness and a genuine meaning. It is a further cliché, or perhaps double cliché, that clichés are to be avoided like the plague.

Clichés are ideas or images or phrases that have become the victims of their own success. They are now wilted and jaded and have long outlived their usefulness. We trot them out without really thinking about it and without considering whether they bear any residue of meaning. Most did once have meaning but it has been lost in – you guessed it – the mists of time. Some still do have a literal meaning, and if you do not know what that is you might misuse it. Often clichés are sterile marriages of two words once put together to great effect and now trapped in a loveless union from which neither can escape. It is sad really. But clichés are tired and lazy, and the best thing you can do for them is avoid them in your stories. Or, to use a cliché, kick them into the long grass.

There are hundreds of examples, but here are some of the most common ones in journalistic usage:

– Acid test
– Blow-by-blow account
– Fingertip search
– Last-ditch/Eleventh-hour bid
– War of words
– Row is brewing
– Silver/magic bullet
– First the good news, now the bad news
– Kick the can down the road
– At the end of the day
– One thing is certain
– Cautious optimism
– Open the floodgates
– Burning issue
– Emotional appeal
– Foreseeable future
– Monotonous regularity
– Pool of blood
– Accident waiting to happen
– Lock, stock and barrel
– Bite the bullet
– Reign of terror
– Grind to a halt
– Too close to call
– Wake-up call
– Win-win
– Lose-lose
– Question mark hangs over
– Fresh twist in the row over
– Violence flared
– Double whammy
– On a knife edge
– Kick into the long grass
– Push the envelope
– Miracle baby/escape/rescue
– Bears all the hallmarks
– Think the unthinkable
– Mercy dash
– Mystery surrounds/shrouded in mystery
– Sea of faces
– Speculation was rife
– Dawn showed the full extent of
– No stone unturned
– Window of opportunity
– Rain failed to dampen spirits
– Level playing field
– Limped into port
– High hopes

– Sifting through the debris/rubble
– Worst-case scenario
– Moving the goalposts
– Game of two halves
– Beg the question.

Almost any phrase containing the words "situation" or "scenario".

Never....

Here are some things that should never appear in your work or anyone else's for that matter.

- Never say "could of", "would of" and "should of". Say "could have", "would have" and "should have".
- Never spell "all right" as "alright".
- Never use the American word "gotten" (even in "ill-gotten gains" – because that's a cliché).
- Never say "passed away" or "passed". Say "died".
- Never use "shared" as an alternative to "said".
- Never use these words unless you are sure you are doing so accurately: literally, ironically, hopefully, basically, miraculously.

12

Storytelling: reporting numbers and statistics

fact-checking…..a world of statistics…..a sceptical approach…..averages…..percentages…..big numbers…..cause and effect…..calculating costs….time frames….."up to"…..comparing like with like….. surveys…..opinion polls…..three case studies…..ten top tips

Journalists are notoriously bad with statistics. They love stories with big numbers in them, but often lack the confidence or expertise to subject data to the same sort of critical analysis that they instinctively apply to other sources of information. As a result, lots of statistical howlers regularly find their way into the news, and audiences are frequently perplexed or poorly served. This is generally the result of a lack of competence in handling numbers, rather than a deliberate attempt to mislead.

It is no longer acceptable, if it ever was, to shrug and say ruefully: "I was never any good at maths". A failure to report statistics properly is a failure of accuracy. You cannot be an effective journalist without a basic grasp of numbers and how they work. But there is nothing to be scared of: a successful approach usually involves nothing more challenging than a bit of common sense and asking a few simple questions about the statistics in front of you. Treated properly, numbers can be powerful and illuminating aids to storytelling. They just need handling with care. But we should not be frightened of them or avoid them because of that. Indeed, there is a whole host of online tools that can help you mine data effectively, and present it in ways that your audiences will appreciate.

Fact checking

The last ten years or so have seen the emergence of large numbers of independent fact-checkers, reflecting concerns about the reliability of information and statistics being presented without proper scrutiny or challenge. The focus tends to be on political fact-checking – analysing the claims and counter claims that make up so much of political discourse. It is a complicated area, in which data, opinion and interpretation are so mixed that they can be next to impossible to disentangle. Fact-checkers strive to present audiences with "the truth" about controversial statistics, but a definitive answer is often elusive. All this underlines how circumspect you have to be in dealing with statistical and other claims.

Not all fact-checking organisations are journalistic, and indeed some devote themselves to challenging the media coverage of politics and other areas of reporting. In the UK, the leading independent fact-checking organisation is a charity called Full Fact. Some news organisations have their own in-house teams: the BBC's Reality Check correspondents often appear on air as well as running a dedicated area of the BBC News website, and *Channel 4* has an online FactCheck feature. *The Guardian* has a Reality Check blog, the *Independent* an InFact feature, and in Scotland, *The Ferret* is an independent media cooperative with its own fact-checking section. Looking at how these organisations dissect and analyse statistical and other claims will give you a useful insight into the sort of techniques involved.

A world of statistics

One reason it is so important to develop some expertise in dealing with numbers is that there is no getting away from them. Almost every story you do will involve some numbers or statistics, especially if you are trying to offer some context. The desire to measure, to impose order and to prove something with figures is an overpowering one in government and in society. Waiting times in A+E. School league tables. Crime figures. Greenhouse gas emissions. Even price comparison websites. Figures and statistics lurk in wait for us around every corner. They wield great influence, because they are used to forecast, to explain past events and to inform policy, as well as helping us make personal decisions about the things we buy and the service providers we choose.

This chapter aims to help you think about numbers as friends rather than foes, allies that offer strong and convincing evidence to back up your storytelling. There will be no complicated statistical theory, just some practical advice and guidance about handling statistics. We are going to look at the contexts in which figures and numbers most frequently crop up in journalism, and at the most common mistakes that journalists make. We will develop a sensible and questioning approach that will alert you to danger and help you to avoid making those mistakes yourself.

The structure and content of this chapter is loosely modelled on a training workshop originally created for BBC journalists. The BBC employs many business, economics and other journalists who handle numbers all the time and understand how they work. But there are hundreds of others who do not have that natural facility or specialist knowledge. The workshop encouraged them to ask the sort of questions that would help them report and present statistics in a responsible and accurate way.

A key figure in helping devise the content was Anthony Reuben, a financial journalist who was to become the first Head of Statistics for BBC News. In 2019, he distilled his thoughts and experiences about statistics in news stories in a book called *Statistical: Ten Easy Ways to Avoid Being Misled by Numbers*. Some of the material in this chapter stems from ideas and examples in that book. Also recommended is another excellent introduction to the subject: *The Tiger That Isn't: Seeing through a World of Numbers* by Michael Blastland and Andrew Dilnot. The details of both can be found at the back of this book.

You may have heard this well-known quotation: "There are three kinds of lies: lies, damned lies and statistics". And there is some truth in the claim that you can prove pretty much anything with statistics. That is one reason they can represent a minefield for journalists. People use all sorts of tricks in presenting numbers, and you need to be ready to spot and defuse them. Only then can you judge the value of the figures, and the strength of the arguments that are founded on them.

Even figures that are offered in good faith by apparently unimpeachable sources can be confusing and difficult to handle. Let us take an ever-topical example on the subject of gender pay gaps – something that is often in the news. If you wanted to establish the average pay gap between the earnings of men and women, there are plenty of reliable sources to explore. An obvious starting place would be the Office for National Statistics (ONS). You would surely be very happy with the reliability of any figures you got from there. You might also take a look at the Equality and Human Rights Commission (EHRC) website. And perhaps check out the Government Equalities Office, which leads for the government on policy relating to women.

All good, official, sound sources. The problem is that when you look at what they have to say about the gender pay gap, you get three different figures, spread across quite a large range.

What is going on? Which of the three figures is correct?

The answer, confusingly and exasperatingly, is that they all are. The discrepancies are explained by the fact that they all do their calculations in slightly different ways. The ONS figure is based on full-time employees only. It excludes part-time workers and overtime. But the Equalities Office includes both, because it says more women than men work part-time, so if you exclude them you get a distorted picture. The EHRC looks at a different kind of average from the ONS. (We'll look at averages in a minute.) So the discrepancies are explained by a different methodology and analysis of the figures.

How are you supposed to reflect this when you come to compile your report? Do you pick one figure and go with that, to avoid confusing your audience? Or report all three figures and let the readers draw their own conclusions? It is not simple. You can imagine a radio debate about the gender pay gap, with three different interviewees each quoting the figure that best supported their argument, and with each of those figures being different. They would all be correct, but the listeners would be left in a state of terminal confusion. The debate would leave them worse informed, not better. The presenter would have to try to explain what was happening. But how could the presenter be expected to know about those different methodologies? And if you were writing a news story on this subject and you had all these figures at your disposal, you would need to indicate to the audience why a seemingly straightforward statistical question prompted such a wide range of answers. That would mean explaining how each figure was calculated. So even figures from official or otherwise reliable sources will often need to be presented with a degree of context.

A sceptical approach

The secret of dealing with statistics successfully at a fundamental level is usually a simple matter of common sense and the exercise of a little healthy scepticism. Not taking things at face value and asking a few obvious questions will help you get to a safe place when you are reporting figures.

Here is a great common sense rule of thumb when you are presented with a claim made on the basis of figures. Ask yourself: is this *likely* to be true? Does it look and feel right? Because if it does not, there is probably something wrong with it. This is one of the golden rules of reporting statistics: if it looks or feels wrong, it probably is wrong. If it looks too good to be true – then it probably is.

Let's apply that test to a real-life example – a front-page lead in one of our most distinguished national newspapers. The headline read:

Public pensions cost you £4,000 a year

The intro below this startling headline read:

> The annual cost to the taxpayer of funding public sector pensions will more than double over the next five years to £4,000 per household, the Office for Budget Responsibility has disclosed.

On the face of it, this looks respectable enough. The source quoted is the Office for Budget Responsibility no less. Should be impeccable. The paper thinks it is a strong enough story to lead on.

But think about it for a moment. Is it *likely* to be true? Does it feel right?

There are different ways of measuring the average annual income of a British employee. Let us take a relatively generous figure of £30,000, and assume a single wage-earner in the household. So if this story is right, each household would be forking out £4,000 a year for public sector pensions out of a total income of £30,000 before tax. Is it likely that this one area, public sector pensions, is going to account for such a huge slice of a person's average income?

Remember our rule. If it looks or feels wrong, it probably is wrong. And if you think about it for only a moment, it certainly does feel wrong.

And it *is* wrong. Not because the figures were being spun, or it was deliberately overwritten. But because the paper made a simple error, and put a decimal point in the wrong place. When the story appeared on the paper's website, it had been corrected, and the headline read rather differently.

Public pensions cost you £400 a year

Oops.

Charts, statistics and datasets are part of your daily source material. So test them as you would any other source. Adopt and adapt the same checklist of questions that we discussed in the chapter on Sources. Look for the information you need to put the story into context and decide its editorial value:

What is the source of this story? A good starting point for scrutinising any information will always be to ask yourself: Who says so? Who is telling me this? Does the person who provided these figures have an agenda or bias that might affect their reliability or credibility?

Is it reasonably likely to be true? Then go back to our fundamental question, which also holds for any situation. Do I believe it? Once again: if it looks wrong it probably is wrong.

How did they produce these figures? Look at the methodology. Do you understand how the statistics have been gathered, presented and interpreted? Does it look sound? The sort of things to be looking for here are whether they are comparing like with like, why they have chosen certain start and end dates and so on. We will explain the variable effects of these factors later.

What might they have left out? Some inconvenient findings perhaps that do not support the central interpretation.

Can I verify or corroborate it? Are there other places I could go for a different perspective or some comparisons or some independent analyses, to help me get a feel for the reliability and value of these figures?

Are the conclusions justified? Do the conclusions follow logically from the statistics, and do they hold water? What are the assumptions and definitions? Do the raw data support the claims? Do the conclusions reflect a partial or selective reading of the results?

In sum:

> Really?
> Who says so?
> On what basis?
> Does it stack up?

With our sceptical hat now jammed firmly down on our heads, we are going to look at some of the aspects of working with numbers that journalists find most difficult, and where most mistakes are made.

Averages

Averages offer a way of making sense of a large mass of statistics. If you can manage and organise your data, you can see patterns, identify trends, draw conclusions and so on. Averages help reduce a large quantity of material into a simple and readily understood proposition. Given that news reporting is often about reducing things to their core essentials, that is obviously very helpful. But averages come with risks attached too. They can have the effect of flattening out or over-simplifying a range of complex figures, and giving an illusion of order and logic where none really exists. But if you are aware of the risks, it is not difficult to avoid them.

One of the problems is that in everyday speech, we use the word "average" to mean "middling", "typical", "ordinary" "the centre ground", "the norm", or something that applies to "most people". In a technical statistical context, "average" may indeed refer to the middle. But very often it won't.

Think about life expectancy. These days we can expect to live much longer than our ancestors. Their average life span might have been 50 or 60 or less, ours is more than 80. But that does not automatically mean that we are now living longer. Figures from earlier periods reflect the high rate of child mortality. Very many babies – perhaps as many as 40 per cent in the early 1800s – died before they reached their first birthday, or later in infancy. If you made it through your first few years, you could expect to live almost as long as people do today. The scale of infant mortality had a massive dampening effect on the overall average life span. If a baby died at the age of one, and an adult died at age 99, the average life span of the two of them put together would be 50. These days, babies have a much greater expectation – more than 95 per cent – of living to adulthood; so since 1820, the overall life expectancy figures have moved steadily upwards. It is not that we are all living longer – but that *more of us* are living longer, and *fewer of us* are dying at a very young age. Because of this one highly distorting factor, comparing average life spans across centuries can be misleading.

Averages are at their most valuable when they reveal what is true for a particular group, or what is most typical of them. So when you are looking at averages provided by other people, say in a press release, you need to be clear from the beginning what group you are dealing with. And you need to know what their starting point was, and how they reached their conclusions.

Different sorts of averages

We talk about averages all the time, but there are three distinct and different sorts of averages. It is important that you find out and understand which definition is being used in each particular instance.

The mean average is what you get when you add up a set of figures and divide by the total number of figures. That is what most people think of when they talk about an average figure. Six people aged 24, 35, 47, 55, 63 and 76 have a combined age of 300. If we divide 300 by 6 we get 50, and that is the **mean** average age of the group – even though none of the group is 50 and only two of them are close to that average.

The median average is the middle number in a range. But with six figures, as in our example above, there is no single middle figure. So we create one, by taking the *two* middle figures – 47 and 55 in this example – adding them together (102) and dividing by 2. This creates a single middle figure, and that figure is 51. So the **median** average of this group is 51. It is the middle number in the range of all their ages. In this particular instance, there is not much difference between the mean and the median. But that is not always the case.

The mode average is used much less frequently than the other two. It is the single most popular figure in a range. There is no mode average in our example, because no figure occurs more than once.

When a past Controller of BBC Radio One was asked in an interview about the average age of listeners to the station he gave three answers – a mean, a median and a mode average.

> The mean average was calculated by adding together the ages of every listener (I am not sure how they managed to do that!) and then dividing by the total number of listeners. The average was 32.

> The median average was calculated by looking at the entire span of ages of listeners and taking the age in the middle of the range. The average was 30.

The mode average was calculated by looking at the ages of every listener, and finding the largest number of people of a single age. The average was 18. In other words, there were more 18-year-olds than listeners of any other single age.

So the average age of a Radio One listener was 18, 30 or 32, depending on which measure you use. That is a very wide differential, and no doubt caused the Controller to scratch his head when deciding what music to play. You can see why you need to be clear which average is being used in the data you are scrutinising as part of a story you are reporting.

Why does everything have to be so complicated? Each of these methods does have value, but each comes with its own caveats and there are circumstances in which one sort of average will be much more robust and revealing than another.

To see how this works in practice, let us take as an example the salaries of a dozen workers in an office, all of whom are on the same grade. To find out the **mean** average salary of the group, you add the 12 salaries together – let us say it comes to £300,000 – and divide by 12. So the **mean** average salary of the group is £25,000 a year. Since they are all on the same grade, there probably would not be big differences between the best and worst paid, and no-one would be earning very much less than or more than £25,000. The mean average is a useful indicator here.

But if we add their manager to the mix – someone who is earning £75,000 a year – the picture changes. The total for the salaries of the original 12 was £300,000. With the manager included, it has risen to £375,000. To get the new mean average we must now divide that new total by 13. It brings the average for the group up to nearly £29,000 – even though none of the original 12 might be earning as much as that. So 12 of the 13 could be earning less than the average income for the whole group. That does not make much sense. That one larger figure which is a long way outside the rest of the range, known as an "outlier", has a distorting effect – such that the **mean** average is no longer such a useful figure when it comes to getting an accurate picture of the group's earnings.

However, a **median** average would be much more useful if you wanted to get a sense of the average salary of this group of 13. The median would be the middle figure in the range. That would be somewhere near £25,000, and would be much the same whether you included the manager or not. A **median** average would give you a more accurate reflection of the pay of the larger group.

Sports fans are obsessed with statistics and performance averages. No sport attracts more statto fanatics than cricket, and a cricket example illustrates this difference between mean and median very well.

In his final series as a player in 2018, the former England cricket captain Sir Alastair Cook scored 376 Test match runs over the span of 9 innings. To find his **mean** average for the series, we divide 376 by 8 (one innings was not complete and so does not count) and we get just under 47. This means he scored a mean average of 47 runs every time he went out to bat. This was a little higher than his international career average, which stands comparison with all the greatest batsmen. In other words, he enjoyed a highly successful series.

But look at his individual scores across the series: 2, 7, 37, 16, 7, 14, 244 not out (this was the innings that was not completed, because he was undefeated), 39 and 10.

You can see from this that he had a run of very low scores, and a single huge score of 244. Take away that exceptional score – the "outlier" – and his **mean** average over eight of his nine innings would have been a paltry 16.5. That does not look so good. It suggests that for most of the tour, he was performing well below his best. His **median** average – the score in the middle of the range – was 14. That better reflects his performance overall. His **mode** average would have been 7, since that is the figure that occurs most often, but that would not be a particularly meaningful indicator in this case.

So depending on which method you use, Cook's series average was 7, 14 or 47. It was either very poor or world class. Cricket fans who wanted him dropped from the team would have pointed to the median figure. Those who wanted him retained would have looked at the mean figure.

In sum, averages are extremely useful, but they can mislead. Bear these points in mind:

– Be clear which sort of average is being used in the figures you are looking at, or by the people you are interviewing.
– Understand that using different sorts of average to interrogate the same set of figures might produce very different results. This can be exploited by those interpreting the figures.
– Understand that an average figure may be statistically sound in the way it has been calculated, but may still be misleading.
– Consider whether applying a different sort of average would suggest a very different – and possibly more accurate – picture.
– Assess which method you think is the most sensible and revealing in the context of the story you are producing.

Percentages

Like averages, percentages are very useful ways of drawing simple conclusions from complex data, and they have the advantage of being readily understood by most people. If you talk about 6 out of 10, or 8 out of 10, then most people know that means 60 per cent or 80 per cent. And vice versa. A quick way of working out percentages is by starting from what 10 per cent would be, or what 1 per cent would be. That is easy to do in your head, and it gives you a base to work from.

So if you were earning £3,000 a year and someone gave you a bonus of £1,500, you could quickly calculate in your head what that represented in percentage terms. Ten per cent of £30,000 is £3,000. You have been given half that, so your bonus is worth 5 per cent.

The most common mistake people make with percentages is in calculating the percentage rise between two figures. Let us say your bonus last year was £300. This year it has gone up to £1,500. By what percentage has your bonus increased?

If your answer is that it is a 500 per cent increase, because £1,500 is five times £300, you have made one of the most common errors in statistics. You have forgotten that your starting point is £300 – last year's bonus – and not 0. So you need to go up in steps of £300, like this:

– Your bonus last year was £300. If you **doubled** that to £600 this year, your bonus would have increased by 100 per cent.
– If your £300 bonus of last year **tripled** to £900, it would have increased by 200 per cent.
– If your £300 bonus of last year **quadrupled** to £1,200, it would have increased by 300 per cent.
– What has actually happened is that it has **quintupled** to £1,500, and so has increased by 400 per cent.

It is correct to say that your bonus this year is five times what it was last year.
It is correct to say that your bonus this year has increased fivefold over last year.
It is not correct to say it has increased by 500 per cent. As we have seen, the rise in percentage terms is 400 per cent.

Another thing to be wary of is the difference between a percentage and a percentage point.

> Think of *percentages* in terms of 100. If your bonus last year was £300 and this year it is £600, in *percentage* terms it has gone up by 100 per cent.

It would be correct to say that your bonus has gone up by 100 per cent.
It would be correct to say that your bonus has doubled.

> Think of a *percentage point* as one (rather than 100). If the Bank of England interest rate is raised from 0.25 per cent to 0.5 per cent, the correct way to describe this would be as an increase of 0.25 (or a quarter) of a percentage point.

It would be correct (but rather misleading) to say that rates have gone up by 100 per cent.
It would be correct – and preferable – to say that rates have gone up by a quarter of a percentage point.
It would *not* be correct to say they have gone up by 0.25 per cent. That is to confuse percentages and percentage points.

Always report both percentages and the actual numbers together. Either figure on its own can be confusing. If you hear that your chances of contracting a particular form of cancer have more than doubled, you will naturally be alarmed. But if you were then given the actual figures, which showed that one in a million people were getting the cancer before, and that figure was now two in a million, you would probably conclude that you had little to worry about. The risk has doubled, certainly. But it has only risen from very very small to very small. The percentage figure on its own is misleading. You need the actual figures as well in order to calibrate the risk.

The opposite is also true. If you were to read that a business was half a million pounds overspent (£500,000), you would think that there was something seriously wrong with the way it was being run. But if you then learned that the company's overall budget was £50 million, then you would realise that the overspend represented only 1 per cent of the total spend. Most businesses would be deliriously happy with a margin of error as small as that.

So you need both percentages and figures in order to understand a story fully. People feeding you statistics will often use only one of them – the one that best supports their argument. It is up to you to look for the other, and see how robust that argument actually is.

Calculating percentages

How do you work out a percentage? Use an online calculator is the easy answer. Failing that, here is a simple way of doing so.

Let us say you have a story about redundancies at a company. The company employs 250 people and is making 35 of them redundant. You want to know what percentage of the workforce is getting the sack.

> **Step 1**: multiply the number of redundancies, 35, by 100 = 3500.
> **Step 2**: divide 3500 by the total number of employees, 250 = 14.

This company is making 14 per cent of its workforce redundant.

You can do this the other way round. You are told that a company employing 250 people is cutting its workforce by 14 per cent. You want to know how many people are losing their jobs.

> **Step 1**: divide the total number of employees, 250, by 100 to find out how many people make up one per cent of the workforce = 2.5.
> **Step 2**: if 2.5 is one per cent, multiply that by 14 to find out how many people comprise 14 per cent = 35.

This company is making 35 people redundant.

Needless to say, there is more than one way of doing these calculations. If you are having trouble, or have a more complex percentage problem, try one of the many instructional videos on YouTube.

Big numbers

Big numbers are getting bigger all the time. We don't talk about deficits in billions these days, we talk about trillions. Where once a millionaire would be considered a rich person, now you need a billion – or several billion – to be considered wealthy. Journalists love big numbers: they have lots of noughts, they sound important, they make lovely headlines. But so often they are not what they seem. Big numbers need to be broken down and looked at in context – as with our imaginary company overspend. This scrutiny can make big numbers look rather smaller than they first appeared.

Millions, billions and trillions

Before we start, let us be clear about the difference between millions and billions and trillions. It is all too easy to say or write one when you mean the other – and indeed to mishear, since the first two sound alike.

A million is a thousand thousand. A billion is a thousand million. A trillion is a thousand billion.

> one million is written as 1,000,000 or 1m. It has six zeroes.
> one billion is written as 1,000,000,000 or 1bn. It has nine zeroes.
> one trillion is written as 1,000,000,000,000 or 1tn. It has 12 zeroes.

This is one reason big numbers can be such a problem. They are difficult to visualise. We know what a hundred quid looks like, but how can we imagine a trillion? We know what a football crowd of 50,000 looks like, but how can we picture a global population of more than 7 billion? Big numbers have to be wrestled into submission if we are to make sense of them for ourselves and for our audiences.

Step 1 to doing that is to ask the question: "Is this really a big number?"

How do you find the answer to that question? Take this headline from an online story from some time back.

National Health Service to lose 50,000 jobs, trade unions say

The intro read:

> More than 50,000 NHS jobs will be lost because of government cuts, a new anti-cuts campaign group says.

This sounds like a big number and potentially a very big story. Health service cuts are always going to be controversial, and 50,000 is an awful lot of jobs. Patients will surely suffer, even die. The figure comes from an "anti-cuts campaign group", so we know that they have an agenda, and it will be in their interest to make the losses sound as big as possible. Let us see if we can find some context that will help us judge exactly how big this number is.

In paragraph two we learn that these jobs will be lost "over five years". So the cuts are not quite as savage as we might first have thought. They will play out over time.

The report was accompanied by some analysis by a health reporter, which provided further valuable context. He reported that the National Health Services (NHS) of the UK had a combined workforce of 1.4

million people. Doing a sum rapidly in your head, you can work out that 10 per cent of that is 140,000 and that 1 per cent is 14,000. If 14,000 jobs comprise 1 per cent of the workforce, the 50,000 in our story represent around 3.5 per cent. If we are cutting 3.5 per cent of jobs over five years, the rate of shrinkage is less than 1 per cent per year.

As the reporter further explained, two years earlier the workforce had *grown* by 60,000 over 12 months. So even if it lost 50,000 jobs over the next five years, the NHS would still be bigger at the end of the process than it had been seven years previously. The loss of those 50,000 jobs will certainly have an impact – but now we know some background, the story does not look anything like as strong as it did when we just had that bald figure alone.

Always look carefully at stories relating to the NHS. For one thing, there is no single NHS, because health powers are devolved around the UK. There are separate health services in England, Scotland, Wales and Northern Ireland. You always need to be clear which you are talking about. If the government pledges to give another £1.5 billion a year to the NHS in England, then that sounds like a substantial commitment. But NHS England has a budget that is heading towards £150 billion a year. So the new money would represent an increase of only 1 per cent – probably less than the rate of inflation. For any figure associated with the NHS to be significant, it has probably got to be really, really big. Ask the question: big – compared with what?

You can see that with a bit of context, a very big number can very quickly look like a much smaller number. With that in mind, let us work through a story and subject it to a little critical scrutiny. This one appeared on the website of a national newspaper.

Town hall bans staff from using Facebook after they waste 572 hours in one month

The story was about a council that was apparently appalled to discover that its staff were between them spending an average of 413 hours a month on Facebook, peaking at 572 hours in one particular month. This was said to be the equivalent of 71 eight-hour days.

That looks like a lot of time on Facebook, and a lot of people wasting time at work. These are big numbers. Big enough for this council anyway. They banned their staff from using Facebook at work.

But *are* they big numbers? Let us investigate.

We will start with the biggest figure – 572 hours wasted on Facebook in one month alone. To give this some context, we would very much like to know something about the culprits – the people who work for the council. How many of these Facebook addicts are there? The story tells us in the second par: the council employs 4,500 people. So what next?

Get the calculator out. A bit of long division is now called for. Rather than work in fractions of an hour, we will find life easier if we convert those 572 wasted hours into minutes, by multiplying by 60. Those 572 wasted hours are 34,320 wasted minutes. Divide those minutes by 4,500, the number of employees, and the answer you get is 7.6.

So in the month of most usage, each employee was on Facebook for an average (a **mean** average) of 7.6 minutes.

That was the worst month. Average usage is said to be 413 hours a month. If we follow the same process for this figure, we work out that 413 hours is 24,780 minutes. Divide that by 4,500, and we have 5.5 minutes of usage for each employee.

This is a monthly figure. Perhaps we can reduce it to a daily figure. Let us say the average month comprises 21 working days. If we divide 5.5 minutes by 21 days to find an average daily usage, we get 15.7 seconds.

So we have now got that very big figure of 413 hours down to an average of less than 16 seconds per person per day. Which is a tiny fraction of 1 per cent of their working day.

We are given two more items of context further down the story. Here is the first:

> Before the ban, staff were allowed to use Facebook and other sites in their lunch breaks or after work.

So far from wasting working time, many staff were behaving in a way that was officially sanctioned. Here is the second:

> Staff can apply to have the site unblocked if they can prove they need it for their job – such as benefit fraud staff carrying out checks on claimants' lifestyles to make sure their status is what they say it is.

So there are some uses of Facebook that are a legitimate part of the workload of some council staff.

With this information and a few very simple calculations, we might conclude that this council does not have much of a problem when it comes to staff use of Facebook. We did not do anything very complicated in order to examine those very big figures and see that they were not so very big after all. We have discovered that the council massively overreacted to what looked like a big problem, but might not have been a problem at all. They created a disgruntled workforce for no good reason. That, surely, is the story that these figures tell – and we found it by dint of asking one question and doing few simple sums.

Cause and effect

A very common error is to confuse cause and effect, or what statisticians call "correlation and causation". What this means simply is that when you have two facts that look as though they *might* be connected, you make the assumption that they *are* connected. You see one set of figures going up, and another set of figures going down, and you assume that one is causing the other.

False conclusions like this offer further evidence of the claim that you can prove anything with statistics. Put any set of statistics in the vertical axis of a chart, and another set in the horizontal axis, and you probably be able to deduce – quite falsely – some sort of relationship between them. A website called *Spurious Correlations* specialises in this sort of exercise, and some of its creations demonstrate how ridiculous these false connections can be. Here are some of the statistics they put together and found that it was theoretically possible to see connections between them, and/or that one was the cause of the other:

> The number of people who drown by falling into a pool correlates with films featuring Nicolas Cage.

> The amount of cheese each person eats correlates with people who die after becoming entangled in their bedding.

> The volume of American crude oil imports from Norway correlates with motorists killed in collisions with railway trains.

There is plenty more nonsense where that came from. It is plainly ridiculous to suggest that there is a real cause and effect relationship between these twinned sets of random statistics.

And yet we fall for many less obvious examples all the time. It is in our nature to try to explain things and make sense of them. We like science, logic, order, regularity, patterns. We do not believe with anything like the same fervour in chance, coincidence or the randomness of events. And yet, when we do come across things that look as though they might be causally connected, the strong likelihood is that any ostensible relationship is simply the result of chance.

Even so, it can be hard to let go of suspected connections. In the town of Bridgend in South Wales, 26 people committed suicide over a period of two years. This was far higher than both the national average and the previous rate of suicide in the town. Most of the suicides were young adults, and all but one died by hanging. There was an understandable general feeling that this phenomenon could not be put down to chance, but that there had to be some explanation behind it, some linking cause for this tragic spike in the number of suicides. All sorts of ideas were put forward – poor social conditions, a "copycat" effect, a "suicide cult". But the police found no evidence to connect the cases and nor did the coroner who presided over the inquests. Instinctively, it was felt that the strikingly high numbers must mean that there was a connection. As far as we know, there wasn't.

In *The Tiger that Isn't*, Blastland and Dilnot describe a simple experiment of throwing a handful of rice in the air and then seeing how the grains lie. They fall randomly, but there are some areas in which many grains cluster together and others with only a few grains. If that was a news story, and each grain of rice was a colon cancer case, say, we would want to know why there were cancer clusters in some areas and not others. But as the book points out, it would be amazing if you threw a handful of rice in the air and it came down perfectly evenly distributed. Some things just happen. Some coincidences are just that – coincidences. Avoid making links that cannot be justified by the evidence – and be on the alert for others who try to do so.

Calculating costs

In our money-oriented society, we are fond of putting a price tag on everything. In news terms, this tendency extends to things on which it is clearly hard to calculate a price – the cost to the economy of heavy snow or some other weather event; of public sector strikes; of an outbreak of flu or coronavirus; a prolonged holiday over Christmas and the New Year. When you see a price put on these, always ask: Where do those figures come from? How are they calculated? Do they mean anything?

Here is an example:

Snow Britain: disruption could cost UK economy £3 billion

This was an online report about the effects of a recent period of bad weather. The cost to the economy, according to the Federation of Small Businesses (FSB), was £3 billion. Or more precisely: it *could have been* £3 billion – not quite the same thing. When we examine how the FSB came to this conclusion, we learn that it was based on the assumption that 20 per cent of people had stayed away from work because of the snow. There was nothing in the story to explain the basis for that assumption. Then we learn that on an average Bank Holiday, 40 per cent of people do not go to work. Bank Holidays were said to cost the economy £6 billion, although we were not told how that figure is arrived at either. So, the logic went, half, as many people stuck at home in the snow must cost half as much – £3 billion.

What are some of these costs? Well, for example, if we stay at home, we eat out of the fridge and do not buy sandwiches says the FSB. Clearly none of this adds up to anything very robust. But the FSB knows the media have an appetite, and they feed it, and get themselves a bit of free publicity in the process. It is a big figure, it comes from a respectable-looking source, and it is duly snapped up.

When a number of public sector unions organised a series of strikes, the media routinely reported that the cost to the economy was £500 million. This was apparently based on an estimate in advance that the action would cost between £280 million and £500 million, depending on the extent of the action. That estimate in itself relied on a number of assumptions, some educated, some guesswork. For example, it was assumed that every single school would be closed as a result of the strikes. And the cost of those closures was based not on how much real money was lost on a strike day, but on a mathematical calculation of the monetary value of a school day. As it happened, several hundred schools remained open, so the actual cost of the action was almost certainly lower than the "worst case" £500 million. But that was the figure that stuck and was used in virtually all reporting of the strikes – before, during and after. These estimates are of dubious value anyway: those £3 billion or £500 million figures are not of any practical use to anyone.

Be wary of accepting figures for the cost of things that cannot easily be costed: the cost of a flu epidemic, the cost of severe weather events, the cost to the health service of an operation or a missed appointment. Ask some questions about how the figures were arrived at, and take a view as to whether the assumptions made were reasonable and whether the figures are really meaningful.

Time frames

With anything that is being measured over a period of time, it is always worth looking at the start date and end date that has been chosen. A start date may be an event: it would be perfectly reasonable to examine the performance of the British economy both before and after the UK's exit from the European Union, in order to make comparisons and draw conclusions about the effect of the change in economic terms. The date of an election that brought a new government to power would also be a rational start date for an examination of various aspects of performance. Sometimes the time frame will be more random, but still seem sensible enough. Comparisons of global temperatures look at one decade against another. There is obviously nothing climatically significant in the turn of a decade, but you need a block of at least ten years to begin to see a consistent trend (some would say 10,000 years). But be on the lookout for what may be artificial start and end dates, because they may have been chosen deliberately to support an argument.

Suppose you were looking at the incidence of youth reoffending over a period of years. Suppose too, that for no obvious reason, there was a big spike in youth reoffending in 2009 and 2010, which by 2011 had disappeared, and the situation had remained stable since then. Think about what we said about the way one or two outlier figures can distort an average.

> If you looked at the average level of youth reoffending over ten years from 2009, you would be including two years of unusually high figures.

> If you looked at the average level of youth reoffending over ten years from 2010, you would be including one year of unusually high figures.

> If you looked at the average level of youth reoffending over ten years from 2011, you would be excluding both those two years of unusually high figures.

In short, you would get very different outcomes depending on which time frame you chose. So when presented with a case that is apparently supported by statistics gathered over a period, always dig a little deeper to see why that particular period might have been chosen, and what potentially distorting factors may have been present during those years.

"Up to"

"Up to 70 per cent off!" say the Sale signs outside the furniture stores. We all know this means that a few items in the store are being discounted by 70 per cent, but by no means all of them. Yet we sometimes forget this when we are writing news stories. Offered a range of figures, we always choose the higher one.

We have already mentioned coverage of a bad weather event in which the costs "could be" £3 billion and public sector strikes in which advance estimates put the cost at "up to" £500 million. In the case of the strikes, that was the figure used thereafter to describe the costs, even though it was based on some things that did not happen (the closure of every school, for example). We tend to go for the bigger figure because it sounds more impressive and makes the story feel more important. But be careful not to mislead.

Take this statement:

> The government says EU citizens are applying for permanent rights to stay in the UK at a rate of be-tween two and five thousand a week.

It would be accurate to report this as:

> Up to five thousand EU citizens are applying for permanent rights to stay in the UK each week.

But while strictly accurate, it would not reflect the actual picture. It implies that 5,000 is the weekly norm, even if it does not actually say so. But in some weeks, there are only 2,000 applications. It would be more accurate – and responsible – to report both figures.

Comparing like with like

Look carefully at figures that involve comparisons. It can sometimes be very difficult to compare things on a genuine like-for-like basis. Say you wanted to compare the performances of the different health services across the four nations of the UK. You would have to satisfy yourself that the figures you were looking at were directly comparable – were based on the same criteria, covered the same timeframe and had been calculated in the same way. That is very unlikely to be the case. Comparisons between different countries in which vastly different circumstances and influencing factors exist are especially risky. It is very difficult to be sure that you are making sound like-for-like comparisons. This was strongly underlined during the coronavirus outbreak of 2020, when repeated attempts were made to compare the relative performances of different countries in combating the virus. Each one had to be hedged with caveats and qualifications. If you want to compare countries, see if you can find someone else who has already done the work for you: there are plenty of big international institutions for whom this sort of thing is meat and drink. Don't forget to attribute the source of any figures you use.

Graphs

Graphs, tables and pie charts are simply different ways of displaying statistics, with the intention of mak-ing them easier to visualise and understand. But again, they can be misleading. A simple chart compares two things by recording one of them on a vertical axis, and the other on a horizontal axis. Look at each axis to see the measurements that have been chosen: they can have a dramatic effect on the look of the results.

Say for example, you wanted to chart the speed with which new cases were rising in an epidemic. The vertical axis might show the rising number of cases; the horizontal axis might show a time frame. If the vertical axis measured from 0 cases to, say, 5,000, and cases were steadily rising from 3,000 to 4,000, that would result in a steep upward line on the graph. But if the vertical axis went from 0 to 20,000, the up-ward line would be much flatter and look much less dramatic.

The same would be true of the horizontal axis. If the measurements there showed rises day by day, then at the height of the infection, again, the upward line might be steep. But if that horizontal line measured cases over a matter of months, or even a year, it would be much flatter. The raw figures would be exactly the same on both axes, and the presentation of them would not be inaccurate in either case: but presenting them in different ways might produce very different impressions about how far and how fast the infection was spreading.

When presented with statistics represented visually in some way, adopt the same questioning and sceptical attitude that we have already discussed – and ask yourself how different the results might look if they were illustrated in a different way. And when you are creating your own graphs, perhaps to illustrate an online story, think carefully about how to present them in a way that reflects the true picture and does not – however inadvertently – create a misleading impression.

Surveys

The very word "survey" should set alarm bells ringing in your head. The figures offered by surveys can be the most suspicious of all, with little to recommend them in terms of statistical analysis. But they offer bright and breezy headlines and many receive prominent news coverage even if there is precious little substance underneath.

Some surveys are based on science, or purport to be, and some on public opinion – those doing the survey have canvassed opinions from members of the public. Both need treating with caution.

In the field of health alone, barely a day goes by without us being presented with the results of a scientific study or survey that assures us that red wine is good for us, that red wine is bad for us, that short bursts of activity are better than more sustained exercise, that fasting two days a week is good for you, that fasting two days a week is bad for you, that a vegetarian diet reduces your risk of certain cancers and so on. They can't all be right. They might all be wrong, or of little statistical value.

Then there is the equally heavy supply of other random surveys based on polling, in which there is a suspicious connection between the interests of those who commissioned the work and the conclusions reached. That is likely to be because of the choice of questions and the way in which they have been asked. If you see a press release headlined "Survey shows chocolate is good for you", the first thing to check is who commissioned it. Don't be surprised if it turns out to be a chocolate manufacturer. Here are a couple of real ones:

> The credit crunch has prompted a dramatic increase in dry cleaning as people buy fewer new clothes.

Who commissioned the survey? A chain of dry cleaners:

> A massive 95 per cent of Britons consider taking a holiday at least once a year as more important than owning a home or having children.

Who commissioned the survey? A holiday company. And by the way: is this likely to be true do you think? Me neither.

That doesn't mean surveys are particularly harmful. But many are of very limited news value beyond an alluring headline, and belong in the waste paper basket rather than in print. Adopt the sceptical approach we outlined earlier, beginning with the same questions. Go back to that checklist:

> What is the source of this story?
> Is it reasonably likely to be true?
> How did they produce these figures?

What might they have left out?
Can I verify or corroborate it?
Are the conclusions justified?

For surveys of opinion, add these questions:

Who paid for the survey? The paymasters will expect the findings to be favourable to them.

Do they have a commercial or other interest in the outcome? If so, the survey is likely to have been heavily weighted in favour of one conclusion before a single person was asked a single question.

How many people did they ask? A normal minimum survey size would be 1,000 people but methods are important too. A survey in which people responded in person in the street is more valuable than one in which people were sent a mass email. Sampling a small group is very difficult, and unless you speak to all of them, is going to be statistically dubious. Say you wanted to do a survey of Premier League football managers. There are 20 of them. With such a small number, you would probably have to interview all of them, or very nearly all of them, before you could confidently draw any conclusions. It would not be good enough to speak to three or four, and extrapolate their views across the whole lot.

Were they the right people? What was the spread/mix? If you want to know whether people prefer coffee to tea, then there is no point interviewing only tea drinkers.

What did they ask them? It is depressingly easy to influence the results of a survey with the choice of questions, and the way in which they are worded to point you to a particular answer. Always look at what people have been asked and see whether you think there was ever a reasonable likelihood of an impartial and dependable outcome.

If you want to see how easy it is to construct a dodgy survey, and understand some of the tricks that are used, check out this site:

http://neurobonkers.com/2012/02/28/how-to-construct-a-bogus-survey/

Anthony Reuben quotes the results of two political surveys carried out by the same polling company in the same month – one for a newspaper, the other for a television political programme. The year was 2008, and the financial crisis was at its height.

In the first survey, respondents were asked about financial bailouts with this question:

Is it right that taxpayers' money should be used to bail out the banks?

A healthy majority, 58 per cent, said no it was not right.

In the second survey, respondents whether or not they agreed with the following proposition:

I support the government using taxpayers' money to stabilise the financial system.

The result this time was that 50 per cent agreed. The same question, asked in two different ways, subtly weighted to encourage different answers.

So always be sceptical. The interpretation of findings will always be a subjective and selective process, so you should never drop your guard. Many respectable surveys are now published in full online, so a good tip is to get under the bonnet of the press release and see if you can find the raw data. You will feel much more confident about the survey if you can check out the methodology and look at the results for yourself. You will often find a story that is much better and more interesting than the one offered by the press release.

Remember: surveys never "prove" or "show" anything. They only "suggest" or "indicate".

Opinion polls

The same is true of opinion polls. They are usually attempts to take the temperature of public opinion on political issues. At their most basic, they ask people which party they intend to vote for at the next election. Beyond that, they may ask a raft of more detailed questions on the issues of the moment. The results are scrutinised eagerly by politicians and the media, even though everyone is fully aware that opinion polls are not always reliable measures of what is really going on with the electorate. They have been known to be wrong, sometimes very wrong. For this reason, any discussion of the latest poll is often preceded with the rider: "of course we must not set too much store by a single poll, but….."

Even so, you can be more confident about the credibility of opinion polls than you can with the typical survey. This is because many polling companies have built up their reputations over many years, and are always open about how they have done their research. You still need to be wearing your sceptical hat though, and asking some questions about the results of opinion polls. The important things to look for are:

Who conducted the poll? There are several reputable polling companies with long track records of conducting polls. If your poll has not been done by one of these, you might want to seek reassurances about who the pollsters are and how they have performed in the past.

Who for? Polling companies are commercial organisations, so they conduct polls only when someone commissions and pays them to do so. Very often this will be a national newspaper. National newspapers have political agendas. We have already noted the tendency of survey results to reflect the opinions of those who commissioned them. So knowing who is paying for the poll is an important piece of context.

How many people were questioned? For a poll that hopes to show what the whole country is thinking, the pollsters must interview at least 1,000 people. So when you report the poll findings, say how large the sample was.

Who were these people? The pollsters are conscious that their results can be badly skewed if they question an unrepresentative sample, or leave out important groups of people. An online poll, for example, automatically excludes anyone who does not use a computer – a significant number of people. The pollsters will often reveal what steps they have taken to "weight" their findings, in an effort to ensure the results are as accurate as possible.

How were they questioned? There are those who think that people are more likely to be honest if they are interviewed face to face in the street than if they are spoken to on the phone or fill in a questionnaire online. You do not need to have an opinion on this – just report how the respondents were questioned.

When were they questioned? Depending on what is going on, the timing of the survey will often be significant. Were people interviewed before the new figures that showed the economy was slowing down significantly? Was the polling done before the Chancellor's Budget speech, or afterwards? Again, in your reporting, make room to say when the polling was done.

What were the questions? You probably will not have room in your report to include all the individual questions and answers, but it is still worth looking at what people were asked. We have already seen how the way questions are phrased can affect the kind of response it receives.

How does this compare with previous polls? Opinion polls are carried out on a regular basis, especially around election time. So over time, a pattern is established and trends may emerge. A newspaper may commission the same polling company to conduct virtually the same survey several times over a period. So it is always worth comparing the new results with previous ones – as long as you are satisfied that you are comparing like with like. If the previous three polls have had the two biggest parties roughly neck and neck, and the new one shows one of them with a ten-point lead, something might be going on which merits further inquiry.

This sounds like a lot of stuff to get in to your report of a poll's findings, but you can condense it into a reasonably short space. Here's a typical example.

> A new opinion poll by Ipsos Mori suggests the Conservatives have a three-point lead over Labour at the start of the election campaign. This is four points down on the same poll a month ago. The company interviewed 1,500 people face to face on Thursday and Friday of last week – after the Labour manifesto launch but before the Conservative launch.

Don't forget:

The "don't knows". These are people who have yet to make up their minds how to vote. It is a mistake to assume that if and when they do make up their minds, their votes will be divided in the same proportions as those who have decided. The bigger the number of undecided, the greater the risk that the poll is not fully representative.

The margin of error. Most polls indicate how much reliance should be placed on their results by stating what they consider to be the margin of error. This is usually 3 per cent either way. So if such a poll suggests that 60 per cent of people intend to vote a certain way, it is really saying that the number is anything between 57 per cent and 63 per cent. This is clearly very important in a close race. A poll that finds a 50–50 split may in fact reflect a 47–53 or a 53–47 split, each of which would produce a very different result. So if the results are as close as that, it is unwise to set too much store by them. Time to resort to the cliché: "too close to call".

Opinion polls sometimes get things spectacularly wrong, which is why the BBC guidelines insist that the results of a single poll should never be the lead story in a news bulletin. In recent years, by far the most reliable political polls have been the exit polls conducted jointly by the main broadcasters on General Election day. The results are released at 10 o'clock in the evening, when the polling stations have closed. They have proved extremely accurate in the past five elections. This is attributed to the fact that people are interviewed on their way out of the polling station. Normally, they are asked some way in advance of polling day which way they are thinking of voting. Many have yet to make up their minds at that stage, and indeed may never vote at all. The strength of the exit poll is that they are being interviewed after they have definitely made up their minds and have actually cast their votes. Further, the pollsters speak to many more people than they would for a conventional poll, and they do their interviews in marginal seats where the results of any election are decided.

Case studies

If you are remotely interested in numbers, how they work and how they are routinely misused, you can do no better than listen to the long-running BBC Radio Four programme *More or Less*. Each week it looks in an entertaining and accessible way at the numbers in the news, and subjects them to critical scrutiny. The results are often revealing. Past episodes are available as podcasts, and if you take the trouble to listen just a few episodes, you will rapidly get into the habit of looking at statistics in an intelligent and questioning way.

With the help of *More or Less*, we are going to apply everything we have learned so far to three real-life case studies. The first two demonstrate how far off course you can veer if you fail to stick to the safe path of gentle scepticism and your checklist of questions. The third is a textbook example of how to apply this approach clearly and effectively.

Case study 1: North Sea cod

This online story from the website of a national newspaper reports some genuinely shocking news:

Just 100 cod left in North Sea

Cod! The fish in our fish and chips! The sub-heading adds the qualifier that we are talking about adult cod, but that hardly makes it any the less shocking.

Before we get too depressed, let us apply the first of our stock questions. Is this likely to be true? Does it sound right?

The answer is surely: no, it doesn't. The task of counting how many fish there are in the sea and working out how old they are must rank as one of the great statistical challenges. But when it comes up with a conclusion as startling – and as improbable – as this, we need to look further.

Our next standard question is: who is telling me this?

The answer is that these figures came from the government. They were the findings of a survey carried out by DEFRA – the Department for Environment, Food and Rural Affairs. That sounds like a pretty good source.

What more do we learn from the online story?

> A survey of catches at European ports has found that fishermen did not catch a single cod over the age of 13 last year. The findings raise concerns for future stocks of cod, which become more fertile as they age. The fish can live as long as 25 years and grow to 6ft. The research was carried out by Defra's fisheries laboratory. Chris Darby, head of the team, said: "Our latest assessments suggest in 2011 there were 600 cod aged 12 to 13 in the North Sea, of which about 200 were caught. None of the catches recorded at North Sea ports around Europe showed any fish aged 13 or over. Analysis of that data suggests there are fewer than 100 such fish in the whole North Sea."

So we have the source – a government department with no obvious agenda – and we have the methodology. Maybe there is something in this after all.

The *More or Less* team were very interested in the cod story, and when they heard that the fishing industry was challenging the figures, they decided to delve a little deeper into it. They featured the claim in their programme and wrote an online story of their own under the heading:

North Sea cod: is it true there are only 100 left?

More or Less traced the first mention of the story back to another newspaper, from where others had picked it up in the incestuous way that journalism works. This is what the programme found:

> The [newspaper] chose to class an adult cod as aged over 13. But that's not merely an adult cod. It's an ancient cod. Cod start to mature at ages one and two and they're fully mature by six. So we shouldn't be surprised that there are very few cod aged over 13 (in fact fewer than 60 have been recorded in the North Sea in past 30 years) just as we shouldn't be surprised there aren't very many humans over 100. So where did the newspaper get the idea that cod reach adulthood at 13? Well in the same article, the paper stated that cod could live to 25, which implies a 13-year-old cod is merely middle-aged whereas in fact it's really, really old.

So the *More or Less* approach was not to question the source of the story – which seemed impeccable – but to look at the methods and premises used in the survey. Then they asked another of our key questions about a statistics story: are the conclusions justified? And if not, can we come up with something more accurate? *More or Less* continued:

> So: just how many "adult" cod are there in the North Sea? Remember, the paper said there were just 100. The right answer? Well, using the same dataset, but with a lower age for an adult cod, the right answer appears to be rather more than 100. 21 million, in fact. And taking this headline at face value, how many cod are there altogether in the North Sea, young and old? More than 100? I should say so. This story estimates their number as……437 million.

By looking at the figures in a rather more rational and realistic way, the programme managed to replace the number of 100 with a new estimate of 437 million. You could hardly have a starker example of the dangers that can lurk in even the most respectable-looking figures.

Case study 2: Implanon

More or Less also looked at a story run prominently a few years ago across the news media. One television news programme made it the lead story.

The report highlighted concerns about a contraceptive device called Implanon.

Implanon is a tube filled with hormones that is inserted into the arm and can prevent pregnancies for up to three years. But the television programme reported:

> more than 1,000 people had complained about it, not only women who had had the implant but also health professionals

> 584 women had reported becoming pregnant even though they had had the device fitted

> nearly £200,000 had been paid out in compensation to people who had become pregnant or been hurt by the implant

> at least 14 women had made compensation claims against their local health trusts.

The report therefore raised serious concerns about the effectiveness of an increasingly popular form of contraception. This looked like a big story. It appeared well founded, and others followed it up. But what about the figures? How shocking were they?

Let us start with the most striking statistic – the 584 women who had developed unwanted pregnancies. That sounds like a lot. But let us ask one of our standard questions: is that really a big number?

To judge that, we would need to know how many women in total were using Implanon, and presumably having no problems with it. *More or Less* took up the story and found that 1.4 million women had used Implanon between 1999 and the time of the television report. That put them in a position to calculate a percentage figure, to see if it painted the same worrying picture. The team calculated that the failure rate of Implanon as represented by those 584 cases out of 1.4 million was 0.06 per cent. In other words, more than 99.9 per cent of those using Implanon were not experiencing any trouble with it. By asking just one question, they produced a very significant piece of context for the story. Those 584 women still have problems that should not be dismissed. But they represent a tiny fraction of the total numbers using Implanon.

What about that figure of 0.06 per cent? Is *that* a big number? Or a small one? How can we judge whether Implanon's results are good or bad?

The obvious way to do so is by comparing the performance of Implanon with other forms of contraception. *More or Less* did a lot of work on that too, and found this:

- The contraceptive pill has a typical failure rate of 8 per cent.
- Condoms have a typical failure rate of 15 per cent.
- Vasectomies have a typical failure rate of 0.15 per cent.

The story that emerges from this is rather different from the one that was reported. It is that although Implanon is not without its problems in a minority of cases, it appears to be a very much more reliable contraceptive than the most widely used alternatives.

And *More or Less* uncovered that by asking just two questions:

> **584 out of how many?** This gave them both the raw figures and the percentage; we always want to know both.
>
> **Compared with what?** This gave them the comparative context to assess the relative merits of Implanon.

Case study 3: Labour's election pledge

The most famously misleading political statistic of modern times was the claim made by the Leave campaign in the run-up to the European Referendum vote of 2016 – the famous "bus" slogan. The Leavers claimed that if the UK came out, then the £350 million Britain paid into the EU every single week would be available for spending on things that were more important, notably the health service. Although this figure was exposed early on as being at best misleading and at worst downright inaccurate, the Leavers kept using it – most notoriously on the side of their campaign bus. Eventually, it stuck in the consciousness of many voters.

During the General Election campaign of 2019, the *More or Less* team were busy looking at some of the statistics being bandied around by the parties, and seeing whether or not they had any credibility. There were two special editions of the programme. One of them looked at the feasibility of Conservative promises that if the party was elected, there would be 50,000 more nurses in the NHS within five years, and 40 new hospitals within ten. In both cases, the programme found that behind those headline figures, things were not always what they seemed.

In the second programme, the team looked at a claim by the Labour Party that its spending plans would represent savings of £6,700 a year for "the average household". They examined this figure in the form of an on-air conversation between the presenter Tim Harford, and reporter Ruth Alexander. This was a brilliant example of applying our sceptical approach in real time. The presenter is in effect asking the questions on our checklist, and the reporter is providing the answers. The results are revealing. Here is a transcript of their on-air exchange:

Presenter
I am puzzled by the definition of "the average household". What does your family have to look like if you are going to benefit from this £6,700?
Reporter
The biggest item on the list is childcare. But to get the full benefit of Labour's proposals, you need to have a two-year-old child in pre-school childcare and another in junior school, to take full advantage of the proposed expansion of the free school meals programme.

Presenter

So what are Labour's childcare proposals?

Reporter

Labour wants to expand 30 hours of free childcare to all children between the ages of 2 and 4 – currently children don't qualify for 30 hours of free childcare until they're 3, and both parents are working. Labour estimates its policy would save an average household almost £3,000 a year.

Presenter

Yes – if that average household has a two-year-old child they want to put into childcare. And what about the school meals?

Reporter

Labour's promising free school meals for every junior school student – so 7–11-year-olds. Currently only those at infant school qualify. This policy only applies in England.

Presenter

Ok, so it doesn't sound outrageous to claim that there are lots of families who'll benefit, but still, having one two-year-old and one kid in junior school – that is not the experience of every single family, is it?

Reporter

It isn't. If you have older children, or no children, you won't get this benefit. It's hard to come up with a precise figure so you have to make an intelligent guess.

Presenter

I know the man to make intelligent guesses. That is Rob Eastaway, the author of *Maths on the Back of an Envelope: Clever Ways to (Roughly) Calculate Anything*. Have we asked Rob?

Reporter

We have. Rob's looked at the ONS figures and told us a good rough estimate would be that there are a bit over 200,000 households like that in the UK. That is to say, with a two-year-old and another child between 7-and 11-years-old.

Presenter

Let's call it 200,000 households. So, Labour's policy would put £6,700 not in the pockets of the average family, but in the pockets of 200,000 households.

Reporter

No. Because to get to the £6,700 figure, Labour says you also need a pair of rail season tickets – so two adults. And the ONS says around 20 per cent of families have just one parent, so we need to take 20 per cent off our estimate, which takes it down to about 160,000 households.

Presenter

The point is not that households have to have two adults, but that they have to have two adults with rail season tickets. How many households have two rail commuters?

Reporter

Not many. Most people only travel by train a few times a year. The Department of Transport estimates that just 6 per cent of commuters travel by train.

Presenter

And what is Labour promising to this 6 per cent of commuters?

Reporter

Cheaper rail journeys. They say they'll bring some rail fares down by a third. They calculate an average household with two season tickets would save almost £2,200 a year.

Presenter

Right, so that's a big sum of money and that contributes to this £6,700 figure – but it's only 6 per cent of these 160,000 households who would qualify. So we're talking about, what, maybe 10,000 households?

Reporter

It's actually less than that. And here we hit the limits of what official stats can tell us. That 10,000 figure includes families where at least one person commutes by rail. But not all rail commuters have season tickets. And remember, to get the full amount here, you'd need a family with two young children and both parents holding a full season ticket.

Presenter

Right. So we could be talking about a couple of thousand families, or maybe just a few hundred. And remind me how many households there are in the UK?

Reporter

27.8 million.

Presenter

And the percentage of them who would enjoy the full £6,700 benefit?

Reporter

Tiny. Certainly much less than a tenth of 1 per cent. And quite plausibly, less than one hundredth of 1 per cent.

This is a classic example of how to unpack a statistical claim. By asking some reasonably obvious and intelligent questions we add more and more context and get a clearer and clearer idea of the value of the figures presented to us. In this case, the conclusion is that although many people would have benefited to some degree from Labour's spending plans had they been implemented, the number of people who would benefit to the tune of the £6,700 figure quoted is…close to zero.

Ten top tips

These examples should have convinced you of the relevance and effectiveness of asking those key questions on your checklist. We will conclude this chapter with some tips taken from the handout distributed to BBC journalists when they had completed the workshops I referred to earlier. If you stand by these, you will navigate this tricky and dangerous area with confidence and without falling into any of the traps that so often bedevil journalists when they tackle statistics.

Look on statistics as your friends, providing you with facts and evidence on which to base your stories. But treat them with caution and respect.

1. Let the statistics drive the story and not the other way about. Taking a theory and trying to find statistics that fit it is a recipe for disaster, and one of the biggest causes of inaccuracy and misrepresentation. Make sure that whoever has provided the figures hasn't fallen into that trap, deliberately or otherwise. Look at both percentages and raw data to get a complete picture.
2. Too good to be true? If a story looks wrong, it probably is wrong. Don't take things at face value, especially if you are not looking at the raw figures, but at how someone else has interpreted them or written them up.
3. Context. Look at the background. What is being measured and over what period of time? Could the chosen start and end dates have an effect on the findings? Remember that many important social and other changes happen over long periods of time. Beware of something that looks like a dramatic shift.
4. Check your source. Is the person who paid for the survey likely to be someone with a vested interest in interpreting findings in a particular way?
5. Look at the methodology. All responsible producers of statistics will tell you how they have been produced, the size of the sample and the margins of error. Beware of people seeking publicity using poor surveys, self-selecting samples or partial selection from someone else's data. For something that affects more than 20,000 people, you'll need a survey sample of at least 1,000.
6. Compare like with like – both over time and between different sources. Just because two sets of statistics look alike, it doesn't always mean you can compare them – methods and samples can differ. Comparisons between different countries are especially difficult.

7. Correlation and causation. Just because two facts are sitting alongside each other and look as though they might be connected, do not assume that they are. There may be no connection between them at all, causal or otherwise.

8. Big numbers and little numbers. Seen in context, each can look very different. A risk going from 0.01 to 0.02 might be a "doubling" but it's still a very small risk. A billion pounds of health spending might sound like a lot, but looks less so if it's expressed as much less than 1 per cent of the total budget. Make sure you look at both the percentage and the raw numbers.

9. Don't exaggerate. To say the cost of something "could be as high as" a large sum might be strictly true but could be misleading if it's a worst-case scenario. The central estimate is the most likely to be accurate.

10. Averages. The "mean" is all the figures added together and divided by the number of figures. It is the most commonly used. The "median" is the middle figure within a range. It often gives a fairer picture. Understand the difference and be clear which you are dealing with.

Part three

Multi-platform journalism

13

The digital journalist: the digital scene and writing for the website

keeping up…..what just happened?…..the internet and social as platforms for news reporting…..what makes a good digital journalist….. your personal profile as a student/freelance…. your personal profile as an employee……writing for the internet…..search engine optimisation…..the digital newsroom: Birmingham Live…..data analytics

The growth and expansion of the internet has spawned a host of new roles and new jobs in journalism. Some are with established news providers that have diversified into digital content; others are with organisations that are products of the digital age, such as *HuffPost* and *YahooNews*. But regardless of where you are working as a journalist, you will probably be expected to contribute to the digital output of your organisation – most obviously by writing for the website, but also perhaps by producing audio and video material or assisting with the running of its social media accounts. This chapter and the next will examine how far the journalism skills you have already amassed can be applied to digital working, and what new capabilities and techniques may be called for.

In this chapter, we set the digital scene and consider what your personal online profile should look like, both before and after you land a job. There are pointers about how you should behave online – whether you are a student, or a reporter/producer already employed by a media organisation. We look at writing for the internet, maximising the reach of your stories, and following and shaping their success through analytical tools. We examine the typical workload of a fully fledged digital journalist.

Keeping up

This is a difficult subject to tackle, because the word "digital" means different things to different people, and the digital economy is not yet fully formed. It is young, dynamic and still developing at speed. It is hard to keep pace with everything that is happening. "Writing online" does not just mean producing material for the website – it takes in chat apps, newsletters and social networks too. Well-established platforms are forever changing direction or tinkering with their offerings, and the character and demographic of their user base can fluctuate too. New players arrive on the scene. Some become massive almost overnight, achieving dizzying success in terms of subscribers and users. Others flatter briefly, and then disappear without trace. It is not easy to predict what will fly and what will crash and burn.

With this in mind, it is important that you try to follow and understand overall digital trends on a continuing basis. Maintaining this kind of overview will undoubtedly improve your job-seeking prospects, and will be valuable to you in almost any journalistic job that you manage to land. Here are three websites that you will find really helpful in this endeavour:

- **The Reuters Institute for the Study of Journalism** publishes a number of papers on a regular basis, of which the most useful in this context is its annual Digital News Report.
- **The Tow Center for Digital Journalism** works with Columbia University's journalism centre in the US, and aims to help journalists shape the future of digital journalism.
- **NiemanLab** is a part of Harvard University in the US. It works to identify the role and nature of journalism in the internet age.

What just happened?

The opening chapter of this book took an overview of the way the journalism industry looks today. Digital journalism is an increasingly influential element of the business, and one of the principal agents of change in the way journalism is produced and consumed. Today's digital scene is the product of 15–20 years of frantic, chaotic and largely uncontrolled innovation and change, beginning in the late 1990s. It is the result of a whole series of different but interlocking and interdependent factors, all coming together at the same time to create a revolution, not only in journalism but in many other industries too. The result is that in many respects, journalism today is barely recognisable from the business of a generation ago. The shockwaves are still being felt, and although a lot of what is happening now could be characterised as consolidation and catching up, they will continue to be felt for years to come.

The process is well documented by Ian Hargreaves in his book *Journalism: A Very Short Introduction*. And for an account of what it was like to be in the hot seat as a national newspaper editor during those turbulent times, read *Breaking News: The Remaking of Journalism and Why It Matters Now* by the former *Guardian* editor Alan Rusbridger.

The key elements in the revolution were these:

- **Convergence** – as the influence of the internet grew, media organisations began to invade each other's territory. Everyone set up their own news websites with varying degrees of enthusiasm, and some newspapers diversified into radio and television too. Journalists learned new production skills: the talk was all of multimedia, multiplatform and multiskilling.
- **Democratisation** – meanwhile in the world outside, the business of creating news and sharing content was suddenly no longer the preserve of journalists, but open to anyone and everyone. Amateur bloggers could reach a big global audience just as easily as professional news providers, and some became highly influential – and rich. Eyewitness reporting became a big part of this open access, with the emergence of what came to be known as "citizen journalism", "eyewitness media" or "user-generated content" (UGC). A thriving market developed for this material among professional news organisations, and very soon the telling of most major stories on mainstream media was reliant on eyewitness media of some form or another. Whenever and wherever something happened, a person with a smartphone was seldom far away.
- **New platforms** – it wasn't long before new platforms and networks made sharing even easier for individual internet users, and threatened to marginalise traditional journalism still further. Google came to be seen by many members of the public as the world's principal provider of news, even though the company employed not a single journalist and simply aggregated the efforts of others – whose individual branding and identity were often lost along the way. Facebook (from 2004) and Twitter (from 2006) provided users with easy and cheap ways to post and share content. Others followed. Not everything people shared was news content of course, but the potential for the news business was immediately evident.

– **Mobile** – the development of smartphones and tablets accelerated the process through the development of Android phones and Apple's iPhone and later iPad, with the facility to download apps – mini software packages that allowed users free or paid access to news from the big providers, and a very great deal else besides. Soon, all the major news providers had apps too.

– **The backlash** – by now all the elements for the digital revolution were in place, and the new world order began to emerge. The main casualties were newspapers, whose income depended on sales of the paper and, to an even greater degree, the proceeds of advertising. When so much was faster and cheaper online – if not completely free – the reasons to buy a newspaper evaporated. Circulations plunged, and scores of smaller titles were merged or closed down. The global economic downturn of 2008 simply made matters worse. A further shock was administered by the coronavirus crisis of 2020. Although technology allowed for the continued production of titles in lockdown by staff working from home, the physical side of the business – printing, distribution and of course sales at retail outlets – was badly hit. Revenue from advertising fell through the floor during the crisis.

– **The legacy** – all of these factors continue to shape and influence a still-evolving industry. Some publishers and broadcasters have proved more resilient and adaptable than commentators had predicted in the way they have reacted to the new realities. The response has not been consistent: some organisations are still moving sluggishly, regarding digital as a secondary activity and secondary priority. Some have kept both plates spinning: two of the world's most popular websites – *MailOnline* and *Guardian Online* – are run by British newspapers, but both have maintained a strong focus on the printed product as well. Others have redefined and reinvented themselves – and turned their priorities on their heads – to become digital first, or even digital only. And as we have noted, newer organisations to emerge in this century have been set up from the start on solely digital lines, or with digital at the centre of their activities.

Even the latecomers to the digital game have now embraced it, some more energetically than others. Yet there remains significant diversity over the best way to make online journalism pay: some offer content free to large audiences and rely on advertising and other commercial tie-ups. Other news organisations have sought to persuade their audiences to pay for online journalism, just as they once paid in droves for printed newspapers. There is probably not a one-size-fits-all solution.

In a digital world, the journey between the creation of the content and its consumption by the user is a very short one. It bypasses all those expensive stages of printing and distribution. As soon as the content is ready, it is sent directly – and instantly – to subscribers, and alerts them to its arrival. And as a bonus, the publisher knows who those people are, what they are interested in, how long they stay on the pages and much else besides – and therefore also has a good idea what it takes to keep them paying their subscriptions. Audience data is key in this new world.

The digital scene that is emerging is vivid, varied and vibrant. All the big media organisations have a strong online and social presence. Through these they interact directly with their audiences, soliciting information and news material, and offering increasingly sophisticated means of directing them to material likely to be of interest to them, or giving them the means to apply those filters themselves. The growth of data journalism is a response to the wealth of potentially newsworthy material that is sitting online if only you have the necessary technical, editorial and visualisation expertise to find, analyse and present it.

At the minute-by-minute end of things, where speed is of the essence, continuously updated live pages enable organisations to cover big stories in a multifaceted way in real time. News offered in bite-sized chunks in a series of linked stories reflects the promiscuity of internet usage, where no one stays anywhere for long. Only selected stories become "long reads" that require more of a commitment from the user. Much effort goes into the design of a story online, and the way the reader will interact with it. That design is not only about pushing the editorial content, but also maximising the potential reach of stories by means of search engine optimisation (SEO) and other hooks. Some articles may also be heavily geared to drive video views or ensure users stay longer on a page – so generating advertising revenue. News organisations will typically operate on several social platforms, with content carefully versioned to suit each one. Editorial decision-making is increasingly informed by algorithms and data analytics that identify trending stories in such detail that you can see how many people are reading an individual story at a given time.

The democratisation of the web is still in evidence with blogging, vlogging, podcasting and personal websites, and the huge volume of news, in its loosest sense, circulated informally, both publicly and privately, within social networks. We have mentioned some of the online-only news providers that have emerged, such as *HuffPost*, *Vice* and *BuzzFeed*. Other digital providers have been created, enjoyed a brief moment in the sun and then disappeared without trace. *BuzzFeed*'s contraction in the UK in 2020 shows how tough the digital market can be. The turnover in media players is much faster than in the past, because the competition for eyeballs is so intense and relentless. Anything that does not find a market quickly is liable to be discarded in favour of something newer and shinier.

At a local level, many small newspapers find themselves in competition with hyperlocal online sites or local community groups on Facebook and elsewhere. As the name suggests, these are able to operate within very small communities of people, geographical or joined by common interests.

What does all of this mean for you, a young journalist at the outset of your career? It means that some of the jobs that gave your predecessors their first step on the career ladder – particularly in local and regional newspapers – no longer exist. However, there are still plenty of them, and they still offer a brilliant practical grounding in journalism when it comes to learning on the job. The radio and television sectors remain strong and also offer great places to learn. But new jobs are coming increasingly from the digital world, with a particular premium being placed on skills like finding stories online, understanding audiences and interacting with them. Junior jobs in online operations tend to involve a fair amount of "versioning" – taking news material that has already been gathered by others, and transforming it into something that fits the platform on which it will appear: a website or a specific social network. Working on digital platforms therefore requires a mix of traditional skills of the sort we have been studying, and some technical skills. That is what we will be exploring in this chapter and the next.

The internet and social as platforms for news reporting

One of the defining characteristics of the internet is speed – the speed at which things are published and the speed with which you can gain access to a world of knowledge. A search engine can deliver you hundreds of thousands of results in a split second. Speed has always been a massive factor in the collection and dissemination of news, and the internet takes that to new levels. But with that speed come downsides. When you are under pressure to publish immediately, it can be hard to insist that you need more time to check stories out fully, to confirm and corroborate the information or to add important context. This is a perennial tension for reporting on any 24-hour platform. On social networks, it can be tempting to make false assumptions based on intense and concentrated levels of user activity, and it is easy to forget that the social community is not necessarily representative of the public as a whole.

The advantages of operating online, however, are great:

- You have access to a gigantic potential audience – far greater than anything you could hope to reach in any other medium. During the coronavirus crisis, a single background article on the BBC News website received more than a hundred million views.
- Your stories are updated and/or rewritten more or less on a rolling basis. There are few hard deadlines: the usual impulse is to publish something quickly, however brief, and then add to it later. But you can also hold a story back, and publish it when you think it will have the most impact.

- The production process is quick: you can report breaking news within a matter of seconds. You don't need the whole story. A single fact in a short headline is enough to start the process.
- In the case of a big or running story, this might become a live blog to which you are adding new material over a period of hours. These live pages allow you to report small details and updates at speed without having to rewrite the story each time. This can be a cross-media exercise – an update on an online story might come in the form of a tweet from one of your news reporters that is transferred directly into the live stream.
- There are no restrictions on length – although you are presenting to an audience with a generally short attention span, so disciplined and tight writing is still desirable. However, data analyses and "long reads" are popular features.
- Your digital outlets can cross-reference and cross-promote each other.
- You have opportunities that have never existed before to interact with the audience and to involve them in the gathering of news as well as the discussion, analysis and sharing of it. You have much more of a sense of how the audience is responding to your published material than you do with other media.
- You have huge resources to track down people, images and non-professional video, and to acquire and verify information and other material recorded by the public.
- You have great opportunities for the imaginative and illuminating "visualisation" of stories – illustrating them with audio, video, charts, maps, infographics and so on. All of these can add to the effectiveness and interactivity of the overall storytelling.
- You can offer a huge range of stories, organised so that they can be found quickly by the reader. And they will remain there for good, part of an online archive that will remain searchable indefinitely.
- You can be incredibly responsive and nimble – analytics will show exactly how many people are reading a story at any given time as well as a range of other data that can inform your decision-making and allow you to make changes in real time.
- You can direct the audience to associated stories and to other parts of the site, and the wider internet.

What makes a good digital journalist?

As an online journalist, you need the core skills that all journalists need, as discussed in earlier chapters, including these:

An instinct for what makes a story
A commitment to clear, accurate, interesting (and legal) reporting
A flair for storytelling
An interest in people
An ability to express yourself clearly
An ability to work quickly under pressure
An ability to brief yourself quickly
An ability to make difficult subjects understandable and interesting
Enthusiasm and commitment.

And here are some skills that are more specific to online journalism, or are perhaps needed to a greater degree in the digital sphere than in other forms of media.

An ability to make rapid judgements about material, and turn round stories at speed

An ability to be flexible – moving quickly from one story to another, or one platform to another

A willingness to learn new technical skills, such as those associated with data journalism

An understanding of online audiences – how they differ by platform and demographic, how they behave and how to reach out to them

An understanding of some of the basics of search engine optimisation and data analytics

An ability to combine text with headlines and images or video

An ability to take full end-to-end responsibility for the presentation of your stories to maximum effect.

Your personal profile as a student/freelance

The internet is highly democratic. Anyone can set up shop there. You can create your own website or be posting your first blog within a matter of minutes. You can establish a presence on a whole host of social networks just as easily. This gives you a massive advantage over your journalistic predecessors, in that you have a public outlet for your work without having to rely on someone else to publish it, and can post pretty much anything you like at any time. As you build your experience and profile – and a portfolio of work – this is an opportunity you should be seizing. You no longer need to wait until you have a job in journalism to start publishing material, so don't delay. What you create may turn out to be your passport to that first job.

Adopt a professional attitude to everything that you publish or post in the digital space. It is always tempting to think that on the internet anything goes, and its informality and chaotic character mean you can afford to let your hair down a bit. This is a dangerous road to go down. The laws of libel and copyright still exist online, and everything you share will last indefinitely – accessible to future employers as well as everyone else. So apply the usual standards and ethics that you would expect to exercise in any other medium. Above all, remember that whatever you publish is potentially being shared with the whole world. As the saying goes: "if you share – it's out there".

Software is available – much of it free – that enables you to create a basic personal website from a template without too much difficulty and with a minimum of technical knowhow. A website, perhaps blog-based, is a valuable vehicle for your journalism, displaying your work to best advantage to tutors, NCTJ examiners and potential employers alike. You can create your own podcasts – there is excellent advice about how to do so at *thepodcasthost.com* You can establish your own *YouTube* channel. In terms of your social media profile, *Twitter* and *LinkedIn* are seen as professional spaces, and offer good shop windows for you.

Think of the work you are publishing as contributions to a multimedia CV that you will be happy to share with potential employers as part of a job application. Give yourself a quality threshold but set the bar within your reach – no one is expecting you to produce outstanding journalism to a professional standard from the outset. Those potential employers will be looking beyond the content for evidence of qualities like energy, enthusiasm, curiosity and imagination.

One or two tips:

– Your site/blog and your social media account are going to be the places you demonstrate your aspirations to be a serious professional journalist. Choose a sensible name and non-jokey email address/ handle that will stand the test of time. A gimmicky or fluffy name may seem like a lot of fun when you start, but you will surely regret it as you progress. If you have a common name, or find someone else has already snaffled your chosen username, then customise it with something that will help identify you, such as "journalist", or "news".
– Choose a suitable profile picture, of the sort that you might add to a CV.
– Use your site as the place where you publish your journalism (and link to it in your profile). Keep your personal stuff about holidays, parties and birthdays somewhere else, or at least in a separate area of your site.
– Make sure there is always some evidence of recent activity on your site/account.

– Be careful to observe the law. You are becoming a publisher, and that means you must abide by the law with everything you publish.
– Pay particular attention to any copyright issues with any images or other materials that you "borrow" for your site.

This is the place where you can begin to develop your online persona and journalistic identity – where you start to find your voice. What you write about is up to you. You might have a special interest that you want to focus on, or you may see yourself as a commentator on a wide range of topical issues. You do not have to write long essays – a blog can be a few short, pithy paragraphs, and will probably be the better for its relative brevity: internet users have a short attention span. You may want to mix up the content between smaller items and those to which you attach more weight, between picture-based posts and something more text heavy. The key thing is to post *something*, and to post regularly so that your site looks dynamic and up to date. There is nothing less inviting than a site to which no new material has been added for weeks. You will build an audience not solely through original content, but also with links/retweets/shares/likes, by setting out the sort of fields you are interested in writing about and by interacting with people who respond to your content.

Social networks are also shop windows for potential contacts and employers. Twitter is a good place to begin, because this is where journalists congregate to share materials and opinions. By following some of them, you will learn a lot about journalism, develop insights into how top practitioners work and also see how they present arguments and communicate on the platform.

Social is a still a dynamic and developing field, so don't be afraid to experiment. Some journalists have had great success in telling stories to a younger audience through *Instagram* or *TikTok*. A recurring theme of this book is always to keep the audience in mind, and that is no different when you are operating in the digital sphere. Think about who you want to reach, and then decide which medium, message and platform offer the best ways of reaching them. Sign up for *LinkedIn*, a professional networking site that gives you potential access to hundreds of thousands of useful and influential contacts. This is also a place for your CV, and somewhere jobs are advertised.

Every social media platform works slightly differently, and they are all changing all the time. *YouTube* is a great place for instructional videos to help you get started. *LinkedIn Learning* (formerly *Lynda.com*) is a particularly useful resource in explaining the workings of different software tools and systems. It is a subscription service, but your course might subscribe to it on behalf of its students. There are more resources listed in the next chapter.

Your personal profile as an employee

Once you are in a job, you need to be even more circumspect about your digital presence, because you are a representative of your company, and everything you do potentially reflects on your employer. It may be that you are expected to share stories using only the corporate accounts. But the chances are you will have your own named social media accounts as well, where you can also share your stories and build a personal presence online. Be careful: a very common slip is to tweet on an official account something that you meant to tweet on a personal account. Some organisations will actively encourage you to use your own accounts to offer insights to your audience about the journalistic process, and shed a little light on how the business of news works. So you might share information on your social accounts about someone you are on your way to interview and what about – which can act as a trail for the story you will be publishing later. You may even get a response with suggestions for questions to ask. Juggling accounts in this way requires you to be smart and disciplined. You may want to be funny and edgy and to allow your personality to come through. But unless you are a big name writer, you do need to be wary of crossing the line between a lively personality and something that feels over-opinionated or lightweight. There can be a fine line between observation and informed judgement (on the right side of that line) and opinion and polemic (on the wrong). This is true of other forms of journalism as well.

Although some companies are relaxed about their staff offering personal opinions and comments on topical issues, and linking to other sites, many will adopt a more cautious approach because of the reputational risk involved. Most will have in-house codes or protocols which set out their expectations. Broadcasters have a legal obligation to be impartial, so do not want that undermined by staff advertising their personal opinions. Wherever you work, people outside will assume that your comments online and elsewhere reflect the views of your employer. Do not put much confidence in a disclaimer on the lines of "I work for X but the views expressed here are my own". It will offer you little or no protection if you step over the line.

Even if you think you are being careful, it is very easy to slip up when you are posting on social media sites. As we have said, the informality of the internet and the huge amount of material circulating there can make it feel as though it matters less. But there are hidden dangers. Even seasoned journalists are regularly caught out with incautious posts that backfire on them in this way.

This is the key advice the BBC gives to staff to try to head off breaches of impartiality and other difficulties when using social media:

– Anyone working for the BBC is a representative of the organisation, both offline and on, including on social media. The same standards of conduct apply in all circumstances.
– Behave professionally, treating others with respect and courtesy.
– Assume that anything you post will potentially reach a worldwide audience (even if privacy settings are in place) and will be viewed critically.
– Don't express a personal opinion on matters of public policy or politics.
– Assume that it will become known that you work for the BBC, whether you declare it or not – identities are easily traced.
– Be aware of what your likes, shares, retweets, use of hashtags and who you follow may say about you and your own opinions.
– There is no distinction on social media between personal and official accounts. Your personal brand is secondary to your responsibility to the BBC. Assume that if you are known to work for the BBC, regardless of what your job is, your views will be taken as representing the views of the BBC. Stating that they are your own views will offer you no protection.
– If you make a mistake, correct it quickly and openly.

And here are some of the specific things they advise staff not to do:

– Do not be drawn into ill-tempered exchanges.
– Do not post when your judgement may be impaired.
– Do not use your BBC status to seek personal gain or pursue/support campaigns.
– Do not criticise your colleagues in public.
– Do not reveal how you vote, or express support for a political party.
– Do not post anything that could not be broadcast on the air.
– Do not sacrifice accuracy for speed – second and right is always better than first and wrong.
– Do not mistake social media networks as accurate reflections of public opinion – your audience is overwhelmingly elsewhere.

None of this means that you cannot maintain a healthy and active presence online and on social media. It just means you must be careful and sensible when doing so. It is usually better to keep your personal and professional stuff separate unless you are on a platform such as *Vice* or *BuzzFeed* that actively encourages you to display a degree of individuality. You just need to understand what the parameters are. When you start a new job, familiarise yourself quickly with the views and policies of your new employer when it comes to your online profile.

Writing for the internet

If you have absorbed the principles and practices set out in the chapters on storytelling, you should have no difficulty writing stories for the web. The core considerations, based on the 6Ws, are the same. What is the story? What is the top line? What do I need to include, and what can I leave out? As with any other form of journalism, your goal is accurate, fair and contextualised reporting, delivered as quickly as possible. You want to produce stories that are written crisply and economically and are attractive to the reader.

That said, writing for the web has its own requirements that distinguish it from other media. You cannot cover a story by simply transferring a television news report to the web, any more than you could put a radio report on the television. The web is its own medium, and demands and deserves a particular approach. It is where everything comes together, as the epitome of both *multimedia* – any combination of text, images, audio, video – and *multiplatform* – accessed via any number of devices. There are specific factors to bear in mind when writing in this environment, notably the techniques that present your story most effectively, and give it the best chance of being found and read.

These days, the websites of most news organisations are pretty sophisticated; stories do not necessarily appear at the top just because they are the most recent, as once was the case. Most have multiple topic pages, some as closely curated as the site's homepage, updated and re-ordered as stories ebb and flow in importance, relevance and popularity. The most viewed pages are often those containing the latest news, because those are the first page users encounter when they go to the site, and because news items are those most commonly looked for on search engines. They will probably browse them first even if they came with the intention of looking for something else. So it is vital that the news stories on that front page are up to date, well written and well presented.

Each news organisation uses a content management system (CMS) to create its online news stories. You should receive training in this when you start work. It will be designed to be simple and quick to use, so you can concentrate on writing the story and adding whatever images, media and links may be needed. You may be working with additional systems that also allow you to search for and import pictures, audio and video as well as other associated stories. These may be integrated into the main CMS.

Thanks to the global reach of the internet, your story has a potential audience running into millions. So the emphasis on accuracy and speed is perhaps greater online than it is on any other journalism platform. A typical initial structure for a breaking news story is a headline and four paragraphs. If it is significant and you want to get it out there fast, it may start as only a single sentence, like an old-style newsflash. Speed is of the essence. You will usually be aiming for a short and coherent initial version of around 75–100 words. And you need to produce it quickly: five minutes is your target, ten at most. A longer version should take no more than 20 minutes.

One of the distinguishing characteristics of working online is that you need to do more than just research and write your story. You must also do whatever you can to make sure it is found and read. Among other things, this may well mean providing a headline and a striking image or video, with a caption if one is required. As we will see when we come to look at SEO, you may also need to think about ensuring your story, and especially its headline, includes the words that users are likely to type into their search boxes.

Your headline and the main image are important ways of attracting readers. Internet users skim content very quickly, so your headline and image offer the best opportunity to catch their eye and encourage them to read the story. There is also evidence that users will share content on the basis of the headline alone, without necessarily reading the full story themselves. Like all the best headlines, yours should make sense on its own, be immediately understandable and avoid jargon or anything else that will encourage the reader to move on. The puns or tease headlines that can be effective in newspapers are best avoided here – not least because they can make your story harder to find via search engines. Generally speaking, online audiences prefer active, descriptive headlines. These are also helpful for SEO purposes and for sharing on social, of which more later. The headline should relate to what is in the intro, or first paragraph, of the story that follows, without duplicating or using the same form of words. It must also be accurate, and not over promise or mislead in its desire to attract attention. Overselling leads to clickbait, and to an audience that will feel cheated.

Above all, of course, the headline needs to fit whatever template you are working in. You may be restricted to as few as 50 characters. But some sites, such as *MailOnline*, have distinctive styles that are quite different, and are essentially the whole intro presented as a headline. You will need to understand the house style and protocols in operation in the place you are working.

House style on some sites is to write an "abstract", sometimes called a "subdeck", as well as a headline. An abstract is a sort of secondary heading that adds another angle to the headline but is not part of the written story. This is part of the house style of the *Guardian* website, for example. Here is an example of a *Guardian* story with headline, abstract, image (or "thumbnail"), caption, and intro:

Hong Kong crisis: at least 300 arrested as China protests grow (headline)

Riot police flood city as pro-democracy groups protest against law criminalising 'ridicule' of Chinese anthem. (abstract)

Image of skirmishes (thumbnail)

Hong crisis: protesters and police clash over new anthem law. (picture caption)

Hong Kong police arrested at least 300 people during day-long protests and skirmishes across the city, as residents railed against controversial legislation aimed at bringing the territory further under Beijing's control. (Intro)

Note that when a story appears on a home page or section page people will only see the above, or less. Images that work well scaled up might not look good when you are only seeing them as a "thumbnail" (that is, a smaller version that sits under or next to a headline).

Remember too that lots of people will only ever view your story on the small screen of a smartphone. This means you'll need to consider how an image will look in various sizes. And it is worth making the effort to find the best image you can. Words are obviously important, but in all digital formats, a striking image makes your story much more shareable, and therefore gives it a much greater potential reach. Look for pictures featuring people rather than general views or buildings, as audiences find these more relatable. Make sure the images are relevant to the story – if not, the reader will feel sold short. Think of the headline, abstract and thumbnail as working together to help you make the most of the material you have, and to maximise the chances that people will stop to read the story when they glance at your homepage or their social media feed.

Once you have your headline, writing a short and concise story in four or five sentences should present no problems for you if you adopt the approach set out in Chapters 9 and 10. The same rules apply – a pithy intro, sources as appropriate, supporting material, and – probably in the last paragraph – as much as you can fit in by way of necessary background. However short the story is, the reader still needs to be able to understand it.

The main pressures on you with a new story are time and space. Although in theory there is no limit on length for a web story, the need for speed will create its own constraints. You may have only a few minutes to produce your story, and may be aiming to include all the essentials in only 100 words or even fewer. The ability to identify those essentials we discussed in Chapter 10 is at a premium.

It is a skill that comes with practice. The process of paring down the material is not unlike that required by a radio news summary, which might contain half a dozen stories, each self-contained but each only around 60 words long. There is a section on writing those summaries in Chapter 16. You can help yourself, as always, by seeing how others do it. Look at online stories constantly to see how they have been constructed, and how they have managed to work within the word count. It is also really valuable to look at how other sites present the same story that you are working on: have they made a better or worse job of it than you?

Sometimes that short version of the story will be all you produce. The most interesting or newsworthy facts will always be in your first paragraph. But as you have more time, and the story develops, it may be worth more, and you can add more detail as you would with any other story – quotes, colour and so on. A big story might be 600 words, with media, graphics and other illustration. It may be supported by linked stories or sidebars. Lesser stories will have lower word counts and less illustration – perhaps 200–400 words. But if the story remains in the news pages, you will probably find that your first, short, version, which contained the essence of the story, will serve you well again. Your quick four-par version could well provide the first four pars of the longer piece.

Not all stories are breaking news that has to be published straight away. If they are not time sensitive, it is worth thinking about how you can improve their potential reach with the timing of their release. Maximum web traffic tends to be around breakfast time, lunchtime and late evening. In the daytime, people are looking for quick updates; later in the day, they may have more time for longer reads, more analysis and more video. On an international site, you can time publication to hit peak traffic in different time zones.

Write as you would for any story destined for print: a new paragraph for each new thought or sentence; active and simple words that tell the story clearly and succinctly. A large proportion of the audience will be using a mobile phone, and short, well-spaced pars help make reading easier. If your story has a number of good angles, think about whether some of them would be better treated as separate, linked stories – say as a profile or backgrounder. This is known as "chunking". A suite of associated shorter stories, say 300–500 words, will often fare better than one long piece of 800 words – and may have more chance of being discovered by the audience. Remember though that all the key elements must be in the main story, because that might be the only one that is read.

Your main task is to get the most out of the material to hand by deciding the best combination of media to tell it. The task becomes harder, but potentially more rewarding, the more options you have. In the early stages of a breaking story, you may have only enough details for a couple of pars of text. As things develop, you will get more details, add images and receive audio and video. Later still, you may be able to add value and context with maps and charts. It is a question of being adaptable to your changing circumstances.

Most stories should have a least one image attached to them – and don't forget you will probably need to write the caption for it. Bearing your mobile audience in mind, look for strong images that do not contain a level of detail that might be hard to pick out on the small screen. Your organisation is likely to have access to an agency photo library, and there will always be plenty of stock shots to choose from. If you must use a stock shot, try to find something that has not been used many times before. You can improve the quality of images in Photoshop, but be careful not to create an image that is misleading as a result – by cropping out an important detail or character, for example. The extent to which you crop the picture and prepare it for publication will depend on your local house style and software. Video should be in short clips, embedded at whatever point in the narrative seems to make most sense. As ever, don't forget possible copyright issues.

Locator maps are often useful, and can be quickly created or retrieved from the archive. As in a newspaper story, crossheads and quote boxes help break up the blocks of text and make the story look more attractive. Lists, bullet points or Q&As also break up a dense body of words and make the story visually more pleasing. Picture galleries of half a dozen images or more are generally well liked by readers. Link your stories to others that cover similar subjects – deep link to specific pages if you can rather than homepages – and promote them on your social accounts.

Your story may well be published with a thread inviting readers to share their own experiences or thoughts about the story. Make sure you monitor these – as with social networks, they offer instant feedback and are a great potential source of case studies or follow-up stories. Respond to comments if you can, ignoring – and reporting to your content editor if warranted – anything unnecessarily provocative or abusive.

Be careful when cutting and pasting from previous stories if you are updating or rewriting. You may be duplicating media and links as well as text, and you must be sure that all of those elements are still accurate and relevant to the new story. If they aren't, remove them from the new version.

Search engine optimisation

Having a digital presence online is not enough on its own. Users have to be encouraged and helped to discover your material. When an internet search can offer hundreds of thousands of results, there is no guarantee users will find their way to your offerings. SEO is about presenting your material online in such a way as to guarantee more prominence in searches, and generally to encourage more traffic to your work. It is also about giving your story a longer shelf life, such that it can still be found long after publication. This is especially important for stories that are less time-sensitive and more evergreen in nature.

When you type in a search on Google, or any other engine, you set in motion complex algorithms designed to find and display all the content that is relevant to your search. So if you as a content provider want your site and your story to appear prominently in the list of results, you need to have some idea about the intent of people searching, and the way in which they search. They are probably not conscious of it, but they do so by means of keywords. Keywords are what people enter into a search engine when they are looking for something. If your story contains those keywords, you maximise the chances of the search engine putting your material high up on its list of results.

As so often in journalism, this means thinking about the needs and wants of the audience, in this case trying to second guess what keywords they might use, and then making sure that those words appear in your story. They should be in the headline, and preferably at the very start of the headline. That is why you see so many online headlines frontloaded like these examples:

> Climate change: two degree target 'unachievable'
> EU talks: 'bad faith' claims on both sides
> Covid vaccine: trials 'encouraging'.

And the example we used above:

> Hong Kong crisis: at least 300 arrested as China protests grow.

A subject followed by a colon, as in these examples, is known as a "kicker".

Most of us tend to start an internet search with something fairly general, and then we refine it when we find it throws up too many results. If you type in generic words like "Russia", "Premier League" or "World War Two", you will be overwhelmed by the volume of results. So you will add qualifying words, or ask the search engine questions designed to take you closer to what you want. And when you do so, you will usually use simple and straightforward words.

If that is how you yourself behave when you are searching, then you have some ready-made pointers about how to create content that the search engines will find and present. In any online story you are writing, think about what keywords a user is likely to type in to find your story – then make sure those words appear in your piece.

Example: imagine there has been a fire at an art gallery called Exclusive Art in Newtown in the fictional county of Anyshire. It is believed one person may have been injured, and some valuable paintings have been destroyed.

You might publish an online story with any one of these headlines:

> One feared hurt in Anyshire blaze
> Precious art goes up in smoke
> Town centre fire destroys paintings.

Now imagine you are a resident of Newtown, or an art lover, or anyone else who might be interested in this story. You hear a rumour about the fire and you open a search engine to try to find more details. What are you going to type in the search box? Probably something like:

> Newtown fire
> Art gallery fire.

Either of these searches would take you to various accounts of the fire – but probably not to any of our three example headlines above. The keywords here are pretty obvious: "fire", "Newtown" and "art". A search using those words would not find any of our three headlines very readily. So if you wanted people to see your story at or near the top of the list of results, you should have written a headline that looked more like these:

> Newtown art gallery fire: one feared hurt
> Newtown fire: art works destroyed.

You would hope that any search engine would find that story straight away. Although you cannot control how high up the list of similar stories yours will feature, you need to give it the best chance you can. The trick is to imagine what keywords your potential readers are using, and then use them yourself. You can use Google Trends to help you with this. It is a free tool that will show you the subjects people are searching for, related search terms and when there is a spike in traffic. Many news organisations, especially the tabloids, use this to inform their publishing choices.

All this means being very disciplined about avoiding the sort of journalese that we looked at in Chapter 11 – those short words that are helpful in headlines but seldom used in normal conversation. Does anyone use the word "blaze" in everyday language? Or any of those other headline favourites like bid, slam, probe, quiz, shock and all the rest? As far as SEO is concerned, they are non-starters. Leave them for the newspapers – or better still, leave them altogether. For online stories, the headline has a specific job to do in helping the search engine encourage the reader to come to your story.

The digital newsroom – "Birmingham Live"

Many digital journalists are largely office-bound (or working from a desk at home), spending at least some of their time reversioning stories that have appeared elsewhere or come in from agencies; corroborating material originating from the public, often via social media; and working on the strong visual presentation of news stories to maximise their effectiveness online. But in most news organisations that are digital only, or taking their digital operations seriously, there is scope for conventional reporting work as well.

A case in point is the *Birmingham Live* digital operation, which runs the website and the social media accounts of what was formerly known as the *Birmingham Mail* – a newspaper. The printed paper is still published under that name (and we look in Chapter 19 at how its dedicated reporters work), but as its online rechristening suggests, the digital team is very much the driver of the overall news operation. It is the *Live* team that deploys most of the reporters in the field, and it is the digital outlets that those reporters are serving in the first instance.

The paper made the switch to a digital first model after calculating that as a commercial operation, it was approaching a tipping point. Income from the printed product was in decline; income from the digital product – through advertising on the website – was increasing. The strategic switch to a digital operation was intended to accelerate that trend until the two lines intersected, and the website (the future) became more profitable than the newspaper (the past). Some print reporters were retained to produce bespoke material for the newspaper beyond that the digital team would be generating – extra sports coverage and longer features, for example. The digital news team concentrates on the website and social accounts, using analytics, research and traditional reporting to build and retain an engaged audience.

For a plan like this to work, you need a healthy audience for your digital products. *Birmingham Live* is part of Reach plc, which has followed a similar policy with many of its other papers. Not everyone has a digital presence as multifaceted and highly sophisticated as this. Most importantly it puts digital first, rather than regarding it as a secondary activity.

The news desk is divided into three separate streams:

- **Breaking news** – speaks for itself: the team constantly updating the news pages with new or refreshed stories.
- **Trends** – again, as the name suggests, this team concentrates on trending topics, driven in part by what data analysis (see below) shows to be the stories and issues of particular interest to the readership. Reporters are extensively deployed to cover social issues, such as poverty, homelessness, public transport and the use of food banks.
- **Social** – this is the team that maintains a dynamic presence on social networks. A substantial presence on *Facebook, Twitter, YouTube* and *Instagram* can be taken as read, but there will be several separate accounts on individual networks, again with the intention of getting the content to the audiences that will be most interested in it. These accounts may be based on an area or locality, or arranged more thematically by subject areas. The subjects do not follow the pattern of old-established specialisms such as health and education. *Birmingham Live* has separate *Facebook* groups for, among others, traffic news, sport, parenting news, court reports, people and politics, Brummie Mummies and news from South Birmingham. New ones are being added all the time, and existing ones are dropped if after a trial period they do not attract enough support.

Everything we have said in previous chapters about the way you work applies to digital reporters as much as it does to print, radio or television reporters. The same basic values apply: the same principles around accuracy, newsgathering, ethical behaviour and storytelling are all just as important. The basic construct of the story is the same: the news line, or main point, covered in the intro, the story developed with quotes and other supporting material, the writing crisp and lucid. The difference lies in the dynamics of the way the material is handled, and in the added onus on the reporter to understand the wider business of effective digital delivery.

The digital reporter working in this kind of environment must have a very clear idea of the totality of the offer, and its requirements in terms of the audience and the overall presentation of the story. Producing a decent report is important, but no longer enough; a broader range of skills is required. *Birmingham Live* and similar operations want reporters with a strong understanding of storytelling in its entirety when it comes to online and social output. To the traditional virtues of curiosity and enthusiasm, the digital reporter adds a good knowledge of what makes a story for individual platforms and – critically – how to present it on each. More than any other means of distributing news, digital journalism is trying to forge a match between the content and the people who will be most interested in looking at it. Digital audiences are fickle and promiscuous – they often read only the first line or two of a story, and they hop between a large number of platforms. It takes a special effort to grab and hold their attention. So the digital reporter needs to understand not only the story in the editorial sense, but also the potential audience for it, how it will be targeted at that audience and how well or badly it is performing. It must be suitable for viewing on a mobile, for example, as well as a laptop and a tablet. All this means thinking in headlines, pictures, videos and other illustrations – in sum, seeing the story as a whole and being involved with the production process beyond the delivery of the written story.

Digital writers in Birmingham are expected to produce stories that include a range of elements:

– **The headline.** In the office, staff talk to each other about stories in headline terms to encourage a culture of thinking about the marketing process. Diary entries are written as headlines. The headline must not only tell the story, but also be designed to help the story reach as many readers as possible – through SEO keywords, or references to specific names or localities.
– **The story itself.** The story itself remains the most important element in the process, even though there are many more elements in play as well.
– **Pictures/videos.** The reporters take their own pictures and videos on their phones, and only occasionally work with staff photographers. They need to understand what images work to best effect, the particular issues around publication on different platforms and how to upload them into the system.
– **"Read More" links.** These direct the reader to other associated material in which they might be interested.
– **Widgets.** These display information that points the reader to other sources through buttons, dialog boxes, pop-up windows and selection boxes among others. They offer the means by which the stories can be localised, flagging the location or subject matter so that they stand the best chance of reaching the appropriate readership.

In sum, the reporter is not simply providing the words, but has responsibility for the whole online presentation of the story in all its various aspects. And this applies across multiple audiences, because big digital news providers are operating so many different accounts. The reporter must therefore have an understanding of what sort of stories do well with the audience that arrives via Twitter, the one that comes through a search and the one that visits the homepage every day. You can track this information through data analytics, which we look at next.

You are not flying completely solo – there will always be editors, copy editors and others to act as a second set of eyes before something is published and to assist with editorial issues and presentation. But the digital reporter arguably shoulders more responsibility than counterparts in other media because of this end-to-end commitment to the story.

At the scene of breaking news

We looked in Chapter 6 at how you operate when you are first on the scene of a breaking news story – sending over some raw material as quickly as possible, to buy yourself the time to go and discover what is happening. Covering breaking news for digital platforms is not dissimilar in its priorities. The first imperative is some sort of image from the scene, which you can send back quickly. You will probably follow this with some pars of description, somewhere between an online story and a live blog. Putting yourself into the reporting helps add to the sense of immediacy and urgency: "I arrived here only a few minutes ago, and as I did so more emergency vehicles drew up, their sirens wailing", and at the end: "I can see some people gathered behind the safety cordon, and I'm going to see if any of them saw what happened", which implies a promise that you will be back shortly with more details – and so encourages readers to stick with you. A burst of video, and some more stills will also be very useful for those back at base who are putting the coverage together: the video can be inserted into your copy, and the pictures can be put into a gallery. And then the cycle repeats itself, with you updating your copy as often as you can, and sending back further videos and images as you are able to get them.

Data analytics

Data analytics is at the heart of the digital newsroom. Through the use of a variety of measuring tools known as metrics, content managers and editors can track the behaviour of individual stories in real time. They use these insights to inform what stories they publish, what prominence they give them and how long they keep them on the site.

There are a number of online analytics providers, of which *Google Analytics* is the best-known free service and *Chartbeat* is probably the best known paid-for tool. Various metrics are offered by Facebook Insights, Twitter Analytics and LinkedIn Insights. Some of these tracker tools provide you with a dashboard – a summary of data about who is coming to your site and what they are doing when they get there. Among other things, analytics will tell you:

> How many people are using your site (unique users)
> How many people are reading a story at any given moment
> What part of the world they are from
> How many readers are new visitors to the site, and how many are returnees
> How many pages/stories they look at on each visit (pageviews)
> What kind of device they are using – phone, tablet, computer
> How they came to the story – from elsewhere on the site, or referred from a social network for example
> How long they are staying with a story (dwell time) before "bouncing" somewhere else (bounce rate)
> The times of day when usage is at its heaviest/lightest
> Which stories are generating most interest and interaction
> When interest in a story suddenly spikes unexpectedly.

This information is anonymised, so that there are no privacy issues around gathering it, and it is aggregated to give an overall picture of the performance of the site, as well as a close focus analysis of individual stories. Analytics give journalists a mass of metrics that explain how users are behaving in general, or at any given moment. A rise or fall in unique visitors will indicate growth or shrinkage. A rise or fall in the number of visits each unique visitor makes will be an indication of loyalty. And a rise or fall in the number of page views per visit is evidence of greater or lesser engagement.

Clicks are not everything. A story might do relatively badly in terms of the number of hits it is getting, but really well in terms of audience engagement – how long users are sticking with it, how many of them choose to share it. A story scoring well in those terms would also be regarded as successful even if relatively few people read it, because it may encourage them to return.

All this is invaluable real-time feedback for anyone publishing material online, regardless of platform. It helps content editors understand what stories are doing well and what stories are under-performing, and gives them the evidence and the opportunity to make alterations and corrections in a timely manner. In this way there is a direct connection between the behaviour of the audience and the actions of the news provider. More broadly, the analytics provide valuable indications about the audience, what kind of stories are of most interest and will generate most response, what kind of content presentation goes down best. This informs strategic decisions about editorial agenda, running orders, presentational style and tactics, branding and much more.

Editors need to strike a balance, however. There will always be a tension between giving the audience what they *want* – which analytics clearly indicate – and what they *need*, by way of more significant news items that are not so obviously appealing. This tension may manifest itself as a straight fight between editorial ambition and commercial imperative – at the extreme, between valuable journalism, on the one hand, and clickbait on the other. All news organisations must navigate a way through this. The mass of information at their disposal from analytics does not replace or supersede the editorial function. It informs it and has an influence on editorial decision-making. The trick is not to be a slave to the data, or to overreact to each small movement of the dial.

Even so, you can make immediate adjustments if, for example, you see a story doing much less well than it should. If a good story appears to be under-performing, perhaps the headline is not appealing enough and needs rewriting. The keywords are missing. Perhaps the story does not work so well on a mobile. Perhaps it is not constructed as well as it should be: a story may be illustrated by a striking gallery of photographs, for example, but users are clicking away before they get as far as the pictures. If so, the pictures need moving further up the story. If a story is performing strongly several days after it first appeared – by which time it would usually have disappeared from the front page of the site – editors will decide to keep it there for longer, and perhaps look for associated or follow-up stories that will ride the wave of that interest.

As a newsroom journalist, you may well have the same access as everyone else to the dashboards that summarise what the analytics are telling your company about the way stories are performing. The editorial judgements about whether or not it is necessary to respond to the feedback, and in what way, will normally be the responsibility of content managers or editors. But it is fascinating to track the performance of your own stories, and it is important that you understand how the analytics work and what they are saying – and how the editor wants to respond. These factors will determine how you present your stories, or how you alter and adapt them to try to attract more traffic and increase their effectiveness.

14
The digital journalist: social media and online research

social media…..the main players…..social media tips….live blogging…..trust, disinformation and fake news…..data journalism….eyewitness media…..advanced digital research…..confirmation and corroboration…..data visualisation…..Post Traumatic Stress Disorder….think digital

In this chapter, we will look more closely at working with social networks and at a number of areas of digital journalism that will help you find, verify and publish your material. If you are already a digital native and feel at home in the digital world, this chapter will help you apply your knowledge and expertise in a journalistic context. It should also demystify some aspects of digital journalism for older journalists who have not grown up with it in the same way, and find it confusing, suspicious and not a little intimidating.

Digital journalism does require some specific skills, most of them around knowledge of the various tools at your disposal, and how to use and get the best out of them. Journalists are not expected to be experts in coding and design, and some technical and graphic design tasks will always require people with a specific background in those areas. But every journalist needs at least a working knowledge of the digital world and what an incredible resource it offers. The more capable and competent you are in this field, the more marketable you become as a potential employee. Many seasoned journalists do not have these skills and find them difficult to acquire, so they are highly prized. If you can demonstrate them, your personal stock will skyrocket. And as time goes by, you will not be able to survive without them.

Social media

Social networks are an integral part of the journalism business, and open up many opportunities for research and communication as well as for the dissemination of news. They also extend the reach of what you have to offer, helping you find audiences that might not naturally be aware of your material and do not use mainstream media sources. The potential is vast, and if your content is presented appropriately, it can reach hundreds of thousands, even millions, of people.

The editorial processes and systems of any modern news organisation should have a social media strategy at their heart. From the moment a story is first discussed and commissioned, even if its principal intended outlet is not digital, the planning of coverage should include consideration of how the story will be presented across a range of digital platforms. That discussion will also recognise that platforms are not generic: each social network is different, and has a different user base and different formatting requirements – and they all change all the time. Your material has to be adapted to take account of these variations.

As a digital journalist, you need to be able to put all of this together in a single end-to-end stream of effort. As seen in the *Birmingham Live* operation we looked at in the previous chapter, digital journalists need not just to find stories and report them but also to help their stories reach the most suitable audience. That means researching the different platforms and studying what forms of content perform well and what less well. You might use social media to source stories, verify what you find, obtain copyright permission for eyewitness media, package your content for different platforms and then actively target a particular audience. It is a multifaceted role that goes far beyond the basic reporting of a story.

Do not be daunted. You are probably already familiar with, and a regular user of, the principal social networks. All you need to do is bring to bear the fundamental journalism skills that you have already learned around newsgathering and storytelling, and apply them in the digital space. As a senior digital journalist on a national news desk told me:

> When I recruit, I am not looking for social media specialists. I am looking for journalists with initiative and imagination. We can teach them all the specific skills they need, and quite quickly. But I would expect them to have a basic understanding of how to check out information posted on social media, of the importance of user-generated content to newsgathering and a grasp of how copyright works. They need to be highly sceptical and be able to ask the right questions to get to the bottom of what's accurate and what isn't.

These are the qualities you would expect of any journalist, and are not specific to the digital world.

The main players

No organisation or individual can be an effective active participant on all social networks. You need to be selective, and to understand who is using each network and how, and what kind of content, in what form, works best on each one. What you post and how you publish depends first and foremost on the strategy of the organisation for which you are working and the sort of audiences it wants to reach. Beyond that, the whole social scene is a moving target: algorithms change in a way that it is not always easy to understand, the way the networks operate is being tweaked and refined all the time and different formats move in and out of fashion. Video is definitely in – but what is the optimum duration of a video report? And should it be a polished and edited report, or something more raw and authentic with a less "produced" feel? The answer today may be different from the answer six months ago. In six months from now it may be different again. Try to keep pace with the way things are going. But more importantly, keep up to speed on your own employer's social strategy on each of the networks on which is it active, and how that strategy evolves and changes over time.

Facebook

Facebook remains by far the biggest player in the field, by virtue of sheer numbers of users – more than 1.5 billion of them, including about half the population of the UK. It is also one of the world's most valuable companies, ranking alongside Amazon, Microsoft, Apple and Google. It owns *WhatsApp* and *Instagram*. In spite of its size, it is worth remembering that many younger people are less active on *Facebook* than they once were, spending more time on (to them) more exciting platforms. Much of the activity on *Facebook* is by older people or families sharing pictures and news: more than 80 per cent of parents on *Facebook* are "friends" with their children. Perhaps further evidence of this profile is that increasing numbers of people look to *Facebook* and other social media for local news. But while big news stories are usually the most shared posts on *Twitter*, for example, *Facebook*'s most popular items tend to be softer, with a greater emphasis on human interest stories or listicles.

As a journalist, you will find *Facebook* a powerful resource if you are looking for people who are not on the radar but who suddenly find themselves caught up in news stories. Their *Facebook* pages will often contain personal details and photographs that might help you build and illustrate your story. You can also use *Facebook* to appeal for people to get in touch if they are at the scene of breaking news stories, such as bad weather, demonstrations or natural disasters. Be aware of potential copyright issues – just because you can see something on the internet does not mean you have the right to copy and publish it. Publishing photographs from *Facebook* or any social networking site without permission will infringe the copyright of the person who took them. It is also potentially an infringement of their privacy – something about which you will remember the ethical codes have a lot to say. In practice, the use of such material does happen, and may on occasion be justifiable. But you would be well advised to refer up and/or consult *Essential Law* before you start helping yourself to pictures without permission.

Media pages on *Facebook* tend to focus less on minute-by-minute news and more on added value – strong words and pictures, extracts from interviews, longer explanatory articles and links to other content. As with all social networks, the visual content is critical – it is the images, still or moving, that draw in the reader. A softer story with limited news value but strong visual appeal will generate positive reactions in the form of likes, comments and shares. Try to keep across the responses you get – they may offer new leads, or may simply help you build a relationship with the audience. People are generally delighted if their comments prompt a direct response from a journalist. Don't forget that your news posts will usually be mixed in with all the personal *Facebook* content people are sharing with their friends and family, so the tone and nature of the news content needs to reflect that kind of ambience.

In terms of both presenting content and finding potentially newsworthy material, think about the audience you are targeting. For example, if you are looking for details of something that has happened in a residential neighbourhood, you will find *Facebook* groups an absolute boon. Look also at the comments people make on the *Facebook* pages of the local newspaper. People see *Facebook* as the easiest way to share information with friends and neighbours.

Twitter

Twitter was founded in 2006 and has more than 300 million users – so by that measure, it is less than a fifth the size of *Facebook* and generates less traffic and smaller audiences than other platforms like *Instagram* and *Tumblr*. Famously, *Twitter* became the favoured means by which President Trump chose to communicate with the rest of the world. Partly, but not wholly because of that, it has gained an unwanted reputation as a place where a great deal of misinformation or fake news is circulated. For that reason, journalists tend to take a sceptical view of it as a news source, using it principally as a tip-off service alerting them to developments that they can check out elsewhere. To be fair, the same is true to an extent of *Facebook* and all social content.

However, some high-profile people such as politicians and celebrities will use their personal *Twitter* accounts to post updates about what they are doing – which of course can be regarded as a first-hand source. Prominent journalists and commentators maintain personal accounts on *Twitter*, and some spend a large amount of their time pontificating there. This has become much easier with the larger character allowance per tweet, and the expedient of spreading your contributions across a series of consecutive tweets. As well as using *Twitter* as a vehicle for their reporting, journalists will also talk about the mechanics of what they are doing and what they are reading, and add insights into how they operate. So it is a good place to be if you want to see senior journalists at work and get a sense of how they go about their business.

This makes *Twitter* a good place to tune into the news conversation, where strong opinions are voiced on topical issues and will often spark a torrent of comments from all sorts of sources, often including well-known names. Articles, still pictures and video clips will be retweeted to prompt or extend the debate. News feeds will include regular updates on running stories, however small the development. Breaking news on *Twitter* is a popular feature – *Sky News* has more than 6 million followers there, *The Guardian* 9 million and *BBC News UK* more than 11 million. As a reporter on a breaking story, you will be posting tweets as you go along on your own account, while observing the protocols and priorities of your employer in terms of the order in which you file. A single tweet does not have to tell the whole story: it can just add an angle or new line to continuing coverage. Your team back at base can use those tweets to add to live coverage on other platforms, or retweet on the organisation's official accounts. So regular tweets can be good means of filing regular copy on a moving story – as well as boosting your profile and the brand of the organisation.

To a degree, it is up to you how active you want to be on *Twitter*. Some love it, but there is a view that if you tweet every small development you lose sight of the big picture, and can end up offering an imbalanced picture over time. It is also a sad fact that a lot of prominent journalists suffer highly unpleasant abuse on *Twitter*, which no one should be expected to tolerate. Take advice from your employer and decide where you want to sit on the spectrum, and then maintain that position consistently so that your followers come to know what they can expect from you and in what circumstances you will be posting.

Be wary of joining debate if it is important for you to maintain a professional neutrality. Plenty of journalists have been caught out expressing too strong or too personal an opinion on people or issues, and found that a disclaimer saying they are speaking only for themselves makes little or no difference. Journalists rarely emerge from a *Twitter* row with an enhanced reputation.

Instagram

Instagram, which is owned by *Facebook*, has more than a billion active monthly users and is a strong rival to *Twitter* in the news stakes. It is one of the fastest growing platforms for news organisations, with features such as stories, where a number of stills and short video clips are put together into a simple narrative, and IGTV where longer video clips can be posted.

Instagram's success is based on the massive popularity of still images and video in the digital space. This is the place – or one of the places – for your most eye-catching content. With great visuals and trending hashtags, your material will do well. Without them, you are unlikely to make much of an impression with this audience. The words take second place, and stories are usually very tightly written. Audiences seem to like consistency in branding terms, so stick to an established style in terms of fonts and video formats. *Instagram* is also more likely to be used by a younger audience, so think about this when considering story selection for the platform.

YouTube

YouTube is an online video-sharing platform owned by Google. It is almost unimaginably large, with hundreds of hours of content uploaded every minute and more than a billion hours of content viewed every day. Users can upload their own video content, create playlists, share and review content and subscribe to other channels. The vast majority of the content is uploaded by individuals, but big media organisations have their own *YouTube* channels. Clearly the broadcasters have an advantage over print publications, because they routinely generate much more video. The BBC has nearly 8 million subscribers, *Sky News* 2.5 million. But the *Daily Telegraph* has well over a million, and both the *Daily Mail* and the *Sun* also have a substantial *YouTube* presence. The content of the *YouTube* channels occupied by newspaper brands tend to be a combination of video they have generated themselves, eyewitness media and reworked agency material.

You can follow *YouTube* channels by subscribing to them, and can set up alerts for when an account uploads a new video. As with other platforms, *YouTube* might be a source of video content when individuals unexpectedly find themselves caught up in the news. As with other online sites, take advice on copyright issues.

LinkedIn

You probably think of *LinkedIn* as a place for networking, making connections and looking for jobs, and you should take full advantage of its potential in all of those areas. Fewer people associate it with news, and not all organisations have a presence there. But those that do perform well – the *Financial Times* (*FT*) has nearly 6 million followers on *LinkedIn*, *BBC News* nearly 7 million and the *Economist* more than 11 million. It is a professional audience – the success of the *FT* and the *Economist* and the nature of the material they publish there reflect that.

Snapchat

Snapchat is a free messaging app, the distinctive feature of which is that the pictures and video ("snaps") shared by users disappear after they have been viewed. It has around 230 million users worldwide sending 4 billion snaps a day, and is popular with young people who find it less formal than *Facebook*.

The ephemeral nature of *Snapchat* content might suggest it is not an ideal site for news, but the lure of that huge teenage audience is too great to be ignored, and there are plenty of news organisations now active on the platform. They offer material with a longer shelf life, specifically aimed at that audience profile. Bear *Snapchat* in mind as a potential source of breaking news images: during the fire at Notre Dame Cathedral in Paris in 2019, the American network *CNN* ran more than a dozen videos from Snapchat users showing the fire from a variety of different perspectives.

TikTok

Opinions are divided as to whether the video-sharing site *TikTok* is worthy of its place on this list, seen from a news context. It is the youngest of the big social networks but it has enjoyed a meteoric rise in popularity. Launched in China in 2016, it soon notched up more than half a billion active monthly users. Attracted by celebrities, many of those users come to the site via their mobiles to create short dance and lip-sync videos. Some of these become viral trends. Two thirds of users are under 30, and *TikTok* has become closely associated with young people looking for more fun than they feel they get on other platforms. Journalists are still working out what sort of content works best on a network that is not an obvious outlet for news, and at time of writing the bigger organisations seem particularly wary of it. The youth of the audience has led to concerns that it has the potential to be exploited by paedophiles and cyberbullies. Added to that are worries about its Chinese ownership and about privacy and transparency. However, everyone wants to attract a younger audience, and *TikTok*'s numbers are so huge that the media may feel obliged to engage at some point.

This list is far from comprehensive. If you are interested in this area, look also at *Tumblr*, *Reddit* and *Pinterest* and at some of the many other platforms and chat apps that appear on a regular basis.

Social media tips

The best social media content is strongly visual, be it still images (or graphs and maps) or video. Video posts on all platforms reach considerably larger audiences than text-only or photo posts.

These tips pull together some of the pointers we have discussed when looking at how to operate both on social media and on the web.

    follow our golden rule of storytelling – simple, straightforward, clear and concise

    always look for strong pictures and video to support your stories and give them maximum appeal

    keep your site/accounts regularly updated, with new material or suggestions for sharing

    if your material does not need to be published/posted at once, think about the best time to release it

    think about which platforms are most suitable for your material, and the sort of people you want to reach

    try different approaches to writing and publishing, and see which seem to generate the best audience response

    interact with the audience if the opportunity presents itself

    use analytics to see how your material is performing – and adapt your approach accordingly.

Live blogging

Live blogging is a means of reporting a story minute by minute in real time – a constant news stream. It does not parcel the story up for the audience in the traditional way – with a considered overview containing a sharp intro and a well-organised compilation of facts, quotes and background information. All those elements may be there, but they are not ordered: they are published in snippets as they happen, building into a stream of continuous coverage over a sustained period. There is no need to reprise the whole story every time you record some new detail, and indeed brevity is very important. This format can be used on news websites and social media accounts. A big sports website may be running a whole host of live blogs at the same time on a Saturday afternoon, allowing users to follow live text commentary (sometimes with stills and video inserts) of any one of a dozen or more football matches or other sporting events. A local radio or television station or a newspaper might run a live blog containing updates on all the stories they are covering on a given day.

Live blogs have the obvious appeal to an audience of immediacy, speed and brevity, and they are extremely popular. They also allow for a single reporting stream to contain contributions from more than one reporter, and more than one platform. And there is also the option (routine in sports coverage) of allowing for comments from the audience.

A live blog on a government announcement about schools, for example, may begin with a series of short extracts from the announcement or a ministerial statement, followed later by quotes from opposition parties. A political correspondent may add observations about the political significance, or the atmosphere in the House of Commons. There may be a short piece of commentary and analysis from the education correspondent. Comments from teaching unions and other interested bodies may follow – perhaps in the form of tweets which are simply imported into the live stream. Readers will be offered links to associated stories or backgrounders. The fact-checking team may scrutinise some of the figures that are being bandied about in the debate. The main points of the story so far will appear at the top of the blog for the benefit of new joiners. All this may continue for as long as the story is still generating new angles and developments.

At their best, these blogs feel fast and dynamic, bringing multiple aspects of a story together in one place. Sometimes, though, they can lack balance, structure and coherence, and make it harder for journalists to exercise their key function of explaining stories and putting them into context.

If you are contributing to a live blog on a big story, the elements you are providing may simply be part of a wider reporting effort, as in the above example. But you might find yourself doing a live blog all on your own – say if you are the only reporter covering a press conference, a big court case or a council debate. This will give you the headache of having to balance the time and effort you are devoting to the live stream with the need to pay attention to what is happening in front of you, and whatever other coverage you will be expected to provide later. How you perform that juggling act will depend on the circumstances and the priorities of your employer. Those reading a live blog want to feel that it is bringing them the very latest developments as quickly as possible. Speed is more important than production values. If it feels a little rough around the edges, that can add to the sense of immediacy. Speed is not, however, more important than accuracy.

Live blogging lends itself to all sorts of stories beyond breaking news. If that is the case, you may have more time to think about gathering still or video images to post alongside your descriptions, and you might be able to offer some analysis and judgements about what you are reporting. Because of the unstructured nature of the format, video can be raw footage that has not been beautifully edited, and will often work better in this style of reporting. The text updates you blog should be just that – updates with a new detail or new quote.

Trust, disinformation and fake news

The more news people read on the internet in general, and social media in particular, the less they seem to trust it. Since trust is the absolute foundation stone for any news provider, this is a cause for concern. The internet is an extraordinary repository of human knowledge, all available at a moment's notice around the clock. That makes it a great tool for journalism, for finding stories, researching them and then publishing them in various forms. But because it is open to all, it is constantly vulnerable to misinformation (shared unintentionally) and disinformation (shared deliberately) and what we have come to know as "fake news".

It is as well to be clear about fake news, since its meaning was wilfully distorted by President Trump and then others to describe any report with which they did not personally agree. That elision should be resisted. Fake news is, as its name suggests, a fiction. It has nothing to do with bad journalism, which is when journalists do not do their jobs properly, or with journalism that makes politicians uncomfortable. It is made by non-journalists and passed off as real news, often in a highly plausible disguise. At first it was just a nuisance; now it is a real menace. Surveys taken in the UK during the coronavirus pandemic of 2020 suggested that almost half of those searching the internet for advice about the disease encountered misleading or inaccurate information. People spread fake news for all manner of reasons, including financial gain, undermining people or groups they don't like, or from a misguided sense of mischief. But the coronavirus survey is just one example of how careful we need to be with material that comes from any but the most unimpeachable of sources. At its most sinister, disinformation is a political weapon used by one state against another, with the intent – and genuine potential – to destabilise and undermine the democratic process.

More encouraging research from the time of the coronavirus confirmed what previous crises have demonstrated-that at times of peril people do tend to turn to sources that they regard as tried and tested. In the UK, that generally means established mainstream media news providers like the *BBC*, *ITN*, *Channel 4*, *Sky News*, the *Times*, the *Guardian* and the *Daily Telegraph*. As was argued in earlier chapters, professional journalism's best bulwark against fake news and disinformation is to concentrate on producing high-quality content that readers and audiences can trust and will turn to. That can be quite a challenge in the crazy world of social.

Data journalism

In Chapter 7, we looked at the different sources from which you can find news and information – not only online, but through developing personal contacts and using Freedom of Information (FoI) legislation, for example. The section on FoI gave a sense of just how much revelatory and newsworthy information is available on open sources. There is a vast and tantalising world of potential news material out there.

Data journalism is about burrowing around and finding it. Often it means uncovering stories in numbers – stories that are often buried away in reports, balance sheets, FOI responses or even football results. News has always been driven by facts and figures, so there is nothing very new about data journalism. Another phrase – Computer-Assisted Reporting – is perhaps a more precise way of characterising it. The difference today is that the volume of data available online is enormous, and the number of stories waiting to be found has also increased exponentially. Data journalism is the process by which you find and tell them – and it has already produced thousands of powerful stories.

Some of the techniques required to dig deep into data banks and interrogate them until you come up with something of interest still require specialist skills. Not everyone combines a facility with spreadsheets, an ability to find their way through some of the farther reaches of the internet and the journalistic instinct to spot and draw out a potential story. Plenty of journalists would rather be out reporting in the field than sitting in front of a computer screen. Accordingly, most big organisations employ specialist data journalists, either full time or for specific investigations. But some aptitude for working in this way is increasingly seen as important for *all* journalists; if you can combine some of these skills with your other journalistic resources, you will find yourself highly valued.

The key skills are:

– Numeracy, and understanding the basic principles governing the handling of statistics (see Chapter 12)
– An ability to search the internet for sources of data
– An ability to work with spreadsheets to organise your data
– An ability to interrogate and analyse the data for potential stories
– An understanding of how to verify and check what you find
– A feel for how these stories can most effectively be told online
– A flair for presentation.

Of course, the key thing is to have an idea of what to look for in the first place. As with all reporting, that means constantly asking questions about stories and coming up with ideas for investigating them further. Look at the big stories of the day, or on your patch, and think about what more you would like to know about them, or what angles have not been fully explored and could be pursued. When big data sets are published, try to think of ways of looking at them that might turn up insights that others have missed. More generally, just keep your eyes open and exercise your natural curiosity. If you are sitting in a traffic jam, think of ways to explore how many years of their lives people spend stuck in traffic, or how much they spend on petrol while not going anywhere, what the overall cost to the economy congestion might be, or what the effect that traffic jams alone might have on greenhouse gas emissions. It is amazing what you can uncover if you are prepared to dive into the deeper waters of the internet. Looking at a number of different data sets from different sources and bringing them together might also yield a story, as long as you are careful not to make assumptions about connections that might not exist. (See "Cause and effect" section in Chapter 12.)

More sophisticated examples of data journalism engage the audience interactively. Here are some websites that do this work, and give a sense of what is possible and how illuminating and fascinating it can be:

Gapminder publishes all its data, so you can follow its methods. It is an organisation that uses data to explain the world we live in. A good example is its plotting of average life expectancy against average incomes.

ProPublica is an independent newsroom that specialises in this type of work. A good example is its analysis of biological studies that compared the rate of animal extinction today to the extinction of the dinosaurs.

Bloomberg has a data graphics section that is full of interesting material – including a data-based analysis of the most dangerous jobs in the US. Spoiler: taxi drivers and chauffeurs came top, ahead of police officers and security guards. That's a cracking story.

The BBC encouraged participation in sport by creating an interactive quiz that was designed to reveal to people what sport they were most suited for – and then directed them to the places near their homes where they could take up that sport.

The Wall Street Journal produced a striking data-based presentation showing the impact of vaccines in treating a number of diseases since 1930.

The simple message is: come up with an idea, do some searching online and see where it takes you.

A familiarity with spreadsheets is very helpful. A lot of the material you are looking at will probably be on spreadsheets, and you may need to create your own in order to manage your material. A knowledge of how to use and perform simple operations with them will take you a long way down the road of data journalism – maybe as far as you need to go. These operations will include an understanding of how to use functions like *pivot tables* and *Vlookup* to filter material, sort it and carry out mathematical calculations that could turn raw data into trends and averages, and expose anomalies. These tools allow you to "interview" or "interrogate" data in spreadsheets as you try different ways of filtering or ordering your findings. It enables you to "clean" data, so that you remove all the material that is not relevant to the line of investigation you are pursuing.

Think of this process as you would if you were a research scientist. There are two basic scientific approaches: start with an idea or proposition and test it from as many different angles as you can, to see if you can prove or disprove it. Alternatively, take some apparently unconnected data and try to impose some sort of order by examining it in different ways, to see if any sort of pattern emerges, or something from which you can start to draw a general conclusion. You can use either of these approaches when looking at data as a journalist. Unlike a scientist, your goal is not a magic formula. It is a news story.

If you have a grasp of computer coding, this could prove extremely valuable within a journalism context. You can create a set of commands that can be used repeatedly with different data sets. This will save you time when you are organising your data, or when you are gathering it in the first place by "scraping" it from the internet. In essence you are writing yourself a little programme that saves you endlessly cutting and pasting or performing the same functions over and over again. There are good Beginner's Guides on the internet, especially on *LinkedIn Learning*. Look at the guides to *R* and *Python* as a starting point.

It is important not to think about data journalism as a discrete activity happening all by itself as a separate part of the newsgathering process. The key word in the phrase "data journalism" is "journalism". The method is one with which you are already familiar: gathering information and then examining it to see if there is a story there. With Google, Excel and others, you can subject that information to extensive analysis – breaking it down by country, region, ethnic group, sector or organising it in any way that reveals something new and interesting. Whatever your source, you are still going to have to subject it to the same sceptical scrutiny as you would with any other story you produce.

None of this means we have abandoned our devotion to the idea that journalism is about people. The numbers can look stark and bald enough in a spreadsheet or a chart, and they need life breathing into them even when you have uncovered something interesting. Very often, those numbers will represent people, or reflect some aspects of the way the world is and how individuals are affected. The raw data may be pointing you to the story, but you are going to need more than that when you come to telling that story. You will need to bring it to life as you would any other story, in three basic ways:

– By delving deeper. The story you have uncovered may offer more follow-up questions than it does answers. You need to do more research, perhaps by other means, such as talking to experts. Not everything is done on a computer. Ask: What are these figures telling me? Why might this be happening? Why is it happening in this locality, or to this particular group of people?
– By introducing the human element that will make your story more relevant and readable. Ask: Who is represented by these figures, or affected by them? Then use social media to track some of those people down so that you can give a real and human face to the bald facts. Talking to people remains one of the best ways of getting and understanding the significance of raw information. The data provides only one of your sources.
– By strong "visualisation" – how you present your story online. More on this later.

Key points about data journalism:

Data journalism is about data, but mostly it is about journalism.

Finding and analysing the data will often be only the first step in your gathering on a story.

Think of data journalism as being about potential human stories rather than pages of figures. Raw data will usually relate to people and human activity.

You **do not** need to have specialist technical skills to be able to do at least some data journalism.

You **do** need to be confident looking at statistics, and how to assess and analyse them.

You **do** need some basic knowledge of spreadsheet programmes such as Google Sheets or Excel, because this is how data can be organised and scrutinised.

If you feel confident – and want to increase your value in the organisation – you can start to teach yourself, or ask for training in, some of the principles and tools that will speed up and deepen your research.

Eyewitness media

Sometimes known also as citizen journalism or user-generated content (UGC), eyewitness media is material provided by members of the public who find themselves at the scene of a newsworthy event. It may be information, but more often than not it is photos or video, usually shot on a mobile phone. Everyone with a smartphone is a potential reporter, and eyewitness media is an integral part of storytelling across all media – broadcast and online outlets in particular. Some of the most striking and memorable images you see in news coverage have been captured by members of the public rather than professional journalists. One of the earliest and most famous examples was footage in 2000 of the supersonic airliner Concorde, on fire and about to crash in Paris, shot through the window of a vehicle driving on a road that ran parallel to the runway. Perhaps the most notorious was the shocking footage of the aftermath of the murder of a soldier in a London street in 2013. Distasteful though it may seem, footage like that can command high prices and spark a media bidding war. But that is the exception: most people who find themselves in possession of newsworthy material do not expect to be paid for it, and are happy to have it used at all, happier still if they are credited on screen. Most of it would not have much market value anyway. There is more about how to go about gathering eyewitness material, and the ethics around acquiring it at the scene of a story, in Chapter 6.

Eyewitness material comes into news organisations in one of three ways:

– **People send it to you.** Newsrooms are inundated with offers of stills or video all the time. The offer may be nothing more noteworthy than a spectacular sunrise, or the effects of a cloudburst sent in by the person who took the photograph in the hope that they will feature as "one of our weather watchers" in the evening forecast. But it may be genuinely newsworthy material that you will be interested in using – perhaps relating to a story that is already running.
– **You find it.** Apart from seeking it at the scene, you can use some of the dozens of online newsgathering tools at your disposal to track down images, video and people – all of them potentially offering something to enhance your telling of the story. This might be material that has been posted online, sometimes anonymously, accompanied by a claim about what it shows. If you think you might want to use it, your priority will be to verify it, and then clear copyright permissions. More on this below when we come to advanced internet searching and verification.
– **You ask for it.** If there is a news story running, or a topical discussion about a particular issue – say, whether or not the National Health Service (NHS) should fund a new drug – you might harness the power of your online reach and social networks to encourage people to get in touch with you to share their experiences and material. You can talk directly to huge numbers of people, asking them for eyewitness accounts or video, views, opinions or personal experiences. This will often deliver great case studies that will illuminate your reporting of the issue. *#Journorequest* is a hashtag UK journalists and bloggers use to post requests for help with specific articles or programmes.

Advanced internet research

We have made reference countless times in this book to the power of the internet as a resource for journalists. To harness its almost limitless potential, and find what you are looking for, you need to know how and where to find it. Knowing how to track down exactly what you need in this infinite well of knowledge is a skill in itself. And if you can do it quickly too, you are ahead of the game.

One of the reasons we often fail to find what we want is that we are looking in the wrong place. Type a vague request into a search engine, and you might get millions of results, not necessarily ordered in a way that will help you. Using advanced search functions will enable you to narrow that search, reduce the number of results and make it more likely that the results you do get will be useful to you. Taking advantage of the refining options offered by search engines, you can reduce those millions of results to something more focused and manageable. It is surprising how few users of the internet take advantage of these functions. Beyond that, there are literally scores of sites and tools to enable you to search the riches of the internet with an incredible degree of sophistication.

Use internet searches in combination with more traditional resources. For example, if you are trying to find people in the locale of an event, use Google Street View to find the names of shops or other businesses in the vicinity. Some will display their phone numbers, but even if they don't, you should be able to find their numbers using an online directory, and then you can call people directly on the phone.

Google

Everyone searches for stuff on Google, but few people know how to get the best out of it. Refining your search is easy, can make you more effective and save you a lot of time.

To hone your search, click *Settings* on the top line and then select *Advanced Search*. Now you can look for pages with or without certain words or phrases, or for exact words. You will see further options to narrow your results by language or region. You can set time parameters, which enable you to produce only the most recent results if that is what you want. If you know something is on a site somewhere but you cannot find it, search the whole site by putting its name into the box marked "*within a site or domain*". Searching by "*file type*" enables you to define what sort of document you are looking for – a pdf report perhaps, or an Excel or PowerPoint document. You can also search blogs and discussion boards that might offer unexpected perspectives and could be of interest. There are some simple Google operations that can also save you a lot of time and effort when searching for things:

https://moz.com/learn/seo/search-operators

Twitter

Twitter has its own Advanced Search facility, but the best way to navigate it is via a free tool called *TweetDeck*, which is owned by *Twitter*. *TweetDeck* is a dashboard from which you can search multiple accounts. *Twitter* is probably the most open of the social networks, and *TweetDeck* enables you to search its users and content in a number of different ways. It allows you to bring all your searches together in one place and manage them so that you do not have to keep inputting the same information. It also enables you to stream what people are tweeting on a breaking news story and the reactions to it – a powerful aid to your newsgathering and a great way to stay abreast of new developments and be alerted to new material.

You might begin your *TweetDeck* search by entering a keyword, but the chances are that this will not refine the search sufficiently – you will still be looking at vast amounts of irrelevant material. So you filter the search in any one of a number of ways – using a date range or time range, looking only for tweets containing images or video, including or excluding retweets and so on. You might be looking for hard information, or you might be searching for eyewitness media or other video/still images that will help illustrate a running story.

Twitter Lists enable you to create groups of users – and you do not have to be following them individually to put them on a list. So if you are interested in a particular news story, or news from a particular location or theme, you can create a list of all the users whose content you think might be of use. You can keep this private if you wish. Creating a list is simple – *Twitter icon > Lists > Create a new list*. But it could well be that someone has already done the work for you. Some good places to look for lists that already exist are *Electionista*, *Tweetminster*, *Reported.ly* and *Storyful*. Alternatively, from the Google search bar, type *site:twitter.com/*/lists* and then, in inverted commas, the subject on which you are seeking a list. If you find the list you want, you can subscribe to it, but you will not be able to add or remove any names from it. Using *Twitter List Copy* you can use it as the basis of a new list of your own, to which you can make changes.

You will now want to add this list to your *TweetDeck* dashboard, which you do via + and "*List*" and then select the list. You can then search your lists – for instance, by combining terms. Put proper names in quotation marks. The basic search principles are these:

1. Keyword A **OR** keyword B
2. Keyword A **AND** keyword B
3. " " – includes an exact phrase, such as "Boris Johnson"
4. () – combines "buckets" of search terms to create a more complex search.

Here is an example of searching using those protocols:

1. **Fire OR smoke OR explosion** – for this to succeed, the tweet you seek must contain **any** of these three search terms. This search is probably going to get a lot of irrelevant posts.

2. **Fire AND London** – for this to succeed, the tweet you seek must contain **both** of these search terms. Its chances are better, but you are still missing lots of other potential phrases being used.

3. **(Fire OR smoke OR explosion) AND London** – for this to succeed, the tweet must contain **one of any** of the bracketed "bucket" of search terms, **plus** London. This is more specific, but may still miss other descriptions of the location.

4. **(Fire OR smoke OR explosion) AND (London OR Soho OR "Oxford Circus" OR "Regent Street")** – for this to succeed, the tweet must contain **one word from the first bucket and one word from the second bucket**. This is the best option, because it allows you to search multiple combinations in one search – particularly vital when you're working at speed.

Once you're happy with your search terms – which you can go back and tweak at any time – the little icon in a box at the top right of the column is also very useful. It looks like something taken from a map of the London Underground, comprising two lines with circles. It offers you a number of options for refining your search, such as showing only tweets with images or video attached, or excluding retweets.

Much of this is intuitive. Proceed by trial and error, and see what searches seem to produce the best results in different circumstances. Most journalists know that *Twitter* is a great tip-off service for spotting trends or possible breaking news, but have little idea of the incredible newsgathering and research power that lies behind it. *TweetDeck* is the most versatile tool available to manage social, and it offers incredibly rich options for newsgathering.

With all *Twitter* use, make sure you understand the different applications of the @*name* and *hashtags*, to be confident that you are reaching the people you want to reach – or, more pertinently, excluding those you do not want to reach. Try *Twitter* first if you are proactively looking for eyewitness media – images and other material associated with news stories that people are posting on their various networks. *Twitter* offers the best searching possibilities – although its geolocation search facility will work only if the location setting on the account is enabled or included in the *Twitter* bio. Unfortunately, the chances are that this will not be the case. If so, search for keywords instead. This involves trying to think what the keywords might be, as in search engine optimisation (SEO). Remember that people who are local to the area you are searching are more likely to use local references – in other words they will tweet the name of a street or district rather than a town or city. They will often use swear words to convey their surprise or horror, so try a few of those. And they will use the first person – so try searching for "I", "we", "me" and "my".

Twitter's "Moments" facility collates a series of tweets from a place or an event.

CrowdTangle

CrowdTangle – which is a free tool for journalists, owned by *Facebook* – describes itself as "the easiest way to keep track of what's happening on social media". It collates data on how your posts, and those of your rivals, are performing. So it is potentially an important element of your organisation's data analytics. But it is also very helpful in finding and researching stories through the concept of "overperforming" posts. Based on the past history of a particular account, *CrowdTangle* monitors more than a million social accounts and highlights the posts that are doing significantly better than might be expected. It alerts you to these posts by email.

To search for content proactively, go to *apps.crowdtangle.com/search* and put a keyword, hashtag or URL into the search bar. You will get the latest related posts from across *Facebook* (including public groups), *Instagram* and *Reddit,* which you can then sort by language, post type, country, timeframes and so on. You can also sort by posts with the most interactions, comments and shares. You are able to search for video content on *YouTube* or native video – that is, video content created on, or uploaded directly to, a social network. The *CrowdTangle* website contains detailed information about to get the most out of the tool.

Facebook

"*Facebook groups*" offer a good way of getting under the skin of what is happening locally or within a community. The groups can be Public, Closed or Secret – which means you should be sensitive and ethical in the way you employ them, since users will often believe themselves to be operating in a safe and confidential space. But the depth of conversation you will find there is often much more textured and rich than anything you will find on *Twitter*. To find a group, type a description in the search bar then hit Enter and select the "groups" tab. You will see Public and Closed groups on this topic. You can view the discussion on Public groups, although if you want to post something yourself, you will need to join. To join a Closed group you will have to ask to be admitted by an administrator.

To search on *Facebook*, select "*Facebook search*" and type in the search. The results show all public posts, and are displayed in chronological order, with the most recent first. Just beneath the search bar, a number of related pages, groups and events will display, which is useful too. However, *Facebook*'s search function is not particularly suited for use by journalists – presenting you with information it thinks a typical user may be interested based on previous posts, pages they like and so on.

A good tool that may help you find what you want on *Facebook* is *who posted what?* which enables you to search keywords on specific dates (and also works on *Instagram*).

Instagram

There are several tools you can use for searching here. A warning about the following list, though: new tools arrive and depart all the time – and a single change of algorithm by the network can render them useless!

– **Mulpix** is an advanced *Instagram* search engine that allows you to use a series of filters to find who and what you are looking for.
– **who posted what**, which also works with *Facebook*, enables you to search keywords on specific dates.
– **Keyword Tool** (also available for *Twitter*) enables you to search via hashtags.
– **GRAMUSER** helps you search for users of video on *Instagram*.
– **mpsocial** is a means of seeing the exact time an *Instagram* post was sent.
– **Wopita** is a web application for the display and analysis of *Instagram* contents that lets you, for example, browse all photographs and videos tagged by keyword, display the most popular hashtags and search users and hashtags.
– **Storiesig** is a means of downloading and saving *Instagram* stories before they are deleted.

Where to find more

This is only a taster of the many tools available for searching social media and what they can do. To find more, and to stay up to date, try these sites:

– **Research Clinic** is the creation of Paul Myers, a world expert in the field of internet research. The site is a goldmine of simple and advanced internet search sites and techniques. However experienced you are online, you will find some of the functions and options simply mind-boggling – and perhaps even a little scary as well. http://researchclinic.net/index.htm

- **The Facebook Journalism Project** offers free training to journalists on how to get the best out of *Facebook* and other social tools. https://www.facebook.com/journalismproject
- **The Google News Initiative** is an effort to collaborate with the news industry, through new products, partnerships and programmes, to help journalism thrive in the digital age. https://newsinitiative. withgoogle.com/training/
- **Journalism.co.uk** is a regularly updated site full of news and tips on digital and social media trends. https://www.journalism.co.uk
- **The Social Media Reporter** is an online guide to helping you get the most out of social media in your reporting, written by the BBC's Cordelia Hebblethwaite. https://medium.com/the-social-media-reporter/welcome-fb6bed033687
- **The NCTJ's (**National Council for the Training of Journalists) **Journalism Skills Academy**, launched in 2020, houses a raft of resources aimed at helping you develop your skills. www.nctj.com/journalismskillsacademy

Here is a real-life example of how some of these search techniques, used in combination with more traditional forms of newsgathering, can come together on a story. In this case, the process was a relatively simple exercise involving *Facebook*, not requiring some of the more sophisticated tools we have just been talking about.

> A national news organisation was working on a horrific story about a number of would-be immigrants into the UK who had suffocated in a container on their journey. A man was arrested in connection with their deaths, but the only information released about him was his name (which was a common surname) and age. It was the lead story for every news outlet, and everyone wanted to find out more about the suspect.
>
> The reporter assigned to the story looked the name up on Facebook, cross-checked with ages, and found a number of possible matches in the age range. After a process of elimination, and a study of information found on the profile pages, one of them emerged as the most likely.
>
> The reporter went to that individual's account and looked for his list of Friends – especially for people with the same surname, who were likely to be family members.
>
> Going through this process of filtering produced someone with the same surname whose profile suggested he might be the father of the man under arrest.
>
> A visit to that individual's Facebook page revealed a lot of material about a local football club, with which it appeared the father was actively involved.
>
> The reporter went to the football club's website, and found that the father was an official of the club. It included his telephone number.
>
> The reporter telephoned the father and was able to obtain all the details he needed for an exclusive story.

Full-time digital journalists will be familiar with all the many social networks and will use many of these tools on a daily basis, moving between one platform and another. It is a chaotic world, but if you can find your way around it you will be at the cutting edge of modern journalism and you will find it exciting, stimulating – and a lot of fun.

Confirmation and corroboration

With so much available online, new roles have emerged in many big newsrooms for journalists whose sole job it is to try to verify sources and satisfy themselves that material is safe to use. It is a kind of detective function that has emerged from the explosion of non-professional video and other content that is published on the internet every day. Often the material in question will be pictures or videos rather than text or verbal statements. Potentially newsworthy pictures are posted online all the time. Before using them, we need to be sure that they really show what they purport to show, and that they were filmed when and where it is claimed they were filmed.

Journalists working full-time on this function are trying to verify material for potential broadcast or digital publication, and to filter out anything the provenance of which looks suspicious. Every day, newsrooms receive thousands of emails, comments, pictures and videos directly from the public, often via their websites and social media platforms. And as we have seen, proactive searching can unearth a great deal of potentially useful information and images. Unless the source is clear and authoritative, everything has to be checked out prior to use. The risks of not doing so are great. Rumours can go viral in no time, images can be manipulated and wrongly labelled and things are taken out of context.

As we have noted in connection with eyewitness media, this material may come to your attention because someone has sent it to you unsolicited, because you have asked for it, or because you have found it as the result of a search. The process of verification follows the same pattern in each case.

You will probably start with the most fundamental point, and question whether or not the site or account that is the source of the material looks genuine. To take a *Twitter* account as an example: look at when the account was first set up, who it follows – and how many followers it has and who they are. Is there a profile picture? How active is the account, and what sort of things does it tweet about? Is it verified by *Twitter* with a blue tick? If you are not satisfied with the answers to any of these questions, you might begin to doubt whether or not it is a genuine account.

The best way to verify video material or images is to speak to the people who claim to have filmed them. Tracking them down is not always easy and sometimes impossible. But if you can do so, ask some of these questions – the sorts of questions you would pose when assessing any source.

> Did you take the photo/video yourself?
>
> Can you give me some details about yourself?
>
> Where are you?
>
> How do you come to be there?
>
> When did you get there?
>
> What did you see?
>
> What can you see now?
>
> What happened before and after filming? Did you capture that too?
>
> How did you record the material?
>
> If need be, can you provide additional information – the make/model of the phone/camera you used, the time of day, the exact location?

If people are really at the scene as they are claiming to be, they will tend to give – or you can ask them for – answers that describe what they can see and hear. This will help convince you that they are genuine. The vaguer their answers are, the more cautious you need to be. A good question is whether they have any other images that they shot at the same time. It would be rather odd if they took only one picture, or shot only one piece of video, if they found themselves in the middle of a dramatic event.

Once you have this information, you can begin to cross-reference it with other sources you may have that might help with corroboration, or use digital tools like *Google Street View* to verify locations. And if you get to the stage of having the material downloaded to your own server, you can get some expert opinion about whether or not the images might have been manipulated or otherwise interfered with.

If the material relates to a breaking news story, you will be doing much of this with one eye on the clock and another on the competition. If there is strong and relevant material floating around online or on social networks, then you will probably not be the only journalist looking at it. You want to be first to discover it, so that you can secure the rights to the material if necessary, but also to be the first to get it to air if it checks out satisfactorily.

There will be times when it is not possible to contact the user directly, or where journalists feel the need to carry out additional independent checks, further to authenticate the material. If so, they can employ a number of other verification techniques that really do reinforce the comparison with detective or intelligence work.

To take a common example: some graphic footage posted online from a conflict zone. Let us say the images were purportedly put there by a rebel faction, claiming to show some fighting that day between the rebels and government forces. The verification team is asked to confirm that the footage shows exactly that, and not something else entirely; and that it was shot that day as claimed. Here are some ways in which the team might try to do that:

> Analyse the images to look for signs of additional digital information, or evidence of manipulation.
>
> Do reverse image searches to see if the images have appeared elsewhere on the web. You can do this using Google Reverse Image or Tin Eye. Hoaxers often post archive material and claim it is new.
>
> Check when the material was uploaded.
>
> See if the video has been shared elsewhere by pasting its unique code (the bit after the v= in the url) into a Twitter or Facebook search.
>
> Check satellite image searches to try to verify the locations shown. Look at local weather reports – does the weather in the images correspond with what the weather was like that day?
>
> Speak to experts in that region, or those who know the story well, to get their assessment of the material.
>
> Use language experts to translate any audio, or suggest whether dialects or regional accents might help locate the footage in a particular region.
>
> Look for other potential locators – car registration plates, telephone numbers on shop frontages – that might help pin down where the material was filmed.
>
> Analyse the social media account from which the story came, checking its credibility, history, interaction and relationship with other users and websites.
>
> Track down other social media profiles of the user. Cross-reference against other verified content and reports from your own journalists and producers, and other news agency sources.
>
> See if there is any other "chatter" or references to the same or similar content on other social media sites or the wider web.

All this can be painstaking work, and it will not always be possible to come to a definitive conclusion. If not, an editorial, judgment needs to be made about whether or not to use the material, and how much information to share with the audience about the checks that you have been able to carry out.

If you are interested in this kind of work, have a look at *Bellingcat*, one of the acknowledged leaders in this field. It is an investigative journalism website that specialises in fact-checking techniques of this sort. It is well worth looking at the site for advice and guides, details of past investigations and the techniques that were employed. Have a look too at *First Draft News*, a leader on anything to do with verification or social media newsgathering. It publishes news, best practice and case studies. Another useful source of advice and tips is *The Verification Handbook*. *Full Fact*, the independent fact-checking organisation, is worth a look too. A short course run by Full Fact and the NCTJ, designed to help you develop your skills in this area, can be found at the NCTJ's Skills Academy.

Data visualisation/visual journalism

Once you have gathered and verified your material, whatever its source, you will want to present it in as effective and engaging a way as possible. This is true of all journalism of course, but the web offers you a variety of opportunities for the multiplatform illustration of stories, and the active engagement of the audience. This is sometimes called "data visualisation" or "visual journalism". Visual journalism generally refers to multimedia or interactive journalism online – from something as simple as a graph or chart to a website where you can click through additional information and video.

The various stages of data journalism – from research and analysis through to publishing a multimedia report online – require a wide range of skills. You will not be expected to have all of them. For big projects, specialist techniques are employed, often requiring the skills of people from several different backgrounds. The Visual Journalism Unit in BBC News, for example, brings together web designers, television designers and journalists to work across both television and digital platforms. It may take a long time to bring a major project to fruition using complex computer graphics, and the resultant material has to work effectively on whatever device the consumer is using – smartphone, tablet or full-size computer screen. Online visualisation and television reporting are coming closer and closer together – a treatment that works on the internet may also form the basis of a well-told television report. If you are working with a professional web content developer, or perhaps briefing them on what you want to achieve, you will want to demonstrate a knowledge of house style and a feel for design through fonts, titles, headlines and labels.

Lesser stories still require illustration, but in ways that may well be within your own capabilities. Illustrating a web report with a still photograph or a gallery of pictures, with an audio or video clip, is relatively straightforward, and is routine practice for online stories and social media posts. With motion graphics, or infographics, you can tell a story by applying text to a slideshow or video – this is very effective for picture-led stories or short backgrounders. Even when there is a heavier dependence on words to carry a story, text can be moved and animated in such a way as to create visual interest and to avoid presenting the reader with big blocks of static text. Beyond that, you may wish to illustrate your story with a simple graph, map or chart in the way you might illustrate a television news report. You will find some ideas on this in the chapters on Television Journalism.

Post-traumatic stress disorder

It has long been recognised that journalists working in war zones or covering natural disasters such as earthquakes and famine are vulnerable to a traumatic reaction – at the time, or in some cases years later. Over the last 20 years, media organisations have become better at identifying the signs and dealing sympathetically with sufferers. Post-traumatic stress disorder (PTSD) can be treated successfully.

But over a similar timeframe, journalists have been developing PTSD even if they have never left the office, because of the extraordinary growth in the volume of graphic images and videos available online. A lot of this is potentially newsmaking material, and journalists have to view and sift through raw, unedited footage, looking for anything that might be considered worthy of inclusion in news output. Some staff – often quite junior – watch disturbing and distressing images over and over again while trying to establish their veracity and to edit out anything too extreme for broadcasting.

If you find yourself working in conditions such as this, it is possible you may experience an adverse reaction, which might be a symptom of PTSD. If you do, or think you might, you should make it clear that you would rather not do work of this nature. There are tell-tale signs to watch out for – not just in yourself but also in your colleagues. Some people will not want to speak out for fear of it disadvantaging them in some way. If you see a colleague struggling but saying nothing, you will be doing them a favour if you do something about it – speaking to them or to a manager.

Some pointers on PTSD:

– **Recognise** if you are at potential risk because of the nature of what you are doing.
– **Understand** that it is an entirely normal human reaction to experience negative emotions as a direct consequence of viewing traumatic images regularly and/or over a period.
– **Realise** that if you feel you have symptoms, you should never feel guilty or ashamed – only human.
– **Control** your exposure by pausing the video periodically and moving away from your desk for a while. Lower the volume if need be. If you know you are about to witness an extreme act of violence, ask yourself whether you really need to watch it in order to gain the information that you need. If this does not help, you must take further action.
– **Act** if you have symptoms of trauma, or any other mental health condition, by talking to someone you trust: a family member, friend, colleague, manager or mental health professional. Never isolate yourself or feel reluctant to express your worries. Being open is the first step to resolving them. Many employers now offer professional counselling; don't feel ashamed about taking it.

The Dart Centre was established to examine all aspects of the reporting of violence, conflict and tragedy. This includes the effects of such reporting on the journalists who are involved in every stage of the process. Dart has carried out specific research on newsrooms and traumatic stress. You will find help, advice and support on its website, at https://dartcenter.org

Think digital

When you are making digital content, think of yourself as a digital content creator. That sounds obvious, but if you are working at the same time in print, television or radio, it is tempting to do no more than add a few tweaks when you come to version your material for digital outlets. The digital space is a medium in its own right, and one that demands and deserves to be thought about in that way. Right from the planning and commissioning stage, through publication and engagement with the audience, try to think like a digital publisher and not like a broadcaster or newspaper reporter who is also knocking off a version for online. Material originally crafted for another medium and not subjected to a full digital overhaul will bomb with the audience. That is also true *between* individual social platforms – a video that appears vertical and square on *Facebook* will look very different on *YouTube*. Your aim is for your content to look native on each platform.

Think visual

Although digital platforms can be used to publish all your material, strong visuals should be your top priority. This is especially true of social media. You want arresting images from the first frame, with plenty of movement and colour throughout. The words can offer effective support, with headlines top and bottom, or burned on to the image.

Think mobile

Your material is going to be consumed on a variety of devices, but mostly on smartphones. That means a bias towards shorter items – though longer can work if the material is strong enough – with subtitles, and with square and vertical video. This optimises the space the video occupies on screen as users scroll through it. It is essential for *Facebook* and *Instagram*. Use subtitles, in case users cannot listen to the audio because they are on the move, or don't have headphones with them. Burned-in subtitles increase the chances that users will stick with a piece.

Think shareable

If you can prompt your audience to share your content with others, you are giving it a huge push in terms of reach. People obviously share something that they like, or that perhaps prompts them to think of the person or group they are sharing it with. They might share something they think is important and which others should see. Heart-warming stories with positive messages encourage a lot of sharing. And subconsciously or otherwise, people tend to pass on material that reflects positively on themselves and their personal values.

Think strategic

There are lot of social media platforms out there, and you cannot sustain an effective presence on all of them, either as an individual or as an organisation. Two or three feels like a maximum, although you might review which they are over time. It is an environment in which astonishing growth rates – and equally sensational declines – are commonplace.

Think audience

As with all journalism, never lose sight of the people for whom your content is intended, what appeals to them and what will attract and hold their attention. That will vary from platform to platform and story to story. On digital platforms in particular, it is important to talk to your audiences in the way they talk to each other. Young audiences in particular can spot a lack of authenticity a mile off when oldsters try to get down with the kids. Become a native for the platform on which you are operating. Your analytics will tell you what does well or badly in terms of sharing, retweeting and page impressions, and you can respond to those indicators.

15
The radio journalist: the radio scene and writing for radio

the radio scene.....BBC radio networks.....BBC news and current affairs programming .....commercial and other services.....radio as a medium for news reporting .....what makes a good radio journalist? .....newsroom roles.....national and international news on local stations.....writing for radio.....twelve steps to a good radio script.....numbers and percentages on the air.....a sprinkle of stardust.....the hate list.....your broadcasting style....getting ready....on the air

We have concentrated in earlier chapters on the business of writing stories for print and online publication. These are the stories you are most likely to be producing in your early days. The precepts and practice of good writing we have discussed also apply to news production in other media such as radio and television. Although there are distinctions that require an understanding of each medium, and a different range of techniques, the core principles of good practice pertain across all branches of journalism. And there is a virtuous circle here: the more you know about broadcast techniques, the more accomplished you will be as an online journalist, where you will be handling video, and to a lesser extent audio, on a routine basis. In the next two chapters we will be exploring radio journalism. They will help you understand more about the nature of radio and the different demands it places on you as a reporter or as a newsroom radio producer.

Radio can sometimes be regarded as a bit old-fashioned or staid compared with the glamour of television or the bracing airs of the internet. If that is what you think, think again. Radio is a massively popular and successful medium. It employs thousands of journalists who would never want to work anywhere else, and as a medium for news it has distinct advantages over print, television and the internet.

When you are working on radio output, you are communicating with an enormous audience. Around 90 per cent of people in the UK listen to the radio every week. That is many millions of people. They have a choice of more than 600 licensed radio stations. And for most of those stations, a regular bulletin of news, sport and weather is a regular feature, usually at the top of every hour.

So there are plenty of employment opportunities for journalists. Radio is huge fun to work in. You can operate on your own or as part of a team, you can be massively creative, and the medium is fast and flexible.

The radio scene

Radio programmes in the UK come from two main sources:

The BBC, which provides a variety of audio entertainment and information, in both music and speech, at UK level, at national level (Scotland, Wales and Northern Ireland) and at local level.

Commercial stations, ownership of which – as in local newspapers – is largely consolidated in a number of large companies. They are music-led for the most part, but also feature news and information, and advertisements.

Of the two principal technical systems by which radio is broadcast, *analogue* has long been the most extensive and widely used. There are four analogue wavebands:

- **FM** the home of most of the major stations.
- **AM** (or Medium Wave) where audio quality tends to be not quite as good as FM, and where you will hear stations such as BBC Radio 5 Live and TalkSport.
- **Long Wave** and **Short Wave,** both little used now. But some stations such as BBC Radio 4, the main speech network, broadcast on both FM and Long Wave frequencies, and sometimes split the two. So if you are a cricket lover, for example, you can listen to commentary of a Test Match on Radio 4 Long Wave, while the regular schedule continues on Radio 4 FM. Some commercial stations do the same, to separate speech and music output.

The second major broadcast system is *digital* or *DAB (Digital Audio Broadcasting)*. Digital transmissions were introduced around the start of the century. Take-up has been slow, but digital listening has now overtaken analogue. In general, DAB offers better and more reliable quality. You still need a DAB-enabled radio to listen to it, but most car radios are digital, and you can also listen through Freeview on your television set or on the internet. Internet streaming means you can listen to any station you like at any time – whether it is in Birmingham or Brazil – live or via a catch-up facility. No longer do you have to be geographically within the relatively small reach of a radio mast. Some stations exist only online.

BBC radio networks

The BBC is a very big player on the UK radio scene. There are five main national radio networks:

Radio 1 – chart, dance, urban, alternative new music. R1 has a commitment to news with a twice-daily programme called *Newsbeat* – a 15-minute magazine with a news agenda and style tailored for this younger audience.

Radio 2 – easy listening music from the 1960s onwards for a mature audience. There is news every hour on the hour 24/7, and some news magazine style programmes, such as the show hosted by journalist Jeremy Vine.

Radio 3 – mostly classical music, but also a wide range of arts-related programming. Carries the least news of any national BBC network.

Radio 4 – speech, drama, comedy, documentaries, with a very strong commitment to news and current affairs programming, which forms the spine of the daily schedule. It occupies several hours of output each day. We will look separately at Radio 4 news content in a moment.

Radio 5 Live – another speech network, led by sports commentaries and sports news and chat, but also with very strong news content.

Digital broadcasting has also given birth to a lot of other BBC stations, including:

- **BBC1Xtra** – contemporary urban music
- **BBC Radio 4 Extra** – repeats of comedy, drama and shows originally broadcast on Radio 4
- **BBC Radio 5 Live Sports Extra** – additional live events coverage supporting the output of 5 Live
- **BBC 6 Music** – alternative music, much of it live
- **BBC Asian Network** – broadcasting to the UK's South Asian communities.

BBC radio news and current affairs programming

The bulk of the BBC's news and current affairs programming is broadcast on Radio 4:

– **Today**: three hours every morning from 0600, Monday to Friday, with a shorter Saturday edition
– **The World at One**: 45 minutes at lunchtime from 1300, Monday to Friday, with a shorter Sunday edition
– **PM**: one hour at teatime from 1700, Monday to Friday
– **The World Tonight**: 45 minutes in the evening from 2200, Monday to Friday.

In addition, there are half-hour news bulletins at 1800 and 2400, with the 1800 versions reduced to 15 minutes at the weekend.

Radio 4 is on the air for around 19 hours a day, and more than a third of that time is occupied by news and current affairs. Even when it is not broadcasting its own programmes in the early hours of the morning, it is carrying the news-heavy BBC World Service. All that requires a lot of journalists – or producers, as they are often called in broadcast news. Beyond that there is a mass of other factual non-news programming made by producers who may well have a journalistic background. This includes the daily consumer show *You and Yours*, the daily arts programme *Front Row* and documentary programmes such as *The Report* and *File on Four*.

BBC World Service broadcasts speech, news and discussion programmes in English and more than 40 other languages. It can be received in the UK, but as its name suggests, its target audience is outside, and it reaches up to 200 million people a week around the world. As you would expect, the news agenda is more international and less UK-focused.

At a local UK level, the BBC has a network of 40 radio stations that were established from the late 1960s, and which collectively cover all of England and the Channel Islands. They range from major conurbations like Birmingham, London, Manchester and Sheffield to more rural/large town services such as Cumbria and Somerset. There are separate national stations in Wales, Scotland and Northern Ireland.

While following the same editorial brief, all these stations are distinctive and different, rooted in their localities and reflecting the character of each area. All have a strong commitment to news and local information such as weather and traffic reports. The overall tone and texture of output is one of friendly companionship, offering a focal point for communities through a mix of speech, music, sport, debate and specialist programmes.

BBC Local Radio claims to reach 15 per cent of adults in England (6.7 million people). Of those, 16 per cent – more than a million people – consume no other radio at all. For some, their local station is their sole source of news.

Commercial and other services

On the commercial side, there are a number of stations that broadcast nationwide, although all stations are of course available via DAB. Among the main players are:

– **Classic FM** – the UK's first national commercial station, on the air since 1992, playing mainly classical music
– **Absolute Radio** – a group of nine stations, seven of which are dedicated to rock and pop music from different decades
– **TalkSport** – sport and news phone-ins and commentaries

– **LBC** – originally the London Broadcasting Company and the UK's first licensed commercial station when it was launched in 1973. It has been available nationally since 2014, and its sister station **LBC News** – a rolling news channel – is also available throughout the UK
– **Times Radio** – launched in 2020, a joint venture between *The Times*, *The Sunday Times* and Wireless Group. Studio-based topical discussions with regular news updates. TalkSport is a sister station, and supplies sports news. Times Radio does not carry advertising, but accepts sponsorship and raises money by encouraging listeners to subscribe to the two newspapers. Its news coverage has been likened in tone and content to BBC Radio 5 Live.

The first commercial stations were LBC Radio and Capital Radio in London, both launched in 1973. Commercial services multiplied, often splitting output on their AM and FM frequencies to play chart music on the one and offer more speech and information on the other. There are now several hundred commercial stations.

From the late 1980s, commercial stations owned by local companies were bought up by larger radio groups. They consolidated content, and broadcast a similar format in many areas – the same content in many cases, thus diluting the "localness" of the stations. The largest operator of radio in the UK is Global Radio, which owns Capital, Heart, LBC, LBC News, Smooth, Classic FM, Radio X and Gold. Wireless Group owns TalkSport and Virgin, and is itself owned by Rupert Murdoch's News Corp. Bauer Radio owns Absolute, Greatest Hits Radio, Jazz FM, Kiss, Magic and Planet Rock.

Because they depend on advertising revenue, commercial stations need substantial audiences, and so tend to be mostly music-based with some news and information.

Community radio stations typically cover a small geographical area with a coverage radius of up to five kilometres (although they also stream online), and are run largely by volunteers on a not-for-profit basis. They can cater for communities or for different areas of interest – such as a particular ethnic group, age group or interest group, religious communities or the Armed Forces and their families. The idea is that rather than talk at its community, the station should become a central part of it. This means creating direct links with listeners, offering training opportunities and making sure that members of the community can take part in the way the station is run. If you are interested in getting into radio, it is a good idea to find out where your nearest community station is and to see if there are any ways in which you can get involved.

Radio as a medium for news reporting

The key assets of radio are speed and simplicity, which, in the business of reporting news, give it a substantial advantage over both newspapers and television. It is able to reach a very large and diverse audience incredibly quickly. Here are some of the strengths of radio:

- Most radio broadcasting is live, so stations can react instantly to breaking news or developing stories.
- The production process is quick: you can receive information one moment and broadcast it unscripted the next, or write it up and have a report on the air within minutes.
- It is always up to date: it is on the air 24 hours a day (in most cases), and you are never far from the next news summary.
- You can take it with you anywhere – any room in the house, in the car, outside, abroad. And you can pick up any station via the internet.
- It is relatively straightforward and cheap to produce from a technical point of view, certainly by comparison to television, which requires a lot more people, a lot more gear, a lot more money and a lot more logistics.

- Radio has a unique capacity to stimulate the imagination. Simply describing a scene or an event and using the power of words and sounds can evoke an image and convey it to listeners, encouraging them to use their own imaginations to do the rest.
- Radio can also be very intimate, creating a relationship with the audience unique among news platforms. When the best broadcasters are asked about their technique at the microphone, when they know many thousands if not millions of people are going to be listening to their voices, they all say the same thing: I imagine I am talking to just one person. They think of it as a normal conversation with a friend in a relaxed setting, not as an declamation to the world through a gigantic public address system.

Here is a catchy slogan from an Irish radio station that neatly captures the benefits of radio as a fast and flexible medium.

You can watch it tonight, you can read it tomorrow, but you can hear it now on Newstalk 106.

What makes a good radio journalist?

As a radio journalist you need the core skills that all journalists need, as discussed in earlier chapters, including these:

Curiosity
A commitment to clear, accurate, interesting (and legal) reporting
A flair for storytelling
An interest in people
An ability to express yourself clearly
An ability to brief yourself quickly
An ability to make difficult subjects understandable and interesting
A good interview technique
Enthusiasm and commitment.

And here are some skills that are more specific to radio journalism, or broadcast journalism as a whole; or are perhaps needed to a greater degree in broadcasting than other forms of media. Many of these skills will also be invaluable in the preparation of podcasts.

An ability to work quickly under pressure
Technical competence – an ability to record, edit and broadcast
An ability to express yourself clearly and fluently on air, both live and with a script
An ability to paint pictures with words
An understanding of the power and potential of natural sounds
An ability to think on your feet
Flexibility – moving quickly from one story to another
Versatility – able to do any job in the newsroom
A good broadcasting voice
An instinctive "ear" for radio.

Newsroom roles

No two stations or organisations are the same, or use the same job descriptions or terminology, but here are some roles that are common to pretty well every radio news operation of any size. Multiskilling is the norm, and smaller stations will run with only one or two people on duty at any one time, sharing most of these duties:

News editor/head of news

– Sets editorial agenda, style and tone
– Has editorial responsibility for fairness, accuracy, legal compliance
– Handles complaints
– The person with whom the buck stops
– Managerial roles (budgets, staff, rotas, training).

Bulletin editor/duty editor

– Hour-by-hour responsibility for news output
– Assigns stories and staff
– Takes in stories from reporters in the field
– Makes the regular calls to the emergency services and others
– Checks the wires, and what the opposition is up to
– Checks for accuracy, legal issues
– Often reads the news on air.

(Senior) producer/broadcast journalist

– Collects information and prepares news stories and summaries
– Conducts interviews, writes voice reports, edits audio, compiles news packages, produces news
    programmes
– Often reads the news on air.

National and international news on local stations

Local radio stations cannot run large national or international reporting networks. Nor do they wish to do so: their focus is their local area. But they still need to report what is happening in the rest of the country and the rest of the world. So arrangements are in place to deliver a supply of national and international news coverage to local stations in a form that can be used as soon as it arrives.

Within the BBC network, this is organised by the General News Service (GNS). The GNS desk at the BBC network news headquarters in London supplies a service to all BBC news outlets throughout the country, and is particularly aimed at the local radio network. It provides written summaries of national and international news that can be read on the air straight off the screen, individual news stories in various forms, voice reports and audio material ("actuality"). Local radio stations add these to their own local items, and so create mixed bulletins of local, national and international news.

Independent Radio News, or IRN, was formed when commercial radio began in the early 1970s. It provides client stations with a continuous service of national and international news, operating in a similar way to the BBC's GNS. The content is produced by Sky News Radio, which, through its contracts with IRN and others, supplies a full service of news, sport, business and entertainment news to almost every commercial station in the UK. A dedicated team of radio journalists based at Sky Centre in London writes, reports, produces and reads the news and sport 24 hours a day. The copy and audio is sent directly to radio newsrooms, and stations can choose whether or not to opt in to the hourly bulletin.

Writing for radio

Now you have an understanding of the general landscape and individual nature of radio, it is time to think about the basics of good writing for the medium. Some of them are the same or very similar to those in other forms of journalism, and some are specific to radio. In the next chapter we will look at the most common radio formats. Here, we will concentrate primarily on the words: how you adapt your writing and employ the techniques that will make your reporting most effective in the medium of radio. The two skills are not discrete: a well-written and well-crafted script will be much easier to broadcast – and much easier to listen to as well.

This is how a former editor of the BBC Radio Newsroom defined the function – indeed the duty – of the radio journalist:

> It is our job to communicate clearly and effectively, to be understood without difficulty, and to offer listeners an intelligent use of language, which they can enjoy. Good writing is not a luxury; it is an obligation.

He saw the job as being about clarity, as you would expect, and the ability to understand instantly what you are hearing without puzzling about what the reporter or newsreader is trying to say. Much of that stems from a natural and imaginative use of the language. Your only conduit of communication is the spoken word, complemented by natural sounds that help convey atmosphere and meaning. Words and sounds are all that you have. There is no printed text for a listener to refer back to. There are no pictures, still or moving. Just the words you choose, and the way in which they are broadcast.

Good writing in all forms of journalism is about finding the words to express precisely what you mean. Those words will usually be short, unambiguous and in common use. Esoteric, multisyllabic words are a barrier to understanding and sound pretentious. Short words in short sentences present the listener or reader with the fewest obstacles to comprehension. All this is doubly true of radio, because the listener has only one chance to grasp the story. Clarity and simplicity are at the heart of a successful radio dispatch or news summary.

Radio is the most direct form of communication we have as journalists. It is an extension of everyday conversation, with the exception that – for the most part – the conversation is one way. We are describing events or explaining a story to the listeners. The listeners cannot respond. They can only listen. And often they are only half-listening: unless they are listening with earphones or air buds, they are almost certainly not giving the radio their full attention. It is on in the background while they are doing other things – driving, cooking, ironing, eating, having a conversation. And since, as we have noted, they have only one opportunity to pick up what is being said, that puts an even greater premium on ease of understanding. If you are not concentrating fully when reading a newspaper you can go back and read a passage again. With radio, once it's gone it's gone.

So the golden rule for writing for radio is to be direct, and to use simple everyday language with concision and precision. You must be concise, because you never have enough space. The script of a whole half-hour radio bulletin would barely fill a couple of pages of a newspaper, so you really do have to keep things disciplined and tight. The message about direct, simple and precise language is one you have heard several times already in this book. Avoid complexity, vagueness and ambiguity. Short sentences containing a single thought work best in basic news reports. Remember that you or someone else is going to have to read the script on the air. The longer and more complicated a sentence is, the harder that will be: you need to draw breath somewhere! Use short words that punch their weight. And the opposite of that, and to be avoided, is complicated language or sentence construction, or something that is not clear, or can be understood two ways. Your scripts must not only be intelligible and understandable – they have to be *instantly* intelligible and understandable.

Here is a real example that demonstrates all of those points. Imagine you are a newsreader. You have been given the following script to read live on air. Try reading it out loud as though you were broadcasting a news bulletin.

> The British Medical Association has criticised a government strategy to tackle childhood obesity in England by asking manufacturers to cut sugar in children's food and drink by 20% and to encourage children to exercise more because it doesn't address issues like television advertising or cheap deals on junk food.

How easy was it to read out? Not very, I suspect. It is not even a straightforward task working out where you might pause to draw breath. How easy would it be for a listener to grasp the detail? Not at all easy.

What is wrong with that script?

– It is too long.
– It is one continuous sentence.
– It contains too many thoughts and subordinate clauses.
– It is hard to read – the writing is not clear.
– It is hard to understand.
– It is ambiguous and potentially misleading. Until you go back and examine it, you are not sure who is asking manufacturers to cut sugar – the government or the British Medical Association.

In other words, it breaks pretty much every one of our rules. Let us see if we can improve upon it and turn this story into a decent script that will work for a radio listener. The simplest first step is to chop it up into shorter sentences, with each one containing a single thought. We have talked before in a print/online context about breaking dense bodies of text into smaller parts. Exactly the same applies to radio. Here is how that sentence might look when broken down in this way:

> Leading doctors have criticised a government strategy to tackle childhood obesity in England.

This is the "news" element of the story, the "top line" or intro. We don't need to spell out here who the BMA are, or give the organisation's name in full. It will hold us up. "Leading doctors" tells us as much as we need to know at this stage. Next:

> The plan asks manufacturers to cut sugar in children's food and drink by twenty per cent, and encourages children to exercise more.

This is the background information you need in order to be able to understand what it is the BMA is criticising.

> The British Medical Association says the strategy ignores issues that cause obesity, like television advertising or cheap junk food.

This is the detail of the criticism, filling out the top line.

Try reading that version out loud. You should find it much easier than the first version, and it should feel more understandable. Why is that? Because although the facts are in the same order, the story now comprises three short elements rather than one very long one, and follows a logical sequence. There are obvious places to pause for breath. As a result it is easier to read and easier to understand. This is almost exactly the same process we went through when breaking down a print story and making it more accessible.

Our improved version is not any shorter. It is actually a bit longer. The first one is 51 words (in a single sentence), the second is 54 (in three sentences). That means it will take an extra second to read. But it is worth it, because we now have a story that makes some kind of sense and which, we hope, can be understood at first hearing.

My word count of 51 assumed that "20%" was three words. It is only one word when written on paper (and in your computer's word count), but it will be three when read aloud. That is one reason I rewrote it in the second version as "twenty per cent". Your production system will calculate the length of your script by counting the number of words, on the basis of three words per second. So writing numbers out in full helps make those timings more accurate. It also makes the script easier to read when you are broadcasting live, and you are less likely to stumble over it. If you have a story involving the sum of ten and a half million pounds, for example, it will be much easier to read aloud if it is written down as "ten and a half million pounds" rather than "£10.5m", or, worse, "£10,500,000".

Here is another real example from a major story of some time ago. Once again, the writer has essentially packed four stories in one sentence.

> The World Health Organisation has declared the coronavirus outbreak a pandemic, as the number of deaths in Italy dramatically increased, a number of other countries announced their first cases and the UK stepped up measures to tackle the virus.

This is a catch-all intro in which the writer has not troubled him or herself to decide which of the four news lines is the most important – and so has simply lumped them all together in one sentence. Some journalists don't mind portmanteau or umbrella intros such as this, setting out all the elements up front and then returning to them one by one. I am not one of them. You might get away with it in a print story, but it does not work for broadcasting. There is too much going on here to allow for instant clarity, and to allow us to grasp all the details as we hear it read to us. Let us give each of those four strands their own sentence:

> The World Health Organisation has declared the coronavirus outbreak a pandemic.

Again, we start with the equivalent of an intro, a clear statement of the news element of the story, the top line.

> The news came as the number of deaths in Italy – the worst-affected country outside China – increased dramatically.

> At the same time, a number of other countries announced their first cases of the virus.

> Meanwhile, the UK has stepped up measures to tackle it.

That process of dismantling and reassembling creates a narrative flow that sounds more natural and is much easier to grasp at the first hearing. Each paragraph is linked to the one before with a conjunction designed to encourage that sense of flow: "the news came as", "at the same time", "meanwhile".

Breaking the story down in this way also makes it less dense. Paradoxically, by taking it to pieces we have made it easier to see it as a whole. Beyond that, the longer and more involved the script, the duller it sounds on the air. There is nothing remotely dull about this story, but the original intro is so wordy that it strips the energy and interest out of it. As with most forms of journalism, being boring is a cardinal sin. If you do not sound enthusiastic about what you are telling listeners, they are not very likely to be very interested in hearing it. Part of that of course is in the delivery on air. But an interesting and lively piece of radio begins with an interesting and lively script.

So use your storytelling skills. As we have said before in many other contexts, think of yourself as telling your story to your mother, or your friends. Use the informal language and speech patterns that you would normally use in everyday conversation. Your scripts need to sound as though they were written for speaking, not for reading. A newspaper report might refer to "Florist Harriet Black, 25, of Nottingham"; that is fine for a written account, but it would sound stilted on radio. Radio needs to reflect the way we speak: "Harriet Black, a 25-year-old florist from Nottingham".

You can use colloquial language by all means, but avoid slang and clichés, and use only images and metaphors that add to the telling and understanding of the story. Don't hide behind them as an excuse not to use your imagination to bring a story to life.

Sometimes you have to work quite hard to convert what people have said or written into a fluent and engaging report. You will come across a lot of people who talk in very eccentric ways, or in ways that do not replicate the way we usually converse with each other. Everything has its own language, shorthand and jargon. When you talk to police officers, councillors and union leaders, you will hear all sorts of official or stilted language that people just do not use in ordinary life. People speaking formally or in an official capacity often feel an inexplicable need to adopt an unnaturally stiff and prolix mode of delivery as if they are giving evidence in court. Official documents are often written in jargon or over-formal language sometimes called "officialese". It is your job to translate them into everyday spoken English.

Try doing that with these examples. They contain the sort of formal, official language that blurs meaning, but which you will often encounter. Rewrite these into simple sentences that feel more natural and newsy and would work for a radio audience. Give yourself a target of no more than 20 words.

> The judge said: 'I am satisfied that having regard to all the circumstances, a custodial sentence for Mr Jones would be appropriate in this case'.

> The police have issued an appeal for potential eyewitnesses who were in the vicinity of the town centre at approximately 2am when an individual was the victim of an assault.

> The union representing workers in the rail industry has issued a statement announcing that it has instructed its members to withdraw their labour from 0600 on Monday in pursuit of its submission for a substantial salary uplift.

> The council is to consider a proposal for the upgrading of the waste drainage infrastructure at a cost of £1,000,000.

Here are some suggested "translations":

> The judge said: 'I am satisfied that having regard to all the circumstances, a custodial sentence for Mr Jones would be appropriate in this case.'

would work better as ......

> The judge told Jones he would be going to jail. (11 words)

In the same way:

> The police have issued an appeal for potential eyewitnesses who were in the vicinity of the town centre at approximately 2am when an individual was the victim of an assault.

would work better as ......

> Police are looking for anyone who saw an attack in the town centre in the early hours of the morning. (20 words)

Note that "in the early hours of the morning" is longer than "at approximately 2am", and is actually less precise: but it sounds more like the way you would talk. You can put in the precise time later in the story. Next:

> The union representing workers in the rail industry has issued a statement announcing that it has instructed its members to withdraw their labour from 0600 on Monday in pursuit of their submission for a substantial salary uplift.

would work better as ......

> Rail workers are going on strike over pay – starting with Monday morning's rush hour. (14 words)

And:

> The council is to consider a proposal for the upgrading of the drainage infrastructure at a cost of £1,000,000.

would work better as ......

> Councillors are to vote on a million-pound plan to improve our drains. (13 words)

Note that each of the "improved" versions is a complete rewrite, not just a rearrangement of the words. We have thrown out the turgid versions with their over-formal language and come up with something much snappier that retains the meaning but conveys it much more economically and with much greater impact and immediacy. Gone are all the words that are vague, or form a barrier to instant understanding – "custodial sentence", "substantial salary uplift", "drainage infrastructure". These do not sound as though they would form a part of everyday normal conversation. "The union has issued a statement announcing that…." can be replaced by the simple phrase: "the union says".

Our overall objective is a written script that, when read aloud, sounds spontaneous and unscripted, and sounds as though it is the way you would describe something in normal conversation as opposed to in prose.

Twelve steps to a good radio script

1. **What's my story?** As with all storytelling, begin with a clear idea of the information you are trying to communicate and what the writing is trying to achieve. Take some time to think about this before rushing in.
2. **What is the best way of telling it?** A short news report will often be a simple narrative – a factual account of something that has happened. Alternatively, it might be something more descriptive, evoking a scene or an atmosphere. You might be trying to explain something complex. In all cases, you are trying to capture the listeners and persuade them to stay with you. Ask these questions:

    > What sort of story is it?
    > What is the best and most effective way of telling it?
    > What is it that I want to say?
    > What do I want the listener to understand about the story?

3. **Write in short sentences using simple, active words.** If your average sentence is more than 20 words, it is too long. For a simple news report, most of your sentences should be short and clear, without too many complicated subordinate clauses or extra thoughts. For a longer, more descriptive piece or passage, you can use longer sentences. But mix them up with short ones to break up the pace and make it easier to listen to. The same goes for your prose writing.
4. **Write for the ear.** The way you write is determined by the way you speak. We want succinct and precise prose that sounds like conversation. Imagine that you are addressing just one person.
5. **Be disciplined.** Keep a firm limit on the number of adjectives you use, being sure that each one is actually adding something to your story. Stay away from journalese and clichés that have long since lost originality or meaning.

6. **Let the story unfold at an easy pace.** Tell it over a series of linked thoughts and sentences. Don't give the whole story in the first sentence. Take it one step at a time, with one thought per sentence. Take the listeners by the hand and lead them through the narrative step by step. This may sound patronising: but do you want to leave your audience confused and disengaged?

7. **Be clear about timelines.** After your opening sentence, or the material you put into your cue or introduction, it is usually best to tell the story in chronological order. This is especially the case when you are describing a sequence of events. It will almost always be easier to describe, and easier to understand, if, after your top line, you start again at the beginning.

You may need to refer back to previous events to add context and background. Always make it clear when you are doing so, and keep the listener informed about where they are.

> The Chancellor has set out new measures to stimulate the housing market. **This morning's** announcement comes after the Bank of England lowered interest rates **last week. Today's** move is seen as........

8. **You do not need to start with the most important or arresting words.** This may seem like an odd piece of advice, given everything we have talked about in connection with creating striking intros in your printed stories – openings that will make readers sit up and take notice. But radio listeners will often miss, or mishear, the first word or two. If they miss a critical bit of information, they will find it hard to catch up. If your script starts: "Rail fares are going up from Monday", but the listener misses the word "rail" the rest of the story becomes meaningless. So although it feels odd, it might be safer to begin "the cost of rail travel is going up from Monday", or, more informally, "If you travel by train, your journey will cost more from Monday". This gives the listener that little bit more time to home in on the story. It is also more like the way you would speak in everyday conversation. We do not hear in the same way that we read. When we are listening to the radio, we tend not to pick out individual words, but rather linked words or phrases.

You should also be prepared to sacrifice impact in favour of helping the listener get a locus on the story. All of these, for example, are perfectly acceptable ways into radio stories that would seldom be used in print:

> In the United States......
> The main teaching union has said.......
> There has been an angry reaction to......
> The government has announced.....
> The Health Secretary has repeated.....

In each case, the listeners are getting an early steer about the story and where it is coming from. They need to understand at once the location of a story, or who is being quoted, or who has made an announcement. It is essential to their understanding and calibration of what follows. Making them wait too long for important detail is poor radio practice. You might feel your scripts sound rather workmanlike and unexciting as a result, compared with the way you would construct a story intended to be read rather than listened to. But think about the medium in which you are working and about the needs of the listeners.

You can also quickly transport them to a new story with a simple signpost: "*Abroad now*, and in Germany.....". "*Here at home*, it has been a day of fluctuating fortunes on the stock market....". "*Health News:* plans have been announced for a programme of hospital refurbishments....". "*In sport:* Manchester United have named an unchanged side to play......"

9. **Help the listener make an instant judgement** about the story. This is an extension of the previous point. Imagine you heard this on the radio:

> A man armed with a rifle has killed one person and wounded six others in a busy shopping centre.

You would probably be quite interested in knowing more. And the first thing you would want to know is *where* this happened. That is going to go a long way to determining how you respond to this story and how interested you are.

Suppose it started like this:

> In Mexico City, a man armed with a rifle has killed one person and wounded six others in a busy shopping centre.

Be honest: you are less interested than you were. It is a terrible thing to have happened of course, but Mexico City is a long way away and this sort of thing is more or less a daily occurrence there.

Suppose it started like this:

> In Paris, a man armed with a rifle has killed one person and wounded six others in a busy shopping centre.

You are more interested now. Paris is not far away, and is somewhere many people will know from personal experience. This feels much closer to home, and you want to know more.

Suppose it started like this:

> In London, a man armed with a rifle has killed one person and wounded six others in a busy shopping centre.

You are definitely engaged now, even if you don't live in London. Shootings in British shopping centres are rare events, and there is always the lurking fear of a terrorism connection. You are likely to be very interested in knowing more about what has happened.

Suppose it started like this:

> In **Your Home Town**, a man armed with a rifle has killed one person and wounded six others in a busy shopping centre.

I guess the point is made. The simple inclusion of the location is a vital piece of contextualising information that instantly helps the listener calibrate the story, and we need to provide that information as early as possible. You can't leave until the end of a sentence information that the listener needs in order to be able to understand the beginning of it.

The same is true of stories that are based on something someone has said. In this example, it is not the location we need to know up front, but the identity of the speaker. Take a look at this sentence.

> The British economy is in decline and thousands of jobs are in danger unless the government takes 'immediate' action.

The first reason this does not work for radio is that listeners cannot hear inverted commas. In a print story, the quotation marks around the word "immediate" would convey to the reader that this story was a quote, based on someone speaking about the economy. Anyone listening to this on the radio would not know that – and might conclude that it was the view of the radio station that the government needed to act. That is the last thing you want the audience to think. As listeners, before we can assess how important a story this is, we need to be told that this is someone's opinion – and we want to know whose opinion it is. If it is a member of the government or someone from the ruling party breaking ranks to criticise their own economic record, it is a big political story. If it is an important industrialist or influential body like the Confederation of British Industry, it is a serious criticism of government policy from an influential source and again, an important story.

But as we read on we learn that it is none of those:

> The former Prime Minister Gordon Brown told the annual conference of the Unite union that emergency measures were needed at once.

With a Conservative government in power, you would expect a former Labour Prime Minister speaking to an audience of trade unionists to be critical. It would be much more of a story if he were saying the government policy was bang on the money and was paving a path to a glorious future. It is not a surprising intervention, nor one that is likely to have much effect on government policy. It is still a perfectly valid news story – but clearly a much less significant one than it might have been had the speaker been someone else.

For this story to work on radio, we must learn who the speaker is right at the beginning, so we do not follow a false scent. This is how a radio version might sound.

> The former Prime Minister Gordon Brown says the British economy is in decline and thousands of jobs are in danger.

> He told the annual conference of the Unite union that emergency measures were needed at once.

Very straight, very factual and not at all showy. It is not going to make the heart race. But it is the proper way to serve a radio audience. The listener has to be given all the important information about the story as soon as possible.

10. **Use the present tense (to begin with).** Radio is all about what is happening now, what has just happened or what may be about to happen. Its immediacy is its key asset. So write with that in mind, and when stories are fresh that will usually mean using the present tense not the past.

> The Environment Secretary says Britain will meet its climate change targets. She's told a conference in......

You can give still more immediacy to the story by emphasising its newness:

> The Environment Secretary says Britain will meet its climate change targets. **Speaking within the last half hour,** she .....

When the story is a few hours old, you might reflect that passage of time with a change of tense. So if the Environment Secretary made her comments in a speech in the morning, then by evening the past tense may feel more appropriate:

> The Environment Secretary has said Britain will meet its climate change targets. Speaking earlier today, she......

So use the present tense for news that the listener is probably hearing for the first time.

> England are through to the World Cup Finals.

is more vivid than

> England have qualified for the World Cup Finals.

11. **Use the active form not the passive.**

> The Prime Minister **has been attacked** by MPs over plans to.....

is the passive form.

> MPs **have attacked** the Prime Minister over plans to.....

is active and sounds more immediate and newsy.

These are not absolute rules, more default positions, especially when you are describing things that have just happened. Sometimes, doing things differently – and ignoring this advice – just feels right and better. If that is your instinct, follow it.

12. **Rewrite and rehearse.** Each time you revise your script, look for ways of simplifying the language. When you are satisfied, *read it out loud* by way of rehearsal. They say talking to yourself is the first sign of madness, but it happens to be the best way of making sure that you have written a script that makes sense, flows well, contains no errors and can be read easily, without any tongue-twisters. Read it through under your breath and don't be embarrassed – it is good practice and a sign that you are serious about producing a script that works for radio.

Numbers and percentages on the air

We have seen that these are a key part of many stories. But use too many of them on the air, and your listener will get lost and fail to understand. So use them sparingly.

It is sometimes preferable – and much easier to understand – to use words rather than figures. So instead of writing 20 per cent, 33 per cent or 75 per cent in your script, say a fifth, a third or three quarters. Choose the form of words that will be most easily absorbed and reflects everyday conversation – even at the cost of removing some details. If the cost of my taxi fare from the station to my home has gone up from three pounds fifty to seven pounds, how would I describe that to you? I would not say: "my taxi fare has increased from three pounds fifty to seven pounds". I would say "my taxi fare has doubled".

Rounding up or down is also acceptable. You can render 965 or 1,023 as "about a thousand" or "just under"/ "just over" a thousand. But don't round up too much. A figure of 68 is "about two thirds" or "around two people in every three", but it is not "nearly 100".

Sometimes the precise number will be required. If the latest figures show inflation stands at 2.4 per cent, then that is the figure to use. It would be absurd to say it has gone up to "nearly 2 and a half per cent" because with inflation, each percentage point is significant. Ditto with interest rates. If the rate was moved back up from a quarter of 1 per cent to a half of 1 per cent, then use those precise figures.

A sprinkle of stardust

A good script and an effective broadcast depend on all the things we have discussed. They add up to the need to bring a story to life for the listeners by vivid and accurate reporting delivered in a language they understand and in a style with which they feel comfortable. There are plenty of acceptable ways of producing a radio script, or doing a live report. You should always be aiming higher than acceptable though, and trying to add a little stardust to your reporting – that X factor that gives it a lift and makes it that much more engaging and easy to listen to. Here is an example from the Style Guide of the Radio 1 news programme, *Newsbeat*.

"Competent" report from the scene of a motorway coach crash:

> The coach was heading to London with a group of pensioners shortly after 8 o'clock. Eyewitness say it appeared to lose control and plough through the central reservation, crashing head-on into a lorry on the opposite carriageway. Firefighters have been examining the wreckage all day. They now think all passengers are accounted for. The police have been checking for clues as to how the crash happened. The motorway has been closed all day and may not reopen until tomorrow.

This is a big and serious story, so you might think that a "straight" account such as this is the most appropriate way of approaching it. I would agree. There is nothing wrong with it. It conforms to most of our basic principles of clarity and simplicity, and does not overdose on adjectives or sensationalise the story in any way. There are strong active words like "ploughed" and "crashing". It would work well for print. But in radio terms, most of the drama and colour has been drained from what is a highly dramatic event. *Newsbeat's* preferred version, with stardust duly sprinkled, goes like this:

> It's normally one of the busiest stretches of road in Britain, but tonight it's empty. Both carriageways are shut. The firefighters you can hear behind me are cutting into the wreckage with special equipment – brilliant light illuminating the scene. I can see at least twenty people measuring the road, collecting debris, looking for clues as to how the coach ploughed through the central reservation and into the lorry on the opposite carriage way. Ten hours after the crash and the smell of petrol hangs in the air. This motorway won't open until tomorrow.

You can see at once how this version brings the crash scene directly to the listener to an extent that the first version does not, and that it does so without sensational or insensitive use of words. The first one was fine, but considering the reporter was actually at the scene, it gave us no real sense of what it was like to be there. The second version does. We have the detail about the brilliance of the lights illuminating the scene, the people collecting debris and the detail about the smell of petrol hanging in the air. The reporter has engaged all his or her senses – sight, sound, smell are all there, and the result is a gripping first-hand account, which takes full advantage of the fact that the reporter is at the location. It paints a vivid picture for the listener without hyperbole or overwriting. It is a very strong piece of radio reportage.

The hate list

Here is a Top Ten of the things radio listeners hate most – and are therefore to be avoided:

– Mispronunciations
– Inaccuracies in reports about the places where they live
– Bad grammar
– Misplaced emphases
– Americanisms
– Jargon, journalese and slang
– Delivery too fast
– Stories that suggest London is the centre of the universe
– Lack of sensitivity ("how do you feel?")
– Over-aggressive interviewing.

Your broadcasting style

As a broadcast journalist, especially in a local operation, you will naturally expect to do a lot of broadcasting – reading hourly summaries, live reporting or producing recorded news packages. Many young journalists worry that their voices will not be good enough. In fact, very few people are incapable of broadcasting competently. Some are better than others of course, but it is not a mysterious gift vouchsafed to a select few: most people can do it. And the range of voices on air is much more diverse than it once was. Verbal idiosyncrasies or regional accents that might once have kept you off the air are now welcomed as evidence that the station is reflecting the breadth and diversity of the audience to which it is broadcasting. Even if your broadcast voice really is not good enough, that does not necessarily disqualify you from a future in radio journalism. There are plenty of non-broadcasting roles, and in larger organisations the number of people on air is actually in the minority.

As a radio reporter, you will expect to provide live contributions to programming, and to file pre-recorded voice reports and longer packages. In a local station, you will probably spend more time reading the hourly news summaries. Most of the advice below refers to that second function – regular live newsreading. But you will find that most of it applies equally to your reporting work.

Ideally, you will have the opportunity at some stage for some professional voice training. This will teach you to control your breathing and read scripts with clarity and authority – the two key qualities of a good broadcaster. Even if training is not available, there are things you can do to develop and hone your microphone technique:

> Listen to as much output as you can (not just news), and try to analyse what makes a good broadcaster – or a poor one

> Ask an experienced broadcaster to take you under his or her wing and run a couple of sessions for you, with advice and feedback

> Listen back to, and analyse, your own work

> Don't try to be someone other than yourself. Your voice is an expression of your personality– allow it to come through, and don't start trying to replicate what you think a radio reporter ought to sound like.

Delivering the news on air successfully requires more than a good voice, important though that is. As ever, preparation lies at the heart of things. Here are the key elements for a successful broadcast.

Getting ready

Arrive in the studio in good time. It is always tempting to keep fiddling with your script until the very last minute, or to take in some new information that has just arrived. You need to be very disciplined about calling a halt to this work and getting yourself to the studio or broadcast point with – at the very least – three or four minutes to spare before you go on air. Here's why:

– If you arrive at the last moment and are flustered or out of breath, your broadcast will be a disaster. However good the material is, you will ruin it with breathlessness or lack of preparation. The listeners do not see the preparation: they only hear the broadcast. So make sure it is as professional as it can be. If you get out of breath, you may be surprised at how long it takes you to recover to the point that you can broadcast properly. When you do, you will be distracted and more liable to stumbling – or "fluffing" as it is called.
– If you are in charge of putting the whole summary or bulletin to air, you will need to be happy that you have all the audio lined up in the right order and ready to go, and that you have tested all the sound levels and established links with any outside sources. This takes time.
– You will have a couple of minutes to run through the script – something you probably will not have had time to do before now. Indeed, you may not even have written all of it, and so are reliant on the ability of colleagues to produce a good readable summary. Reading it quickly aloud under your breath will expose sentences that are too long to read easily, typos and other simple errors, unusual names and other unfamiliar words that you might have difficulty pronouncing when you get to them. There will be times when you will have no option but to read a script that you have not seen before ("sight reading"), but you should avoid this if you can.

Take care with pronunciation. Mispronouncing local place names is the number one loathing of a local radio audience. Wherever you are working, there will be local pronunciations of names that might be different from the way they look on paper. Do you pronounce the county town of Shropshire as "Shroosbry" or "Shrowsbry", for example? In some cases it may be a matter of taste, but if not, and you get it wrong, you will very soon hear about it. Make sure you are aware of local idiosyncrasies of pronunciation. This is part of your commitment to basic accuracy.

If you are suddenly presented with strange names from faraway places, it might be possible to avoid using them altogether. Should an unfriendly colleague present you with a late script that says: "In South Africa, animal poachers have shot dead four park rangers at a reserve in Leeupoort Vakansiedorp, a hundred miles north of Pretoria", then it is fine for you to cross out the name altogether and just say "at a reserve in the north of the country" or "at a reserve a hundred miles north of the capital, Pretoria". The name will not mean anything to your audience and is not critical to their understanding of the story, so don't torture yourself trying to master the correct way of saying it. But have a word with your colleague when you go back to the newsroom.

Warm up. You need to get both your voice and your body ready for broadcast, if you are to sound confident and relaxed on air. Choose whatever breathing exercises or voice exercises work for you – gargling, singing and reciting rhymes are all favourites. Whichever it is, make sure some sounds are coming out of your mouth before you start broadcasting, so that your voice is warmed up and ready to go, and you won't begin by saying two words and then having to stop to clear your throat.

In terms of your body, again, go with whatever works for you. Stretch, shake your shoulders, yawn – anything that will help you feel loose and relaxed.

Warming up is also about preparing to deliver an on-air performance, which is what you are going to do. If you are on the early turn or the graveyard shift, it can be hard to summon up much energy or enthusiasm, especially if the material has become stale and over-familiar to you. But you absolutely must make the effort. At all times your broadcasting must be bright, alert, engaged and interested. You need to be able to switch on that on-air persona, however jaded you happen to be feeling at the time. It is the very least you owe to your listeners. If you fail to prepare yourself to perform properly, it will be very evident to anyone who is listening – and they are unlikely to be impressed.

Sit up straight. Make sure both feet are on the ground and that your backside is in the back of the chair. You do not have to be ramrod stiff – your delivery will sound stiff too, and a bit distant. But you should adopt a certain uprightness of posture to avoid going too far the other way, to make sure that you are correctly placed for the microphone and that you are within easy reach of all the buttons you are going to be pushing during the summary. The design of the desk should facilitate this. Once on the air, you don't want to be moving around too much.

Food and drink. Have a drink of water before you go on the air, and have some to hand – preferably not ice-cold – to sip during the audio clips or in case of last minute dryness. Keep liquids well away from the technical equipment. Avoid eating biscuits or anything else that might leave you with a rogue crumb in your throat at the moment of broadcast.

Have a complete script. Whether you are reading from paper or the screen, make sure that your script is legible and complete, and that you haven't left half the pages on your desk in the newsroom or accidentally deleted a section of text. The script should include the station intro and outro – that is, the words the station uses to get into and sign off from its news output. Make sure your own name is written in. It sounds absurd, but if you are nervous, or everything is happening in a hurry, you can literally forget your own name.

Punctuation. If you have a hard copy and are not reading off screen, you will find it very helpful to mark your script at the places you can pause and take a breath. You will normally take a breath after a full stop, and a shorter one, if needed, at another punctuation point such as a comma or semi colon. You can highlight these on a printed script by writing forward slashes on the script at your pause points. You can do the equivalent on screen by inserting more spaces at the pause points. If it is evident that there is too long a gap between the slashes and spaces, you may need to tweak or rewrite the sentence to make it easier to broadcast. It sounds terrible if you run out of breath before you reach the end of the sentence. Take a good breath before starting and between stories, and try to breathe easily and steadily throughout. You want the listener to feel as though you are in conversation, and that you are telling them a story, so the more natural you can sound the better.

The microphone. Get some advice about the optimum distance between your mouth and the microphone in the set-up in which you are working. That will usually be two or three inches, depending on how loudly you speak. Too close and you will start "popping", which means your "p" and "b" sounds – called "plosives" – will distort. Too far away and you will literally sound distant. Be aware that some microphones can pick up sounds other than your voice, so be careful not to bang the desk for emphasis or fiddle with your pen while you are reading. Paper rustle is another hazard – turn the pages of your script as quietly as you can. Metal watchstraps, rings and bracelets can all make distracting noises.

Headphones. Always wear them. If you are reading and someone else is operating the desk, you will need them anyway to be able to converse via talkback. If you are on your own, you will need to be able to hear the content of the audio clips, since the loudspeakers in the studio will be turned off. Headphones may also help you identify when you are popping, or making any other noises that are being picked up by the mic.

On the air

There has been plenty of emphasis in this book about the need to write and broadcast as you would speak in everyday conversation. That holds true for radio broadcasting. But of course it is not a conversation in the literal sense: you are talking, but no one is responding. You will often be delivering important and serious news. So although your broadcasting style should still aim to be friendly and approachable, you are bound to introduce a certain degree of formality as well.

Don't shout

You are speaking into a microphone, the function of which is to amplify your voice. So there is no need to shout. Talk at your normal level, and project only as much as you would in a normal conversation with someone sitting opposite you, say at a distance of four or five feet.

Don't rush

If you are nervous, you will start to gabble. You will speed up, make mistakes and the meaning of what you are saying will be lost. Although the pace may change slightly from story to story, aim to speak at an even speed throughout, the usual norm for which is about three words a second. You will know the durations of your audio clips, and your computer will automatically calculate for you how long it will take you to read your script, based on that speed. If your script is too long, even if by only a few seconds, cut it until it is the right length. Do not try to cram 2'15" of content into a two-minute slot. It will sound hurried and will lose authority. Do not put yourself under pressure by going into the studio with more material than you have airtime for.

Hitting the right words

We have already spoken about the need to run through a script in advance to identify the pause points – places where the script naturally gives you the opportunity to take a breath. Just as important is identifying which words or phrases need to be stressed. Stressing does not mean speaking more loudly. It means putting a particular emphasis on a word that is important. As with so much else, the stresses should follow the natural cadences of everyday speech.

The words you emphasise will depend on the story and the sense of each sentence. If it helps, you can put a line under the words that need to be stressed, but if you have already marked your script with slashes to show the punctuation points, there is a danger that you will confuse yourself with too many instructions.

To hit the right words, you need fully to understand the story you are reading, and which words are significant. If you hit the wrong ones, you will sound as though you don't know what you are talking about, or don't care, and you will destroy the effectiveness of even the best-written script. You will also annoy the listeners; poor delivery is another thing that makes them shout at the radio. Rehearsal time, and reading the script out loud before you broadcast will really help – particularly if the script has been written by someone else.

If your script contains direct quotes, don't forget that the listener cannot see inverted commas and so needs to be given a signal. You can provide this by pausing very slightly on either side of the direct quote, and lifting your voice to read the direct speech. If you think there is any danger of the listener being left in any doubt about what is in quotes and what is not, you can add the verbal equivalent of inverted commas: *the situation was,* **as she put it***, bad and getting worse;* **she described the situation** *as bad and getting worse; the situation was,* **in her words***, bad and getting worse.* That way the listener is clear that you are quoting someone directly and not making any sort of editorial comment yourself.

Tone/inflection

Getting the tone right is important for exactly the same reason. It shows your understanding of the sort of story you are reading, and it sends a signal to the listener about the character of that story. Your general delivery is going to be friendly and relaxed, but you are clearly not going to employ exactly the same tone of voice for each story. The script contains the words that you say, but it does not tell you how to say them. It is up to you to glean from the story the appropriate tone for delivery. The lead story in a summary will generally be about something important or serious, and the last story will generally have a more upbeat feel to it – whether it is a funny "and finally" item or a weather forecast or sport story. You don't need to overdo it by reading the first story at a funereal pace and the last one with exaggerated cheerfulness: the gap between the two extremes of tone may not be all that wide, because you want to sound professional throughout. But your tone should make a nod to the content that you are reading.

Make sure your voice and intonation match the nature of the story. If you have two stories next to each other that demand too great a change of gear – say the death of a family in a car crash followed by a new world record for eating hard-boiled eggs – then either change the order of the stories, or cushion the transition by leaving a longer pause between the two stories. Do not try to bridge with a phrase like "on a lighter note". That will sound crass and insensitive.

Enunciation

We have noted that most voices and accents are suitable for broadcast as long as they are clear, and easy to understand. That is not an excuse for sloppy enunciation. Avoid these in particular:

> *Febry*
> *Home Sekertry*
> *Pry Minister*
> *Chooseday*
> *Northern Island* – especially given that politicians often refer to "the whole island of Ireland".

Fluffs

Rare indeed is the broadcaster who never makes a slip or stumbles over a script. If you misread something when you are recording a report, that is not a problem because you can simply do it again. Make sure you edit out the overlap afterwards. If you fluff when you are broadcasting live, then keep calm and carry on. Simply pause, and then go back and pick up the sentence at the point you left it. If it was a really bad fluff, or if you coughed, for example, then you can acknowledge that by inserting a simple "I'm sorry" or "excuse me" before carrying on reading. If it was a mispronunciation or a misread that actually contained a mistake – if you said "million" when you meant "billion", for example – then you need to correct yourself before carrying on: "I'm sorry, that should have read *three **billion** pounds*". Whatever you do, keep going. Try to put it behind you and not to lose your concentration. You will be in danger of fluffing again almost immediately because your mind is still on your previous mistake. The same thing happens when you have had to negotiate a particularly difficult name in the script. You rehearse it, and when the time comes, you read it flawlessly. You are so relieved that three seconds later you trip up at a point where there is no obvious danger. Keep your head and keep your focus.

However desperate the situation is, one thing you must never do is swear, or express your frustration in graphic terms. Assume that your mic is on and that people can hear what you are saying at all times. A time of particular danger is at the very end of your summary, when you hand back to the main programme. If something has gone wrong, it is tempting to vent as soon as you think you are off the air. Don't do it. Your mic may still be live and you may still be broadcasting.

The same is true when you are recording a piece. If you stumble and need to take a sentence again, just pause, say "overlap", and start again. Don't curse or express frustration. The danger is that if you fluff and then swear, you will accidentally leave that in when you tidy up the piece, and it will be broadcast on air. You would be surprised at how often this happens. It is a good reason for making sure that you leave yourself time after your editing to listen through to the whole piece from beginning to end to be absolutely sure that it is clean.

Breakdowns

The same coolness is required in dealing with technical problems. You introduce an item, press Play, and nothing happens. Or the wrong piece of audio comes out. Or the whole system crashes and you can't play anything. Or you cross to a live reporter and cue them in, and there is a lengthy silence because of a communications glitch. The same rules apply as for fluffs:

> Don't pretend it didn't happen
> Apologise, and if necessary explain
> Move on
> Stay calm.

A cool head is vital because you are still live on air and you have to make it to the end of your broadcast somehow. The show must go on. How you react will determine how the listeners react. It may seem like an absolute disaster to you, but listeners actually rather like it when things go wrong, and are usually pretty tolerant as long as gaffes are handled competently. It reminds them that radio is a live medium and most of the time it is delivered seamlessly.

Here is an example. You read this cue: *The Prime Minister has announced a new initiative to tackle the problem of homelessness and street sleepers. At a news conference this morning, he said it was time to get to grips with what he called "a national scandal"* You then press Play to start a clip of the Prime Minister speaking. Instead, we hear someone talking about a film actor who has just died.

You realise at once that you are playing the wrong clip. What to do? You stop the clip at once and say: "I'm sorry, that very clearly wasn't the Prime Minister. We'll try to bring you his comments a little later". Then you move to the next story.

Here's another scenario. You read this cue: *The Prime Minister has announced a new initiative to tackle the problem of homelessness and street sleepers. At a news conference this morning, he said it was time to get to grips with what he called "a national scandal". We're crossing live now to our political correspondent Paul Jones, who was at the briefing. Paul, what is this new plan all about?* You have selected Paul as a live outside source, but you hear nothing. After a second or two, you say: "Paul Jones, can you hear me?" but still nothing comes back. So you simply say: "obviously a problem with the line to Paul there, we'll try to come back to him later". Then you move on to the next story. You are not disguising the fact that things have not gone according to plan, but you are not making a big deal of it either. Nor will the listeners: they are used to it.

Be yourself

Your voice is by definition personal to you, so do not try to change its character when you are in broadcast mode. We have talked about the overall effect you are trying to achieve: friendly but authoritative, warm but professional. Adapt your voice to those requirements, but do not imagine that you have to become a different sort of person once you have the headphones on and the microphone is live in front of you. Although you are impartial about the news, you cannot and should not try to stop your personality coming through, as long as it remains professional and controlled. Do not imitate others, or try to sound the way you imagine radio reporters are supposed to sound. Going down that route will often lead you to develop a sort of sing-song delivery which goes up and down and actually sounds very inauthentic. If you think you are in danger of falling into this habit – or someone else warns you of it – the basis of the problem may lie in the script. When each story is only two or three sentences long, it is very easy to fall into a formulaic approach, with the result that all stories look – and therefore sound – pretty much the same in structural terms. Even within a story of only 60 words or so, there is plenty of scope for a mixture of short sentences and long, and the other techniques that can break up the pattern and pace, and allow you to use inflection to produce something that is easy to listen to. A good on-air delivery is founded on a good script.

16

The radio journalist: news summaries and radio reporting

As a producer or reporter on a radio station, you can expect to produce a variety of different forms of output. But all the various formats conform to the principles we have already discussed. Many radio producers spend most of their time in the office, helping with the production of programmes – by booking and handling guests, for example – or preparing the regular news updates. Only a minority get out and about with their recording devices, making news packages or providing live reports into programmes.

In this chapter, we will look at the architecture of radio news, and examine each of these different forms in turn. We will also explore the techniques involved in gathering material for a radio report, and how that report is assembled.

The news summary

Most stations offer a summary or bulletin of news at the top of every hour. Many also do a short summary on the half hour, and some do headlines on the quarter hour at peak times. But the hourly summary is the staple and the spine of most stations, whether they are music-based or speech-based, or a mixture of the two. For some music stations, the hourly news summary is the only news output there is, produced by a small team working exclusively in an office. Writing a lot of different stories briefly and quickly, cutting clips and assembling a coherent summary of news – and then doing the same thing an hour later, and again an hour after that – are core skills for any radio journalist. The better you are at it, the better you will be at almost every other element of making radio.

The hourly summary will vary in length from station to station, and even within the daily schedule. On some stations, the summary is just a script read out by a newsreader or presenter with no audio or voice reports illustrating any of the stories. Such a summary is referred to "a straight write" or "a straight read". That is, however, quite unusual: if the summary is anything longer than a minute, you will generally find that at least one or two of the stories are illustrated with audio in some way.

You would normally expect to include five or six stories in the average two-minute news summary, perhaps more. So by a process of simple maths, that means you have roughly 20 seconds per story. If you think of three words per second as a default rate of delivery, that is about 60 words for each of your stories.

That is an average. They don't all have to be the same length – indeed, if you can vary the lengths, you will improve the pace and feel of the whole thing.

That count of 60 words amounts to two or possibly three sentences at most. My last paragraph was 90 words – so 60 is quite a miserly allowance. You can see at once that, as with other forms of journalism, one of the key skills of radio news is economy of writing – boiling the story down to its essentials while presenting it in an easily understood and engaging conversational style.

At least one story may be illustrated by a reporter voice piece (VP) or, more likely, a piece of audio, called a clip, cut or soundbite. In a short summary, clips are more favoured than voice reports for the simple reason that they are shorter. You can extract a perfectly workable and useful clip of someone making a coherent point in ten seconds of audio, or "actuality" as it is sometimes called. For a voice report to say anything worthwhile is going to take at least 20 seconds, and even at that length it won't be adding much detail. This is why you tend not to hear reporter pieces in short news summaries – they take up too much space and reduce the number of stories you can fit in to your time slot.

However, *any* illustrative material is going to add to the time it takes you to tell that particular story. That means less time for the other stories – which in turn means they have to be written even more tightly, and/or that there will be fewer of them. So there is a continual trade-off between illustrating stories to keep the summary sounding bright and pacy, and maintaining the story count – that is, the number of stories in each summary.

The more stories you include, or the more audio you use, the livelier your summary will sound. But be careful. If you make your stories too brief, or read them too quickly, you may end up with something that doesn't tell the audience very much or, worse, is practically meaningless. If the summary is too busy and too crowded, and moves at too breathless a pace, the listener will find it hard to take everything in.

Here are some of the key things to bear in mind when you have the task of producing an hourly news summary over a period of several hours.

The stories you select for your summary, and the way you write them, will vary according to your audience

When deciding what stories to include in your summaries, think – as always – about your audience. Who are they? How old are they? What are their interests? Why are they listening to this station? Look for stories that you think will fit their profile. That does not mean that you select only stories that are of interest to them. They still need to hear all the main stories of the day. But it might mean that you give greater prominence to, and report in more detail, those stories you think might be of particular interest to your core audience.

Most summaries will be a mix of local, national and international news. Your summary might reflect all three of those, and it might also include lighter items such as sport, arts or human interest stories. It may be the station style to end each summary with a brief weather forecast, or travel report. There are no hard and fast rules. For an audience listening to local radio, a good strong local story will usually trump most other news. For national news stations, UK stories will usually be of greater interest than something happening on the other side of the world. But it all depends on the news of the day – no two days are the same, and the circumstances are always variable.

If you are working for a local station and there is not much local news about, try to create a local feel and relevance by finding a local angle – such as what your own MP has to say about the big story of the day, or what local business organisations think about national economic news. Or see if you can write a version of the story that brings out the local interest.

Take this story:

> Rolls Royce have announced details of a new aero engine for short-haul aircraft. They say it will be quieter and up to twenty per cent more fuel-efficient than existing engines. The new engine will be built at the company's factory in Derby, guaranteeing jobs at the plant for at least ten years.

If you were writing that story for a national news outlet, the impressive environmentally friendly features of the new engine would probably be the story:

> Rolls Royce have developed a new engine for short-haul aircraft that is 20 per cent quieter and more fuel-efficient than existing engines.

But if you were working for a radio station in Derby, you would be much more interested in the fact that the new engines were to be made at your local factory. You would be more likely to write the story like this:

> Thousands of workers at the Rolls Royce aero engine factory in Derby have been told their jobs are safe for at least ten years, thanks to a revolutionary new engine for short-haul aircraft.

Think of the audience, and what is likely to be of most interest to them.

Juggle your running order

You can make the whole summary feel different from the previous one simply by changing the order of the stories, or dropping one or two of them and introducing new ones. Changing the running order, even if the stories themselves are essentially the same, will help vary the pace and make it sound different. You won't change the entire summary every time, and you will usually need to include the big story or stories of the day every hour.

Change the top story whenever you can – even if you are only moving the same stories around, it will go a long way to making your summary sound different from the previous one. You do not always have to lead on the big story of the day. Think of each summary as an update on what has happened in the last hour or so, rather than a review of the most important news of the whole day. That means you might lead on a story that is not massively significant, but to which you give more prominence simply because it has only just happened, is new to the audience and perhaps has a local feel.

Watch out for clashing stories next to each other in the order, or having too sudden a change of mood and tone between one story and another. That can sound crass.

Keep refreshing the stories hour by hour

You find yourself on a shift that requires you to write a succession of hourly summaries. None of the stories is changing very much, and not much in the way of new material is coming in. You will probably start to get bored with the stories you have. The listeners might be getting bored too – quite a lot of people have the radio on in the background all the time, and they do not want to hear exactly the same summary over and over again.

So avoid running the same stories in the same form hour after hour. If nothing much is happening, there are simple ways of making things feel a bit different. One of the simplest is just reordering the sentences of each story. You could go back to the original story and replace some of the details in your last version with some different information. Or you could try to make it sound fresher by moving it on in the way you introduce it – perhaps by looking forward to the next development. It is all about making it sound as though things are happening, even if it is really pretty quiet.

Look for ways to update or advance stories by bringing in a reaction, a different angle or a new development, or simply rewrite the story so that it doesn't sound the same as the previous version. Give a new story energy by emphasising its freshness: "Reports are coming in…..", "we've heard within the past hour…..". Promise that you will keep listeners up to date: "we'll bring you more details as soon as we have them….", "more news on that in our next summary…."

This is particularly important in the early morning, a time when radio audiences are at their largest but when the news is not moving much – the day's events have yet to unfold. Some of the stories may still be hanging over from yesterday, but you need to try to give them renewed topicality if you are still running them. Your audience does not want to wake up to yesterday's news. So rather than opening a story with a reprise of yesterday's big court acquittal, make it feel like a "today" story by starting with something like: "Kevin Strong is waking up a free man this morning after being found not guilty of………" If the council passed a controversial planning application last night, start your report today with "Newtown residents are coming to terms this morning with the prospect of two new twenty-storey blocks of flats in the town centre". If people are saying largely the same things as they have said before, then they can be made to sound newer if you say they are "renewing their warnings" or "stepping up their calls for action", or "putting the government under further pressure". They may be the same stories, but with a little imagination you can make them sound different and fresher without exaggerating or straying from accuracy.

Keep the story count up

No story should be longer than three sentences. Longer, and within the format of a short summary it will start to drag, and it will squeeze the time you have for other stories. It is a tall order to pack all the details of a big and complicated story into just a few seconds, so don't try. Concentrate on the most recent developments and avoid too much history. Think of it as a headline, which by definition is a short sharp summary of the story. That headline can be your way into a brief summary story, which you then build on with a couple of further sentences of detail. As we have seen countless times, the ability to reduce a story to its bare essentials while keeping it self-contained, comprehensible and clear is a fundamental journalistic skill, and it is never more in evidence than in the production of radio news summaries.

Make sure you understand the stories

This should be obvious, but if you are reducing every story to no more than about 20 seconds, it is tempting to skimp on your reading of them. You know you will not have the room to include more than a few details, so you just take in the first few lines. This is a lazy attitude, and must be resisted. The more you read into a story and make sure that you understand it, the better equipped you are to find new angles, to produce a crisp and readily understandable version of it and to create slightly different versions each hour.

If you are picking up where someone else has left off, at a change of shift, for example, don't just duplicate what your predecessor has written. Go back and check the original source material if you can. Not only will you be satisfying yourself that the story is accurate, you will probably find another way of presenting it that will help make the next summary sound fresh.

Summaries are short.....

.....but that does not mean they can be less good, or require less care. Pride yourself on producing a clear, interesting and fresh-sounding summary. Each story will be self-contained and brightly written and will include the essentials the audience needs to understand it. It will also sound different from the version of an hour before. Avoid repetition of words or phrases, either within the summary or over a run of hourly summaries.

The best way of absorbing all this is to listen to it in action. Sample news summaries on a number of stations, and listen to a succession of summaries on a single station, to see how each is moved on from the one before.

Cutting clips

If the station house style is to include audio in the summaries, that will usually be done by way of a clip of actuality. It may be known by different names in different places, but actuality is simply audio of someone who is not one of your reporting staff – a "real person". So it could be a short excerpt from an interview or a speech, for example.

Cutting clips can be a frustrating process. Sometimes you find just the clip you want, with the speaker making exactly the point you are looking for, but you cannot use it because it is too long. Or perhaps the inflections are wrong – such that when you isolate the clip, the audio ends with the speaker on an upward inflection that will sound as though you have cut them off in mid-thought.

You may think you have found exactly what you want and then the speaker fails to finish the thought neatly, and sets off in a completely different direction. Some people talk in a rapid stream of consciousness style that makes it hard to discern where one sentence or one thought ends and the next one begins. This makes it very difficult to extract a coherent 10–15 second clip from them. It is a process of trial and error, and you will soon get the idea of what clips work, and what don't. Use your ear and your judgement. Err on the side of caution – if your edited clip doesn't sound quite right to you at the first hearing, don't keep listening to it until you have persuaded yourself that it is acceptable. If it didn't sound right to you the first time, it will not sound right to the audience either.

You can make internal edits within a clip, or bring together two sections from different parts of an interview to make one new clip. But be careful that the result makes sense, and that you are not distorting what the speaker was saying, but are representing it fairly. And make sure that the edit, or join, "works" in a technical sense and sounds natural. You can try remaking a tricky edit several times to try to get it right; but if after a number of attempts it still does not sound natural, move the edit point to more convenient place earlier or later in the audio – or abandon that clip and find another. Remember to include a breath at each join – either the breath after the last word of the first part of the clip, or the breath before the first word of the second part. If you cut both breaths out, the edit will sound nonsensical. If you leave both breaths in, the pause will be too long, and the speaker will sound as if they are gasping.

An office-bound summaries team can generate some of its own material by conducting audio interviews by phone or videolink. When you are recording material in this way, you will learn to look out for possible clips as your interviewee is speaking. In those circumstances, you have the chance to ask a question again until your interviewee gives you a version you can use. Don't be afraid to ask the same question more than once, and tell the interviewee why you are doing it. A lot of the people you interview will have been through the process many times before and will know what is involved. They will not be surprised or fazed if you say to them: "the point you made about x seems really important, but the answer you gave me was rather long – could I put the question again, and ask you to make the point a little more briefly?" Obviously you can't always do this with less experienced people, or if the circumstances make it a tactless thing to do – someone who has had something bad happen to them, for example. Use your judgement.

You do not want the audio to carry basic information that is better placed in the cue. Your ideal clip will contain description or colour that enhances the story, or gives a reaction to it, and therefore adds some value to the basic facts. Suppose you are looking for a clip from this interview with a fire officer at the scene of a big incident:

POSSIBLE CLIP 1 We got the call soon after midnight, and we were here within seven minutes. Once we had assessed the situation we brought in backup, and we now have eight appliances here. About 40 people are involved in the operation at the moment.

POSSIBLE CLIP 2 The building was well alight when we arrived and looked as though it might collapse, so one of our first priorities was to make sure that no-one was inside and that the area was cleared. At first we had a report that people were trapped, but this turned out not to be the case and everyone was accounted for.

POSSIBLE CLIP 3 Well, yes, it's an issue. Because it is a chemical factory, there is obviously the added danger of an explosion and so we are having to tread very carefully. It's a very….it's a massive fire, one of the biggest we have had to deal with in recent years. So obviously we have to….we are taking every precaution. My first priority is the safety of the fire and rescue teams who are doing such a courageous job here. I need to go now, but I will try to update you later.

These are all potential clips.

Clip 1 is factual and not really what you are looking for in a clip. It contains a lot of useful information about the scale of the incident, but that is something you would probably want to include in your introduction to the clip.

Clip 2 is definitely an option – you have the strong description of the scene that confronted the fire crews and the need to make the area safe. The line about them wrongly thinking someone was inside does not really go anywhere because that situation was resolved. It would be a different matter if there *were* still someone inside the building.

Clip 3 looks by far the best option. It is strong and describes a situation of ongoing hazard and drama – and it carries a tribute to the heroism of the firefighters. We will edit out the preamble "well, yes it's an issue", which is probably in response to a question, and which just holds us up while adding nothing. We can edit out the false starts to two of the sentences ("It's a very….." "So obviously we have to…..."). And we will remove the promise of a later update.

That leaves us with:

> Because it is a chemical factory, there is obviously the added danger of an explosion and so we are having to tread very carefully. It's a massive fire, one of the biggest we have had to deal with in recent years. We are taking every precaution. My first priority is the safety of the fire and rescue teams who are doing such a courageous job here.

It still looks a bit long. That's no problem. You can just take the first or the last part of it. Or cut this bit out of the middle:

> It's a massive fire, one of the biggest we have had to deal with in recent years.

If you do that, you end up with a good strong evocative clip of about the right length for your summary:

> Because it is a chemical factory, there is obviously the added danger of explosion and so we are having to tread very carefully. We are taking every precaution. My first priority is the safety of the fire and rescue teams who are doing such a courageous job here.

You also have at least one alternative clip that you might decide to use in the next summary an hour later, to ring the changes.

Not everyone talks with the admirable precision of our fictional fire chief. There are lots of ums and ers, "you knows" and false starts. If you have time, and it works technically, you can take these out – a process known as "de-umming". You are not distorting the meaning of what was said, you are doing it for production purposes to make the clip cleaner and more effective. It is possible to overdo it. If you clean someone's words up too much, the result can sound oddly robotic and artificial. Use your judgement about what sounds most natural.

If someone has refused to do an audio interview but provided a written statement, you can turn that into an audio clip by having one of your colleagues voice it up. "The company declined to be interviewed, but provided this statement, read by one of our producers."

Writing into clips

When you are writing your introduction to an audio clip in your script, the key thing is to make sure you give the listeners all the information they need to understand it. We mentioned this in the last chapter, and will return to it when we come to consider cues for voice reports.

Who are we about to hear from? What is their handle on the story? Witness? Spokesman? Commentator? Someone reacting, or giving an opinion?

Help the listeners prepare for what they are about to hear by giving some hint of what the speaker is going to say, or what their mood is.

"The Labour MP John Brown said he was angry about the decision" will be a good way of setting up a clip of John Brown sounding angry. "The Liberal Democrat MP Jane White said the government couldn't be trusted with the Health Service" will be a good way of setting up a clip in which Jane White criticises government health policy. Avoid lame cues such as "this is what the Labour MP John Brown had to say", or "Liberal Democrat Jane White reacted like this" which sound feeble and waste space.

Make sure the cue and the clip work together. Since the cue must include all the information we need to understand what follows, that might mean prior explanation of something we are about to hear. Suppose you wanted to use a clip of a scientist saying this:

> The next moves in space exploration may involve returning to the moon. We have so much still to learn about the moon, and whether it's NASA or Roscosmos or someone else who gets there first, I think that will be a tremendously exciting development.

Listeners may or may not know that NASA is the American space agency and Roscosmos is the Russian equivalent. If you want to use this clip, you need to help them by explaining in advance. Your cue into this clip might say something like:

CUE: Professor Jack Green of Oxford University predicted a new race to the moon between the American and Russian space agencies.

CLIP: The next moves in space exploration may well involve returning to the moon. We have so much still to learn about the moon, and whether it's NASA or Roscosmos or someone else who gets there first, I think that will be a tremendously exciting development.

In the same way, alert listeners to anything out of the ordinary they are about to hear, such as background noise, so that they are not surprised or distracted by it.

On a crackly telephone line, she told us the relief convoy had still not arrived

Amid wild cheering, he said he felt vindicated by the verdict

With the celebrations in full swing behind him, the coach was understandably elated:

Cues and voice reports

Only larger stations have the budgets to employ full-time radio reporters, and they are much sought-after jobs. Elsewhere, reporting is regarded as just one of many skills required of a multitasking broadcast journalist. Some stations never use reporters for live or recorded updates on stories, for the simple reason that they don't employ any dedicated reporters. For small stations, or those that play mostly music, the only news output is the hourly summary, produced in the office from a variety of sources by a very small production team – perhaps no more than one or two people at any given time. They may receive feeds of audio and other material from a shared source, but they do not have the resources to report from location or do much of their own newsgathering.

But where there is a commitment to longer news bulletins of anything up to half an hour – as on BBC Radio 4 at six o'clock and midnight – you have space for more detailed reportage. The format of those long bulletins is a number of headlines followed by a sequence of cues, or introductions, each leading into either a clip of actuality or a VP of around 60–90 seconds by one of the reporters. Less important stories will be "straight writes", typically of 15–20 seconds, with no accompanying audio.

The audio report, variously called a voice piece, VP or voicer, therefore comes in two parts: *the cue*, which is read by the newsreader or presenter; and *the report itself*, live or pre-recorded. The cue, or introduction/ lead-in/intro – different companies use different terminology – sets the piece up; the report itself, by the correspondent or reporter, gives more detail and builds on the information that is in the cue. It is very important to see these as two elements of the whole: they must be made to work together.

Each has its own functions. Let us talk about the cue first.

Functions of the cue:

the cue tells the listener what the story is about

This is of course its primary function, and in that sense it serves the same purpose as a print intro. The cue contains the key facts in just the same way – the only difference is that it's written for radio, and thus to be listened to rather than read. But it must convey the core information. If you had only the cue and no VP, you should still have enough information to understand the gist of the story.

the cue sets up the piece that follows

The information contained in the cue must complement what we are about to hear in the report. It must set up and lead naturally into the voice report or clip of actuality that the listener is going to hear next. That means giving the listeners all the information they need to understand the report that is coming next – as we have already discussed when talking about setting up a clip. The cue should not repeat words, phrases or information that are going to appear in the piece. The cue and the piece must work together in harmony. If they don't, the result will sound clumsy and clunky.

the cue sells the story to the listener

In this respect it is again like a print story. The cue should try to draw in the listeners and make them want to find out more about the story. That means using the same active and engaging language that we have talked about in other contexts.

Do not confuse a cue with a headline. They are not the same thing. Think of it as the intro, the top couple of sentences in a news item.

Always start by writing the cue

As a reporter, when you come to write your piece, you should always start by establishing what information is going to be in the cue. You and the presenter or producer must agree an outline of what the cue will contain. This is about basic communication between members of the team. If you start writing your report without knowing what is in the cue, there is a danger that it will overlap with or otherwise fail to dovetail with your piece. You might also put so much of the story into your report that there is nothing left to put in the cue. Drafting the cue helps you focus on the story that you are about to tell. It helps you make sure that when you come to write the piece, you don't repeat anything that the audience will already have heard. And it helps you make sure you don't refer to something the audience has *not* heard, and which might therefore be confusing.

If you are the producer compiling the bulletin, you will need to agree cue material with the reporter in order to be able to produce a final polished cue that seamlessly sets up the piece. You can rewrite it if you wish, to make it fit better with the rest of your bulletin, but the draft that the reporter has produced will give you the basic material that needs to be included.

Here are two common examples of where it can go wrong:

Bad practice 1: Cue and piece repeat the same information.

CUE: The latest inflation figures show that prices rose by 2.3 per cent in October, the biggest increase for six months. John Smith reports:
JOHN SMITH VOICE PIECE BEGINS: "Inflation rose by 2.3 per cent last month. That's the biggest rise for six months........"

That is an obvious example of the cue and the piece not working together, and you can imagine how horrible that would sound to you as a listener if you heard it on the air. If John Smith and the person responsible for the cue had spoken to each other in advance, this could not have happened. Here is an example of how the cue and piece could work better together for that story.

CUE: The latest inflation figures show that prices rose by 2.3 per cent in October, the biggest increase for six months. John Smith reports:
JOHN SMITH VOICE PIECE BEGINS: "These figures are worse than expected, and reflect increases in fuel prices last month......"

Here we have the cue and the piece working together, with the VP building on and adding to the information that was in the cue. There is no overlap. Note that the cue does not change – it contains the main news line of the story. The difference is in the way the VPs start. The second VP does not repeat what we have already heard but takes that as a starting point to develop the narrative further.

Bad practice 2: Cue does not set the piece up properly

Now the opposite problem. The cue doesn't tell you enough to understand the voice report that follows. Here's an example:

CUE: New measures to help tackle the rising problem of obesity come into force next week. More details from Jane Smith:
JANE SMITH VOICE PIECE BEGINS: "Mr Robinson said he had no doubt that the requirement for labels to carry more calorific information would bring about a big improvement in the nation's health. He told the House......"

If you heard this, you could be forgiven for thinking that these were two completely different stories. What are these measures? Who is Mr Robinson? What house? What is the connection between cue and piece?

To fix this, we need to put more information into the cue:

CUE: The health secretary Michael Robinson says he has no doubt that new measures to tackle the rising problem of obesity will help improve the health of the nation. Jane Smith reports:
JANE SMITH VOICE PIECE BEGINS: "The measures come into force next week, and the government clearly has high expectations for them. Mr Robinson told MPs….."

Again the solution is by thinking of them as linked elements, working together to tell a story in an effective way. Although starting the story with a name and job title is not very exciting, it does give the audience the information needed to understand and assess the piece in the way we discussed in the last chapter, and it means the reporter can dive straight into the detail of the story without having to explain who Michael Robinson is. Indeed, we do not even need to repeat his first name because we have already heard it.

So while as a reporter you will be anxious to crack on with writing the script that you are going to record, always make time to work on the cue first. Collaboration between reporter and producer is vital if you are to produce a seamless piece of radio journalism.

The cue may seem like a mechanical device – and it is. But that does not mean it has to be perfunctory or dull. It is a piece of broadcast news like any other, and as we have said, it also has the job of selling the story to the listener. A striking quote or a few morsels of telling detail can bring it to life and demand attention for the rest of the item.

And as always, remember that the listener has only one chance to absorb it, and so your language must be simple, attractive and accessible. Don't clog it up with adjectives, acronyms and numbers. In sum, give the cue the attention and crafting it deserves. It is vitally important to effective storytelling on the radio and in its own small way it is an art form.

The written cue will often contain some technical information, not for reading on the air but for the benefit of the person who will be in technical charge of putting the programme to air. This includes the name of the person we are about to hear, the duration of the piece and the first and last words. When it is on paper, it may look a bit like this:

CUE: The health secretary Michael Robinson says he has no doubt that new measures to tackle the rising problem of obesity will help improve the health of the nation. Jane Smith reports:
SMITH: (name of reporter) 44" (duration of report)
IN: "The new measures….. (first words of report)
OUT: …….remains to be seen" (last words of report).

Broadcasters use single and double inverted commas as shorthand to denote minutes and seconds. So a piece that is a minute and a half long will be written as 1'30".

Make sure than anything that is likely to become dated or overcome by events is in the cue and not in the VP. It is the work of a few seconds to alter a cue, which will always be read live. But a VP needs to be re-recorded if it falls out of date, and you may end up having to drop it altogether if you don't have time to do that, or the reporter has gone home.

Functions of the VP

So, we have set up your voice report now: the piece you are going to write and then record for broadcast. Like the cue, your piece is going to attempt to do one or more of a number of things:

– **Describe** what has happened, adding detail to the bare bones set out in the cue.
– **Explain** what has happened.
– Set out the **background and context.**
– Indicate **why it is important**.
– Suggest **what might happen next**.

There are various factors to be borne in mind, some of them specific to the story, some of them external factors that will determine how you proceed. These are the things you need to take into account when sitting down to write your piece.

External factors include the questions to which you will always need the answers when preparing any piece of journalism: *how much?* and *what's my deadline?*

The person editing the programme or bulletin in which your piece will feature will usually be the one to tell you how much time you can have. They will give you a time duration, not a word count. Remember to establish whether the time you are given is just for the piece, or for the cue and piece combined. Once you have your duration, you can start to develop an idea of the shape of your piece, what you have time to include – and must include – and what you can leave out if time is tight. Even when you are pressed for time, you should take a few moments to decide exactly what the role of your piece is within the bulletin, what its shape should be.

Your deadline will usually be the transmission time of the bulletin for which you are writing. But don't write all the way up to the clock. You need to leave time to have your script approved and make any changes that are required, to record and save it in the appropriate technical location for transmission and to make any journeys that may be necessary – for example, if your desk is two floors away from the place where you will be recording the piece. Never leave yourself so short of time that you need to hurry from one place to another before recording. A piece delivered when you are out of breath always sounds horrible.

There are other external factors to bear in mind as you approach the writing of the piece:

– If you are working on a big story, yours might be one of several reports covering a variety of angles. You need clear guidance from your editor on the purpose and parameters of your particular piece, to avoid overlapping with other material.
– You might also be asked to include some actuality in your piece – typically one or two clips. You will need to find out how to get hold of these, and possibly edit them yourself. Then you will have to write into them in exactly the same way as you would if you were introducing them in a summary, bearing in mind everything we have already said about cues and writing into clips.

Within those parameters, and once you know exactly what is expected of you, it then becomes a straight-forward piece of writing which follows exactly the same rules as most other forms of newswriting, with the addition of the considerations we have discussed with relation to radio.

Writing your VP

The first thing to consider, as you might expect, is what sort of piece you are going to write. It may be serving one or more of a number of different purposes.

– **A basic news report.** A piece in which you describe something that has happened. This is the most likely format for an "action" story such as a motorway accident or a round-up of weather damage, or for breaking news, when there is a premium on finding out the basic facts of a story as soon as possible. When events are actually unfolding, the analysis can wait until later.
– **A background piece.** This might be where your analysis and context come in, looking in more detail at a story that has happened and seeking to explain it and give your audience the information to understand it better.

It is of course perfectly possible to combine both of these in a single piece.

– **An update piece.** You may be describing the latest developments in a story that has already been running for some time. You will probably be starting with the new material (although most of it might be in the cue), but you need to think about how much the audience will already know about the story, and how much you need to remind them of what has already happened.
– **A colour or close focus piece.** A purely descriptive piece that might be a report of something that you have seen yourself, and which, for example, helps bring home to the audience the effect in human terms of the bald headline. So reportage of a flood or famine that has killed many people can be given power and potency by a detailed report of the effects on a single village or family.

Be careful not to attempt to do too much: not every piece needs a lot of background; not every piece needs you to offer a judgement. Often you will want to make room for the colour, the telling detail or a striking phrase. There won't always be room for everything: decide what is the most important for a piece that is interesting and attractive as well as informative.

It is important that you start well and finish well, so that your story engages the audience from the off and also has a discernible beginning, middle and end. You might want to send an early signal about the story and where it is going, why it is important and why people should want to listen to it. You can structure your piece in a number of ways: by starting straight in with the latest news, for example, or by setting out first how important it is. A lot of this is about your own style, personal preferences and the way you see your story.

Here is the information for a typical story that will help us explore those options.

> Conservative MP John Black has resigned after opponents exposed inaccurate statements in his election literature. He apologised to his constituents, saying his behaviour had fallen short of the standards they were entitled to expect. He had claimed to have a number of academic qualifications to which he was not entitled. His departure presents a difficulty for the government because they have only a small majority in the House of Commons. It is also an embarrassment for them, because he is the third of the party's MPs who has been forced to resign for one reason or another in the last six months.

If you were given this material and asked to write a short VP, you could legitimately present your report in any one of at least four different ways.

In each case, the content of the cue would be the same: the news line is that John Black has resigned for making inaccurate statements. From there, you have a choice of approaches:

Approach 1 Simple narrative storytelling, starting from the beginning and following the chronology. The cue tells us that Mr Black has resigned and why. Here is your report:

> In his promotional literature at the last election, Mr Black claimed to have a distinguished academic record. But opponents have claimed that most of these qualifications were bogus.
>
> Mr Black admitted the inaccuracies and apologised to his constituents, saying his behaviour had fallen short of the standards they were entitled to expect.
>
> He is the third MP in the last six months to be forced to resign for one reason or another, and his departure further reduces the government's Commons majority.

Approach 2 Simple narrative storytelling, but starting this time with the latest detail, and then recapping. The cue tells us that Mr Black has resigned and why. Here is your report:

> Mr Black has apologised to his constituents, saying that his behaviour had fallen short of the standards they were entitled to expect.
>
> He admitted inaccuracies in his promotional literature at the last election.
>
> In his literature, Mr Black claimed to have a distinguished academic record. But opponents have claimed that most of these qualifications were bogus.
>
> He is the third MP in the last six months who has been forced to resign for one reason or another, and his departure further reduces the government's Commons majority.

Approach 3 The political context. If you were a political reporter, you would probably be most interested in the wider implications of this story. So you could begin with a strong statement about its significance. The cue tells us that Mr Black has resigned and why. Here is your report:

> Mr Black's departure is a severe blow to the government, whose majority in the Commons is already wafer thin. It will now find it even harder to get its legislative programme through.
>
> It is also a serious political embarrassment – he is the third MP in the last six months who has been forced to resign for one reason or another.
>
> In his promotional literature at the last election, Mr Black claimed to have a distinguished academic record. But opponents have claimed that most of these qualifications were bogus.
>
> Mr Black admitted the inaccuracies and apologised to his constituents, saying that his behaviour had fallen short of the standards they were entitled to expect.

Approach 4 Another politically angled way in would be to start by putting the story into the context of recent events. The cue tells us that Mr Black has resigned and why. Here is your report:

> Mr Black's departure is a serious political embarrassment – he is the third MP in the last six months who has been forced to resign for one reason or another.
>
> It is also a severe blow to the government, whose majority in the Commons is already wafer thin. It will now find it harder still to get controversial legislation through.
>
> In his promotional literature at the last election, Mr Black claimed to have a distinguished academic record. But his main opponent has claimed that most of these qualifications were bogus.
>
> Mr Black admitted the inaccuracies and apologised to his constituents, saying that his behaviour had fallen short of the standards they were entitled to expect.

There is nothing wrong with any of these versions. They all carry the key facts and a degree of context. Even though the order in which the information is presented is different in each case, all are perfectly accurate and acceptable. They show that even within the confines of a very short voice report, you have a number of approaches at your disposal.

You will have this breadth of choice with very many of the stories you write, in whatever medium. The approach you take will depend on how your editor sees it, what sort of story you think it is, how new some of the detail is, the context and how important you think the story is. If you think it is very significant, a strong opening sentence straight after the cue that indicates as much can be very effective. It doesn't have to be long or detailed: Opening your piece with: "This is very unwelcome news for the government" or: "This is the biggest overhaul of the system for more than twenty years" can be effective in providing a context for the detail that will follow. In the end, it boils down to what feels right and most appropriate for the moment you are writing the story, and your own personal style and preferences.

With any approach, try to organise your material into a logical sequence. All of the examples above do that – in each case, every paragraph contains a single thought, and they are all easy to follow. Remember the truism about a radio listener having only one chance to absorb what is being reported. Your script should have a logical flow to it, including any detail that is important to the telling of the story or the audience's understanding of it. If you move between timeframes, make sure you take the audience with you.

Once you are into the business of actually writing, all the usual rules apply.

> Write for the ear, not the eye, and follow the patterns of everyday speech.

> Write conversationally, even it sounds a little less urgent and dynamic. It is what the medium requires.

And as with most journalism:

> Use simple language and simple sentences.
> Break up the pace with a mixture of shorter and longer sentences.
> Avoid jargon: if you must use it, make sure you explain it.
> Don't use too many long words or adjectives.
> Try to produce a clear narrative.
> Attribute your sources.

The reporter package – gathering the material

The main ingredient of radio news and current affairs reporting that we have yet to look at is the package or wrap. This is a fuller and lengthier report than a VP. It affords you more time to tell the story, with probably at least two interviewees and some sort of natural sound to give it an atmosphere and sense of location. The package is made up of a series of clips or sounds, tied together by a series of scripted links. Such a report could be anything from 90 seconds to 5 minutes or even more.

The typical radio package of around three minutes could take one of a number of forms. It might be a longer and more in-depth report on the story of the day, pulling together developments and including clips of some of the main players in the story. Or it may be a feature – designed to fulfil just the same function as a print feature by concentrating less on hard news angles and more on detail, background, colour and the human element – helping the listener get under the skin of the story. It may not be "newsy" in the conventional sense, but it might well cast a different perspective on a current news story, say by giving a view from the ground about how a recession or social trend is actually affecting people. This sort of feature lends itself to a creative and imaginative approach, and will usually involve a lot more work and thought – and production skills – than a news voicer that is put together at speed to meet a bulletin deadline.

As with any story, preparation is key, so unless it is a brand new story, start by making sure you understand how the latest developments will affect the story so far. Get a handle on the main issues at play, researching the background and context, and being aware of what has been reported already – especially by your own programme or station. And because this is a piece of radio, you will need to think about good locations in which to record, and good sources of natural sound.

If you are doing an on-the-day story, find out what audio material is already around, or is expected as the news day develops. Even if you want to avoid using something that has already been aired, you might find there is some valuable unused material that will help you come at the story from a slightly different angle.

Then get out of the office. Head for a location that is near enough for you to have time to assemble material, edit it and get it back to base before your deadline. If you are not producing a piece on the day, but have more time to assemble it, then obviously you can venture further afield. Either way, you want to reduce the amount of material that is recorded in a studio, with your voice introducing a series of clips that are lacking in atmosphere. Such a piece may be competent – but it also risks being dull.

For news packages, all the interviews you do will probably be quite short, because you know you will not have room to include much of them in your piece. You will be cutting the interviews into short clips, and will use no more than one or two from each interviewee. We looked at interviewing in greater depth in Chapter 8.

This means each clip must be worthy of its place in your piece, and you need to be thinking about this all the time you are doing the interview. Ask yourself:

> What is the key ground I want this interviewee to cover? What is their role in my package?
> Is the interviewee making these points in a way that I can use in the package? Is he/she speaking succinctly, understandably and in such a way that I will be able to find one or two strong clips?

If your interviewee is not being succinct and understandable, you need to keep at it until you get what you need. Ask open questions that cannot be answered with a straight yes or no – those responses are no good to you at all.

As we have said, if the interviewee is not delivering, keep asking the same questions until you get something that you want. You can, and should, explain why you are doing this. As we have noted, that means saying something like: "that was a great point, but your answer overall was a bit long: can I ask you the question again and ask you to make your answer a bit shorter?" This will not feel rude if you do it nicely and your interviewees will probably cooperate unless they are in a bad mood or a big hurry.

Look for self-contained answers, complete sentences that you can lift out and use as clips. You can school your interviewees by asking them to respond in this way. For example, imagine this exchange as part of an interview you are doing:

YOU: What sort of effect is this going to have on your business?
INTERVIEWEE: Exactly, good question. As I said before, who knows where we are going to end up? But it's not looking good.

If you are looking for a clip, you will know as soon as you hear this answer that it will not be much use to you when you come to the edit. It will not stand up on its own as a clip. If you had to use this in your package, you would have to include the question as well and run the whole thing. You might try to snip out "as I said before", because it refers to something the listener is not going to hear in the package. It would not be a great clip, including the question eats up extra time, and you would have much more flexibility if you encouraged your interviewee to reply with a complete sentence. If you explain why you want them to do this, you will usually find them cooperative. So your conversation might go like this:

YOU: What sort of effect is this going to have on your business?
INTERVIEWEE: Exactly, good question. As I said before, who knows where we are going to end up? But it's not looking good.
YOU: Do you mind if I put that question again, and ask that you reply with a complete sentence, such as "the effect in my business will be…..". It will just make it a lot easier for me to edit what you are saying – and it will make you sound better! And if possible, can you not refer back to something you said earlier in the interview, as I might not be using that.
INTERVIEWEE: Ok, sorry.
YOU: Please don't apologise. It's not what you said, it's just the way that you said it! Thank you. Here we go then. I'll put the question to you again. What sort of effect is this going to have on your business?
INTERVIEWEE: It's too early to say exactly what the effect on our business will be, but the signs are not good at the moment, so all we can do is sit tight and hope for the best.

You now have a useable self-contained clip that gives you much more flexibility and economy when you come to the edit.

The kit of parts for a conventional radio package will usually include two or three clips of different interviewees with some sort of natural sound. Other commonly used elements are vox pops, archive material, and one or more standuppers, or "as lives", by you reporting on location. A standupper might be descriptive: "I'm standing here at the location of yesterday's flood, and I'm looking at a scene of absolute chaos". It might be a link: "after talking to John Brown in the shopping precinct, I'm taking the short walk down the High Street to speak to someone with a very different view of the issue…". Or it might contribute an editorial thought

> as you look around the area it isn't hard to see why it has acquired a reputation for a range of social problems. Young people say there are no jobs, no prospects and nothing to do except get into trouble.

Record plenty of standuppers – they can be very useful when you come to assemble your piece, especially if you want the whole report to sound as though it comes from the location; and if you don't use them, you have not lost anything. Note how all of these examples transport the listener to the scene – the flood site, the High Street, the deprived area.

Example

Here is an imaginary story. You hear that there has been a bad case of fly tipping in a field outside a village on your patch. You make some calls and discover that council workers are in the business of removing it. You go to the scene as quickly as you can, and find that council diggers are shovelling the rubbish into trucks, while some of the villagers look on. The field adjoins a churchyard.

We will consider first what material you will want to gather, and then later we will think about how to put it together into a radio package. In this example, your course of action is relatively obvious. You will want to record the following as elements in your piece:

> Sounds of the diggers at work. That is the best natural sound on offer. Record plenty of it.
>
> A standupper with that noise in the background, describing what you are seeing. Put in plenty of detail: what sort of rubbish is it? This might offer a clue as to who dumped it. Describe also what you are smelling, because the rubbish is giving off an unpleasant aroma. That will help convey the scene to your listeners.
>
> The villagers. You can interview one or two of them separately, or together as a group. You will want to ask them what they know about how the rubbish came to be dumped, how long it has been there, whether it has happened before.
>
> You find a council foreman at the site and interview him about the problem. When did the council hear about it? How? Do they know who was responsible? Is this a regular problem for the council? You may find that the person on the ground does not want to speak to you and refers you to the council press office instead. You will want to ask the press office if someone will go on the record to talk to you about the problem and how much it costs the council to tackle it – an environmental health officer perhaps, or the chair of the relevant council committee.
>
> You go to the church and find the vicar, so you interview her as well. You will ask her similar questions to those you put to the villagers.
> The diggers stop work. You record some contrasting wild track: all that can be heard now is birdsong.

You might want to do a bit of research about the penalties for fly tipping, which would be a useful element of your piece.

In quite a short space of time you have assembled the material for a very nice radio package. We will look later in the chapter at what your report might sound like.

In that example, the business of gathering material was relatively straightforward. You were able to find everything you wanted at the same location, and you did not have to make a lot of calls before leaving the office to find people and arrange to meet them. It is not always as easy as that. Here are some practical thoughts about the gathering of material outside the office.

Before you leave

– Do some research. Print useful articles or facts to take with you.
– Make lots of calls. You will save yourself masses of time if you know where you are going and how to get there, and have found some interviewees in advance and made arrangements to meet them.
– Check that your recording device and any other gear is working. Change the batteries and/or make sure you have spares.
– Check that you have the necessary mics, shields, cables and leads, stands, memory cards, headphones and anything else that you will need. Rolls of sticky tape and waterproof insulating tape will often come in handy.
– Check that you are not going to record over some previous material that you do not want to lose.

In the field

– Test that your recording device is working.
– If you are going to be recording against a background of natural sound, do a number of tests to make sure that you have got the right balance between your voice, and that of your interviewee, and the background.
– Record at least a minute of natural sound, sometimes called background, atmos (atmosphere) or wild track. You may need this in the edit, perhaps to help cushion the link between two pieces of audio of different quality.
– Get physically close to your interviewees. During the interview, you want to move the microphone as little as possible between yourself and the person you are interviewing. If you are too far apart, there is a danger that the start/end of one contribution will be slightly off-mic – and in the worst case, is rendered unusable as a result. If you cannot get close, make sure that the mic is always close to the interviewee rather than you: it is more important that you capture the answers than the questions.
– Get your interviewees to say a few words before you begin the interview proper, to make sure that you are recording at the appropriate sound levels. The standard question is to ask them what they had for breakfast. The answer will be neutral, and it helps relax them.
– Do not let your interviewees go before you have listened back and satisfied yourself that you have recorded them successfully.
– Record a number of standuppers, or "as lives", on location, as in our example above. Try several versions of the same one, perhaps at different lengths. These are the radio versions of a television piece to camera, in which you describe what you can see or what has happened. They give your piece a strong sense of location in a way that links read out in a studio cannot, and they give energy to the whole. It may be that you use very few of them, sometimes none of them. That doesn't matter – if you have them, you have given yourself options. If you do not have them, you have boxed yourself in unnecessarily. Try to make your standuppers sound natural, conversational and spontaneous.
– If you feel confident enough, try writing and recording your links on location as well. You can script and record then and there, and assemble the piece later. This breaks our rule about editing the clips first and writing your script second, and as a result it will not always work, because your links might not fit with the edits you later make. But if it does come off, your package will sound much tighter, engaging and more coherent.

Natural sound

As we have noted a number of times, natural sound is vitally important in making your material come to life, making it interesting to listen to and in conveying to the listener a sense of what is really happening and what it was like to be there. Always have an ear cocked for it. Sometimes it will be obvious – music, people shouting, say at a sports event or a demonstration. Simple actions such as a knock on a door, uncorking a bottle or opening a newspaper will produce sounds that add interest and authenticity to your piece. You need to develop an ear and an instinct for it. Just recording the noise and atmosphere in the situation you are in can give you a few seconds of background conversation or noise that you can drop into your piece at some point. It can be tempting to start your piece with someone answering the phone saying "Smith's Motors, can I help you?" or something similar – which has the advantage of the early introduction of a "real" voice which immediately conveys the location. But this has become a cliché and is best avoided. Close your eyes and listen. There are sounds all around you – birdsong, traffic, the buzz of people talking. If you develop an ear for it, you will find there are many possibilities. It is all there and available, and it will lift your work enormously. And, incidentally, it is vitally important in television pieces as well. Developing a feel for natural sound and using it well will make an enormous difference to the quality of your reports.

If you are going to lay natural sound under part or all of your report, it works well to bring up the sound a second or two before we hear the first speaker – and to fade it out again after the final words at the end. You can even bring the actuality up under the last couple of seconds of the cue, to prepare the listener for the atmosphere. Add these instructions to your script if you are going to record with the help of a sound engineer or studio manager, so that they know what you want them to do.

CUE: ......the march wound its way along the Embankment and culminated in a rally in Trafalgar Square. The atmosphere was noisy but good humoured. Our reporter (FADE UP ACT) John Smith joined the marchers:
INSERT: SMITH/ACT DUR: 1'15"
STARTS ON 5" OF ACT
IN: "It was an impressive display of unity......
OUT: ....clear message to the government" (FADE OUT ON ACT).

The reporter package: putting it together

When you have gathered all your material, it is time to talk to the programme editor about what you have got and how to make the best and most effective use of it in your report. The editor may want to listen to some of your material, or may be happy for you to describe what you have and then suggest ways in which the piece can be assembled. The editor may also decide that you don't have enough material, perhaps because an important perspective has not been reflected. If you cannot cover that in your script, you may find yourself setting out once again to fill that gap with another interview.

Either before or after this conversation, make a point of listening back to everything you have recorded. You may be able to do this on the bus or train on your way back to the office (but not while driving). It will not sound exactly as you imagined it or remembered it – it may be better, it may not be as good. Either way, this is the point at which you are starting to make concrete decisions about what clips to cut and how to cut them, and how they fit into the narrative flow of your piece. In order to make good decisions, you need to be fully across all your material.

You will be editing for a number of reasons:

– To reduce the mass of your material to the length you require for your piece
– To extract the best and most pertinent material for the telling of your story

– To tighten up the actuality by removing unwanted words, hesitations and repetitions, so that it flows well
– To enable you to cover all angles within a limited running time
– Depending on the variety of your material, to enable you to create a sound picture of your story that
    will appeal to and resonate with the audience.

Editing requires a certain ruthlessness. You will almost always have more material than you need, and if
the audio is strong, you will find it a wrench to sacrifice some of it. The more you have recorded of course,
the bigger this task will be. You can make it easier by not over-recording. If you know you are looking
only for a short clip, call a halt to the interview when you have got what you need. Even if you think you
might be running two or three minutes of your interview, you will not want to record for more than five
or six minutes: even then you will potentially have twice as much as you need. There are no rules here –
some of your questions might be to elicit information such as names and job titles, and the answers might
never be intended for broadcast. Or you might have to prolong the interview if you are not getting just
what you want. If you go into the interview with a clear idea of what you hope to achieve, it will help
focus your questions and save you recording more than you are ever going to be able to use.

We have noted that it is perfectly acceptable to create a clip or clips by taking short extracts from several
different answers to make a composite or hybrid clip that performs the editorial task you require. The key
thing is to be satisfied that in this process you are maintaining the sense of what the interviewee said, and
are not in any way distorting or misrepresenting their comments.

Sometimes you will have to accept that an edit you would like to make does not work for technical reasons.
For example, if the background noise changes substantially during the course of the interview, it may sound
odd if you create a clip made up of a few words from near the beginning and some more from near the end.
You can overcome this problem if you have taken the precaution of recording plenty of wild track. You can
lay the wild track underneath the clip, and it may then smooth out the junction and sound fine.

Another potential problem with a hybrid clip is that the sound levels are different in each of the component parts. The interviewee may start to talk more loudly or more quickly as he or she becomes animated. You might have had to pause the interview, or move to a different location in the middle of it.
To fix this, you will have to experiment in the studio, trying to balance the levels through the desk until
you have something that you are happy with. If you are not happy though, abandon the attempt. Lots of
great clips are unusable because of irreconcilable levels, inflections, interruptions and a myriad of other
reasons. However much you want the edit to work for editorial reasons, admit defeat if it does not work
for technical reasons. A duff edit is immediately obvious to the listener. It is distracting and suggests that
your quality threshold is not as high as it should be.

Once you have decided what audio you plan to use, edit the clips *before* you start thinking about your
script. The content of the audio, and the order in which you run your clips, will dictate what information
is included in each link of your script. The script is the most flexible part of the package. It is completely
within your control, and is the means by which you are going to move between your various pieces of
audio, writing seamlessly into and out of them in the way we have already discussed. It is also the part of
the piece that will carry the information that is not in the audio.

For these reasons, it is always best to assemble all your clips, fully edited and ready to go, before you start
on the script. You will then be in a position to time them all, and so know exactly how much time you
have for the script, which will be in effect a series of links between the clips. You will be surprised how
little time you have. In a three-minute package, your audio clips may add up to more than two minutes.
That doesn't leave you very much time for script, especially as each link has to introduce the next clip.
This is not necessarily a bad thing: you want the audio to carry the package as much as possible and to
be the main element of it. You do not want acres of script when there is far more interesting material to
be heard. Some reporter packages do not feature the reporter at all – they are made up solely of a series
of sounds or clips stitched together in such a way as to tell the story without the need for the reporter's
intervention. But even if that is not the case, the room you will have for your links is likely to be very

tight, requiring – as always – clear, simple and concise writing. This underlines why it is important to assemble all your audio first. If you write your script first and then cut the clips, you will find that your piece is twice as long as you want it to be, and then you have to begin the tiresome process of hacking it back or – more likely – starting all over again.

With all that in mind, let us return to our package about fly tipping in a local beauty spot. You have brought all your material back to the office and are now putting it together. You follow exactly the process just described – listening to what you have recorded, selecting and editing your clips, writing the links that will lead the listener from one clip to the next and then recording the whole thing. Your structure might look something like this:

Element 1: sound of diggers

Element 2: your standupper, in which you describe what is happening

Element 3: a link into your first piece of actuality. You might have had the foresight to record this at the scene, but if not, you can record it back at base. Something like: "watching the clear-up were residents of the nearby village. One of them, Barbara Jones, told me the fly tippers came regularly, always late at night"

Element 4: Clip of Barbara Jones

(You could follow this with another clip from a villager)

Element 5: a link to a clip of the vicar. "Only a stone's throw away is the historic medieval church of St Thomas. The vicar Anne Barnes, spoke of her sadness at the sight of all the rubbish"

Element 6: Clip of Anne Barnes

Element 7: a link to the council official. "Back at the clearing operation, I spoke to environmental health officer Gordon Fox about the problem of fly tipping"

Element 8: Clip of Gordon Fox

Element 9: Closing thought from you to finish the piece. You might possibly end with a few seconds of your birdsong, which you could write into with a line like: "The diggers have done their work, but the fly tippers may well be back. For now though, peace returns to this lovely spot."

You will see from this example that most of the piece is taken up by the people involved in the story, and the natural sounds. You have only a few short links to explain what is happening, and even then, each link has work to do in introducing the next person we are going to hear from. The fact that in a three-minute package you might have barely a minute of script is a good thing – the more real people and natural sounds we hear the better. But it does underline the point about the need to write very economically, and to make every word count. It also demonstrates why it is best to cut the clips before you start to write the script. Until you know what is in the clip, you cannot write into it appropriately.

When you have finished editing and scripting, but before you record, take an overview of the elements – your draft cue, your draft script and your clips. As ever, ask yourself some obvious questions before proceeding:

Editorial questions:

> Do my cue and piece work together?
> Have I told the story well?
> Have I answered the questions the listener wants answered?
> Have I covered the ground/perspectives?
> Have I left out something that really should be included?

Quality questions:

> Is this piece going to sound engaging?
> Have I made the most of natural sound?
> Have I extracted the best clips?

Do all the edits 'work'?
Do my links work with the clips that they introduce?
Is my piece the duration I was asked for?

Once you are satisfied with the answers to these questions, it is time to record your links and put the package together – which will often be the quickest and most straightforward part of the whole process. When you have finished, always listen to the whole thing through from beginning to end, to make sure you have not left in any bad edits or overlaps by mistake, or had any small stumbles that you did not notice when recording.

Other techniques

This is the basic format of a typical feature. But you can play with it in a number of ways and achieve effective results by using different techniques.

– You can get your interviewees to introduce themselves as a way of giving structure to the piece. For this to work, they all need to use the same form of words: "I'm Sandra, and I live in Newtown"; "I'm Alan, and I live in Oldport". Or, more formally: "My name is Andrew Jones and I am sales manager for Johnsons Widgets", "My name is Joan Roberts and I am sales manager for Betta Bikes". You run the introductions and then the clips of them making their points.
– You can set your interviewee up in advance and then introduce them "as live". Say you are doing a piece on a new shopping mall and you are going to walk around describing it and then interview the mall manager. You have the manager standing by, ready to go. You record a standupper in which you talk about the mall and then you say: "I'm joined now Darren Smith, who is the manager of the new mall. Darren, thanks for talking to me – all ready for the big opening on Saturday?" And you keep recording while Darren answers. This technique can give a strong sense of place and works well, but like so many things in broadcasting, if it is to sound spontaneous and unplanned, it needs to be carefully organised and walked through in advance. This would also work as a live treatment.
– If you are reporting from a place where there is a lot of natural sound – a music festival for example – you may be able to remove your own voice from the package altogether, and just use a montage of sounds mixed with clips of interviewees who introduce themselves.
– Some reporters like to break up a clip, which can work well. Example:

INTERVIEWEE: We employ more than 60 people on this production line.
REPORTER: Simon Bell is head of production at the factory
INTERVIEWEE: It's a 24-hour operation and we work on the basis of…….

If you use this technique, you are bending one of our rules – about not leaving until the end of a sentence any information that the listener needs in order to understand the beginning of it. In the example above, we hear from Simon Bell before we know who he is and what he does. It works only if we do not have to wait very long to get that information. But it is best to avoid this technique in a short news report.

All of these techniques also work with television reports. The radio package is a flexible beast, so use your imagination and try new ways of doing things. Too many radio packages sound the same – link, clip, link, clip – and they seldom need to. Natural sound will always help, but you can play with different structures and formats too, depending on the nature of the story.

Live reporting

Live reporting is a whole separate skill. You are the reporter at the scene of a story, connected by your phone or other means to the team producing a live programme back at base. The on-air presenter introduces you and throws to you for your report, or to explain what is going on in a brief conversation between the two of you. This latter is called a two-way, or a down-the-line (DTL) interview. It can be nerve-wracking: the technology lets you down, your mouth dries up, your mind goes blank. But once you get used to it, you will find, as most radio reporters do, that it can be the most fun and exciting part of the job.

A typical two-way will be around two or three minutes long, which in radio terms is quite a decent period of time, and one in which you can convey a lot of information. The presenter will probably ask three questions in that time, the first of which will usually be: "what's the latest?", "what's happening there?", "what can you see?" or something along those lines. Your answer will be fairly obvious. You also have the opportunity here to locate yourself at the scene of the action and show that you have been doing some journalism: "I've been speaking to some of the neighbours, and they told me...." "fire officers here are telling me that it will be some hours yet before they have the blaze under control", "I was prepared for the scene of devastation here, but not for the smell that pervades everything...."

The second question might ask you for more details, or it might take you into the background or context of the story. The presenter will not so much ask a question as invite you to provide the context that is needed: "remind us how we got to this point", or, "the roots of this dispute go back some months I understand", or "this is not the first time concerns have been raised about safety at the site". This is where you will sketch in the information the listener needs in order to make sense of the story – in exactly the same way as you would in a scripted VP. In order to be able to do so, you will need to have done some research on the story before you set off and when you arrived at the scene. The listener is relying on you to tell the story in its entirety.

The final question might well look ahead: "what happens next?" or "what's the next step?" You will often be in a position to offer a view on where the story might be going in the next hour or day or further ahead. But be careful not to speculate, or offer an opinion as to how events may develop. That is not your job. You can say something *factual* – "the next move is likely to come on Thursday when the two sides meet again.....", and you can offer a *judgement*: ".....though on the basis of what we have been hearing today, they remain a very long way apart". But do not offer an *opinion* "there is no chance of a settlement that will avert a strike". If you do so, you are overstepping the mark and turning into a commentator, which goes well beyond your remit as a reporter.

It may be that you will have had time to discuss in advance, either with the presenter or with the production team, what questions you will be asked, and what you are likely to say in your answer. It is useful to be able to do this, because it means you are less likely to be wrong-footed by an unexpected question – to which you might not know the answer – and the whole thing should flow more smoothly and naturally. If there is an area of questioning that you want to avoid for whatever reason, now is the time to flag it.

If you are unfortunate enough to be asked a question from left field, which you are in no position to answer, you have two choices. You can either say "I don't know the answer to that", which is perfectly acceptable if it is something that you would not reasonably be expected to know, such as events that are happening somewhere else; but if you feel that this would be a lame response, and that you really ought to be able to answer it, then resort to the old trick of diverting the conversation back to ground where you feel safer: "I'm not entirely sure about that, but I can tell you that.......", "I think the question here most people are asking is actually....". With luck, the presenter will realise he or she is taking you somewhere you do not want to go, and take the hint with the next question. On no account try to busk it or guess the answer to a question: it is unprofessional and very dangerous. Better to admit ignorance than to hazard a guess and be caught out.

Remember that a two-way is supposed to sound like a normal conversation – which again is much easier if you have had the chance to run through it in advance. So use the words and phrases you would use in normal speech and avoid long answers. Practice answers of no more than 30–40 seconds. Try to make the whole thing sound as spontaneous and unrehearsed as possible – reminding yourself that the best way to do that is to rehearse and plan as much as possible. If it helps, jot down a few notes or reminders to yourself of things you need to say – as you are on the radio, no-one will see you referring to them. But do not make them too wordy or detailed, or you will sound forced and unnatural and listeners will be able to tell that you are reading something. Of course if you *are* reading something – an extract from a statement or report, for example, or some quotes from a lawyer in a court case you are covering – then it is perfectly fine to read verbatim from the text or from your notes. Just make sure you are clear with the audience that you are doing so.

Don't worry if your delivery is not absolutely perfect – if you pause, or have to start a sentence again. That is what ordinary conversation is like, and as long as you stay calm you will sound fine. Obviously you want to be as polished and coherent as possible, but sounding natural means that you have some latitude. Relax.

If you want to hear live reporting in its best and purest form, tune in to the sports coverage on any radio station. You do not have to be a sports fan to be able to hear and marvel at the techniques and style of the best sports reporters. If you hear some bad ones, that will only make you more admiring of the majority. Because live reporting is what they do almost all of the time, they develop an absolute mastery of it and offer fertile ground for learning for any young radio journalist, not just those who aspire to be sports reporters themselves.

Live locations

If you are the scene of a breaking story, you will naturally want to get as close to the heart of it as you can. But this can create all sorts of hazards for live reporting. The last thing you want is for something to happen that cuts you off when you are in full flow to a live audience. Here are some obvious hazards:

- **Your phone.** Unless you are using it to do the two-way, switch it to silent for a few minutes. You don't want it going off mid-interview, especially if you have a distinctive ring tone.
- **The weather.** If you are doing a story about bad weather, intervention by strong winds or rain while you are speaking might be an effective part of your reporting. If the weather is bad but is not the story, choose a location where you are unlikely to be caught out by a sudden cloudburst.
- **Loud background noise.** Again, this could be part of the story – if you are at demonstration say, or a sporting event. But even then, you don't want the background noise to be so loud that you cannot make yourself heard over the din. Look for a spot where the background atmosphere will come through on air, but not at such a volume that the listener cannot hear what you have to say.
- **Disruption.** If you are in the middle of a story where feelings are running high, then as a live reporter you are potentially in a vulnerable position. You may find yourself being jostled, shouted at (possibly with obscenities) or heckled. All of these are likely to affect your performance, and some may result in the studio bringing the item to an abrupt end. If you think there is any danger of this happening, move to a place where you feel more secure, while still being within range of the action. In extreme circumstances, you might suggest to the studio that they pre-record your contribution so that if there is a problem it does not go out on the air.
- **Place of danger.** The story you are covering may present a degree of danger to people in the vicinity, including you. The immediate aftermath of a bomb explosion, for example, or an earthquake; a terrorist attack; rioting. You should have extensive training before you are exposed to anything that puts you in physical danger in this way. If you attempt to report live – as you will want to do if you are at the heart of a story – you may well be putting yourself in a great deal more danger. No two-way – no story – is worth a risk to your life or well-being, so don't do it. Sometimes discretion really is the better part of valour. You are unlikely be operating on your own in these circumstances, but if you and your team are put under pressure to broadcast or work in conditions that you consider too dangerous, you should and must refuse, and remove yourself to a place of safety.

Driving the desk

If you work in a local radio station, you will be expected to understand most aspects of the production process. That is one reason it is a wonderful place to begin a career in broadcast journalism – you get the chance to do everything, often at quite an early stage, and you become a seasoned and well-rounded radio journalist very quickly. On a reporting shift, you will source and record your own material and cut clips, you will know how to record your links in a self-op facility or at the desktop, and how to edit the whole package together ready to be broadcast.

A self-op facility is a single soundproofed space containing all the equipment one person needs to record and broadcast a piece and put it into the playout system. It may also allow you to put yourself live on the air if it is linked to the main output studio.

A larger **studio** consists of two spaces linked by a large window: the studio itself where the presenter sits, and which will usually contain at least two or three more seats and mics for guests; and a control room, or "cubicle" where the programme is recorded and/or put to air by a multiskilled producer or sound engineer. This is where the studio console and mixer are located, with various channels that enable the engineer, or whoever is running the desk, to select the presenter, pre-recorded material on a playout system and guests calling in from outside the studio. Some of these desks will double as self-op studios for single person operation.

A self-op facility or a full studio may be fully computerised, with touch-screen functions taking the place of faders, buttons and all the other paraphernalia of the conventional transmission desk. It may be a combination, retaining the traditional desk but with computerised playout and other functions. In recent years, radio desks have become ever smaller and simpler, and it does not usually take long to pick up the principles of operation. Your organisation will be using one of several computerised playout systems in which audio is logged, labelled and managed, and in which you can create a playlist for the next summary or bulletin. Jingles, idents and all the other furniture of a radio station will be in there too. You will write your scripts in the system, and will have the option of reading them directly off screen if you prefer, or if you do not have the time to print them beforehand.

No two desks or playout systems are exactly the same, but the principles generally are, and modern desks are straightforward and intuitive in their operations. Make sure you get the training you need to carry out the technical responsibilities that are expected of you, and observe and practice until you are confident that you know your way around the desk and the other technical facilities in the place you are working. It will feel daunting and difficult to begin with, but if you make sure you have everything explained to you properly at the outset, you will find that with practice you are soon able to operate efficiently and with confidence.

17

The television journalist: the television scene and picture gathering

the television scene.....the terrestrial schedule.....24-hour news.....current affairs programming.....
television as a medium for reporting news.....what makes a good television journalist.....newsroom
roles.....the nature of television news..... .....gathering pictures.....working with a camera operator.....
working as a videojournalist.....other sources of pictures......top technical tips

The television scene

Television news bulletins were introduced in the 1950s, and gradually became the dominant medium for news and current affairs reporting. During the Second World War, and at other times of national crisis, families had gathered round the radio. But after the first great television event – the Queen's Coronation in 1953 – it was to television that people would turn in their millions for events such as Churchill's funeral, the 1969 moon landings and football World Cups. The power of pictures, brought in live by satellite from all over the world, was irresistible. In the modern age, much of that viewing takes place online – although big events can still generate enormous audiences for conventional television news broadcasts. Video reigns supreme. Nothing else has the impact or potency of something we can witness with our own eyes.

Until the last years of the 20th century, television news was delivered in carefully edited and packaged formats known as "built" bulletins. They were broadcast at set times of the day – lunchtime, teatime and mid to late evening – and were typically half an hour in length. The big players were the BBC, with its main bulletins at six o'clock and nine o'clock, and Independent Television News, or ITN, which provided coverage to the ITV network, principally through the celebrated *News at Ten*. Supported by regional bulletins, these programmes enjoyed a duopoly for many years and attracted very large audiences. When there was a big story, it was not unusual for the news bulletins to be the most-watched programmes of the day.

When continuous television news channels emerged, pioneered by Cable News Network (CNN) and Sky, it was not long before pundits began to predict the imminent demise of the built bulletin. Why, they asked, would anyone want to sit down in front of a news programme aired at a time of the broadcasters' choosing, when they could switch on for updates at any time of the day or night? It seemed a rational question, especially when the BBC and ITN joined the party with the launches of *BBC News 24* and the *ITN News Channel*.

But it did not happen. Continuous news channels often struggle to attract significant audiences outside times when big stories are breaking, and audiences have continued to display an appetite for a well-produced and edited digest of the day's news, delivered with expertise, flair and style. Although viewing figures have been in shallow but steady decline over the years, the bulletins cling tenaciously to their slots in the schedule (the BBC evening news now being at ten o'clock rather than nine) and still deliver very respectable audiences. The same is true of the half-hour regional bulletins broadcast at teatime by both the BBC and ITV.

So the mixed economy has survived. Into the brew more recently has come the explosion in online news consumption, in both text and video forms. As things stand, the built bulletins, the continuous channels and the online offers co-exist, with audiences switching between them – and using radio news services too – to find the information they want in the format they want and at the time they want.

The online picture is examined in Chapter 13, although much of what follows here will also apply to digital journalists whose role incorporates videojournalism. In the next two chapters, we look at the practical techniques and craft skills you need to acquire in order to become a good television journalist. The goal of many aspiring journalists is to appear on television as a reporter or the presenter of a news or current affairs programme. But as with radio, there are also plenty of highly skilled, demanding, senior and responsible jobs that do not require you to appear on camera.

The terrestrial schedule

In terms of built programmes, the daily menu offered by the main free-to-air channels (the "terrestrial" channels) has changed little over the years. The BBC still offers substantial news bulletins at one o'clock, six o'clock and ten o'clock. ITV News, produced by ITN, has equivalent programmes at half past one, at half past six and at ten o'clock – where it is in direct competition with the BBC. Both networks offer regional news programmes of varying lengths, the main offerings being half an hour of regional news on ITV at six o'clock and the same for the BBC at six thirty. It is these teatime programmes – national and regional – that attract the largest audiences.

For years it was thought that there was no audience in the UK for television news programmes at breakfast time. In the US, the breakfast shows are widely viewed and very influential. But the British were a nation of radio listeners when it came to the early mornings. Even so, both the BBC and ITN plunged into early morning television broadcasting in 1983. Breakfast programmes, usually with a lighter, more relaxed feel – presented on sofas rather than from behind desks – have been a staple of the early morning schedule ever since.

The BBC also identified an appetite for a late-night current affairs programme, with news-making interviews and a deeper investigation of the stories of the day. So in 1980, *Newsnight* was born, and is still broadcast five days a week on BBC2 at around half past ten.

Meanwhile new channels were emerging, each of them having to decide how big their commitment to news would be, and what sort of news and current affairs programmes to offer. In 1982, Channel 4 became the UK's fourth freely available channel, joining BBC1, BBC2 and ITV. Its principal news offer is the multi-award-winning *Channel 4 News* (produced by ITN), which goes out at seven o'clock in the evenings, with a duration of 55 minutes from Monday to Thursday, and shorter editions on other days. The programme is a mixture of hard news coverage and more in-depth current affairs reporting – leaning more towards *Newsnight* in its format than the more structured style of the television news bulletins.

A little later, in 1997, Channel 5 became the fifth terrestrial analogue broadcaster. It broadcasts early evening news bulletins, also produced by ITN.

So the traditional television news bulletin is still alive and kicking on the mass audience free-to-air terrestrial channels, offering a daily mix of packaged news and – on BBC2 and Channel 4 – a degree of added scrutiny of the day's events.

24-hour news

Audiences have a wide range of digital news channels to choose from, broadcasting 24 hours a day. Although still not available to some viewers without the requisite television sets or subscriptions, they can be streamed via the internet. The principal 24-hour news channels are:

– **Sky News** was the first UK-based round-the-clock news channel, launched by Rupert Murdoch in 1989 and with a high reputation for its rapid responses to breaking news.
– **BBC News Channel** was launched as *BBC News 24* in 1997. The channel provided the first domestic competition to Sky News. It was followed by the *ITN News Channel*, but that venture did not survive and was closed down five years later.
– **CNN** (Cable News Network) is an American-based channel, which was the first in the field when it was launched in 1980. It has a US-facing channel and a global network, CNN International.
– **BBC World News** is the BBC's international 24-hour news channel, broadcasting to audiences around the world outside the UK. It was launched in 1991 and is owned and operated by the commercial arm of the BBC – in other words, it is not funded by the licence fee. This is because the licence fee is paid by audiences in the UK, and the output of BBC World News is targeted at viewers elsewhere.
– **BBC Parliament** broadcasts live and recorded proceedings of both Houses of Parliament, The Scottish Parliament, the London Assembly, the Northern Ireland Assembly and the Welsh Assembly.
– **France 24,** broadcasting in English and three other languages, is the French equivalent of BBC World News, aiming at an overseas viewership.
– **Bloomberg Television** is a global television channel specialising in business and financial news. It was launched in 1994.
– **Al Jazeera** is an Arabic channel owned by the government of the Gulf state of Qatar. It was launched in Arabic in 1996, but now broadcasts in a number of other languages, including *Al Jazeera English*, created in 2003. As you would expect, its programming has a strong Arab perspective, although the station claims to be both independent and impartial.
– **RT,** formerly known as Russia Today, is funded by the Russian government and presents the news from an overtly Russian perspective, reflecting the views of the Kremlin. As such, it is seen by some as a propaganda tool of the Russian government, and Ofcom has frequently found it to be in breach of the Broadcasting Code requirements on impartiality.
– **China Global Television Network**, formerly *CCTV International*, is an English-language channel produced by the state-owned Central China Television. In 2021 Ofcom withdrew its licence to broadcast on the grounds that it was owned by the Chinese government, and thus breached ownership rules.
– **Fox News Channel** was launched in the US by Rupert Murdoch in 1996 to reflect a conservative political standpoint. It has often been seen as a mouthpiece for the Republican Party, although it strongly rebuts allegations of bias.
– **MSNBC** is a pay channel providing news coverage from *NBC News* – one of the three big American networks (with *CBS* and *ABC*). It is seen by some as politically left leaning, in other words, the opposite of *Fox News*.
– **News UK TV** (owned by Rupert Murdoch) and **GB News** (fronted by former BBC presenter Andrew Neil) are new UK news channels launching in 2021. Both are expected to adopt a strongly political approach.

Current affairs programming

In addition to this mix of built news bulletins and 24-hour news channels, there is a wide range of documentary, investigative and current affairs output known as "long-form programming". These programmes devote their whole half hour or hour of running time to the detailed examination of a single topic. The best-known programmes in the UK are the BBC's *Panorama* and Channel 4's *Dispatches*, but there are many other strands and one-off investigations. The BBC broadcasts *Question Time* on Thursday evenings – an hour of topical debate with a panel of politicians and other prominent figures in front of a live audience.

Television as a medium for reporting news

The key asset of television is moving pictures, which give it a substantial advantage over both newspapers (stills only) and radio (no pictures at all). Online apps and social networks also make substantial use of video, but a well-crafted television news report in which striking images are married to a strong script remains incredibly powerful, and can provoke strong emotions in an audience.

Television cannot boast some of the advantages that we identified for radio. The production process is not as quick or as simple; it is not as portable; and it lacks the same intimacy.

Television's power lies in its ability, through pictures, to remove obstacles between the viewer and the story. Where pictures are available, the viewer can be made an eyewitness to events. Television has a unique ability to convey what an event or experience is like, by the simple expedient of presenting the images directly to the audience. Great pictures, well used, can make viewers feel a wide range of emotions – anger, sadness, elation, sympathy, indignation. They take us straight to the heart of the action – the heat of a battle, a pioneering medical procedure, the effects of a famine, the destructive power of an extreme weather event. They take us to peoples and places of which we know little, and have the power to expand our horizons, and to learn and understand the effect of events happening near and far. This is why television is such an enduring and dominant medium in general, and as a vehicle for reporting the news in particular. A print journalist can describe something on paper, and illustrate it with still photographs; a radio journalist can describe something on air, and illustrate it with natural sound; but a television journalist can simply run the pictures and say: "Look. This is what is happening, and this is what it is like".

This paean to television presupposes that you always have great pictures at your disposal. But often this will not be the case. The hard truth is that television is not always the best medium for conveying ideas and information. When it comes to pictures of floods, or earthquakes or dramatic events, or live sport, nothing can beat television for putting viewers in the front row to see for themselves. But on any given day it tends to be more prosaic stories that make up a large proportion of the news. The performance of the economy. The length of hospital waiting lists. A political argument about social care. A court case, with no cameras allowed inside the courtroom. These are the bread and butter of the news agenda, and yet they offer little or nothing in the way of memorable images. They are hard to illustrate in a way that is interesting or engaging – especially if they are stories that crop up again and again: National Health Service (NHS) funding, for example. These are stories that are "picture challenged" as the saying goes. They do not offer any images on a plate waiting to be edited into a news report. It is up to the reporter and producer proactively to think of ways of illustrating these stories in creative ways that will turn them into good pieces of television reporting. A huge amount of time in any television news operation is spent trying to compensate for a lack of pictures in this way.

What makes a good television journalist?

Television journalists need the core skills that are a requirement for all journalists, as discussed in an earlier chapter – including these:

Curiosity
Clear, accurate, interesting (and legal) reporting
A flair for storytelling
An interest in people
An ability to express yourself clearly
An ability to brief yourself quickly
An ability to make difficult subjects understandable and interesting
A good interview technique
Enthusiasm and commitment
Technical understanding and aptitude.

And here are some skills that are more specific to television journalism, or broadcast journalism more generally; or are perhaps needed to a greater degree in television than other forms of media.

The ability to work quickly

Technical competence: many television reporters are videojournalists – able to record, edit and broadcast

The ability to express yourself clearly on air, live or with a script

The ability to marry words and pictures to best effect

The ability to think on your feet

The ability to work effectively in a small team – or alone

Flexibility – moving quickly from one story to another

A good broadcasting voice

A good on-screen persona

The ability to sound natural and conversational

An instinctive 'eye' for television.

As with radio, do not assume that you can appear on television only if you have a perfectly modulated voice and are either dazzlingly beautiful or exceptionally handsome. Your suitability for a reporting role in front of the camera will depend on how many of the above qualities you can demonstrate, rather than on what you look like. And only a minority of television journalists actually appear on the air.

Newsroom roles

No two stations or organisations are the same, or use the same job descriptions or terminology, but here are some roles that are common to pretty well every television news operation of any size:

Editorial staff

Programme/channel editor

– Sets the editorial agenda, style and tone.
– Makes the key decisions about running orders and content.
– Has editorial accountability for fairness, accuracy, legal compliance.
– Handles complaints.
– The person with whom the buck stops.

Senior duty editor

– Is the editor's right-hand person.
– Will edit some editions of the programme.
– Is a key point of contact with all those working on the programme.
– Looks after the running order, checks timings, spellings, etc.

(Senior) producer/broadcast journalist

– Coordinates production of individual programme items.
– Makes sure items are finished on time and in broadcastable form.
– Sources video – agency, library, archive, etc.
– Commissions graphics.

Technical staff

Camera operator

– Shoots the pictures for the piece (and will sometimes edit them as well).
– Sets up and shoots live inserts from location.

Picture editor

– Edits programme items at base, working with reporter and producer.

Graphic designer

– Designs graphics for individual items and other programme elements.

Studio director

– Is a point of contact between editor and technical team.
– Drives programme on air.

Transmission team (TX)

– Ensures items are ready for playout, and that live outside sources are up and running.

Vision mixer

– Changes the shot that appears on screen, on the instructions of the Director.

Before reading this chapter, and the next one, you would find it helpful to read the corresponding chapters about radio journalism. Although there are obvious differences between radio and television, many of the features and principles are the same. Some core elements are common to all forms of broadcast journalism – some indeed are common to all news formats and platforms.

Not all good radio reporters are proficient at television, and vice versa. But if you have a clear understanding of the similarities and differences, there is no reason you should not develop into a fully competent broadcast journalist, equally at home in either medium.

The nature of television news

In radio, our storytelling tools are words and natural sound. Given the power of pictures, it is easy to forget that both of these are also critically important in television. The job of the television journalist is to ensure that the words and sounds are working in harmony with the pictures. They must complement each other, not fight each other. They are partners in the overall enterprise: just because you have good pictures to illustrate a story, that does not mean you can afford to be slipshod with your script; and if you don't have good pictures, it will not be good enough to throw any old images on the screen while you deliver your words of wisdom.

As always, put yourself in the position of your audience. Like radio listeners, television viewers have only one chance to grasp the story. And because they are using their eyes as well as their ears, the potential for distraction and confusion is all the greater. Clarity and accessibility are as vital in television news reporting as anywhere else – and it is often that much harder to deliver them.

Writing a television script requires even more economy than radio, because sometimes the pictures will be able to carry the story on their own, with little or no input from the reporter. If the pictures are telling the story, there is no need for speech. Knowing when to pause and say nothing is an important skill in television storytelling. A script for television does not need to – and should not – describe what the viewer is seeing: that would be superfluous, distracting and probably irritating. The script needs to guide the viewer along the way, punctuating the pictures, sewing them into the narrative – and simply saying the equivalent of: "look at this", and then backing off while the viewer does just that.

Here is a simple example of how radio and television might tackle the same story in ways that suited each medium. This is a fictional despatch from a reporter covering a conflict overseas, who comes across a refugee camp:

RADIO REPORTER: "The camp has grown from nothing to a vast size in the space of a week. Now there are tents as far as the eye can see. But there is nowhere near enough shelter for the several hundred bedraggled and frightened refugees who have fled the fighting and gathered in this remote spot. They have little by way of food and water, and no medical supplies. Everyone asked us if help was coming."

TELEVISION REPORTER: *(Pictures from inside of vehicle approaching the camp)* "A bend in the road and suddenly, there is the camp. *(Pictures of the tented village)* A week ago, this was a barren and deserted piece of land. Look at it now. *(Pause while we take in the pictures)* Makeshift shelters offering scant protection from the heat of the day and the cold of the night. *(Shots of refugees out of doors)*. And not enough cover for everyone. They are hungry and thirsty, and many are sick." *(Pictures of refugee making rudimentary meal with a few ingredients)* "This will be the only meal of the day for Shola and his family" *(Shots of Shola talking to reporter, with natural sound)*. "Like everyone else, Shola wants to know if help is coming."

The point should be self-evident. Both pieces contain almost exactly the same basic information. The radio reporter has to describe for listeners everything he or she is seeing. The radio piece would have some natural sound in it too, the noises of the camp. The television reporter can afford to let the pictures do the work, and the words just help them along. The phrases *"look at it now"* and *"this will be the only meal of the day for Shola for this family"* spoken over pictures of preparations for a meal, are good illustrations of how this is done. Those script lines would not work on the radio.

Good writing is just as important in television as it is in all other forms of journalism. It is just a different sort of writing. Pictures still need the support of well-chosen words, no matter how strong they are. Even great pictures can be enhanced further by a great script. In television, good writing is not only about choosing the words that say exactly what you want to say; it is also about choosing the words that respond to and reflect the images that the viewer is seeing at the same time.

As with most other forms of journalism, the "right" words are typically short and in everyday use. Long or unusual words are a distraction and expose you to the probably justifiable charge that you are showing off. It is worth repeating one of this book's mantras: short words in short sentences present the viewer with the fewest obstacles to comprehension. Clarity and simplicity are the roots of any successful television report.

To emphasise the fact that this is true of all broadcast journalism, I am going to reprise in full a paragraph from an earlier chapter on radio. All of it applies just as strongly to television:

> You need to be direct, and to use simple everyday language with precision. Avoid complexity, vagueness, ambiguity. Keep it simple – one thought per sentence. Short sentences work best in basic news reports. Remember, you or someone else is going to have to read them out, so the longer and more complicated they are, the harder that will be: you need to draw breath somewhere! Use short words that punch their weight. And the opposite of that, and to be avoided, are complicated language or sentence constructions, something that is not clear, or – worse still – something that can be read two ways. Your scripts must not only be intelligible and understandable – they have to be <u>instantly</u> intelligible and understandable.

One of the most common faults of television reporters is to load their pieces with too much information and too many thoughts, taking insufficient account of what the viewer is seeing. This is called "writing over the pictures". There is no real relationship between what the viewers are seeing and what they are hearing. What you are aiming to do is to write *to* the pictures, not *over* them. Your report is not the place to demonstrate how much you know about the story, or to describe all the various angles and perspectives. Your job is to sift out the most important information; to render it as simply, as clearly and as comprehensibly as you can; and to fit that with the pictures available. Your decisions about what to leave out are as important as your decisions about what to put in. If a script becomes too complicated, the viewer will not be able to follow it. If it lurches halfway through from one point to a completely different one – known in the trade as "a handbrake turn" – it is likely to leave the audience puzzled and confused. If you find yourself using words like "meanwhile" or "at the same time" or "in another development", you are probably about to change the subject, and start talking about a different angle of the story. Be satisfied that this is the right and logical thing to do, and that it works with the pictures. And be satisfied that the audience will be able to follow your thought processes easily.

It is always tempting to squeeze in one extra fact or thought, to cover off another angle. Resist. An old rule of thumb for television news is to decide the key point you wish to convey, and then make sure that point is repeated at least three times: in the cue, in your script and also perhaps in a clip of speech, or actuality – often called "sync" in television – or your piece to camera. That way the audience is being offered a simple and clear idea, and having it explained and built upon through the course of the piece. This is summed up in the old adage:

> Tell them you're going to tell them, tell them you're telling them, then tell them you've told them.

Gathering pictures

Don't even think about starting to write your script until you know what pictures you have at your disposal. If you do, you will certainly write too much, and by definition, what you are writing will not relate to what people are going to be seeing on the screen. Cut the pictures first, and then script to them. Pictures are paramount – so picture gathering is as important as information gathering in television reporting.

Ideally, most of the pictures you use will have been shot by you or one of your colleagues. You may work as a videojournalist (VJ) and therefore be expected to do your own filming and editing. Depending on the size of the organisation you are working for, and your role within it, you may be fortunate enough to be working with a professional camera operator. If you are able to return to base to put your piece together, you may be able to work with a professional picture editor too. Some camera operators, especially those who work primarily on location in the field, combine both these functions, and are often referred to as "shoot-edits".

We will look at ways of operating in both of these scenarios – with a professional, and as a VJ.

Working with a camera operator

If you are lucky enough to be working with a dedicated camera person, and maybe even a producer as well, then think of your team as exactly that – a team. Both of you, or all of you, need to understand and agree the nature of the story that you are collectively trying to tell, and what pictures you will need to tell it in the best way possible. The pictures may present themselves to you without you having to work too hard – if you are sent to the scene of a fire, for example. But even then, you are going to need a range of shots in order to assemble the necessary kit of parts for a strong report.

The quality of the pictures will make or break your piece, so you must think hard about what you want them to achieve. Then you need to communicate that to whoever is working with you. Discuss the nature of the story with them, and the sort of mood or feeling that you want the pictures – and by extension the piece as a whole – to convey. Too many reporters make the mistake of thinking that the camera operator knows what is required, and just let them get in with it. From a technical point of view of course, camera operators do know exactly what they are doing, and many will have well-developed journalistic and production instincts as well, born of long experience. But they do not want to second-guess you or – worse – be treated as though they are just the technician while you are the star of the show. They deserve your respect. They are the ones who are going to be supplying the raw materials of your piece. They need to be included and communicated with and to understand fully what it is that you are hoping to achieve with your report. They will know much better than you how to secure the pictures that will contribute so much to that report; so take advantage of – and bow to – their knowledge and expertise. Share your thinking with them, and listen respectfully to theirs. They will have plenty of ideas about how to gather the best material. All this is also true if you are the producer in the team rather than the on-screen reporter.

Working with a camera operator also liberates you to attempt far more ambitious things than you would be able to achieve on your own. Pieces to camera (PTCs) are the most obvious examples of this. If you are working alone, it will be hard to produce a PTC that is anything more than a static shot from a fixed position – possibly outside a building some way from the action. You might be able to produce a selfie PTC with a smartphone, but it is difficult to create something that looks professional. With an independent camera, you can get closer to the story and "walk and talk" – moving around more to illustrate it. Your camera operator can start the PTC on you and then pull out and/or pan around. Or vice versa. Your camera can be a long way off – in the age of drones, a *very* long way off – and then zoom in and pick you out in a crowd of people or some other news location as you deliver your PTC. Again, discuss and take advice about what will work best – and what will fit best in the context of the story you are telling.

In the same way, your camera operator can film you going about the business of reporting: knocking on the door of someone you want to interview, approaching people for their views or generally reacting to the situation in which you find yourself. This kind of activity, in which you are in vision, and therefore making yourself part of the story is called "reporter involvement". It is difficult to achieve if you are holding the camera as well as doing the reporting. Reporter involvement can be useful in increasing authenticity and giving the viewer a strong sense that you are reporting from the very heart of things. But it can be overdone. You are the reporter, but you are not the story. Don't put yourself in every shot.

Working as a VJ

Now suppose you are on your own, having to shoot the pictures yourself and without any of the very considerable advantages of working with a dedicated camera operator. You need to be doing all the thinking yourself now: what is the story, what are the pictures I need and how can I get them within the limitations under which I am working? The answer is to try to think as a professional camera operator would.

What you need

A video camera. You can film on your smartphone, and its size and portability make it a useful camera in some situations. But it has its limitations. Close-ups (CUs) are difficult to do well, for example. You will produce something much more polished and better looking with a basic camera. There are plenty on the market and most are capable of producing a professional-looking result. The very basic ones are sometimes referred to as "point and press" cameras because that is all they require you to do: point the camera at the image and press Record. These cameras will have default settings designed to work in most situations and to make it hard for you to go too far wrong. You are probably looking for something a little more sophisticated than this – a camera that has those default settings, but also the means to override and adjust them manually as you become more competent and confident. The main thing is to feel comfortable with the equipment you are using. The more you use it, and the more you experiment, the more comfortable you will become.

Batteries, memory or SD cards. Make sure you have fully charged batteries and spares and formatted cards to record your material.

Stabilisation. Some cameras have inbuilt stabilisation which is useful for handheld work, but might need to be switched off if you are using some other form of stabilisation. There are various options here, depending on the task.

– **A tripod**, as the name suggests, is a three-legged stand which can be used as a platform or base for the camera, so that you do not need to be holding on to the camera all the time. You will usually use it for your interviews. It is also handy for shooting a PTC if you are on your own. The tripod is collapsible for carrying, and can be adjusted for height and angle.
– **A monopod** is a single-legged (and therefore not free standing) camera support which affords you stabilisation if you are moving quickly between shots and haven't the time or space to keep moving the tripod You attach the camera to the monopod and extend its leg until the camera is at about eye level. When you are ready to shoot, stabilise the camera by leaning the monopod against one of your legs.
– **A gimbal** is an attachment for the camera that allows you to produce a stable shot when you are moving around – say trying to film someone who is walking or running.

Sound. Because the camera is all about pictures, it is easy to overlook the importance of obtaining good quality audio. If you do overlook it, you may be in trouble, because poor quality sound is one of the few things that you cannot fix in the edit. If you want to use the audio recording from the camera for a radio report, you may find that once separated from the pictures, the sound quality is not as good as you would like. To make sure you record audio of an acceptable quality, make sure you have a lavalier mic, also known as a lapel mic or clip mic. They usually come with a clip to allow for attachment to the clothing of the interviewee. The mic has a lead that is either routed directly to the camera or, more likely, runs to a small radio frequency transmitter that can be hidden in a pocket or fixed to a belt.

The elements of a television news report

When you film your report, you will be looking for a range of shots:

For scenery or detail – as opposed to individuals – the shots are more or less self-explanatory:

– **The close-up (CU)** – homing in tight on the detail
– **The medium shot (MS)** – revealing more detail of the scene

– **The long (or wide), shot** – taking in the general surroundings to give a view of the overall context
– **The general view (GV)** – establishes the location – often the exteriors of buildings inside which the story is happening out of range of the cameras (such as court buildings).

Range of shots of a person:

– **The big close-up (BCU)** – very close, the face filling the screen
– **The close-up (CU)** – faces, hands or other points of detail
– **The medium close-up (MCU)** – showing head and shoulders
– **The medium shot (MS)** – showing the top half of the person featured in the story, from head to hips, showing hands and head
– **The medium long shot (MLS)** – showing the subject from head to knees
– **The long shot (LS)** – the whole person, head to toe.

These are not universal terms, but are generally understood by most organisations. They all refer to the distance between the camera and the subject of the shot.

Another range of descriptions refers to the height of the camera relative to the scene:

– **The top shot** is a bird's eye view of the scene.
– **The high shot** shows the scene from the front, looking down.
– **The level shot** is in line with the subject's eyes.
– **The low shot** shows the scene from below eye level.
– **The low-level shot** is the view from the ground.

When you are thinking about the shots you need, always keep in mind an idea of what the end product – your final report – is going to look like. This gives you a much better chance of gathering all the necessary material, with the full variety of shots, rather than find too late that a vital element is missing.

A typical television news report is made up of some or all of these video components:

– Sequence(s)
– Action and reaction
– Close-ups
– Detail
– Atmosphere and natural sound
– Set-up shots
– Clips
– Piece to camera.

Sequences

The basic building block of your piece in picture terms is the sequence. A sequence is a story within a story that gives your piece a narrative focus. It is the element of the story that brings it home to the viewer, personalises it and makes it relatable and understandable. People are at the heart of television reporting just as they are in print and radio. The human touch is what audiences relate to most, and it is how they make sense of stories that might otherwise seem too difficult and remote.

You need to think carefully about sequences when you are tackling a story that does not obviously offer much in the way of pictures. The answer will very often be to identify a person or people in some way affected by the issue you are covering in your report, and telling their stories as specific examples of the general thrust of the story. If you have time, this might involve a degree of research and pre-filming, so that you have assembled a lot of material in advance. More on pre-filming below.

A sequence is built by putting together a variety of shots to create an interesting narrative – literally, a sequence of actions. Let us take a very basic example of someone going into a shop to buy a loaf of bread. Here are some of the shots you might like to have for a sequence telling this story:

> Wide exterior shot of subject approaching and entering shop
>
> Medium shot of subject entering shop seen from the inside
>
> Medium shots of subject greeting shop owner and owner responding
>
> Tracking shot of subject heading to bread counter
>
> Close up of range of loaves on sale
>
> Big close up of subject selecting one
>
> Medium shot of subject taking loaf to counter
>
> Medium shot of counter seen from behind subject, showing both subject (from the rear) and shop owner, as transaction takes place
>
> Close up of payment being made
>
> Reverse of the opening two shots, as the subject says goodbye and goes to the door, followed by exterior shot of him leaving.

You might choose to shoot this in a number of different ways, but this would be one way of doing it. These shots would also work in a social media version of your story. Reading that list, it is quite easy to imagine what that sequence is going to look like when it is edited together. You will also realise at once that if you want to get a shot from the outside – of the subject entering the shop – and a shot from the inside – of the subject coming in – you are going to have to get the subject to perform this action at least twice. That is a small insight into the amount of setting up and cooperation required for even the most straightforward of sequences. Do not underestimate the length of time it can take you to assemble all these moving parts.

The other thing that might strike you is that this adds up to quite a lot of shots to create only a few seconds of television. It shows how important it is that you think through the entire sequence in advance. Without one or more of the shots listed above, the sequence would be harder to put together, or would not be as good as it might be. You might have hours of material but still lack the components you need to make the perfect sequence.

To help with the editing, hold your shots when filming for what might feel a lot longer than necessary. The typical length of time between shot changes in a television news report is about five seconds (much less in the US). To make sure that you have a useable five seconds of a particular shot, hold it for at least twice that time. The same idea applies with a panning shot (taking in a panorama) or zooming in on a detail. Hold the shot steady for a few seconds while it establishes itself in the eye of the viewer, then do the pan or zoom and then hold the shot again as it settles in a final position. Moving too quickly can leave the viewer feeling queasy. Moving the camera around too quickly so that the eye is never able to settle on one image is known as "hosepiping".

Armed with your kit of parts, you are in a position to put together a picture sequence of perhaps 15–20 seconds, featuring some natural sound around which you can script a report which introduces our subject, explains the story being illustrated and then perhaps widens the story from the specific to the general. Maybe in this case the story was that the village shop was in danger of closure, and that it was a lifeline for a number of people who relied on it for basic supplies or human contact. How you construct the piece as a whole is something we will address in more detail in the following chapter, but a sequence such as this might lead easily into a clip of the subject or the shop owner talking about why the shop is having to close.

It boils down to giving yourself as many options as possible when you come to put the piece together. As part of this, avoid filming all your shots from eye level. Look for angles – you can add extra interest by filming from above or below, from one side or another. As ever, don't overdo it and make it look too arty or too tricksy – that sort of thing has its place, but is generally not appropriate for a straight news report. It will distract the viewer and look out of place. You are filming a short news report, not creating high art.

Action and reaction

Your action shots will be the ones that actually tell the story. If you are reporting something that's happened – a road crash, say, rather than the release of a report – the pictures should suggest themselves to you fairly obviously. But bear in mind what we have just said about variety. Even if your pictures are going to tell the whole story for you, you will still need a range of shots from a variety of distances and angles. This will enable you to build a textured and watchable report. If all your pictures look the same, in terms of their composition, your report is going to feel one-paced and much less vivid.

With almost every story, it will be necessary for you to gather reaction. This might be a basic human response, or it might be an informed opinion about the issue you are reporting.

Close-ups

CUs of people are the things that will really make your story resonate with the viewer, and it is almost impossible to gather too many of them. CUs of faces, especially the eyes, will give a clear insight into how the subject is feeling, whether acting or reacting, and the audience will respond accordingly. Be sensitive to the situation – it will sometimes feel intrusive if you get your camera too close to someone who is visibly distressed. You may get great pictures, but your viewers will have a sense of intrusion, and not like it. If you can, and if it is appropriate, ask the subject for permission to come closer to them. If it is refused, you must back off. You can carry on filming and can still get strong shots from a distance by adjusting your lens. The use of a camera with a zoom is very useful for this. Even so, do not forget you may be filming someone who is upset or worse, and a degree of tact, empathy and basic decency is required.

Detail

In the same way, an eye for detail is invaluable while you are filming, and will also be highly effective in conveying an atmosphere. This is true of all forms of reporting. Look out for the way people are reacting – perhaps when they are unaware the camera is on them. Catching them laughing, putting their hands to their mouths in shock, interacting – all of these will speak volumes about how people affected by a story are feeling and reacting, and will convey far more than any script line can.

Be aware too of your surroundings. If you are filming in someone's home, for example, look for the little touches that will convey something about the way they live – a group of family photographs perhaps, a cat stretched out asleep in the sun, a hand-embroidered cushion. These details allow the viewer to build an instant idea of the environment. The more you develop an eye for this sort of thing, the better your picture-gathering will be, and the better your finished work will be.

Even unpromising situations such as press conferences, meeting rooms or platform speeches can be enlivened by some imaginative use of camera angles, or a scrutiny of the scene around you. You can film the audience from the speaker's point of view, for example, and get good reaction shots – are they paying rapt attention or falling asleep? There will nearly always be something that catches your eye, which will add colour and definition to your piece and help carry the audience with you.

Atmosphere and natural sound

Everything that we said about this in relation to radio applies just as much to television, often even more so. Again, you can almost never have too much, so always get more than you think you will need. If there is a continuous sound at the location, such as music or a public address system, children in a school playground or even just traffic noise, record a good chunk of it on its own so that you have an extended piece of audio. You will find this very useful when you are editing your piece, as it will give you space to pause in your script, and to join seamlessly different pictures whose junctions might otherwise feel clunky and unnatural.

Always take a few moments to stop and listen to the sounds around you. Some are so expected and familiar that we filter them out and are hardly aware of them. Record at both close quarters and at a distance to maximise your options in the edit. It will often be a good idea to record sound separately on a radio mic, which may well provide better quality than the mic on your camera. This is essential if you are being expected to provide both a radio report and a television report. As we have noted, the sound quality from a television camera mic will often be fine when it is heard in conjunction with watching pictures, but may be of marginal broadcast quality on its own.

Set-up shots

Set-up shots, or establishing shots, are the pictures by which you introduce people who are about to feature in the piece. So before we hear from the minister, or the bereaved parent, we see them engaged in some activity that gets the audience ready to hear from them.

It can be difficult to make these look natural, and there are many hackneyed ways of setting up interviewees in this way. MPs are seen crossing the road from the House of Commons (presumably on their way to be interviewed by you). Bereaved families are seen leafing through old photograph albums. Although these may feel like the least important pictures in your piece, you are going to present them to an audience, so try to create an establishing shot that looks credible and natural and not too obviously artificial.

Cutaways

Cutaways are the shots you need to help you make an internal edit in a piece of video, typically a clip of someone speaking. If you simply cut out the words you do not want, you will be left with a jump cut, in which the point of the edit will be visible to the viewer. You will want to avoid this if you can. The simplest way to do that is to cover the join with other pictures, so that the subject is briefly out of vision as we cross the edit point. You can create these visual bridges in a number of ways:

– **The "noddy"** is not an option for a VJ, because it involves having a second camera on the reporter as well as the one that is filming the interviewee. If do you have this option, you can insert some brief pictures of the reporter responding to what the interviewee is saying – which is usually done by nodding the head; hence the name. If there is only one camera, it is acceptable to shoot the noddies afterwards and cut them in at the edit.

– **The two shot** again requires the availability of a camera to pull out and show both interviewer and interviewee. If it is shot from slightly behind the interviewee, we will not be able to see their mouths moving and so the cut can be made without appearing to be out of sync.

– **The cut-in** involves shooting some detail in a big CU – typically showing the interviewee moving their hands or gesticulating. You can cut a second or two of these pictures into the clip to cover the edit point.

Cutaways seldom look natural but often cannot be avoided.

Architecture

This is a rather sarcastic way of referring to pieces that feature a lot of external shots of buildings. They are also sometimes called general views, or GVs. If these shots are part of the story – "this is the square in which the attack took place" then they are fine; but too often they are a poor substitute for better pictures that are lacking. This happens most often when you know where the story is happening – an important meeting perhaps, or a court case – but you are not allowed to film inside. This is why so many PTCs are done outside buildings: because the reporter wants the audience to know that he or she is at the scene of the story, but this is the closest they can get to it. Their shortcomings can be disguised to an extent with a script line – "in this building behind me, the fate of the company is being decided", "this is as close as we are allowed to the crime scene". They often cannot be avoided, but a piece that relies too heavily on exterior views of buildings is unlikely to make for very compelling viewing.

Clips and piece(s) to camera will be looked at in more detail in the next chapter.

Other sources of pictures

It may be that you are able to shoot your entire piece on location on the day, and have no need for any other elements at all. This is a good position to be in, but it is also quite unusual. If you are in a hurry, or if you are tackling a story that is very difficult to illustrate, you may have to look elsewhere for the images that will carry your story.

Pre-filming. This is done by you or a colleague, in advance of the broadcast of your piece. In the case of publication of a big report, for example, you will normally have a few days' notice of publication date. You may even be given an indication of the contents, either through an off-the-record briefing or a press release with an embargo date, which gives you some detail on the understanding that you do not use any of it until publication day. If you have this kind of notice, you can find the case studies that you need and either film a sequence with them in advance or make sure that they are available to you for filming on the day.

Library or archive pictures. These pictures will often be your first port of call. This is essentially previously transmitted footage that is available for using again. You can expect to have access to your organisation's previous news coverage of your story, and probably to the original raw material that went into it, known as "rushes". The rushes will usually be much more useful, because they have not already been edited into another piece, and so you have more material to work with, and more flexibility. It may also be the case that previous news reports have been recorded on a single track, or "leg", which means you cannot remove the voice of the original reporter – or if you do, you lose the natural sound as well. That makes it very difficult for you to make effective use of the material. The rushes will give you more options when you come to reuse them for your piece.

The library or archive will also have a selection of "stock shots" – generic shots of stories that crop up a lot – such as traffic jams or planes taking off or landing.

Library material is clearly less powerful than anything that has been shot on the day, unless of course it depicts specific previous events and you want to remind viewers of them. But some footage looks much the same, whether it was shot six weeks ago or that morning. The same stories crop up again and again, and it is hard to make today's shots of hospital wards or doctors' surgeries or school classrooms or residential homes look very different from all the previous occasions you have gathered similar material. But if you are obliged to use these pictures, try to extract the best value you can from them. A series of generic shots randomly stuck together while you intone some words of script will not make for very attractive viewing. Shots used in this way are sometimes described as "wallpaper", and this is a term of disparagement. So don't give up just because you are having to use something that has come out of the library: make the best you can of it. CUs from the library material may often work better than anything else.

It is always worth checking that there will not be any problems with rebroadcasting library material. If you use very old pictures of, say, a medical environment, it is possible that someone in the pictures has subsequently died, in which case you might cause unnecessary distress by re-using the pictures as wallpaper in an unrelated story. You also need to check for any copyright issues, which you should do before using any pictures that have not been shot by you or someone else within your organisation. Depending on the context, you might have to add a caption on the screen making clear that the pictures are library, or saying when they were shot.

Historical footage. It is sometimes also known as Archive, confusingly. If it predates colour television – footage from the Second World War, for example – it is sometimes referred to as "black and white". This is specific footage of important news events of the past, which you may want to use to illustrate a story today – if you are doing an anniversary piece, for example. Old newsreels are brilliant for this. But this kind of material can be a minefield because so much of it is protected by copyright, and you cannot use it without paying a fee. (The same is true of a lot of sports footage, which is in the possession of television rights holders.) It is very important that you check the copyright position before you use any of this material – regardless of how easy it is to find on the internet. If you breach copyright, your employer will be left with a large bill and will not be best pleased with you.

Agency/partner pictures. Most broadcasting organisations have contracts with news agencies that deal in pictures. In exchange for a subscription, the broadcaster has access to all the material filmed by a news agency. A lot of this will be basic news material on the big stories of the day – finance ministers filing into an important meeting, the President boarding an aircraft, Cabinet ministers walking into Number Ten – which means television news makers do not have to send their own teams to every event. Agencies may also offer stock shots and archive material. Agencies will send out regular updates of the shots that are available on the day. These are known as "dope sheets".

Public service broadcasters in Europe exchange pictures and facilities as members of the European Broadcasting Union, with the European News Exchange (ENEX) fulfilling the same function for commercial broadcasters. Broadcasters may sometimes agree to work together on major events such as Royal weddings, pooling their resources and sharing pictures to ensure the widest possible coverage.

Your company may also have strategic partnerships with other major broadcasters, deals by which pictures are exchanged under a protocol drawn up between the parties. In the UK for example, the BBC, ITN and Sky each has mutual arrangements with one of the big American channels.

Video News Releases, or VNRs. They describe material that is provided by companies or others showing some aspect of their operation that they want to publicise – a sort of illustrated press release. Companies may even circulate video interviews; say with their Chief Executive talking about plans for the future. They use these as an alternative to allowing journalists independent access to the Chief Executive. Most media organisations are extremely reluctant to use this material, since they have had no control over what has been filmed, and of course have not been given the opportunity to question the boss directly. They might feel more relaxed about footage that showed a process – such as a computerised graphic sequence provided by a space agency, showing how a space explorer sends back images, or gathers samples from the surface of a planet. If VNR is used, it is usually accompanied by a signal on screen as to where it has come from.

Graphics. The speed with which they can now be generated and a massive expansion in what is technically possible make graphics an attractive element of storytelling and are especially helpful if you are short of pictures. They are a great way of tackling statistics-heavy stories, and are also a key feature of storytelling online. Some pieces are made up almost entirely of graphics – and are branded as such, with a reporter live in a studio talking in front of a big screen.

Sophisticated graphics require trained and skilled designers, but if you do not have access to a professional in-house team, you may still be able to create some graphics for your piece using some of the basic tools that are available online. You need not be too ambitious with the design or the movement of the graphic, but you should be able to create simple charts and diagrams, and page templates on which you can place pictures and quotes. This latter is especially useful in court reporting, when you want to report key evidence verbatim but will not have been able to film in court and so have few pictures to cover the piece. You can get quite a long way on your own, but if you are expected to produce your own graphics, seek some professional tuition at the outset, and check if there is a house style to which you need to conform.

Maps. Locating a story, or giving it some geographical context, will be useful information for the viewer – and will be a great help if you are short of pictures.

Surprisingly few people have a reliable knowledge of the geography of the UK, let alone the rest of the world. So maps are very often a very useful, indeed necessary, addition to your storytelling toolbox. Again, they are relatively easy to create by use of any one of a number of tools.

Stills. You can use a static image such as a still photograph to create a moving image. A still of a missing child or an escaped prisoner might be pretty much all you have to illustrate your story. Rather than show it on screen for ten seconds (which will seem like a very long time), you can create a "move" on your editing software, in which you zoom slowly into the image or out of it, or both. It is still only a single image, but you have added motion that the eye will follow and make the ten seconds feel much less. You can also film a move with a camera.

Visual metaphors. Not a technique to be employed with any sort of hard news story. But when you cannot think of any way of illustrating your story, such as with a backgrounder or explanatory piece, or as a way of tackling something more conceptual, then it can be effective. Daily current affairs programmes such as *Channel 4 News* and *Newsnight* use this technique very frequently, but it requires a lot of creativity and is not easy to do well. In essence, it means coming up with a metaphor to explain your story and filming images that fit the metaphor. An obvious, but rather clichéd example might be a weather metaphor: your piece starts with pictures of a darkening sky and a script that talks about storm clouds gathering over whatever story you are covering. A series of pieces to camera is a way of extending a metaphor through script rather than images. It can become tiresome if over-extended, and is hard to pull off. It is also very difficult to do on your own – you probably need a producer or dedicated camera operator in order to make it work. You are probably well advised not to try it on your own to start with, and certainly not without approval or input from your editor or an experienced producer.

Top technical tips

This chapter is not a technical workshop, and no substitute for proper training in camerawork, nor for experience in the field. As with the rest of the book, it aims to alert you to the issues involved, offer you some principles to set you off in the right direction and help you avoid getting into difficulties. In that spirit, here are some technical pointers to help when you are gathering pictures on your own.

Contrast

When it comes to dealing with contrast – different shades of light – the camera is no match for the human eye. Even so, today's cameras and smartphones will do a good job in balancing the different shades to make what you are filming look as close as possible to what you are seeing. It helps to keep the sun behind you as you film. You can try shooting directly into the light, but it requires a higher level of skill. Avoid using extra lights to try to compensate – they simply add another degree of difficulty.

Focus

Focus is critical for all storytelling, and again, the camera's automatic settings should sort out most of your problems for you. Remember though that, like poor audio quality, out-of-focus pictures cannot be fixed in the editing process, so it is vital that you get the focus right at the point of filming.

B roll

This is a term given to the extra shots you will often need to help glue the piece together in the edit. Gather a good selection of wide, mid and CU shots of the environment in which you are filming or the people you are filming. You may need them for the final report. This does not just mean spraying the camera round to pick up some random GVs. CU shots are just as important, if not more so, and they are the shots that add character and quality to the storytelling. Shoot from different vantage points to increase your options.

The 180 degree rule

This is one of the important principles of film-making. Put simply, it states that two characters in a piece – in other words, the interviewer and interviewee, or interviewees – should remain in the same visual relationship to each other throughout. This maintains the continuity of the conversations the interviewer is having in all interviews. If the interview is shot from a number of different angles, you might end up with the interviewer on the left and the interviewee on the right in one shot, and the other way round in another. Breaking this rule is called "crossing the line", and it has a disorienting and confusing effect on the viewer. So if filming a variety of shots of an interview, say for use as cutaways, keep interviewer and interviewee in the same physical positions in relation to each other.

Framing, and the "rule of thirds"

Another basic principle of photography and film-making. Think of your image as being divided into nine equal boxes, with two lines coming down vertically and two lines going across horizontally. Focus your subject at one of the intersections of those lines. This prevents you placing the subject right in the centre of the screen, and moves the focus slightly to one side. This has the effect of drawing the viewer's eye into the shot and making the whole look more balanced. For a wide shot, locate the horizon one third of the way down the picture, not in the middle.

Shoot for the edit

As always, keep the edit in mind when you are gathering your pictures, to be sure that you have enough shots and a sufficient variety of shot. This is particularly important for a sequence. Err on the side of length with your shots, filming several seconds on either side of the action that you want to record. This will help you achieve an edit that looks seamless.

Saving and labelling

When you have finished filming, make sure that the recording has worked, and that your material is saved, clearly labelled and uploaded on to a computer, so that it cannot be lost or accidentally erased. Your shoot is not complete until you have done this, no matter how late it is and how tired you are. You do not want to lose the fruits of your labours by accident.

Don't wait until you are using your camera on a real story before trying some of these things. Take your camera out as often as you can, and experiment with different angles and distances and practice getting a range of shots, or a collection of shots that could be used to make a sequence. Watch sequences on television news programmes, concentrating on the number and variety of shots that have been used. You will soon discover what works and what doesn't, and how to avoid the pitfalls. Better to work things out while practising than when you need to produce a story for broadcast. When you have recorded some practice material, find the time to look at it again afterwards and try to analyse what worked well and what didn't. Try to imagine that you will have the job of editing this material into a real news piece – or better still, do the edit for real. Have you got enough material? Have you got the right range of shots? Can you use the pictures you have shot to create a sequence, or to tell the whole story? What is missing?

If you are filming on a smartphone, the same thing applies. Record as many shots as you think you need to construct your sequence or piece, and edit them on any form of software that allows you to add a track, or voice over. There is more on this in the section on Mobile Journalism in Chapter 20. Not only does this sort of trial and error make you better practised and slicker at gathering and editing material, it is also a very good way of teaching yourself what works well and what does not.

18

The television journalist: continuous news and television reporting

In the last chapter, we looked at some of the issues specific to television journalism, and then concentrated on the gathering of pictures. In this chapter, we will go through some of the formats employed in television news, and then consider the editing and production process – what you do with those pictures, and how you marry them to the words to create a fully integrated report. We will also look at pieces to camera (PTCs), and the issues and techniques associated with live reporting.

The architecture of television news

There are relatively few different ways of packaging words and pictures in a television news operation. The traditional built bulletins that still command the biggest audiences – programmes like the BBC's *Six O'Clock News* or ITV's *News at Ten* – follow a basic formula that has not changed much over many years. These half-hour digests of the big stories of the day are usually anchored by a single presenter sitting at a desk. They start with a set of headlines and trails, and then tackle around eight to ten stories in the form of edited reports from correspondents, each about two minutes long, and preceded by an introduction, or cue, read by the programme presenter. There will usually be some live elements, with correspondents reporting from the scene of breaking stories, or offering analysis and perspectives that add value to the packaged report. At some point there will be a handful of lesser stories, each covered with around 15 seconds of pictures accompanied by two or three sentences of words, or track. These stories may be grouped together, so that the presenter moves from one to the other without reappearing in vision in between. They are sometimes known as "wipe sequences" because of the visual device used to move between them, in which one story appears to wipe the previous one from the screen.

Regional news programmes at teatime – also half an hour in length – follow a similar pattern – headlines and trails, introductions to programme items with live contributions too. Within that, there is a wide variety of presentational techniques: some have a single presenter, some have two; some are presented from a "soft" area such as a sofa, some from behind a desk; some have longer features, particularly in the second half of the programme; most have weather forecasters and sports reporters who are part of the presenting team and interact with the main presenters. A quick online tour of regional programmes at 1800 (for ITV shows) and at 1830 (for BBC regions) offers a good sense of the range.

Other daily news shows – those at breakfast time, or the news and current affairs shows such as *Channel 4 News* and *Newsnight* – have more freedom and flexibility than the straight news bulletins, and use a wider range of presentational forms, often with more than one presentation point in the studio. Much of the content is live, largely in the form of single interviews or discussions; but the recorded reports will usually be longer and have a huge amount of creativity and imagination devoted to them. They might use reconstructions featuring actors, music or sophisticated graphics in a way that would not be considered appropriate for a straight hard news report.

What all these have in common is an aspiration to use the medium to its full effect, using words, pictures, graphics and studio presentation to create a bright, informative and engaging programme.

Continuous news channels operate in a rather different way, but are still recognisably a part of the same news family. Because they are on air all the time, they have fewer constraints and an altogether looser format. If a story breaks, they can cover it live and stay with it as long as they think it is of interest and value. If things are quieter, each channel has a basic structure which is iterable – that is, it can be re-peated (with refreshed content of course), allowing the channel to broadcast round the clock without attempting to reinvent the wheel each day.

This structure will usually be built around a summary of the main news at the top of the hour, and headlines or very short summaries at various other points during the hour. There will be regular slots for business, sport and weather and – late in the evening – reviews of the following morning's newspapers. Even when stories are not developing very much, channels will try to make them sound fresh by pursuing new angles, and interviewing different guests and correspondents. But there is not time to produce a whole new set of edited reports every hour, and so the same pieces will probably run two or three times over a period of a few hours until they are out of date or have been superseded by a newer version. Pack-ages may receive several airings at slow news times, which are through the small hours of the morning, mid-morning and mid-evening.

News summaries and wipe sequences

The summaries that kick off each hour on continuous channels, and the shorter items of news that appear in the built bulletins, are produced in much the same way. Different organisations have different termi-nologies for these items. Here are some of the variations:

– A sequence of pictures with words read by an out-of-vision presenter is known in ITV as a **ULAY** (un-derlay), by the BBC as an **OOV** (out of vision) and by Sky as an **LVO** (live voice over).
– A sequence of pictures appearing on screen while the presenter is interviewing someone live (corre-spondent or guest) is known in ITV as a **FLOAT** or **ULAY**, in the BBC as a **FLOAT** and by Sky as an **OLAY** (overlay).
– A free-standing clip that is not part of a packaged report is known in ITV as **SOT** (sound on tape) by the BBC as a **CLIP** or **SYNC** or **ACT** (actuality) and by Sky as a **GRAB**.

Note that sometimes the presenter is in vision for the first few words of these brief items, before the switch to pictures. So if you are asked to produce a short news item, you need to know whether the whole story will be covered by pictures, or only part of it. If your presenter is in vision reading the first sentence of the story, and then the programme cuts to pictures while he reads the rest of it, then obviously you will need fewer pictures. If the story is in the middle of a wipe sequence, and the presenter reads straight on from one item to the next without being seen on screen, then you will need enough pictures to cover the whole of the text of the story.

Once you know this, and what sort of duration you are aiming for, you need to go and look at all the avail-able pictures. For a story of 15"–20" in length you are looking for three or four good shots – more than that, and it will look too frenetic and jumpy. Ideally, you would like a mix of different sorts of shot, but that is not essential if the nature of the story takes you in a different direction. If it was a piece about the extent of flooding after heavy rain, for example, a series of aerial or wide shots might illustrate the story better than a succession of close-ups. Don't forget about natural sound: just because the item is shorter, that does not mean you don't need to consider using that. A snatch of sound can add impact.

Make sure that you have enough pictures to cover your script, and some more for insurance. The presenter may stumble and start a sentence again, and you don't want the pictures to run out before the presenter reaches the end of the story, leaving a blank screen. One way of avoiding this is to put a freeze on the final frame of your last shot as a sort of buffer, so that the viewer will not be looking at a blank screen if the presenter falls behind the pictures.

Having cut your pictures, time them so you know how long you have for the script, or track, that you will then write to accompany them. As with all your work, use simple and direct language, and make sure the words work with the pictures. Allow the pictures to lead the script so that the viewer is taken through the story easily and naturally. If you find yourself struggling, it may be because the shots are not in the optimum order. Try switching them round.

Packages/VTs

The cue

Everything we said about the radio cue in Chapter 16, and about its relationship to the piece that follows, also holds good for television. When you have done the necessary work with your pictures – of which more in a moment – you are ready to start writing. And, as in radio, always begin with the cue. This is the introduction to your coverage of the story, so like any intro it must tell the viewer what the story is about. Like a radio cue, it needs to set up the report that follows. It also has an element of salesmanship about it: it is trying to draw viewers in and make them want to find out more. If you do not know what information is in the cue, you cannot make a sensible start in the scripting of your package, and there is a danger of duplicating information – or worse still, missing out key elements. So always draft your cue first or, if someone else is working on the cue while you cut the piece, agree with that person what information the cue is going to contain, so that you can account for that in your script.

Writing the cue should also help focus your mind on some of those basic questions that you should be thinking about before embarking on the writing of any story. What is the story? What is today's angle? What do I want my piece to achieve? What do I need to include? What can I leave out?

The piece/package/VT

A recorded television news report is usually called "a piece" or "a package" or sometimes "a VT" (harking back to the days of videotape). Once you have agreed what information is to be included in the cue, you can start thinking about the structure of your package. As ever, you will also want to know in advance the duration that has been allocated to you by the programme editor, and the deadline – the time by which you must have it ready to go to air. A very rough rule of thumb is that it will take you around an hour to edit a minute of a television news package. Make sure you build in enough time at the end for someone to view and approve the piece once it is finished, and for making any changes that are required. It makes bulletin editors understandably jumpy if the first time they see a piece for which they are accountable is when it is going out on the air. Remember that it takes longer to make changes to a television piece than it does in radio. But because a television package is built up one component at a time, if you are working at base you can ask your editor to come and look at what you have done so far, even if you are only part way through the edit. This will make the editor feel more comfortable that all is going according to plan, and it will make you feel more confident that you are on the right lines.

So, armed with knowledge of the cue material, the duration and the deadline, you can begin work in earnest on the content and structure of the piece. Your report is likely to attempt to serve some or all of a number of purposes:

- **Describe** with words and pictures what has happened, building on the basic material provided in the cue.
- **Explain** what has happened, setting out the background and context.
- **Indicate** why it is important.
- **Suggest** what might happen next.

Just as with radio, you need to think also about what sort of piece you are producing:

- **A basic news report.** A piece in which you simply describe something that has happened. This is the most likely format for an "action" story such as a traffic accident or a round-up of weather damage; or for breaking news, when there is a premium on finding out the basic facts of a story as soon as possible. When events are actually unfolding, the analysis can wait until later.
- **A background piece.** This might be where your analysis and context come in, looking in more detail at a story that has happened and seeking to explain it and give your audience the information to understand it better. Clearly, it will be harder to find the right pictures to go with your exposition.

It is of course perfectly possible to combine these if you have the allotted time and the pictures you need to cover them:

- **An update piece.** You may be describing the latest developments in a story that has already been running for some time. You will probably be starting with the new line (although most of it might be in the cue), but you need to think about how much the audience will already know about the story, and how much you need to remind them of what has already happened.

Be careful not to attempt to do too much: not every piece needs a lot of background; not every piece needs you to form a judgement. Often you will cut back on the words in order to let the pictures breathe. You will want to make room for colour, the telling detail or a striking phrase that someone has used. There won't always be room for everything: decide what is the most important for a piece that is interesting and attractive as well as informative.

This is the point at which your thinking diverges from that you employ with a radio package. Because with television you have that all-important extra dimension with which to achieve the desired effect: the pictures.

However important the story is, and the words that you use to report it, the pictures are the dominant feature of all television packages. Viewers watch first and listen second. They must be at the heart of your thinking through the whole process of creating your report. It is still vital that you decide up front what your story is. This is not just a judgement about the story on its own – the strength or otherwise of your pictures will be factors in your thinking. Once you have decided, your job is to select and order the images and other elements that will tell that story most effectively. The pictures will suggest to you the structure of your piece. So in terms of the way in which the information is presented, a television piece and a radio piece on exactly the same story may be put together in completely different ways.

If you are going to let the pictures influence how you construct the piece, as you should, the first thing you need to do is view them all. Have a look at everything that is available to you, whether it is your own footage, relevant pictures shot by someone else, agency, archive or library material. When doing so, bear a number of things in mind:

– **Identify the strongest images.** Often, but not always, you will want to start your piece with these. But they might not illustrate what you consider to be the main news points that you want to convey in the early part of the package. There may be need for a trade-off between these two things.
– **Think about the overall volume of pictures** you have. Even a two-minute package will devour a large number of images and shots, and it will often be the case that you don't have enough visual material to sustain the length of piece you are aiming for. If that is the case, suggest to your editor that you make the piece shorter. This may feel instinctively like an odd thing to do, but it is always the right call. It is not a reflection on the importance of the story, or on your abilities. Less is often more: running the piece at a duration that suits the amount of good visual material at your disposal will always produce a better and sharper piece. Pictures stretched over a longer piece they are not strong enough to sustain will feel dreary and lifeless. Just because you have been given two minutes does not mean you have to fill two minutes if you do not have the pictures to do so successfully. Your editor will think more highly of you if you suggest cutting your piece to 1'30" or 1'45" if that is a more natural length for the material available. To repeat: this is nothing to do with the significance of the story, and everything to do with the materials to hand when you think about how best to present it to the audience.
– **Think about whether the pictures available allow you to build the sequences** we discussed in the previous chapter: mini stories such as case studies within the overall report. In order to build a sequence, even one of only about 20"–30", you will need a good range of shots and quite a lot of them. If you don't have them, the sequence might not work at all and you might have to abandon it in favour of a more general approach.

With a clear understanding of the material at your disposal, you can start to build the structure. The inverted pyramid approach that we discussed in the context of a newspaper or online story does not work for us here. You may be able to start with the most important facts, add others and then add context and background, as per the pyramid concept. But the chances are that the pictures will suggest a different approach. And you need to sustain the viewer's interest all the way through the piece: you are looking to produce a well-rounded and crafted piece of storytelling, in which the end is as important as the beginning. The concept of a piece that can be cut from the bottom to save space is not appropriate here.

Your piece will typically contain a number of different elements:

– **The "news" pictures** that tell the story
– **A sequence** or sequences that enhance the storytelling through examples and case studies
– **A clip** or clips of interviewees
– **A piece to camera (PTC)**
– **Library, stock or archive footage,** depending on the nature of the piece and the availability of pictures.

The trick is to take these building blocks and fit them together in one continuous flow, so that each element makes the transition seamlessly and naturally into the next, as your words and the pictures work together in close harmony. Although you may not be presenting the information in chronological order, the structure will have a logic to it that guides the viewer through in an easy and understandable way.

To ensure that the pictures have the lead role in this process, cut them first and add the track afterwards. You can do this in stages. So, for example, cut an opening sequence of pictures that are going to get you to your first clip/interviewee. When you are satisfied that you have that sequence in good shape, write and record the words that will go with it, and put the two together. The first 20″ of your piece is now complete and you can move on to the next element. It is much easier to write words to edited pictures than to cut pictures to a preset script, and it makes for much better television too. This approach is also most likely to extract the maximum value from any natural sound you may have – sound effects or a couple of words of dialogue that you will want to retain. When you have noted where the natural sounds are, you can script around them accordingly. If you write the script first, you will find yourself trampling all over them.

The primacy of the pictures does not mean that the words are not important. They are going to be delivering plenty of information. But they need to be responsive to what the viewer is seeing. If the pictures literally tell the story, you may need very little by way of script. If they are introducing us to a character who is going to be a part of the story, then the script needs to sketch in some of the background.

Here are some examples of how those two scenarios might play out in practice. First, a forest fire:

PICTURES: Wide shots of blazing forest
SCRIPT: Out of control and destroying everything in their path
PICTURES: More shots of fire spreading rapidly; **natural sound** of burning
SCRIPT: Fanned by strong winds, the flames move across the ground at terrifying speed
PICTURES: Houses in path of fire
SCRIPT: This village lies in the path of the flames. People here have been told it's too dangerous to stay
PICTURES: Residents packing up vehicles and leaving
SCRIPT: They grab what possessions they can, and head to safety further inland
PICTURES: Firefighters tackling flames; **natural sound** of hoses and shouted orders
SCRIPT: The firefighters are struggling against impossible odds. They do their best, but they cannot stop the relentless advance of the flames
CLIP of interview with fire chief.

The script here refers at each point to what we are seeing, and adds more detail that we cannot see: the strong winds, the warning to residents, where the residents are going and so on.

The first sentence is important. It can start with a descriptive statement that supports the pictures – as the above example does: "Out of control and destroying everything in their path". Or it could make an overarching point: "These are the worst fires in half a century". The pictures here would allow of either approach.

It has become fashionable to start television pieces with short, terse statements lacking a main verb. The example above does this. It can be very effective in setting a mood or tone, getting the attention of the viewer and giving a sense of the pictures without describing what we are seeing. But like everything else, if overused and over-dramatic it can become hackneyed. Use the construction when it works, but not for every piece that you do.

Look for ways of expressing facts in a way that will make the story more relatable, and maintain interest. So

> These are the worst fires for half a century

could be "humanised" to:

> No-one living here can remember anything like this.

Or better still, attach the thought to a real person (who would need to be seen in the pictures of course):

> Neil Strong has lived here all his life. He's seen many forest fires. But nothing like this.

Note that most of the sentences in our script here are short and uncomplicated and use bold, active language. The pictures are very strong; the viewer just needs leading through them. They do not need a cumbersome or heavy-handed script.

Note also the difference between a television script and a radio script. When the pictures are good, short sentences allow you opportunities to pause to allow them to have maximum impact. In some cases they will barely be sentences, more terse phrases that add to the effect of what we are seeing on the screen. This staccato approach does not work with everything: weaker pictures need more help. But when they are strong, the reporter steps back and lets them do the work. You could be even more spare than in the example above:

> Forest fires. (Pause) An annual hazard here. (Pause) But seldom this early. (Pause) And seldom this ferocious.

Not a verb in sight, but it is a good way of extracting maximum effect from strong pictures. No one actually *talks* like this, though – so this kind of scripting would not work on the radio. There are no pictures to look at there, and you are attempting to replicate the rhythms of normal conversation. And that means verbs, and complete sentences. A radio version might begin like this:

> There are forest fires here every year – but they seldom arrive this early or strike with this level of ferocity.

Our television piece begins with the strongest pictures available. Your natural inclination is to do this, and it is a good instinct – you want to get the story off to a strong start and to engage the viewer. But it is not compulsory. If you have a very strong sequence of pictures, you may want to build up to them. This will often be the case if the pictures are graphic and potentially distressing: you want to lead the viewers up to them and prepare or warn them for what they are about to see. You might also hold your best pictures back if they are, as it were, the punchline of the story, and you want to build the tension by working your way up to a big reveal. The choice is yours, but your default will probably be to start with what you think is your best material.

Now, a much softer piece about a group of fathers who attend classes in hairdressing, so that they can style their daughters' hair. This has charm, but nothing like the savage picture power of the fire story. So it starts with a sequence:

PICTURES: Wide shot of room in which a number of men are standing behind their seated daughters, arranging their hair into various styles; natural sound of chatter
SCRIPT: This is a hairdressing school – for dads
PICTURES: Close-up of face of one father concentrating, moving to a big close-up of his hands arranging an elaborate plait in his daughter's hair
SCRIPT: It teaches fathers how to do a task usually left to mum
PICTURES: More close-ups of combing, plaiting, braiding
SCRIPT: They learn how to comb, plait and braid their daughters' hair
PICTURES: One daughter looks at hair in mirror: natural sound of her reaction
SCRIPT: The results meet with approval from a very demanding clientele
PICTURES: Another father (Jack) working on his daughter's hair
SCRIPT: The class was Jack's idea. Having had his daughter's hair professionally styled for several parties, he decided he'd like to have a go himself
PICTURES: Jack talking to Maria. We can hear their voices but not what they are saying
SCRIPT: He enlisted expert help from stylist Maria, and soon found other dads keen to try their hand
PICTURES: Wide shot of room full of activity; natural sound
SCRIPT: They say it helps their relationship with their daughters and gives them a valuable shared activity.

CLIP from interview with Jack or Maria.

A room full of people is not the most promising source of pictures, but here it works well because, unlike the forest fires with its big dramatic wide shots, this story is best filmed around close-ups showing the dexterity of the fathers and the intricate styling of the hair. It has a nice opening sentence, picking up on the fact that fathers styling the hair of their daughters is rather unusual – a point made crisply in a mere seven words. The pictures then continue to illustrate while the script unfolds the story. There is natural sound and good range of characters, some of whom we are going to get to meet later in the piece – Jack and Maria and Jack's daughter.

It is more important than ever to get a lot of big close-ups when you are shooting in a confined space. In this example, faces and hands and hair are obvious and good options, and you can also try doing something with mirror images. The more close-ups you have, the more storytelling options you are giving yourself.

Even though the piece is based largely on medium or close-up images, it begins, as the first one did, with a wide shot that sets the scene. This is sometimes called the establishing shot and is the most common way of getting into a piece, with both pictures and script giving us the context of the story that is to follow. You can start with close-up images, but the viewers will take longer to process what they are seeing, and may be too distracted by the image to concentrate on what they are being told. In essence, you are choosing between starting with the general picture and moving to the specific, or the other way round. See what the pictures suggest to you as the best course.

These are two very different stories – one very strong with powerful pictures, the other very gentle and less newsy, and thus reliant on close-ups and a mellower form of storytelling. In each case, though, the principle of picture-led production is clearly on show. Let the pictures carry the story, while the script offers complementary supporting information but does not duplicate the information we are getting from the pictures.

In both of these examples, you have decent material to work with. In very many cases, you will find that you do not have very good pictures, or any pictures at all. While some news subject areas naturally lend themselves to picture treatments, very many do not: economic and business stories, for example. Even an "action" story like a plane crash can be hard to illustrate in the very early stages, when you have no pictures and may not even know what type of plane has gone down. We talked in the last chapter about what to do when stories are "pictorially challenged" – using maps, graphics, library and archive, for example, or preshooting where the circumstances allow. But even if you are successful in finding enough pictures for your piece, they may not be very exciting, and certainly lack the appeal to draw the viewer in from the first frame.

When your pictures need help, your script can often provide it. However nondescript the images are, there will usually be something that you can pick out to get you started. I am reminded of a television report of a multimillion dollar deal in the City of London, where the best of a bad bunch of news pictures were of a group of half a dozen business executives in suits smiling outside the building where the deal had been signed. The correspondent was faced with the unenviable task of launching his piece on the basis of this unpromising fare. So he picked out a detail. He noticed that one member of the group was wearing a particularly bright tie. He wrote an opening script line under the pictures that began: "The man wearing the loud tie and the big smile has good reason to be happy. He's just signed a deal that made him a very rich man". This is a classic case of making bricks without straw. Suddenly the man in the suit is a person, the viewer looks at his tie and his smile, and (we hope) wants to know more about how he came to be so rich. We don't notice how feeble the pictures are. A clever bit of scripting has surmounted the problem.

There are other little tricks like this that can lift ordinary material a notch or two. Most of them are based on creating some kind of atmosphere or interest, or picking out some detail like the loud tie, and making a feature of it. Look for a clever or ear-catching phrase that will make the viewer take notice. Include time references to create the sense of action and a narrative. Make every effort to include snippets of natural sound, give them space and write round them imaginatively.

In terms of your general writing style, the basic rules that we have established and returned to many times before all continue to apply. Write short, clear sentences without subordinate clauses. A working rule of thumb of about 15–20 words per sentence is a good guide, fewer if you can. If you look at all the examples above, you will see that most of them are a dozen words or fewer. You are talking, so write in the same conversational and idiomatic manner as you speak, and as you would in a radio script. Your words are there to be listened to, not read, so make them sound natural. As always, avoid jargon, clichés, acronyms and complicated words.

Above all, resist the temptation to write over every frame of the pictures. Pictures need room to breathe, and so does natural sound. If you are given two minutes for your piece, assume that your track will be barely half that. By the time you have included a couple of clips and a piece to camera, you will be lucky to have room for much more than half a dozen short sentences to carry the whole burden of the story. Be ruthless about evicting all extraneous material and stick with the main point of the story and the key things you want to convey; if you start worrying that you haven't covered off certain angles or perspectives, your script will get longer and woollier and the piece will suffer as a result. So write simply and economically, and don't crush the pictures under a heavy weight of verbiage.

That in turn should enable you to deliver your script in a relaxed and natural manner. Because delivery too is important. If your script builds in pauses, working round natural sound and referring to what the viewer is seeing – all of which it should be doing – then you need an actor's sense of pacing and timing to a much greater extent than is required in other forms of journalism. Read your scripts out loud to yourself before you record them: if the words sound like something to be read rather than spoken, then rewrite them. And each time you rewrite, try to make the script shorter rather than longer.

Reporter involvement

The PTC is the most obvious way in which you personally are associated with your piece, as the audience sees you on screen delivering your verdict on a story. But there are other ways in which you can insert yourself in the piece, generally referred to as "reporter involvement". All are legitimate, but as we said in the last chapter, it is important not to overdo them. In a longer programme in which the reporter is conducting an investigation, there will be a great deal of reporter involvement as we follow the course of that investigation. In a two-minute news report, there is less scope for this and an excess of it will feel inappropriate. The reporter should be careful not to make the story about himself or herself. Reporter involvement is perfectly acceptable, but it must enhance the storytelling and not get in the way of it.

Here are some examples of reporter involvement:

– **Set-up shots.** Reporter seen interacting with interviewee (chatting, walking along with them, looking through documents together, having a cup of coffee) as a way of introducing a clip from the interview
– **Reporter at work on gathering news.** Reporter knocking on door of elusive interviewee and asking them to open up. Reporter working through paperwork or conducting internet search. Reporter attempting to doorstep or snatch comments, perhaps as part of media scrum ("are you going to resign, minister?"). Reporter asking a question at a press conference
– **Reporter at the scene of the story.** Reporter in helicopter looking out over affected area (floods, droughts, etc.). Reporter being shown scenes of suffering/damage by relief workers. Reporter talking to victims about what has happened to them.

You will recognise all of these from the television news reports that are broadcast every day. Each can be said to have an editorial purpose, and it can add to the effect of a piece if we see and hear the reporter

engaged in journalistic activity and reporting on the spot. The accompanying voice track may emphasise the reporter's first-person involvement in the story. But if there is no editorial reason for reporter
involvement, then it is as well to avoid it. We do not want to see the reporter in every shot, becoming a
distraction and a barrier between the viewer and the story.

Pieces to camera

For some reporters, the PTC is the most important part of the whole package, for the obvious reason that
this is the time they appear on screen. This is the most common example of reporter involvement. The
PTC is actually an important element of most television packages, for a number of reasons:

– A PTC will often show the reporter at the location of the story. This adds credibility and authority to
   what is being said, because the reporter is on the ground and describing things that he or she has
   personally witnessed or found out.
– A PTC allows the reporter to offer a judgement or further insight to the basic reportage, giving the
   viewer a greater sense of the context and significance of what is being described, and perhaps suggesting what may happen next. Again, this gives authority and substance to the piece, especially if
   the reporter is a specialist, whose knowledge and experience will add value to the basic storytelling.
– A PTC, or even a series of PTCs, can offer a production solution if a story is lacking in any meaningful
   pictures.

Whatever purpose the PTC is fulfilling in a particular piece, it is important that it actually adds something
to the reporting, and is not simply a piece of cosmetic showboating. A PTC may occupy 20 per cent of the
time devoted to the whole report, so it needs to be worthy of its place. A vacuous PTC that looks gratuitous
and has nothing to say is a waste of valuable time and can be irritating to the viewer. The PTC should always contain some sort of information, context or insight that complements the rest of the piece.

Where should it go?

The conventional place for a PTC is at the end of the report, where it offers the opportunity to sum up
and add extra value. But it does not have to be there. It could appear at the very start of the piece, setting
up what follows. This can be especially effective if the reporter is live at the scene of a breaking story and
wants to convey the immediacy and drama of what is happening straight away, before the recorded report
winds back the clock and takes us through the story from the beginning. These days it is fashionable for
an opening PTC to be done live, if resources and other considerations permit. There may still be a PTC
at the end of the piece too, a "top and tail" arrangement in which the recorded material is sandwiched
between two live elements. The "tail" might be a two-way – an exchange between reporter and presenter.

The PTC can also form a useful function within the main body of the piece, as a bridge between one
thought or location and the next. For example: "That's the way they see things on this side of the border.
(*Reporter seen crossing from one side to the other*). I crossed to the other side, and a very different picture
emerged". This is a simple but effective join between two distinct elements within your piece, which
takes the viewer with you as you move from one to the other.

Where should I record it?

The location of your PTC is important and needs to be relevant to the story. As possibly the longest
single element of your piece, it needs forethought and planning. It might not always be possible to get

close to the action, and very often the best you can do is record your piece outside the building where the action is taking place. You see this every day with political reports – where the reporter will be in Downing Street or near the Houses of Parliament – and court cases, where it is not possible to film inside the court building. If you are the scene of a developing news story, there may be a police cordon that prevents you getting close to the heart of the action. You have to make the best use of whatever is available.

You can make a routine outside location feel a little more interesting, immediate and relevant by referring to what is going on behind you: "this is as close as the police are allowing us to come to the scene. Just a few yards from where I'm standing they are beginning a detailed investigation into what has happened." "The courtroom in the building behind me was packed as the trial began." "Here at Number Ten, urgent meetings are expected to continue late into the night as the government decides how to respond to the crisis."

Beware a location that feels irrelevant or out of date. A PTC or live report outside a darkened courthouse from which everyone went home hours ago does not add anything to your piece. With a bit of imagination, it will usually be possible to find a location with some sort of connection to the story. Locations around your own place of work can sometimes serve the purpose: a PTC in which you are seen seated at your desk in the middle of going through a lengthy printed report; a PTC in an edit suite in which you are watching incoming footage; a PTC next to a wall or other blank space onto which you can later project some graphics or quotes. These have the advantage that you don't have to travel far to record them – very important if you are pushed for time.

What do I say?

As noted, the content of your PTC depends on the function it is serving within your piece, and whether it is going to go at the beginning, in the middle or at the end. The conventional PTC is a medium shot of the reporter, framed loosely enough for the viewer to be able to see the story location in the background, in which the reporter delivers around 15" of thoughts about the story. There is nothing wrong with that format, but it can be varied in any number of ways to add interest and effect. By all means try something a little different: but make sure that there is some form of editorial purpose behind it.

This is particularly true if you are planning to move around. You will often see a PTCs in which the reporter is picked out walking up a busy street while talking, before suddenly coming to a standstill and unburdening himself or herself of their great thoughts. This may add a degree of visual interest (though not much) but there is no editorial reason for it and most of the time it just looks false and forced. The viewer wonders idly where the reporter is going, and why, their concentration waning in the process. If you have no reason to move, then stay put.

If, on the other hand, you *do* have a reason, then go for it. A simple example:

> (Reporter walking up one side of a suburban street) "The houses on this side of the street back directly on to the railway line, and the owners are eligible for grants for double glazing and sound-proofing to their properties. But over on this side…" (Reporter seen crossing road) "……the houses are just too far away from the line to qualify for grants. They say it's just as noisy here, and the ruling is unfair."

Here the reporter is using the PTC to illustrate the key part of the story and the physical movement is completely justified editorially.

As we mentioned in the last chapter, you can use a zoom in or out on a PTC to give a sense of scale, assuming you are working with a camera operator and not self-shooting. But if you do, make sure there is a point to it. A PTC which begins with a close-up of you and then comes out to reveal you as just a face in a crowd may have a pleasing effect, as may the opposite move, but unless your script offers some editorial explanation, it just looks tricksy and pointless.

A "moving" PTC can also be used to demonstrate or describe something with a prop such as a piece of machinery. See "walk and talk" below. The use of drones opens up a whole world of possibilities.

With any PTC in which you attempt something a bit out of the ordinary, make sure that you shoot a more straightforward version as well. This is your insurance if, when you come to the edit, you decide that your more creative effort does not work for whatever reason. Having a back-up piece gives you confidence to try different approaches, safe in the knowledge that you have a fallback position if they don't come off. It is sometimes difficult to know whether they have been successful or not until you come to the edit and look at the PTC with all the other material at your disposal. If you don't need your "safety" PTC, you have not lost anything. But it might just get you out of a hole. And if you are asked to rework your piece to freshen it up for a later bulletin, a different PTC will often be a helpful means of doing so.

When you are planning a more conventional PTC, summing up the arguments or offering judgements, the key rule is to make sure that you have something to say. PTCs which do the equivalent of concluding "the arguments seem set to continue for some time to come" or "there for the moment the matter rests" or "only time will tell" are bland and unimaginative and tell the viewer nothing. Your PTC should aim to add more information, more background or some thought about where matters lie and what may happen next – or some combination of any or all of these. But if you have nothing useful to say, and no interesting location from which to say it, then question whether your piece actually needs a PTC at all.

With all PTCs, the usual rule of simplicity applies. You cannot do a complicated analysis or summarise opposing arguments in the space of 15" or so, so don't try. Decide on what single point you want to make, and concentrate on that alone. The less complicated and detailed your PTC, the better it will be.

How do I remember what I want to say?

Your PTC is probably going to be delivered directly to the camera, so you will need to be able to deliver it fluently and naturally without reading from a script. It is fine to use your notebook as a prop if you wish, especially if you are going to quote something verbatim, such as a key phrase from a speech or some evidence from a court case. But in general, you will be committing your 50 words or so to memory.

Different reporters use different techniques. Some write their PTCs out in full and then learn them. This has the advantage of ensuring that you say just what you want to say, but it can make your delivery sound unnatural and forced. Some write out their script and place it next to the camera and simply read it out. This only works if you have excellent eyesight and for a straightforward PTC with no movement, where the reporter never deviates from looking down the barrel of the camera.

For most, it is a question of sketching out what you want to say, working up a few key phrases that help express that, and then doing some rehearsing. While the camera operator is setting up, it is a common sight for the reporter to be walking around some distance off, head down, muttering away as he or she practices what they are going to say. You want to create the illusion that you are having a spontaneous conversation with the viewer, and so you want the PTC to sound natural and unforced. As with so much of broadcasting, you will only be successful in creating this sense of speaking off the cuff if you do plenty of preparation beforehand. You can make yourself a few guidance notes to get you started, with perhaps some handy phrases designed to help you achieve the conversational and spontaneous effect you are looking for. The *way* you express yourself is as important in its own way as the editorial content. Only when the two are in harmony can you produce an effective PTC. As we shall see, the same is true of live reporting.

When the time comes to record your piece, do not be discouraged if you don't get it right first time. In fact, it would be surprising if you did. It might take you a few takes to warm up, to get a complete grip on what you are going to say and to deliver it fluently in one go. Your camera operator will expect this and will be tolerant of a few false starts and stumbles that require you to go back to the beginning and start again. However, you will not necessarily get better or more fluent with each attempt, and patience may be strained if the number of takes starts to creep up too much. The more practice you have, the better you will be, but you can also iron out a lot of potential difficulties if you use the period of preparation well, and have a clear and well-rehearsed idea of what you want to say and how you are going to say it before you step in front of the camera.

When you have recorded the PTC, play it back as soon as you can to make sure you have not inadvertently made any editorial mistakes and to make sure you are happy with the way it looks.

Walk and talk

Some PTCs fall into the category of what is variously described as "walk and talk", "action rant" or "show and tell". In the age of continuous news channels, this has developed into a separate technique and a discrete means of storytelling. As a VJ, it is unlikely you will have many opportunities to try it, because you really need someone else to be holding the camera. It might just be feasible using a selfie stick, but be prepared not to use it if it doesn't work.

As the name suggests, a walk and talk is a piece in which the reporter, in vision, leads the viewer around a location followed by the camera operator, describing what can be seen, inviting the viewers to see it for themselves. The same technique can be used to describe a process or protocol – such as how a piece of machinery or a production line works. The studio-based reporter "explainer" package with graphics, sometimes called "the big screen", is a related form of the idea.

A walk and talk might be anything from a few seconds to a couple of minutes in length. A short one can double as a PTC, a longer one can be an effective alternative to a news package. The most obvious examples are filmed by reporters at the scenes of news stories, the camera following them as they pick their way over wreckage or rubble, describing what they are seeing, audibly directing the camera towards images so that the viewer can see them first hand, sometimes stopping to interview people affected by the story or those assisting with rescue or relief work.

Although the best pieces look very spontaneous and natural, they are nearly always the result of meticulous planning and preparation. The reporter and the camera operator must work in very close cooperation, agreeing in advance where the reporter is going, setting up and positioning the people to be interviewed along the way, deciding where to pause and at what points the camera will leave the reporter and focus on what the reporter is seeing or pointing at. The reporter will often give the camera operator guidance as part of the commentary "and if we bring the camera round to look in this direction, you can see....."

A good walk and talk needs a confident and fluent reporter; a willing and enterprising camera operator; and a high degree of preparation, communication and cooperation between the two of them. It is not something a multiskilled reporter can attempt on his or her own.

Live reporting

In the age of 24-hour news, the ability to report live is an essential skill. Many television reporters (especially sports reporters) spend much more time broadcasting live than they do producing packaged news reports.

Much of what we have said about PTCs applies equally to a live report:

– Find a good location.
– Know what you want to say.
– Don't try to cover too much ground.
– Use simple, easy-to-understand language.
– Try to look and sound relaxed, natural and conversational.

To which we might add:

– Be clear with the programme production team at base what you can and can't do, and what they expect
     of you and when.

And as we have had occasion to say very many times before: the secret to delivering all of this successfully
is forethought and preparation.

Location

Everything we said in the section above on PTCs, about selecting a location with editorial relevance,
applies equally to live reporting from location. But there are other factors to bear in mind too, more practical than editorial. We touched on some of these in the section on live reporting for radio.

A PTC may be shot in just a few minutes, but a live location may be one where you will spend several
hours, maybe even days, reporting on a regular basis as your story develops. So it is important that it is
safe and secure and sustainable over a period. If you are lucky, you may have a production team, even a
professional safety adviser, to help with the selection and security of a location.

Apart from looking for a location with a good live shot in the background, the key things to think about
are people and the weather. Both can be unpredictable.

It will be tempting to get as close as you can to the scene of your story. But getting too close could expose
you to risk if large numbers of people suddenly start moving in your direction. To some, the sight of a
television camera is like a red rag to a bull, and you might find yourself in a very uncomfortable situation
if they start to surround and harangue you. Even relatively harmless activities like standing behind you
while you are on air, pulling faces or displaying placards, will be distracting at best, and may feel threatening. Find somewhere that feels safe even if it is a bit further away, with a way out if you need to leave
in a hurry. Somewhere above ground level may be a good option. A roof may give you a good wide shot
and attractive background to your story. But it may feel less attractive if the weather is changeable. You
don't want to be broadcasting in a gale or in the pouring rain – unless you are doing a story about the
weather. Make sure you have a large umbrella with you, preferably displaying the name of your company,
but failing that with no branding at all.

Communication

A high degree of communication between those at the live location and those running the output in the
studio is absolutely vital. There are basic things you will need to know: When do they want their next live
two-way with you? How long do they want? Are there any new developments of which you need to be
aware? And there are things that they need to know from you: Is the story moving? Do you have anything
new to say? Is anything expected which would make it a good time or a bad time for them to cross to you?

Then there is the detailed communication that is needed for each individual contribution. *You* want to know: Who is the presenter? What questions am I likely to be asked? Can you tell me what will be in the introduction/cue before you come to me? *They* want to know: What questions can we usefully ask you? Is there anything we should be avoiding? What are our cue words for playing in clips or pre-recorded material you sent earlier?

If you have a conversation, or conversations, along these lines, you are in a good place to start planning your time and what you are going to say. Perhaps you have half an hour before you are next going to be on air. That gives you time to grab a bite to eat or a drink, or make some calls and try to find out more about what is happening with the story. You know that you are going to be asked two or three questions, and you have a good idea what those questions will be – indeed, you will probably have suggested them. So you can begin to prepare what you are going to say. You might make some brief notes of the things you want to be sure to include. You might think of one or two striking phrases that will make your reporting more vivid and interesting. You will want to check your appearance before you go on air to make sure nothing is out of place that will distract the viewer. And you will want to prepare yourself to perform: a piece of live television is a performance, and you want to appear both knowledgeable and authoritative about your story, but also enthused by it and eager to convey that enthusiasm to your audience.

Content

What you say in your live contribution will depend of course on the story and what you know about it. As with radio two ways, the first question is likely to be something straightforward, asking you for the latest details, or anything new that you have to report. You will be expected to include some background and context at some stage, and perhaps suggest when we can expect more details or developments and what they might be. None of this should present any particular problems to you, as you will have been across the story for some time, and indeed, it may not have changed much since you were last on air. If you are covering some event known about in advance such as a speech, a press conference or a demonstration, you may find yourself doing quite a lot of previewing – talking about the event before anything has actually happened. You may feel that on occasion you are not doing much more than filling space, treading water until you have something tangible to report. But that is all part of continuous news broadcasting, and if you have done your homework and armed yourself with plenty of background information, you should not have much difficulty talking round the story while you are waiting for the action to unfold.

The usual rules apply:

– Think about what you want to say, and what information and insights you want to include.
– Break that material down into manageable chunks. Don't try to pack too much detail and too many thoughts into each answer: the viewers won't follow you, and you will sound rushed and confused.
– Try to restrict yourself to one, or at most two, points per answer.
– Keep your answers tight – 30"–40" is a reasonable length to aim for, although of course not all your answers have to be the same length. You will find you can say quite a lot in that time. Once you get past 45" you are in danger of losing the viewer's attention or straying off the point you are trying to make.
– If the studio wants to signal to you that they want you to end your contribution, you will hear a voice on the talkback saying "wrap" or "ten seconds" or just "ten". This is a sign to you that you have ten seconds to wind up whatever you are saying and bring your thoughts to an elegant conclusion. So it is important that you understand what ten seconds feels like, and how much you can say in that time. It does not sound long, but it is actually plenty long enough for you to come to a halt in an organised and unhurried way. This basic skill is one that many reporters never master. They either come to an abrupt halt in mid-sentence, or carry on regardless for another half a minute. Teaching

yourself how to wrap up in ten seconds can be done easily with a stopwatch and a little practice. It is well worth the effort.

– Use simple words and everyday speech, and try to talk as if the interview is really no more than a conversation between you and the presenter. A good way of doing this is to pick up the wording of the question with the first words of your response.

– Remember that you are the reporter at the scene, the eyes and ears of the viewer. So use the first person, singular or plural: "I've just come from the square where the demonstrators are gathering......"; "I've just spoken to the main organiser of the event, and she told me......"; "From here we can see the weather rolling in from the east, and more rain is forecast"; Tell the audience things they cannot see or hear: "it is now bitterly cold", "the smell of smoke is still hanging in the air", "the mood feels threatening". All of this reinforces the sense of place – that you are reporting directly for us from the scene. It humanises the exchange of what can sometimes be quite dry information.

– Remember that you are performing, and always sound engaged and enthusiastic about what you are saying and describing. Unless you inject some energy into your delivery, you will come across as underpowered or uninterested.

– Remember not to assume knowledge on behalf of the viewer. This may be the fifth time you have done a live report on this story, but you cannot assume that your viewers have heard any of the previous four. Or if they have, that they have absorbed or remembered much from them. Treat the fifth as though it is the first, although you can refer back to your previous contributions: "when you were with us here an hour ago, the square was deserted; now it is filling up very rapidly".

Walking

In a conventional down-the-line interview, you will look steadfastly at the camera all the way through. (If this is pre-recorded for some reason, it is known as an "as live".) But you can turn and point or move if the circumstances warrant – and provided whoever is behind the camera is completely aware of what you are going to do. Any such move, however straightforward, needs to be discussed and rehearsed beforehand if it is to look slick and natural as opposed to wooden and clunky.

A simple example would be if you were talking to the presenter, but wanted to share with the viewer the scene behind you. You might say something like: "let me give you a taste of how things look here in the square as the crowds gather". While you are doing that, you will naturally turn to one side and might gesture with your hand. The camera operator moves from the focus on you, following your hand and then offering a wide shot of the scene. You will keep talking while the viewer is looking at this shot, even though you are by now out of vision. And then you do the whole procedure in reverse: the camera comes back to you, until we are back to you reporting directly at the lens in a medium close-up.

This is a simple procedure, and you will have seen it executed dozens of times. But it still needs talking through and rehearsing if it is to come off to its best effect. And if you are going to be walking somewhere during the two-way, more practice is required. As with a PTC, make sure that you are walking for a reason – that we are going to see something or meet somebody, that you are going to come to a place that relates to your storytelling and that you are not just moving around randomly. You will probably say a few words before you start moving, then set off slowly so that the camera – and the viewer – can establish where you are and then follow you. It is a simple enough manoeuvre for you to do, but it requires a lot of skill from the person behind the camera. The only way to make sure it works is by an agreement on what you are going to do and then as many rehearsals of the moves as you need or have time for.

Interviewing

It may be that the destination of your walk is a person you have arranged to interview as part of your slot. This person will not be a professional broadcaster and so will need briefing on what to expect. Talk them through in advance exactly what is going to happen and position them in such a way that the camera can see them over your shoulder, with both their eyes visible. If you have a group of guests, arrange them in an angled line so that you can move down the line with the camera following you. If they are standing in a circle, your camera operator will be in a world of pain.

Floated pictures and clips

The editorial team in the studio may ask you to talk over some pictures that they have cut, or in and out of some clips. Those clips may even have been quarried from interviews that you yourself have done earlier in the day.

In both cases, the video will be played in from the studio and although you will be able to hear the audio, you will not be able to see anything, so to that extent you are flying blind. To make this work, you will need very clear information from the studio.

If they have some pictures that they intend to run – or float – while you are talking, you need to know what those pictures show and how long they will be running. You will not be able to talk in detail to the pictures if you have not seen them, but you will be able to refer in general terms to what you know the audience will be seeing. You will usually hear the studio say "on pictures" to indicate that they have started running the float, and that is your cue to start talking about the things you have been told the images show.

To talk in and out of clips requires more of an exchange of information on either side. This is another instance where communication is vital so that both ends of the operation have a crystal-clear understanding of the plan of action. *You* will need to know who is speaking in the clip or clips, and anything relevant about them – their job title, and/or the reason they are associated with the story. You also want to know what they are saying in the clip, how long it is and what the last words are, so that you know when it is time for you to pick up again when they have finished speaking. It is then your job to work out a form of words to introduce that clip. What *the studio* needs to know is when to start playing it. So when you have roughed out your introduction, you must tell the studio the words to look out for that will indicate to them that they need to run the clip.

Here's an example. You are reporting from the scene of a train crash. The programme team at base has done an interview, and they want you to talk into and out of a clip of it in your next live two-way.

> **They tell you:** the interviewee is George Jones, he is a rail safety expert and he is saying that signal failure is the likeliest case of the crash. The clip is 15" long, and ends with the words "that will be the job of the inquiry".

> **You tell them:** you will cue in the clip by talking about the possible cause, and they should start playing the clip when they hear you say "he told us what he thought might have caused the crash".

> **Live on the air, you say:** "Although everyone here at the scene is concentrating on the rescue operation, thoughts are already turning to the possible reasons for the accident. Earlier, we spoke to rail safety expert George Jones and he told us what he thought might have caused the crash".

> **That is the studio's cue to play in the clip.** You listen to it for 15" and when you hear Mr Jones say: "that will be the job of the inquiry", you know it is finished and so you pick up again where you left off and say something like: "Rail safety expert George Jones. I've been talking to rescue teams here, and they are telling me......"

Expect the unexpected

If something goes wrong during your live interview, be prepared to ride with it. The chances are that none of the following things will happen, but they can and do on occasion. The important thing is to acknowledge them and try to handle them as calmly and as professionally as you can. On no account pretend that they are part of some overarching plan, or that they are simply not happening.

Here are some of the problems that can befall the live reporter:

You suddenly find that you cannot hear what is being said to you in your earpiece

Your instinctive reaction will be to start fiddling with your earpiece. The studio will notice that and realise that you might have a problem. They will alert the presenter. Don't say anything, because your mic will probably still be on, so your plaintive "I can't hear you" might interrupt whatever the presenter is saying. You have little alternative but to stand there looking at the camera – don't move, you may still be in vision on screen – and hope either that your sound comes back, or that the programme switches to another item.

Someone starts to move you along from your location because you are in the way. Members of the public try to disrupt your broadcast

These are situations in which clearly matters are moving outside your control, and the sooner you are able to hand back and get off the air the better. If you are in physical danger, you need to protect yourself, and there is the possibility of bad language or unpleasant scenes being broadcast. Again, you would hope that the studio would be quick to pick up that you have a problem and switch to another item. If not, try to keep cool and say something like "I think we are about to be moved on from this location, so for the time being let me hand you back to the studio", or "our position here is coming under pressure from some of the demonstrators, so for now let me hand you back to the studio". It is easy to say and hard to do, but your aim is to keep your cool and hold the fort until you are off the air.

The presenter asks you a question you were not expecting and cannot readily answer

I can do no better here than quote from one of the texts I recommend to broadcast journalists: *The Television News Handbook* by Vin Ray. Details are at the back of this book.

Ray notes that there can sometimes be a tension between reporters sweating in the field against a host of logistical and editorial problems, and presenters who have all sorts of stuff going on in their earpieces all the time and have several plates spinning as they try to keep the programme running smoothly. That can mean that presenters are not always as well briefed as they would like to be, and can ask hapless reporters in the field questions for which they are not prepared and do not know the answer.

If this happens, one trick is to deflect the question: "That's something a lot of people here would like to be able to answer" before moving on to safer ground. Another is ignore the question altogether, and try to get the interview back on to the expected track: "I think the *real* question here is whether….." An alert presenter will realise what has happened and take the reporter's cue.

A presenter may ask you for your opinion on some aspect of the story. It might be something benign – "how long is the hearing expected to last?" – but it may be an invitation to you to comment on some aspect of the story you are reporting. As with all your work, be careful not to express your own opinion. In a live setting, it is all too easy to wander into the realms of speculation or comment. Offering judgements is fine: "it looks as though there are still plenty of disputed areas, and these talks are likely to continue for some time yet. The points at issue seem to be these….." This kind of information and background helps the audience, and you are not expressing a view one way or the other. If asked for an opinion, deflect. So in the unlikely event that your presenter says: "the government has got this completely wrong, hasn't it?", you would answer along these lines: "their critics would certainly say so, but ministers argue……" Or, to flip it: "the government would strongly deny that, but their critics say…." If you are going to report opinions, make sure they are attributable to someone, and not to yourself.

Here is Vin Ray's Top Ten list of the complaints reporters make about presenters, in order of frequency (some of which, it must be said, are no fault of the presenter):

1. They ask you to describe what you cannot see, where you are not located and where you have not been.
2. They do not appear to listen to the answer given.
3. They steal the first thing you told them you were going to say and use it in their introduction.
4. They ask questions that include the answer.
5. They repeat the same question in a different form.
6. They introduce you in the wrong location.
7. They include inaccurate statements in the question.
8. They ask long mumbled questions down a distant line.
9. They make a statement rather than asking a question.
10. They get your name wrong.

As a television reporter you will no doubt have cause to vent about some or all of these problems somewhere along the line. Then you become a presenter and start to see the world in quite a different way.

19
The print journalist

a changing role.....case study 1: the weekly newspaper....case study 2: the regional newspaper.....case study 3: the national newspaper.....conclusions

A changing role

Is there such a thing as a print journalist any more? The UK still has an active and varied – if declining – newspaper and magazine industry, but fewer and fewer of the journalists it employs work solely for the printed product. Almost all are also expected to produce content for websites, apps or social media accounts. Even the job title is disappearing, as those working across media in this way are increasingly known as content producers or digital producers. In some large newspaper groups, a content editor may have oversight and responsibility for a group of titles, and merged content teams might also work across a range of publications within the group.

This reflects both cost cutting and the wider shift of priorities, referred to frequently in this book, away from physical copies and towards greater digital content. More and more news organisations are undergoing radical organisational change, with digital-led operations and increased working from home, fully or part time. All are at different stages of this journey, but pressing on is the only option. There is no going back.

There is still a role, however, for print journalists, even if they need multiplatform skills too. The National Council for the Training of Journalists' (NCTJ's) most recent analysis of *Journalists at Work* – quoted in the Preface to this book – found that more than half the working journalists in the UK were primarily engaged in producing material for publication in print. They may be doing other things as well, and the tide of history may be against them, but this is still a very large and active sector of British journalism. So it remains important to understand how print journalism works – not least because so many of the core skills apply across all journalistic platforms.

The first journalistic activity that many courses address is how to construct the basic unit of journalism: a straightforward news report, of the sort that might appear on a website or in a newspaper. It is an exercise that offers an ideal model for learning the first principles and practice of reporting. Whichever career path you follow, the ability to produce an accurate, factual and crisp written account is the foundation from which everything else can flow. Once you have mastered these fundamentals, you have a firm base from which to diversify into different sorts of writing on different platforms. We looked at this process in detail in Chapters 9 and 10.

In the traditional print newsroom production model, the reporter is assigned a story by the news editor or content editor. Once the story is written, it goes back to that editor. If approved, it then passes to the sub-editors. Their job is to prepare it for publication: correcting any errors, doing any necessary rewriting,

writing the headline, making sure the story fits the design of the page and the hole allotted to it by the chief sub-editor, and generally polishing the look of the story within the page.

The role of the reporter in this production process is therefore in the early stages – gathering the necessary information and then writing the story. Once the newsdesk is happy with it, the reporter and the story part company. The story proceeds through other stages on its way to eventual publication while the reporter moves on to the next assignment.

In this model, which is how most newspaper newsrooms functioned right into the 21st century, and in some cases still do, the story passes through several pairs of hands – the reporter, the news editor, the chief sub-editor and then the sub-editor, and probably the editor or deputy editor as a final pair of eyes. Some of them may handle it more than once. At each stage there is a level of scrutiny and checking designed to ensure that the finished story is as accurate and as well presented as possible.

New technology and financial pressures have meant that this model no longer works for many newspapers. Processes have been streamlined, teams merged, entire layers stripped out. A story passes through fewer stages in its life cycle, and so there are fewer checks and balances, fewer opportunities to spot and weed out errors. Priorities change, and producing a story for print may be secondary to publishing it online. This puts an added onus on the reporter to make sure the story is right in the first place. Of course, you will always want to do everything you can to deliver a story that is properly researched, accurate and well-written. That should always be your goal. But because the distance between the reporter and publication is generally shorter today than it once was, your ability to do that is more vital than ever.

Different newspapers have responded to the challenges of digital in different ways, and there is no longer any typical model. So this chapter looks at three contrasting examples of how things are developing in the print world, and how the role of the print journalist is affected in different ways. We look at a local weekly newspaper, where the emphasis is still very much on the printed product rather than the website content. We look at a national paper with a very highly developed online presence, but a working model in which journalists work on either the paper or the website, and there is little overlap. And we look at a regional digital-first operation in which most of the journalists concentrate on the online content, and a small dedicated team works separately to produce the printed paper, using a significant amount of material that was originally written for the website.

These examples offer a cross-section of the different organisational models that currently co-exist, and demonstrate that the role of the reporter is different depending on where you are working. What they have in common is that they are all moving away to a greater or lesser degree from the model of a single printed product – a model that functioned for well over 150 years before the arrival of the internet.

Case study 1: the weekly newspaper. The *Maidenhead Advertiser*

The *Maidenhead Advertiser*, known locally as the 'Tiser, was founded in 1869 and is based in the Berkshire town of that name. It is published on a Thursday, and has a circulation of around 15,000 – some distributed free, some paid for. Its sister papers, the *Windsor and Eton Express* and the *Slough Express*, are also produced in the Maidenhead office, with common content where the geographical patches overlap. The Windsor and Slough papers are published on a Friday. Overall the circulation area spreads from Reading in the west to Heathrow Airport in the east, and from Marlow in the north to Ascot in the south. It's a large area.

The *Advertiser* is unusual, in that it is an independent paper with the status of a charitable trust, run by a family who have owned the paper for almost the whole of its existence. It is not part of any of the big conglomerates that between them own hundreds of titles – although it is printed on a Newsquest press in Oxford.

Maidenhead is a riverside town on the Thames, 25 miles west of London and with good transport links east and west via the M4 and M40 motorways and a regular rail service. These links, and its proximity to Heathrow Airport only 12 miles away, are the source of many of its regular stories – Crossrail, motorway widening, Heathrow third runaway. Its closeness to Windsor gives it a strong interest in Royal stories, and it enjoyed a brief period in the national political spotlight while its MP, Theresa May, was Prime Minister. Another big running story is the regeneration of the town centre and the development of new housing.

The *Advertiser* is large by weekly paper standards – its standard size is 72 pages per issue. That will include anything up to 40 pages of news, with another five pages of leisure and lifestyle and 8–10 pages of sport. The reporting staff comprises an editor, deputy editor, chief sub-editor, around half a dozen reporters and two or three sub editors, not all of them full time. Each of the reporters has a local patch to cover, with a dedicated page to fill each week, as well as contributing to the main news pages. The paper needs well over 100 stories a week to fill all those pages, and each reporter is expected to produce about five page leads per week. These stories will be around 300 words in length, though more space will be made available if need be.

As an independent, the paper does not have the resources of some other local papers. It does not have a subscription to the Press Association news feed, for example. This means everything in the paper is generated in-house, which puts a lot of pressure on the editorial team. Everyone has more than one job: the editor at time of writing, James Preston, writes the motoring column; his deputy writes about film. The Chief Sub is also a sports reporter. The Chief Reporter mentors the junior reporters. The paper is lucky in one respect, in that its office is still in the town centre. So many local papers have found themselves banished from the hearts of their towns to soulless industrial estates on the outskirts. A central location means the reporters find it easier to get out of the office to do their reporting. That can depend on staffing – if one or two reporters are ill or away, it puts significant extra pressure on the others and reduces their scope for getting out of the office.

The working week is built around the two press days – Wednesday for the Maidenhead paper, Thursday for Windsor and Slough. The top team tries to pace the effort through the week, in order to avoid a chaotic pile-up on press day. That means getting the less demanding stories, or those that will not change before publication day, out of the way as early as possible. The reporters will try to write those stories and fill their patch pages as soon as they can, and certainly by Monday. The sub-editors will also try to finish those pages in good time, and leave them on hold for any necessary updating later in the week. That clears the decks for a concentrated effort on the front 15–20 pages in the final couple of days.

Upcoming stories that are known about are registered in the diary and assigned by the editor. Reporters are also expected to generate their own material. Ideas are discussed at news meetings most days of the week. The local council – the Royal Borough of Windsor and Maidenhead – delivers plenty of stories each week, and reporters cover most of the evening committee meetings. They expect to work at least one evening a week and do a weekend duty every five to six weeks. Wednesday and Thursday are busy days as the clock ticks down to the 6pm deadline, when the paper is sent in the form of pdfs to the printers in Oxford.

The *Advertiser* has managed to retain most of the checking stages that help eliminate mistakes and make corrections before they get into the paper. Once written, stories are sent to a "Copy In" basket. The editor reads every story himself, making corrections and asking for clarifications. Then he puts the stories in a "Copy Ready" basket, which is when the sub-editors start work on putting them into the pages. The subs work with pre-designed templates – "page shapes" – but are able to change and redraw them as they wish. When the pages are finished, the editor looks at them again and asks the reporters to check pages as well, as a further insurance against mistakes. As James Preston says: "It can be a really good story, but if there's a typo in the headline no-one cares about the story". The pattern of production is going through a period of evolution, and moving to a system under which reporters type their stories directly into the page shape, as happens at some other local newspapers. This streamlines the sub-editing stage, although some worry that it dilutes the capacity to spot mistakes and rectify them.

The reporting staff on the paper are young – under the age of 30. Some will stay for extended periods; others take the traditional career view that a year or two on a weekly is a good stepping stone to other things. When a vacancy arises it is advertised. The typical recruits may come direct from an NCTJ-accredited university course, or have done their NCTJ Diploma as postgraduates. If they don't have shorthand at the speed of 100 words per minute, they are expected to acquire it rapidly. Shorthand is not optional. James Preston says: "It's absolutely essential. For a fast-paced newsroom to work, you need people who can turn copy round fast". Some of his young reporters are training for the NCTJ's senior level qualification, the National Qualification in Journalism (NQJ).

The paper does not expect its graduate recruits to have a lot of experience, but it likes to see evidence of work experience, or work produced and possibly published during the university or college course. Your NCTJ portfolio will be a help here. Journalistic prowess is tested at the interview with a practical exercise, such as producing a story based on a poorly written press release. Young reporters are not expected to be the finished article, and they are given advice and feedback at every stage. Most common faults are as these: a tendency to over-write, and a failure to come up with enough ideas for follow-up stories, new angles, Freedom of Information (FOI) request suggestions or finding a local twist on a national story. These are all things we have addressed in this book.

There is some photographer cover, but reporters are expected to take their own pictures when out on a story, transfer them into Photoshop from their phones and crop them ready for the sub-editors. Picture spreads sell papers and are a useful way of filling pages if the news is in short supply. There is also an online market for video footage if the story warrants it.

The *Maidenhead Advertiser* has a "digital-first" approach, in that the top news stories will appear first on the website. With the paper coming out only once a week, this makes obvious sense. At least half a dozen news stories are published on the site each day. There is also a presence on *Facebook* and *Twitter*. Reporters are encouraged to develop their individual accounts as well as contributing to those of the paper, and social networks are an effective way of interacting with the audience and delivering regular stories. Although the stronger stories get their first outing online, the main editorial effort still goes into the newspaper. Very strong stories may be held back, or appear online in only partial form, so that they can be given a bigger showing in the paper. Some of the online material is behind a paywall however, which means extra effort is required beyond the simple business of breaking a story. James Preston says: "we break stories online, but for those who want to pay we have to give them something that adds value". This may be longer or more detailed versions of the reports that appear in the paper.

If you are a reporter with a story to break, your first duty is to get it out online. This can be done directly, but it usually passes through a second pair of hands. After that, you update your social accounts, and then set about developing the story for its appearance in the main paper later in the week. A story that appears online on a Monday cannot appear in substantially the same form in the paper on a Thursday. It needs moving on with reaction or a new angle.

A commitment to accuracy is taken as read. "We drill it into reporters from the start", says Preston, "but we expect them to get it right first time. I really hate having to print corrections, even for minor things". This extends to spelling and grammar. "Some students really struggle with points of grammar. 'Its' and 'it's' seems to be a particular problem. People notice and they comment online."

The thing about reporters that annoys him most? "They won't pick up the phone! They say 'I've sent them an email', but emails are easy to ignore. Picking up the phone is much quicker and easier, but for some reason they don't like doing it."

Case study 2: the regional daily newspaper. The *Birmingham Mail*

The *Birmingham Mail* is published six days a week, covering Birmingham and the surrounding area. It has a circulation of about 15,000. There is also a weekly paper, the *Post*, and a Sunday paper, the *Sunday Mercury*. All three are produced in the Birmingham newsroom – although the sub-editors have the technical capacity to work from home. Many split their working week between home and the office. One lives nearly 200 miles away and works remotely all the time. As one sub-editor observes: "you can put a newspaper together on the moon as long as you've got the kit". During the coronavirus crisis, those remote working methods were tested to the full in all newsrooms.

The papers are owned by Reach plc, formerly Trinity Mirror, the UK's largest commercial publisher of national and regional titles. It also owns the *Daily Mirror*, the *Daily Express* and the *Daily Star*, and a number of large regional newspapers as well as many weekly titles.

Reach has made a conscious decision to embrace the digital revolution and has rebranded and reordered its operations to reflect that. The sign on the office door says *Birmingham Live* rather than *Birmingham Mail*. The printed papers form an important part of the operation, but the emphasis has shifted decisively towards the web and social networks. *Birmingham Live* has more than 30 accounts across social media platforms. In Chapter 13, we looked at what life is like as a digital journalist on *Birmingham Live*. Here we are concentrating on the work of those reporters working for the newspaper only.

This radical change of emphasis and focus away from print and towards digital has put Reach ahead of many of its counterparts in the rest of the UK. Others are already treading this path, and it is very likely that in the future, most if not all of the rest will follow.

The creation of *Birmingham Live* has had profound effects on the *Mail* and its sister papers, and by extension the reporters who work for them. For one thing, there are far fewer of them. The reporters who cover the main stories of the day are all employed by the *Live* operation. The newspaper has around half a dozen dedicated reporters of its own, who are directed at stories that will add value for the paper. They are expected to go and find those stories themselves. They are looking for off-diary pieces that might make longer news reports, sometimes called news features, or double-page spreads for the paper. This means that they are less troubled than most reporters by the tyranny of deadlines. Most of their stories will not be done from start to finish on the day, because they do not have an urgent news peg. The on-the-day news is being handled by the *Live* reporters. A piece done by a *Mail* reporter on a Monday, for example, might not appear in the paper until Thursday.

Nor are the reporters expected to version their stories for the website or any other part of the *Live* operation. It is up to the *Live* team to take the stories written for the newspaper and turn them into material that works for the digital audiences. In its turn, the *Mail* relies on the *Live* operation to deliver the news stories of the day. Here the process works in reverse, because that material has been designed for web and social publication, and will not usually be suitable for transferring directly into the pages of the paper. So the small team of subs working solely for the paper spend much of their time adapting or rewriting that copy and turning it into newspaper stories.

The *Mail* news editors have other resources at their disposal, beyond the work of the *Live* reporters: the news being generated in other parts of the Reach empire, and the Press Association news feed. The whole operation also benefits from a number of recent industry initiatives to improve reporting in neglected areas: there are six Local Democracy Reporters funded by the BBC under a national scheme, and two Community News Reporters paid for by a *Facebook* programme managed by the NCTJ. The *Live* operation is also supported by Google through its Laudable project, under which local news publishers work collaboratively on business models for podcasts and audio in local news.

The *Mail* pages are usually designed by the subs from a basic framework, once they have assembled the stories and the pictures in a form with which they are happy. They do not use pre-designed page templates as some other papers do, preferring to design the page around the available material rather than shoehorn a story and picture into a fixed design. An average day will see them filling about 20 pages of news and perhaps 8 of sport. The paper is being put together late into the evening, and does not go to press until about 11 o'clock, so there is plenty of scope for including late-breaking stories.

The dedicated *Mail* reporters have no responsibility to provide material for the digital platforms. They write for the paper only. They do not do on-the-day stories, or "spot news" as it is sometimes called. They will usually be senior reporters chasing off-diary stories on their own initiative. These might be 400–600 words for a page lead, perhaps rising to 1,000 words for a double-page spread. There are staff photographers, but the reporters are expected to take their own pictures if staffers are not available. They keep the desk informed of what they are doing, and they file their material direct to the sub-editors who are therefore the "second pair of eyes" in terms of checking and reworking the copy. This means there is only one checking stage between the reporter and publication, although sub-editors everywhere are generally a pretty rigorous bunch and demanding of high standards.

The *Mail's* reporters will usually have a couple of years' experience under their belts – typically at weekly newspapers or local news agencies, and preferably with an NCTJ qualification. The qualities the paper looks for are those that every junior reporter should be aspiring to. Here are some of the comments the senior managers made: they may remind you of things you have read in other chapters.

> People must have ideas. You can't come into a newsroom and expect to be given stories. We expect people to come to interviews, and to work, with loads of ideas for stories. We say: 'tell us your best ideas, the most important questions to ask and the people to answer them'.

> Reporters need to have an idea of the story beyond the words. They need to be aware of how their stories can be dressed up. No picture – no story. No headline – no story. It's important that they think pictures all the time. We sometimes get frustrated about their picture selection.

> They must understand our demographic. We cover many deprived areas, so stories around those issues always do well.

> Good journalists are also students of journalism. They read what other journalists are writing.

> At a junior level, we don't interview many people who haven't already had something published of their own such as a blog or some sports reporting.

> We're looking for enthusiasm, curiosity, a knowledge of news – what makes a good story and how to pitch it.

> We want people with some knowledge of current affairs and who understand what we do and are aiming for.

Case study 3: the national newspaper. The *Daily Mail*

The *Daily Mail* is the second largest of our national newspapers in terms of circulation (after the *Sun*, which it sometimes claims to have overtaken), selling just under a million copies a day. There are separate Scottish and Irish editions. Although like most newspapers, its sales are declining – by around 5 per cent a year – it has fared better than many of its competitors. The paper appears in a tabloid format and is aimed at the middle of the market – that demographic sometimes called "middle England" or "middle Britain". This is not a geographical reference, but is usually taken to mean aspirational middle-class people, politically in the centre ground or a little to the right of it. The *Mail* itself occupies this ground and advises its readers to vote Conservative at General Elections. These readers are typically in their 50s and 60s. The *Mail* caters for a younger market with *MailOnline*, one of the most-visited newspaper websites in the world. Unusually, the newspaper and the website are produced separately under different editorships, and cater for different audiences.

For the newspaper, the focus of activity in the early part of the working day is the newsdesk, where a team of four or five are at work early assembling a news list of the stories of the day. These stories will come from a very wide variety of sources, the most important of which are the paper's own reporting staff; other newspapers; television and radio output; news websites; the Press Association schedules and other agency material.

If you are a reporter working on the *Mail*, this is the time of day to pitch your story to the newsdesk. They are actively looking for material at this time, ahead of the morning editorial meeting. Later in the day, they become absorbed in the delivery of the stories and the production of the paper, and are less receptive to lengthy pitches. So if you want to sell a story idea, pick your moment. Remember there is no better time than on a slow news day. If the pace of news is slack, the premium on good ideas for news stories is much higher. So don't give up if things are slow. See it as an opportunity to fill the vacuum.

While the list of stories is being assembled, the newsdesk is talking to its reporting staff and getting them started on the stories that are likely to feature in the following day's paper. There is a group of specialist correspondents with expertise in politics, health, science and so on: they will be offering ideas and following up on those stories in which the desk is interested. The same process is happening with the "district" staff – reporters based around England covering regions such as the North West, the South West, the Midlands and Yorkshire. On top of that, there will be six to ten general reporters on duty in the building, waiting to be sent out on stories or to expand and rewrite agency copy.

The news list is just that – a list of the day's stories summarised in one line each and fitting on to a single page of A4. At the *Mail*, they prepare five such lists every day: for UK news, for foreign news, for City and financial news and for sport. The fifth is prepared by the picture desk, and is a list of the images available to support the stories on the other lists. The availability and quality of pictures are important features of the editorial decision-making process. A weak story might make it into the paper if the pictures are strong. A decent story might struggle if the pictures are weak. Pictures are as significant to newspapers as video is to television news; they are an integral part of the storytelling, and the element that makes the story most attractive and interesting to the reader or viewer.

The lists are ready for 11.30, when there is a meeting in the editor's office to run through them and discuss the stories of the day. At this stage, decisions are not being made about the relative merits of the stories, where they will appear in the paper and how they will be treated. The focus is much more on looking at the totality of what is around. The *Mail* has a voracious appetite: on a typical day, there will be 25 news pages to fill, not including the business and sports pages. That means finding 25 stories that are strong enough to be page leads, and another 50 or so stories besides. On the day of my visit, the news lists contained around 75 stories, about 40 of which appeared in the following day's paper.

As the day wears on, the focus shifts to the actual production of the stories. Once they are written, ideally by mid-afternoon, they are delivered into a "news basket" on the newsroom computer system. The newsdesk takes the first look at them. They may go back to the reporter if there is something missing, or something they want to check or don't understand. They may do some rewriting and tidying up if they think it is necessary. Not every story comes to fruition of course: some of them don't "make" if they turn out not to be true or not strong enough to warrant pursuing further. Others will prove stronger than first thought. And new stories are appearing all the time. These changing circumstances are discussed in regular verbal or email exchanges between newsdesk and reporter. Once the reporters have filed their stories, they are assigned others, or will look for more stories, for that day or later in the week.

By early afternoon, the focus of activity is shifting from the gathering of the news to the process of deciding what is going into the paper and where. The newsdesk briefs the night editor on what to expect, and the picture editor gives the night editor a detailed briefing on what pictures are available to illustrate the various stories. At another editorial meeting at 15.30, there is a further discussion, and after that the business of creating the next day's paper begins in earnest. The night editor is now joined in the newsroom by other senior editorial figures, making decisions about the relative merits of stories and where they should appear. Individual stories are handed over to sub-editors who will check them, rewrite where necessary, cut to length, commission any illustrative or design features they want and write a headline. Each page is gradually signed off, and the first edition is usually ready for printing by around 2145 in the evening. Throughout the whole of this time, new stories are coming in, and either being rejected or taking the place of those no longer considered strong enough. On the day of my visit, around 20 stories that were not on the radar by the time of the afternoon meeting broke later and were included in the next day's paper. So early to mid evening is a time of high productivity, quick thinking and decision-making and rapid adaptation to changing circumstances. It is not a time when the desk will welcome calls from you unless they are directly relevant to the stories that are then in production.

From the point of view of the reporter then, the key things are:

to offer your story, or be deployed on a story, as early as possible, certainly by late morning

to file your story in good time, preferably by mid to late afternoon

to ensure your story is accurate and properly researched: the newsdesk is entitled to expect that this will be the case

to flag up any legal issues you think might arise from your story, which can then be checked with the duty lawyer in London

to note future stories of which you may be aware, or follow-ups, for inclusion in the diary.

Most of the reporters employed by the *Daily Mail* will be seasoned and experienced hands. Working as a reporter on a national daily will not usually be your first job. However, the *Mail* does run its own trainee scheme, which recruits new young journalists. An NCTJ Diploma is a big advantage for applicants. For those who don't have a Diploma, the paper will arrange some training and shorthand lessons. All reporters are expected to have shorthand.

Although landing a trainee job at the *Daily Mail* is a huge achievement, it does mean that you have to take extra care with your work. This is a powerful national newspaper, and the effect of any errors you make will be magnified. The paper gives its trainees the opportunity for some slightly less exposed experience by sending them on secondment to the Irish or Scottish editions for a few months, or spending time with a district reporter. Working on copytasting and forward planning shifts in the main newsroom is another good way of absorbing experience and seeing at close quarters how the senior professionals go about their business.

I asked several senior members of the *Mail's* editorial team for their observations about the work of reporters, both trainee and fully fledged. I asked what mistakes reporters made most frequently, and what most irritated newsdesk and sub-editing staff. Here are some of their responses: again they echo points made in earlier chapters.

I hate reporters who, if they don't know much about a story, lack the willingness to check it out and research it properly.

There is no excuse for filing inaccurate copy. When the stories reach us they should be copper-bottomed and iron-clad.

I don't like slang or Americanese. The Mail is about accessible journalism but that doesn't mean we don't like good writing. We take pride in a well-written paper.

I have to rewrite intros more often than not.

It is an unforgiveable sin not knowing what is in your own paper. You should know the context of your story in terms of what our previous coverage looks like.

Too often reporters don't seem to know what the *Daily Mail* audience is. Young, highly educated metropolitan reporters have got to understand they are writing not for their friends but for a different audience entirely.

Think about the context of your story in Daily Mail Land in order to make it relatable to your audience.

Stick to your word count. A page lead is around 600 words. A picture story is about 300 words. I have one reporter who shall be nameless who is incapable of filing less than 1,000 words. So I have to start off by cutting nearly half the piece.

The people who drive me mad are those who don't read their own stories in the paper. They don't see what has been changed and so they make the same mistakes [breaches of house style] over and over again.

It is understandable that younger reporters do not get cultural references to things that happened before they were born. But if you don't get it, find out properly. Don't cut and paste ten pars of Wikipedia.

This last point came up several times in conversation. The context was a story that day about a long-running row between two famous pop singers of the 1970s and 1980s. Their names would have resonated strongly with *Mail* readers, but a young reporter could be forgiven for not having heard of either of them. If assigned the story, it would be a part of their research to find out, and to try to give the story its proper context. This is not done, as the senior *Mail* editor said, by cutting and pasting from Wikipedia. Nearly all the *Mail's* readers would have known of these two singers, and would immediately spot anything in the story that did not ring true.

Conclusions

Are there any general conclusions to be drawn from these three examples, representative of the main categories of British newspaper? Putting aside the variations of size and scale, each has a slightly different set-up, and there is a different relationship in each case between the printed newspaper and the online content. This reflects the varied nature of digital absorption across the print sector. What they have in common though shines clearly through the comments of senior journalists in each operation – and has nothing to do with the changes brought on by digital: a continuing commitment to the traditional values of good journalism, and an impatience and exasperation with journalists who fail to demonstrate those fundamental values.

In particular, they talk about accuracy, thoroughness and an understanding of the nature of the newspaper, the website and the readership. These are basic virtues that we discussed in the very early chapters of this book. They are not theoretical: they reflect the practice that is followed in every newsroom every day, and that you will be required to follow as a working journalist. They apply across the board, whether a paper is forging ahead with a digital-first approach, or whether it is still – for now at least – operating in a more traditional way.

20

The mobile journalist: the freelance journalist

the mobile journalist…..equipment…..recording audio on a smartphone…..recording video on a smartphone…..still images….working from home…..the freelance journalist…..pros and cons….. starting out…..something for nothing?…..money…..tax…..copyright.

This chapter looks at different aspects of working on your own – as a self-contained multimedia operator, as a journalist working from home (WFH) and as a freelance. All these ways of operating have their attractions and their disadvantages.

Mobile journalism – or MOJO – is a feature of all kinds of news reporting. The capabilities of the smartphone mean you can record and edit all sorts of content without the need for a lot of cumbersome and expensive gear. All organisations make use of lightweight technologies, even if only as part of a larger operation. A mobile phone is often used as a second or even third camera on a television shoot, for example, even if the main camera is a piece of high-end kit being used by a professional camera operator. But some journalists have taken these possibilities a step further and work *only* with a mobile phone, supported by a laptop and a few accessories. They are called mobile journalists. They are still staff reporters, rather than freelances, but they work self-sufficiently.

Working from home is increasingly common, and requires you to have the technical equipment and connections to work as effectively from your house as you would in the office. It also requires a degree of self-discipline and a temperament that allows you to work alone for much of the time without feeling isolated and stressed.

Freelance journalists are self-employed, marketing their services either by working casual shifts, or selling features and other work to a range of publications. Entering the freelance world can be daunting, but some people enjoy being their own boss and find that the freelance option is the best fit for their lifestyle.

The mobile journalist

Wherever you are working, you will often use your mobile phone as a camera, an audio recorder or a video recorder, to provide material across the media. This may be through choice, it may be of necessity. As a mobile journalist, this is the way you work all the time. Mobile journalists film and record entire features, sometimes entire programmes, using only the phone and a number of accessories designed for use with a mobile. They can also edit on the phone, but for anything more complicated than a simple clip, most prefer to download the material to some form of editing software and work on a laptop.

In terms of how the material is gathered, the process is very similar to that for other platforms, particularly when it comes to recording audio and video. If you want to try your hand at mobile journalism be sure to read the chapters about radio and television journalism first. They cover the fundamentals of handling audio and video. In terms of principles and practice, much of what is described there also applies to working solely with a smartphone. The editorial process of coming up with the ideas and developing them, then gathering material and constructing your piece is unchanged.

MOJO is highly appealing for young journalists. You probably already have the phone, so your only additional expenses are data charges and the costs of subscribing to whatever apps you feel you need to make yourself completely self-contained in production terms. Today's phones are incredibly versatile, and that gives you the precious gift of independence. If you have a great idea, you can go out and pursue it on your own without a commission, without assistance and at very little cost. Even if you do not have a ready market for it, the practice will be invaluable – and you can self-publish it on *YouTube* or *Vimeo* and share it on your website and on social media. If you are looking for a job, a body of work built up in this way can form an invaluable part of your CV. Even if your prospective employers are not looking to hire a mobile journalist as such, they will be interested in the range of skills you have amassed while creating your stories. And the ability to show initiative and to find and deliver your own stories is always greatly sought after.

But it is not as easy as it might sound. Going solo can be liberating and encourage your creative juices to flow, but it also means that you have to do everything yourself. You do not have anyone to shoulder the burden of any part of the process, or to act as a sounding board. You have to come up with all the ideas and organise all the logistics. Thinking about your story, warming up your interviewees and setting up your kit all at the same time require a high degree of concentration and organisation.

Equipment

Although a smartphone (iPhone or Android) is in theory pretty much all you need for gathering content, there are some accessories that will make your work a very great deal easier. They are usually small and portable and most full-time mobile journalists reckon that everything should fit into a rucksack. Lugging a load of heavy and cumbersome kit around defeats the object of the exercise. Here are some of the things you might want to pack into that rucksack.

– *Phone charger*
– *Auxiliary power pack*
– *Spare memory cards/SIM cards/plenty of memory, depending on what sort of phone you are using*
– *Casing rig with handles* – a case your smartphone can fit into, to allow you to hold it steady while you are filming
– *Lenses* – different lenses can be clipped over the phone's existing camera to give you a wider range of options – everything from wide group shots to close-up detail
– *Collapsible tripod* – so that your phone can be self-standing and stable during filming
– *Selfie stick* – to increase your range and variety of shot
– *Foldable keyboard* – to attach to your phone if you need to write scripts on location
– *Headphones* – to reassure you that the recording is working, and to give you an idea of the sound quality
– A *separate mic* – will give you better audio quality than that offered by the phone's own inbuilt mic. This is especially true if you are recording video at the same time, which means that your phone will be some distance from the source of the sound. The quality of the audio will suffer, and may not be good enough for radio broadcasting. You can attach the mic to the casing via a "shoe" – in effect creating a miniature rig
– *Windshield* – if using a separate mic

– A *battery-operated gimbal* – allows you to film on the move and to pan up/down and left/right or tilt up and down

– When you have gathered your material, you will probably need some *software*, which you have to pay for, to increase functionality – for publishing, or if you want to do more sophisticated editing.

Recording audio on a smartphone

– Make sure the phone is fully charged.

– Put your phone into *Airplane* or *Flight* mode before you start recording, and turn on the *Do Not Disturb* feature. This will stop your phone making unwanted noises if someone calls or messages you while you are recording. You will need to reverse the process afterwards if you are sending your material straight away via wifi.

– Your smartphone will have an inbuilt microphone. Find out where it is – in the case of the widely used iPhone, it is at the base of the device. Keep your hands clear of it. To record yourself, hold the phone to your ear, as you would when making a call, or horizontally under your chin. Do not hold it horizontally next to your mouth, as it is likely to distort.

– If you are interviewing someone by phone, try to persuade them to record themselves on their own phone while they are talking, and then send the audio to you afterwards. Then you have both ends of the interview in good quality and can edit them together.

– As with all audio recording, look for an external environment or one indoors with a soft acoustic, such as a furnished room with carpets and curtains. Recording in large or empty rooms or kitchens with wooden floors can create the impression of an echo on the recording.

– Use the windshield when outside if need be. If you don't have one, try using a sock or soft material like a handkerchief. If you don't have a separate mic but are unhappy with the sound quality, try using the mic that is on the headphones that came with the phone.

– If you are using an iPhone, there is an app for recording audio called "Voice Memos". Although serviceable, it does not allow you hear or monitor what you are recording. So you must listen back straight away to make sure your recording is there, and that you are happy with the quality.

– To set levels on an iPhone, hit the red button to begin recording, and you will see a waveform on your screen, which will move up and down depending on the loudness of the audio. If it is too high or too low, your only way of adjusting it is to move the phone closer to, or further away from, the source of the audio.

– On iPhones, a yellow box at the bottom of the screen enables you to locate start and finish points ("ins and outs") for audio clips. Use *Trim* to save the audio *within* the yellow markers as a clip. To make an internal edit, use *Delete* to *remove* the area inside the yellow markers. There is no *Undo* facility, so you might want to save your recording by tapping the three dots on the screen to make a duplicate before you begin editing.

– If you want to explore beyond the capabilities of Voice Memos, there are other apps with much more functionality such as *Audio Memos*, *Voice Record Pro* and *Ferrite*, which can build mixed, multitrack audio packages.

Recording video on a smartphone

– Make sure the phone is fully charged.

– Clean the lens.

– Put your phone into *Airplane* or *Flight* mode before you start recording, and turn on the *Do Not Disturb* feature. This will stop your phone making unwanted noises if someone calls or messages you while you are recording. You will need to reverse the process afterwards if you are sending your material straight away via wifi.

– Put the screen on maximum brightness so that you do not misjudge the exposure.
– Make sure you have enough storage. Video files quickly become very large. Five gigabytes is a good minimum.
– Decide which ratios you are going to use. Landscape mode is a default for traditional video. But some social networks will require square or vertical ratios. If you have a choice, you will generally get better results with the phone held horizontally rather than vertically.
– In a dark environment, turn on the room lights or move closer to natural light.
– If you don't have any steadying device such as a case, tripod or gimbal, try to keep the phone stable by leaning against a wall or pillar, or holding it firmly with both hands.
– The lens on the back of the camera is of a better quality than the one on the front. But the front camera can be preferable for a piece to camera (PTC) because you can frame your shot more accurately and see what it looks like as you are filming. The danger of using the back camera for a PTC is that you cannot see whether or not the shot is properly framed, and you will not know until you review it afterwards.
– When recording a PTC, look at the camera lens and not the screen. Remember that you are not having a conversation on the phone, you are filming a piece of video for a news report. Project clearly and make sure you deliver with energy and expression. Otherwise your PTC will feel underpowered.
– There are options for different shots, such as slow motion or time lapses. Both require you to film over a longer period. If you use the zoom function, you might lose some clarity of image.
– If using an iPhone, go to *Video* and tap *Edit* to make a clip. Move either end of the yellow trim window to set your in and out points. Tap *Play* to review and then tap *Done* if you're happy. If you aren't, tap *Revert* to go back to the original.
– To go further than this basic top and tail option it is advisable to turn to one of many third-party apps on the market.

To send your video to someone else, the best tool to use is *Telegram*. Unlike other messenger apps, it allows you to send video in an uncompressed form and to operate across several devices, rather than being tied to a single device.

Still images

– Clean the lens.
– Check in your *Settings* the format your photo will be taken in. On an iPhone you will usually select *most compatible*.
– Use Landscape as a default – although for social media you can use Portrait too.
– The phone's automatic settings will find a good focus, level of brightness and exposure. By tapping on the screen you can make any tweaks that you think will improve the shot.
– You can zoom by putting two fingers on the screen and widening them out, but be aware that you may suffer a loss of focus in the process.
– Use *High Dynamic Range (HDR)* mode when there is contrasting light and shade in the same shot.
– If you don't have any steadying device such as a case, tripod or gimbal, try to keep the phone stable by leaning against a wall or pillar, or holding the phone firmly with both hands.
– Gently tap the shutter release button to take a photo, or hold it down to take a burst of photos – numerous images in quick succession from which you can choose the one you like best.
– Panoramas taken with the phone held upright show much more of your location than the landscape photo. Turn the phone horizontally or scan upwards to show more of a tall building.
– When it comes to sharing your photos, options include email, social media and cloud sharing sites. What you see on your device will depend on the apps you have, and services you have signed up to.

Working from home

You do not have to be a mobile journalist or a freelance to work from home, part or all of the time. WFH was becoming more prevalent in journalism before the coronavirus pandemic, but government lockdowns accelerated the trend. Employers discovered that more of the production process could be done remotely than they had perhaps realised. Many journalists with access to the right software, communicating via any of a number of video-conferencing tools and other channels such as Slack, can operate at home pretty much as they do while in the office. Increased WFH is part of the long-term consequences of the virus. For example, three quarters of staff at the *Daily Mirror* and *Daily Express* now work from home permanently

Managers have in the past been suspicious of allowing staff to work from home, believing that they would not work as hard or as conscientiously when left to their own devices. In fact, studies have shown that productivity can actually increase with home working. For some people, the danger of WFH is an inability to switch off – working too much rather than too little.

The advantages are obvious. The biggest will probably be waving goodbye to the daily commute, which will save you huge amounts of both time and money. It also offers the chance of greater flexibility, so you can work around the school run for example, or a daily exercise session. Depending on the production process in which you are working, you might be able to adjust your working hours to suit your metabolism – if you are a morning person or an evening person, for example.

There are downsides too: journalists are a gregarious bunch and most enjoy the cut and thrust of life in the newsroom. WFH can be a solitary experience if you live alone or are going to be spending large parts of the day working alone. You will miss the company, and might feel stressed and anxious. It may be possible for you to arrange to spend part of the week in the office and the rest WFH.

If you are going to be spending any amount of time WFH, make sure you set yourself up properly to do so as efficiently and easily as possible. This goes far beyond having the right technical equipment and a secure internet connection. It is about looking after your physical and mental health and well-being.

Ten top tips:

> set up a dedicated workspace where you can operate without distractions. Even if you live alone, the kitchen table is not a practical idea. Setting up in a study or a spare room, or even a dedicated work area within a living room will help you differentiate between work space/time and non-work space/time.

> if you live with others or have a family, discuss with them how to make it work, and set some boundaries.

> make sure you can work comfortably and ergonomically, with a proper adjustable chair. The monitor should be at eye level and about an arm's length in front of you, with the keyboard/mouse comfortably to hand.

> when you are WFH, you lose all the daily milestones of office life – the journey to and from work, meetings, meal breaks and so on. So create new ones: have your working day mapped out such that you can do what needs to be done, but also have time to eat and take some exercise.

> don't spend hours in front of the computer screen. Take regular short breaks to stretch and walk around – 5–10 minutes every hour.

> to avoid confusing your sleep patterns, get up and go to bed at roughly the same time each day. When you get up, get washed and dressed as though you were going to work – don't spend the whole day in your night clothes. When you have finished for the day, stop reading emails and checking your phone and do something else to help you wind down, especially in the hour or so before you go to bed. It is easy to feel that you must be 'on' all the time: you don't.

> regulate your meal times. It is very tempting to spend the whole day snacking from the fridge. Prepare your meals in advance, have set times for meal breaks and do not eat at your desk.

drink plenty of water and go easy on the caffeine.

crucially, **stay in touch with your colleagues.** They will probably be feeling the same as you. Talk over the phone if you can rather than by email, and take part in any organised video calls. It is important to retain your connection to your mates and to the mother ship.

If you are struggling, tell someone about it. Do not suffer in silence. If WFH does not suit you, try to avoid it.

The freelance journalist

Journalists come to freelance careers by a number of different routes. Most often, they have first worked as full-time journalists for some time, and decided to branch out on their own. As a freelance you control when, how and how much you work. You can decide to work in one of two ways: as a casual, doing shifts with a number of organisations and being paid by the day; or as a writer or multimedia producer selling ideas and having them commissioned, again by a range of outlets. In this model, you are paid by the piece.

Anyone can set themselves up as a freelance journalist without an NCTJ Diploma or any other form of formal training. In practice, it is hard to get shifts and to sell your material if you do not have any experience, professional qualifications or profile to fall back on. For those who want to start their careers as freelances, it is advisable to build up a body of work online, as discussed in Chapter 13. You can create a portfolio of self-published work that will serve as a kind of CV when you pitch your ideas to potential commissioners.

An alternative, and difficult, path is to earn money by dint of establishing a high-profile online presence and developing a reputation as an influencer, vlogger, podcaster and so on. The difficult bit is not so much attracting an audience, but persuading people to pay for what you are providing – or possibly pay to advertise on your site. For a site that specialises in serious journalism, this is very hard to pull off. For something more lifestyle based, the chances may be higher. But it is a high-risk strategy, and you would be well advised to have a contingency plan in case you could not make it pay.

Newsletters are an increasingly common addition to the means by which a freelance can self-publish to a defined audience and bring in some income, perhaps by subscriptions. But again it is a risky strategy, and almost certainly not a way to make a living on its own.

Before you embark on a freelance career, do some calculations. Work out how much you need to earn in a year to meet all your outgoings – food and drink, rent, car, tax and other bills. Think also about how much time you can, or want to, devote to work: whether you want to work full time or part time, during the week only or at weekends, during the day only or evenings and overnights. Then try to come up with a strategy that has a good chance of delivering on those two separate – and sometimes conflicting – sets of priorities. The freelance world is unpredictable, so this is not easy to do. But if you think you can pick up some casual shifts, you will know the daily rate and can work out how many shifts you would need to do in order to pay the bills. If you hope to survive by selling individual pieces of work, it would be wise to have some potential commissions already in place, or the contacts that give you confidence that you will get them. Do some research about who pays what for freelance work. If your sums don't add up, or demonstrate that you will have to work much harder than you would ideally like in order to make them add up, then perhaps a freelance career now is not the right choice. It may be at a later date, if your circumstances and priorities change.

Pros and cons

Some people love the freedom and independence of being a freelance. Others are terrified by the uncertainty and lack of security it involves. Before embarking on this path, weigh up the pros and cons.

Advantages

You are your own boss – you decide what work you do and when you do it.

You are free of rotas and people telling you what to do.

You work with subject matter that you find interesting.

You develop a range of different outlets for your work.

You might find time to take on other interesting, non-journalist work, as part of a broader portfolio.

Disadvantages

You are at the whim of commissioners who will often reject your offers for what seem like fatuous and thoroughly unconvincing reasons, or who do not reply at all.

You find it hard to turn down work because you don't know where the next commission is coming from.

You are vulnerable to feast or famine: too much work at any given time, or too little.

You do not have a salary, so no reliable, regular income. You are paid when people decide to pay you.

You might have to pitch a lot of ideas to a lot of people in order to secure sufficient commissions.

You will spend a frustratingly large amount of your time making contacts, submitting ideas, negotiating rates of pay, chasing late payments.

You are running a business: you need to keep receipts, maintain records, submit invoices, fill in tax returns.

You are working alone: it can feel like a solitary business.

The conclusion you reach after weighing one list against the other will be a matter of personal preference. Does it sound like an exciting challenge or an intolerable risk? Only you can decide. But it should be obvious from both lists that there are certain qualities you will need in abundance to prosper as a freelance – realism, enthusiasm, energy, patience, motivation, persistence, resilience among the most prominent.

Starting out

In practical terms, the taxman will want you to have an employment status as a freelance, in order to see how much you are earning from your work. You can establish yourself as a sole trader or go further and set up a limited company. Both are relatively straightforward to do. You will want to open a business bank account to help organise your finances and keep them separate and transparent.

You will find it valuable to talk to someone else who has already been there and done it. Most freelancers will be happy to help you and give you advice as long as they do not think you are likely to invade their turf or pre-empt their ideas. There are online communities for freelance journalists, where you can exchange experiences and ask for guidance and support. You can find a list of them, and a lot of other very valuable advice about setting yourself up as a freelance, at journalism.co.uk

Journalism.co.uk runs a freelance database with more than 400 members and offers perks such as a branded email address and discounts on training courses. The National Union of Journalists (NUJ) also manages a directory for its freelance members. There are many other websites carrying news and information about the practice of freelance journalism. The NCTJ encourages all its students to remain part of its alumni community, and to take advantage of the skills development resources available at its Journalism Skills Academy.

You will have already decided what sort of journalism you want to do, and what sort of subjects you want to specialise in. Your next step is to investigate the market. What sorts of publications or websites specialise in those areas, and therefore offer you the best commissioning prospects? You probably have more chance of work on smaller or specialist publications than on national or high-profile titles, at least until you are established.

Now it is the time to get yourself out there. Find out who commissions for those publications and get in touch with them. They are interested in ideas more than anything, so have plenty to offer – do not make contact just to say that you would like to work for them. The critical part of the whole process is coming up with ideas and then pitching them successfully to editors or commissioners. This is examined in detail in Chapter 21.

Something for nothing?

When you are trying to gain a foothold or curry favour with a commissioner, you might be tempted to offer to provide something without being paid for it. Resist if you can, unless you think you are getting some kind of benefit in return – an experience that you would not otherwise get, or some formal or informal training. Otherwise you can look a bit desperate and set an unfortunate precedent for your future dealings. Low pay is better than no pay at all. If you can, hold out for commissions from people who will pay you rather than those who won't. There is an element of self-worth involved here. You are providing a professional service for someone who has an appetite for it. If they want it, they should be prepared to pay for it.

Money

If you manage to secure a commission, you will want to know how much you are going to be paid for it. You need not and must not be embarrassed or self-conscious in asking about this. It is your livelihood after all. If it is left to you to raise the subject, do so in as natural a way as you can. If you sound nervous, needy or tentative, commissioners might try to beat you down on price. In reality they probably have a bit of flexibility, so you should be thinking instead of nudging the fee upwards. It will be helpful of course if you are already a proven performer, and have successfully done work for them in the past. Either way, have some idea before you start what you think would be a reasonable rate, given the publication and the time and effort that you will need to devote to the commission. A fee of £100 might be acceptable for something that takes you only a few hours, but not if it involves a week's work.

Some publications have fixed rates. Your journalism contacts might have details of the rates certain titles routinely pay. But these might still be negotiable. If it is clear that your piece is going to take a substantial amount of time, or involve you in significant expense, then that needs to be part of the conversation.

Agreeing a price is one thing, getting the money paid is often quite another. You will become increasingly irritated by the amount of time you have to waste chasing money from people who cannot be bothered to pay you on time, or are too inefficient to do so. Bouncing round between commissioners, PAs and accounts departments is no one's idea of time well spent, but it is very much a part of the freelance's lot.

Submit your invoices promptly, and include a request for payment within 30 days. If you find you have a lot of money outstanding, set aside a certain amount of time every week to chase it systematically.

Accountancy may not be your strong point, but you do need to manage your finances carefully. The money may come in only spasmodically, but it will go out on a regular basis as you pay your bills, so it is useful if you have some sort of cushion so that you are not engaged in a perpetual and highly stressful balancing act.

Those outgoing bills may include premiums for health insurance and sickness cover, in case you have a period in which you are unable to work. You will not have a company pension either, so it is worth considering what provision you can make for yourself in that area too.

Tax

You can appoint an accountant to submit your tax return for you, but if you would rather not go to the expense you will have to do it yourself. If you have never done this before, you are probably rather apprehensive about it, but it is actually not as complicated as you might fear. You need to tell the taxman that you are self-employed and check out the guidance on the HMRC website. There is a helpline too. Again, your network might be able to help with advice if you are struggling.

The tax you pay will be worked out on a simple calculation based on what you have earned after your expenses have been deducted. So you need to know what constitutes a legitimate expense – office space, stationery, technical equipment, travel and so on. Then you have to be rigorous about keeping records of anything you intend to claim for. Retain receipts for anything that could conceivably count as a business expense and keep a log in a spreadsheet or accounts package. Keep the receipts themselves in one place, with a note attached to each to remind you of when you incurred the expense and what it relates to. You need to keep everything for six years.

Put money aside to pay your tax bill when it comes, and also to pay your national insurance contributions. If you earn more than around £80,000 a year, you will have to register for VAT.

Copyright

Part of the agreement between you and the person who has commissioned you should be an understanding about copyright. You own the copyright of anything you produce, so when you give someone the right to use your work, make sure you know the full extent of that permission. If someone wants to feature your work online as well as in a printed magazine, for example, you need to agree to that – and you should be thinking about negotiating a higher fee. Take advice and try to operate on your own terms: you are not obliged to submit unquestioningly to theirs.

Part four

Specialist practice

21

The feature writer

a world of opportunity…..different sorts of features…..features and news reports…..development of a feature: the idea, the pitch, the research, the structure…..the beginning – the intro….. different sorts of intros….. the middle – the body….. the end – your conclusion….. developing a writing style…..top tips for writing features

Most journalists start their careers as reporters, a role that calls for many of the core skills that are regarded as essential to good journalism in whatever form. That view is strongly reflected in the syllabus of the National Council for the Training of Journalists (NCTJ) Diploma. With those skills in the bag, however, you are free to follow your preferences in all sorts of different directions. The hurly-burly of life in the newsroom, turning out multiple news stories against the clock, is not for everyone. Many find longer-form journalism, which often requires more thought and deeper research, is more to their taste. If the minute-by-minute maelstrom of breaking news holds no charms for you, life as a feature writer has an obvious appeal. Having more space to play with, and longer to prepare and present your material, can feel like something of a luxury after the organised chaos of the newsroom. You can write with more freedom and inject more of yourself into your work. The same is true of broadcasting, where some journalists work exclusively on producing longer features, and indeed whole programmes, away from the immediate news of the moment.

A world of opportunity

There is no shortage of opportunity for good writers. All newspapers carry large numbers of features, and their weekend sections and supplements – covering travel, lifestyle, property, arts, motoring, personal finance and others – have a very heavy features content. News websites too have found that audiences want more than a simple diet of straight news.

Anyone who has ever seen the satirical BBC news show *Have I Got News For You* will also be aware that for every hobby, trade or pursuit, however niche, there is a specialist magazine. The UK has an enormous and varied magazine market, with something like 2,800 separate titles, some of them with circulations that newspaper editors would give their right arms for. It is claimed that around 80 per cent of the adult population – more than 40 million people – consume some printed magazine content each month, with many also reading magazines online. This consumption is spread across the generations, although female readership is notably larger than male. That might explain why magazines devoted to women's interests represent the dominant sector of the market, a long way ahead of the next most popular categories, leisure interests and country pursuits. The biggest individual best sellers are TV listings magazines.

Magazines have been hit by the general decline in sales that has also afflicted newspapers over a long period. But it is still a vast market, and many magazines enjoy a close relationship with their readers. Those readers may have had to fork out the price of a paperback book to buy their monthly issue. But they seem not to begrudge it. They enjoy what they read, feel a connection to the magazine and believe they get from it something that they cannot get elsewhere.

It all adds up to a strong demand for features in magazines and newspapers – which in turn means a strong demand for good feature writers. Some are in-house staff; but very many are freelance and write for any publication that will commission them. If you want to be a feature writer, whether on general topics or on a particular area of interest, then there are suitable publications – and potential commissions – out there waiting for you. And if you want to be a freelance, an option considered in Chapter 20, there are plenty of places for you to try your luck.

Different sorts of features

A feature is, broadly speaking, a piece of editorial content that isn't a news report. Within that generalised description, features can fall into any one or more of a large number of categories. Some straddle the gap between news and features.

Backgrounders or **explainers** are very often "news features", complementing the main news report by adding extra information or description for which there is no room in the principal piece. They add context and texture to the overall coverage. Very often these are not long pieces, but boxes or panels which typically include extra quotes, Question and Answers (Q&As) that explain the story, historical and future timelines and so on. In these forms, they may be produced by the news teams rather than feature writers.

Investigative features are longer reports that might run into several thousand words, reporting the outcome of a story the writer/publication has been working on over a long period.

Reportage will usually be an eyewitness description of a news event or some associated aspect of it. Again, it may be written by the news reporter who was there. But very many features describe the aftermath or consequences of the event, either at the time or later, and these are often the work of feature writers. A travel feature is essentially a piece of reportage.

Interviews or **profiles** of people in the news, or celebrities, are a staple of the features market. For an interview, you clearly need to speak to the subject. A profile can be produced without the cooperation or involvement of its subject, using research and conversations with people who know them.

A-list interviewees I categorise these separately because such interviews are often very tightly controlled and managed, and the journalist has little room for manoeuvre. There might well be a commercial agreement between the publisher and the celebrity – or more likely, the celebrity's promotional team. Magazines like *Hello!* and *OK!* are prepared to spend tens of thousands of pounds for exclusive access to the homes of celebrities, or to their weddings. Copy approval will often have been agreed, and the resultant feature is often little more than an uncritical puff in the middle of a mass of glossy photographs. Only genuine A-listers can demand and secure this level of control.

Colour pieces, which may or may not be linked to a news report, attempt to convey the feel and atmosphere of an event. The writer is a detached observer, although the piece can be written in the first person or the third person. If you are commissioned to write a colour piece, you have licence to wander round with your eyes and ears open, soaking up the atmosphere, observing how people are experiencing an event and forming your own impression. A colour piece is an eyewitness description by a writer who is on the lookout for the small occurrences and tiny details that will bring the article to life. These small touches will often provide you with a mass of material for your piece, including your intro. They will usually involve people of course, and are to be found in:

– An incident, be it unusual, amusing or sad, that helps sum up the mood of the occasion
– How people behave and interact – again, not necessarily the key players at the heart of an event, but bystanders at the fringes
– What people say – ditto. Scraps of overheard conversations can often capture the feel of the event sounds and smells – your piece will probably be accompanied by pictures, but they cannot convey what the noise – or the silence – was like, or the smell.

General features may be written about a whole range of different genres and subject: lifestyle, leisure activities, travel, all aspects of the arts, sport and so on.

Analysis or **"think pieces"** invite you to go more deeply into a subject, and possibly express an opinion of your own – or perhaps to reflect the opinion of the editor or publisher. This might be a regular personal column, or a one-off opinion piece for a newspaper's opp ed pages. Don't imagine, however, that you are going to become a columnist straight away. While it is a widely held ambition, securing a regular opinion slot in a major news media outlet takes skill, experience and probably a bit of luck. But if this is an ambition for you in the longer term, study how others do it, and hone your "voice".

Reviews will also offer an opportunity for you to set out a subjective view of a film, television programme, car or restaurant. Papers often commission **previews** as well.

How to... pieces are very popular. "How to Lose 8 Pounds in 8 days"; "How to guarantee a stress-free holiday"; "How to survive the office party"; "How to make your own Christmas decorations"; "How to amuse your kids this Bank Holiday weekend"; "How to spot whether your partner is cheating on you."

Lists or **Listicles** are based on much the same idea – an attractively packaged look at a subject in the form of a list. Very prevalent online, where they were popularised by *BuzzFeed*. Most days will see a "best of...." or "worst of" list of some sort or another, and lists can take many other forms: "20 Things You Never Knew About....."; "10 must-see sights in Paris"; "Step by Step Guide to a Healthier You"; "Your 7 Day Programme to beat that bulge". They are often subjective and might be tongue-in-cheek or amusing. The presentation of the information is usually relatively straightforward and obvious.

Q&As, or Question and Answer pieces, are those in which you give information about a subject by posing some imaginary questions and then providing the answers. It is the equivalent of an FAQ, or Frequently Asked Questions page on a website, and will often appear as a panel attached to a story, as mentioned above. It is an economical and effective way of conveying a lot of information or explaining the fundamentals of a complicated story.

Features and news reports

If we compare and contrast the nature and functions of these feature formats with those of a basic news report, we will find that they have much in common:

– **Both** are written with the needs and interests of the readership in mind.
– **Both** want to grab the attention of the reader from the beginning. The feature might take longer to exert its grip. Once it has done so, it must sustain that interest right through to the end of the piece. Think of a feature as a form of short story.
– **Both** want the reader to finish the piece feeling better informed and having enjoyed the experience of reading it.
– **Both** will have people and human interest at their core.
– **Both** can describe events and examine why they happened, why they are important, what their implications might be. Feature formats that directly undertake this role include backgrounders, explainers, analysis, Q&As and think pieces.

– **Both** seek to increase interest by the inclusion of colour, but the feature offers much greater scope to do this, with more room for interesting detail that it would not be considered necessary to include in a news story.
– **Both** look for a conversational style that picks out the words and the natural rhythms that we all use. **But** hard news must observe a certain formality of style and structure that does not apply to the feature writer.

It is clear, then, that more unites than divides them. But contrasts become evident when we consider the treatment and the execution.

Length

A feature of 750–1,000 words or more allows you to delve more deeply into a subject than you are generally able to do in a news report, giving a broader and more textured view of it and bringing in more perspectives.

Pace

In keeping with this, features tend to move along at a more leisurely pace than news reports. It is hard to maintain a sense of urgency and immediacy over a longer stretch, and you would not want to do so – it would be too exhausting an experience for the reader. You have the same duty to keep readers interested, but rolling out the story in a more leisurely manner does not mean they will be any the less engaged.

Content

There is not the same imperative in a feature for the rapid delivery of key facts. You might not need too many "news facts" at all, depending on the nature of the piece. A colour piece or a descriptive piece may rely more on your powers of observation and expression than on conveying hard information.

Your voice

A news report will normally be a dispassionate and impartial presentation of the facts. You keep yourself and your own opinions out of it. With a feature, you can allow yourself more latitude. This can include writing in the first person or making references to yourself, some humour or whimsy, even some engaging ramblings off the beaten track. That doesn't mean you have a licence for self-indulgence, woolliness or overwriting. But a feature is a different kind of reading experience, and you can take advantage of the opportunities it offers to be creative and imaginative.

Structure and style

That same latitude applies to structure. Remember the inverted pyramid model that serves you well for news – with the most important information summarised at the top, followed by background, quotes, context and further detail in diminishing levels of importance. You will seldom adopt that approach to writing a feature. You can start your narrative at almost any point. There is no right or wrong way of writing a feature. How you choose to do it is up to you – and your features editor or commissioner.

Comment

News stories do not permit you to voice your own opinions. Many forms of feature actually require you to do so. If you are writing a review, for example, of a book, play, film, car or restaurant, then the whole point is that you offer a subjective opinion. A feature based on an interview with an individual may allow you to convey something about what you thought of them or how they came across to you. A think piece or an opinion piece also requires you to take a position and to support it by argument – possibly, if you are writing an editorial or "leader" column, not an argument you personally agree with!

Human interest

Assuming you are not working for a technical publication, your storytelling should always be through the medium of people and their experiences. The subject could of course be yourself, if your piece relates something that has happened to you, or your own opinions.

Humour

A feature can attempt to entertain in a way a hard news piece seldom can, by stylistic devices and humour, for example.

Development of a feature

The idea

In this context, the word "idea" embraces both the subject and the proposed angle of the piece. If you suggest a piece about housing issues, say, or "something on Russia", your features editor will be entitled to say: "That's a big subject. What aspect of it and what angle did you have in mind?" If you don't have an answer, you will feel rather foolish.

In your early days as a staff writer, you will probably be told what to write about. Your ideas may be canvassed at an editorial meeting, but features editors tend to know what they want and commission accordingly. Even so, you should regularly be coming up with your own ideas and suggestions for features. However definite their views are, commissioning editors love ideas, and there is a lot of satisfaction in having yours adopted, and then – if you are fortunate – being able to research and write the piece yourself. Even if your idea is not pursued, it may be that there is somewhere else you could publish it, as a blogpost, for example.

Writers of fiction are always asked by their readers: "where do you get your ideas from?" They are often stumped for an answer. It is hard to identify how and why ideas and images pop into our heads, and there is not much point trying to offer detailed advice about how to come up with great ideas. But if they do not automatically spring forth unbidden, there are things you can do and places you can go that will encourage the flow. Your journalistic curiosity should mean that you are open to new thoughts, trends and information all the time, with your antennae attuned to anything that might be turned into a feature. Here are some tips to help you nudge the process along.

– Make a note of ideas as you have them, however vague or ill formed they are at that stage. You can go back to them later and see whether they are worth filling out. This way you will have several embryonic ideas on the go at any one time, and will never be short of an answer if a features editor asks you out of the blue: "have you got any ideas for me?"

– Cut out anything you see in a newspaper or magazine that you think might be turned into an idea. It might be only a small news item or a throwaway reference that has the potential for further exploration. You can print something you see online, or save the link to it.

– Look at the sorts of stories that are being commissioned by your target publications, and think about the potential for following them up, revisiting them at a later date or taking a story in a different direction.

– Letters pages, radio phone-ins and the chat on social media give you direct access to members of the public and a hotline to what they are thinking and talking about. These will very often lead you to viewpoints and perspectives that you had not considered before, and which you can investigate.

– Keep your eyes and ears open, and remain receptive to ideas. They may come from the most workaday sources – such as the experiences of your friends and family, or things that you overhear. An idea might easily come from a conversation you hear on the bus, or something one of your friends says to you on an evening out. Think of the rhetorical questions we all ask all the time: "Why is it so difficult to get hold of a decent X these days?" "Do you ever get the feeling that……?" "Why is everyone so crazy about Y?" "You never hear anything about Z these days – whatever happened to her?" Maybe other people are thinking the same things and asking themselves the same questions. It sounds trite, but the answers might give you the subject for a feature. It is the job of a journalist to answer the questions that people are asking. Keeping yourself open to the reception of ideas is a big part of the process.

– Many of your ideas will come from the news of the day, and from doing plenty of reading, watching and listening. As a journalist you are, as a matter of course, keeping up with what is going on in the world. You have access to a vast amount of information from a wide range of sources. There is stuff happening all the time, and you can take almost any story or topic and come up with a feature idea connected to it. A good idea that is topical will always be well received. This could be:

a closer look at a current news story and the circumstances behind it. Often a news story will be a symptom of a wider issue: you can look at the wider issue in a feature, explore and throw light on it. This works just as well in reverse: if the news story of the day is about the wider issue, your feature can look at what it means to people in their everyday lives, with human interest and case studies.

an interview with one or more of the people involved in a story. This doesn't have to be done on the day the story is in the news – it could be weeks, months or even years later. Everyone has a story to tell, and an individual angle, and reflections after a passage of time can be an effective way of revisiting a story.

a preview of a story that is coming up and that is likely to be of interest.

anniversaries and other news pegs that offer an opportunity to revisit a story and find new things to say about it. Look ahead as far as you can – it takes time to research and write a feature, so if you are pitching an idea that is pegged to an event the following day, you are putting yourself under pressure to deliver your feature within 24 hours.

a secondary piece supporting the main news story and adding more background, such as facts and figures or historical context, that helps the reader understand the story better and more fully.

a case study that puts a story into a human context.

a piece that takes a small snippet of news and builds it up into a larger story.

an interesting – and possibly provocative – take on a story of the day.

The possibilities are infinite. Your ideas certainly don't have to be associated with the news reports of the moment, especially if your specialty is lifestyle issues, popular culture or the like. But you will find the news a steady source of ideas and inspiration if you are stuck. Test this with any news report by listing five relevant questions that are suggested and have not been answered by what you have read or heard. You can develop a feature idea that answers some or all of those questions.

The best ideas of course are those that are original. Try to suggest a piece or an angle that has not been looked at before, or not in the way you propose to treat it. Check first that it *is* original – and that the same subject or treatment has not already been done by your target publications in the previous few months.

The pitch

You will need to do a little research ahead of pitching your idea – enough to enable you to talk persuasively about what your piece will contain and what angles it will cover. You can do something more in-depth once you have secured the commission. This applies whether you are a staff writer or a freelance.

You need to be sure that the piece you have in mind will be of interest to the intended audience – and by extension, suitable for the publication for which you are working, or to which you are offering the idea. That requires an understanding of the sort of material it usually publishes, the way that material is structured – there will usually be a house style – and the kind of audience it is catering for. Look at a few recent issues to see the sort of thing it is interested in, and the way in which it likes its features presented. A great idea is of little value if it does not appeal to the proposed market.

If you are a freelance, you will probably be pitching via email. The amount of detail you include will depend on whether or not you are already known to the commissioning editor and have an established relationship. If so, you might need nothing more than a brief outline of your proposed piece, the way in which you want to present it, the angle you propose to take, what you would expect it to include. If necessary, you can flesh the idea out, perhaps with a follow-up telephone conversation.

If you are pitching cold to someone who doesn't know you, you will need to do work a little harder:

– Make sure that you are sending your pitch to the right person. If you don't, it will probably go astray and might end up in the bin without even being looked at. Get the person's name and title right. The names of senior magazine editors and their email addresses are usually published in each issue.
– Say a little bit about yourself – your background, experience and any reason that you would be a good person to write about this subject. You might have some special knowledge of it, have good contacts or have written about it before. This helps establish your credentials in much the same way as you would seek to do when applying for a job.
– Give a short and succinct summary of your feature idea, and why you think it is worth doing.
– Give some of the detail we have already mentioned – proposed format, angle, content, plus what interviewees it might require (and whether or not you have already set any of them up), and a suggested length.
– Offer only an outline of content, without giving too much away. It is not unheard-of for editors to snaffle an idea and put one of their staff writers on it, squeezing out the poor freelance.

That adds up to quite a lot of information. But be aware that features editors get a lot of offers and will always be pressed for time. So your total pitch should not occupy more than the equivalent of a page of A4, less if possible. Don't include it as an attachment if you want it to be read.

Your pitch is going to demonstrate something about your writing style, so avoid being too stiff and formal. Adopt a friendly and relaxed tone, without being presumptuous or over-familiar.

Some publications helpfully publish details of the sort of ideas they are interested in, and the way they like a pitch set out. If they take the trouble to offer guidance, they will expect you to take the trouble to follow it. The *Press Gazette* has run a series of features entitled "How to Pitch", each one containing the views of a commissioning editor. You can find a number of these articles online.

The research

You have had your idea, and you have managed to find someone who wants to run your feature. Now the real work begins.

Most substantial features require a large amount of research. Even if your piece is going to be based on one or two key interviews, you still have to find the ideal interviewees, and discover some way of making contact with them and persuading them to cooperate. That can be surprisingly time-consuming. Once they have agreed, you will need to research their backgrounds by way of preparing for the interview.

Your first port of call for all sorts of research will probably be the internet. It is a rich, diverse and inexhaustible source of information. You still need to assess your sources carefully – there is plenty of unreliable and questionable material out there, and the last thing you want to do is repeat as gospel something that turns out to be opinionated, ill-sourced and tendentious. As we have discussed before, it is really important that you use the internet with discrimination, and with a full awareness of the pitfalls that await the incurious and the unwary. For help with searching online, refer to Chapter 13.

Most things you search for will offer you a Wikipedia page. Wikipedia is a seductive resource because it seems to offer exactly the information you want and in an easily accessed and readily digestible form. But use it as a pointer or a signpost to other more authoritative sources rather than relying on it as a source in its own right. Wikipedia articles usually include the references on which they are based, so you have the opportunity to find your way to primary sources that give you more confidence. If you find something of interest on Wikipedia, make sure you confirm it from some other source before using it.

This is not to single out Wikipedia for criticism, especially as it is such a brilliant resource in many ways. But you need to adopt a sceptical attitude to plenty of materials on the internet. This applies in particular to sites that are in essence open to anyone and everyone to vent their possibly rather ill-informed opinions. Blogs, social networks, message boards and comment threads would come under this heading.

A lot of the online material you might like to read will often be behind a paywall – such as academic papers, newspaper and magazine articles, archive material. If you are not prepared to pay, you will have to resort to other methods of research.

The power of the internet makes it easy to forget that there are plenty of other places to find things out, some of them just as quick and more reliable. Reference books can be invaluable, but make sure they are up to date. Beyond that, do not underestimate the value of the telephone. When the phone and the library were all that journalists had in those dark days before the worldwide web, they proved to be more than adequate methods of gathering information.

The advice here is similar to that we gave in the chapter about newsgathering for news stories. Use press offices, charities, media centres (the Science Media Centre, the Education Media Centre), government resources (the Office for National Statistics) and many more to find your way to the information and the experts you need. It may take a few calls for you to track down the person with exactly the knowledge you are looking for, but pursuing them with phone calls rather than through the internet can often be a lot faster and produce better results. Don't forget that you may need to speak to some subject experts as part of your background research. You will want to pick their brains for a lot of the background and context that you need, even if you never have any intention of quoting them directly in your final piece.

The interviewees

Reviews or opinion pieces apart, the key element of most features is the people you speak to and what they tell you. If you are writing a profile of an individual, it is pretty obvious that you want to interview them and people who know them or have an opinion about them. If you are writing about a subject or an issue rather than an individual, it is worth taking time to find the ideal interviewees, with the right level of knowledge and credibility. Finding these people and arranging to meet or speak to them will often be the most time-consuming element of the entire process. If you are writing a descriptive or colour piece, your interviewees may simply be the characters you meet along the way. A good feature writer must be an effective interviewer. Techniques around interviewing are examined in detail in Chapter 8.

The treatment

Once you have your commission and have done your homework, you need to decide on the structure of your feature. The business of organising your material and deciding how to present it is just the same as the process of ordering a news report, even if the final product is going to look very different. The rest of this chapter will concentrate on the options you have, and the way you go about putting your piece together.

The beginning – your intro

Now you have gathered all your material, make the time to read it through and marinade in your mind for a bit. You want to begin writing with a clear idea of the purpose or thrust of the piece as a whole, and the means by which you will realise that concept. See if some ideas or themes emerge. Think about the appropriate tone for the whole. Mull over a number of possible treatments or ways into the piece. Decide what is your strongest material and what is dispensable. It might help clarify your thoughts to outline your ideas to a friend and see what they think is the most interesting element of your story, as a simple piece of market research engaging a potential readership.

Your first paragraph does not need to get straight to the point with the immediacy and economy of a news report. But it is designed to serve the same purpose: securing the attention of your readers and making them want to read on. In some ways that is harder to do with the longer format. You can come at a feature from any angle and using any one of a large number of techniques, some of which we are about to examine. Because your story will often start quite gently and unfold over a succession of paragraphs, it can be more difficult to engage readers straight away. As we shall see, many writers seek to overcome this by adding a little mystery or intrigue at the outset of the piece as a lure to the reader.

In a news report, the intro usually refers to the opening paragraph alone, where the story is condensed and "sold" to the reader. With a feature, the intro may comprise several paragraphs, depending on the approach you take. There isn't even a rule of thumb about how long your intro should be – it can be very short, very long or anything in between. It will often require a lot of time and effort to get it right, and you may have several goes at it. Don't worry. The importance of the intro means it is worth that investment of time, and once you have cracked it, everything else will come much more easily.

There are two main ways of getting started:

– *"Newsy"* In Chapter 10, we spent a lot of time discussing intros for hard stories. You can adopt this approach for your feature as well if you wish. A feature reader can be drawn in by a short and snappy opening sentence just as much as by an intro that gradually unpacks itself over several pars. For a "news feature" – a longer piece closely linked to one of the day's big stories – a businesslike intro similar to that of a news report may be more appropriate. A very big story might have a number of supporting features linked to it: a backgrounder, an explainer, a fact box, some statistical analysis. They are all part of the coverage of the main story, and so should not feel too tangential or discursive.
– *Delayed drop.* Again, we have already encountered this format as one that is also frequently used for hard news stories. It is perhaps the most common method of starting a feature. The first par is used to set the scene in some way. The "nub", or "nut", of the story is then revealed further down. When a drop intro is employed on a news story, the reader does not usually have to wait long for the nub – typically there will be one paragraph of setting up, followed by disclosure in the second paragraph. In a feature, the drop may be a lot longer, and indeed, there might be several pars of building up interest and tension until we get to the nub. A lot of the structural techniques below are variations on this basic idea of the drop, in which a situation is teed up for the reader, and then resolved. Like an expert comedian, the writer sets up a situation and then delivers a well-timed punchline that pulls everything together.

Different sorts of intros

The examples used in this following section are all genuine, and were gathered from national newspapers and a selection of magazines over a single weekend. This is a good exercise if you want to be a feature writer. Consume as many features as you can – or at least their openings – to see how experienced professionals do it, and to analyse what works best. Choose the presentational technique that is best suited to the story you want to tell and those who will be reading it. Your writing should go where the material leads you.

If you spend some time looking at examples, you may also be struck by how variable the quality is. In order to gather the handful I have quoted below, I looked at well over a hundred features. Quite a number of them were overwritten and self-indulgent, falling lazily into a formulaic approach that left me with absolutely no desire to read on. Because there are fewer rules, it is tempting to think that anything will pass, and can be put down as "style". Never allow yourself to get into this way of thinking. The other side of this coin is that in my weekend survey, I ended up reading a lot of features on subjects about which I had previously had not the slightest interest. So well and so artfully were they presented that I found myself reading on in spite of myself. That is the effect for which you are always striving.

Note that some of the intros I have quoted here could easily have been listed in a different category: some of these techniques overlap. They are selected not because they are good or bad, but because they illustrate the various techniques and options at your disposal.

Tease

Most drop intros are teases of one sort or another, as they try to pique your interest, to intrigue you and to draw you in to the story. The opening line is normally a single statement that looks innocent enough and yet prompts readers to ask all sorts of questions, the answers to which they will find only by reading on.

Examples

When someone asks if you want to see their cellar, the answer for anyone with only a rudimentary cinematic knowledge has to be "No, thanks".

It is the middle of the night. The children have been traveling for hours, first by plane, then by bus, taken to a country some have never heard of, where they don't speak a word of the language.

In the wild manly environs of wolf and cougar country, in a cosy, wooden-slatted family home, an American man in a tank top and Bermuda shorts swings energetically upside down from the first-floor banister in a yoga sling.

The telephone sat in the dormitory hallway, and when it rang it might have been for any of the residents – young women in their teens and early 20s, all students at the University of Chicago......But sometimes the voice at the end of the line would ask for "Jane".

Amid the dozens of A-list celebrities and social media Titans gathered in isolated splendour on the Sicilian coast last summer, the interaction between two of the more camera-shy guests went largely unnoticed.

Description

With a descriptive opening, you are in effect starting with colour. Your intro sets the scene, describing a place or something happening which takes the reader into the environment in which your story is set. The introduction of a person, or people, invariably makes the narrative more interesting and relatable. A description needs some elegant writing or some interesting detail, or both, and it must be relevant to the rest of the story – as you will make clear when you come to the nub. Many travel features use this technique. Some pieces are wholly made up of description.

Examples

A perfect Somerset winter's day. Sunlight gilded the roofs of the quiet village of Rowberrow, once a mining hub where men dug calamine for making brass.

Gazing out at a cold, bright winter sky, only the rising steam interrupted my view of the rolling Ardennes hills, framed by the twisting branches of bare trees.

We meet in room 701 of the Monte-Carlo Bay Hotel. It is a big room, which is good, for he is a big man: 6ft 2in and more than 16 stone. He smiles as he stretches out his hand.

Me Me Me!

Many features are written in the first person, as they reflect the opinions or experiences of the writer. If you had a regular column, you would expect to write in the first person most of the time. The same would be true of any piece that required you to offer a subjective opinion – a travel feature or theatre review, for example. Beyond that, you would normally write in the third person. However, some writers are notably reluctant to exclude themselves from the piece, particularly with features based on interviews. Presumably they think it adds an air of credibility or authority to the piece and signals to the reader: "I really did interview this person and believe me, I asked some pretty searching questions". Be careful not to over-indulge however. If the story is not about you, then resist the temptation to make it about you – as in this example:

Examples

I'm at the bar of a boutique hotel in Kensington, waiting for classical guitarist Milos to arrive.

This might be fine if something happened to the writer while she was waiting, or if, say, she was nervous or apprehensive about the impending meeting for some reason. But it didn't and she wasn't. She seems to think the most interesting person in this impending encounter is herself rather than Milos.

"So," I say to my wife, "I've been asked to write about happiness peaking when we hit 47.2 years of age".

It was during the pouring of my first pint that I began to realise that at the Commercial Hotel in Knaresborough they do things a little differently. Standing at the bar, I was briefly texting my whereabouts to a friend. "You'll have to put that phone away", the barman told me. "This is a digital detox pub".

I would not let it defeat me. It had been sitting on top of a cabinet in our upstairs hallway, just outside our bedroom, for days.

Han Chong is fresh from his SS20 New York fashion show when we meet at his Hoxton studio. "I came back and had a party", he laughs emphatically.

Introducing a character

Start off by introducing us to someone who is going to be central to your piece, and tell us something about them, so that we can immediately start to take an interest in them. This is often a way into a TOA or TOT piece. These acronyms stand for *Triumph over Adversity* and *Triumph over Tragedy* – stories of how people fight back to overcome illness or some other setback, and the subjects of very many features. You will recognise the genre.

Example

James Padot has been union all his life. For decades, the pipe-fitter relied on his trade union to steer work his way on grand construction projects across the Midwest and to ensure he was paid decently enough to feel he had a stake in the American dream.

Eighteen months ago, Kevin Sluman was out on his boat trawling for fish in the Bristol Channel, delighted to have his son Aaron back from London and working alongside him in the summer sunshine.

Author Jacqueline Woodson lives in a quintessential Brooklyn brownstone with her partner, two children, a cat and two huge friendly dogs.

The character does not have to be someone of whom we have never heard. The technique works with well-known people too – especially if we immediately learn something about them that we did not already know:

When he's not acting, Sir David Jason loves nothing better than tinkering in his 'man cave' – fixing things, assembling, building, inventing. "I'm fascinated by how things work", he says.

You need a lot of energy to interview Dev Patel. At one stage he is so enthusiastic about a point he is making that he stomps on a coffee table in the central London hotel room where we are sitting.

From gold-patterned wallpaper and velvet upholstery to peacock feather fabric, there is barely a corner of Leith Clark's glamorous Victorian house that isn't filled with rich, dramatic shades.

Quotes

Starting a news story with a quote is generally frowned on in hard news reporting, especially in broadcast media, because we need to know who is talking before we can make any sense of what was said. The narrative of a feature unwinds at a slower pace, and it is perfectly acceptable to begin with a quote, as long as it is arresting or intriguing. The fact that the reader does not know who is speaking might actually add to the mystery and appeal. If need be, the reader is prepared to wait to find out who the speaker was and what the circumstances were.

Examples

"Bella, I know it's not the point, but where is your jumper from?"

"I passed out. I couldn't walk." The godfather of alternative comedy is describing the disease that almost ended his career.

"Yes I am a workaholic", says the writer, actor and comedian David Walliams, trying to explain why he never seems to stop.

"I am so happy I get to bring some British banter to Victoria's Secret", says Londoner Leomie at the launch of the Incredible Bra and Bombshell Paradise Fragrance.

Anecdotes

An anecdote is often only another form of *description* or *introducing a character*, but it can be a very effective way of getting into a feature. Obviously there needs to be some point to it, in relation to the purpose of the piece as a whole. But a story that is funny or touching is an excellent way of grabbing your readers by the lapels and persuading them to read on.

It will work best when told in the first person. That doesn't necessarily mean that you are the subject of it. It can be an anecdote told to you by one of your interviewees, which you then quote in direct speech. "I was walking along minding my own business", John Brown recalled "when suddenly the most extraordinary thing happened".

Examples

In the early 1990s, Tom Stoppard had his first conversation with his mother about being Jewish. All four of his grandparents had died in the Holocaust. His mother, Martha, had never wished to talk about those times. But finally, she did.

The night terrors came often but Harry Olmers remembers only one of his dreams. "I was standing facing my mother. We did not talk to each other, we just looked. There was a brick wall being built between us and it got higher and higher until....until I could no longer see her."

Ever since Prince Alfonso von Hohenlohe rolled up in a Rolls-Royce Phantom and decided to build the Marbella Club for his aristocratic friends in 1954, this southern Spanish beach town has been synonymous with swishness.

Almost 50 years ago, when I was 25, I was at the heart of what was the only coup d'etat executed by British Army officers in living memory.

Snuggled on my daughter Nina's bed, we had finished one story when she reminded me that good dads always read more than one. I sighed inwardly.

Killer fact

Knock your readers off guard, or draw them into the piece, by starting with a fact or statistic, often quite starkly presented, that will serve to introduce the subject of your piece. This works well for news features.

Examples

Germany has 83 state-subsidised opera companies – one for every million of its citizens.

The average Briton over the age of 65 has been on 114 holidays.

A question

Starting with a question that (presumably) you propose to answer in the course of your piece can get you off to a good start. But the question needs to be fairly simple and precise, and it needs to be one the reader would be interested in having answered. You will often see pieces that start: "Have you ever wondered what it would be like to.....", when all too often the reader's answer is likely to be a single word in the negative. A good way to skirt this risk is to answer the question as quickly as possible.

Examples

Could you still fit into the trousers you wore when you were 20?

Can the stories we tell ourselves about disease and illness change the way we experience them? Is there a good way to approach the end of life?

Have your children got eco-anxiety? How would you know if they had?

What makes your home a happy one? The findings of a new study might surprise.

Are the UK's cities on course to become family-free zones? The latest figures suggest so.

Who is the least likely royal to become a latter-day fashion pin-up?

Question and Answer

As we have already mentioned, a Question and Answer piece, in which you give information about a subject by thinking up your own relevant questions and then giving the answers, is a good way of conveying a lot of information in quite a small space. It may not need an intro at all.

Chronological narrative

This is storytelling at its simplest. You start at the beginning and describe events in order as they happened. This format is also often used for TOA/TOT features. A narrative of this sort is likely to build up to the main point of the piece, which we do not discover until we are some way in. But it doesn't have to. An alternative approach is to *start* with the key event and its consequences, and then go back to the beginning, in the way that countless novels do. The intro or the opening sentences of such pieces can often be very matter-of-fact, and seem to be doing little to try to sell the piece. It is going to be a slow burn. In essence, the writer is saying to the reader: "I have a great story for you here. Make yourself a cup of tea, settle down, read on and enjoy". Note that all of these examples begin with a time reference, which is very effective as a scene setting device.

Examples

On July 11, 1944, Winston Churchill was shown evidence provided by four escapees from Auschwitz of the mass murder of Jews at the extermination camp.

It was November nine years ago, and the very end of the growing season, when we took possession of Hillside.

The night in question – as with most nights in the ambulance service – began like any other midweek shift.

Back in June 2013, the political department of Unite, Britain's most powerful union, produced a confidential report for its executive.

On July last year, not long after sunrise, George King-Thompson, then 19, became the first person to "free climb" the tallest building in western Europe: the Shard.

"Our reporter tried his/her hand"

There is a whole genre of personalised features in which the writer is the hero of the piece. Typically, the role of the writer will be as some sort of guinea pig. A feature about giving up smoking, for example, might be written as a first-person account by the reporter of his or her own efforts to kick the habit. A feature about a new diet craze might be based around the writer trying it out and reporting the results. This format can be applied in hundreds of different situations, accompanied of course by pictures of the writer suffering in the cause of their craft. A piece such as this would be written in the first person, but that does not mean you cannot include interviews, quotes and background in the usual way.

One thing that should be evident from all these examples: you can sell and write a feature about absolutely anything.

The middle – the body

The feature may not conform to the inverted pyramid format of the news report, but it has the same basic component parts: a striking start, although that may be a few paragraphs long; and the main body in which much of the key information is conveyed, by a combination of quotes and supporting information. Beyond that, the feature should also deliver a sense of completeness, and have a good ending to bring the reader to a satisfactory conclusion, by bookending or other means.

The body is the engine room of the story, carrying the main narrative or information elements of the feature. As with news reporting, you will find that once you have solved the knotty problem of your intro, everything else begins to fall into place. You have got into the story, now it is a question of telling it. You have at your disposal the same elements you use in news reporting – quotes, colour, context – and how you employ them and in what proportion depends on the nature of the piece and what you want it to say. Try to make the piece flow smoothly, without any rough edges and jarring inconsistencies of style. Each paragraph should lead naturally to the next without crashing gear changes that seem forced, and disrupt the easy flow of your narrative. The old adage about imagining how you would tell the story to someone in conversation is useful in this context too.

This approach holds good with any sort of story, be it a description of life on the streets for homeless drug addicts, or a portrait of someone who collects Victorian postcards. Whatever the story is, think hard about how you want to tell it. After all, you are marshalling a lot of material and you have multiple options as you decide how to present it. It takes time. Do not expect to produce a 1,000-word feature in twice the time it takes you to write a 500-word news report. It is a miniature work of literature, and it will take longer as you change things around until you are happy that you have got it just right. Even then, your features editor is very likely to come back to you to request some changes.

In a feature that is dependent on interviews, or perhaps a single interview, you will use more quotes than you would in a news report. Many will be direct quotes. A run of three or four pars of quotes one after the other is not unusual if you think they serve your purpose, reveal something about the interviewee or allow them to develop a thought or argument in some way. A run of several pars without any quotes might also be appropriate if you are developing a descriptive narrative, and perhaps including some background, some of your own reflections, or describing the interviewee's gestures or facial expressions.

Be careful not to lose your discipline and shape by overwriting or self-indulgence. You may have more space, but economy of expression and the right choice of words are just as important in feature writing as they are in news reports. Your sentences can be longer and more complex, but don't overdo it. Ditch the purple prose, and don't show off. You can use unusual or lesser-known words that you would not consider putting in a news story, but make sure you are using them correctly and that your readers will know what they mean.

Here is a review that demonstrates what happens when you ignore this advice:

> Prepare for a fresh outbreak of Les Mis mania. In bringing the £200 million refurbishment of his eight theatres, which began in 2004, to a rousing finale with the opening of the Sondheim – the Queen's Theatre, renovated to the tune of £13.8 million and renamed after the American living legend – producer Cameron Mackintosh has created a playhouse so beautiful it's an attraction in its own right.

As dogged as the remorseless police inspector Javert in Victor Hugo's 1862 masterpiece, and as devoted to doing good as the (reformed ex-con) hero Jean Valjean, Mackintosh – who had a crucial hand in developing Les Miserables in the first place alongside composer Claude-Michel Schonberg and lyricist Alain Boublil, and has closely supervised this architectural project too – deserves his own round of grateful applause.

There is another 500 words of this. The first nine words are fine, but after that it is pretty much unreadable. The writer knows a lot about his subject and is determined to show us just how much by cramming extra information into every reference seemingly without any thought to what the result is likely to be as a reading experience. That second paragraph is a single sentence, with its subject – "Mackintosh" – hopelessly weighed down by the burden of verbiage it is being asked to support before and after. You have to read each sentence several times to even begin to understand what it is saying and digest all the references. This is a writer who needs to reconnect with some of the disciplines of simple uncomplicated prose.

The body of the feature needs to sustain the mood or the voice that you have established at the outset. You may have quotes from half a dozen interviews that you would like to include, or more anecdotes and examples than you could possibly find room for. Even though you will have much more room than in a news report, there will still be decisions to be made about what you include and what you leave out, and the way your story can be developed to maximum effect.

One of the big decisions you will often have to make, as will be evident from the examples quoted above, is whether or not to include yourself in the piece – insights into your own life and experiences if they are relevant to the subject, descriptions on your interaction with your interviewees, and your own opinions and impressions. Whether or not you feature yourself will depend on the kind of piece it is and whether you or your features editor thinks it is appropriate. If you already have a profile, and your style is built around this kind of personal approach, then you will naturally want to employ the same technique. If you do not have such a profile, and there is no obvious role for you personally in the feature, then keep yourself out of it.

The end – your conclusion

News pieces sometimes have to be slashed back in a hurry if there is not enough room for them in the page, or something new happens that demands extra space. News reporters therefore present their copy in such a way that the least important and most easily removed material is at the end of the story. That way, if their story is subsequently cut two thirds of the way through, readers are not missing anything vital, or anything that they need in order to be able to understand the story.

That is not the case with features. You should think of the piece as a whole, with a beginning, middle and end, and try to bring it to a neat and elegant conclusion. Look for a final thought or observation or quote – a "pay-off" – that pulls the whole thing together.

There are a number of ways of achieving this.

return to the main point of the story or argument, and bring everything full circle by taking the reader back to the place from which you started. This practice is known as 'bookending'. You might pose a question in the first paragraph and answer it in your last.

summarise the arguments or perspectives that we have read about in the piece, and tie them up with a final thought.

call your readers to action – if your piece has been about an issue where a response is needed, make clear what needs to be done and by whom, or warn about the consequences of inaction. You will probably want to put this into the mouth of one of your interviewees, rather than assigning yourself this crusading (and non-neutral) role.

look to the future, finishing with some thoughts about what the next developments could be.

a strong quote that picks up one of the key themes or characters of the piece is a good way to finish.

finish with a throwaway line or a little sting in the tail designed to leave the reader with any one of a number of emotions: guilt, pleasure, amusement, puzzlement, anger, reflection and so on.

Developing a writing style

If the writing of news reports can sometimes seem formulaic, the feature gives you plenty of opportunities to develop your writing style and find your voice. That sudden freedom can feel slightly daunting, but think of it as liberating rather than threatening. The more you write, the more you will develop a way of working, a creative process and a style that is distinctively your own, and with which you feel comfortable. But you must also be prepared to be flexible. You can expect to produce all sorts of different sorts of pieces, on different subjects, possibly for different publications, sometimes at short notice. One size will not fit all. The same approach will not always work, but part of the enjoyment of writing features is meeting the creative challenge posed by dealing with different sorts of material for different markets.

Developing your personal style comes with time, and you need to give yourself the space to allow it to happen. There are things you can do that will speed you on the way:

- **Know your market.** Always think about who you are writing for. We saw when we discussed the pitching process how important it is to understand the readership – what sort of people they are, what they are most likely to be interested in. Carry that thought process into the writing of the piece. Put yourself in the minds of the readers of your piece. You do not want to baffle them with complicated concepts, or patronise them by talking down to them.
- **Try different things.** The longer format gives you more latitude than a news report in all sorts of way. Experiment with different approaches. Don't be afraid to step outside your comfort zone and try something new. Think about your material and see what sort of presentation it suggests to you.
- **Rewrite.** The beauty of allowing yourself to try different approaches is that you can always cross them out and start again if they don't work. You should always re-read your work with a critical eye, remembering once again what your intended audience is likely to make of it. Revision should be about making things tighter and smoother – not longer and more elaborate.
- **Seek feedback.** If your piece has been commissioned, you will certainly get some feedback – and if it is not what the commissioner had in mind, that feedback might be quite robust. Aside from that, ask people you know and trust to read your work and give you their candid opinion of it. You should seek and welcome any sort of feedback, however critical. It is an important element of your learning and development as a writer.
- **See how others do it.** Reading as widely as you can will always be helpful, and you will subconsciously absorb a lot along the way. This is not about copying the style of another writer, but about understanding how they achieve an effect. Specifically, read the work of others in your field, and try to analyse what makes a good or a poor piece.

If you try too hard to cultivate a certain style, especially if it is one that does not come naturally to you, it will feel mannered and artificial. Follow your instincts and see where they take you. Let the words come naturally and don't force them. Don't show off either. If you labour too obviously for an effect, or indulge yourself in over-ornate writing, you will distract the readers from the narrative and irritate them.

Re-read your work with an unsentimental eye. If you see something you feel doesn't work, try to analyse why it doesn't work and where it feels discordant. If you can put your finger on the wrong notes, you will fix it more quickly and you will not repeat the mistake. But have confidence in yourself and your writing. Within the confines of good grammar, there are very few rights and wrongs.

It is tempting to think that style is about fancy words and elaborate phrase making. It is not, not in journalism at any rate. The simplicity and clarity that you have been urged to seek in all your writing is just as important in features as it is in snappy news reports. It may be a different form of journalism, but it is still journalism. One of the best-known comments about style was made by the Victorian poet Matthew Arnold:

> Have something to say and say it as clearly as you can. That is the only secret of style.

Others enjoin you to try to write as you would talk, an idea that we have encountered time and again in this book. In all journalism there is a narrow gap between the spoken and the written word, in the sense that the colloquial and informal style that characterises the best journalism derives from the natural cadences and rhythms of everyday speech. In broadcast journalism of course, there is no gap at all. The best way of seeing how successful you are at writing in this way is to read your work out loud. You will hear all sorts of things that you had not noticed on the page.

One of the most famous proponents of the plain and simple approach was George Orwell, both a novelist and a journalist. He summarised his thoughts in a celebrated essay entitled *Politics and the English Language*:

1. Never use a metaphor, simile or other figure of speech that you are used to seeing in print.
2. Never use a long word when a short one will do.
3. If it is possible to cut out a word, always cut it out.
4. Never use the passive when you can use the active.
5. Never use a foreign phrase, a scientific word or a jargon word if you can think of an everyday English equivalent.
6. Break any of these rules sooner than say anything outright barbarous.

Orwell also said:

> A scrupulous writer, in every sentence that he writes, will ask himself at least four questions, thus: 1. What am I trying to say? 2. What words will express it? 3. What image or idiom will make it clearer? 4. Is this image fresh enough to have an effect? And he will probably ask himself two more: 1. Could I put it more shortly? 2. Have I said anything that is avoidably ugly?

This excellent advice holds good for everything that you write, of whatever sort and for whatever medium. It is a very good place to start, as you begin to experiment with your writing. As with all your other journalistic output, keep it clear, keep it simple. But as you grow in confidence, feel emboldened to add a little colour to the plainness. Try your hand at various techniques: a short sentence, or several short sentences, followed by a longer one; or vice versa. A paragraph that builds tension, which is then resolved with a smart conclusion. Extended metaphors (Orwell only advised us not to use hackneyed and overused metaphors and similes; there is nothing wrong with coming up something fresh of your own) or a bit of word play perhaps. Try things out and see whether or not they come off. But, to repeat: in the end you are looking for a style that suits you and with which you feel at ease, not one you have copied from somewhere else and which feels laboured and not natural to you.

We should not really talk about style on its own, because although important, it is simply the vehicle that allows you to present your material and tell your story. Content is king. Style is not more important than substance. As Matthew Arnold advised: "have something to say". If you feel uncertain about content or approach, let your readership be your guide. Try to tune yourself to their wavelength: who are they, what do they like, what will make this a pleasing and informative reading experience for them?

When your feature is complete, you want it to be a well-written, informative and entertaining read. You may have given yourself free rein to experiment, but you will have done so within a certain looseness of structure. There are *some* rules. Your feature will:

- Have an accurate, grammatically sound and authentic narrative, using simple and direct language, and avoiding over-complexity in its sentence structure.
- Have a logical flow that links each paragraph fluidly with the next, and tells the story at an appropriate pace.
- Create an overall effect that will elicit a response from the reader: laughter, excitement, interest, persuasion, inspiration.

Top tips for feature writing

Here in summary are some more specific tips about how to achieve all that:

- Get off to a strong start.
- Strive to pinpoint the exact word(s) to convey your meaning.
- Use simple, familiar words.
- Some of your sentences can be long – but make sure that the writing is clear, the meaning is quickly absorbed and the reader will not be held up trying to work out what you are trying to say.
- Help create a sense of flow with linking words or thoughts that join paragraphs. Use conjunctions like "but" or "yet", or start a paragraph with a thought that picks up directly from the back of the previous paragraph.
- Avoid clichés and over-worn phrases, especially in descriptive passages.
- Use active language not passive, and try to maintain the right pace (which does not necessarily mean a fast pace).
- Avoid digressions, unless there is a reason for them.
- Try to write as you speak – it will help you develop a more natural and relaxed style.
- Do not leave the reader with unanswered questions.
- When you rewrite, try to make the piece shorter not longer.
- Ask for and take notice of feedback.
- Read as much and as widely as you can, to see how others do it.
- Look over your work for evidence of failure to do any of these – and amend accordingly!

Note how many of these tips would apply equally to news reporting. Features are not a separate and discrete branch of journalism. They simply offer a different, and richly rewarding, medium for storytelling.

22

The court reporter

different courts.....deciding what to cover.....who can I talk to? .....who can't I talk to?.....what can and can't I do in court?.....stages of a criminal trial.....the details you will need.....inquests....challenging the court.....requests not to report a case.....live blogging from court.....writing your story

This chapter gives you practical advice about how to approach the job of reporting court cases. It is intended to complement *Essential Law for Journalists* and not to be a substitute for it. *Essential Law* is the place to go for the knowledge you need to pass your NCTJ law exams in media law and regulation, and court reporting. This chapter is your guide as you head to the courts to apply that knowledge.

Criminal proceedings in the courts furnish news organisations with scores of strong stories. Reports of court cases are popular with all audiences – print, online and broadcast. Yet the number of specialist court and crime reporters is in long-term decline, and news editors often send a general reporter to cover cases. You could be that reporter. They also rely heavily on local news agencies to do their court reporting for them. You could be a reporter with one of those agencies. So you need to be ready to tackle a court case at short notice.

Different courts

If you are assigned a case to cover, it is likely to be in one of these three courts:

– **Magistrates' Court.** All criminal cases begin here, and 95 per cent of them are dealt with here too. Only the more serious ones are sent to a higher court for sentence, or for trial by judge and jury. The magistrates themselves, occasionally still known by their older title of Justices of the Peace (JPs), are volunteers and not legal professionals. They will typically sit as a panel – or "bench" – of two or three, one of whom is the chair. Advice on the law and procedure is provided by a legal adviser, or clerk. A district judge also hears cases on his or her own in the magistrates' court.
– **Crown Court.** Cases go to the Crown Court if they are too serious to be heard by magistrates, or if the magistrates feel the crime deserves a sentence beyond the limit they are allowed to impose. In some circumstances, defendants can elect to have their cases heard before a jury in the Crown Court. The court also hears appeals against decisions made by magistrates. The cases are presided over by a judge who decides on matters of law, advises the jury and ensures that the trial is conducted fairly. If the defendant is found guilty, the judge decides the punishment.

– **Coroners' Court.** It is in these courts that inquests are held – inquiries into the cause of suspicious or unexplained deaths. These are very often newsworthy. The court is presided over by a coroner – a former lawyer who might also have some medical expertise. Sometimes a jury is sworn in to decide how someone died. The court does not express an opinion about who if anyone might be criminally responsible – that is the role of the criminal courts.

You might also find yourself at one of these hearings:

– **County Court.** The county courts deal with civil, or non-criminal, matters. Cases are brought not by the Crown Prosecution Service (as in a criminal trial) but by individuals who feel their rights have been infringed. This might be businesses trying to recover money they are owed, people seeking compensation for injuries or landowners seeking orders to stop people trespassing.
– **Tribunals.** All sorts of appeals and disputes are heard by tribunals, which are conducted in a more informal way than cases in the courts. Employment tribunals, often involving appeals against allegedly unfair dismissal, are often a source of good stories.

The most serious or important cases are heard in the **High Court**, which also hears appeals against decisions made in the lower courts.

If you are covering a case, you will usually do so in person. But during the coronavirus pandemic, some courts began hearing both civil and criminal cases remotely, with participants able to join via videolink. This might signal a trend for the future. You make a written application to the court to be given access and are sent a web link that enables you to sign in. What you can see depends on where the camera is pointing, but you should have a general view of the courtroom and be able to hear and follow proceedings. Participants in the case, such as vulnerable witnesses, may themselves be appearing via videolink, and some of the lawyers might be doing so as well. Although these facilities make it possible for you to cover cases without actually attending, they do need organising in advance, and following the trial can be difficult. It is not uncommon for documents to be referred to in court but not read out, so part of the job entails requesting access to papers that have been laid before the court – which you are entitled to see.

Deciding what to cover

You may be sent to court to cover a specific case that you know is about to start. You find out what courtroom has been assigned to the case, check what time it begins, and off you go. Life is a lot more problematic if you are sent to the courts simply to scout around and see if you can pick up some stories. You could well be spoilt for choice. In some towns and cities, there may be a dozen or more magistrates' courts sitting at any one time, and several Crown Courts too. You can only be in one place at a time. Trying to decide which case to follow is very difficult.

There are some things you can do to narrow the search a little. Your starting point in the magistrates' court is the court list, setting out the cases to be heard in each courtroom. You can arrange to have these lists emailed to you. They give you the basic information about each case: the name, address and date of birth of the defendant, the charges and the number of the courtroom. Cases will not necessarily be heard in the order in which they appear on the lists.

A lot of cases in the lower court are heard in a matter of minutes. A defendant may be asked to enter a plea, before being remanded in custody and sent to the higher court. Hearings are often adjourned to a later date to give the parties more time to prepare. Unless it is such a big case that you want to record every stage of it, these hearings will not be of much interest to you.

There might be a dedicated court dealing with the "overnights" – people who have very recently been arrested and charged by the police and need to be produced at court for a first appearance. These cases are at a very early stage and are unlikely to be concluded. They may be worth a short report, depending on the offence. There will be dozens of other cases that you can discount at once – things like minor driving offences or non-payment of the television licence fee. None of these will deliver you a story unless there is something unusual about them, such as someone well known being caught speeding.

More promisingly, some court lists have a separate category of "likely guilty pleas". These are worth looking at. If the defendant pleads guilty, there is a strong chance that the case will go ahead and be concluded in one day. That means you will have a full case to write up. Look for the acronyms NGAP and GAP on the court list – short for Not Guilty Anticipated Plea, and Guilty Anticipated Plea.

There are other things to look for on the magistrates' court lists. The most obvious is the seriousness of the offence, although as we have said, the more serious it is, the more likely it is to be dealt with by the higher court. Keep an eye out for cases in which there is more than one defendant, and look at what they are charged with. Look too for cases in which a single defendant faces a series of charges. Each charge may be relatively minor on its own, such as shoplifting, but if the accused is facing multiple charges it could make a good story. Look at the ages of the defendants. Most elderly people are relatively law abiding, so if the defendant is over 70, say, and the charge looks interesting, it might be worth a look. Disputes between neighbours are common, and provoke the most extraordinary behaviour, even by the otherwise respectable older generation. A row between neighbours over an overgrown leylandii overhanging a boundary can trigger a sequence of events that – since it has ended up in the courts – will be well worth reporting.

There are daily lists for the Crown Court too, which give the name of the defendant and what kind of a hearing it is going to be – a plea, a sentence, a bail application or a full trial. A search of the defendant's name might reveal an earlier appearance in the lower court, which may in turn give you more detail of the charges and the nature of the case. If you learn that a senior judge is sitting, or that a senior barrister (Queen's Counsel, or QC) is appearing, that might be an indication that it is a significant case.

Who can I talk to?

If you have not been to the court before, make sure you arrive in plenty of time. There may be security checks to go through, and you will need to get a sense of the geography of the building. Whether Victorian piles or ultra-modern glass palaces, court buildings can be very hard to find your way around. For both magistrates and Crown Courts, there may be a list caller, who will be able to give you the names of magistrates, lawyers and the time any cases in which you are interested are due to be heard. There might also be a court office where you can check details of pending cases, sentences and remand dates. If a case has been adjourned, the caller/office can let you know the new date, and if a case has been concluded, they will tell you the outcome. Find out where the court office is, and whether or not there is a press room you can work in.

You should behave professionally and respectfully in court. Dress appropriately, do not consume food, stand up when the judge or magistrates enter and leave, and if you need to leave the court during a case, do so as quietly as you can.

If for some reason you have missed a case that sounds interesting, you can write up a basic version of it from the details on the list and from what the court office tells you about the outcome. It will be a short and factual account without much colour but it will mean that you have covered it. It is dangerous to try to put together a fuller retrospective account once the case is over. If you were not there in person to hear what was being said, it is not worth the risk of trying to piece together a fuller report afterwards.

Mistakes are easily made and can get you into trouble. If you missed the case, just report the basic facts: who was charged with what, how they pleaded and what the verdict was – plus the sentence, in the event of a guilty finding.

You can speak to other court officials too. Some legal advisers or clerks are more helpful than others, but they should be prepared to explain points of procedure if you are struggling to follow what is happening. Solicitors and barristers from either prosecution or defence may also help if you ask them, though they are not obliged to do so. Police officers will sometimes give you a steer on a promising case. This is where it helps if you are a regular visitor to a court and your face is known. You will see the same lawyers, court officials and police officers on a regular basis, and can develop a relationship with them. Most barristers like to see their purple oratory quoted in the media, and may be willing to speak to you after a case and fill in any gaps you may have missed in their address to the court. It is also worth listening closely to the judge's summing up at the end of a trial. A punctilious judge will review all the evidence that has been heard in the case, so if you missed any of it, this is a second chance to pick up extra details and fill the gaps – as well as getting a steer on the evidence the judge considers worthy of greatest weight. Judges sometimes make a copy of their sentencing remarks available to the media.

It is not a good idea to talk to defendants or witnesses during a case (see the Editors' Code), but you can do so afterwards if you wish. People who have been acquitted may be only too happy to talk to you and explain how they were almost the victims of a terrible miscarriage of justice. They may even seek you out. If there is a conviction, you might get a police comment about the case, although this will often come from the press office rather than officers on the ground. Police liaison officers will sometimes be helpful in arranging for reporters to talk to victims or their families after a trial, if they wish to speak to the media. We have all seen television pictures of impromptu press conferences being held outside the court buildings, but this tends to happen only in the highest profile cases. That does not mean you cannot go looking for reaction yourself if you feel it would add to your story.

The other group of people you can usefully talk to you are your fellow reporters, if there are others covering the same case as you. You may be working for different organisations, but there is less competition inside the courtroom because you all have access to the same material. Once the case is over of course, it is a different matter. But there is often a camaraderie among court reporters, and you will usually help each other out if someone cannot read their writing or their shorthand, or if there is a key quote that you all want to be sure you have got down right. If this sort of cooperation feels uncomfortable, remember that the day will certainly come when it is you who needs the favour.

Who can't I talk to?

This is a much shorter list. As we have said, you should not approach people involved in a case before or during a trial – except possibly to ask them if they will speak to you afterwards. Remember that the codes forbid you to offer them money for their story. Nor should you approach any of the magistrates or the judge in a case. On no account should you approach a member of a jury at any time.

What can and can't I do in court?

When you go into a courtroom, the first thing to establish is where you are going to sit. If the press box or press bench is not clearly indicated, you can ask a court usher or clerk. With older Victorian courtrooms, acoustics are a problem, and if you find you cannot hear what is being said, you might have to ask if you can move – or just move anyway. If you are sitting a few rows behind a barrister speaking quietly and with their back to you, it can be hard to follow what is being said. Don't wait until it is too late to move discreetly to somewhere you can hear, avoiding the obvious no-go areas.

You can have your laptop or tablet with you in court and your mobile phone too. You cannot use the phone to make or receive calls (turn it to silent) but you can use it to report what is happening by text or tweet or live blogging. Some courts do not like to see mobile and other devices in a courtroom, but you are within your rights to have them and should stand your ground if challenged. It helps if you use them as unobtrusively as you can.

Here are some of the things that you must *not* do:

– Take photographs or video of anything in the court or the court precincts. What constitutes "precincts" is not fully defined, but is usually taken to mean anywhere inside the building or internal spaces like courtyards. Photographs or video of defendants, witnesses and lawyers entering and leaving court buildings are commonplace and are generally tolerated.
– Make or receive calls on your phone in the courtroom.
– Make any audio recording of proceedings.
– Make any sketches inside court: if you need these, they have to be done outside the courtroom, from memory.

Stages of a criminal trial

Here is the typical progress of a criminal case once it comes to trial.

– Preliminary legal arguments
– Jury sworn in (if a Crown Court case) and given instructions by the judge
– Opening statement by the prosecution, setting out the case against the defendant
– Prosecution case outlined in detail, including the calling of witnesses. The evidence of a witness can simply be read out if it is not in dispute. Otherwise, witnesses appear in person to be examined by the prosecution and then by the defence
– Defence case outlined in detail, including the calling of witnesses. Defendants themselves do not have to give evidence if they do not want to do so. As above, agreed evidence can be read out in court. Otherwise the defence lawyer examines the witnesses, and the prosecution can do so as well
– Prosecution closing speech
– Defence closing speech
– Judge sums up, advising the jury on points of law and going through all the evidence that they have heard, emphasising the issues the jury should concentrate on
– Jury sent out to consider the evidence, before returning to the courtroom to announce a verdict
– If the verdict is not guilty, the case is over and the defendant is free to go
– If the verdict is guilty, the judge decides on the sentence, at the time or at a later hearing.

The details you will need

You will need to make a lot of notes during a trial. If you have shorthand, this is where it really comes into its own – indeed, you may struggle without it. You will need an accurate note of the following:

Defendant's name, age, address, occupation and any other details you are able to glean – marital status, children etc. You can record what they are wearing and how they behave in court if you think it is relevant.

Name of judge or chair of the magistrates.

Names of prosecution and defence lawyers.

Names of witnesses, and any other details you are able to find out about them – especially if their relationship to the defendant or victim is relevant.

Defendant's previous convictions and any other offences that are being taken into consideration.

The arguments made by the prosecution and defence lawyers. Because they are attempting to convince and persuade the jury, their speeches will often be littered with memorable quotes.

Details of evidence given by witnesses. Again, look for good direct quotes.

Verdict and sentence, and remarks made by the judge.

Reaction in public gallery, if any.

Inquests

Inquests nearly always produce a story for the simple reason that they consider the circumstances of a death – something in which it is human nature to take an interest. Because they are about exploring what happened rather than apportioning blame, the atmosphere in a coroner's court is often more relaxed than at a criminal hearing.

As with the courts, coroners publish early details of inquests – they are supposed to do so seven days in advance. They are obliged to make public the time and place of the inquest, the name and age of the deceased and the date and place of death. It is likely that the death will already have been reported as a news story, so you can do some homework about the case before you go along to the hearing.

The coroner takes evidence from a variety of sources, as the criminal courts do. Perhaps the most important evidence comes from the pathologist who has carried out the post-mortem examination on the dead person. They will often give detailed (and sometimes graphic) evidence of what they discovered, and what that suggests about the probable cause of death. The coroner asks the questions, although relatives of the dead person will sometimes hire a lawyer to ask questions on their behalf. Even if they don't, the coroner will often invite them to raise any questions they would like answered.

As in the criminal courts, an inquest will not always be completed in one sitting. There will often be an "opening", often lasting only a few minutes, during which the coroner will hear evidence about the time and place of death and the formal identification of the body. The case will then be adjourned for a full hearing at a later date, allowing for a funeral to take place without further delay. An opening might last only a few minutes, and you will not normally report it unless it is a high-profile case.

At the end of the inquest, the coroner or the jury will reach a decision as to the probable cause of death. It used to be said that the coroner *recorded* a verdict and the jury *returned* a verdict. This terminology survives, but these days it is often reported as *a conclusion* about the cause of death.

There are a number of possible conclusions: death by natural causes; accidental death; death in a road traffic accident; death by misadventure; drug-related death; death from industrial disease; unlawful killing; suicide. If the evidence is insufficient to allow a conclusion to be reached, an "open verdict" is recorded. If the coroner adds some comments to the conclusion, this is known as a "narrative verdict." An example might be recommendations that safety or other measures be put in place to ensure that the circumstances that led to the death could not be repeated.

Although you are legally allowed to report all the details you hear at an inquest, for reasons of sensitivity, you will need to be judicious about what you actually include in your published report. That is especially true of deaths by suicide. Refer to the Editors' Code.

Challenging the court

Even courts can get procedure wrong, and there may be occasions when you feel the need to challenge their decisions or ask for reporting restrictions to be lifted. If someone under the age of 18 is convicted of a particularly serious crime, for example, you can ask the judge to agree that his or her name be made public, rather than being concealed on account of age. You may have the support of the prosecution in this. In other cases, you may feel that reporting restrictions being put in place are not justified. If there are other reporters covering the case, you can act jointly. The best way to raise this is by speaking to the clerk, or asking one of the court ushers to pass a message for you. You may be asked to stand and explain the reason for your request. If you are seriously worried about the way things are going, consult your editor.

Even if you think a judge has got it wrong, you must abide by a reporting restriction until it has been overturned. Breaching a court order is a serious matter, a criminal offence where strict liability rules apply. In other words, how you came to breach the order is irrelevant. In theory, you or your editor could face a fine or even a jail term.

Requests not to report a case

It is not uncommon for people to approach reporters after a hearing and ask them not to report a particular case. If anything, this makes it more likely that you *will* report it, in order to demonstrate that you have not yielded to undue pressure. If it is a minor matter that you were not going to bother with anyway, there might not be an issue. But if not, you must never agree to supress your reporting. Be careful – people can become aggressive, and even threatening. Your best response is to say that it is your editor, and not you, who decides what is published, and you will pass on their comments, with any reasons they may have for the request. Always tell your editor or news editor about any such approaches.

Live blogging from court

As noted, you are allowed to use your phone for live reporting from the courtroom, as long as you do it as discreetly as possible. What form that reporting takes will depend on your newsdesk. They may want you to send them updates, which they will process themselves and publish on the web or via social media. You may have the facility to publish directly on to a live blog page on the website. They may prefer a string of tweets.

However you file, the fact that you are allowed to do so presents you with a dilemma, because you cannot do two things at the same time. If you are texting updates, you are not listening to the evidence and making notes of what is being said. You might miss a key point or quote. So it is a balancing act. But in all but the shortest trials, there will be periods when not much is happening – say if legal points are being discussed, or when one witness leaves the witness box and another is sworn in. So you can pick your moments to send updates without jeopardising the full report that you will be filing when the trial is over. And when it comes to the verdict at the end of a trial, your messages can be short and to the point: maybe only a word or two – "guilty", "not guilty", "five years" and so on. If these posts come at the end of a series of others, anyone following the case needs no more information than this.

For a really good and gripping example of live blogging from the closing stages of a murder trial, go here:

https://www.birminghammail.co.uk/news/midlands-news/live-mylee-billingham-murder-father-15167220

Writing your story

There is never a time when care and accuracy are not important in journalism, but court reporting requires the highest possible standards. The stakes are high: get something wrong and you – or your editor – could find yourselves in contempt of court, with little in the way of legal protection. You must take care over every detail, and be confident that you understand the protocols and other requirements of the law as it relates to the media and reporting of the courts. Make sure you hold on to your notes of cases for several months.

Beyond that, you are in the familiar business of storytelling, and court cases frequently throw up very strong stories that will have a big appeal for most audiences. As with all your other reporting, you are looking for a strong introduction, and some good colour and quotes. Within that well-known framework, there are some details that you *must* include in any court report:

> *The name of the court.*
>
> *The name and other details of the defendant.* It is important to include the address and any other identifying details. This helps avoid confusion with other people who have the same name as the defendant, or live in the same area.
>
> *The offence or offences with which they are charged.* Do not rely solely on the court list. Charges can be dropped or added. Listen to the charges that are actually put to the defendant in court.
>
> *The plea.* State whether the defendant pleaded guilty or not guilty. (Note: the past tense of "plead" is "pleaded" – not "pled".)
>
> *The verdict.* State whether he or she was found guilty or not guilty.
>
> *The sentence (if there has been a conviction).* Sentencing can sometimes be postponed until a later date. If that is the case, say so.

If the case is adjourned, say so and give the reason and new hearing date if you have them.

All of these things must feature in every court report you do, however short, and whatever platform.

When quoting lawyers, make sure it is clear which side of the case they are on. "John Smith, *prosecuting*, ….." or "for the *prosecution*, John Smith ….." . Ditto "Jane Jones, *defending*…." or "for the *defence*, Jane Jones….." You will want to report both sides of the case in roughly equal proportions. If the trial lasts more than a day, your report on the first day will deal almost exclusively with the prosecution evidence and the defence will hardly get a look in. If this happens, make sure that your report on Day 1 ends with the words "the case continues" to indicate that we have not yet heard both sides of the story. And make sure that the balance is righted when the defence gets its turn the following day. If you start reporting a case, you must make sure that the eventual outcome is reported too. If you don't, you may well find yourself on the receiving end of a complaint of unfairness, especially in the event of a "not guilty" verdict.

With all of this detail to record, it is sometimes hard to write a story that does not feel rather stilted and formal. This can be exacerbated by the legal system's love of jargon and orotund language. As with all jargon, do what you can to render it into everyday spoken English. A few examples:

> Entered a plea of guilty = admitted, or pleaded guilty
> Knowingly and with intent = deliberately/ intentionally
> Occasioned = caused
> Pending = until
> The accused = the defendant, or – preferably – their name
> Was in possession of = had
> Witnessed = saw.

Do not let any of this stand in the way of the colour and vividness of the case. Courtrooms are often the settings for incredible human drama, and should be treated like any other story when it comes to deciding what goes into your intro and what the best quotes and angles are. Remember you are writing a news story rather than an official record of court proceedings. Compare the approaches in these two versions of a fictional court case:

Version 1

James Green, 34, of Parsons Lane, Newtown, was sentenced to seven years in prison at Newtown Crown Court yesterday after being found guilty of causing actual bodily harm.

The court head that Green had attacked two men in a pub where more than twenty people were watching a football match featuring his home team, Tottenham Hotspur.

Sarah Simpson, prosecuting, said Green had drunk more than ten pints of beer and several glasses of whisky when he launched what she called "a frenzied drunken attack" on fellow drinkers during an argument after a Tottenham player was sent off.

Version 2

Spurs fan James Green was jailed for seven years yesterday for "a frenzied drunken attack" while watching football in a pub.

Green saw red after a Spurs player was sent off, and two men were seriously hurt in the fracas that followed. Newtown Crown Court heard that he had drunk more than ten pints of beer and several whiskies.

In sum, you need to be especially careful about reporting court cases. You must conform to the laws relating to media coverage, and your story must contain a number of mandatory elements. But beyond that, the technique is exactly the same as that you would employ with any other news story. Look for the telling detail, the most arresting angle. And of course the headline or top news line. This will often be the outcome, but it could come from any element of the case. You could get your news line from:

– **The sentence**: "Pensioner banned for speeding"
– **The verdict**: "Accountant guilty of tax fraud"
– **The defendant (or anyone else in the case) if they are well-known**: "Film star fined for drunken outburst" "Man jailed for stealing from soccer star"
– **The nature of the crime**: "Banker crashed best friend's sports car" "Man stole 200 rare birds' eggs"
– **The time and place**: "Naked groom arrested on stag night" "Bank robbed during Easter break"
– **Mitigating circumstances**: "Husband topped 100 mph taking sick wife to hospital" "Driver went on drinking spree after girlfriend dumped him".

Let your journalistic instincts for the story dictate how you write up your case. You must be accurate and comply with the law. But this does not have to be a straitjacket that prevents you from producing a lively and readable account of the case.

23
The political reporter

Politics affects us all. It is the subject of, or a feature of, all sorts of stories across every branch of the news media.

Local government

On any local or regional outlet, whatever the medium, you are likely to find yourself covering stories either directly or indirectly associated with local government. Councils in the UK are responsible for many aspects of our everyday lives, from schools to street lighting, from social services to planning and much else besides. They have the power to raise money through the council tax to add to the cash they receive from central government. This money pays for transport, highways, police, fire, libraries, leisure and recreation, rubbish collection and disposal, environmental health and trading standards. So the decisions they make have a direct and significant effect on the lives of everyone covered by their jurisdiction.

Some of the issues they have to deal with may seem minor, such as the frequency of rubbish collections or dogs fouling public parks. But these issues are of great importance to residents, who want to read and hear about them from local newspapers – whether in print or online – and on local radio. Local authorities are therefore the source of many of the stories you will work on at a local, regional or occasionally national level.

Like all elected officials, councillors are accountable to the voters, and it is part of the job of the media to keep those voters informed about how they are doing. Sadly, there has been a steady decline in the reporting of local government in many areas over recent years. This is a great shame. It means many good stories are not being told, and it represents a weakening of that journalistic purpose of scrutinising the activities of those in positions of power – especially those spending public money – and holding them to account. There is a ray of light, however. The Local Democracy Reporter Service, funded by the BBC through the licence fee, was a positive effort to redress the balance, and saw the appointment of 150 journalists dedicated to council reporting. It has already paid dividends, producing literally thousands of stories for local media.

Reporting local government is like all other reporting in most respects, but it does require a degree of familiarity with the mechanics of how things work, and this may vary from one authority to another.

The purpose of this chapter is to offer some practical advice and tips about how to approach the reporting of this particular area.

The structure of local government

First, a brief reminder of the different sorts of meetings that you might find yourself sent to cover. As you will know from *Essential Public Affairs*, the structure of local government is different in each of the four nations of the UK, and varies from area to area.

In most of **England**, there are two sorts, or tiers, of council: county councils and district councils – with responsibility for council services split between them. County councils look after education, social services and waste disposal. District councils are responsible for rubbish collection, housing and planning applications.

Some urban areas have single-tier authorities known as unitary authorities that provide all the services in their areas. The biggest cities and their areas, such as Greater Manchester and the West Midlands, have single-tier metropolitan district councils. London has 32 boroughs and an over-arching authority.

The picture is simpler in **Scotland**, where there are 32 local authorities, or councils, providing services including education, social care, waste management, libraries and planning.

There are 22 unitary authorities in **Wales** covering planning, education, libraries, environmental health, refuse, housing and social services.

There are 11 local councils in **Northern Ireland** covering a similar range of activities.

Councils typically have a network of separate committees, each with specific responsibilities such as social services, housing or planning. Although you will cover full meetings of the council, some of the best stories will come from committee meetings.

Parish, or town councils are at the bottom of the democratic structure. Even if you do not attend their meetings, it is well worth keeping in touch with the chair or clerk about what is going on at this very local level. Although they mainly make recommendations, they are good for taking the temperature of local feelings on things like planning applications, and stories that start small at this level will often develop into something more significant. It is good to get in at the ground floor on such stories.

Day-by-day reporting

As with so many areas of grass-roots journalism, the secret of success lies in the range and quality of your contacts. If you are reporting your local councils regularly, you will want to be able to contact any of your local councillors at any time – and make it clear that you want them to contact you if they have anything they consider might be newsworthy. Make yourself known to all of them if you can. There is much more party politics in play in councils these days, so always be aware of the party perspective or political loyalties of the councillor you are dealing with. Most will be reluctant to stray too far from the party line, but they might speak to you off the record if there are policies they are particularly unhappy with – or if they just like a good gossip. Independent councillors have no one to answer to but themselves, and will be often be a good source of information. They offer a counterpoint to the narratives that come from the rival parties, but they have no direct inside knowledge of what the ruling party is up to.

Get to know council press officers too. Many of them will be former journalists who have at one time done the job that you are doing now. But they too have an agenda, so you need to look carefully at their press releases, as you would any other press release, rather than taking them at face value.

Council officers – the people who advise councillors and make recommendations, and who actually implement the council's decisions – are obviously very good contacts. Chief executives and directors of finance can be very valuable sources. Less senior officers may be apprehensive or suspicious about talking to you, but those you are able to cultivate over time will be very helpful. Even if they will speak to you off the record only, they can be invaluable in explaining complicated policy issues to you. You will sometimes get more and better information from figures further down the chain, such as planning officers.

Stories will come to you in many ways. In some cases it may simply be a case of following up on something from a council meeting. You may hear a snippet or a throwaway line at a meeting, or see something buried in the paperwork that you think is worth further inquiry, and which you pursue separately. Members of the public who see or hear your name in association with a story will contact you directly to tell you of similar instances, or to describe their own experiences. If your name appears against a story about street lighting in one area, you will find people from other areas contacting you to tell you about the state of the lighting where they live: one story can be a spark for others. Councillors too will start to come to you with stories once you have established yourself as someone who is interested in reporting local issues. You can examine public records of the council accounts, and the expenses being claimed by councillors. The letters pages of newspapers, local radio phone-ins or *Facebook* community groups may alert you to local issues of which you were not aware – and provide you with potential contacts and interviewees. And so on. Once started, you will find plenty of material and plenty of stories. You can be encouraged by the fact that these are matters close to the hearts of your audience, and that by covering them, you are helping fulfil one of the most important democratic functions of journalism.

Council politics

Depending on the political make-up of the council you are covering, some stories will be about the politics alone, or will have a strongly political element. Tensions will run particularly high in the run-up to the May elections, or if the ruling party has only a small majority, or no majority at all. You need to be sure that your reporting is impartial and that you always gather a range of comments and views on each story. You do not want to be accused of following the agenda of one party, or not subjecting all parties to the same scrutiny and rigour. Remember to treat your sources with scepticism – if a councillor comes to you with a red-hot tip-off, it may be a great story, but you should pause and think about their motivation, as well as checking out what they are telling you.

Council meetings: paperwork and previews

As with so many assignments, the secret to council reporting is preparation and planning. These days, most councils and their committees publish the agendas of their meetings, and most of the supporting documentation, at least a week in advance – sometimes longer. This gives you the opportunity to get a head start on some of the issues that will be coming up, to research them thoroughly and perhaps to write some of them up as preview pieces.

So if you know you are going to be covering a meeting, your first task is to go through the paperwork and look for potential stories. They will not always be obvious: council officers are not employed for their news sense, and use officialese, convoluted sentences and technical language that can make the paperwork difficult to understand. It is a code that you have to crack. With time and practice you will learn to penetrate the acronyms and the verbiage, and tease out the interesting and potentially significant stories. This of course is part of what you are accustomed to doing in other areas of journalism: it is simply a matter of applying your skills to this area.

You should make a point of going through *all* the documents – even the Appendices, because quite often that is where the story is buried. Each report is written by a named officer, so you can contact them if you want more information.

In your reading, you are looking in particular for:

upcoming decisions, especially those involving spending, that might have substantial or controversial consequences

planning applications that may be controversial – and most of them are. Even apparently minor ones can arouse mighty passions and produce good human interest stories

new developments in stories that have been running for some time

decisions that might represent a change in policy or changing allocation of resources

anything offbeat or interesting that might make a colourful story.

Many council meetings are routine and much of the business is, to be candid, not very interesting from a journalistic point of view. Few members of the public exercise their right to attend. So look out for anything that might offer something out of the ordinary to enliven proceedings. Find out which councillors sit on this particular panel or committee – are they known for their strong views, or usually good for a colourful quote? Is there a guest speaker of some sort, or someone submitting a petition? Is one of the council officers due to give a presentation at the meeting? If there is a controversial planning issue to be discussed, scores of residents may turn up to lobby councillors, both in favour of an application and against it. These meetings can get very rowdy and heated. The committee will allow members of the public to make short representations to them ahead of the discussion – usually limited to one or two representative submissions of about three minutes each. Any or all of these might give you a strong story.

On reading through the papers, you may find two or three stories that you or your newsdesk think are worth previewing – in other words writing stories that look ahead to what will be happening: "councillors will decide next week whether to spend fifty thousand pounds on….." You can call some of the councillors involved to see if they will give you a quote in advance. Some may not want to talk to you ahead of the meeting, but they might be prepared to give you some background and a steer off the record as to whether they think the decision will be a controversial one, and how the vote might go. You can follow up locally with people likely to be affected by the decision – many of whom will not even be aware that it is about to be resolved by the council.

Most councils pride themselves on their transparency, and publish a lot of material online. But individual council officers will probably be reluctant to talk to you directly unless you have cultivated a relationship with them. They will probably refer you to a council press officer, who should be able to point you in the right direction. If they are reluctant to give you extra information to which you think you are entitled, you can submit a Freedom of Information (FOI) request. This can take a few weeks to deliver a response. Before you go down this route, double-check that the information you are seeking is not already available somewhere on the council's website.

As in all forms of journalism, you will find having the right contacts extremely valuable. If you are covering local government issues on a regular basis, you will find that you are talking to some councillors quite frequently – especially if they are the chairs of committees, for example, or cabinet members with special areas of responsibility. They are very useful sources for you. If you get to know them well enough to be able to call them out of hours, and they trust the integrity of your reporting, you will be able to secure quotes at short notice and get a lot of background material and context that will give you a better understanding of the story.

At the meeting

So much for your preparation. What about the meetings themselves?

Again, as ever, a little preparation goes a long way. Arrive in plenty of time, so that you can get yourself organised before the meeting starts. With some councils, you will be able to walk straight into the room where the meeting is being held. With others, you will be asked to wait until you are collected and taken to the room just before the meeting starts. Check that there are no new documents that have been submitted since the paperwork was published.

If you are not familiar with the venue, identify yourself to someone who looks as though they are helping set up the meeting, telling them you are a reporter and asking if there is a designated area for the media. Make sure you are happy with where they put you: if you have to get up during the meeting, say to chase someone you want to speak to who is leaving early, you need to be sitting somewhere that allows you to do that without disrupting proceedings – near the door, for example. So if the place you are offered is not to your liking, ask to move somewhere else. You can always sit in the public gallery if you wish.

You will need to know the policy of the council when it comes to recording, taking pictures and reporting direct from the meeting from the meeting via social media. Not all of them have the same protocols. Some will make clear their position within the paperwork, with a notice such as this one, taken from a council website. Note that most of this applies to anyone attending the meeting, not just reporters:

Mobile technology and filming – acceptable use

Those attending for the purpose of reporting on the meeting may use social media or mobile devices in silent mode to send electronic messages about the progress of the public parts of the meeting. To support this, County Hall has wifi available for visitors – please ask at reception for details.

Anyone is permitted to film, record or take photographs at council meetings. Please liaise with the council officer listed in the agenda prior to the start of the meeting so that those attending the meeting can be made aware of any filming taking place.

Use of mobile devices, including for the purposes of recording or filming a meeting, is subject to no disruptions, distractions or interference being caused by the PA or Induction Loop systems or any general disturbance to proceedings. The Chairman may ask for mobile devices to be switched off in these circumstances.

It is requested that if you are not using your mobile device for any of the activities outlined above it be switched off or placed in silent mode during the meeting to prevent interruptions and interference with PA or Induction Loop systems.

Thank you for your cooperation.

This particular council takes the view that you can do pretty much what you like as long as you do not disrupt proceedings or interfere with the sound systems. Not all are so liberal. Make sure you are aware of the rules at the meeting you are attending – and that you have found out what the wifi password is before the meeting starts.

Ideally your seat will be at a desk or table, so that you can set your equipment out in front of you. You probably will not be offered a printed agenda, so unless you have printed it yourself in advance, you will want to have the agenda open in front of you on your laptop. This leaves your phone free for posting on social media and for making a recording of any part of the proceedings that you think is worth capturing – also for social media use, or simply so that you can listen later and make sure you have your quotes right. You can also use your phone to take still or video pictures of anything untoward, such as a disturbance in the public gallery.

The council will usually make and publish a recording of the meeting, but it is unwise to rely on it. Some recordings are of dubious quality and hard to decipher when you are listening back. They might only be made available several days after the meeting has finished, which is of no use to you. A webcast though should be quickly accessible, and if you know that there is one available, you will feel more confident about leaving the meeting for a few minutes if you need to do so to find a potential interviewee. You know you will be able to listen back to what has happened in your absence.

The meeting will be run by the mayor or council/committee chair. They will normally sit with council officials, who will advise them on policy and background, and speak to papers in their name. The individual councillors will speak when invited to do so by the chair. If you are not familiar with the councillors, and they don't have name cards in front of them, you will find photographs of them on the council website which should help you identify them. Other councillors will refer to them by name, so you will usually be able to work out who is who. If you are covering a committee meeting, there will be a relatively small number of members, so you can make a list of them in advance and work out who is who as you go along. Failing all that of course, you can ask after the meeting. The same is true of any council officers or members of the public who speak during the meeting. Remember though that members of the public who address the meeting on a given issue are probably interested only in that one issue, and will leave once it has been discussed. So if you want to speak to them for whatever reason, you have to be ready to leave the meeting for a while and catch them on the way out.

How many social media updates you post, and how much time you devote to making notes and concentrating on what is going on in front of you, will depend on the nature of the debate and the level of interest your audience is likely to have in it. Councillors will often be posting live updates themselves, so it is a good idea to follow them online and see what they are saying. Do not be surprised to find that they are also following you, and that something you post is picked up and perhaps even referred to later in the debate. You will also get used to hearing references to previous reporting that you or others have done on the subject in hand.

If you have done your homework in advance and earmarked the items you think might be newsworthy, you should find it easy to decide what stories are worth writing up. Some items can develop unexpectedly during the debate, if there are strongly opposing views. Do not try to take a verbatim account – make sure you have the main points – including the final decision – and some good colourful direct quotes.

Writing your stories

As we said at the start of this chapter, the decisions councils take affect many aspects of our daily lives. Remember that when you come to write up your story. Your readers will not want a dull account of a council discussion. They want that discussion turned into a readable account that is relevant to them.

This means avoiding where you can some of the off-putting jargon of a council meeting. Concentrate on the outcome and effect of the discussion and describe it in relatable terms:

> Councillors on Newtown Council's finance committee voted last night to approve proposed increases of three per cent in next year's council tax.

Would be more interesting written as:

> Newtown residents will have to pay more for local services next year, with council tax bills going up by three per cent.

Make sure your report is fair and balanced, with quotes and perspectives from both sides of the debate. When you quote councillors, always give them their titles and make sure you report their political affiliation, and probably the name of the ward they represent as well: "Councillor Jack Brown (Liberal Democrat, Bankside) said ......"

Make sure that your report makes clear the outcome of the debate – whether a motion was passed or defeated, or a decision adjourned until a later date. You may need to double-check exactly what was decided. This may seem odd, but sometimes it can be very hard to work out how items have been resolved, especially as the chair or officers may well use jargon such as "defer and decide" to wrap up the discussion, or there is an agreement that a controversial item be "taken back" to committee for further discussion. If you are not sure what that means, go and ask someone afterwards. Never feel embarrassed about asking these questions, even if it is something as basic as clarifying what was actually decided. If you are not sure, you cannot write an accurate and well-informed story, you will get things wrong and you will sell your audience short. Remember that decisions made in committee might not necessarily be final, but have to go to the full council for final sign-off.

Filing your stories

When the meeting is over, you may find that you have several stories worth reporting. Some will be self-contained, in the sense that with the paperwork and what you have heard in the debate, you have all the material you need to write the story. In other cases, you may feel the need to speak to councillors or others who were not at the meeting, for information and comments that will ensure that you report the story properly and reflect all appropriate points of view. You can hang about after the meeting and try to buttonhole councillors, but be aware that sometimes meetings end with what are called "Part Two" agenda items from which the press and public are excluded, so you might have to wait quite a long time for them to finish.

You may also wish to speak to councillors or press officers if there are elements of the debate that you did not understand, or areas in which you feel you need more detail.

Councillors are wont to bandy statistics and make claims during their speeches. Although you can quote them of course – making sure you attribute – you will often feel the need to check out some of these figures or statements. This is especially important if they have come up with something striking that you intend to include as a significant element of your story – or even to make the top line. Councillors are no more reliable than anyone else when it comes to the use of statistics to support their arguments, and they are also capable of making honest mistakes in the handling of data. You can ask them afterwards where they got their figures from – you may be able to verify them yourself online; and/or you can ask a press officer about them, to see if the figures are robust.

Some county councils hold their meetings during the day, but many other councils and committees meet in the evening, and so will finish quite late. Having decided which stories you want to write, you then need to decide when to file them. This will depend on a balance between two things:

– Whether you have all the information you need to write your story – as above. If you need to gather further detail and comments, you are probably not going to be able to do that until the following day
– Your deadline. This is something you need to discuss with your newsdesk. You may well be in a position to talk to the desk and make a preliminary decision in advance of the meeting. Even if you file a story for the website as soon as the meeting is over, it is possible that it will not be processed and published until editorial staff come to work the next morning. If you are working for a newspaper with an approaching deadline, or for a broadcast outlet, you may be under pressure to produce something more quickly.

If you have already published a preview of something that was coming up for debate, you will usually want to do a follow-up story to report what actually happened at the meeting. Sometimes the lively or hostile response generated by a preview story can result in the council removing the item from the agenda while they think again about whether to proceed. If you discover they have done that, you have yourself a story.

A story that is appearing in a newspaper or website will ideally be illustrated with a picture – and in the case of the latter, perhaps some video. Pictures taken at meetings are unlikely to be very interesting unless there has been an unexpected development such as an intervention from the public gallery. So you need to think about pictures that could be used to accompany your story. Sometimes a picture of the building, road, park, shopping centre or whatever has been discussed will serve this purpose. Your office may well have suitable stock pictures on file. If not, you might have to go and take some yourself.

Much of this will apply to the first few meetings you cover. As you do more, you will learn how to read the paperwork with a more educated eye, you will develop more knowledge of local issues, you will know the names of councillors and many of them will have become regular contacts.

National government

It is unlikely that you will be reporting from a national Parliament or Assembly at the start of your career, although if you develop an interest in local government, this might well be a logical next step. Your early links to central government will probably be through your local Member, or Members, of Parliament (MP). MPs are very valuable contacts. They are always keen to speak to their electorate through local media, and so will usually be very willing to speak to you. They want the voters to know that they are active in Parliament and doing a good job on behalf of their constituents. They will nearly always be good for a quote on national or local issues, and almost anything they have to say will be newsworthy. They may proactively keep you in touch with what they are doing at Westminster – where they stand on the big issues, or causes that they are actively trying to promote.

If you want to move from covering local politics to the national stage, try to make a name for yourself as someone who is interested in political stories and can find them. Putting in FOI requests is one way of doing this, as is perusing some of the vast number of documents published by *gov.uk* and *parliament.uk* You may find something that others have missed. Attend as many political events as you can – debates, speeches, conferences: many of them are free, and you will make some useful contacts. As ever, coming up with good story ideas is one of the best ways to get noticed by potential employers.

The job of a political correspondent based in Westminster extends far beyond reporting what happens in the House of Commons or House of Lords. True, there are set piece occasions in the chamber that will make big news stories, such as ministerial statements or debates on current issues, or close votes; and of course, there is the weekly political theatre of Prime Minister's Question Time. Select committees are powerful bodies that often tackle topical issues and take evidence from prominent people, some of whom may be in the eye of whatever the current storm may be. They are a good source of stories.

But much of your work will be done away from the chamber, around the corridors and committee rooms of the Palace of Westminster. The building itself is something of a warren, and there are some areas that are off limits to journalists, so one of your first tasks is to find your way around and learn some of the short cuts. A friendly colleague is probably the best person to help with this, and generally to show you the ropes. This will also involve discovering the day's order of business, what parliamentary resources are available to you, what committees are sitting in what rooms and so on. It is worth investing in a copy of *Vacher's Parliamentary Companion*, which contains the names and contact details of those in the political arena across the UK's parliamentary institutions, as well as an updated calendar of political events and news from the UK and EU parliaments and assemblies. It is a paperback book, published four times a year to reflect the constant changes in government roles and responsibilities, so you will need to buy a new edition every so often. There are several online sites carrying this information, and these are always up to date; but it may not always be convenient for you to go online to check a simple fact in a hurry.

Political journalists work within a "lobby" system that gives them privileged access to government briefings. These are mostly off the record – which is why so many political stories quote unnamed "government sources". Not every publication or political journalist has access to the lobby – online news media are all excluded – and the lobby system has always had its critics from those who see it as an unaccountable closed shop. More US-style televised briefings from Downing Street may answer some of these criticisms. But most political journalists are in constant search of exclusive stories, and are unlikely to abandon time-honoured practices of off-the-record conversations and informal briefings.

Nowhere in journalism is a good contacts book more valuable than at Westminster. MPs love gossip as much as journalists do, and many political stories come from the conversations that go on in the bars and restaurants in the streets around Parliament. Much of your time as a political reporter is spent in talking to ministers and MPs, trying to find out what is going on behind the scenes and get the first whiff of a potential story. You will find that that contacts you made in your local or regional reporting days will be extremely useful to you when you start reporting from Westminster. If you already know two or three MPs, or even more, you have the ready-made beginnings of a political contacts book, with the advantage that you are building on relationships that already exist. Many seasoned and long-serving political correspondents continue to rely heavily on contacts they made in their early days of reporting from a town or region.

It is also worth talking to Special Advisers, or SPADS, a relatively new phenomenon that has transformed the working practices of political journalists over recent years. They represent a whole new tier of communication – go-betweens for relaying to journalists what ministers are thinking or doing. Some have become extremely powerful, and much better known than many ministers in the Cabinet. Remember that they are there to push a political perspective and agenda, and see you as a useful vehicle for doing so. A useful vehicle is not something you necessarily want to be, great though they are as contacts; so exercise the usual discrimination and scepticism in your dealings with them.

For an inside account of a SPAD in action, read *Power Trip: A Decade of Policy, Plots and Spin* by Damian McBride.

A lot of your work will be done on the phone. But one advantage of what is sometimes called "the Westminster village" is that everyone is physically present within a small area, taking in the Palace itself and the nearby blocks that house the offices of backbench MPs. If you wander around, you will bump into people and can chat to them and see if you can get any interesting news lines from them. Ministers are harder to pin down. They spend more of their time in their Whitehall departments and unless you are close enough to them to call them directly, you will probably need to go through a press officer to gain access to them.

Much of your reporting might be about the pure politics of government tactics and personalities, who is in favour and who is in trouble. But remember that, like local authorities, governments make decisions that affect all aspects of our lives, from how much tax we pay to how they choose to spend it. Those decisions are probably of more interest to your audience than "in" stories about MPs and parties jockeying for position and advantage.

In order to report the stories on the political agenda, you will find yourself having to know something about a large number of areas. This might include some basic knowledge of economic theory, and the way the big parties approach the management of the economy; some familiarity with the workings of public services like health, education, pensions and social care; and an idea of the main global issues of the day and where the UK stands in relation to them. This means constant reading around your subject and an ability to brief yourself rapidly if an issue suddenly comes to political prominence.

To keep up with what is happening at Westminster, look at Red Box, a daily political briefing from *The Times*, with a regular podcast. You have to pay a subscription for print or digital access. The daily morning newsletters from Politico, at https://www.politico.eu/newsletter/london-playbook/ are also essential reading for the political classes. Each of the political parties has its own website, and you will need to understand where each of them stands on any given issue.

Some tips for political reporters:

– Learn the language of Westminster. You will have been introduced to much of it in the Public Affairs syllabus, but now you will be seeing and hearing it in action and it will become part of your daily routine. You will often need to explain the intricacies of the political and parliamentary processes to your audience in simple and understandable terms. Do not assume that they have much prior knowledge.
– Treat statistical claims with care. Remember all the cautions and caveats we examined in Chapter 12. Facts and figures are bandied about with abandon in the political arena, and are almost always open to challenge or interpretation. Handle with care.
– Listen carefully. A change of direction or a change of opinion can be signalled very subtly. You need to listen hard for the nuances. Sometimes this will be a case of comparing something being said now with what was said before, and looking for tiny changes of emphasis or choice of words. Be prepared to go back and find out what was said before.
– You will have many informal conversations with all sorts of people. Very often they will not want to be quoted directly. Always be clear whether you being told something unattributedly or not. It is essential to know whether your interviewees are talking on or off the record. See Chapter 7.
– Remember the audience. It is easy to get immersed in the ins and outs of Westminster politics and personalities, and to lose sight of the issues that really matter to your audience.

24
The specialist reporter

At some stage in your career, you may decide that you want to specialise in one particular area of journalism. This may be a form, such as feature writing, or radio documentaries. It may be a particular medium. Or it may be a subject area such as politics, health, sport, business, lifestyle or culture. It might be a combination of all of these.

Specialist journalists add value because they have expert knowledge of their subjects and the communication skills to share it in a readily understandable form. They make sense of complicated issues and offer informed judgements. They provide depth, texture, background and explanation, helping audiences understand and make their own informed assessments about what is going on in the world.

Most specialists are journalists first and specialists second. In other words, they train and work as general reporters at the start of their careers before deciding to concentrate on a particular area. It is unusual, but not unheard of, for people with specialist knowledge and expertise but no journalistic background to become journalists. You will read of one striking example of this below.

There is no set path to becoming a specialist. Many find they drift into it by writing about a particular subject over a period, either because they are asked to, or because one story leads to another and they suddenly find they have become the go-to reporter in that field. What you specialise in will also depend on your particular interests, knowledge, background and preferences – and on happenstance.

Because there are no hard and fast rules, and it is hard to generalise, this chapter consists of contributions from a number of distinguished specialist journalists. Between them they cover a broad range of specialist subjects across media, and their personal profiles are equally varied. You can read more about their individual career paths at the end of the chapter. Before that, they share their own stories and experiences, and offer advice to those who aspire to set out along this route. In doing so, they also restate and underline the importance of many of the messages that are contained in this book.

Was there anything in your background that led you to your chosen specialism, or helped you make a success of it?

Roger Harrabin, Environment Analyst, BBC News

– When I started reporting the environment there was only one environment specialist in the UK. The excellent Geoffrey Lean – then of the *Observer*– said: "In those days I would see the whole UK environment press pack every morning when I looked in the mirror".
– There was huge appetite within the BBC for my stories, although some of the old guard considered them to be a bit hippyish. Things have changed now.

Eleni Courea, Political Reporter, The Times

– I've long had a fascination with British politics (slightly oddly, as I grew up in Cyprus – I used to watch old PMQs on YouTube). I went on to study politics at Cambridge, although paradoxically my course covered barely any British politics. So I don't think it [a degree in your specialism] is at all a prerequisite.

– What helped the most was perhaps running my college politics society – we organised regular panel debates with some high-profile figures and my job was to write to them and get them to agree to come. That process was actually pretty similar to firing off emails to potential sources and interviewees as a journalist.

– The other thing I did while at university and which helped was an internship at the *Spectator*. It lasted only a week but involved plenty of writing, so it gave me a real flavour of what political journalism was like.

Paul Kelso, Business Correspondent, Sky News, former Sports Correspondent

– Knowing a lot about your brief is essential but it's an inevitable by-product of doing the job and comes with time. More important is a grasp of the tenets of journalism. They don't change regardless of the subject.

– I always loved sport and great sports writing, but being able to recall Cup Final results is of little use if you don't think about what questions to ask, can't record the answers correctly and can't express the essential issues clearly.

Jeremy Laurence, former Health Editor, the Independent

– My father was a doctor. I took science A levels. Between school and university I worked in upcountry hospitals in Uganda. The experience made a deep impression on me. I have returned to Africa many times since, chiefly reporting on the HIV/Aids pandemic.

Adina Campbell: Community Affairs Correspondent, BBC News

– My current role was advertised a few months after I joined network news. I never intentionally set out to work in community affairs but by then I'd covered many stories which involved speaking to people who often felt marginalised and sidelined. My job is to get more of their voices on mainstream programmes and tell their personal stories. I strive to build trust and good relationships with people I meet and that's helped secure interviews. As a black woman I know how it feels to be in the minority and overlooked.

Simon Walters, Assistant Editor, the Daily Mail and former Political Editor, Mail on Sunday

– A lifelong interest in current affairs. I was brought up to be curious, enthusiastic and fair-minded.

Will Gompertz, Arts Editor, BBC News

– I had everything and nothing required for my BBC job. I didn't tick any of the official boxes (no degree, no previous experience, etc.), but I ticked most of the unofficial ones (senior arts world connections, sector knowledge and experience, written for national newspapers, curiosity, articulate, enterprising).

Emily Beament, Environment Correspondent, PA Media

– Though my qualifications in the area are limited to an A level in Social Biology, the environment has always been something I've been passionate about, and I think that's true for a lot of reporters in the sector. We had to choose a specialist area as part of our City journalism course, and it seemed a natural choice to select environmental reporting.

– My year in Dublin, where I was part of a reporting team of six, gave me the opportunity to carve out a bit of a niche in environmental stories which I was then able to use as evidence of my interest in the sector for my PA interview for the environment correspondent job.

Chris Morris, Reality Check Correspondent, BBC News, former foreign correspondent

– I studied history and international politics, so I always had an interest in foreign affairs and diplomacy. That pushed me towards foreign journalism. Languages are important – but I certainly wouldn't describe myself as a linguist. I think curiosity to find out more about the world is the most important quality you need to succeed. The level of specialism you choose to acquire is really up to you.

How and why did you make the move from a generalist role to a specialist one?

ROGER HARRABIN: On the *World at One* the editors just let me get on with anything that I thought looked interesting. It produced good radio, and it got on air.

ELENI COUREA: I very much started out as a specialist – writing for a trade magazine about science policy – and simply moved from one specialism to another. I've never worked as a generalist reporter. I'd say that starting out as a specialist by taking that same route is a really good way to break into the industry. Traditionally local papers were where cub reporters cut their teeth but, sadly, that is now a much harder route to follow because they have suffered years of financial hardship and declining circulations. I think trade magazines have largely replaced them in that function.

PAUL KELSO: In my first newsroom, specialisms were seen as a way of separating yourself from the herd, of avoiding the inevitable slow-days as a reporter on the cab rank, of developing contacts and story ideas and themes. They had status, and titles beneath their bylines. (Also, being a Sports Correspondent brought sensational lifestyle benefits.)

JEREMY LAURENCE: When I started in the mid-1970s, most journalists learned on the job. There were two routes in: either get a job on a local paper and hope to make the leap to Fleet Street from there; or get a job on a specialist magazine, develop an expertise and make the leap that way. I chose the latter.

ADINA CAMPBELL: It was timing. My job came up unexpectedly and by that point I'd worked on dozens of national stories and built up a great number of contacts. Up until this point in my career I'd been a "jack of all trades" so to speak, and worked on any story thrown my way. When this job was advertised I saw it as an opportunity to focus on diverse audiences and bring their stories to light. Working as a specialist means having an extensive contacts book as well as providing deeper analysis and understanding about your subject area.

SIMON WALTERS: I enjoyed being a municipal reporter on my local paper. Moving on to national politics seemed a natural progression.

WILL GOMPERTZ: Becoming a specialist does not mean ceasing to be a generalist. It means hyper-contextualisation, deep sector knowledge and an unrivalled black book of contacts (who will actually pick up the phone to you). The advantage of specialising is focused reporting around which you and your readers/viewers can build a relationship. The disadvantage is the risk of getting boxed in, finding the specificity limiting not liberating.

EMILY BEAMENT: I was keen to get a specialist job to enable me to have more autonomy over my work and to really get into a subject. It was also a natural career progression within PA for general reporters to go for and secure specialist jobs. I had previously made it known within PA I'd be interested in the environment role if the opportunity arose. When the job came up there was a formal interview process.

CHRIS MORRIS: In some ways I've always been a specialist. Being a foreign correspondent means you know more about the country you're based in than almost anyone else in your organisation. You are their eyes and ears in a place that can suddenly, and often unexpectedly, lead news bulletins around the world. I got a lucky break to get a foreign posting early in my career (to Sri Lanka) and when you get the opportunities you have to make the most of them.

I also spent a total of nine years on two postings covering Europe and in particular the EU and how it works. So I spent a lot of time studying the relationship between the UK and the rest of Europe. When the Brexit referendum loomed into view, I was in a better position to try to explain what was happening than most people at the BBC.

Were there any difficulties you had to overcome along the way – prejudice, lack of qualifications, lack of opportunity?

ADINA CAMPBELL: I've always had a strong work ethic because growing up I had it drummed into me that education was a ticket to success. I've been fortunate to have plenty of opportunities along the way and support from colleagues. However, I know many people who haven't, and who felt gender, class or race were factors. Funnily enough some of the prejudice I've faced has been from people I've interviewed who don't expect to see a black female news correspondent. That's part of the ongoing problem we're facing in society – lack of representation in newsrooms and on-screen.

ELENI COUREA: The biggest obstacle to getting into political journalism is the sheer competitiveness of the field, which leads to people having to do lots of unpaid experience in order to make their CV stand out. Work experience and internship schemes have become more formalised but traditionally, it was often the case that you'd have to have connections in the media in order to secure them.

Because of the way the sector works a good way to get into it is to freelance or to get shifts on papers that can then become a springboard for a job. This was an obstacle to me because coming from Cyprus, I didn't have anywhere to stay in London (or even in the UK) long term if I were to go down that route – although I did occasionally stay with friends to do one-week internships and the like. I wanted to rent in London and get a job that gave me the steady income I needed to do that, so that's why I got a job for a trade magazine. I really learned a lot from that and recommend it as a route to anyone else in the same position.

The next challenge was to get from being a reporter for a little-known trade magazine to getting into one of the national papers or broadcasters. I must have applied for more than 100 jobs and graduate schemes with national newspapers before I won the Anthony Howard Award [see below] – the vast majority of which I never heard back from. That process of constant rejection can be incredibly dispiriting but I found that persistence eventually pays off, particularly if you get feedback wherever you can about how to improve your applications.

I was lucky enough never to face any serious prejudice or discrimination during all this, but it's certainly not an uncommon problem. There are increasing numbers of excellent mentorship schemes for people trying to break into journalism, and I really recommend applying to these as a way to get support and advice for what to do in those situations.

How did you go about acquiring the knowledge you needed to become effective in your specialism? How easy did you find it? How long was it before you felt you could speak with authority about your special subject? How did you manage in the meantime?

ROGER HARRABIN: I read papers and listened a lot. My degree is in English so I obliged scientists to explain issues to me with great simplicity. In some ways my lack of knowledge was a handicap, but in other ways it turned out to be an asset – because it forced scientists to explain it to me in words the general public could understand. I could then explain to the public.

Of course, since then I have learned a thing or two about the science. My background also gives me a slightly different take on science. I see stories through the prisms of uncertainty and risk, rather than top-down scientific wisdom.

ELENI COUREA: To get on to the Anthony Howard Award you have to submit a 5,000-word essay setting out what you would investigate during the course of the year. That in itself takes a lot of thought and research and forces you to make some judgements and decisions that prepare you for a year in political journalism.

That said I found that I've learned the vast majority I have needed to so far just by being on the job. From the beginning I started scheduling coffees with MPs, parliamentary assistants and whoever else I could find in that world, and I was also sent around the country to do vox pops and get a sense of how people felt about politics at that time. I attended lobby briefings, party conferences and watched how colleagues sourced and pitched stories. Soaking all that up is the only way of acquiring the knowledge you really need to be a political journalist. Learning the "theory" – for example, reading books about British politics – is definitely useful, particularly if you're writing analysis or opinion pieces in which you can compare with and draw on the past, but it's definitely not as important as that practical experience.

I can speak with some authority on the subjects I report on now but I definitely still have a lot to learn. The thing is that when you're writing a story or speaking on the radio or TV you need to do so in a way that's understandable to a well-informed but non-specialist public, which means you don't have to really get down into the weeds. I'd say that reporting on Westminster politics is unique in the sense that it changes and evolves in a way you need to constantly keep up with. Governments and opposition parties work in different ways depending on the context of that time and who's in charge of them.

PAUL KELSO: Read everything. In every sector the specialist media is packed with expertise and excellence. Those journalists already doing the job – the opposition – are your guides to what you need to know to navigate the field. On many days they will all be doing variations on the same story. Keep an eye out for those who are doing it differently, and most of all those with their own stories. Try to work out where they are getting them from. The goal is exclusive material but you cannot get there overnight. You need to understand the wheel before you can reinvent it.

Read the important books too. Historical context is important if you are going to pull off the trick of sounding convincing to others before you've convinced yourself.

For the first few months you are going to be feeling your way but no more than as a general reporter. The knack of daily journalism is working out what you need to know, and who can tell you. A specialism gives you the precious virtue of time on the same stories. Very often you will not know the answer to the questions. The key is knowing who does, and to get them to answer your call.

Speak to everyone. I draw up a list of the people that matter in the field, as far as it's possible, from the relevant Government department (but don't get bogged down in Westminster) to the key agencies, regulators, media-friendly experts and speakers. If you are lucky, the fact you work for a credible outlet will open the door for you. If not, be persistent. Buy the coffee, ask all your questions, listen hard and get a mobile number.

Learn enough of the jargon to sound convincing to insiders but don't use it on-air or in print. In a really complex and broad field like health, or business, it's impossible to get across everything. There will be things you didn't even know were a thing until they are a story you're asked to cover – the unknown unknowns. But that list gets shorter the longer you cover a beat, and every subject has its tropes: the company collapse in business; the NHS winter crisis; the doping scandal in sport. Cover one and the next one is easier. You know where it's likely to go.

Accept it is not going to be an overnight process. It will take six months before you have the measure of a subject, and it might take two years before anyone can really judge if you are any good at it. But at the start make a virtue of your ignorance. You can ask all the stupid questions that can be devastating. Within months you will be too self-consciously well-informed to risk it.

And once you have worked it out, guard against becoming institutionalised. In my first newsroom there was a specialist who may have known more about his given subject than anyone before or since in the history of journalism. But very often, when the newsdesk approached with a request, he would sneer at the suggestion, cite an historical precedent that proved this was not a story, and if it was certainly not one worthy of his time. You have to want to report the stories, even the boring ones.

JEREMY LAURENCE: I started on *GP* magazine, a weekly magazine for doctors. I spent my 40-year career writing about health. Like most journalists, I still worry whether I am speaking with authority.

ADINA CAMPBELL: I try to spend as much time as I can off-camera speaking to people at the heart of my stories so I can build a better picture of what they're experiencing. The interviews are equally important but those "off-the-record chats" are also fundamentally insightful. I try to do lots of background reading especially during quieter spells or in my own time. I also attend as many community events and gatherings as I can which take up many evenings and weekends. A significant part of the job involves what you don't see on air.

SIMON WALTERS: Self-taught, learned on the job. It took many years to grasp the subject but I have always been interested in politics so it was a pleasure. Learning how to craft a story was much harder and took many years. I managed by trying hard to overcome my shortcomings. It was not easy.

WILL GOMPERTZ: You have to live your specialism. Anything less than total immersion and you risk missing stories, uneven reporting and making editorial mistakes. A minimum six-month period dedicated to getting across the specialism is essential. But that is just priming the canvas, the real work is the daily reading, researching, enquiring, digging, visiting, talking and thinking about the stories/areas within the specialism on which you are working. That never stops. Not even on holiday.

EMILY BEAMENT: One of the great things about the environment sector is there were a great many organisations with people who can talk with knowledge and passion about what they do, and could provide me with information.

Early on, I made efforts to arrange visits to conservation projects, sustainable farming schemes, etc., to educate myself about issues, and I still think it's very important to get out of the office and see for yourself what is going on.

I gained access to scientists through the facilities the Science Media Centre provides, including briefings and one-to-one interviews. When unsure of an issue, I have asked the advice of more experienced or specialised journalists in the environmental "press pack", and I'm always – to this day – reading around the subject, exploring it through reading studies – even if I don't write about them – and other people's articles and analysis. Twitter is a good source for this, when posted by credible sources.

CHRIS MORRIS: When you arrive on a new foreign posting you're immediately immersed in a new country and a new culture. It is 24/7 learning and that makes it easier to get up to speed quickly. You have to have the confidence to speak with authority, even if there are plenty of things you don't know.

Don't forget the vast majority of the audience you're writing or broadcasting for are not experts or specialists, unless you work for a specialist trade publication. They rely on you to know enough to speak to them in ways they will find useful. There are plenty of experts who would make terrible journalists because they speak as though they're writing a PhD thesis.

If you wanted to move from one specialism to another, or to a non-specialist role, how easy would that be to achieve? Would your specialist knowledge be an asset, or do you feel as though you are so identified with your current role that it would be difficult to break out?

ROGER HARRABIN: I would find it very painful and difficult to move to another specialism – I've been doing this one for so long. What's more, I'm covering the biggest story in the world. Who would want to give that up?

ELENI COUREA: I think I'd be in a good position to move to another specialism if I wanted to, because the contacts and knowledge you get from reporting on politics are generally very valuable. There is certainly a lot of precedent for political journalists moving to jobs reporting on defence or security matters, for example.

I also think that I would be well equipped to move to a non-specialist role because I'd have developed the main skills I needed to succeed in that, such as versatility and resourcefulness. Politics is a very complex and competitive specialism where you're competing with dozens of other extremely talented journalists for scoops. It's one of the most challenging areas you can be in.

PAUL KELSO: One of the challenges of moving specialisms is that the better you are at your existing job, the harder it might be to convince yourself and others that you can change course. There are risks, but being a victim of your success is better than the alternative, and you will get credit for trying to take on a new challenge.

I underestimated the challenge of shifting from newspapers to broadcasting, but it would have been impossible had I not moved in a familiar specialism. Shifting from sport to health after 14 years was almost as disorientating, and the biggest challenge was convincing myself I could do it.

I've been asked how I could possibly convert a specialism in sport to health, or business. My answer is that it is all *journalism*. The real specialism you have is reporting.

The key thing to remember is that you are only *covering* a subject, you are not *doing* it. I was no more asked to carry out hip surgery as a health correspondent than I was to score goals for England as a sports reporter.

JEREMY LAURENCE: I remained a health reporter for my whole career. I did feel I was so identified with the role it would have been difficult to break out. I have watched colleagues with the necessary talent who have successfully broken out. But I have also watched colleagues who tired of their specialisms, tried to break out, and crashed and burned. I never have tired of writing about health, fortunately – and am still doing it today.

ADINA CAMPBELL: I believe my journalistic skills are interchangeable and transitioning wouldn't be too difficult. I've worked in many roles over the years and would like to think my overall experience would put me on the front foot for most jobs in journalism. I managed to move from health to community affairs seamlessly. The core skills were there, as I knew the demands of the job. I just had to re-focus and build a more detailed understanding of the specialism.

SIMON WALTERS: Having spent 40 years as a political reporter it would be hard to switch. On the other hand, there is no great difference in writing a typical political news story and any other news story. Specialist commentating is a different matter.

WILL GOMPERTZ: If you're any good at your specialism you will become synonymous with it and therefore moving on to another area could be difficult. However, if that new area is closely associated with your current specialism, such as politics and economics, the move can be seamless. But going from sport to education might be tricky. That doesn't necessarily mean you're stuck, though. Other opportunities within a specialism will open up, both in journalism and beyond.

EMILY BEAMENT: I've been at PA as environment correspondent for 13 years, and I can't envisage moving out of that role into a wholly different specialism or non-specialist role.

CHRIS MORRIS: Moving from one specialism to another is certainly possible. As I said before, that's what you do as a foreign correspondent when you move from one country to another.

I think there are different models for being a successful foreign correspondent. One is to have studied, say, Mandarin at university and to have a PhD in Chinese studies. You are a recognised expert. Another is to say (as I did when posted to Turkey): I've never been there, it's a blank sheet of paper for me and I'm going on a voyage of discovery. I will take the audience with me as I discover more about this country/specialism – starting from scratch.

Obviously if you have succeeded in mastering one specialism (or reporting on one country), it helps convince editors that you can do it again reporting on something/somewhere else.

How do you find being a specialist?

ROGER HARRABIN: I love it. I'm part of a local, national and international debate. Scientists, policy people and members of the public engage me to talk about my work. It's an immense privilege – especially working for the BBC where I can tell stories in the way I think they should be told.

ELENI COUREA: I find my specialism extremely rewarding. I am incredibly fortunate to be reporting on major events and decisions that shape the future of the country – I never felt that more strongly than during the parliamentary wranglings over Brexit between 2017 and 2019. But more broadly, political journalism gives you unparalleled access to senior politicians, advisers and policymakers, and that is an immense privilege.

PAUL KELSO: A specialism gives you focus and certainty. It helps you define your targets and gives you a guaranteed route to getting on TV or in the paper. It allows you to develop knowledge and contacts and analytical skills, and to break stories that get attention. If you do it well, and for long enough, stories may even start to come to you, rather than having to be pursued endlessly.

Winning the respect of experts and new peers is deeply rewarding, as is the moment when commissioning editors no longer know more than you about the subject.

JEREMY LAURENCE: I like it. And it has advantages. As a specialist reporter in the newsroom, you are expected to come up with your own stories – so you can pursue your own agenda (up to a point). As a general reporter you must do the newsdesk's bidding – you are cannon fodder in their hands. And specialist reporters are (or were) better paid.

There is also security: if you should lose your job, a specialism can give you a means of earning a living as a freelancer. Health and Finance are said to be the best (i.e. most lucrative) specialisms for freelancers.

ADINA CAMPBELL: I feel I have ownership and authority of my specialism. Being a specialist means you have more control editorially and produce more considered stories. Occasionally when there's a big breaking story that I'm particularly interested in, I miss the adrenaline of being involved and being part of that news cycle. However, those moments don't happen often because we are a busy team.

SIMON WALTERS: Endlessly fascinating and rewarding.

WILL GOMPERTZ: It works for me. My specialism is arts and culture, a beat that is endlessly fascinating, story-rich and incredibly broad: there's an arts or culture angle to almost any story. All of which is good news for me, because I can't imagine the sport or legal desk getting in touch any time soon!

EMILY BEAMENT: I find being a specialist extremely rewarding and interesting. I get to tell really important stories, use my knowledge to inform and engage people, and meet interesting people and see fascinating things.

Having done this job for more than a decade, I sometimes think there's nothing new under the sun, but then a new angle to a story, or a new story altogether, comes along and reinvigorates me. My longevity in the role also gives me a perspective to see how things are changing over time and use that to inform my stories.

CHRIS MORRIS: I love it, and probably wouldn't have stayed in journalism so long if I had spent my whole career as a general reporter.

On the other hand, I'm not sure I'd want to have spent 30 years focusing on the same issue. But for some people that's the most rewarding thing to do.

In other words it's horses for courses; you have to know what works best for you and how you function best as a journalist, and try to plan your career accordingly. Knowing your weaknesses is definitely a strength.

Of what you learned in your early career, what has stuck with you and been of most value to you as you developed into a senior journalist?

ROGER HARRABIN: I joined the *Coventry Evening Telegraph* without journalist training and had to wait six months for a three-month NCTJ course. The course was very helpful, but before that I floundered painfully trying to translate my English degree into journalistic copy. I was helped out by Gerry Hunt who had been a trainee before me. He took me through the business of news writing step by step and later went on to a senior role at the *Mail*. Thanks, Gerry.

ELENI COUREA: I think my first job, which I did for nearly two years, taught me what was most essential – how to write clear, clean copy quickly; how to cultivate sources and find stories; how to identify spin; and never to turn my nose up at any task or job. I've never done an NCTJ or formal journalism qualification, but I'm about to start doing one part time now that I work at the *Times* – so I'd say that it's ultimately very useful for any journalist. Lots of jobs require knowledge of at least shorthand and media law.

PAUL KELSO: My training was largely on the job but the skills I did learn, including shorthand, I've relied on throughout my career. Whenever I've switched specialisms I've tried to apply the same journalistic standards.

Without question I learned more working as a general reporter than at any other stage of my career. It is the essence of news journalism and the most fun. You genuinely do not know what each day will bring, you get a huge variety of experience – the car crash, the murder trial, the weather story – and, if you are lucky, you find yourself first on the scene of big stories that resonate for years. Everything else you do in your career is an adaptation of the fundamental skills required to make sense of a news event at pace, with clarity, brevity and the appropriate tone.

Irrespective of the subject, what really helped when I set out as someone with no formal training was having read newspapers obsessively. There was always one on the kitchen table when I was a kid and as an adult I read a wide variety by choice and habit. Whether it's text, audio or video, knowing the style and the tone of the outlet you plan to work for is invaluable.

JEREMY LAURENCE: I worked for the student newspaper at university. Everything I know about journalism I learned then. It was the only training I had. After that it was learning by doing.

ADINA CAMPBELL: Keep it simple when writing scripts.

How would I explain this to my best friend over coffee before broadcasting live?

Tenacity is key even when it seems like a story is hard work; sometimes those stories can be the most rewarding later down the line.

It's either all or nothing. Always do a story justice and never be half-hearted about it. Don't broadcast a story until you have the right voices and all the evidence.

Listen! Don't feel like you have to constantly interject of prompt someone while doing interviews. Some of your best material can come after a long pause.

SIMON WALTERS: My training consisted of a six-month NCTJ course for school leavers in Cardiff. It was perfectly adequate. I was content to learn the rest on the job. I was fortunate to work with more experienced journalists who guided me.

WILL GOMPERTZ: There is no substitute for doing the job. It's like driving, you only really learn after passing the test and you're out on your own. Everything you have known or done feeds into your journalism, but the most valuable lessons I've learned are: be persistent, listen (really listen), work incredibly hard on your questions because a great question can lead to a great story and don't forget if you want someone to read/watch/listen to your story you have to use your writing skills to bring it to life.

EMILY BEAMENT: From my City course, I still use my shorthand every day at work, and the lesson about how to write a good intro!

When I was a trainee, a senior journalist told me: "At PA, you have to be two things: you have to be fast and you have to be right. But if you can only be one of those things, you have to be right". I think in today's fast-paced, online, 24-hour news world, that advice applies well beyond PA.

CHRIS MORRIS: I never did any formal training as a journalist, so initially experience gained on the job was the most valuable thing for me. At the start of my career I spent about six months in the BBC World Service newsroom, which in those days had a very particular way of doing things. But it taught me how to write accurately, quickly and concisely.

Mentors are always useful, both inside and outside your own company. Never be afraid to ask questions or ask for advice. It might not be the right advice for you, but it will always help inform the decisions you make.

What advice would you give to a young generalist journalist thinking of concentrating on a special subject, or area of journalism?

ELENI COUREA: My view has always been that developing a specialism, regardless of whether it is politics, is immensely rewarding. That's particularly the case when you're the sort of journalist who's passionate about getting scoops. You are much better positioned to do so if you've built up expertise in a subject and made lots of contacts you talk to regularly within it. I'm sure there's lot to enjoy about the versatility of being a generalist reporter but I think that anyone who's thinking of developing a specialism won't regret doing so.

PAUL KELSO: If you are lucky, specialist journalism allows you to pursue your passion and to make a difference. If you get the chance, take it, but bear in mind it is – with luck – a long career, and you don't have to do the same thing forever. It is possible, I hope, to become credible in more than one field.

JEREMY LAURENCE: Do it. Once you get into it, anything and everything is interesting.

ADINA CAMPBELL: Contact someone who is doing the job already and ask them loads of questions. Don't be afraid to send them an email even if you haven't met them before. Most people are kind and will get back to you. Find out how they got to where they are and what they typically do in a day.

You also can't read enough about stories in your interested specialism.

Critique reports that interest you and think about how you would cover them differently.

Find or ask for a mentor.

Remember why you decided to become a journalist in the first place.

SIMON WALTERS: Make the most of any journalistic opportunity that arises. The skills required to be a good journalist are broadly applicable to generalists and specialists. Accuracy, fairness and a sense of mischief, hard work, curiosity, respect not deference – and learn to write clearly.

WILL GOMPERTZ: Only go into a specialism if you have a genuine interest in the area. Check out the competition, and learn from what they do well and what they do not do well. Learn. Give it your all. Everything else will look after itself. The world needs specialist journalists. Experts play a vital role in a healthy democracy.

EMILY BEAMENT: If you have an interest in a subject, try to be proactive about developing your knowledge and coverage of it. Pitch ideas (though be careful of stepping on specialists' toes) or volunteer if opportunities in that area come up – for example, helping cover a conference, event or major story, or data crunching on an investigation.

As a specialist, you can find yourself writing about subjects that are really important or which people really care about, such as the environment.

If that's the case, I think it's important to be mindful of the responsibility you have to engage and inform readers on things that really matter and can have a huge impact on their lives.

CHRIS MORRIS: Always have a specialism up your sleeve. It doesn't have to define your career, but it certainly can't do you any harm. I sometimes talk to sixth formers about journalism as a career and often get asked questions along the lines of "Should I study physics or journalism?" My answer is always "do the physics – have the ability to tell me something I don't know". You can study journalism later, or you can learn on the job. And if you stay curious, you can pick up new specialisms as your career progresses. You're never too old to learn something new!

The specialists

Roger Harrabin, Environment Analyst, BBC News

I trained on the *Coventry Evening Telegraph*. Over seven years, I did a wide range of jobs including council correspondent, sports sub-editor and page designer for a women's colour magazine. I joined *Thames TV* as a script-writer/sub and was very miserable behind a desk. I freelanced in Fleet Street as a sports sub on the *News of the World*. In 1986, I joined BBC Radio London, then moved to Radio 4 *World at One* and *PM* programmes. The *Today* programme later created a roving role for me, and I travelled the world widely – mostly focusing on the environment and related issues. In 2009, BBC News created the role of Energy and Environment Analyst so that I could work on television and online as well as radio.

Eleni Courea, Political Reporter, *The Times*

I've been working on *The Times* staff as a political reporter since 2020. I got the job after winning the Anthony Howard Award, which gives young people the opportunity to spend a year working in the lobby – among the group of journalists who have unrestricted access to the Houses of Parliament and daily No 10 briefings. Before starting the Award, I worked as a reporter for two sister trade magazines called *Research Fortnight* and *Research Europe*, writing about science policy and universities. That was my first job after university, and I spent nearly two years there.

Paul Kelso, Business correspondent, Sky News

My first job in journalism was at the *Guardian* in 1995. I was staggeringly fortunate. It was the only place I ever wanted to work and I got to learn my trade from some of the people I most admired. After a spell on features and then the sports desk, I joined the paper's trainee scheme as a reporter in the newsroom. In 2003, I became Sports Correspondent, a specialist role covering sports news, loosely defined as the back-page stories that made it on to the front pages. In 2008, I joined the *Daily Telegraph* as Chief Sports Reporter, a similar role that took in the London 2012 Olympics, and in 2013 I became Sports Correspondent of *Sky News*. In early 2017 I was appointed Health Correspondent, and in 2019 became Business Correspondent.

Jeremy Laurance, Freelance Health Writer

My first job was in weekly specialist magazines – *GP*, *World Medicine*, then *New Society* (social policy) and *New Statesman*. My first job on a national paper was as Health Correspondent for *The Sunday Times*. Later I spent 5 years as Health Correspondent on the *Times* and 16 years as Health Editor, the *Independent*.

Adina Campbell, Community Affairs Correspondent, BBC News

After graduating from Cardiff University with an English Literature degree, I stayed to do a Postgraduate Diploma in Broadcast Journalism. I spent weekends and holidays freelancing as a newsreader at local radio stations across South Wales and the South East of England. After gaining my MA, I worked in commercial radio and secured my first full-time job as a broadcast journalist at a radio station in Cheltenham. I left after six months to join a bigger news team in Oxford.

I joined the BBC in 2008 as a news reporter for BBC 1Xtra and Radio 1 Newsbeat in London. Aged 23, this was my dream job and I spent the next four years travelling across the UK as a roving reporter filing stories for those programmes. During the same period, I became a television presenter for a BBC Two show *Revealed* and made documentaries for a teenage audience. In 2013 I left network news and become a regional television reporter with the BBC South Today news team in Oxford.

I moved back to London and joined network news in 2017. My roles included working as a health, education and general news correspondent. In 2018 I became the BBC's Community Affairs Correspondent.

Simon Walters, Assistant Editor, the *Daily Mail*

I did not go to university. I started as a reporter with the *Evening Mail* in Slough, at the age of 19. I became Press Association Parliamentary reporter in 1978, and after six years moved to the *Sun* as a political reporter. In 1994 I became Political Editor of the *Sunday Express*, and later its Deputy Editor. I was Political Editor of the *Mail on Sunday* from 1999 to 2018 and am now Assistant Editor (Politics) of the *Daily Mail*.

Will Gompertz, Arts Editor, BBC News

I left school at 16 and started out stacking shelves in a supermarket (surprisingly enjoyable), progressed to selling records at Our Price, holiday camp entertainer and finally stage hand in a West End theatre. Next, a job as a runner in a production company, then I founded a specialist visual arts publishing company, sold it for quite a lot of money and bought a fast car. The Tate Gallery hired me: I thought I'd stay six weeks and was there for seven years. I published, produced, wrote and managed. I took a course in stand-up comedy for an article in the *Guardian*, which developed into an Edinburgh Fringe show (*Double Art History with Mr Gompertz*). The BBC wanted an Arts Editor. I got the job.

Emily Beament, Environment Correspondent, PA Media

I did a BA degree in English literature, followed by a Postgraduate Diploma in newspaper journalism at City University in London. From there I joined PA on their news trainee scheme, a three-year programme. I started with a year in Yorkshire, focusing largely on page production/regional newswire/

Teletext/early digital news provision. Then I had six months in London as a general news reporter, followed by a year's placement as a general news reporter in Ireland, before coming back to London to complete my traineeship. I got a job with PA as a general news reporter in London and a little over a year later the environment correspondent job came up and I went for and got it.

Chris Morris, Senior Correspondent, BBC Reality Check

I have worked for the BBC for 30 years, and mostly as a foreign correspondent with postings to Colombo, Washington DC, Istanbul, New Delhi and twice to Brussels. For part of the time I was based in big bureaux, and for part of the time I was a one-man band working largely on my own. Both are useful learning experiences. When I returned to the UK at the end of 2016, my in-depth knowledge of the way the EU worked meant that I was put on the Brexit beat. That led to the BBC's new Reality Check team, fact-checking and analysing many of the claims being made.

This book summarised in two pages

If you have the instincts of a journalist, your eyes will have lit up at the sight of this chapter heading. It is an enticing prospect, offering as it does the opportunity rapidly to absorb the key contents of this book without having to go to the trouble of reading it. Needless to say that is not its purpose. But even if you take away nothing but the contents of the next couple of pages, then your visit will not have been entirely in vain.

In putting this book together and then revising and preparing it for publication, I have repeatedly been struck by the frequency with which the same themes and messages crop up, regardless of what platform, medium or element of the journalistic process is under discussion. This brief summary is an attempt to bring them all together in one place. The exercise serves to emphasise the point made in the Preface: that although journalism is changing and heading off in many new and different directions, the basic precepts remain the same. The core values, ethics and standards of the best journalistic practice are immutable. They do not change, even if the environment in which they are applied changes fundamentally. If professional journalism has a future, it will be because people recognise and appreciate that these values, ethics and standards are still being respected and adhered to – and are worth paying for.

Accuracy

A commitment to getting things right lies at the heart of everything you do as a journalist, and extends to the smallest detail of what you broadcast or publish. Without it, you are wasting your time. Seemingly minor mistakes can be the most damaging to your reputation, and that of your employer. When it comes to getting things right, there is one simple rule: check, and check again.

But accuracy is about more than just getting the facts right. It means making sure you are producing fair, proportionate and balanced reporting, striking the right tone and getting the right emphasis.

Audiences

Everything you produce as a journalist is destined for an audience – a reader, listener or viewer. You need to have these people constantly in mind. The needs of that audience will be different depending on where you are working, and you need to understand what those needs are, and to adapt your approach accordingly. In these days of sophisticated data analytics, we know more about our audiences than ever before – who they are, how old they are, where they live, what they are interested in, what they are not interested in, what they are looking for in their news consumption. Although what audiences want and what they need are not always the same thing, it is important to tailor what you offer them in the light of what you know about them. They are the consumers and the customers. It is your job as a journalist to serve them. One of the BBC's many mantras is: "audiences are at the heart of everything we do".

People

Most news stories are about people – what they have done or said, what has happened to them, how they feel and so on. Always look for the human element. Featuring people is the means by which we make our stories relatable to the audience, and illustrate and explain them in a way that is engaging and effective.

Planning and preparation

Journalism can be a breathless business, and the clock is unforgiving. But however pushed you are, even a small amount of time thinking about what you are doing or trying to do will never be wasted. As you become more experienced, you will do this automatically and without having to think too much about it. A few moments spent asking and answering the most basic questions about your sources or your story will always save you time later, because it will make you more organised and focused on what you are doing. This book is full of tips and checklists that encourage you to prepare the ground before you start work, usually with sets of very simple questions like: What is this story? Have I got everything I need to tell it? What do I want to say? Is it of interest to my audience? What do they already know about it? What do they need to know in order to understand it? What is the most effective way of presenting it?

Simplicity

KISS – Keep It Simple, Stupid – is your watchword. However complicated your story is, and whatever the medium in which you are working, use clear, direct, simple, precise, unambiguous, everyday language. This is not about patronising the audience. It is about conveying clearly what you want to say by means that they will understand and find easy to absorb.

News insights

A final checklist! This is from a handout prepared by the BBC College of Journalism and entitled News Insights: Top Tips. It is a great summary of the messages of this book.

1. Accuracy is critical: be sure of your facts.
2. Keep your writing simple and concise.
3. Never underestimate your audience's intelligence.
4. Never overestimate your audience's knowledge.
5. Be transparent and clear about what you know.
6. Consult the editorial guidelines and remember the law.
7. Know the mandatory referrals [to more senior editorial figures] by heart.
8. If you intrude into anyone's personal life, have a clear editorial justification.
9. Cultivate contacts and know when to double-source your facts.
10. Make contingency strategies in case your plans don't work out.

Further reading

General

Journalism: A Very Short Introduction

Ian Hargreaves

OUP 2nd Edition 2014

The Universal Journalist

David Randall

Pluto Press 6th Edition 2021

Breaking News: The Remaking of Journalism and Why It Matters Now

Alan Rusbridger

Canongate 2018

Journalism: Principles and Practice

Tony Harcup

Sage 3rd Edition 2015

The 21st Century Journalism Handbook: Essential Skills for the Modern Journalist

Tim Holmes, Sara Hadwin and Glyn Mottershead

Routledge 2012

News and Journalism in the UK

Brian McNair

Routledge 2009

Power without Responsibility: Press, Broadcasting and the Internet in Britain

James Curran and Jean Seaton

Routledge 8th Edition 2018

Mass Media, Politics and Democracy

John Street

Red Globe Press 2nd Edition 2010

The NCTJ Journalism Skills Academy is a training platform for journalists at every stage of their career. You can study towards formal qualifications, have access to free video resources, undertake short skill-specific courses and test your knowledge in interactive quizzes.

https://www.nctj.com/Journalism-Skills-Academy/about-journalism-skills-academy

The BBC Academy provides training and development material designed to support BBC staff and the wider industry in good broadcasting practice. Search for 'journalism' on the Academy website.

https://www.bbc.co.uk/academy/en/

Ethics and law

Mc Nae's Essential Law for Journalists

Mark Hanna and Mike Dodd

OUP 25th Edition 2020

Journalism Ethics and Regulation

Chris Frost

Longman 3rd Edition 2011

The Ethical Journalist

Tony Harcup

Sage 2007

Public affairs

Essential Public Affairs for Journalists

James Morrison

OUP 6th Edition 2019

Freedom of Information

Freedom of Information: A Practical Guide for UK Journalists

Matt Burgess

Routledge 2015

Your Right to Know: A Citizen's Guide to the Freedom of Information Act

Heather Brooke

Pluto Press 2nd Edition 2006

Interviewing

Interviewing for Journalists

Joan Clayton

Piatkus 1994
Interviewing for Journalists
Sally Adams with Wynford Hicks
Routledge 2nd Edition 2009

Writing and reporting

English for Journalists
Wynford Hicks
Routledge 4th Edition 2013
Writing for Journalists
Wynford Hicks with Sally Adams and Harriett Gilbert
Routledge 3rd Edition 2016
Reporting for Journalists
Chris Frost
Routledge 2nd Edition 2010
Mind Your Language: Writing with Impact for Broadcast News
Christina McIntyre
Independently published 2018

Feature writing

Writing Feature Articles
Brendan Hennessy
Focal Press 4th Edition 2006
Feature Writing for Journalists
Sharon Wheeler
Routledge 2009

Statistics

Statistical: Ten Easy Ways to Avoid Being Misled by Numbers
Anthony Reuben
Constable 2019
The Tiger That Isn't: Seeing through a World of Numbers
Michael Blastland and Andrew Dilnot
Profile Books Main Edition 2010

Maths on the Back of an Envelope: Clever Ways to (Roughly) Calculate Anything

Rob Eastaway

HarperCollins 2019

Humble Pi: A Comedy of Maths Errors

Matt Parker

Penguin 2020

The Art of Statistics: Learning from Data

David Spiegelhalter

Pelican Books 2020

Digital

The Online Journalism Handbook: Skills to Survive and Thrive in the Digital Age

Paul Bradshaw

Routledge 2nd Edition 2018

The Social Media Reporter: A Guide to Using Social Media for Newsgathering

Cordelia Hebblethwaite

https://medium.com/the-social-media-reporter

The Data Journalism Handbook: How Journalists Can Use Data to Improve the News

Edited by Jonathan Gray, Lucy Chambers and Liliane Bounegru

O'Reilly Media 2012

Writing on the Wall: Social Media – The First 2000 Years

Tom Standage

Bloomsbury 2013

Mobile and Social Media Journalism

Anthony Adornato

CQ Press 2017

Broadcast

Essential Radio Journalism

Paul Chantler and Peter Stewart

A & C Black 2009

Radio Production

Robert McLeish

Focal Press 5th Edition 2005

Broadcast Journalism

Andrew Boyd

Focal Press 5th Edition 2001

The Television News Handbook

Vin Ray

Macmillan 2003

The Broadcast Journalism Handbook

Gary Hudson and Sarah Rowlands

Routledge 2012

Understanding Broadcast Journalism

Stephen Jukes, Katy McDonald, Guy Starkey

Routledge 2017

Shorthand

NCTJ Teeline Gold Standard for Journalists

Marie Cartwright

Heinemann 2009

Best books/memoirs about journalism

There are many brilliant autobiographies and other books by journalists, many of them also reflecting on the nature of journalism itself. Here is a selection:

My Paper Chase

Harold Evans

Abacus 2009

Flat Earth News: An Award-winning Reporter Exposes Falsehood, Distortion and Propaganda in the Global Media

Nick Davies

Vintage 2009

Hack Attack: How the Truth Caught Up with Rupert Murdoch [the story of the phone hacking scandal]

Nick Davies

Vintage 2015

No Expenses Spared [the story of the MPs' expenses scandal]

Robert Winnett and Gordon Rayner

Bantam Press 2009

Dear Bill

WF Deedes

Pan 1997

Andrew Marr

My Trade

Macmillan 2004

Nick Robinson

Live from Downing Street

Bantam Press 2012

Nick Robinson

Election Notebook

Bantam Press 2015

A Day Like Today

John Humphrys

Collins 2019

Shooting History: A Personal Journey

Jon Snow

Harper Perennial 2005

On the Front Line

Marie Colvin

Harper Press 2012

Airhead: The Imperfect Art of Making News

Emily Maitlis

Penguin 2019

Index

Printed in Great Britain
by Amazon

39970131R00258